FOURTH EDITION

Writing for Life

Paragraphs and Essays

D.J. Henry
Daytona State College

PEARSON

Boston   Columbus   Indianapolis   New York   San Francisco
Amsterdam   Cape Town   Dubai   London   Madrid   Milan   Munich   Paris   Montreal   Toronto
Delhi   Mexico City   Sao Paulo   Sydney   Hong Kong   Seoul   Singapore   Taipei   Tokyo

Executive Editor: Matthew Wright
Program Manager: Katharine Glynn
Development Editor: Erin Dye
Senior Product Marketing Manager: Jennifer Edwards
Executive Field Marketing Manager: Joyce Nilsen
Media Producer: Marisa Massaro
Content Specialist: Laura Olson
Media Editor: Kara Noonan
Project Manager: Donna Campion
Text Design, Project Coordination, and Electronic Page Makeup: Cenveo® Publisher Services
Program Design Lead: Heather Scott
Cover Designer: Studio Montage
Cover Illustration: View of Bogliasco—Alex Tihonov/Getty Images; Hand and Smart Phone-rvlsoft/Shutterstock
Senior Manufacturing Buyer: Roy L. Pickering, Jr.
Printer/Binder: RR Donnelley/Roanoke
Cover Printer: Phoenix Color/Hagerstown

Acknowledgments of third-party content appear on pages 670–672, which constitute an extension of this copyright page.

PEARSON, ALWAYS LEARNING, and MYWRITINGLAB are exclusive trademarks owned by Pearson Education, Inc. or its affiliates in the United States and/or other countries.

Unless otherwise indicated herein, any third-party trademarks that may appear in this work are the property of their respective owners and any references to third-party trademarks, logos, or other trade dress are for demonstrative or descriptive purposes only. Such references are not intended to imply any sponsorship, endorsement, authorization, or promotion of Pearson's products by the owners of such marks, or any relationship between the owner and Pearson Education, Inc., or its affiliates, authors, licensees, or distributors.

Library of Congress Cataloging-in-Publication Data

Names: Henry, D. J. (Dorothy Jean) author.
Title: Writing for life : paragraphs and essays / D.J. Henry.
Description: Fourth edition | Boston : Pearson, [2017] | Includes index.
Identifiers: LCCN 2015045206 | ISBN 9780134021690
Subjects: LCSH: English language—Composition and exercises—Study and teaching (Higher) | Rhetoric—Study and teaching (Higher) | Creative writing (Higher education)
Classification: LCC PE1404 .H3975 2017 | DDC 808/.042076—dc23
LC record available at http://lccn.loc.gov/2015045206

Copyright © 2017, 2014, 2011 by Pearson Education, Inc. All Rights Reserved. Printed in the United States of America. This publication is protected by copyright, and permission should be obtained from the publisher prior to any prohibited reproduction, storage in a retrieval system, or transmission in any form or by any means, electronic, mechanical, photocopying, recording, or otherwise. For information regarding permissions, request forms and the appropriate contacts within the Pearson Education Global Rights & Permissions Department, please visit www.pearsoned.com/permissions/.

10 9 8 7 6 5 4 3 2 1—V082—19 18 17 16

www.pearsonhighered.com

Student Edition ISBN 10: 0-13-402169-X
Student Edition ISBN 13: 978-0-13-402169-0
A la Carte Edition ISBN 10: 0-13-396032-3
A la Carte Edition ISBN 13: 978-0-13-396032-7

MyWritingLab™ Online Course (access code required)
for *Writing for Life, Paragraphs and Essays 4e,* by D. J. Henry

MyWritingLab is an online homework, tutorial, and assessment program that provides engaging experiences for today's instructors and students.

Writing Help for Varying Skill Levels

For students who enter the course at widely varying skill levels, MyWritingLab provides unique, targeted remediation through personalized and adaptive instruction. Starting with a pre-assessment known as the Path Builder, MyWritingLab diagnoses students' strengths and weaknesses on prerequisite writing skills. The results of the pre-assessment inform each student's Learning Path, a personalized pathway for students to work on requisite skills through multimodal activities. In doing so, students feel supported and ready to succeed in class.

Respond to Student Writing with Targeted Feedback and Remediation

MyWritingLab unites instructor comments and feedback with targeted remediation via rich multimedia activities, allowing students to learn from and through their own writing.

- When giving feedback on student writing, instructors can add links to activities that address issues and strategies needed for review. Instructors may link to multimedia resources in Pearson Writer, which include curated content from Purdue OWL.
- In the Writing Assignments, students can use instructor-created peer review rubrics to evaluate and comment on other students' writing.
- Paper review by specialized tutors through Tutor Services is available, as is plagiarism detection through TurnItIn.

Learning Tools for Student Engagement

Learning Catalytics

Generate class discussion, guide lectures, and promote peer-to-peer learning with real-time analytics. MyLab and Mastering with eText now provides Learning Catalytics—an interactive student response tool that uses students' smartphones, tablets, or laptops to engage them in more sophisticated tasks and thinking.

MediaShare

MediaShare allows students to post multimodal assignments easily—whether they are audio, video, or visual compositions—for peer review and instructor feedback. In both face-to-face and online course settings, MediaShare saves instructors valuable time and enriches the student learning experience by enabling contextual feedback to be provided quickly and easily.

Direct Access to MyLab

Users can link from any Learning Management System (LMS) to Pearson's MyWritingLab. Access MyLab assignments, rosters, and resources, and synchronize MyLab grades with the LMS gradebook. New direct, single sign-on provides access to all the personalized learning MyLab resources that make studying more efficient and effective.

Proven Results

No matter how MyWritingLab is used, instructors have access to powerful gradebook reports. These reports provide visual analytics that give insight to course performance at the student, section, or even program level.

Visit www.mywritinglab.com for more information.

Brief Contents

Part 1 Getting Ready to Write

| CHAPTER 1 | Preparing to Learn about Writing | 2 |
| CHAPTER 2 | Thinking Through the Writing Process | 18 |

Part 2 Using Patterns of Organization to Develop Paragraphs

CHAPTER 3	Understanding the Paragraph	50
CHAPTER 4	The Descriptive Paragraph	68
CHAPTER 5	The Narrative Paragraph	86
CHAPTER 6	The Process Paragraph	100
CHAPTER 7	The Example Paragraph	116
CHAPTER 8	The Classification Paragraph	132
CHAPTER 9	The Comparison and Contrast Paragraph	148
CHAPTER 10	The Definition Paragraph	162
CHAPTER 11	The Cause and Effect Paragraph	176
CHAPTER 12	The Persuasive Paragraph	190

Part 3 How to Write an Essay

CHAPTER 13	Understanding the Essay	204
CHAPTER 14	Effective Titles, Introductions, and Conclusions	228
CHAPTER 15	Using Patterns of Organization to Develop Essays	238
CHAPTER 16	Research Strategies and Resources	290

Part 4 The Basic Sentence

CHAPTER 17	Nouns and Pronouns	322
CHAPTER 18	Adjectives and Adverbs	346
CHAPTER 19	Verbs	364
CHAPTER 20	Subjects, Verbs, and Simple Sentences	388
CHAPTER 21	Compound and Complex Sentences	402

Part 5 Editing the Basic Sentence

CHAPTER 22	Editing Run-ons: Comma Splices and Fused Sentences	420
CHAPTER 23	Editing Fragments into Sentences	438
CHAPTER 24	Editing Misplaced and Dangling Modifiers	458
CHAPTER 25	Editing for Subject-Verb Agreement: Present Tense	468

Part 6 Revising to Improve Expression

CHAPTER 26	Revising for Sentence Variety	490
CHAPTER 27	Revising for Sentence Clarity: Person, Point of View, Number, and Tense	510
CHAPTER 28	Revising for Parallelism	524
CHAPTER 29	Revising for Effective Expression	538

Part 7 Punctuation and Mechanics

CHAPTER 30	The Comma	554
CHAPTER 31	The Apostrophe	564
CHAPTER 32	Quotation Marks	572
CHAPTER 33	End Punctuation: Period, Question Mark, and Exclamation Point	582
CHAPTER 34	Capitalization	590
CHAPTER 35	Improving Your Spelling	598

Part 8 Reading Selections   610

Detailed Contents

Preface　　xvii
Acknowledgments　　xxiv

PART 1　Getting Ready to Write

CHAPTER 1
Preparing to Learn about Writing　2

What's the Point of Preparing to Learn about Writing?　3
　One Student Writer's Response　4
Adopt the Attitude of Learning　5
　Use Positive Self-Talk　5
　Be an Active Learner　5
　Trust Your Teacher　5
Create a Study Plan　6
　Gather Your Tools　6
　Set Goals　6
　Take Action　6
Connect Writing and Reading　8
Use the Reading Process to Strengthen Your Writing　10
Use the Flow of the Reading-Writing Interaction to Strengthen Your Writing　12

Create a Portfolio of Your Work　14
　What Is a Portfolio?　14
　What Should I Include in My Portfolio?　14
　What Is a Reflective Journal Entry?　14
　What Is the Best Way to Set Up My Portfolio?　15
Academic Learning Log MyWritingLab™　17

CHAPTER 2
Thinking Through the Writing Process　18

What's the Point of the Writing Process?　19
　One Student Writer's Response　20
Assess the Writing Situation: Topic, Audience, and Purpose　20
　The Topic: What You Write　20
　The Purpose: Why You Write　22
　The Audience: Who Reads Your Writing　24
Use the Writing Process: Prewrite, Draft, Revise, and Proofread　28
　Prewrite　30
　Draft　42
　Revise　44
　Proofread　46
Academic Learning Log MyWritingLab™　48

PART 2: Using Patterns of Organization to Develop Paragraphs

CHAPTER 3: Understanding the Paragraph — 50

- What's the Point of a Paragraph? — 51
  - Three Levels of Information in a Paragraph — 51
- Identify the Three Parts of a Paragraph — 56
- Compose a Topic Sentence — 58
  - Narrow the Topic — 58
  - Write the Topic Sentence — 60
- Use Logical Order — 61
- Develop Relevant and Adequate Details — 62
- Use Effective Expression — 63
  - Word Choice — 63
  - Sentence Structure — 64
  - Grammar — 64
- Analyze the Effectiveness of a Paragraph — 65
- Academic Learning Log MyWritingLab™ — 67

CHAPTER 4: The Descriptive Paragraph — 68

- What's the Point of Description? — 69
  - One Student Writer's Response — 72
  - The Writer's Journal — 73
- Compose a Topic Sentence — 74
- Use Logical Order — 76
- Develop Relevant Details — 77
- Use Effective Expression: Concrete Word Choice — 78
- Use Description in Your Academic Courses — 80
- Workshop: Writing a Descriptive Paragraph Step by Step — 81
- Writing Assignments MyWritingLab™ — 85

CHAPTER 5: The Narrative Paragraph — 86

- What's the Point of Narration? — 87
  - One Student Writer's Response — 88
  - The Writer's Journal — 89
- Compose a Topic Sentence — 90
- Use Logical Order — 91
- Develop Relevant Details — 92
- Use Effective Expression: Vivid Verbs — 94
- Use Narration in Your Academic Courses — 95
- Workshop: Writing a Narrative Paragraph Step by Step — 96
- Writing Assignments MyWritingLab™ — 99

CHAPTER 6: The Process Paragraph — 100

- What's the Point of Process? — 101
  - One Student Writer's Response — 102
  - The Writer's Journal — 103
- Compose a Topic Sentence — 104
- Use Logical Order — 105
- Develop Relevant Details — 106
- Use Effective Expression: Vivid Images — 108
- Use Process in Your Academic Courses — 109
- Workshop: Writing a Process Paragraph Step by Step — 110
- Writing Assignments MyWritingLab™ — 115

CHAPTER 7
The Example Paragraph — 116

- What's the Point of Examples? — 117
  - One Student Writer's Response — 118
  - The Writer's Journal — 119
- Compose a Topic Sentence — 120
- Use Logical Order — 122
- Develop Relevant Details — 124
- Use Effective Expression: Parallel Language — 126
- Use Examples in Your Academic Courses — 127
- Workshop: Writing an Example Paragraph Step by Step — 128
- Writing Assignments MyWritingLab — 131

CHAPTER 8
The Classification Paragraph — 132

- What's the Point of Classification? — 133
  - One Student Writer's Response — 134
  - The Writer's Journal — 135
- Compose a Topic Sentence — 136
- Use Logical Order — 137
- Develop Relevant Details — 138
- Use Effective Expression: Controlled Sentence Structure — 140
- Use Classification in Your Academic Courses — 142
- Workshop: Writing a Classification Paragraph Step by Step — 143
- Writing Assignments MyWritingLab — 147

CHAPTER 9
The Comparison and Contrast Paragraph — 148

- What's the Point of Comparison and Contrast? — 149
  - One Student Writer's Response — 150
  - The Writer's Journal — 151
- Compose a Topic Sentence — 152
- Use Logical Order — 153
- Develop Relevant Details — 154
- Use Effective Expression: Use of Coordination and Subordination — 156
- Use Comparison and Contrast in Your Academic Courses — 157
- Workshop: Writing a Comparison and Contrast Paragraph Step by Step — 158
- Writing Assignments MyWritingLab — 161

CHAPTER 10
The Definition Paragraph — 162

- What's the Point of Definition? — 163
  - One Student Writer's Response — 164
  - The Writer's Journal — 165
- Compose a Topic Sentence — 166
- Use Logical Order — 167
- Develop Relevant Details — 168
- Use Effective Expression: Sound Structure and Vivid Images — 170
- Use Definition in Your Academic Courses — 171
- Workshop: Writing a Definition Paragraph Step by Step — 172
- Writing Assignments MyWritingLab — 175

CHAPTER 11
The Cause and Effect Paragraph — 176

- What's the Point of Cause and Effect? — 177
  - One Student Writer's Response — 178
  - The Writer's Journal — 179
- Compose a Topic Sentence — 180
- Use Logical Order — 181
- Develop Relevant Details — 182
- Use Effective Expression: Correct Use of Words — 184
- Use Cause and Effect in Your Academic Courses — 185
- Workshop: Writing a Cause and Effect Paragraph Step by Step — 186
- Writing Assignments MyWritingLab — 189

CHAPTER 12
The Persuasive Paragraph — 190

- What's the Point of Persuasion? — 191
  - One Student Writer's Response — 192
  - The Writer's Journal — 193
- Compose a Topic Sentence — 194
- Use Logical Order — 195
- Develop Relevant Details — 196
- Use Effective Expression: Use of Subjective Words to Persuade — 198
- Use Persuasion in Your Academic Courses — 199
- Workshop: Writing a Persuasive Paragraph Step by Step — 200
- Writing Assignments MyWritingLab — 203

PART 3: How to Write an Essay

CHAPTER 13
Understanding the Essay — 204

What's the Point of an Essay? — 205
  One Student Writer's Response — 206
The Five Parts of an Essay — 206
The Levels of Information in an Essay — 208
  Titles, Introductions, and Conclusions Express General Ideas — 208
  Thesis Statement — 208
  Types of Supporting Details — 208
  Levels of Supporting Details — 209
The Traits of an Effective Essay — 211
  A Clear Point: Main Idea or Thesis Statement — 211
  Logical Order — 213
  Relevant Details — 218
  Effective Expression: Using a Thesaurus — 220
Workshop: Writing an Essay Step by Step — 221
  Academic Learning Log MyWritingLab — 226

CHAPTER 14
Effective Titles, Introductions, and Conclusions — 228

What's the Point of Effective Titles, Introductions, and Conclusions? — 229
  One Student Writer's Response — 230
Compose Effective Titles — 231
Compose Effective Introductions — 233
Compose Effective Conclusions — 235
Academic Learning Log MyWritingLab — 237

CHAPTER 15
Using Patterns of Organization to Develop Essays — 238

What's the Point of Using Patterns of Organization to Develop Essays? — 239
  One Student Writer's Response — 240
Develop Your Point in a Descriptive Essay — 240
  One Student Writer's Response — 241
  Writing Assignments MyWritingLab — 244
Develop Your Point in a Narrative Essay — 244
  One Student Writer's Response — 245
  Writing Assignments MyWritingLab — 248
Develop Your Point in a Process Essay — 248
  One Student Writer's Response — 249
  Writing Assignments MyWritingLab — 252
Develop Your Point in an Illustration Essay — 253
  One Student Writer's Response — 253
  Writing Assignments MyWritingLab — 257

Develop Your Point in a Classification Essay	258
One Student Writer's Response	258
Writing Assignments MyWritingLab	262
Develop Your Point in a Comparison and Contrast Essay	263
One Student Writer's Response	263
Writing Assignments MyWritingLab	267
Develop Your Point in a Definition Essay	268
One Student Writer's Response	268
Writing Assignments MyWritingLab	272
Develop Your Point in a Cause and Effect Essay	273
One Student Writer's Response	273
Writing Assignments MyWritingLab	277
Develop Your Point in a Persuasive Essay	278
One Writer's Response	278
Writing Assignments MyWritingLab	282
Develop Your Point in an Essay That Combines Patterns	283
One Student Writer's Response	283
Writing Assignments MyWritingLab	288
Academic Learning Log MyWritingLab	289

CHAPTER 16
Research Strategies and Resources — 290

What's the Point of Research?	291
One Student Writer's Response	292
Find and Evaluate Sources	292
What Kind of Information Do I Need?	293
Where Can I Find the Information I Need?	293
How Can I Know the Information I Find Is Reliable or Trustworthy?	298
Avoid Plagiarism	300
Develop Your Reading/Writing Strategy for Research	306
Master the Basics of MLA	307
In-Text Citations	308
Works Cited Page	309
MLA Formats for Non-Web Sources	310
MLA Formats for Web Sources	314
Sample Student Research Essay	317
Writing Assignments MyWritingLab	320
Academic Learning Log MyWritingLab	321

PART 4 The Basic Sentence

CHAPTER 17
Nouns and Pronouns — 322

What's the Point of Nouns and Pronouns?	323
One Student Writer's Response	324
Recognize Types and Uses of Nouns	324
Identify Count and Noncount Nouns	327
Identify Articles and Nouns	328
Identify Pronouns and Antecedents	329
Make Clear Pronoun References	329
Correct Faulty Pronoun References	330
Make Pronouns and Antecedents Agree	332
Correct Faulty Pronoun Agreement	333
Clearly Use Pronoun Case	336
Editing Assignments MyWritingLab	343
Academic Learning Log MyWritingLab	345

CHAPTER 18
Adjectives and Adverbs — 346

What's the Point of Adjectives and Adverbs?	347
One Student Writer's Response	348
Understand the General Functions and Purposes of Adjectives and Adverbs	348
Use Adjectives: Forms, Placement, and Order	350
Participles Used as Adjectives	350
Nouns and Verbs Formed as Adjectives	351

Placement of Adjectives	352
Order of Adjectives	353
Use Adverbs	355
Use the Degrees of Adjectives and Adverbs: Absolute, Comparative, and Superlative	356
Absolute	357
Comparative	357
Superlative	357
Master *Good* and *Well*	360
Editing Assignments MyWritingLab™	362
Academic Learning Log MyWritingLab™	363

CHAPTER 19
Verbs 364

What's the Point of Verbs?	365
One Student Writer's Response	366
Identify the Three Basic Tenses of Verbs	366
Identify Regular and Irregular Verbs in the Past Tense	367
Regular Verbs in the Past Tense	367
Irregular Verbs in the Past Tense	368
Differentiate Key Verbs in the Past Tense: *To Have, To Do, To Be*	370
Identify the Purpose of the Past Participle	371
Past Participles of Regular Verbs	372
Past Participles of Irregular Verbs	373
Use the Present Perfect Tense (*Has* or *Have* and the Past Participle)	376
Use the Past Perfect Tense (*Had* and the Past Participle)	378
Use the Passive Voice (*To Be* and the Past Participle)	380
Distinguish among Three Commonly Confused Helping Verbs: *Can, Could, Would*	382
Editing Assignments MyWritingLab™	385
Academic Learning Log MyWritingLab™	386

CHAPTER 20
Subjects, Verbs, and Simple Sentences 388

What's the Point of Subjects, Verbs, and Simple Sentences?	389
One Student Writer's Response	390
Identify Types of Subjects	390
Identify Types of Verbs	392
Linking Verbs	392
Action Verbs	393
Helping Verbs	394
Compose the Simple Sentence	395
Distinguishing between a Fragment and the Simple Sentence	395
Locate Subjects and Verbs to Identify Complete Thoughts	397
Understand the Prepositional Phrase	397
Find the Prepositional Phrases	397
The FIL Process	398
Editing Assignments MyWritingLab™	400
Academic Learning Log MyWritingLab™	401

CHAPTER 21
Compound and Complex Sentences 402

What's the Point of Compound and Complex Sentences?	403
One Student Writer's Response	404
Recognize Types of Clauses: Independent and Dependent	404
Compose a Compound Sentence	405
Three Ways to Combine Independent Clauses into a Compound Sentence	405
Compose a Complex Sentence	409
Placement and Punctuation of a Dependent Clause within a Complex Sentence	412
Compose a Compound-Complex Sentence	414
Editing Assignments MyWritingLab™	417
Academic Learning Log MyWritingLab™	419

PART 5 Editing the Basic Sentence

CHAPTER 22
Editing Run-ons: Comma Splices and Fused Sentences — 420

- What's the Point of Editing Comma Splices and Fused Sentences? — 421
  - One Student Writer's Response — 422
- Identify Comma Splices and Fused Sentences — 422
- Identify Five Ways to Edit Comma Splices and Fused Sentences — 424
- Editing Assignments MyWritingLab — 435
- Academic Learning Log MyWritingLab — 437

CHAPTER 23
Editing Fragments into Sentences — 438

- What's the Point of Editing Fragments? — 439
  - One Student Writer's Response — 440
- Recognize the Difference Between a Sentence and a Fragment — 440
- Edit or Revise to Correct Seven Types of Fragments — 442
  - Phrase Fragments — 442
  - Clause Fragments — 450
- Editing Assignments MyWritingLab — 456
- Academic Learning Log MyWritingLab — 457

CHAPTER 24
Editing Misplaced and Dangling Modifiers — 458

- What's the Point of Editing Misplaced and Dangling Modifiers? — 459
  - One Student Writer's Response — 459
- Edit Misplaced Modifiers — 460
- Edit Dangling Modifiers: Two Revision Tips — 462
- Editing Assignments MyWritingLab — 466
- Academic Learning Log MyWritingLab — 467

CHAPTER 25
Editing for Subject-Verb Agreement: Present Tense — 468

- What's the Point of Editing for Subject-Verb Agreement? — 469
  - One Student Writer's Response — 470
- Understand the Basics of Subject-Verb Agreement — 470
- Create Subject-Verb Agreement Using *To Have, To Do, To Be* — 472
- Create Subject-Verb Agreement Using Subjects Separated from Verbs — 476
- Create Subject-Verb Agreement Using Singular or Plural Subjects — 477
  - Create Subject-Verb Agreement Using Indefinite Pronouns — 477
  - Create Subject-Verb Agreement Using Collective Nouns — 479
  - Create Subject-Verb Agreement Using *Either-Or/Neither-Nor* — 480

Create Subject-Verb Agreement Using Fractions, Titles, and Words Ending in –s ... 482
Create Subject-Verb Agreement Using Subjects after Verbs ... 483
Create Subject-Verb Agreement Using Relative Pronouns ... 485
Editing Assignments MyWritingLab™ ... 487
Academic Learning Log MyWritingLab™ ... 489

PART 6 Revising to Improve Expression

CHAPTER 26
Revising for Sentence Variety ... 490

What's the Point of Sentence Variety? ... 491
   One Student Writer's Response ... 491
Vary Sentence Purpose ... 492
   Four Purposes for Sentences ... 492
Vary Sentence Types by Combining Ideas ... 493
   Combine Two or More Simple Sentences into One Simple Sentence ... 494
   Combine Ideas Using Compound and Complex Sentence Types ... 503
Vary Sentence Openings ... 504
   Adverb ... 504
   Prepositional Phrase ... 504

Vary Sentence Length ... 505
Editing Assignments MyWritingLab™ ... 507
Academic Learning Log MyWritingLab™ ... 509

CHAPTER 27
Revising for Sentence Clarity: Person, Point of View, Number, and Tense ... 510

What's the Point of Sentence Clarity? ... 511
   One Student Writer's Response ... 512
Use Consistent Person and Point of View ... 512
   Three Points of View ... 512
   Illogical Shift in Person ... 513
Use Consistent Number ... 515
   Illogical Shift in Number ... 515
Use Consistent Tense ... 516
   Illogical Shift in Tense ... 517
Editing Assignments MyWritingLab™ ... 521
Academic Learning Log MyWritingLab™ ... 523

CHAPTER 28
Revising for Parallelism ... 524

What's the Point of Parallelism? ... 525
   One Student Writer's Response ... 526
Use Parallel Words ... 526
Use Parallel Phrases ... 528
Use Parallel Clauses ... 529

Punctuate for Parallelism	532
Editing Assignments MyWritingLab™	535
Academic Learning Log MyWritingLab™	537

CHAPTER 29
Revising for Effective Expression — 538

What's the Point of Effective Expression?	539
One Student Writer's Response	540
Use Concise Language	540
Use Active and Positive Language	543
Use Concrete Language	545
Use Creative Expressions: Similes and Metaphors	548
Use Fresh Language	549
Editing Assignments MyWritingLab™	552
Academic Learning Log MyWritingLab™	553

PART 7 — Punctuation and Mechanics

CHAPTER 30
The Comma — 554

What's the Point of Commas?	555
One Student Writer's Response	556
Use Commas with Items in a Series	556
Use Commas with Introductory Elements	557
Use Commas to Join Independent Clauses	557
Use Commas with Parenthetical Ideas	558
Use Commas with Nonessential and Essential Clauses	558
Use Commas with Appositives	559
Use Commas with Dates and Addresses	560
Identify Other Uses of the Comma	560
Editing Assignments MyWritingLab™	562
Academic Learning Log MyWritingLab™	563

CHAPTER 31
The Apostrophe — 564

What's the Point of the Apostrophe?	565
One Student Writer's Response	566
Use the Apostrophe to Show Ownership	566
Use the Apostrophe to Form Contractions	568
Recognize Common Misuses of the Apostrophe	568
Editing Assignments MyWritingLab™	569
Academic Learning Log MyWritingLab™	571

CHAPTER 32
Quotation Marks — 572

What's the Point of Quotation Marks?	573
One Student Writer's Response	574
Follow General Guidelines for Using Quotation Marks	574
Format and Punctuate Direct Quotations	575
Punctuating Direct Quotations	575
Format and Punctuate Dialogue	576
Applying Appropriate Formatting	577

Use Direct and Indirect Quotations	578
Punctuate Titles	579
Editing Assignments MyWritingLab™	580
Academic Learning Log MyWritingLab™	581

CHAPTER 33
End Punctuation: Period, Question Mark, and Exclamation Point — 582

What's the Point of End Punctuation?	583
One Student Writer's Response	584
Use the Period	584
Use the Question Mark	585
Use the Exclamation Point	586
Hints for Use of Exclamation Points	586
Editing Assignments MyWritingLab™	587
Academic Learning Log MyWritingLab™	589

CHAPTER 34
Capitalization — 590

What's the Point of Capitalization?	591
One Student Writer's Response	591
Rule 1: Capitalize the first word of every sentence.	592
Rule 2: Capitalize the pronoun *I*.	592
Rule 3: Capitalize the first letter of the first words in written greetings and salutations (for example, *Dear friends*, or *Best regards*).	592
Rule 4: Capitalize principal words in titles of publications.	593
Rule 5: Capitalize the first letters in all essential words in proper nouns.	594
Rule 6: Capitalize the first letter of the title of a person when the title precedes the person's name.	595
Rule 7: Capitalize proper adjectives. Proper adjectives are formed from proper nouns.	595
Editing Assignments MyWritingLab™	596
Academic Learning Log MyWritingLab™	597

CHAPTER 35
Improving Your Spelling — 598

What's the Point of Improving Your Spelling?	599
One Student Writer's Response	599
Five Steps to Improve Your Spelling	600
1. Use a Spell Checker	600
2. Use a Dictionary	600
3. Use Mnemonics	601
4. Track Spelling Errors	601
5. Use the Writing Process to Improve Your Spelling	602
Rules for Improving Your Spelling	602
Recognize Vowel and Consonant Patterns	602
Understand How Suffixes Are Used	602
Add *–s* or *–es* to Nouns and Verbs to Form the Plural	604
Double the Final Consonant in Words with One Syllable	604
Double the Final Consonant in Words with More Than One Syllable	604
Drop or Keep the Final *E*	605
Change or Keep the Final *Y*	605
Understand How Prefixes Are Used	606
Choose *ie* or *ei*	606
Recognize and Correct Commonly Misspelled Words	607
Editing Assignments MyWritingLab™	608
Academic Learning Log MyWritingLab™	609

PART 8 Reading Selections

What's the Point of Reading to Write? 611

Effective Strategies for Responding to Reading Selections 612
- How to Annotate a Text 612
- How to Write a Summary 613
- A Reading Strategy for a Writer 614

Nineteen Reading Selections 615

Description
Niagara Falls
Rupert Brooke 615

Maya Lin's Design Submission to the Vietnam Memorial Competition
Maya Lin 618

Narration
Latino Heritage Month: Who We Are . . . And Why We Celebrate?
Luis J. Rodriguez 620

Confessions
Amy Tan 623

Process
Managing Stress in College
Rebecca J. Donatelle 625

Camping Out
Ernest Hemingway 629

Illustration
Don't Call Me a Hot Tamale
Judith Ortiz Cofer 632

Football's Bloodiest Secret
Buzz Bissinger 634

Classification
The Fundamentals of Forgiveness
D. J. Henry 636

I Am Enough
Melissa Guitron 640

Comparison–Contrast
The Talk of the Sandbox; How Johnny and Suzy's Playground Chatter Prepares Them for Life at the Office
Deborah Tannen 643

The Loss of Juárez: How Has the Violence in Juárez Changed Border Culture?
Sergio Troncoso 647

Definition
What is Poverty?
Jo Goodwin-Parker 650

Cool at 13, Adrift at 23
Jan Hoffman 653

Cause–Effect
Through Young Eyes
Michael S. Malone 655

Why We Crave Horror Movies
Stephen King 658

Persuasion
Nobel Lecture—The Nobel Peace Prize 2014
Malala Yousafzai 660

Hungry vs. Healthy: The School Lunch Controversy
Bonnie Taub-Dix 665

Argument
Can Virtual Classrooms Beat Face-to-Face Interaction?
Libby Page 667

Text Credits 670
Photo Credits 671
Index 673

Introducing the *Writing for Life* Series

Writing for Life, a two-book series consisting of both a sentences and paragraphs book and a paragraphs and essays book, answers the question students often ask about why they should learn to write well—"What's the point?" *Writing for Life* does more than motivate students; it teaches them to take charge of their own learning and helps them transfer the strategies they currently apply to reading visuals to the tasks of reading and writing text.

New to This Edition of *Writing for Life* . . .

More Grammar Exercises

- In response to reviewer requests, our grammar exercises have been expanded to offer more opportunities to apply their skills through additional exercises. The exercises for punctuation and mechanics now appear in MyWritingLab for easy student access and completion.

- The grammar chapters have been reorganized to move students from basic sentence-level concerns to issues of style. This new, more-natural progression makes content both easier to find and easier to assign in sequence.

New Readings

- Seven new readings have been added to Part 8, including "Niagara Falls by Rupert Brooke, "Managing Stress in College" by Rebecca J. Donatelle, "The Fundamentals of Forgiveness" by D. J. Henry, "Cool at 13, Adrift at 23" by Jan Hoffman, "Nobel Peace Prize Lecture, 2014" by Malala Yousafazai, "Hungry vs. Healthy: The School Lunch Controversy" by Bonnie Taub-Dix, and "Can Virtual Classroom Beat Face-to-Face Interaction?" by Libby Page.

- Three student writers contributed paragraphs to illustrate the patterns of organization.

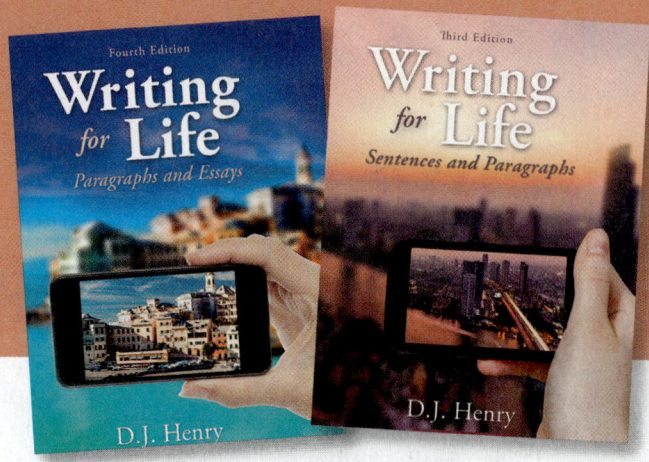

New Supporting Media and Deeper MyWritingLab Integration

- New videos on the writing process, the reading process, and creating portfolios help students with different learning styles understand these key concepts.

- Our two chapter-closing activities, "Writing Assignments" and "Academic Learning Logs," can now be completed in MyWritingLab and sent directly to instructors' gradebooks.

- The *Writing for Life* MyWritingLab etext course now contains an appendix on portfolio creation and use.

Streamlined Approach to Learning Outcomes

- The learning outcomes now appear on the first page of every chapter and tie directly to the headings in the chapter. These learning outcomes help students focus on the key skills that they will develop in the chapter, and provide them with a measure to test their mastery.

- Unit Review exercises enable students to test their mastery of each learning outcome in that Unit. These Unit Review exercises are available in MyWritingLab.

Modified Design

- *Writing for Life*'s revolutionary design has been tweaked to appear more sophisticated where appropriate and easier to digest at-a-glance.

Features of Writing for Life

How Does Writing for Life Effectively Motivate and Prepare Students for Success?

The focus of Writing for Life is apparent in the comprehensive and systematic approach to learning it provides by motivating and preparing students; engaging students with high-interest topics and meaningful visuals; establishing purpose and clear statements of learning objectives; offering relevant applications; and meeting today's students where they are.

WHAT'S THE POINT? is a motivational teaching strategy that addresses the basic question on most students' minds: *Why do I need to know this?* The question and the instructional answer establish the student writer's purpose for studying the chapter. Sample student responses in think-aloud format model critical thinking.

OVERALL INSTRUCTIONAL VOICE establishes a clear, direct, respectful tone that honors adult learners.

EMPHASIS ON ACTIVE LEARNING motivates students to become active learners who assume responsibility for their learning, who reflect upon their progress, and who can and will improve their writing skills.

WRITING ASSIGNMENTS create realistic writing situations that direct students to consider audience and purpose as they employ the writing process. Additional assignments provide topics and situations relevant to "Everyday Life," "College Life," and "Working Life." These Writing Assignments can also be completed online through MyWritingLab.com.

HIGH-INTEREST TOPICS such as tattoos, stress, obesity, eating disorders, pop culture icons, fashion, movies, music, relationships, natural disasters, heroes, and current events engage student interest and foster self-expression.

How Does Writing for Life Engage Students with Illustrations and Visuals?

HIGH-INTEREST VISUALS stimulate interest, clarify concepts, and facilitate student responses. Several visuals are brought to life with new animations accessible through the MyWritingLab/etext course.

PHOTOGRAPHIC ORGANIZERS activate the thinking process, introduce and illustrate a pattern of organization, and stimulate prewriting activities. A set of photographs is arranged in a concept map that illustrates the structure of a particular pattern of organization.

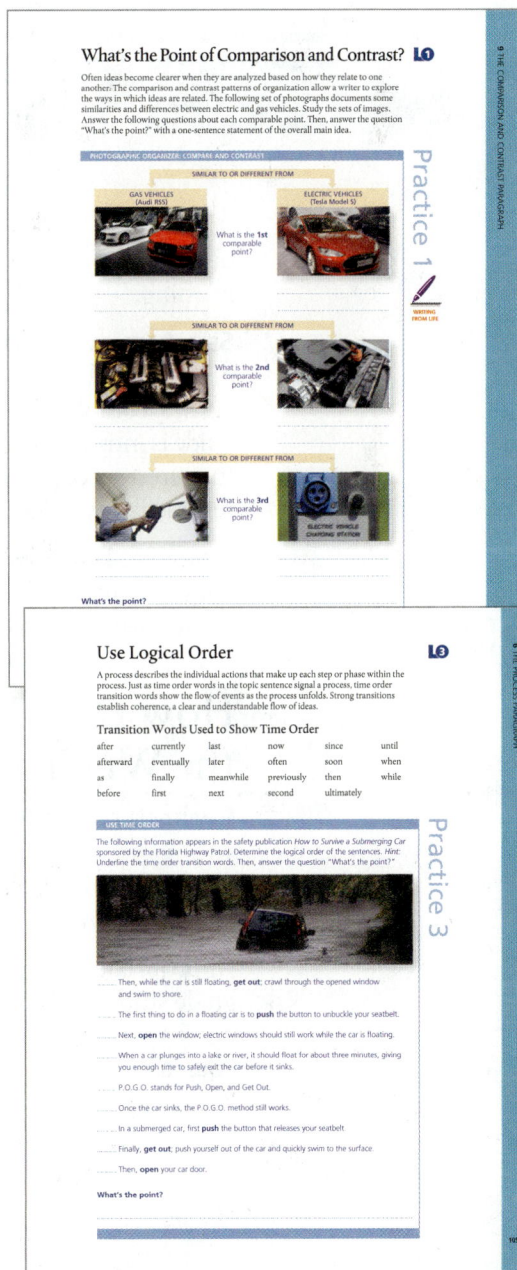

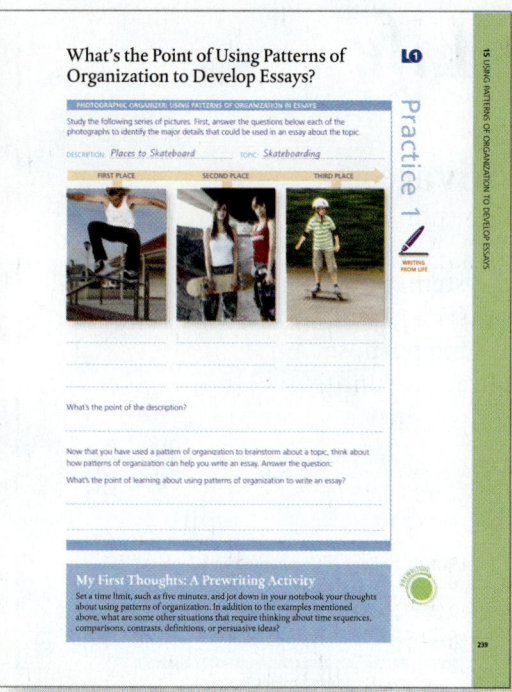

VISUAL LEARNING ACTIVITIES introduce and facilitate writing assignments; concept maps, charts, graphs, and annotated examples enable students to "see" the concept clearly.

VISUAL INSTRUCTION offers annotated visuals with color-coded highlights that make key concepts jump off the page. Concepts and rules are further defined, explained, and illustrated with charts and graphs.

How Does *Writing for Life* Provide Students with Purpose and Core Learning Objectives (Outcomes)?

LEARNING OUTCOMES are statements that specify what learners will know or be able to do as a result of a learning activity.

PREPARING YOURSELF TO LEARN ABOUT WRITING in Chapter 1 teaches students to evaluate their attitudes, identify learning outcomes, generate a study plan, and create a portfolio that helps them "to track growth . . . organize work . . . and think about" their learning and their writing. Simple and easy-to-follow advice guides students to use checklists, reflective questions, and journal entries as they think about their writing and what they are learning.

SELF-ASSESSMENT TOOLS AND GUIDES include learning outcomes, reflective questions, behavior and attitude surveys, guidelines, checklists, scoring rubrics, and journal entries, complete with examples and explanations. For example, a paragraph scoring guide is introduced and explained and followed by a practice that asks students to score a set of paragraphs using the scoring guide. These activities transfer the responsibility of learning and assessment of learning to the student.

ACADEMIC LEARNING LOGS are end-of-chapter activities that tests students' comprehension of the chapter's instruction. These activities can be completed online at MyWritingLab.com.

How Does *Writing for Life* Engage Students with the Writing Process?

EMPHASIS ON THE PROCESS is embedded in instruction throughout the textbook. The writing process is introduced and illustrated in Chapter 2 with a two-page spread of a four-color graphic with explanations of the entire writing process: Prewriting, Drafting, Revising, and Editing.

Appropriate writing process icons appear throughout the textbook as signals to guide students through the writing process of particular assignments. Additionally, book-specific writing process videos can be found within the MyWritingLab/etext course.

WORKSHOP: WRITING A PARAGRAPH STEP BY STEP guides students one step at a time through the writing process from prewriting to editing, and each phase is highlighted with a writing process icon, so students know what they are doing at each point in the process, how they are to do it, and why it is important.

THE WRITING SITUATION is explained and illustrated in Chapter 2 in discussions and engaging activities about how the relationships among topic, audience, and purpose impact the creation of a piece of writing. Writing prompts are realistic writing situations based on everyday life, college life, and working life. These writing prompts stimulate role playing and critical thinking skills and illustrate the importance of *Writing for Life*.

DIRECT INSTRUCTION follows a logical order to best ensure comprehension and foster student ownership of the material. Each lesson moves systematically through three distinct phases: before learning activities, during learning activities, and after learning activities. Before, during, and after learning activities make excellent portfolio entries that foster student self-assessment.

TEXT STRUCTURE is covered extensively at every level, including word, sentence, paragraph, and essay levels. Lessons systematically guide students to consider the types and structures of words, phrases, and sentences; patterns of organization; levels of ideas; traits and function of a main idea; major supporting details; minor supporting details; parts of the paragraph; and parts of the essay. Writing prompts encourage students to adapt text structure to realistic writing situations.

How Does *Writing for Life* Drive Grammar Instruction and Key Applications to Connect with Today's Student?

STUDENT MOTIVATION, always vital, seems to be even more crucial when it comes to mastering grammatical concepts. Unfortunately, too many times, grammar instruction is met with apathy and dread. Grammar has purpose. It's worth the effort to learn it. The purpose of instruction is to foster confidence and mastery. The core features of this text—designed to inspire and motivate—have been adapted to match the nature of instruction for grammatical concepts.

GRAMMATICAL CONCEPTS are comprehensively covered in an approach that combines an illustrated handbook with intensive practice. Examples are clearly annotated visuals with color-coded highlights that make key concepts jump off the page.

GRAMMAR IN ACTION directly addresses some of the most commonly occurring errors in student writing. A specific common error is discussed in the context of a particular pattern of organization. In the last phase of the step-by-step instruction of the Workshop, students study a

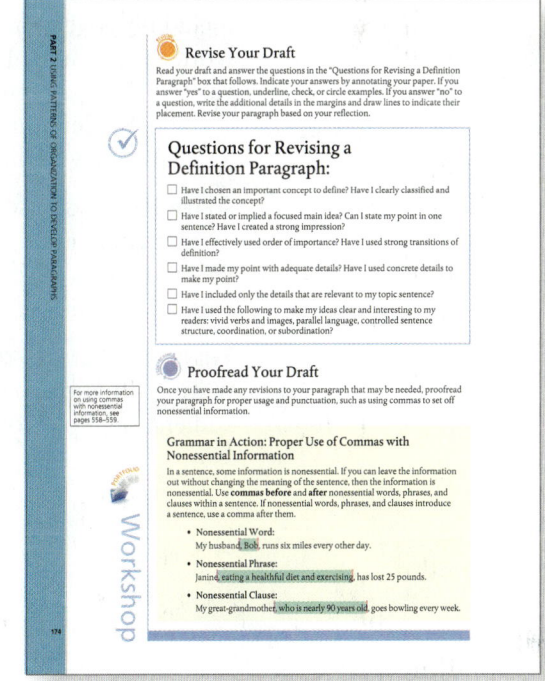

grammatical concept and then proofread and edit a sample piece of writing to ensure correct application of the concept. The correlation among chapters and grammar concepts are as follows:

Chapter 4	Descriptive	Dangling and Misplaced Modifiers
Chapter 5	Narrative	Unnecessary Shifts in Verb Tense
Chapter 6	Process	Eliminating Fused Sentences
Chapter 7	Example	Using Commas in a Series
Chapter 8	Classification	Eliminating Comma Splices
Chapter 9	Comparison/Contrast	Commas after Introductory Elements
Chapter 10	Definition	Commas with Nonessential Information
Chapter 11	Cause/Effect	Commonly Confused Words
Chapter 12	Persuasion	Consistent Use of Point of View

Reading Selections

We know that reading enhances our ability to write well. Therefore, the major emphasis within the in-book reader is the connection between reading and writing.

UNDERSTANDING THE CONNECTION BETWEEN READING AND WRITING This section opens with an attitude and behavior survey that asks students to reflect about their individual reading and writing experiences. Then, it explains the benefits a writer gains from reading, illustrates in a chart the similarities between reading and writing, and offers a practice that models the connection between reading and writing skills. Finally, the section closes by emphasizing the thinking processes students can use to make the connection between reading and writing. Students learn how to annotate a text, summarize a text, and read like a writer.

READING SELECTIONS include 19 high-interest essays, both contemporary and classical, as models of effective writing. Topics cover a wide range of subjects including poverty, culture, careers, and race relations. All reading selections include word count, Grade Level, and Lexile score. The tone and purpose of these essays vary and include distinctive voices such as Amy Tan, Stephen King, and Deborah Tannen. Students are directed to annotate the text and maintain a vocabulary journal of new or difficult terms they encounter.

AFTER READING DISCUSSION QUESTIONS: MEANING, STRUCTURE, AND EXPRESSION focus student attention on four basic traits of an essay: Central Idea, Relevant Details, Logical Order, and Effective Expression. Many of the activities associated with each reading can be completed in the MyWritingLab/etext course.

THINKING PROMPTS TO MOVE FROM READING TO WRITING offer two fully developed writing situations based on the reading. These prompts ask students to consider audience and purpose as they form a response to what they have read.

Developmental Writing Resources

Instructor's Manual for *Writing for Life: Paragraphs and Essays* (0-13-396038-2), by Steve Yarborough, is a practical supplement useful in any classroom setting. The *Instructor's Manual* includes a summary of each chapter as well as sample syllabi to assist with designing a course around *Writing for Life: Paragraphs and Essays*. There is also a complete discussion of how to use each chapter in the classroom, including supplementary assignments and class discussions.

Test Bank for *Writing for Life: Paragraphs and Essays* (0-13-396023-4), by Steve Yarborough, contains multiple-choice and true/false questions designed to test each student's comprehension of every chapter.

See the Instructor's Manual for a complete listing of supplements available for *Writing for Life*.

BREAK THROUGH
To improving results

MyWritingLab™ Online Course (access code required) for *Writing for Life, Paragraphs and Essays* 4e, by D. J. Henry

MyWritingLab is an online practice, tutorial, and assessment program that provides engaging experiences for teaching and learning.

MyWritingLab includes most of the writing assignments from your accompanying textbook. Now, students can complete and submit assignments, and teachers can then track and respond to submissions easily—right in MyWritingLab—making the response process easier for the instructor and more engaging for the student.

Respond to Student Writing with Targeted Feedback and Remediation

MyWritingLab unites instructor comments and feedback with targeted remediation via rich multimedia activities, allowing students to learn from and through their own writing.

Writing Help for Varying Skill Levels

For students who enter the course at widely varying skill levels, MyWritingLab provides unique, targeted remediation through personalized and adaptive instruction, freeing up more class time for actual writing.

NEW! Learning Tools for Student Engagement

Learning Catalytics
Generate class discussion, guide lectures, and promote peer-to-peer learning real-time analytics using Learning Catalytics—an interactive student response tool that uses students' smartphones, tablets, or laptops to engage them in more sophisticated tasks and thinking.

MediaShare
MediaShare allows students to post multimodal assignments easily—whether they are audio, video, or visual compositions—for peer review and instructor feedback. In both face-to-face and online course settings, MediaShare saves instructors valuable time and enriches the student learning experience by enabling contextual feedback to be provided quickly and easily.

Direct Access to MyLab

Users can link from any Learning Management System (LMS) to Pearson's MyWritingLab. Access MyLab assignments, rosters and resources, and synchronize MyLab grades with the LMS gradebook. New direct, single sign-on provides access to all the personalized learning MyLab resources that make studying more efficient and effective.

Visit www.mywritinglab.com for more information.

Acknowledgments

The publication of a text like this requires the effort and sacrifice of many people. I would like to begin with a heartfelt expression of appreciation for the Pearson English team. *Writing for Life* has afforded me the opportunity to work with and learn from a talented group of people. I thank the editorial team for giving me the opportunity to partner with Dorling Kindersley (DK), whose design so beautifully appeals to visual and verbal learners. Matt Wright, Executive Editor, is a wonderful partner to whom I am indebted and grateful. I have been fortunate to work with developmental editor, Erin Dye. I also extend my deepest gratitude to Heather Brady, whose contributions to this series as writer and editor are of immeasurable value.

I would like to acknowledge the production team for *Writing for Life* beginning with Kathy Smith from Cenveo, Inc., who served as copyeditor and project coordinator. I am also grateful to Ellen MacElree and Donna Campion, Production Managers. And I would like to acknowledge Dustin Weeks, Senior Professor of Library Sciences, Daytona State College, for his contributions of writing samples for student activities, and Steve Yarborough, Bellevue Community College, for composing the Instructor's Manual. I wish to thank the following students for the honor of working with them; I am so proud of their contributions to this edition: Hannah Davis, Joshua Hartzell, and Kuei-Ti Lu.

Finally, I would like to gratefully recognize the invaluable insights provided by the following colleagues and reviewers. I deeply appreciate their investment of time, energy, and wisdom: **Terry Clark**, *City Colleges of Chicago*; **Nelda Contreras**, *Brookhaven College*; **Jay Lewenstein**, *Imperial Valley College*; **Tim Parrish**, *Rockingham Community College*; **Kimberly Pope**, *South Mountain Community College*; **Libby Stapleton**, *Angelina College*; **Vanessa G. Uriegas**, *Southwest Texas Junior College*; **Kelly Wilkes**, *Columbus Technical College*; **William M. Young**, *Oglala Lakota College*.

I would also like to continue to thank the reviewers of past editions for their insights and advice: **Wes Anthony**, *Cleveland Community College*; **Nina Bannett**, *New York City College of Technology CUNY*; **Liz Barnes**, *Daytona State College—Main*; **Carolyn Barr**, *Broward College*; **Craig Bartholomaus**, *MCCKC—Penn Valley*; **Elisabeth Bass**, *Camden County College*; **Kathleen Beauchene**, *Community College of Rhode Island*; **Nicholas Bekas**, *Valencia Community College*; **Tina L. Bennett**, *Wichita State University*; **James Bernarducci**, *Middlesex Community College*; **Linda Black**, *St. John's River Community College—Orange Park*; **Kay Blue**, *Owens Community College*; **Randy Boone**, *Northampton Community College*; **Brad Bostian**, *Central Piedmont Community College*; **Patricia Bostian**, *Central Piedmont Community College*; **Aaron Bradford**, *American River College*; **Kathy Britton**, *Florence Darlington Technical College*; **Tracy Brunner**, *Broward Community College*; **Jeff Burdick**, *Willow International College Center*; **Cheryl Cardoza**, *Truckee Meadows Community College*; **Jessica Carroll**, *Miami Dade College—Wolfson*; **Cynthia Cash**, *Southwest Tennessee Community College*; **Gail Harrison Charrier**, *Delaware Technical and Community College*; **Karen Chow**, *DeAnza College*; **Terry Clark**, *Kennedy-King College*; **Jennifer M. Condon**, *Iowa Central Community College*; **Kennette Crockett**, *Malcolm X College*; **Susan Cunningham**, *Ohlone College*; **Kathy Daily**, *Tulsa Community College*; **Sharon Davidson**, *Baton Rouge Community College*; **Nancy Davies**, *Miami Dade College—Homestead*; **Brenda K. DelMaramo**, *Thiel College*; **Marjorie Dernaika**, *Southwest Tennessee Community College*; **Denise Diamond**,

College of the Desert; **Marianna Duncan,** *Angelina College;* **Cynthia M. Dunham-Gonzalez,** *Seminole Community College;* **Marie G. Eckstrom,** *Rio Hondo College;* **Margot A. Edlin;** *Queensborough Community College, CUNY;* **Kim Edwards,** *Tidewater Community College;* **Cheryl Elsmore,** *Antelope Valley College;* **Gwyn Enright,** *San Diego City College;* **Laurie Esler,** *Southern Wesleyan University;* **Cathy Fagan,** *Nassau Community College;* **Karen Feldman,** *Seminole Community College;* **Robert Ficociello,** *SUNY Albany and Middlesex Community College;* **Catherine Fraga,** *Sacramento State University;* **Deborah Fuller,** *Bunker Hill Community College;* **Paul T. Gallagher,** *Red Rocks Community College;* **Maria Garcia-Landry,** *Palm Beach Community College—North;* **Lois Garrison,** *Tacoma Community College;* **Tom Ghering,** *Ivy Tech Community College of Indiana;* **Wendy Goodwin,** *Miami Dade College—Homestead;* **James Gray,** *St. Petersburg College;* **Jeremy L. Griggs,** *Lewis & Clark Community College;* **Judy Haisten,** *Central Florida Community College;* **Denise Haley,** *Bunker Hill Community College;* **Cynthia Halstead,** *Broward Community College;* **Beth Hammett,** *College of the Mainland;* **Greg Hammond,** *New Mexico Junior College;* **Anna Harrington,** *Jackson State Community College;* **Beth Hashemzadeh,** *Bluefield State College;* **Julia I. Hoesel,** *Iowa Central Community College;* **Ken Holliday,** *Southern State Community College;* **Tai L. Houser,** *Broward College—North;* **Kalpana M. Iyengar,** *St. Mary's University;* **Richard Johnson,** *Kirkwood Community College;* **Peter Kearly,** *Henry Ford Community College;* **Christine Kling,** *Broward College—South;* **Helene Kozma,** *Housatonic Community College;* **Catherine Lally,** *Brevard Community College—Cocoa;* **Valerie Lazzara,** *Palm Beach Community College—Lake Worth;* **Angela Leeds,** *Brevard Community College;* **Reginald Lockett,** *San Jose City College;* **Erin Lofthouse,** *City College of San Francisco;* **Dana Thiry Dildine Lopez,** *Eastern New Mexico University-Ruidoso;* **John Luukkonen,** *TCI College of Technology;* **Joseph Marshall,** *Villa Julie College;* **Erin T. Martz,** *Northern Virginia Community College;* **Carl Mason,** *UMass Lowell;* **Anna Masters,** *Brookhaven Community College;* **Dr. James S. May,** *Valencia Community College—East;* **Charlene McDaniel,** *Cincinnati State Technical and Community College;* **Diane McDonald,** *Montgomery County Community College;* **Judy McKenzie,** *Lane Community College;* **David Merves,** *Miami Dade College, North Campus;* **John Miller,** *Normandale Community College;* **Rosemary Mink,** *Mohawk Valley Community College;* **Kelley Montford,** *Colorado Technical University;* **Dave Moutray,** *Kankakee Community College;* **Andrea Neptune,** *Sierra College;* **Julie Nichols,** *Okaloosa–Walton College;* **Sandra Offiah,** *Daytona State College—Main;* **Kelly Ormsby,** *Cleveland State Community College;* **Elizabeth Patterson,** *Melton–Delta State University;* **Jay Peterson,** *Atlantic Cape Community College;* **Dawn Pickett,** *Blinn College;* **Diane L. Polcha,** *Tulsa Community College, Southeast Campus;* **Jesus Quintero,** *DeAnza College;* **Jennifer Ratcliff,** *North Central Texas College;* **Brian L. Reeves,** *Tomball College;* **Dana Resente,** *Montgomery County College;* **Charlotte Teresa Reynolds,** *Indiana State University Southwest;* **Leigh Ann Rhea,** *Calhoun Community College;* **Doug Rigby,** *Lehigh Carbon Community College;* **Elizabeth Robbins,** *University of Alaska Southeast;* **Tina Royer,** *Folsom Lake College;* **Brian Ruffino,** *Brookhaven Community College;* **Sara Safdie,** *University of California, San Diego;* **Rebecca Samberg,** *Housatonic Community College;* **Justina M. Sapna,** *Delaware Technical and Community College–Owens;* **Lisa Sapra,** *Folsom Lake College;* **Tracy Schneider,** *Solano Community College;* **Albert C. Sears,** *Silver Lake College;* **Cherise Shane,** *Community College of Philadelphia;* **Sharon Shapiro,** *Naugatuck Valley Community College;* **Deneen Shepherd,** *St. Louis Community College, Forest Park;* **Rachel Shreve,** *Palm Beach Community College—North;* **Carmen Simpson,** *St. Petersburg College—Clearwater;* **Cynthia J. Spence,** *College of the Desert;* **Jac-Lyn Stark,** *Bunker Hill Community College;* **James Suderman,** *Okaloosa-Walton College;* **Holly J. Susi,** *Community College of Rhode Island;* **Chae Sweet,** *Hudson County Community College.* **Nanette Tamer,** *Villa Julie College;* **Etheline Thomas,** *Delaware Technical & Community College—Wilmington;* **Joseph W. Thweatt,** *Southwest Tennessee Community College;* **Tara Timberman,** *Rowan University;* **Trisha Travers,** *Penn State University—Abington;* **Thomas Treffinger,** *Greenville Technical College;* **Sharisse Turner,** *Tallahassee Community College;* **Christopher Z. Twiggs,** *Florida Community College at Jacksonville;* **Cynthia M. VanSickle,** *McHenry Community College;* **Linda VanVickle,** *St. Louis Community College–Meramec;* **Maria Villar-Smith,** *Miami Dade College—Wolfson;* **Kymberli G. Ward,** *Southwestern Oklahoma State University;* **Michael T. Warren,** *Maple Woods Community College;* **Jeff Westfall,** *Skyline College;* **Kathleen G. White,** *Bellevue Community College;* **Margie Wilkoff,** *St. Petersburg College;* **Rachael Williams,** *West Georgia Technical College;* **Jilani Worsi,** *Queensborough Community College;* **Elizabeth Zarubin,** *City College of San Francisco.*

PART 1
GETTING READY TO WRITE

1 Preparing to Learn about Writing

LEARNING OUTCOMES

After studying this chapter you will be able to:

① Answer the question "What's the Point of Preparing to Learn about Writing?"

② Adopt the Attitude of Learning

③ Create a Study Plan

④ Connect Writing and Reading

⑤ Use the Reading Process to Strengthen Your Writing

⑥ Use the Flow of Reading-Writing Interaction to Strengthen Your Writing

⑦ Create a Portfolio of Your Work

In countless situations in life, preparation is essential to success.

Even a trip to the grocery store requires some planning in order to get all the items necessary to feed a family and run a household in the most economical way. A careful shopper may create a menu, check the pantry and make a list of what is needed, read the ads for sale items, or clip coupons. In short, an effective shopper thinks about the outcome or goal of each shopping trip before going shopping.

Just as a wise shopper prepares to shop, a wise student writer prepares to learn about writing. Writing is an essential life skill, and learning to write well allows you to express yourself, influence others, succeed in college, and compete in the job market. By starting your academic career with this writing course, you are preparing for success. You are laying a sturdy foundation for writing for life. If you are like many others, you may have a few qualms about writing, but take heart! With the right attitude, an understanding about the connection between reading and writing, and a study plan, you *can* learn to write well. Get ready to learn about writing!

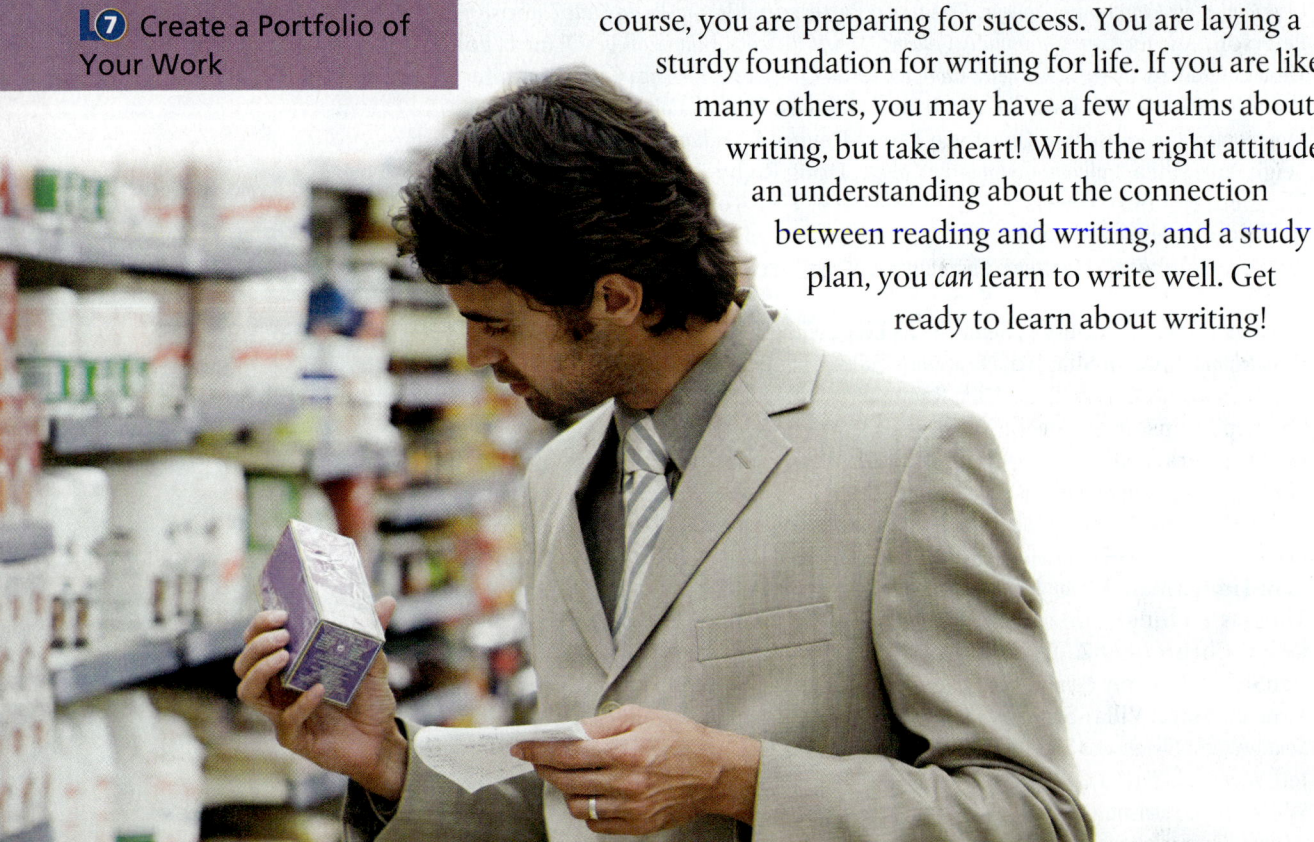

What's the Point of Preparing to Learn about Writing?

Like any other worthwhile endeavor, learning requires preparation. Preparation usually involves selecting a goal, adopting an attitude for success, setting aside time to accomplish the task, gathering tools or supplies, and planning a course of action.

PHOTOGRAPHIC ORGANIZER: PREPARING TO LEARN

The following pictures represent one student's effort to prepare to learn about writing. Write a caption for each photograph that identifies her efforts to prepare to learn.

What is this?

What is this?

What is this?

What is this?

What's the point?

WRITING FROM LIFE

One Student Writer's Response

The following paragraph records one student's efforts to prepare to learn about writing. As you read the paragraph, underline specific steps he took that you might use as well.

Prepared to Learn

(1) I began preparing to learn about writing on the first day of class. (2) First, I read the course syllabus, which listed the books and materials I needed; later that day, I bought everything listed, and I brought everything I needed with me to every class. (3) I found three people who wanted to learn as much as I did so we formed a study group. (4) We helped each other a lot throughout the whole semester. (5) If one of us was sick, we made sure he or she got the notes and assignment for that day, and we read each other's papers to make sure they made sense and didn't have any careless errors. (6) I also used a daily planner to record assignments and set aside time to study and write. (7) I arrived a few minutes early when possible, so that when class began, I was prepared to get to work. (8) I have to admit I had to work on my attitude. (9) I was so shy and afraid of sounding silly that asking questions in class was really hard, so for a while, I stayed after class to ask my questions, but eventually, I gained enough confidence to ask them during class. (10) I also had to learn how to deal with feedback on my papers. (11) I worked so hard on each essay, yet for a long time, my papers came back to me with grades and edits that showed I still needed to improve. (12) It took a while for my hard work to pay off, but I was determined to succeed. (13) I am proud to say, all my preparation and hard work paid off. (14) Not only did I earn an "A," but I also improved my ability to write.

As you prepare to learn about writing, take some time to evaluate yourself as a student writer. Think about your attitude, ways you can become an active learner, your relationship with your teacher, your study plan, and how you will track your growing writing abilities. The more you reflect and the more you prepare, the more likely you are to learn about writing and to become an effective writer.

Adopt the Attitude of Learning

Use Positive Self-Talk

Many people have negative thoughts going through their minds that constantly repeat "I can't" phrases: "I can't write… I can't spell." Often these attitudes are the result of a prior negative event. A basic step to success is changing that script in your head. Replace "I can't" thoughts with "I can." Then, take steps to prove that you can. For example, instead of believing "I just can't spell," think, "I can use a spell checker," or "I can make a list of words I often misspell and memorize their correct spellings." Success begins in your mind!

Be an Active Learner

Come to class. Be on time. Sit where you can see—and be seen. Take notes. Ask questions. Do your work—on time! Make connections between assignments and learning outcomes. Apply what you learn. Seek help. Find a study partner. Take responsibility for your own learning. The more you do, the more you learn!

Trust Your Teacher

One of the toughest tasks in a writing class is accepting feedback on your writing. Think of feedback as a form of coaching from a personal trainer. A personal trainer assesses your strengths and needs, creates an exercise program, and corrects your form to ensure that you make progress. Likewise, your teacher is your writing coach who offers expert advice. So accept feedback as helpful advice. Take note of those errors, study the rules, and revise your work. Turn feedback into an opportunity to learn!

ADOPT THE ATTITUDE OF LEARNING

Read the following reflection written by a student that records how she feels about writing and why. On a separate sheet of paper, write a letter to the student, giving advice to help her overcome her anxiety.

> The very thought of writing an essay and turning it in for a grade makes my stomach churn. I have pretty painful memories of writing classes. In one class, the teacher gave my paper back by handing it to the person in the front of the row to pass back. Everyone in my row got to see the large red "D" at the top of my paper and all the red marks pointing out each one of my errors. I never could bring myself to read the comments, and I was too embarrassed to ask questions. It didn't seem to matter, anyway because I just can't write.

L3 Create a Study Plan

A vital part of preparing to learn about writing is creating a study plan.

Gather Your Tools

Foster success by preparing a study place that is equipped with all the tools you will need: reference materials such as your textbook, a dictionary, a thesaurus, magazines, newspapers, and other reading materials of interest to you; pens (blue or black ink), pencils, and paper; a stapler and a 3-hole punch. Optional items include a computer and a printer. In addition, you will need a 3-ring binder to hold the teacher's syllabus, handouts, assignments, class notes, textbook notes, and lab work. Be sure that you bring your textbook, binder, pens, and pencils to class every day.

Set Goals

Students who set goals reduce stress, improve concentration, and increase self-confidence. Use the following guidelines to set effective goals. *Aim high:* Demand your best effort. *Write goals down:* Recording goals makes them clear and important. *Be specific:* Instead of writing "Stop procrastinating," write "Study English on Monday, Tuesday, and Wednesday evenings between 7 and 9 o'clock." *Be positive:* Instead of writing "Don't make stupid errors," write "Use commas properly." *Set priorities:* Rank goals based on need so you can pace your work. *Set daily goals based on larger goals:* Break a larger goal such as "Understand how to use semicolons" into a series of steps such as "Study the rule, take notes, and do the exercises; then, proofread my paper for proper use of semicolons."

Take Action

Turn your goals into action steps by setting up a time schedule for your study. The following study plan is easy to use and flexible, and it will help you set long-term, intermediate, and short-term goals.

SAMPLE STUDY PLAN	
Long-Term Schedule:	Record ongoing weekly commitments such as job hours, class meetings, church, and so on, for the entire semester.
Intermediate Schedule:	Make a short list of the events taking place and the tasks to be completed in your class (or classes) this week. Make a fresh list each week, as these activities will change from week to week: Writing assignment Tuesday; Math quiz Tuesday; Chapter 3 in English by Wednesday.
Short-Term Schedule:	Make a to-do list on your smartphone every morning (or the night before), listing your daily schedule. Be specific! Then, check off each goal as you accomplish it. Monday: 9:00–9:30 Revise writing assignment; 12:00–12:30 Review math for quiz; 3:30 Return books to library; 7:00–9:00 Read first 30 pages of Chapter 3 for English.

Practice 3

CREATE A STUDY PLAN

Complete the following chart to create your own study plan. Discuss your plan with your class or in a small group. How will your plan change throughout the semester?

MY STUDY PLAN	
Long-Term Schedule:	
Intermediate Schedule:	
Short-Term Schedule:	

Practice 4

ADOPT THE ATTITUDE AND BEHAVIORS OF LEARNING

Complete the survey. Then, on your own paper, answer the following question: "What can you do to improve your writing attitude or behaviors?"

Writing Attitude and Behavior Survey	Strongly Agree	Agree	Disagree	Strongly Disagree
1. I enjoy writing.				
2. I respond to teacher feedback.				
3. I enjoy sharing what I write with peers.				
4. I appreciate the chance to revise.				
5. I want to improve my writing.				
6. I have a quiet, well-equipped study place.				
7. I always come to class prepared.				
8. I complete assignments on time.				
9. I read and study to improve my writing.				
10. I manage my time wisely.				

L04 Connect Writing and Reading

Writing and reading are closely related thinking processes. Writing is the process of expressing meaning with written symbols. Reading is the process of getting meaning from written symbols. A writer (author) sends a message, and a reader (audience) receives a message. An effective writer thinks about what the reader needs to know. An effective reader thinks about the writer's purpose. Thus, writing and reading rely on and strengthen each other. Reading and writing work together as an ongoing exchange of information.

The Reading-Writing Cycle: Exchange of Information

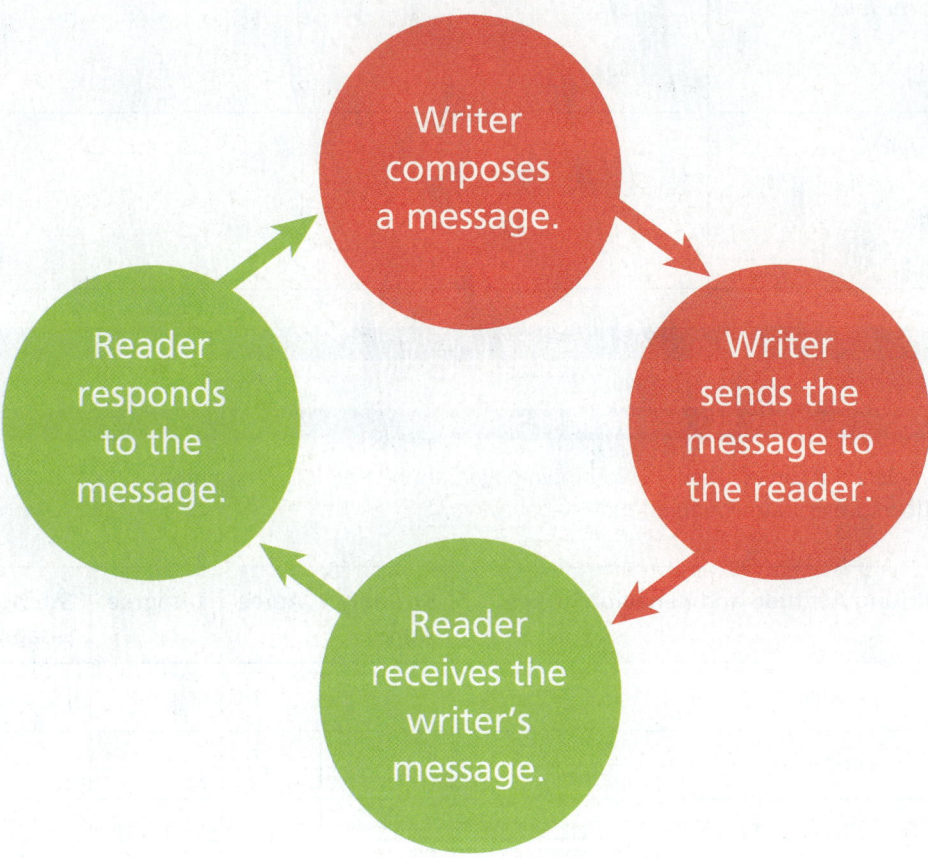

Reading benefits a writer in many ways. For example, by reading, a writer gains the following:

- New vocabulary
- Different opinions on a topic
- Details that support an opinion
- Varying ways to apply writing techniques
  - Ways to use fresh or creative expressions
  - Ways to organize ideas

The more you read, the more you know and the more you have to write about.

A major similarity between reading and writing is that each is a thinking process best accomplished in specific stages. Careful thought before, during, and after reading a selection or writing a piece improves your ability to do both. The following chart correlates the stages of the reading and the writing processes.

The Thinking Process Connects Reading and Writing		
Thinking	Reading	Writing
Before	**Preread:** Ask questions and skim the text; note headings, words in bold or italics, or graphics; predict the author's audience, purpose, and point.	**Prewrite:** Ask questions and skim details to discover your audience, purpose, and point for writing; read for information to use in your writing.
During	**Read:** Comprehend the writer's purpose and point with the use of key words, main ideas, and supporting details. **Apply fix-up strategies:** Use context clues to understand new words; reread a few sentences or a paragraph; make a mental picture of the point.	**Draft:** Express your purpose and point through the use of key words, main ideas, and supporting details. **Revise:** Rephrase or reorganize ideas to clearly support your point; help readers to see your purpose and point; use details to create a mental picture for your reader.
After	**Reflect and Record:** Adjust your views based on new information gained through reading; write in response to what you have read; restate the writer's main points; agree or disagree with what you have read.	**Edit and Publish:** Create an error-free draft that expresses your new insights and skills as a writer.

CONNECT WRITING TO READING

In your notebook, describe the process you use to write. Then, describe the process you use to read. Discuss the following questions with a peer or in a small group.

1. How are your processes similar to or different from the ones described in the chart?

2. How can you use the connection between reading and writing to improve as a writer?

Practice 5

L5 Use the Reading Process to Strengthen Your Writing

Watch the Video on mywritinglab.com

Reading is a thinking process composed of a series of phases. The process is recursive; that is, the reader may loop or combine any of the stages at any point during the process. The following graphic illustrates the highly recommended **SQ3R** reading process.

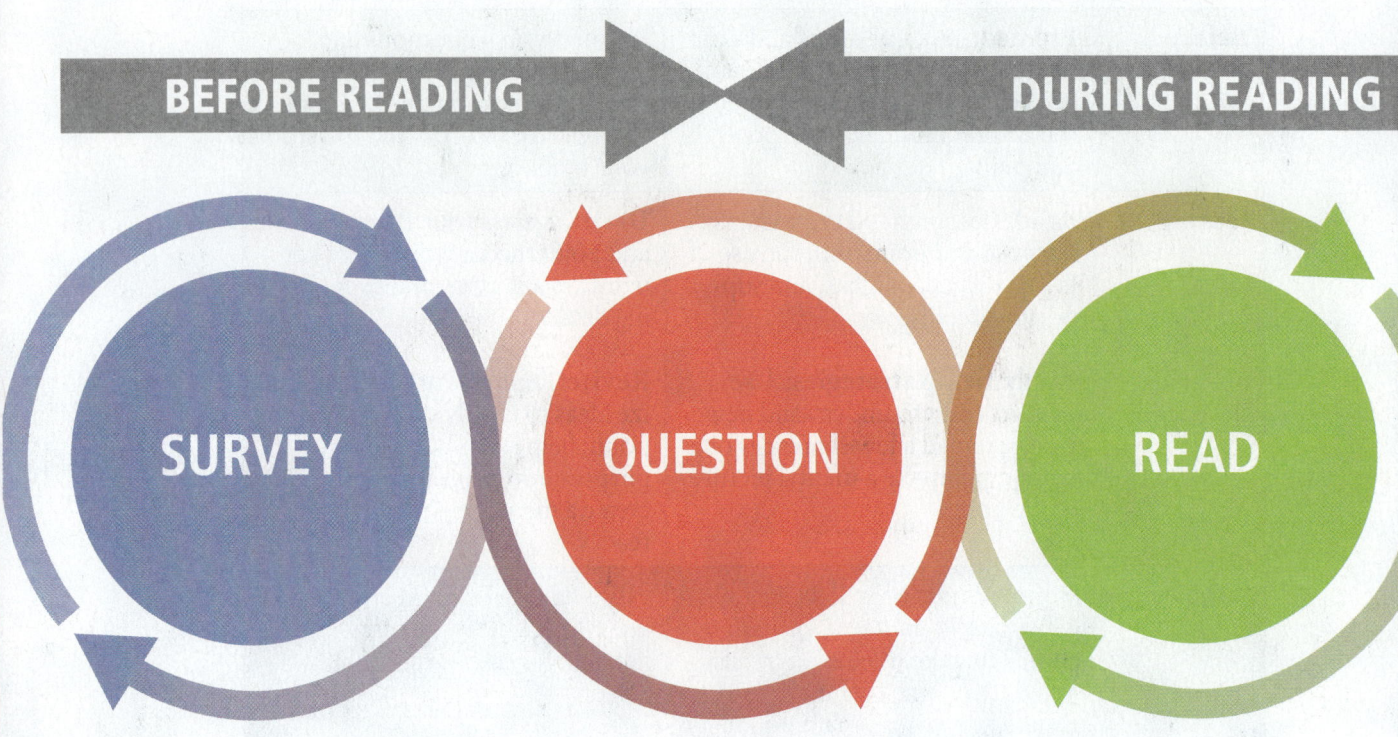

BEFORE READING → ← **DURING READING**

SURVEY — Skim the selection to note the following: titles, sub-headings, key terms in bold or italic type, graphics, pictures.

QUESTION — Ask the following: What is the topic? What do I already know? What is the author's purpose? How are the ideas organized? What is my purpose for reading?

READ — Read to answer questions; adjust pace based on difficulty; reread to understand.

Practice 6

CONNECT WRITING TO READING

Go to the reading selection on page 643 in Part 8. Assume you are taking a college class in business, and you have been assigned this reading as part of your required work. In addition, your professor has indicated this material will be covered in an essay question on the unit exam. As you read the selection, follow the steps for SQ3R as listed in the graphic. Then, write a paragraph that states the author's most important ideas. Write a second paragraph that records your personal opinion about what you have read.

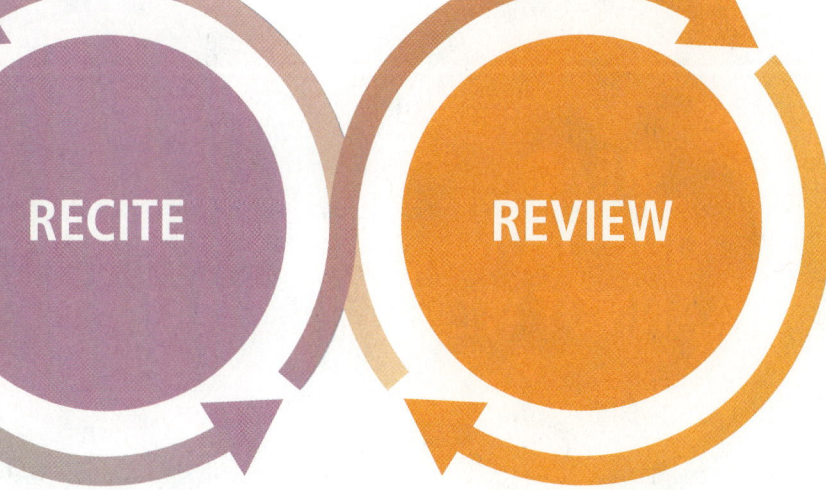

AFTER READING

RECITE: Annotate the text; underline main ideas; circle key terms; record questions and short summaries in margins; restate ideas out loud.

REVIEW: Review questions based on headings; review new words; connect new ideas to prior knowledge; write a response.

CONNECT WRITING TO READING

Working with a peer or small group of classmates, answer the following questions:

1. How is each chapter in *Writing for Life* based on SQ3R?
2. How will using SQ3R to study this textbook help you improve as a writer?
3. Besides this textbook, what else can you, as a writer, read?
4. As a writer, how would you use SQ3R to get information from a magazine or newspaper?
5. How could you use SQ3R to edit a peer's paper?

Practice 7

L6 Use the Flow of the Reading-Writing Interaction to Strengthen Your Writing

Watch the Video on mywritinglab.com

In the next chapter you will learn in depth about the writing process, and throughout the rest of the textbook, you will apply the writing process to your own writing. As you learn and apply the writing process, your writing will benefit if you use the flow of the interaction between reading and writing. At times, your professor may ask you to respond in writing to an assigned reading. At other times, you may choose to read independently to seek out ideas for your own writing. The following graphic and text suggest how to use the flow of the interaction between reading and writing. Also keep in mind that you can use the flow between reading and writing as a way to study this or any other textbook.

A Reading/Writing Strategy

PREREAD: SURVEY/QUESTION → **READ: QUESTION/ANNOTATE** → **PREWRITE: RECITE/REVIEW/BRAINSTORM**

Preread: Survey/Question

- Create questions based on a survey of titles, headings, bold/italic terms, and visuals.

Ask:

- What is my prior knowledge of this topic?
- What is my purpose for reading?
- Who is the intended audience?

Read: Question/Annotate

- Continue to ask/record questions.
- Underline main ideas.
- Circle new or key words.
- Highlight key supporting details.
- Restate ideas out loud.

Ask:

- What prior knowledge can I use to make inferences about the text's meaning?
- What evidence allows me to make those inferences?

Prewrite: Recite/Review/Brainstorm

List, cluster, or outline topics based on your survey; leave room to fill in details during reading. Record predicted answers.

- Freewrite to analyze prior knowledge, purpose for reading, and audience.
- Freewrite a first response to the text.
- Take notes/Recite ideas: Record main ideas in your own words.
- Add supporting details from the reading to the list, cluster, or outline of key topics.
- Brainstorm/list topics from the reading to respond to in writing.
- Identify the intended audience of your writing.
- Compose an outline of ideas for your written response.

DRAFT YOUR RESPONSE

REVIEW AND REVISE YOUR DRAFT

PROOFREAD

Draft
- Read your annotated text.
- Freewrite a response based on the completed list, cluster, or outline of key topics and details.
- Compose a thesis statement for your response.
- Compose an introduction, body, and conclusion of your response to the reading.

Review and Revise Your Draft
- Review your draft for clear use of wording, details, and organization.
- Annotate your draft with needed revisions.
- Rewrite your draft based on your review and annotations.

Proofread
- Reread your draft to identify/correct errors.
- Annotate your draft with needed corrections.
- Create and publish a polished draft.

USE READING TO STRENGTHEN YOUR WRITING

Work with a group of peers. Predict ways you can use the interaction between reading and writing to strengthen your writing.

Practice 8

L7 Create a Portfolio of Your Work

To ensure that you learn about writing and to develop writing skills, you need to track your strengths, your needs, and your growth. A portfolio enables you to organize your work and think about what you are learning.

What Is a Portfolio?

A portfolio is a collection of **all** the work you do as a writer organized in a notebook or electronic folder. Your portfolio shows your hard work and your growth because its contents document how much time and effort you put into your writing. A portfolio allows you to assess your own strengths, needs, and goals.

What Should I Include in My Portfolio?

Your portfolio may include class notes and activities, textbook notes and exercises, grammar tests, lab activities, reflective journal entries, and drafts of your writing. By collecting and organizing your work, you are better able to reflect upon your strengths and needs. As a result, you are able to achieve specific learning outcomes as a writer. For example, to prove mastery of the writing process, you should file in your portfolio all the prewrites, drafts, and final copies of your writings. In addition, the lessons, practices, workshops, and learning logs in this textbook are tied to specific learning outcomes. The heading of each practice identifies its learning outcome. The learning activities in *Writing for Life* are excellent entries for your portfolio.

What Is a Reflective Journal Entry?

Reflective journal entries are tied to the idea of "self-evaluation." In this type of journal entry, you reflect upon your "writing process" and your "writing progress." A reflective journal entry is an informal piece of writing in which you analyze some aspect of your work as a student writer. In each of the chapters about writing paragraphs, you will read a writer's journal that records this kind of thinking. By writing your own reflective journal entries, you can track and overcome your writing barriers.

Reflective Journals: Self-Assessment

Critical Thinking Questions

To deepen your critical thinking about the feedback you have received, your reflective journal entry should also answer the following questions:

- [ ] What steps did I take to write this piece? Did I prewrite, write, revise, and proofread? Do I need to spend more time on any one step?

- [ ] Which of my errors are proofreading errors? What steps will I take to catch these proofreading errors on my next piece of writing?

- [ ] Which of these errors results from the need to study a certain rule? Where can I find this rule? How much time do I need to learn this rule? How will I study this rule (take notes, complete exercises)?

What Is the Best Way to Set Up My Portfolio?

Many students purchase a 3-ring binder and tabbed dividers to section off different types of study and writing tasks. Be sure to date and label all work. You can also collect your writing files in organized folders on your computer.

All work that is turned in for feedback should include the following information: At the top of the first page and flush with the left margin, place your name, your professor's name, the course name or number (include the section number if the course has multiple sections), and the date you're turning in the paper, each on a separate line with double-spacing throughout.

> Iama Writer
>
> Dr. Richards
>
> ENC 001: Section 32
>
> September 24, 2015

All independent work that is created for your notebook or portfolio should be labeled with the date and by the type of work or learning outcome.

Oct. 9, 2015 Outcome: Self-Evaluation
Reflective Journal Entry for Narrative Paragraph

Oct. 10, 2015 Outcome: Structure, Reading-Writing
Comma Splices, Chapter 22, pp. 422–437

Oct. 12, 2015 Outcome: Structure, Reading-Writing
The Process Paragraph, Class notes

The point of labeling is to help you see and discuss your strengths, needs, and growth as they occur in real time.

Practice 9

CREATE A PORTFOLIO OF YOUR WORK: REFLECTIVE JOURNALS

Create a reflective journal entry for your portfolio. Think critically about your prior writing experience by answering the following questions. Describe what you actually do as a writer, not what you think others expect you to do.

1. What types of writing do you compose (such as text messages, Facebook postings, tweets, e-mails, academic essays, and so on)?

2. What steps do you usually take when you write an academic essay?

3. Do you take the same steps to write a text, posting, tweet, e-mail, and academic essay? Why or why not?

4. Based on your prior experience (such as teacher feedback on essays or grammar tests), what are your most common or recurring grammar errors?

5. How often do you read, and what do you usually read (textbooks, newspapers, magazines, blogs, fiction books, websites, and so on)?

6. If you do not read often, explain why.

Practice 10

CREATE A PORTFOLIO OF YOUR WORK

Write an e-mail to a classmate who was absent. Explain the portfolio process. Explain how portfolio assessment will improve your writing skills.

Academic Learning Log: Chapter Review

QUESTIONS FOR PREPARING TO LEARN ABOUT WRITING

To test and track your understanding of what you have studied, answer the following questions.

1. What are some of the materials and supplies needed by a writing student?

2. What are the three attitudes of learning discussed in this chapter?

3. What three general steps can you take to create a study plan?

4. What are the four phases of exchanging information in the reading-writing cycle?

5. What is the reading process represented by SQ3R?

6. What is a portfolio?

7. What is included in a portfolio?

8. What is a reflective journal entry?

Complete the Post-test for Chapter 1 in MyWritingLab.

2 Thinking Through the Writing Process

LEARNING OUTCOMES

After studying this chapter you will be able to:

L1 Answer the question "What's the Point of the Writing Process?"

L2 Assess the Writing Situation: Topic, Audience, and Purpose

L3 Use the Writing Process: Prewrite, Draft, Revise, and Proofread

The writing process has four stages: prewriting, drafting, revising, and proofreading.

Writing develops, records, and communicates your thoughts to other people. Careful writers rely on the writing process to discover, organize, and record information in response to a specific writing situation.

What's the Point of the Writing Process?

The following photographs document some of the situations in which we use writing in our everyday, college, and working lives. Write a caption for each picture that includes a reason for writing well in that situation. Then, state the point of writing well.

PHOTOGRAPHIC ORGANIZER: REASONS TO WRITE

WRITING FROM LIFE

What's the point of writing well?

My First Thoughts: A Prewriting Activity

Set a time limit, such as five minutes, and jot down in your notebook your thoughts about the importance of writing. Do not let your pen or pencil stop, even if you must repeat ideas. Keep writing until the time limit is up.

One Student Writer's Response

The following paragraph is one writer's response to the question "What's the point of writing?"

> Writing is important for several reasons. Everyone knows you have to write a lot in college, so having strong writing skills means you learn more and earn higher grades. Writing is also important on the job. A manager or business owner has to write all kinds of reports and letters. You have to write to make sense and make yourself look good to your customers. In everyday life, strong writing skills can help you say what you mean without being misunderstood. Nowadays, with text messages, e-mails, and Facebook, you are always writing something. So you have to be able to think fast and not write things that could ruin your reputation. Also, in everyday life, you can post a comment to an online article or write a letter to the editor of a newspaper.

L2 Assess the Writing Situation: Topic, Audience, and Purpose

When you write, you develop a point about a topic to fulfill a purpose for a specific audience. To develop your point, you need to think about two aspects of writing: the writing situation and the writing process.

A piece of writing develops in response to a specific **writing situation** that is composed of the **topic** (your subject), the **purpose** for writing (your goal), and the **audience** (your reader).

TOPIC — What you write
AUDIENCE — Who reads your writing
PURPOSE — Why you write

The Topic: What You Write

When writing about situations in our personal lives, we may choose to compose a letter of complaint to a business or an e-mail to a friend. Often in these circumstances, the topic of our writing naturally emerges from our need to communicate. However, when writing for college, many of us face writer's block in our search for a topic. You can break through writer's block by building a topic bank for college writing.

The following thinking guide can help you generate a bank of topics.

The Writing Situation Step by Step:
Topic

Build a bank of topics by listing ideas in a special section in your notebook. Use the following prompts to create several lists:

- [ ] Write down the major topics of importance in a specific course (such as biology, psychology, history).
- [ ] Find interesting or important current events.
  - [ ] Topics most often covered in magazines and newspapers
  - [ ] Controversial topics from television (such as news and talk shows)
  - [ ] Topics about which you want to learn more
  - [ ] Topics about which you feel deeply
  - [ ] Hobbies and personal interests
- [ ] Share your lists with your classmates; use class discussion to generate more ideas.
- [ ] Review and expand your list on a regular basis.

As you continue to build your bank of general topics, read, read, and read some more. Read newspapers, magazines, and textbooks for additional topics. Many textbooks provide writing topics at the end of sections or chapters; in addition, headings and subheadings of chapters or sections are excellent sources of topics for your writing.

ASSESS THE WRITING SITUATION: TOPICS

Skim a newspaper, a magazine, and a textbook and write a list of five topics from each one. Then, share your list with your class or in a small group.

TOPICS FROM A NEWSPAPER: _____

_____

TOPICS FROM A MAGAZINE: _____

_____

TOPICS FROM A TEXTBOOK: _____

_____

The Purpose: Why You Write

Good writing focuses on a goal or purpose. Your writing will flow much more easily when you write with purpose. The following chart presents four basic purposes for writing.

Informative

When writing informatively, your purpose is to share, explain, or demonstrate information.

EXAMPLE:
An **informative essay** that explains the steps of photosynthesis to your reader; a paragraph that answers an exam question about the major causes of stress.

Persuasive

When writing persuasively, your purpose is to change your reader's opinion or call your reader to take action.

EXAMPLE:
An **argumentative essay** that convinces your reader to begin a physical fitness program; a letter to the editor that argues in favor of a law that bans texting while driving.

Expressive

When writing expressively, your purpose is to share with the reader your personal opinions, feelings, or reactions to a topic.

EXAMPLE:
An **expressive piece**—a poem, short story, or personal essay, for example—that expresses your view about a social problem such as poverty or drug abuse.

Reflective

When writing reflectively, your purpose is to record your understanding about what you have experienced or learned.

EXAMPLE:
An **informal essay** that explores what you think is significant about a current event; a journal entry that discusses the strengths of a paper written by you or a peer.

The following thinking guide can help you identify your purpose in writing.

> ## The Writing Situation Step by Step:
> ### Purpose
> - [ ] Annotate the lists in your topic bank to indicate possible purposes for each topic: Beside each one write **I** for informative, **P** for persuasive, **E** for expressive, or **R** for reflective.
> - [ ] Generate four sets of topics based on different purposes for writing, using "The Writing Situation Step by Step: Topic" box on page 21 to guide your thinking.
> - [ ] Select one topic for each of the four purposes and complete the following statements:
>   - [ ] This topic will inform the reader about…
>   - [ ] This topic will persuade the reader to…
>   - [ ] This topic will express…
>   - [ ] This topic will reflect upon…

Practice 3

ASSESS THE WRITING SITUATION: PURPOSE

State the purpose of each of the following topic sentences. Discuss with your class or in a small group how a writer's purposes may be combined in certain situations.

1. My experience and education make me an excellent candidate for this job.

2. Adult stem cell research should be funded by the government.

3. The gentle breeze, the lapping water, and the dappled shade soothe the human soul.

4. Eating disorders fall into several categories based on their symptoms.

5. Based on my unit exam, I need to review the following topics.

The Audience: Who Reads Your Writing

When we take part in a conversation, we know exactly to whom we are speaking, and we adjust our tone, word choice, and examples to match the situation. For example, contrast how you talk with a friend with the way you talk to the dean of your college. Audience has the same impact in the writing situation.

Assume that you have chosen to write about the topic of marijuana. What main points do you want each of the following audiences to consider about this drug? Use the blanks below each picture to record your ideas.

The following thinking guide can help you identify your audience.

The Writing Situation Step by Step:
Audience

- [ ] Choose a specific topic and purpose for writing.
- [ ] List the traits of your audience that are relevant to your topic and purpose:
  - [ ] Age
  - [ ] Gender
  - [ ] Education level
- [ ] If you are writing for a general audience of mixed traits, identify the main traits most relevant to your topic and purpose.
- [ ] Identify three or four points about the topic of most interest to a specific audience.
- [ ] Choose several key words to describe your topic and hook the interest of a specific audience. Use a thesaurus to find the words best suited for your audience.

ASSESS THE WRITING SITUATION: AUDIENCE

Based on your first thoughts about the audiences represented by the four pictures on page 24, write a brief response to the following questions. Then, discuss your answers with your class or in a small group.

- What are the most important traits of each audience represented by the pictures?
- Did your main points differ based on the audience? Why or why not?
- Will your word choice or examples differ based on the audience? Why or why not?

Practice 5

ASSESS THE WRITING SITUATION: AUDIENCE

Each of the following four pieces of writing appeals to one of the audiences depicted by the photos on this page. Write the letter of the piece of writing in the picture that shows its audience.

A. Scientists funded by the National Institute on Drug Abuse (NIDA), a federal government agency, have found that the damage to the brain's thinking abilities that results from smoking marijuana can last up to 28 days after an individual last smoked the drug.

B. Marijuana use today starts at a younger age—also, today stronger forms of the drug are available to you. Marijuana use is a serious threat—do not use it!

C. Under the influence of marijuana, you can forget your best friend's phone number, watch your grade point average drop like a stone, or get into a car accident.

D. Welcome to the Mothers Against Drugs speaker series. During today's speaker panel, we'll investigate the fascinating facts about marijuana. You may have heard it called pot, weed, grass, ganja, or skunk, but marijuana by any other name is still a drug that affects the brain.

When student writers are asked "Who is your audience?" most reply, "The teacher." Of course, the teacher is your immediate audience, and you must carefully consider his or her expectations. However, many teachers understand the value of writing to a real-life audience. College is preparing you for success in life. You are learning to write for life.

ASSESS THE WRITING SITUATION: TOPIC AND AUDIENCE

The following writing prompts apply an academic topic to a real audience.

Write the name of the college course(s) for each prompt and describe the traits of each audience. Discuss your answers with your class or in a small group. Talk about how each audience affects the writer's choice of words and details.

1. Write a letter to the editor of a newspaper that supports or opposes a political candidate.

COURSE(S): ....

AUDIENCE: ....

....

2. Write a report for the school board that explains the benefits of smaller class sizes.

COURSE(S): ....

AUDIENCE: ....

....

3. Write an e-mail to a classmate explaining the five steps for problem solving.

COURSE(S): ....

AUDIENCE: ....

....

4. Write a memo to a new, young employee at a fast food restaurant that explains how the cost of his insurance is based on his age.

COURSE(S): ....

AUDIENCE: ....

....

L3 Use the Writing Process: Prewrite, Draft, Revise, and Proofread

Writing is a process that comprises a series of phases or steps. The process approach focuses on the writer, the way writing is produced, and how the writer can improve his or her personal writing process. The process approach is recursive; the writer may loop or combine any of the stages at any point during the writing process. The key outcome at the end of the process is a published piece of writing. Throughout each stage, think about the relationships among your topic, purpose, and audience.

PREWRITE — Plan or rehearse

DRAFT — Get ideas down in a preliminary form

During the prewriting stage, you create a plan for your piece of writing.

This phase of writing is made up of the following steps:

- Decide on a topic.
- Determine your purpose for writing.
- Gather information.
- Generate details by using clusters, lists, and freewrites.
- Organize the details into an outline.

The rest of this chapter covers specific prewriting techniques.

During the drafting stage, you create a draft of your writing.

This phase may include the following steps:

- Determine who is your audience.
- Choose a format (such as an essay or a letter).
- Create an introduction, body, and conclusion for longer pieces.

Chapters 3–12 guide you through the entire writing process as you learn how to write paragraphs.

REVISE
Take another look at your work

PROOFREAD
Prepare the piece for publication

PUBLISHING

During the revision phase, you fine tune the ideas in your essay. After you have written a draft, allow some time to pass so that you can examine your writing with fresh eyes.

This phase includes the following steps:

- Delete details that are not relevant.
- Add details to ideas that need more support.
- Reorder ideas for clarity.
- Insert transitions between details for a smooth flow of ideas.
- Replace vague or weak words with vivid, strong words.
- Write a new draft if necessary.

Parts 5 and 6 cover specific skills to consider while revising.

Watch the Video on mywritinglab.com

During the editing phase of the writing process, you polish your draft so your reader will not be distracted or confused by careless errors.

This phase includes correcting errors such as:

- fragments
- fused sentences
- shift in tenses
- spelling
- punctuation

Part 7 covers the skills to consider during editing.

Watch the Video on mywritinglab.com

Prewrite

Have you ever stared at a clean sheet of paper with a blank mind, unable to think of how to start a writing task? Or, have you ever had so many ideas that they jumble up in chaos so that you can't even begin to write? Finding those first few words to put on paper can grind a writer's thinking process to a complete halt and cause writer's anxiety.

Some level of anxiety about writing is often a sign that you care about doing well. However, in excess, writer's anxiety can become a barrier. The first step to overcoming writer's anxiety is to understand why you feel anxious and how your anxiety affects your writing. Identifying the causes and effects of your writer's anxiety makes it easier to overcome.

▲ Students writing an exam

Practice 7

USE THE WRITING PROCESS: PREWRITE BY SELF-EVALUATION OF WRITER'S ANXIETY

Complete the following survey to identify the causes and effects of your writer's anxiety. Then in your writer's journal, discuss the following: your level of writer's anxiety; the main causes of your anxiety; the main effects of your anxiety on your writing.

Causes of Writer's Anxiety	High/Often			Low/Never		
I worry about my grade.	6	5	4	3	2	1
Deadlines make me nervous.	6	5	4	3	2	1
I feel pressure to excel.	6	5	4	3	2	1
I fear failure.	6	5	4	3	2	1
I am competitive by nature.	6	5	4	3	2	1
I am distracted by my personal life or social issues.	6	5	4	3	2	1
My professor seems intimidating.	6	5	4	3	2	1
The writing assignment seems irrelevant or boring.	6	5	4	3	2	1
In the past, I have received harsh criticism on my writing.	6	5	4	3	2	1
Effects of Writer's Anxiety						
I put off writing assignments until the last minute.	6	5	4	3	2	1
I get writer's block and cannot think of ideas.	6	5	4	3	2	1
I am unable to understand the writing assignment.	6	5	4	3	2	1
I think about my anxiety more than I do the assignment.	6	5	4	3	2	1
I turn in assignments late or not at all.	6	5	4	3	2	1

Even the best writers experience writer's anxiety now and then. Although no cure-all for writer's anxiety exists, prewriting fuels thinking, triggers the writing process, and fires past the block. Experienced writers have learned to spend time thinking about what they are going to write before they begin drafting.

In general, writing occurs long before you pick up your pen or your fingers touch the keyboard. **Prewriting** includes reading, listening, discussing, and thinking about your topic before you write a rough draft, capturing your prewriting thinking on paper. It allows you to explore ideas and plan your strategies without worrying about polishing them.

> **Prewriting** is the act of generating, exploring, developing, and roughly organizing ideas. Prewriting can help you choose a topic, narrow a topic, and put details related to a topic in logical order.

The rest of this section guides you through five prewriting techniques:

- Asking Questions:
    The Reporter's Questions
    Reflective Questions
- Freewriting
- Listing
- Concept Mapping
- Outlining

As you write for life, try out each one. Combine a few to stretch your thinking. Experiment with all of them. Discover which one(s) best suit you as a writer or in a particular writing situation.

Asking Questions

Asking questions helps you identify a topic and develop details about it based on thoughtful insights. Asking and answering questions helps you discover both what you already know and what you need to learn about the topic. Your goal as a writer is to share a point or main idea about a topic. Usually, a main idea or point is made up of the topic and the writer's opinion about the topic. Two types of questions enable you to explore topics and your opinions about those topics: the reporter's questions and reflective questions.

THE REPORTER'S QUESTIONS

To describe a newsworthy event, effective reporters gather the facts by asking six basic questions:

- Who?
- What?
- When?
- Where?
- Why?
- How?

At first, the answers to these questions may help you identify and narrow a topic that grabs your interest; once you have narrowed your topic, these questions also yield many details of support for your topic.

REFLECTIVE QUESTIONS

Reflective questions also help you discover your purpose for writing by revealing your attitude toward a topic. By using these questions to reflect, identify, and add your opinion about a topic to your writing, you can also narrow a writing topic that is too general.

Although reflective questions will vary based on the writing topic, the following three questions are good examples of some reflective questions that you can use to explore your views about most topics.

- What is the significance of this topic?
- Who should be interested in this topic?
- How can I best express my point to those who do not agree with me?

Asking and answering questions before writing will also guide you to make logical decisions about which details to select and highlight when you do begin to write.

Practice 8

USE THE WRITING PROCESS: PREWRITE BY REFLECTION ON TOPIC AND AUDIENCE

Assume you are writing a report on the power of propaganda for a social science class. Discuss the following poster designed to address a proposal by an oil company to drill offshore near Daytona Beach, Florida. Use the reporter's questions and reflective questions to brainstorm your first thoughts.

Reporter's Questions:

Who is the intended audience of the poster?

What is the relationship between this image and the issue?

How might offshore drilling pose dangers or benefits?

Reflective Questions:

What do I need to know about offshore drilling?

Should propaganda be used to influence the public?

When you are ready to explore ideas about a topic on paper, the following thinking guide can help you use questions as a prewriting technique.

The Writing Process Step by Step:
Prewriting by Asking Questions

Use the reporter's questions to identify a topic, purpose, and audience.

- [ ] What? - [ ] Why? - [ ] Who?

Use the reporter's questions to generate details about the topic.

- [ ] When? - [ ] Where? - [ ] How?

Use reflective questions to identify attitudes and generate additional details about the topic.

- [ ] What are my attitudes or feelings about this topic?
- [ ] What are my audience's attitudes or feelings about this topic?
- [ ] Why is this topic important?
- [ ] How will my audience respond to my point?
- [ ] How can I make this topic interesting and relevant to my audience?

USE THE WRITING PROCESS: PREWRITE BY QUESTIONING

Assume you are a reporter at the scene of a car accident. Using the box "The Writing Process Step by Step: Prewriting by Asking Questions," write a list of questions to identify your point and generate details. Share your ideas with the class or in a small group.

USE THE WRITING PROCESS: PREWRITE BY QUESTIONING

Ask questions to brainstorm your first thoughts about one of the following topics:

- Road Rage
- Graffiti
- Drug Abuse
- Positive Thinking
- Workplace Stress

Freewriting

During **freewriting**, you record your thoughts as they stream through your mind. The key to this brainstorming strategy, like all prewriting activities, is to turn off the critic inside your head. At this point, no thought is wrong, off base, or silly. The idea is to warm up your thinking muscles, flex your creativity, and set your ideas free. The following thinking guide can help you use freewriting as a prewriting technique.

The Writing Process Step by Step:
Prewriting by Freewriting

- [ ] Set a time limit, such as ten minutes, and write whatever comes to mind as fast as you can, without stopping at all.
- [ ] If you get stuck, write the same word or phrase until a new idea comes along. Do not stop writing. Do not worry about wording, organization, or grammar. Later in the writing process, you will organize and polish your ideas—tell that critic inside your head to pipe down for now.
- [ ] When the time limit is up, read what you wrote and underline interesting ideas.
- [ ] Use one of the ideas you underlined as a starting point for a focused freewrite. A **focused freewrite** occurs when you freewrite about a specific topic you have chosen or been assigned.

Practice 11

USE THE WRITING PROCESS: PREWRITE BY FREEWRITING

Read the following two freewrites. Discuss with your class or in a small group how ideas develop using freewriting and focused freewriting. What are the advantages of freewriting? What are the disadvantages?

Okay, the essay is due in two days. The topic is my choice, and I have no idea what to write about. My mind is a blank. Dr. Reese says just start writing and don't stop and pretty soon something will come to you. No luck yet. Okay, what's going on in the world? Lots of people looking for work not many jobs are out there that's why I'm in school to get prepared for a good paying job. But life isn't all about work. Sure I want a good job, but I don't want a job that takes it all out of me. I want time for family and fun, too. I love to travel. If I won the lottery, I would spend a lot of time traveling. <u>My favorite vacation was snorkeling in the Florida Keys.</u> It would be so much fun to snorkel other places like in Hawaii and Australia.

Focused Freewrite

When I was a boy, my family went to the Florida Keys on a snorkeling vacation. That vacation remains one of my favorite memories. My brother and I were like prunes we were in the water so much. The water was the prettiest, clearest blue-green you've ever seen. You can see all the way to the bottom. And the fish and coral are so colorful. We watched schools of colorful fish shimmer in the water as they darted around. They varied from yellow with black stripes, to neon green, to brown speckles. Did you know that coral is a living thing? And it grows in all shapes and colors. Some look like purple fans waving in the current. Others look like grey brain matter. And others look like electric orange honeycombs. I'll never forget when we saw a shark. My brother kept screaming "shark, shark." But his screams were muffled sounds of panic because he was screaming into his snorkel. Boy, we made it back to the boat in record time. Dad said he never knew we could move so fast. What a great time we had!

USE THE WRITING PROCESS: PREWRITE BY FOCUSED FREEWRITING

Step 1: Choose one of the following topics and freewrite for five minutes. Ask and answer the reporter's and reflective questions before you begin freewriting.

- Popular Music

- Useful Technology

- Reality TV

- An Influential Person

Step 2: Read your freewrite and highlight ideas. Write a focused freewrite for an additional five minutes using the idea(s) you highlighted.

Listing

A common way to brainstorm ideas is to **create a list.** If you have a free choice of topics, then create a topic bank: List ideas about which you want to learn more or topics about which you already know something and that you enjoy discussing. To create a list of topics for an academic course, look at the table of contents, the index, and the glossary of your textbook. Use these resources to create a list of topics based on what you will be studying throughout the semester. If you already have a topic, then create a list of everything that comes to mind as you think about your topic. Write your list as quickly as you can. Just as in freewriting, quiet your inner critic. Once you make a thorough list, then you can organize your ideas.

The following thinking guide can help you use listing as a prewriting technique.

The Writing Process Step by Step:

Prewriting by Listing

- [ ] Write a topic at the top of your page.
- [ ] List ideas as quickly as possible in the order that they occur to you.
- [ ] Use words or short phrases.
- [ ] List all ideas that occur to you; reject nothing.
- [ ] If you run out of ideas, choose one idea you have already recorded and begin a new list about that idea.
- [ ] Review your list and group ideas into logical relationships.
- [ ] Label each group of ideas as possible points of development for a piece of writing.

Practice 13

USE THE WRITING PROCESS: PREWRITE BY LISTING

Prewriting for an academic course: The following lists are based on the table of contents of two textbooks. Identify the academic courses to which each list is related. Then, brainstorm a list of additional writing topics based on an idea from each list.

COURSES: ....

COURSES: ....

List 1

Mass Media and Politics
The Power of the Media
Sources of the Media
Bias in the Media
Freedom versus Fairness

New Lists of Additional Ideas

List 2

Coping with Stress
Eating Smart
Maintaining Proper Weight
Keeping Fit
Controllable Health Risks

New Lists of Additional Ideas

Prewriting for Business Writing: Assume you have just been given two weeks' notice because your company is downsizing and eliminating your job. To locate job opportunities, take the following steps:

Step 1: Go to your favorite job search site (for example, your local newspaper likely has listings online).

....

....

....

Step 2: Choose one of the advertised positions and list the skills needed to compete for the job.

....

....

....

Step 3: List the skills you already possess that qualify you for the job.

....

....

....

Step 4: On your own paper, repeat steps 2 and 3 for each of the jobs you listed in Step 1.

Practice 13

Concept Mapping

Concept mapping, also known as **clustering** or **webbing**, creates a visual picture of the relationships among the ideas you generate. Think of what you already know about a map. Someone can tell you how to get somewhere, but it is much easier to understand the directions when you can study a map and see how each road connects to other roads. Likewise, a concept map shows how a topic connects to supporting details—how each idea connects to another idea and how the main idea connects to supporting details. Sometimes, as you use a concept map, the idea that first occurred to you might be a great example for a supporting detail. Rarely do ideas occur to us in a logical order. Concept mapping helps a writer figure out the logical order of ideas. Chapters 4 through 12 will show you how to adapt concept maps to specific writing situations and thought patterns.

The following thinking guide can help you use concept mapping as a prewriting technique.

The Writing Process Step by Step:

Prewriting by Concept Mapping

- [ ] Draw a circle in the middle of your page and write your topic in the circle.
- [ ] Write a word that relates to the topic, circle the word, and connect it to the topic circle with a line.
- [ ] Repeat this process so that a set of major supports radiates out from the topic circle.
- [ ] Write a word that relates to one of the major supports, circle it, and connect it to that major support circle.
- [ ] Repeat this process for each of the major supports to create clusters of minor supports.

Practice 14

USE THE WRITING PROCESS: PREWRITE BY MAPPING

The writer of the following paragraph used a concept map to brainstorm ideas. Read the paragraph. Then, recreate her concept map by filling in the appropriate blanks with ideas from her paragraph. Discuss how the concept map differs from her final draft.

> Ballroom dancing can have many positive effects. The most obvious of these is physical fitness through exercise. Your body becomes more toned and that, in turn, can make you feel better about your appearance. However, several other less obvious effects are just as important. First, confidence is a big factor in dancing. It takes a lot of confidence to dance in front of people, or even to go out onto the floor and dance with someone you do not know very well. For someone who does not have a lot of self-assurance to begin with, dancing causes them to quickly build up their confidence. Next, improved coordination, balance, and posture are a few more positive effects of ballroom dancing. Practicing patterns in

each dance forces you to develop better coordination as you try to get the steps in the right order. Technique makes you develop better balance and posture as you focus on holding your frame while performing the correct steps. Another subtle but important effect is a better understanding of the different types of rhythm in music. Listening to songs over and over again as you practice your dances and having to understand the timing in each one makes you aware of the various rhythms that exist among different types of music. A final and very beneficial effect of ballroom dancing is relieving stress. If you enjoy dancing, it can become a huge help in relieving stress. Dance is a fun challenge and a welcome break from your hectic day. Therefore, there are various benefits caused by dancing that, when combined, create an enjoyable pastime for anyone.

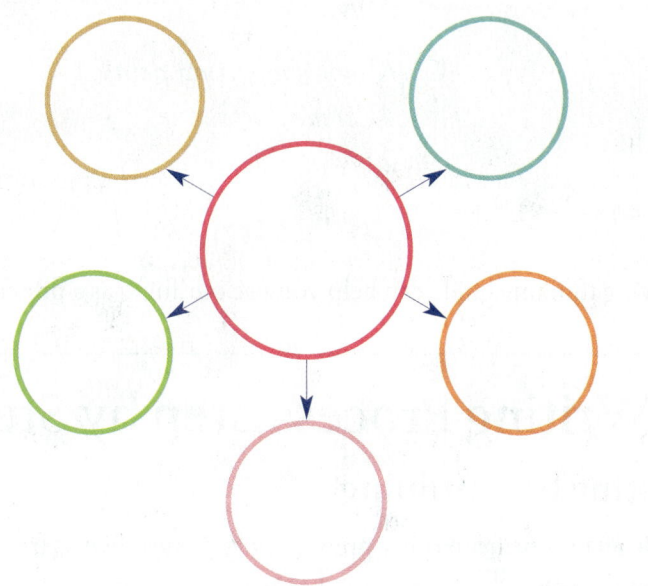

Outlining: A Writing Plan

In addition to brainstorming first thoughts, a prewrite also organizes ideas into a writing plan. A concept map is one way to create a writing plan because it shows the flow of ideas among the topic, major details, and minor details. An outline is another way to create a writing plan. An **outline** lists ideas in blocks of thought, as shown in the following outline for a paragraph.

Main Idea Statement: Topic Sentence

- A. *Major supporting detail*
  1. *Minor detail*
  2. *Minor detail*
- B. *Major supporting detail*
  1. *Minor detail*
  2. *Minor detail*
- C. *Major supporting detail*
  1. *Minor detail*
  2. *Minor detail*

The following thinking guide can help you use outlining as a prewriting technique.

The Writing Process Step by Step:

Prewriting by Outlining

- ☐ Create an outline from other prewriting activities such as freewrites, lists, and concept maps.
- ☐ List and identify each item with Roman numerals, capital letters, Arabic numerals, and lowercase letters, in that order, to show the flow of ideas, as illustrated below:

  I. Main Idea
      A. Major supporting detail
          1. Minor supporting detail
              a. Subpoint

- ☐ Place a period after each numeral or letter.
- ☐ Capitalize each item.
- ☐ For topic outlines, state each item with a word or phrase.
- ☐ For sentence outlines, state each item as a complete thought.

USE THE WRITING PROCESS: PREWRITE BY OUTLINING

The following reflection and concept map was created by a student during the prewriting phase of an assignment. Complete the outline with ideas from the concept map.

Laura's First Thoughts:

I am going to write about the topic "My Ideal Mate," and my classmates are my audience. I am going to focus my topic by discussing three traits of an ideal mate and how my boyfriend is a perfect example of an ideal mate. My purpose is to let the reader know what a great boyfriend I have.

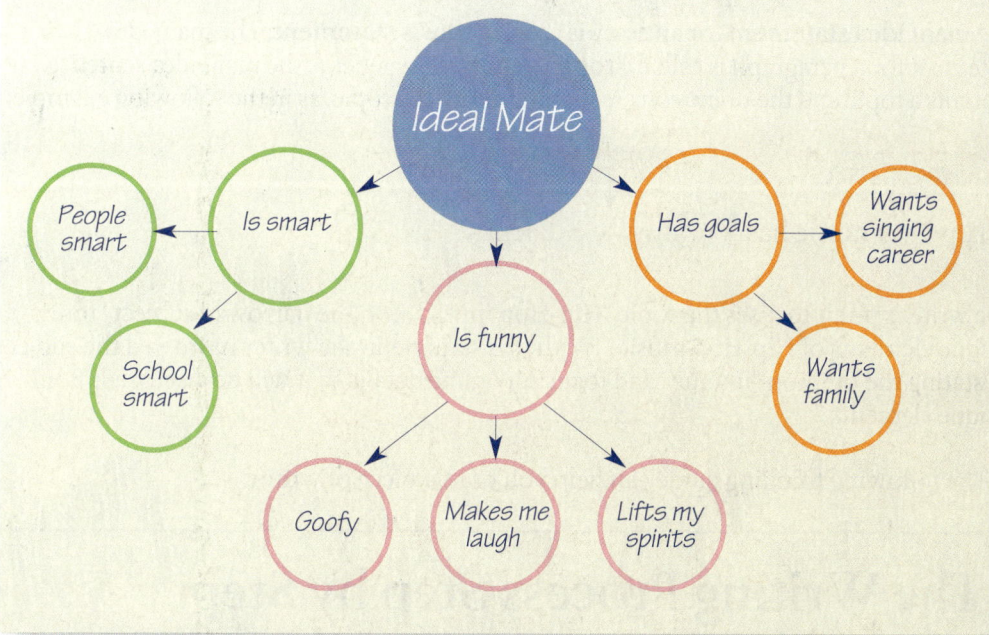

Main idea statement: My boyfriend Kelly is my ideal mate.

A. _____

   1. He excelled in high school and college.

   2. _____

B. Kelly is funny.

   1. _____

   2. He keeps me laughing.

   3. _____

C. Kelly has goals.

   1. He is working toward a singing career.

   2. _____

Draft

The **drafting** stage of the writing process may include several tasks, depending on the writing situation. An essay or letter may require the drafting of an introduction, a main idea, supporting details, and conclusion. A stand-alone paragraph may require only a main idea and supporting details.

> **Drafting** is putting your ideas into sentences and paragraphs.

Compose a Main Idea

The **main idea statement** for an essay is called a **thesis statement**. The main idea statement for a paragraph is called a **topic sentence**. In general, the main idea sentence presents a topic and the point you are making about the topic, as in the following example:

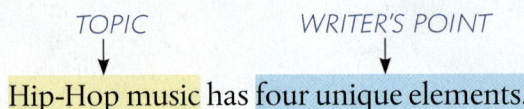

Hip-Hop music has four unique elements.

The writer's point focuses the topic "Hip-Hop music" into the narrowed subject "four unique elements of Hip-Hop music." With this statement, the writer narrowed the subject by stating the opinion "unique" and focusing on the details that will be discussed: "four unique elements."

The following thinking guide can help you draft a piece of writing.

The Writing Process Step by Step:
Drafting

☐ Write your main idea in a complete sentence.

☐ As you write a thesis statement or topic sentence, assert an idea instead of announcing your topic. Avoid the following announcements:

- "I am going to write about…"
- "My paragraph (or essay) is about…"
- "My topic is…."

☐ As you write your first draft, do not worry about issues such as spelling and grammar.

☐ Generate major and minor details to support your main idea.

☐ As you write, include new ideas as they occur to you without self-criticism or editing before you have a complete draft; this first draft does not need to be perfect. You will use the revision process to evaluate details for logic and relevance once your draft is complete.

☐ Use the first draft to discover how your ideas flow and fit together.

☐ Resolve to write multiple drafts to produce your best work.

Practice 16

USE THE WRITING PROCESS: DRAFT BY STATING THE MAIN IDEA

Revise the following main idea statements so they are more effectively expressed. Identify the hint you used to revise each one. Discuss your work with your class or in a small group.

1. I am going to write about how the automobile costs too much, pollutes the environment, and traps us in isolation.

   Hint:

2. The annoying and rude manners of people while talking on cell phones in public places.

   Hint:

3. Minimum wage is a controversial issue.

   Hint:

Write a Draft of Your Paragraph

A draft of a paragraph or essay is the result of careful thought based on prewriting activities. Creating a first or rough draft allows you to get a working copy of your ideas that can be improved upon during the revision process.

Practice 17

USE THE WRITING PROCESS: COMPOSE A TOPIC SENTENCE AND A DRAFT

Step 1: Choose a topic from a previous practice exercise and compose a main idea statement. (Remember that your **main idea statement** is also called a **topic sentence** if you are writing a paragraph. If you are writing an essay, your main idea statement is also called a **thesis statement**.)

Step 2: Write a draft using your own paper.

AUDIENCE AND PURPOSE:

TOPIC:

WRITER'S POINT:

MAIN IDEA STATEMENT (TOPIC SENTENCE OR THESIS STATEMENT):

Revise

Now that you have gotten your ideas on paper, you can review your work to make sure your paragraph offers a focused, unified, well-supported, and coherent chunk of information. As you revise your draft, review and apply what you have learned.

> **Revising** is re-seeing your work through the eyes of your reader. Revising is reworking your draft for clarity, logic, interest, and credibility.

The following thinking guide can help you revise a piece of writing.

The Writing Process Step by Step:
Revising

- ☐ Read your draft out loud (either on your own or to a peer). This is an easy way to identify parts of your draft that may be unclear or awkward.
- ☐ Make sure your main idea is stated clearly in a topic sentence or thesis statement.
- ☐ Make sure that the details in the body of your paragraph or essay fully support your topic sentence or thesis statement.
- ☐ Make sure every sentence in a paragraph relates to your main idea so that a reader can easily follow the logic of your ideas.
- ☐ Move information as needed into the most logical order.
- ☐ Add transitions as needed to clarify the relationship between ideas.
- ☐ Add details and examples as needed to strengthen or clarify the main idea and supporting points.
- ☐ Replace vague words and details with vivid and precise expressions.
- ☐ Delete irrelevant details.
- ☐ If your paragraph or essay draft seems to end abruptly, add a concluding sentence (or paragraph, if you are writing an essay), restating and summing up your main points.

USE THE WRITING PROCESS: REVISE

Read Laura's first draft of her paragraph "My Ideal Mate." Then, complete the activity that follows. Share your work and thoughts with a small group of your peers.

> ### My Ideal Mate
>
> (1) My ideal mate is a man who is intelligent, funny, and goal oriented. (2) Kelly, my current boyfriend, has all of these wonderful traits. (3) Kelly has to be one of the smartest people I know. (4) He excelled academically in high school and college. (5) He is not only book smart but is people smart also. (6) He knows exactly how to keep the people he loves protected and safe from this cruel world. (7) Kelly has to be the funniest person I know. (8) If we didn't have fun and goof around, our relationship would be boring. (9) He can be serious when necessary, and like everyone, has his dark days. (10) Whenever I am down about something, he is the one to make me overcome the sadness and laugh. (11) The most important trait of all though is that Kelly is goal oriented; he knows what he wants out of life. (12) He has a plan to succeed. (13) Not too many guys know what they want. (14) Kelly wants to become a professional musician, have a family, and earn enough money to support his family. (15) All of these traits make Kelly my ideal mate.
>
> –Laura Bender, English Student

1. Locate the topic sentence by underlining the topic once and the writer's point about that topic twice.
2. Cross out any details that are not related to the topic sentence.
3. Circle any ideas that need more examples to fully support the main idea.
4. Choose three words to revise; cross out the words you chose, and above them, write stronger, more vivid words. Use a thesaurus.
5. Insert the following transitions where they best show the logical flow of ideas: *First, In addition, Finally*.

USE THE WRITING PROCESS: REVISE

Review a draft you have written. Annotate or mark your paragraph with the changes you need to make, and write a journal entry about your revision. Do you need to brainstorm more details for certain ideas? Identify those ideas and describe or explain the kinds of details you need. Do you need to use a thesaurus to improve word choice? List and discuss the words that need to be replaced. Based on your review, revise to create a new draft of your work.

Proofread

Once you have revised your paragraph, take time to carefully proofread your work. Publishing a clean, error-free draft proves you are committed to excellence and that you take pride in your work. Many student writers struggle with common errors, and every writer has her or his own pattern or habit of careless errors. To create a polished draft, a writer masters the rules of writing and edits to eliminate careless errors.

> **Proofreading** is preparing your work for publication.
> Proofreading is correcting errors in punctuation, capitalization, mechanics, grammar, and spelling.

The following thinking guide can help you proofread a piece of writing.

The Writing Process Step by Step:
Proofreading

- [ ] Allow some time to pass between revising and proofreading.
- [ ] Read your work one sentence at a time from the *end* to the *beginning*. Reading your work from the end to the beginning allows you to focus on each sentence.
- [ ] Read again from the beginning with a blank sheet of paper that you slide down the page as you read so that you focus on one sentence at a time, covering the rest of the text.
- [ ] Use a highlighter to mark mistakes.
- [ ] Proofread more than once; focus on one type of error at a time.
- [ ] Proofread for the types of errors you commonly make.
- [ ] Use word processing spell checkers carefully (they don't know the difference between words such as *there, their,* or *they're*).
- [ ] Use a dictionary to double check your spelling.
- [ ] Have someone else read over your work.

USE THE WRITING PROCESS: PROOFREAD

The following draft by a student writer reveals her struggle with two common errors: pronoun agreement and subject-verb agreement. The box on the next page sums up the rules for pronoun agreement and subject-verb agreement and includes correct sentence examples. Read the rules and examples in the box, and then use them as a guide to correct the same kind of errors in pronoun agreement and subject-verb agreement in the student's draft.

Student draft

> Procrastination
>
> (1) Everyone deal with procrastination from time to time in some way, shape, or form. (2) Procrastination is not as simple as it seem. (3) It is the body's way of coping with one's emotions, thoughts, and

attitudes. (4) Delaying any given action to a later time may indicate several conflicts. (5) For example, often a person stay at the same dead-end job due to fear of the unknown. (6) They fear the possibility of being faced with something difficult, a task at which they might fail. (7) Sometimes procrastination stem from the fear of achievement. (8) Oddly, a certain type of person may actually fear success. (9) For them, success leads to more responsibility. (10) Other reasons for procrastination may be anger, rebellion against authority, or the need to blame others for one's own unhappiness. (11) To overcome procrastination, a person need to apply a little discipline and willpower. (12) The most popular method is to complete the task as soon as possible. (13) Another method is also simple. (14) They are as simple as having a to-do list, a little checklist, like a grocery list that can minimize distractions.

Pronoun Agreement

If a noun is singular (*I, you, he, she,* or *it*), then the pronoun that refers to the noun must be singular. If a noun is plural (*we, you, they*), then the pronoun that refers to the noun must be plural.

Subject-Verb Agreement

If a subject of a sentence is singular, then the verb and object of the verb must be singular. If the subject of a sentence is plural, then the verb and object of the verb must be plural.

Correct:

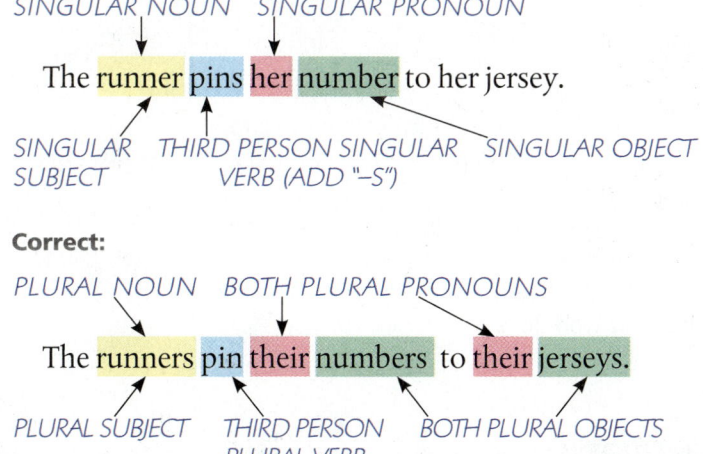

Correct:

PLURAL NOUN   BOTH PLURAL PRONOUNS

The runners pin their numbers to their jerseys.

PLURAL SUBJECT   THIRD PERSON   BOTH PLURAL OBJECTS
                 PLURAL VERB

Practice 20

Academic Learning Log: Chapter Review

THINKING THROUGH THE WRITING PROCESS

To test and track your understanding of what you have studied, answer the following questions.

1. A piece of writing develops in response to a specific situation that is composed of the _____, the _____ for writing, and the _____.

2. The four basic purposes for writing are _____, _____, _____, and _____.

3. The four phases of the writing process are _____, _____, _____, and _____.

4. The writing process is _____: Any step can be repeated as necessary.

5. Several prewriting techniques are _____, _____, _____, and _____.

6. Drafting is putting your ideas into _____ and _____.

7. Revising is _____ your work through the eyes of your reader.

8. Revising is reworking your draft for _____, _____, _____, and _____.

9. Proofreading is preparing your work for _____.

10. Proofreading is correcting errors in _____, _____, _____, and _____.

11. What did I learn about the writing process?

12. What about the writing process do I need to continue studying or working on?

Academic Learning Log: Chapter Review

Complete the Post-test for Chapter 2 in MyWritingLab.

3 Understanding the Paragraph

PART 2 USING PATTERNS OF ORGANIZATION TO DEVELOP PARAGRAPHS

LEARNING OUTCOMES

After studying this chapter you will be able to:

1. Answer the question "What's the Point of a Paragraph?"
2. Identify the Three Parts of a Paragraph
3. Compose a Topic Sentence
4. Use Logical Order
5. Develop Relevant and Adequate Details
6. Use Effective Expression
7. Analyze the Effectiveness of a Paragraph

Think about how a train links cars together to carry people or products to a specific destination. A paragraph links ideas to carry a message to a specific audience. A paragraph is a well-planned sequence of sentences joined together to convey a main point.

A paragraph allows a writer to express clearly and powerfully one main idea about a narrowed subject. A well-written paragraph can express a valid consumer complaint, a compelling reason to be hired, a sincere apology to a loved one, or a concept tested by a written exam in a college course.

What's the Point of a Paragraph?

A paragraph is a well-thought-out chunk of information. A writer narrows a topic into a focused main idea, selects enough relevant details to support the main idea, and organizes these supporting details in a logical flow of information.

Three Levels of Information in a Paragraph

The following flow chart shows the three levels of information within a paragraph.

Subject
- A narrowed topic

1. Main idea
- Is often stated as a topic sentence
- Explains the author's one main point about the subject
- Is a more general statement than any of the supporting details

2. Major detail
- Explains the main idea
- Provides primary support to the main idea
- Is more general than a minor detail

3. Minor detail
- Explains a major detail
- Provides secondary support to the main idea
- Is the most specific idea in the passage

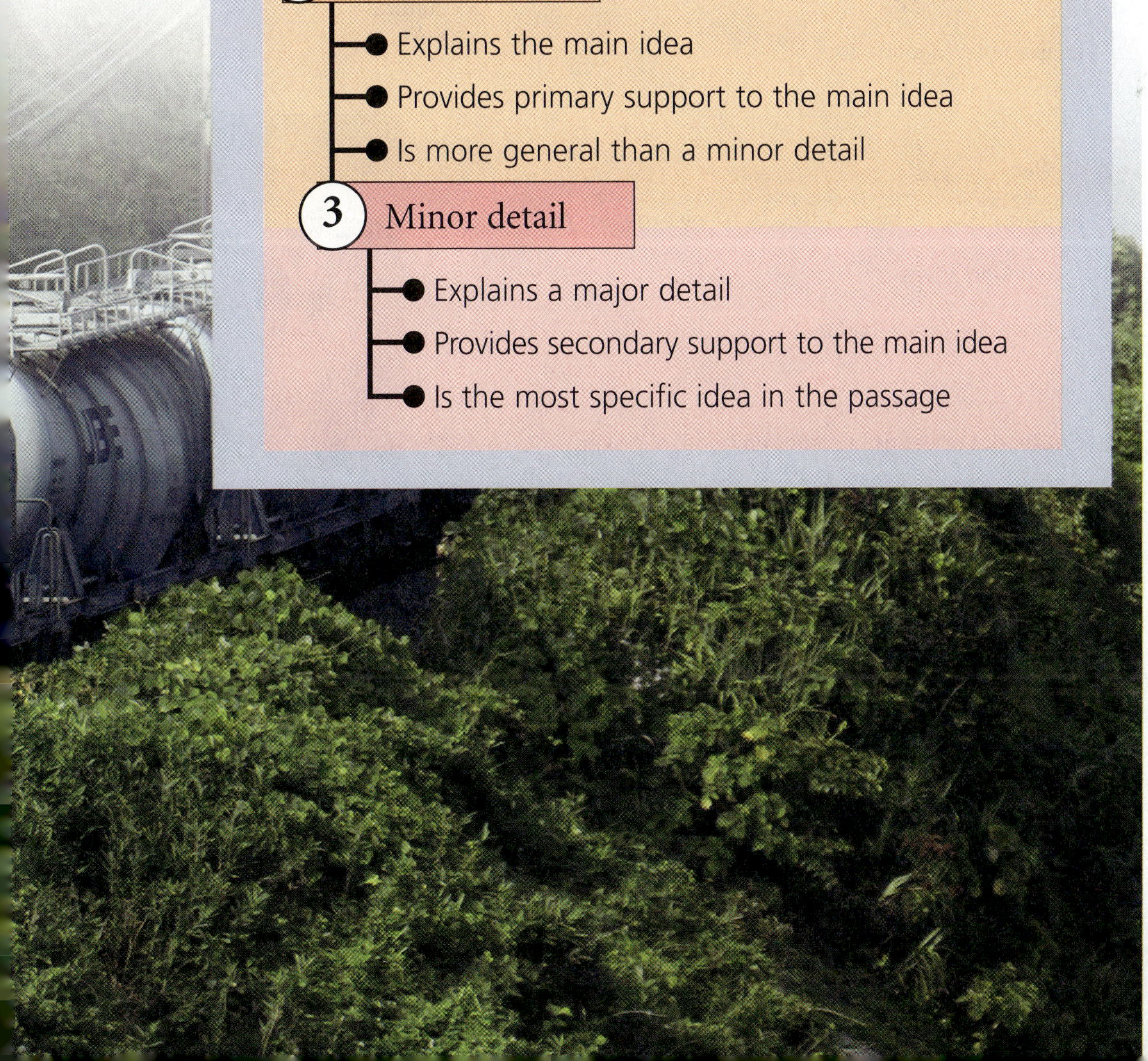

Practice 1

PHOTOGRAPHIC ORGANIZER: LEVELS OF INFORMATION

Study the following outline based on an article about types of tattoos. In the blanks, identify each piece of information as the main idea, major supporting detail, or minor supporting detail.

Four Types of Tattoos: Narrowed topic

Four major types of tattoos are amateur, professional, traumatic, and cosmetic. _____

A. Amateur _____

   1. Cause: often one color, unevenly applied, created by someone at home using needle and ink, soot, or charcoal. _____

   2. Examples: loved one's name; gang tattoo _____

B. Professional _____

   1. Cultural _____

      a. Cause: placed by members of certain cultural groups to symbolize cultural heritage and identity _____

      b. Example: Maori tattoos _____

   2. Modern _____

      a. Cause: placed by a "tattoo gun" by experienced, working artists _____

      b. Example: Tattoo parlors _____

C. Traumatic _____

   1. Cause: dirt or debris becomes embedded in skin _____

   2. Examples: road rash, explosion from fireworks _____

D. Cosmetic _____

   1. Cause: placed by a cosmetic specialist as permanent makeup or camouflage _____

   2. Example: eyeliner _____

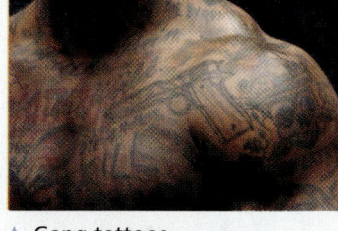
▲ Gang tattoos

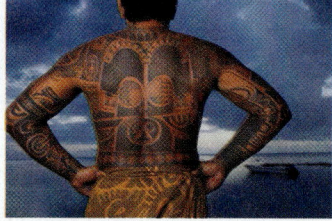
▲ Cultural

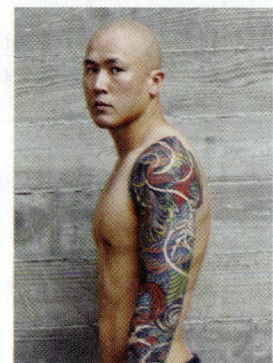
▲ Modern

▲ Permanent makeup

Practice 2

IDENTIFY LEVELS OF INFORMATION

Read the paragraph developed from the previous outline. Circle the main idea. Underline the four sentences that state the major supports. Then, in your own words restate the three levels of information in a paragraph.

Four Types of Tattoos

(1) While tattoos come in all sorts of forms, experts divide them into four fundamental types. (2) The four main types of tattoos are amateur, professional, traumatic, and cosmetic. (3) The first type, the amateur tattoo, is often one color, unevenly applied, and created by someone at home using a needle and bottle of India ink, soot, or charcoal. (4) Amateur tattoos are often simple designs such as a loved one's name or a gang's symbol. (5) The second type, the professional tattoo, may be either a cultural tattoo or a modern tattoo. (6) Cultural tattoos often symbolize the values of a specific ethnic group. (7) For example, the Maori people of New Zealand create tattoo designs that honor their cultural heritage and identity. (8) Modern tattoos are created with a tattoo gun operated by trained, working artists. (9) Modern tattoos reflect the personal values or interests of the person being tattooed. (10) The third type, the traumatic tattoo, occurs when dirt or debris becomes embedded beneath the skin. (11) Two common examples of traumatic tattoos are road rash from a fall or accident and an explosion from fireworks. (12) The fourth type, cosmetic tattooing, takes the form of permanent makeup or camouflage. (13) A tattoo specialist applies permanent makeup such as eyeliner, lip liner, rouge, or permanent eyebrows. (14) Many people use cosmetic tattooing to cover a birthmark, blemish, or older tattoo.

—Based on T.A. Cronin, Jr., "Tattoos, Piercings, and Skin Adornments", *Dermatology Nursing Journal,* 2001 Oct.13(5): 380–383.

What are the three levels of information in a paragraph?

IDENTIFY LEVELS OF INFORMATION IN A PARAGRAPH

Read the following paragraph. Then, fill in the sentence outline with the main idea and missing supporting details.

Why We Explore: Human Space Exploration

(1) Humanity's interest in the heavens has been universal and enduring. (2) Humans are driven to explore the unknown, discover new worlds, push the boundaries of our scientific and technical limits, and then push further. (3) In this new era in space exploration, NASA has been challenged to develop systems and capabilities required to explore beyond low-Earth orbit. (4) Destinations include the International Space Station, translunar space, near-Earth asteroids and eventually Mars. (5) First, NASA will use the International Space Station as a test-bed and stepping stone for the challenging journey ahead. (6) On the International Space Station, we will improve and learn new ways to ensure astronauts are safe, healthy, and productive while exploring. (7) And we will continue to expand our knowledge about how materials and biological systems behave outside of the influence of gravity. (8) Second, exploring in translunar space will provide unprecedented experience in deep-space operations. (9) Translunar space is the vast expanse surrounding the Earth-moon system. (10) In translunar space, NASA can research galactic cosmic radiation—potentially the most threatening element to humans exploring deep space—and develop strategies that may also lead to medical advancements on Earth.

(11) Third, by visiting asteroids, we can look for answers to some of humankind's most compelling questions, such as: how did the solar system form and where did the Earth's water and other organic materials such as carbon come from? (12) Asteroids are believed to have formed early in our solar system's history—about 4.5 billion years ago—along with our sun and the planets. (13) In addition, future robotic missions to asteroids will prepare humans for long-duration space travel and the eventual journey to Mars. (14) Finally, Mars has always been a source of inspiration for explorers and scientists. (15) A mission to our nearest planetary neighbor provides the best opportunity to demonstrate that humans can live for extended, even permanent, stays beyond low Earth orbit. (16) The challenge of traveling to Mars and learning how to live there will encourage nations around the world to work together to achieve such an ambitious undertaking.

—Adapted from "Why We Explore", NASA, 2013.

Main idea (Topic Sentence): _____

A. Major support: NASA will use the International Space Station as a test-bed and stepping stone for the challenging journey ahead.

  1. Minor support: _____

  2. Minor support: And we will continue to expand our knowledge about how materials and biological systems behave outside of the influence of gravity.

B. Major support: _____

  1. Minor support: _____

  2. Minor support: In translunar space, NASA can research galactic cosmic radiation—potentially the most threatening element to humans exploring deep space—and develop strategies that may also lead to medical advancements on Earth.

C. By visiting asteroids, we can look for answers to some of humankind's most compelling questions, such as: how did the solar system form and where did the Earth's water and other organic materials such as carbon come from?

  1. Minor support: _____

  2. Minor support: _____

D. Major support: _____

  1. Minor support: _____

  2. Minor support: The challenge of traveling to Mars and learning how to live there will encourage nations around the world to work together to achieve such an ambitious undertaking.

L2 Identify the Three Parts of a Paragraph

A paragraph is a series of closely related sentences that develop and support the writer's point about a narrowed subject. Often, the paragraph serves as a building block for a longer piece of writing such as an essay, since an essay is composed of two, three, or more paragraphs. In many situations a writer can make a point through one well-developed paragraph. Sometimes, a writer provides a stand-alone paragraph with a title. In addition to a title, a paragraph has three basic parts:

A Beginning:
An introduction of one or more sentences: A topic sentence that states the author's purpose and main point

A Middle:
A body of major and minor details that support the topic sentence

An Ending:
A conclusion of one or more sentences that reinforces the author's purpose and main point

The following graphic describes the function of each part of a paragraph and shows the general format of a paragraph.

Title:
Use Key Words or a Phrase to Vividly Describe the Point of Your Paragraph

Introduction:
An introduction is usually one or more sentences that explain the importance of the topic or give necessary background information about the topic.
<u>Your topic sentence states your narrowed subject and your point about the subject.</u>

Body:
The body of a paragraph is made up of a series of sentences that offer major details in support of your topic sentence. If needed, provide minor details that support the major details. Link sentences within the paragraph with clear transitions so your reader can easily follow your thoughts.

Conclusion:
The conclusion restates or sums up your paragraph's main idea in one or more sentences.

IDENTIFY PARTS OF A PARAGRAPH

The following student essay by Adam Stewart illustrates the use of a title and the three parts of a paragraph. Underline the topic sentence. Circle each of the three parts of the paragraph: Introduction, Body, and Conclusion. Provide a title for the paragraph.

▲ Ambitious worker

▲ Mediocre worker

▲ Lazy worker

(1) Although everyone has to work at one point in his or her life and a strong work ethic is looked upon very highly, unfortunately not all workers understand the importance of hard work and a good attitude. (2) Depending upon which category they represent, workers are judged by their coworkers and employers. (3) Three different types of workers make up the workforce, and each type works toward a very different future. (4) First, the ambitious worker comes to work on time, has a good attitude, stays on task, and is always willing to help in any way. (5) Supervisors and coworkers highly value the work ethic of ambitious workers because they always get the job done and do it well beyond expectations. (6) The second type of worker is satisfied with mediocrity. (7) This type of worker comes to work on time, but he or she is not always on the required task. (8) Mediocre workers do what is required and nothing more. (9) Employers and coworkers tolerate mediocre workers because even though they don't always have a good attitude, the job does get done and usually meets expectations. (10) The third type is the lazy worker, also known as the slacker. (11) Everyone hates the slacker. (12) Slackers consistently show up late, rarely accomplish the required task, and continuously try to get the rest of their coworkers off task as well. (13) The slacker, looking for the easy way out, rarely meets expectations. (14) In conclusion, the ambitious workers will be the leaders and high-wage earners; the mediocre workers will likely remain at some dead-end jobs; and the slackers will probably be fired from job after job, never rethinking their work ethic.

An effective paragraph is **focused**, **logical**, **detailed**, and **well expressed**. A writer (1) composes a topic sentence; (2) creates logical order; (3) develops relevant and adequate details; (4) uses effective expression through the purposeful choice of words, sentence structure, and grammar.

L3 Compose a Topic Sentence

A focused main idea presents a narrowed subject and the writer's controlling point about the narrowed subject. The controlling point often indicates both the writer's opinion and a pattern of organization. A topic sentence states the focused main idea in a complete sentence.

Narrow the Topic

Use the following suggestions to guide your thinking as you focus a general topic into a narrowed subject or topic.

- Narrow the topic based on your **opinion**. An opinion is expressed by using words such as *amazing, alarming, beautiful, best, likely, should*, or any other word that states personal values, judgments, or interpretations. Use questions, freewriting, mapping, listing, or another brainstorming technique to discover your opinion about a topic.

    Example: **General Topic**   **Narrowed Subject**
    　　　　　　　Seatbelts   Seatbelts can be dangerous
    　　　　　　　 Seatbelts save lives

- Narrow the topic based on a **pattern of organization**. A writer may use a pattern of organization to narrow a subject and generate details. Patterns of organization are also used to develop, organize, and express a main idea, major details, and minor details in a logical order. The following list provides a few examples of patterns of organization and signal words for each one.

Pattern of Organization	Signal Words
Space Order	above, below, next to, underneath, behind
Time Order	first, now, then, before, after, process, use
Example	for example, exemplify, includes, such as
Classification	types, kinds, levels
Compare/Contrast	similar, likewise, just as / however, in contrast
Cause/Effect	source, origin / results, impact

    Example: **General Topic**   **Narrowed Subject**
    　　　　　　　Graffiti   The effects of graffiti
    　　　　　　　 The types of graffiti

- Combine topic, opinion, and pattern of organization to generate a narrowed subject.

    Example: **General Topic**   **Narrowed Subject**
    　　　　　　　Seatbelts   Three reasons seatbelts can be dangerous
    　　　　　　　 Proper use of seatbelts saves lives
    　　　　　　　Graffiti   The negative effects of graffiti
    　　　　　　　 Graffiti: A type of artistic expression

Practice 5

FOCUS A TOPIC INTO A NARROWED SUBJECT

Combine the topic with an opinion and pattern of organization signal words to narrow the topic. In the blank items, practice narrowing topics of your choice.

1. GENERAL TOPIC: Health Issue: Weightlifting

   OPINION: positive   SIGNAL WORD: effects

   NARROWED SUBJECT: _____

2. GENERAL TOPIC: A Public Figure: Hillary Clinton

   OPINION: admirable   SIGNAL WORD: traits

   NARROWED SUBJECT: _____

3. GENERAL TOPIC: Historical Place: Gettysburg

   OPINION: most decisive battle in history   SIGNAL WORD: scene

   NARROWED SUBJECT: _____

4. GENERAL TOPIC: Business: Saving Money

   OPINION: smart   SIGNAL WORD: steps to

   NARROWED SUBJECT: _____

5. GENERAL TOPIC: Health Issue: Cancer

   OPINION: _____   SIGNAL WORD: _____

   NARROWED SUBJECT: _____

6. GENERAL TOPIC: _____

   OPINION: _____   SIGNAL WORD: _____

   NARROWED SUBJECT: _____

7. GENERAL TOPIC: _____

   OPINION: _____   SIGNAL WORD: _____

   NARROWED SUBJECT: _____

8. GENERAL TOPIC: _____

   OPINION: _____   SIGNAL WORD: _____

   NARROWED SUBJECT: _____

Write the Topic Sentence

Once you have focused a topic into a narrowed subject with your opinion and a pattern of organization, you are ready to write a complete sentence to state the main idea. Each of the following topic sentences offers a subject and a controlling point: a **topic** narrowed by the writer's **opinion** and a suggested **pattern of organization**.

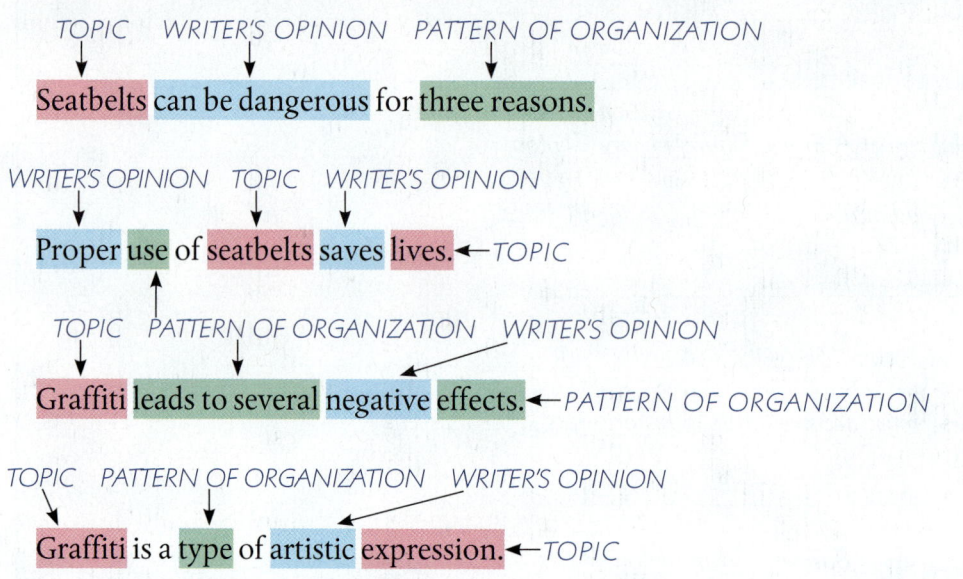

WRITE A TOPIC SENTENCE

Write topic sentences for each of the following narrowed subjects.

1. Narrowed Subject: Benefits of Weightlifting

   TOPIC SENTENCE: _____

2. Narrowed Subject: The Admirable Traits of Hillary Clinton

   TOPIC SENTENCE: _____

3. Narrowed Subject: Gettysburg: Scene of the Most Decisive Battle in History

   TOPIC SENTENCE: _____

4. Narrowed Subject: Smart Steps to Saving Money

   TOPIC SENTENCE: _____

Use Logical Order

Use a writing plan to establish a logical order for details and a clear flow of ideas. A writing plan includes one or more of the following elements.

A Pattern of Organization As discussed on page 58, a writer uses a pattern of organization to arrange major details and minor details in a logical order. The following chart provides a few examples of patterns of organization and signal words for each one (see Chapters 4–12 for in-depth instruction about patterns of organization and signal words).

Patterns of Organization	Signal Words
Description (Space order)	above, below, next to, underneath, behind
Narrative/Process (Time order)	first, now, then, before, after, next, stage
Example	for example, exemplify, includes, such as
Classification	types, kinds, levels
Compare/Contrast	similar, likewise/however, in contrast
Cause/Effect	source, origin/results, impact, reasons
Persuasion	must, should, ought to

Order of Importance Often, a writer decides upon and arranges details according to his or her opinion about the importance of the details, known as **climactic order**. Usually, climactic order moves from the least important point and builds to the paragraph's climax, the most important point.

Order of Topic Sentence Often the controlling point of the topic sentence divides the subject into chunks of information. The order of the ideas in the topic sentence often reflects a pattern of organization or an order of importance for details.

CREATE LOGICAL ORDER

Read the following paragraph from a college textbook. Underline the topic sentence. Circle the pattern of organization's signal words. Then, identify the type of logical order used by the author.

> (1) Interpersonal communication is a continuous series of processes that blend into one another. (2) For convenience of discussion we can separate them into five stages. (3) During the first stage, we sense, we pick up some kind of stimulation. (4) Next, we organize the stimuli in some way. (5) Third, we interpret and evaluate what we perceive. (6) Then, we store it in memory, and finally, in stage five, we retrieve it when needed.
>
> —Adapted from DeVito, *The Interpersonal Communication Book*, 10th Ed., (Upper Saddle River: Allyn & Bacon, 2005) p. 91.

Type of Logical Order: _____

L5 Develop Relevant and Adequate Details

Relevant and adequate details support and develop the main idea.

Relevant details explain and support only the writer's point. Once you narrow a subject into a focused main idea, you then include only those details that relate to your opinion and pattern of organization.

Check for Relevant Details

Apply the following questions to each detail to see if it is relevant to a main idea. If the answers are "no" to these questions, then the detail is most likely irrelevant and should not be included as a support.

- Does the detail reinforce the writer's opinion?
- Does the detail carry out the pattern of organization?
- Does the detail support the main idea?
- Does the detail support a major detail?

Adequate details offer in-depth explanations and supports for the writer's opinion and pattern of organization. In-depth support of a main idea often requires both major and minor details. Major details directly support the main idea. Minor details support and explain the major details (review the chart on page 51 of this chapter).

Check for Adequate Details

Apply the following questions to see if you have adequate details to support your main idea. If the answer is "yes" to these questions, then additional details are most likely needed to fully support the main idea.

- Is more information needed to explain the writer's opinion?
- Is more information needed to carry out the pattern of organization?
- Does a major detail need a minor detail of support or explanation?

Practice 8

DEVELOP RELEVANT AND ADEQUATE DETAILS

Read the following rough draft of a paragraph. Cross out the irrelevant detail. Underline the point that needs more information to adequately support the main idea.

A Winter Wonderland or Winter Escape Vacation?

(1) Many families take advantage of winter break to vacation together. (2) A winter-time vacation offers distinct choices in activities and clothing. (3) On the one hand, fresh snow offers opportunities for skiing, sledding, snowmobiling, snowboarding, or ice skating.

(4) Of course, the family will need to plan on packing additional special clothing. (5) On the other hand, a family may prefer to escape winter in a tropical climate. (6) Balmy beaches offer plenty of fun options such as sunbathing, snorkeling, surfing, and swimming. (7) And the family can travel light. (8) In the tropics, all they really need are their swimsuits and a few causal clothes such as shorts, t-shirts, and sandals. (9) Of course, many people just stay home.

Use Effective Expression

Effective expression enhances the writer's purpose through the precise choice and use of words, sentence structure, and grammar.

Word Choice

Precise word choice communicates exact meaning. Writers choose words that effectively communicate tone, purpose, and order. For example, strong transitions and signal words clue the audience into the logical order of the writer's thoughts. Another example of effective expression is the clear and consistent use of pronouns. In addition, words chosen for their emotional or visual impact create strong images in the reader's mind and carry out the writer's purpose.

Ineffective Expression

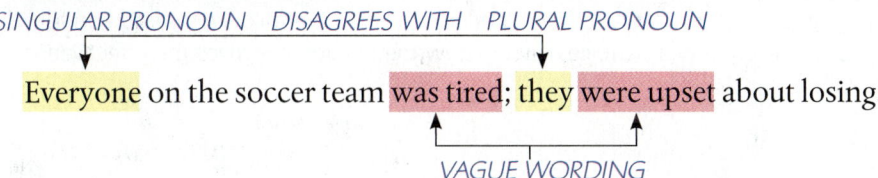

Effective Expression

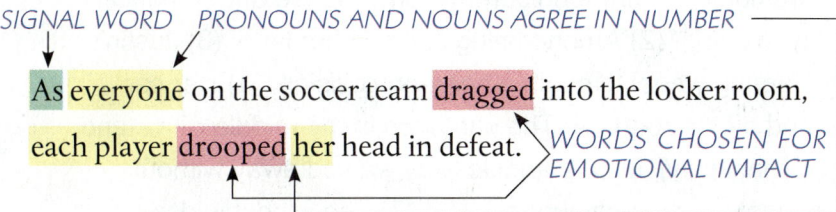

Sentence Structure

Effective expression uses a variety of sentence types to express ideas in clear and interesting statements. (You will learn more about sentence structure in Chapters 20–21.)

Simple Sentences:

Michaella had been out of school for years. She was insecure about her abilities.

Complex Sentence:

Michaella, who had been out of school for years, didn't want to fail.

Compound Sentence:

She studied for two hours every day; as a result, she earned a 4.0 GPA.

Compound-Complex Sentence:

Michaella studied for two hours every day because she didn't want to fail; as a result, she earned a 4.0 GPA.

Grammar

Grammar is a tool of effective expression. Writers use grammar to clarify and polish ideas. Grammar includes a wide variety of language rules such as the following: tense, agreement, and punctuation. (You will learn more about grammar throughout your studies in this text.)

Practice 9

USE EFFECTIVE EXPRESSION

With a small group of your peers, revise the underlined parts of the following paragraph for effective expression through word choice. Discuss how the revision improves the effectiveness of the paragraph.

A Frightful Moment

(1) Justine was driving her friend Jeremy to his house after a concert last Tuesday evening. (2) An oncoming car <u>is</u> in her lane. (3) Justine jerked her steering wheel to avoid a head-on collision. (4) Her car spun 360° and off the road. (5) The car <u>lands</u> in the middle of a stand of trees. (6) Thankfully, Justine and Jeremy walked away without injury; unfortunately, <u>their</u> car was totaled. (7) The windshield <u>is broke</u>. (8) The rear-end of the car <u>wraps</u> around a tree. (9) <u>Its</u> trunk was shoved into the backseat. (10) Because of that frightful moment, Justine <u>was</u> still afraid to drive.

Analyze the Effectiveness of a Paragraph

Many student writers benefit from using a scoring guide. A scoring guide identifies and describes levels of writing effectiveness. The following scoring guide describes the traits of an effective paragraph as discussed in this chapter: A score of "5" indicates a highly effective paragraph. In a small group of your peers, discuss the differences between a "5" paragraph and a "3" paragraph.

Scoring Guide for a Paragraph

5 A focused main idea presents the narrowed subject and the writer's point, and suggests a pattern of organization. Relevant and in-depth details convincingly support and develop the main idea. Strong transitions indicate careful ordering of details based on a logical pattern of organization. Effective expression enhances the writer's purpose through the precise choice and use of words, sentence structure, and grammar.

4 A focused main idea presents the narrowed subject and the writer's opinion, and suggests a pattern of organization. Relevant and adequate details support and develop the main idea. Clear transitions indicate an order of details based on a logical pattern of organization. Effective expression carries out the writer's purpose through the competent use and choice of words, sentence structure, and grammar.

3 A focused main idea presents the narrowed subject and the writer's opinion or a pattern of organization. Relevant details offer enough support to develop the main idea. Occasional transitions indicate the use of a pattern of organization, but details are not always logically ordered. Expression does not interfere with the writer's purpose, even though occasional errors in use and choice of words, sentence structure, and grammar occur.

2 The main idea presents a general subject or a broad opinion. Details are generalized statements or lists that do not offer enough information to support the main idea. Weak or misused transitions and confused order of details indicate little use of a pattern of organization. Weak expression interferes with the writer's purpose through frequent errors in use and choice of words, sentence structure, and grammar.

1 The main idea presents a vague, weakly worded opinion about a general subject. Details are missing, superficial, or rambling. Lack of transitions and illogical order of details indicate no use of a pattern of organization. Confused expression interferes with the writer's purpose through pervasive errors in choice and use of words, sentence structure, and grammar.

Practice 10

EVALUATE THE EFFECTIVENESS OF A PARAGRAPH

Use the scoring guide to assign a score to each of the following paragraphs written by students about the following topic: *An Important Lesson Everyone Should Learn*. Be prepared to discuss your reasons for each score.

.... Life is full of changes and drama. Never know what is going to happened next step. With ups and downs I had learn lot of things. At this point of our life you cannot trust anyone. You learn more about life everyday. Experience make us learn something new and give us a lesson what we should expect next. My life was full of thrill but it's good to have something like that in your life. How life has teach me a good lesson and how you can learn something from my experience. I want to tell others that never give up in your life, never think that life is ending when u loose something out of your life, because it's always a hope that bring your confidence back. Never depend on others not even your close family. Trust yourself and you will make it. Success never comes easy it's always tuff ways to find it. Unless you don't give up life goes on.

.... A friendly attitude can bring us more reward than a frown any day. We all need to learn the importance of a smile. Before I learned this lesson, I didn't know how to react at work to a disgruntled person or a grumpy coworker. In fact, most of the time I would simply call on a supervisor for help. Unfortunately, this move made me seem incapable of handling a problem on my own. Then one day, someone smiled at me for no reason. A friendly face in the crowd made me feel good. If one person with a smile on her face could make me feel lighter, then a smile might be a powerful way to change how other people felt. Over the next few months, I smiled at every person who looked in my direction, even the nastiest of patrons. As a result, most people were friendlier towards me, and I even felt better about myself. I also became easily able to handle those pesky daily problems. I wish more of us could learn that we have the opportunity to change the world within in us and outside of us, when we smile.

.... Everyone should learn an important lesson in life. Some lessons about being honest. Everyone should learn honesty. Parents teach honesty. Don't shoplift. Don't cheat on tests. Don't lie to friends, even white lies. Everyone should learn kindness. Parents and friends teach kindness. Peers are not kind to them. Too many school yard bullies hurt people. If everyone learned important lessons in life, they would be better off.

.... My mom taught how to deal with stress. As a young child, I was diagnosed with attention deficit disorder. This condition makes many every day situations very stressful. So mom taught me three things that have helped me reduce stress. First, she taught me to think ahead. For example every evening, I lay out my clothes for the next day. Planning what I want to wear the night before saves me time and gives me one less thing to worry about in the morning rush to get out the door. Second, she taught me to be organized. Not only do I plan what I am going to wear, but I make a daily list of assignments and appointments so I know exactly what I need to do and where I need to be. I also keep a backpack filled with supplies such as bottled water, healthy snacks, pen, paper, or any other item I might need. Finally, mother taught me to ask questions and take notes. Asking questions and taking notes keep me focused on a task and keeps my mind from wandering in a million different directions. I am grateful that my mom taught me how to reduce stress. I bet everyone would be better off if they could learn what my mom taught me about coping with stress.

.... Steeling is wrong! Unfortunately not everyone knows this. If every one respected others' property as they do there own we would have less chaos. If everyone that was caught steeling had a good beating put on them I am sure they would second guess doing it again, I am not saying that is how this problem should be resolved but I think it would work. Whether you are a child or a full grown adult I believe this concept should be stressed, let alone it is against the law. The world would be a better place if no one stole, and we would all have more respect for each other and there property.

Academic Learning Log: Chapter Review

WHAT HAVE I LEARNED ABOUT PARAGRAPHS?

1. The three levels of information in a paragraph are the _____, _____, and _____.

2. The three parts of a paragraph are a _____, a _____, and an _____.

3. The beginning of a paragraph includes a _____, the _____, and the _____.

4. The middle or the _____ of the paragraph offers major and minor details in support of the topic sentence.

5. The ending or conclusion of the paragraph reinforces _____.

6. An effective paragraph is _____, _____, _____, and _____.

7. A topic sentence states the focused main idea in a _____.

8. To establish logical order, a writing plan includes one or more of the following elements: a _____, order of _____, and order of _____.

9. Relevant details explain and support only the writer's point; _____ details offer in-depth explanations and supports for the writer's point.

10. Effective expression enhances the writer's purpose through the precise choice and use of _____, _____, and _____.

11. **How will I use what I have learned about the paragraph?**
    In your notebook, discuss how you will apply to your own writing what you have learned about the paragraph.

12. **What do I still need to study about the paragraph?**
    In your notebook, discuss your ongoing study needs by describing what, when, and how you will continue studying the paragraph.

MyWritingLab™

Complete the Post-test for Chapter 3 in MyWritingLab.

4 The Descriptive Paragraph

LEARNING OUTCOMES

After studying this chapter you will be able to:

1. Answer the question "What's the Point of Description?"
2. Compose a Topic Sentence
3. Use Logical Order
4. Develop Relevant Details
5. Use Effective Expression: Concrete Word Choice
6. Use Description in Your Academic Courses
7. Write a Descriptive Paragraph Step by Step

A description is an account that creates a vivid mental image.

The ability to describe people, places, or objects accurately is a useful life skill. Whether you are talking with a stylist about the exact hairstyle you want, sharing a funny or startling scene from your day with a friend in an e-mail, or reporting on the structure of a plant cell for a biology class, you will use description to make your point.

> "As they turn to the sheer descent, the white and blue and slate color, in the heart of the Canadian Falls at least, blend and deepen to a rich, wonderful, luminous green. On the edge of disaster the river seems to gather herself, to pause, top, lift a head noble in ruin, and then, with a slow grandeur, to plunge into the eternal thunder and white chaos below."
>
> RUPERT BROOKE, FROM "NIAGARA FALLS" *Westminster Gazette*, 1913

What's the Point of Description?

In a descriptive paragraph, the writer uses sensory details such as sights, sounds, smells, tastes, feelings, and textures to create vivid images in the reader's mind. An experienced writer relies on sense memories of a specific experience to evoke these details. In addition, the writer often uses spatial order to create a clear visual image of a person, place, object, or scene: the location or arrangement in space from top to bottom, bottom to top, right to left, left to right, near to far, far to near, inside to outside, or outside to inside.

Every day, we experience rich sensory details from television, movies, music DVDs, and daily life. Think of a scene that grabbed your attention recently. What is your main impression of the scene? What are several details that make this impression so vivid or memorable?

Description also may include or suggest time order because a person, place, or object usually appears in a situation, or an incident usually occurs or suggests a scene.

Descriptive transition words signal that the details follow a logical order based on one or more of the following elements:

1. The arrangement in space of a person, place, object, or scene

2. The starting point from which the writer chooses to begin the description

3. The time frame as relevant to the description (see Chapter 5 for information about time order)

Getting a mental picture of the person, place, object, scene, or situation helps a writer discover his or her point about the subject being described. Study the following photograph of a popular destination for travelers: SeaWorld, San Diego, California. Use your sense memory of this or similar scenes to call up sensory details. Fill in the graphic with captions that capture the particular details of specific locations at SeaWorld. Then, answer the question "What's the point or impression you are trying to make?" with a one-sentence statement of the overall main idea.

Source: Hannah Davis' Personal Picture; July 2011 in SeaWorld, San Diego, California.

A Where is this detail in the scene?

....

What are the sensory details?

SIGHT: ....

SOUND: ....

SMELL: ....

TASTE: ....

TOUCH: ....

B Where is this detail in the scene?

....

What are the sensory details?

SIGHT: ....

SOUND: ....

SMELL: ....

TASTE: ....

TOUCH: ....

C Where is this detail in the scene?

....

What are the sensory details?

SIGHT: ....

SOUND: ....

SMELL: ....

TASTE: ....

TOUCH: ....

D Where is this detail in the scene?

....

What are the sensory details?

SIGHT: ....

SOUND: ....

SMELL: ....

TASTE: ....

TOUCH: ....

E Where is this detail in the scene?

....

What are the sensory details?

SIGHT: ....

SOUND: ....

SMELL: ....

TASTE: ....

TOUCH: ....

My First Thoughts: A Prewriting Activity

Brainstorm about the images you just studied. Set a time limit, such as five minutes, and write in your notebook about the images you just studied and the details you generated. Write as quickly as you can without stopping. Getting your first thoughts about a topic on paper is an excellent way to overcome writer's block and set your mind to thinking.

One Student Writer's Response

Read the following paragraph written by student Hannah Davis that describes her view of a popular performance at SeaWorld, San Diego, California. Read the description and the explanations; complete the activities in **bold** type in the annotations. Then, read the writer's journal entry about her experience writing the paragraph.

Spatial Order: The phrase "Outside the arena" establishes spatial order. **Circle four more words or phrases that indicate spatial order.**

Relevant Details: Relevant details describe aspects of the scene to support the point. **Draw a box around two additional details that support the author's point.**

Effective Expression: Sensory details such as "ocean blue color—crisp and clean looking" create a vivid mental image. **Double underline 3 more sensory details.**

Main Idea: The main idea is the author's point about a topic. **Underline the author's point about her topic SeaWorld.**

SeaWorld, San Diego, California

(1) Sheer excitement and enthusiasm bubbles throughout the crowd at the famous SeaWorld in San Diego, California. (2) Audience members stare excitedly towards the stage, where so much action takes place. (3) Outside the arena, a male performer, representing the corrupted antagonist, is dressed in a predominantly black wetsuit with a Mohawk of colorful fire on his head. (4) Both hands are thrust up into the air and he holds a flamboyant red and yellow flag in his right hand. (5) Facing the crowd, an intense look covers his face. (6) To his right stands the protagonist, dressed in a vibrant yellow suit. (7) His stance is strong, his body erect, and in his right hand is the same red and yellow flag. (8) Inside the arena, the water is a mesmerizing ocean blue color—crisp and clean looking. (9) To the left, two dolphins have jumped completely out of the water, idling horizontally in midair. (10) Their two bodies, a deep gray color, glisten intensely in the afternoon sunlight. (11) Towards the right are two more beautiful dolphins. (12) These two have also jumped completely out of the water, bodies completely vertical. (13) The contrast between the two groups is absolutely phenomenal. (14) In the middle stage stands a handful of human performers all dressed in loud performance wetsuits. (15) Everyone holds their arms high in a V-shape as if welcoming the dolphins out of the water. (16) Behind the performers, the beautifully articulated set stands in various shades of blue colors representing waves, and various golden and orange colors representing the sun. (17) The dolphins, the performers, and the excited crowd all created a thrilling spectacle at SeaWorld in San Diego, California.

The Writer's Journal

PEER EDITING

The student writer of "SeaWorld, San Diego, California" completed the following reflection to record her thinking about her use of details. Read her writer's journal that describes a few key choices she made as she wrote. Then, in the given space, answer her questions about her use of details in her paragraph. Work with a peer or a small group of classmates.

SPATIAL ORDER: When starting to write, for me, there is almost always a blatant block. I cannot get the first sentence down. My solution is to put words on the paper and keep going; even a simple "sum up" sentence, which states what is happening in the scene, helps to get words to come out. I decided to start at the bottom of the photograph and work upwards because of the audience. What helped me write was deciding where to start (i.e., the bottom of the picture) and then choosing things that popped out at me. For example, I started with the audience and decided to write about them like I was one of them; excitement is a big feeling at SeaWorld, so I wanted the readers to feel that excitement and vibrancy from my paragraph. I had to imagine I was back at SeaWorld, telling a blind individual about what was going on in front of me.

Was the order of my ideas clear? Should I have started somewhere else, like the top or the left side?

Writers use descriptive paragraphs to make a point through the vivid details they observe and share about a person, place, object, scene, or situation. To make a point by describing details, a writer often relies on spatial order transitions and sensory details. At times, a writer also uses time order to describe an experience.

L2 Compose a Topic Sentence

When you write a description, you limit your topic to concrete details based on sight, sound, smell, taste, and touch. Your opinion or attitude about the subject you are describing is your point or main idea. In a description, your main idea may also include logical order signal words; other times, the logical order is implied without including the signal words.

For example, the first of the following two topic sentences includes (1) the topic, (2) the writer's opinion about the topic, and (3) spatial order signal words. The second topic sentence only includes (1) the topic and (2) the writer's attitude about the topic.

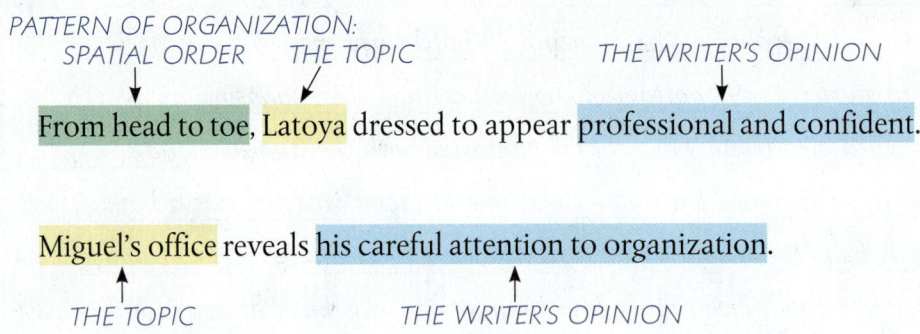

PATTERN OF ORGANIZATION:
SPATIAL ORDER → THE TOPIC → THE WRITER'S OPINION

From head to toe, Latoya dressed to appear professional and confident.

Miguel's office reveals his careful attention to organization.
↑ THE TOPIC   ↑ THE WRITER'S OPINION

Practice 2

COMPOSE A TOPIC SENTENCE

Practice creating topic sentences. The first two items present a topic, an opinion, and logical order signal word(s). Combine the ideas in each group to create a topic sentence for a descriptive paragraph. Then, complete the practice by composing your own topic sentences.

1. TOPIC: (a favorite place) *Grandmother's kitchen*

   OPINION: *Offered a haven of old-fashioned country warmth*

   LOGICAL ORDER SIGNAL WORDS: *A small room at the rear of the house*

   TOPIC SENTENCE: _____

2. TOPIC: (a treasured possession) *The handmade well-pump lamp*

OPINION: *is an eye-catching and whimsical family treasure*

LOGICAL ORDER SIGNAL WORDS: *implied: such as*

TOPIC SENTENCE:

3. TOPIC: (a useful product)

OPINION: *Sleek, lightweight, flexible, easy to use*

LOGICAL ORDER SIGNAL WORDS (AS NEEDED):

TOPIC SENTENCE:

4. TOPIC: (a person of character) MY MOTHER (or father, brother, sister, friend, etc.)

OPINION: *kindness*

LOGICAL ORDER SIGNAL WORDS (AS NEEDED):

TOPIC SENTENCE:

5. TOPIC:

OPINION:

LOGICAL ORDER SIGNAL WORDS (AS NEEDED):

TOPIC SENTENCE:

L3 Use Logical Order

Once you have chosen a topic and focused on a main idea, you are ready to generate and organize details. To organize visual details, spatial order transition words are helpful during the prewriting phase as well as during the drafting part of the writing process. During prewriting, spatial signal words such as *top*, *middle*, or *bottom* can be used as headings to list details. During the drafting stage, explicitly stating spatial transition words creates a picture in your reader's mind of how your subject is arranged in space. Strong transition words establish coherence, a clear and easy-to-follow flow of ideas.

Transition Words Used to Signal Visual Description

above	at the top	beyond	farther	left	right
across	back	by	front	middle	there
adjacent	behind	center	here	nearby	under
around	below	close to	in	next to	underneath
at the bottom	beneath	down	inside	outside	within
at the side	beside	far away			

Practice 3

USE SPATIAL ORDER DETAILS

Determine the logical order of the following details taken from Maya Angelou's autobiography *I Know Why the Caged Bird Sings*. Hint: Underline the words that signal spatial order. Complete the exercise by answering the question "What's the point?"

_____ And when they put their hands on their hips in a show of jauntiness, the palms slipped the thighs as if the pants were waxed.

_____ When they tried to smile to carry off their tiredness as if it was nothing, the body did nothing to help the mind's attempt at disguise.

_____ In the store the men's faces were the most painful to watch, but I seemed to have no choice.

_____ Their shoulders drooped even as they laughed.

—*I Know Why the Caged Bird Sings*, copyright © 2009 by Maya Angelou, (New York: Random House)

What's the point Maya Angelou makes with her use of spatial details?

_____

Develop Relevant Details

A writer narrows a topic into a focused main idea by generating descriptive details that answer questions such as *who, what,* and *where*. As a writer brainstorms, the thinking process brings to mind many sensory as well as spatial details. A writer evaluates the relevance of each detail and uses only those that illustrate the main idea. Some relevant details describe the appearance of a person, object, place, or scene; other relevant details explain the author's opinion about the topic. Many descriptive details appeal to sight, sound, smell, taste, and touch. A **concept map**, or **graphic organizer**, helps in several ways. First, the graphic can prompt your thinking, memory, and creativity. In addition, the graphic helps to order ideas as they occur to you. A graphic organizer also allows you to visualize the details and determine if you have enough to make your point. Irrelevant details do not explain, support, or illustrate the focused point of the paragraph. In addition to the graphic organizer, writers use the revision process to double check details for relevance and to eliminate irrelevant ones.

During the prewriting phase, a writer naturally generates irrelevant details. In fact, an effective writer evaluates the details and uses only those that support the main idea. All descriptive details should work together to create a strong, unified impression, a mental image of the author's main point.

Concept Chart: Description						
TOPIC: Latoya and professional attire for a job interview						
WHERE	SIGHT	SMELL	SOUND	TASTE	TOUCH	
Top: Hair	hair gathered and smoothed into a neat and stylish twist					
Face	light touch of blush and lip gloss; small gold earrings		calm, assured tone of voice			
Middle: Blouse and Jacket	white dress cotton button-up collared shirt; dark blue jacket with a rich pin stripe				firm handshake	
Skirt	below the knee; dark blue, A-line					
Bottom: Shoes	dark blue, polished, low heels, attractive					

Practice 4

DEVELOP RELEVANT DETAILS

The following paragraph develops the ideas recorded in the graphic organizer about Latoya and her professional attire. Circle the main idea. Underline the spatial signal words and the sensory details. Cross out the two details that are not relevant to the main idea.

Dressed to Impress

(1) Latoya Bond had been job hunting for months; finally, she landed an interview with a company that she was eager to join. (2) Latoya felt confident that she was well qualified for the position. (3) After all, she was one of the three final candidates chosen from over 100 applications, yet she also knew the importance of making a good impression. (4) From head to toe, Latoya dressed to appear professional and confident. (5) Latoya gathered her hard-to-manage curls into a neat and stylish twist. (6) To complement her no-nonsense hairstyle, Latoya used makeup sparingly but effectively. (7) A little black mascara on her lashes, a touch of blush across her cheeks, and bit of tinted lip balm brought attention to her interested eyes and her earnest smile. (8) She would also be sure to speak with a calm and assured voice. (9) The neatly pressed collar of a white cotton shirt contrasted nicely with her tailored blue pinstriped jacket. (10) Her dark blue A-line skirt reached to just below her knees. (11) Latoya finished her outfit with a flattering pair of blue low-heeled pumps that matched her briefcase and purse. (12) She would offer her prospective employer a firm handshake. (13) Latoya looked as professional and confident as she felt.

L5 Use Effective Expression: Concrete Word Choice

Precise word choice communicates exact meaning. Words chosen for a specific emotional or visual impact create strong images in the reader's mind and carry out the writer's purpose. As you move through the writing process, think about the impact you want to have on your reader. For the greatest impact, choose concrete and precise words and phrases instead of general or vague expressions. Choose words that *show* instead of *tell*. Consider the following examples.

General or vague words that tell:

This property has curb appeal.

Concrete words that show:

This beachfront cottage charms potential buyers with its colorful garden, wrap-around porch, and ocean view.

Practice 5

USE EFFECTIVE EXPRESSION: CONCRETE WORD CHOICE

Each item below presents a general sentence using vague words. The phrase in parentheses before each sentence—(A customer to a mechanic) in item 1, for example—describes the speaker of the sentence and the person hearing it. Revise each sentence to eliminate vague wording. Consider the point of the writing situation; express ideas with words that have concrete and precise meanings for a specific impact. Discuss your revisions with your class or with a small group of peers.

1. (A customer to a mechanic): My car makes a funny sound sometimes.

2. (A student commenting to his or her companion): The restaurant was disappointing.

3. (A weather reporter to a commuter): The weather is pleasant (or horrible).

4. (A staff assistant to Technology Support): The printer is broken.

5. (A customer to a restaurant manager): The service and food were poor.

Use Description in Your Academic Courses

Many college courses in subjects such as literature, composition, history, psychology, ecology, and biology use description. As you study these subjects, you will read descriptions of historical places, influential people, natural elements, and scientific experiments. In addition, you will write descriptions to learn or demonstrate what you have learned.

Practice 6

USE DESCRIPTION IN A HISTORY ASSIGNMENT

Student writer Jean Powell composed the following descriptive paragraph about an important historical site for a report in her American History course. Complete the following activities: (1) Insert appropriate transition words in the blanks; (2) underline the words or phrases used to create sensory details; (3) discuss the point of her report with a small group of peers or with your class.

(1) The Vietnam Memorial is made up of two black granite walls joined in a wide-angled V shape. (2) A study of just one of the walls reveals the significance of the memorial. (3) A polished black granite slab stretches hundreds of feet long. (4) At its highest tip, it stands 10 feet tall and then tapers to a height of 8 inches at its end point. (5) Its low tip points _____ the Lincoln Memorial. (6) _____ its polished face are the carved names of service men and women who gave their lives during the Vietnam War. (7) Starting at the highest point on the first panel, thousands of names are listed in chronological order. (8) The high polish of the black granite reflects the image of the world _____ the wall. (9) The reflection of earth, sky, and visitors are seen along with the inscribed names. (10) On the wall, the present and the past mingle. (11) A path runs _____ the base of the wall so visitors can walk the path to read the names. (12) Many create pencil rubbings or leave tokens such as flowers, flags, and personal notes. (13) To the side of the path, a wide grassy park adds to the sense of serenity. (14) The memorial is a quiet place where one can come to terms with loss and grief. (15) Its tranquility is a fitting memorial to a controversial war that cost so many their lives.

▲ The Vietnam Memorial

Workshop: Writing a Descriptive Paragraph Step by Step

Prewrite Your Paragraph

The activities below will walk you through the steps of the prewriting stage of the writing process: choosing a topic, focusing your point, and generating and organizing relevant details.

Choose Your Topic

The following activities are designed to help you choose a topic.

1. Create a bank of topics. Use the suggested headings and either brainstorm or list as many topics as you possibly can. Don't analyze your thoughts; just jot down topics as quickly as they occur to you. Compare your bank of topics with those of your classmates.

   - The Scene of an Accident
   - A Nature Scene
   - A Pop Icon
   - An Advertisement
   - Emotions (such as fear)

2. Reread the freewrite you composed based on the photograph of SeaWorld. Underline ideas that could be used for a descriptive paragraph. Map out the logical order of details.

3. Select a photograph of a special place. Write captions, brainstorm sensory details, and freewrite about the photograph. Remember to ask "What are the sensory details and how are the details arranged in space?" and "What's the point?" as you generate ideas.

Focus Your Point

Think about a prewrite you have composed for a descriptive topic. Underline or generate words that suggest your values, opinions, or attitudes about what you described. Think about what strikes you as important about your subject. Consider your audience. Who would be interested in this information and why? Choose a purpose. Write a list of adjectives and sensory details that relate the essence of what you are describing. Use a thesaurus and choose several vivid words to express your thoughts. State in one sentence the point of your description.

AUDIENCE: _____

PURPOSE: _____

SENSORY DETAILS: _____

WHAT'S THE POINT? _____

Generate and Organize Relevant Details

Using the ideas you have already recorded and the concept chart for a description, generate and organize sensory and spatial details that support your point. (*Hint*: Fill in the "Where" column with spatial signal words such as *left, right, near, far, above*.)

Concept Chart: Description					
TOPIC:					
WHAT'S THE POINT?					
WHERE	SIGHT	SMELL	SOUND	TASTE	TOUCH

Write a Draft of Your Paragraph

Using ideas you generated during the prewriting phase, compose a draft of your paragraph. Return to the prewriting process at any time to generate additional details as needed. Use your own paper.

Revise Your Draft

Once you have drafted a description, read the draft and answer the questions in the "Questions for Revising a Descriptive Paragraph" box on the next page. Indicate your answers by annotating your paper. If you answer "yes" to a question, underline, check, or circle examples. If you answer "no" to a question, write needed information in the margins and draw lines to indicate placement of additional details. Revise your paragraph as necessary based on your reflection. (*Hint*: Experienced writers create several drafts as they focus on one or two questions per draft.)

Questions for Revising a Descriptive Paragraph:

- [ ] Have I stated or implied a focused main idea? Have I created a strong impression? Can I state my point in one sentence?
- [ ] Is the logical order of the details clear? Have I used strong transitions to indicate spatial order? Time order?
- [ ] Have I created a vivid mental image through the use of sensory details?
- [ ] Have I made my point with adequate details?
- [ ] Do all the details support my point?
- [ ] Have I chosen concrete words to make my point?

Proofread Your Draft

Once you have made any revisions to your paragraph that may be needed, proofread your paper to eliminate unnecessary errors, such as dangling or misplaced modifiers.

> For more information on dangling or misplaced modifiers see pages 458–467.

Grammar in Action: Eliminate Dangling or Misplaced Modifiers

Modifiers are words and phrases that describe other words. A **dangling modifier** occurs when a writer uses a modifier without including the word that the modifier describes.

- **Dangling modifier**

  INCORRECT: Entering the museum of shrunken heads, my stomach lurched with queasiness.

  (THE MISSING WORD IS "I": IT WAS I, NOT MY STOMACH, THAT ENTERED THE MUSEUM.)

- **Revised sentence**

  CORRECT: As I entered the museum of shrunken heads, my stomach lurched with queasiness.

A **misplaced modifier** occurs when a writer separates the modifier from the word it is describing.

- **Misplaced modifier**

  INCORRECT: Scattering in a million directions, Tyrone hustled to scoop up the spilled ball bearings.

  (THE BALL BEARINGS SCATTERED, NOT TYRONE.)

- **Revised sentence**

  CORRECT: Tyrone hustled to scoop up the spilled ball bearings scattering in a million directions.

PROOFREAD: DANGLING AND MISPLACED MODIFIERS

Edit the following student paragraph to eliminate one dangling modifier and two misplaced modifiers.

The Amazing Ruby Falls

(1) The caves at Ruby Falls are one of the wonders of the world, eerie yet intriguing. (2) Our tour group was a small one of about ten people. (3) We all piled onto an elevator, stuffy from all the bodies and stinking like a dirty sock, to sink 250 feet underground. (4) We exited the elevator, gasping for air because of the lack of oxygen and the dampness of the cave. (5) The cave was dark with barely any light. (6) We wore helmets mounted with lights. (7) I looked like a real spelunker. (8) We saw stalactites hanging from the ceiling and stalagmites growing up from the ground. (9) The columns, drapes, and flow stone were phenomenal. (10) We walked through an onyx jungle flowing with layers of limestone. (11) The massive monuments were smooth and damp. (12) Some were slimy like a snail. (13) Water trickled from the ceiling in my hair and down my face, a kiss from the cave. (14) We squeezed through stone pathways littered with rock shapes resembling everything from bacon, to a dragon foot, to a form that looked like New York City, all natural. (15) We came across a huge formation; that appeared to be lifelike; the ice sickle stalactites looked like they could break free and assault us. (16) A breathtaking formation that appeared to be lifelike. (17) The caves are amazing.

Writing Assignments

MyWritingLab™
Complete this Exercise on mywritinglab.com

Considering Audience and Purpose

Study the photographs at the beginning of the chapter. Assume you are a manager at SeaWorld, and the community leaders have asked you and other interested parties for needed safety improvements at the theme park. Suggest and describe one or more specific safety improvements.

Writing for Everyday Life

Assume you are separated from your family or loved ones during a holiday or a special occasion. Write a letter in which you describe a significant element of the event. For example, describe the decorations of the season or event, a bride's dress, a favorite birthday gift, or the spread of food at a party or dinner. Choose words that reflect one of the following: (1) approval and enjoyment or (2) disapproval and disappointment.

Writing for College Life

Assume you are writing a report in your psychology class about how a person's mood is reflected in the clothes he or she chooses on any given day. Describe an outfit that reflects an individual's mood.

Writing for Working Life

Assume you have invented a product that will make life much easier; also assume that the Small Business Association finances the production and marketing of useful new inventions. Write a paragraph describing your product to submit your idea to the Small Business Association.

MyWritingLab™
Complete the Post-test for Chapter 4 in MyWritingLab.

5 The Narrative Paragraph

LEARNING OUTCOMES

After studying this chapter you will be able to:

1. Answer the question "What's the Point of Narration?"
2. Compose a Topic Sentence
3. Use Logical Order
4. Develop Relevant Details
5. Use Effective Expression: Vivid Verbs
6. Use Narration in Your Academic Courses
7. Write a Narrative Paragraph Step by Step

Narration is an account of events told in chronological order to make a specific point.

All of us love a good story. Think of a good story that you have heard, read, or watched on TV or in a theater.

A good story is about personalities or characters, whether real or imagined. A good story is full of vivid action and details. A good story makes a point.

A writer uses narration to tell a story to make a specific point. Often we tell stories to warn about dangers, to teach important lessons, to record important historical events, or to amuse and entertain each other. Narration is a chain of events. These events unfold in chronological order—the order in which they occur. Thus, details follow a logical order based on time. The writer presents an event and then shows when and how each of the subsequent events flows from the first event. In addition to relaying an event, a writer also uses vivid actions and details to show the point of the story. Vivid details may include specific sights, sounds, smells, tastes, textures, feelings, and actions.

What's the Point of Narration?

Getting a mental picture of an event helps a writer to discover the point he or she wishes to make. The following sequence of photographs documents a series of events that took place in the life of Malala Yousafzai over the course of several years. Study each photograph in the timeline. Write a caption that states the topic of each picture. Then answer the question "What's the point?" with a one-sentence statement of the overall main idea.

PHOTOGRAPHIC ORGANIZER: NARRATION

FIRST EVENT

What happened?

◂ Student standing by a destroyed school, Mingor, Pakistan, 2010

SECOND EVENT

What happened?

◂ Malala Yousafzai, gunshot wounded, is moved to hospital, 2012

THIRD EVENT

What happened?

◂ Nobel Peace Prize lecture, 2014

What's the point?

TOPIC SENTENCE:

WRITING FROM LIFE

My First Thoughts: A Prewriting Activity

Set a time limit, such as five minutes, and write in your notebook about the images you just studied. Do not let your pen or pencil stop. Even if you must repeat ideas, keep writing until the time limit is up. Let the ideas flow freely. Getting your first thoughts about a topic on paper is an excellent way to kick-start your writing process.

One Student Writer's Response

The following paragraph offers one writer's narrative inspired by photographs of Malala Yousafzai. Read the narrative paragraph and the explanations; complete the activities in **bold** type in the annotations. Then, read the writer's journal that describes a few key choices she made as she wrote.

Chronological Order:
Chronological order is established with the phrase "in the moment." **Circle five more words or phrases that indicate time order.**

Main Idea:
The main idea is the point of the narration. Notice the topic is Malala Yousafzai. **Underline the author's point.**

Vivid Verbs:
Vivid verbs such as "refuses" create a mental image and emphasize action. **Double underline three more vivid verbs.**

Relevant Details:
Relevant details describe events to support the point about Malala's courage and determination. **Highlight two more details that support the point.**

Malala Yousafzai's Courage and Determination

(1) All of us, at some point in our lives, face great loss or overwhelming barriers to our goals. (2) Often, in the moment of such challenges, we want to give up or give in to hopelessness. (3) Malala Yousafzai's story shows us how to overcome loss with courage and determination. (4) Malala Yousafzai, born on July 12, 1997, in Mingora, Pakistan, became an activist, speaking out for girls' education. (5) At the time, a Taliban edict had banned girls' education and resulted in the destruction of hundreds of schools. (6) In 2009, at the age of 11, she wrote *Diary of a Pakistani Schoolgirl*. (7) First published on *BBC Urdu* online, her diary records the impact of the ban on her and her classmates' education. (8) Immediately after her public stand, the Taliban issued a death threat against her. (9) On October 9, 2012, a militant shot Yousafzai in the head. (10) The gunman boarded her school bus in her hometown Swat, called her out by name, and fired three shots. (11) Two of her school friends were also wounded. (12) Miraculously, Malala survived the shooting and consequently, became known worldwide. (13) She used her notoriety to speak out on the importance of education. (14) In 2013, *Time* magazine named Malala Yousafzai one of the most influential people in the world. (15) Then in 2014, she was awarded the Nobel Peace Prize, becoming the youngest person to ever receive the award. (16) In the face of death and the tyranny of the Taliban, Malala revealed her courage and determination, and she refuses to stop fighting for what she believes is right. (17) Malala has dedicated her life to her cause, saying, "It's a second life, people have prayed to God to spare me and I was spared for a reason—to use my life for helping people."

The Writer's Journal

PEER EDITING

The student writer of "Malala Yousafzai's Courage and Determination" completed the following reflection to record her thinking through the writing process. Read her writer's journal that describes a few key choices she made as she wrote. Then, in the given space, answer her questions about her use of details in her paragraph. Work with a peer or a small group of classmates.

LOGICAL ORDER: *When I read over my first draft, I noticed that the paragraph didn't really flow smoothly. I had used cause and effect and addition transition words instead of time order words. So I revised to include chronological transitions because this is a narrative. For example, the time order signal phrase "Immediately after" replaced the cause and effect signal phrase "As a result of," in the sentence describing her public stand, and the signal word "then" replaced the addition signal word "and" in describing what happened to her in 2014.*

Does the paragraph flow smoothly now? Which transitions are most effective? Are more time order transition words needed? Where and why?

A narrative tells a story. The story illustrates the writer's point or main idea. To make a point by telling a story, a writer relies on the use of time order transitions, relevant sensory details, and vivid word choice.

L2 Compose a Topic Sentence

When you choose to write a narrative, you limit your topic to the details of a specific event based on time order. Most likely, you also have an opinion or point of view about the event. Your opinion or attitude about the event is your point or main idea. Many writers of narrative paragraphs create topic sentences to state the points illustrated by the events.

For example, the following topic sentence contains (1) the topic, (2) the writer's opinion about the topic, and (3) the pattern of organization used to organize details.

Aaron Ralston bravely survived a five-day ordeal.

TOPIC IS AARON RALSTON

WRITER'S OPINION IS STATED WITH THE WORDS "BRAVELY" AND "ORDEAL"

PATTERN OF ORGANIZATION: NARRATION TIME ORDER IS ESTABLISHED WITH THE PHRASE "FIVE-DAY ORDEAL"

This example illustrates the relationships of the topic, the author's opinion, and the pattern of organization in this particular topic sentence. Note that the word "ordeal" suggests both time order and the writer's opinion.

Practice 2

COMPOSE TOPIC SENTENCES

Practice creating topic sentences. The following items present a topic, an opinion, and time order signal word(s). Combine the ideas in each group to create a topic sentence for a narrative.

1. TOPIC: Jeff Gordon

   OPINION: squeaked to narrow victory

   TIME ORDER SIGNAL WORDS: during the last few laps of the Daytona 500

   TOPIC SENTENCE: _____

2. TOPIC: honesty

   OPINION: I learned the value of

   TIME ORDER SIGNAL WORDS: during my first job interview

   TOPIC SENTENCE: _____

Use Logical Order

Once you have selected your topic and focused on a main idea, you are ready to generate additional details and organize your ideas into a logical sequence based on time order. Each event in a narrative is developed by describing the individual actions and details that make up that event. Just as time order words in the topic sentence signal a narrative, time order transition words also show the flow of events as they unfold in the narrative. Strong transitions establish coherence, a clear and understandable flow of ideas.

Transition Words Used to Show Time Order

after	during	later	previously	ultimately
afterward	eventually	meanwhile	second	until
as	finally	next	since	when
before	first	now	soon	while
currently	last	often	then	

USE TIME ORDER SIGNAL WORDS

The following paragraph was first published by Linda M. Hasselstrom in *High Country News* to explain her choice for self-defense. Fill in the four blanks with appropriate time order signal words based on the logical order of ideas.

A Peaceful Woman Explains Why She Carries a Gun

(1) As I drove home one night, a car followed me. (2) It passed me on a narrow bridge _____ a passenger flashed a blinding spotlight in my face. (3) I braked sharply. (4) The car stopped, angled across the bridge, and four men jumped out. (5) I realized the locked doors were useless if they broke the windows of my pickup. (6) I started forward, hoping to knock their car aside so I could pass. (7) Just _____ another car appeared, and the men hastily got back into their car. (8) They continued to follow me, passing and repassing. (9) I dared not go home because no one else was there. (10) I passed no lighted houses. (11) _____ they pulled over onto the roadside, and I decided to use their tactic: fear. (12) Speeding, the pickup horn blaring, I swerved as close to them as I could _____ I roared past. (13) It worked: they turned off the highway. (14) But I was frightened and angry. (15) Even in my vehicle I was too vulnerable.

—Hasselstrom, Linda M. "Why One Peaceful Woman Carries a Pistol," in *Land Circle, Fulcrum, Inc.*, 1991. Used by permission of Fulcrum Inc.

L4 Develop Relevant Details

A writer narrows a topic into a focused main idea by generating details that answer questions such as *who, what, when, where, why,* and *how*. A writer evaluates the relevance of each detail and uses only those that illustrate the main idea. Some relevant details show the action of the event; other details explain the author's opinion about the event. Relevant details also often include sensory details, which appeal to sight, sound, smell, taste, and touch. These vivid details work together to create a mental image of the author's main point. During the prewriting phase, a timeline can help a writer organize ideas as they are generated. Study the following concept map that was used to generate details about the topic "Aaron Ralston's Ordeal."

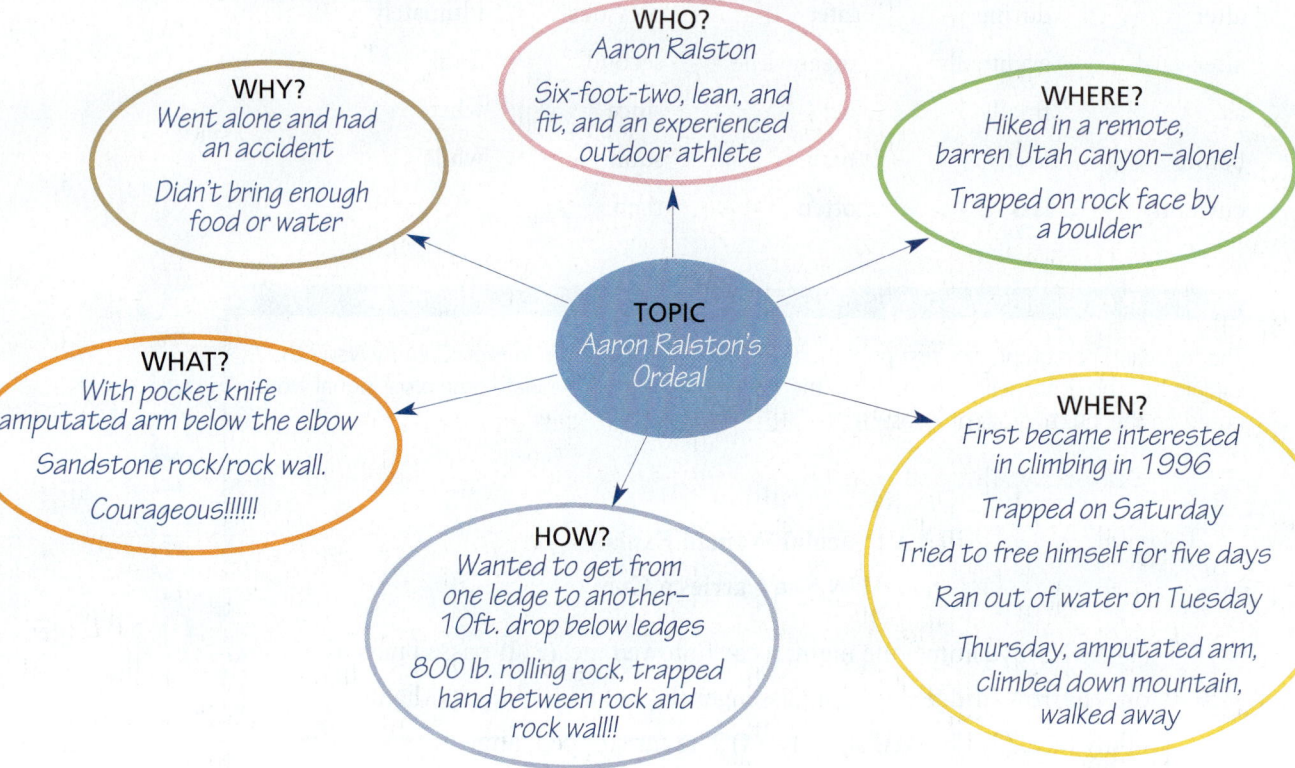

DEVELOP RELEVANT DETAILS

Using the details in the concept map above about the topic "Aaron Ralston's Ordeal," complete the timeline below to show the proper time order of events.

1. _____
2. _____
3. _____
4. _____
5. _____

During the prewriting phase, a writer naturally generates irrelevant details. In fact, an effective writer often produces far more details than can be used to make a specific point. Irrelevant details do not explain, support, or illustrate the focused point of the paragraph. Often, writers use the revision process to double check details for relevance and to eliminate irrelevant details.

DEVELOP RELEVANT DETAILS

The following paragraph develops the ideas recorded in the brainstorming list about Aaron Ralston. Circle the main idea. Underline the relevant sensory details. Cross out the two details that are not relevant to the main idea.

The Courage to Survive

(1) Aaron Ralston courageously survived a five-day ordeal. (2) Ralston began his ordeal Saturday morning when he made an attempt to climb over a ten-foot drop between two ledges. (3) Suddenly, an 800-pound rock roared down upon him from above. (4) He quickly scrambled to get out of its path in time. (5) In the next second, the mammoth stone trapped him on the barren rock face. (6) The boulder had smashed and pinned his right hand between it and a sandstone wall. (7) Six-foot-two, lean, and fit, Ralston is an experienced outdoor athlete. (8) He first became interested in climbing in 1996. (9) For five days, Ralston chipped away at the boulder with a pocket knife. (10) Finally, on Tuesday, he ran out of his meager ration of food and water. (11) By Thursday rescue seemed unlikely, so Ralston, parched with thirst, made the gutsy decision to amputate his own hand. (12) Knowing his flimsy pocket knife would not cut through bone, he used the force of the rock to snap his bones just below the elbow. (13) Then after applying a tourniquet, Ralston cut through his own muscles, veins, and arteries. (14) Once he completed the hour-long amputation, he rappelled down the mountain. (15) At last, a haggard Ralston hiked out of the canyon.

L5 Use Effective Expression: Vivid Verbs

Show, don't tell! Some of the verbs most commonly used by student writers belong to the *to be* family of verbs. However, *to be* verbs such as *am*, *is*, *are*, *was*, and *were* are vague and lifeless. They *tell* instead of *show* action, as in the following sentence: *Ivan was angry*. This sentence tells us about Ivan's emotion, but it doesn't show how he acts when he is angry or how his anger fits into the flow of events.

A writer draws a mental picture for the main idea through the use of vivid verbs.

Vivid verbs show the action that is taking place:

Ivan stomped to the trash can and hurled the report into it.

THE VERBS "STOMPED" AND "HURLED" ARE BIASED WORDS. ANOTHER WITNESS MAY HAVE CHOSEN OBJECTIVE LANGUAGE TO DESCRIBE IVAN'S ACTIONS:

Vivid verbs reflect the author's opinion:

Ivan walked to the trash can and tossed the report into it.

Vivid verbs express sensory details:

Ivan snorted with contempt.

Many writers dedicate one full revision to focus on word choices.

Practice 6

USE VIVID VERBS

Revise each of the following sentences by using vivid verbs to replace *to be* verbs such as *am*, *is*, *are*, *was*, and *were*.

1. The coffee was hot.

2. Ryanne was injured during the race.

3. Michael Phelps was the winner of 18 Olympic gold medals.

4. We were so excited; we were screaming and jumping all around like lunatics.

5. I am afraid of my next door neighbor's pit bull.

Use Narration in Your Academic Courses

Many college courses in subjects such as history, psychology, composition, and literature use narration. As you study these subjects, you will read narrations of historical events, case studies, short stories, and novels. In addition, you will write narratives to demonstrate what you have learned. For example, an essay exam may ask you to relate the key events of a major war or the important events in the life of an influential person. Some college writing assignments ask you to draw upon your personal experience and relate it to what you are learning.

USE NARRATION IN AN INTERPERSONAL COMMUNICATION ASSIGNMENT

Read the following information from a college communications textbook. On a separate sheet of paper, write a response to the writing assignment, given in the last sentence of the text.

Ethics in Interpersonal Communication

(1) Because communication has consequences, interpersonal communication involves ethics, a moral aspect of right or wrong. (2) It is believed that there are certain universal ethical principles: you should tell the truth, have respect for another's dignity, and not harm the innocent. (3) In the U.S. legal system, you have the right to remain silent and to refuse to incriminate yourself. (4) But you don't have the right to refuse to reveal information about the criminal activities of others that you may have witnessed. (5) Psychiatrists and lawyers are often exempt from this general rule. (6) Similarly a wife can't be forced to testify against her husband nor a husband against his wife. (7) In interpersonal situations, however, there aren't any written rules so it's not always clear if or when silence is ethical.

(8) What would you do? (9) While at the supermarket, you witness a mother verbally abusing her three-year-old child. (10) You worry that the mother might psychologically harm the child, and your first impulse is to speak up and tell this woman that verbal abuse can have lasting effects on the child and often leads to physical abuse. (11) At the same time, you don't want to interfere with a mother's right to say what she wants to her child. (12) Nor do you want to aggravate a mother who may later take out her frustration on the child. (13) Write a short narrative that illustrates what you would do in this situation.

L7 Workshop: Writing a Narrative Paragraph Step by Step

Prewriting for Your Paragraph

The activities below will walk you through the steps of the prewriting stage of the writing process: choosing a topic, focusing your point, and generating and organizing relevant details.

Choose Your Topic

The following activities are designed to help you choose a topic.

1. Create a bank of topics. Use the suggested headings and either brainstorm or list as many topics as you possibly can. Don't be critical of what you write; just get as many topics written down as quickly as possible. As you think of new topics, add them to the list. Compare your bank of topics with those of your classmates.

   - Heroes
   - Health
   - Pop Culture
   - Memories

2. Generate ideas with a freewrite. Choose one of the topics from your topic bank and think of an event related to that topic. Write about the event for ten minutes without stopping. Include sensory details: sight, sound, smell, taste, and touch.

3. Select a photograph of a special event. Write a caption, brainstorm topics, and freewrite about the photograph. Remember to ask "What happened?" and "What's the point?" as you generate ideas.

Focus Your Point

Read a freewrite you have generated for a narrative. Underline words that suggest your values, opinions, or attitudes about the event. Think about what interests you about the event. Use a thesaurus and choose several vivid words to express your thoughts. Identify your audience and purpose. Write a list of vivid verbs that show the actions that occur during the event. State in one sentence the point of the story you are going to tell.

AUDIENCE:

PURPOSE:

VIVID VERBS:

WHAT'S THE POINT?

Generate and Organize Relevant Details

Using ideas you have recorded so far and the timeline graphic, generate and organize details that support your point.

What's the point?

TOPIC SENTENCE: ....

....

....

What happened?

1.
2.
3.
4.
5.

 ## Write a Draft of Your Paragraph

Using the ideas you generated during the prewriting phase, compose a draft of your paragraph. Return to the prewriting process at any time to generate additional details as needed. Use your own paper.

 ## Revise Your Draft

Once you have created a draft of a narrative, read the draft and answer the questions in the "Questions for Revising a Narrative Paragraph" box that follows. Indicate your answers by annotating your paper. If you answer "yes" to a question, underline, check, or circle examples. If you answer "no" to a question, write additional details in the margins and draw lines to indicate their placement. Revise your paragraph based on your reflection. (*Hint:* Experienced writers create several drafts as they focus on one or two questions per draft.)

Questions for Revising a Narrative Paragraph:

- ☐ Have I stated or implied a focused main idea? Have I created a strong impression? Can I state my point in one sentence?
- ☐ Is the logical order of the events clear? Have I used strong transitions to indicate time? And space?
- ☐ Have I made my point with adequate details?
- ☐ Do all the details support my point?
- ☐ Have I used vivid verbs to keep my readers interested in what I am saying? Have I used sensory details to make my point?
- ☐ What impact will my paragraph make on my reader?

Proofread Your Draft

Once you have made any revisions to your paragraph that may be needed, proofread your paragraph to eliminate careless errors such as shifts in verb tense.

For more information about verb tense see pages 510–523.

Grammar in Action: Unnecessary Shifts in Verb Tense

Verb tense tells your reader when an event occurred. "Sandra laughed" is past tense. "Sandra laughs" is present tense. "Sandra will laugh" is future tense. A shift in tense for no logical reason is confusing to the reader.

- **A Shift in Verb Tense**

  INCORRECT

  Monica sighed loudly, rolled her eyes, and stomps off angrily.

- **Consistent Use of Tense**

  CORRECT

  Monica sighs loudly, rolls her eyes, and stomps off angrily.

EDIT FOR TENSE SHIFTS

Edit these sentences for unnecessary shifts in tense.

1. Raul works two jobs and attends a community college. He wanted to become a registered nurse and join the Peace Corps.

2. Joe and Jarvonna had a wonderful first date. Joe makes reservations at the Japanese Steak House. After dinner, he surprises her with tickets to watch her favorite team, the Orlando Magic, play the Miami Heat. On the way home, Jarvonna suggested stopping for coffee. Losing track of time, the two talk for hours.

....

....

....

Writing Assignments

MyWritingLab™ Complete this Exercise on mywritinglab.com

Considering Audience and Purpose
Study the sequence of photographs of Malala Yousafzai at the beginning of the chapter. Assume the pictures are to be used to document her achievements on a website designed to increase awareness about her fight for girls' education. Write a narrative that will be recorded as a voice-over and heard as the pictures flash on the screen.

Writing for Everyday Life
Assume you or someone you know recently took action in an emergency situation. Write a paragraph for a letter to a friend relaying the event as it unfolded. Choose words that reflect one of the following: (1) approval of a courageous act or (2) concern for a foolish act.

Writing for College Life
Assume you have witnessed an important historical event such as the invention of the wheel, the first flight into space, landing on the moon, the last battle fought in the Civil War, or 9/11. Write a paragraph for a local paper documenting the event as it occurred.

Writing for Working Life
Assume you are filing for worker's compensation for an injury that occurred on the job. Write a paragraph for a report to your supervisor in which you record the events as they occurred.

MyWritingLab™
Complete the Post-test for Chapter 5 in MyWritingLab.

6 The Process Paragraph

LEARNING OUTCOMES

After studying this chapter you will be able to:

- **L1** Answer the question "What's the Point of Process?"
- **L2** Compose a Topic Sentence
- **L3** Use Logical Order
- **L4** Develop Relevant Details
- **L5** Use Effective Expression: Vivid Images
- **L6** Use Process in Your Academic Courses
- **L7** Write a Process Paragraph Step by Step

A process is a series of steps, occurring in chronological order.

Every day we repeat countless processes, from cooking a meal to flossing our teeth. Effective use of processes allows us to perform efficiently in every aspect of our lives. In our personal lives, we follow specific processes to file our taxes or enhance our health. In our professional lives, most of us go through an interview process to secure a job and an evaluation process to get a raise. In our academic lives, we follow set procedures to enroll in classes, learn, and achieve high GPAs.

A process may describe the steps necessary to complete a task such as changing a tire, downloading a new app, or creating a web page. A process may also describe the phases, stages, or cycle of a recurring event such as the phases of the moon, the stages of human development, or the cycle of grief. To write a process paragraph, a writer identifies and explains the logical time order of the individual steps or stages in the task or cycle. An effective process paragraph also relies heavily on concrete descriptive details and vivid images so the reader can mentally see the process as it unfolds.

What's the Point of Process?

Visualizing a process helps a writer discover his or her point about the procedure. The following sequence of photographs documents a series of steps in a set of Pilates exercises called "spine stretch and roll like a ball." Study each photograph in the timeline. Write a caption that briefly describes each picture. Then, answer the question "What's the point?" with a one-sentence statement of the overall main idea.

PHOTOGRAPHIC ORGANIZER: PROCESS

STEP ONE — What is happening?

STEP TWO — What is happening?

STEP THREE — What is happening?

STEP FOUR — What is happening?

What's the point?

WRITING FROM LIFE

Practice 1

6 THE PROCESS PARAGRAPH

My First Thoughts: A Prewriting Activity

Set a time limit, such as five minutes, and write in your notebook about the images you just studied. Do not let your pen or pencil stop. Even if you must repeat ideas, keep writing until the time limit is up. Let the ideas flow freely. Getting your first thoughts about a topic on paper is an excellent way to overcome writer's block and set your mind to thinking.

One Student Writer's Response

The following paragraph offers one writer's point about the set of exercises depicted in the photographs. Read the process paragraph and the explanations; complete the activities in **bold** type in the annotations. Then, read the writer's journal entry that records decisions made during the writing process.

Main Idea:
The main idea is the point the author is making about the topic. The topic is "an exercise sequence." **Underline the author's point about this topic.**

Chronological Order:
The transition "First" signals time order. **Circle four more time order signal words.**

Effective Expression:
Vivid details such as "sitting tall and straight … as if you were sitting next to a wall" creates a mental picture for the reader. **Double underline three more vivid descriptive details.**

Relevant Details:
Relevant details explain specific steps that build strength and flexibility. Strength is required to curve the spine and pull in the stomach. **Draw a box around a step in the process that builds flexibility.**

Spine Stretch and Roll Like a Ball

(1) "Spine stretch and roll like a ball" is an exercise sequence that builds strength and flexibility in the core area of your body supported by the spine. (2) First, assume the proper starting position. (3) Begin by sitting tall and straight on your mat as if you were sitting next to a wall. (4) Open your legs slightly wider than hip-width apart, placing your heels on the outside edges of the mat. (5) Pull your navel up and in. (6) Extend your arms at shoulder height parallel to your legs and flex your feet, pressing through your heels and pointing your toes toward the ceiling. (7) Next, tighten your buttocks and round your torso up and over. (8) Continually press your lower back behind you and scoop in your abdominals. (9) As you deepen the curve of your spine, press your navel further in as if it could kiss your spine. (10) Imagine your body forming a U-shape. (11) Once you are fully extended, hang your head between your shoulders, and hold the stretch. (12) To roll like a ball from this position, bend your knees and draw both ankles toward the core of your body and balance on your sit bones. (13) Grasp an ankle in each hand; pull your feet close to your buttocks, and place your head snugly between your knees. (14) Imagine your body taking the shape of a small, tight C. (15) Then, inhale and roll back. (16) As you roll, keep your feet close to your body and your head tucked between your knees. (17) Roll until you are balanced on your shoulder blades, but do not roll onto your neck. (18) Throughout the roll, maintain your C-shape and keep your navel pressed into your spine. (19) Finally, exhale as you roll back into your starting position.

The Writer's Journal

PEER EDITING

The student writer of "Spine Stretch and Roll Like a Ball" completed the following reflection to record his thinking through the writing process. Read his writer's journal that describes a few key choices he made as he wrote. Then, in the given space, answer his question about the main idea of his paragraph. Work with a peer or a small group of classmates.

MAIN IDEA: *Even though I really like this topic, I know a lot of people just aren't into exercise. As I reread the paragraph, it sounds like I am only talking to people who already care about exercise, but I really want to inspire everyone to exercise.*

How can I make my topic interesting to people who need to exercise but don't?

A process shows how to do something or how something works. To describe a process, a writer uses chronological order (also called time order), relevant concrete descriptive details, and vivid images.

L2 Compose a Topic Sentence

When you write a process paragraph, you limit your topic to a specific set of details based on time order. Most likely, you also have an opinion or point of view about the process, and this opinion or attitude is your point or main idea. A topic sentence states the point or purpose of the steps, directions, or phases.

For example, the following topic sentence contains (1) the topic, (2) the writer's opinion about the topic, and (3) the pattern of organization used to organize details.

The topic is "grief." The writer's opinion is stated with the phrase "emotional work" and time order is established with the phrases "the six phases" and "in progress."

> The six phases of grief represent an emotional work in progress.
>
> PATTERN OF ORGANIZATION: TIME ORDER — TOPIC — AUTHOR'S OPINION — PATTERN OF ORGANIZATION: TIME ORDER

This example illustrates the relationships of the topic, the author's opinion, and the pattern of organization in this particular topic sentence. Note that the phrase "the six phases of grief" combines the topic and the pattern of organization.

Practice 2

COMPOSE TOPIC SENTENCES

Practice creating topic sentences. The following items present a topic, an opinion, and time order signal word(s). Combine the ideas in each group to create a topic sentence for a process.

1. TOPIC: Test-taking anxiety

   OPINION: can be overcome

   TIME ORDER SIGNAL WORDS: in several steps

   TOPIC SENTENCE: _____

2. TOPIC: Checking the oil and changing the oil in a car

   OPINION: easy and quick

   TIME ORDER SIGNAL WORDS: process

   TOPIC SENTENCE: _____

Use Logical Order

A process describes the individual actions that make up each step or phase within the process. Just as time order words in the topic sentence signal a process, time order transition words show the flow of events as the process unfolds. Strong transitions establish coherence, a clear and understandable flow of ideas.

Transition Words Used to Show Time Order

after	currently	last	now	since	until
afterward	eventually	later	often	soon	when
as	finally	meanwhile	previously	then	while
before	first	next	second	ultimately	

USE TIME ORDER

The following information appears in the safety publication *How to Survive a Submerging Car* sponsored by the Florida Highway Patrol. Determine the logical order of the sentences. *Hint:* Underline the time order transition words. Then, answer the question "What's the point?"

_____ Then, while the car is still floating, **get out**; crawl through the opened window and swim to shore.

_____ The first thing to do in a floating car is to **push** the button to unbuckle your seatbelt.

_____ Next, **open** the window; electric windows should still work while the car is floating.

_____ When a car plunges into a lake or river, it should float for about three minutes, giving you enough time to safely exit the car before it sinks.

_____ P.O.G.O. stands for Push, Open, and Get Out.

_____ Once the car sinks, the P.O.G.O. method still works.

_____ In a submerged car, first **push** the button that releases your seatbelt.

_____ Finally, **get out**; push yourself out of the car and quickly swim to the surface.

_____ Then, **open** your car door.

—*How to Survive Your Worst Nightmare!*, Florida Department of Highway Safety and Motor Vehicles, Copyright © 2008 State of Florida.

What's the point?

L4 Develop Relevant Details

As a writer narrows a topic into a focused main idea about a process, the thinking process brings to mind many details of time and space. A writer evaluates the relevance of each detail and uses only those that illustrate the main idea. Some relevant details show the action of the process; other details explain the author's opinion about the process. Relevant details also include powerful descriptive and sensory details. These details work together to create a vivid mental image of the author's main point about the process. During the prewriting phase, a timeline can help a writer organize ideas as they are generated. Study the following timeline that was used to generate details about the phases of grief.

The Six Phases of Grief

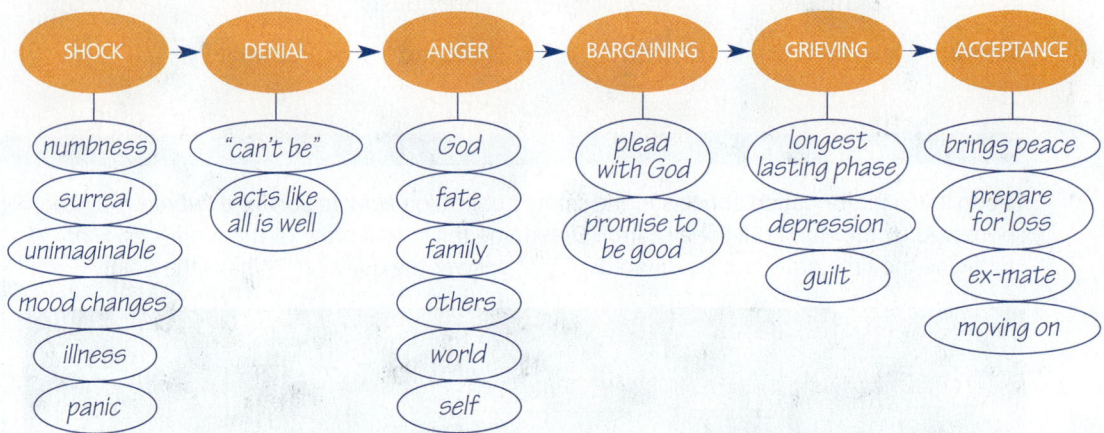

DEVELOP RELEVANT DETAILS

Assume you are going to write about the major stages of the human life cycle for a college psychology course. Create a timeline similar to the one above for the stages of grief. Compare your timeline with that of a peer or a small group of classmates.

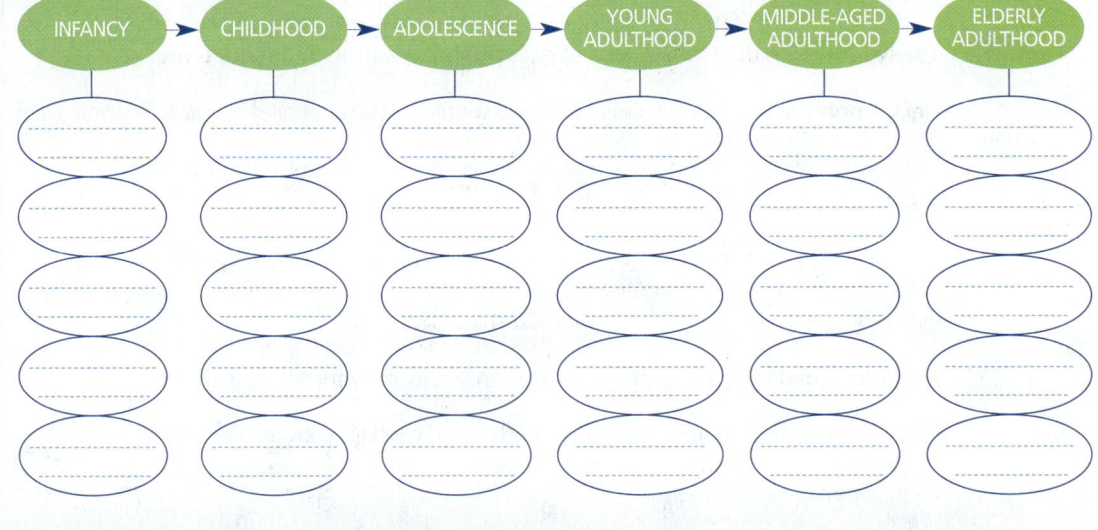

During the prewriting phase, a writer naturally generates irrelevant details. In fact, an effective writer often produces far more details than can be used to make a specific point. Irrelevant details do not explain, support, or illustrate the focused point of the paragraph. A careful writer uses the revision process to double check details for relevance and to eliminate irrelevant details.

DEVELOP RELEVANT DETAILS

The following paragraph develops the ideas recorded in the brainstorming list about the six phases of grief. Circle the main idea. Underline at least three concrete details. Cross out the two details that are not relevant to the main idea.

 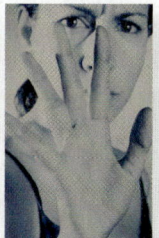    

1. Shock   2. Denial   3. Anger   4. Bargaining   5. Grieving   6. Acceptance

The Phases of Grief

(1) In her book, *On Death and Dying*, Dr. Elisabeth Kübler-Ross explains the phases of grief we experience when we learn that a loved one is terminally ill. (2) The six phases of grief represent an emotional work in progress. (3) The first phase is shock. (4) During this initial phase, we experience a fog of numbness; life seems surreal as it crumbles around us, and the chore ahead of us seems unimaginable. (5) Throughout the second phase, denial, we work hard to erect the illusion that recovery is possible or that life is still normal. (6) We simply think, "This can't be happening to me." (7) Once we move past denial, we then grapple with the third phase of grief—anger. (8) We aim our anger at God, fate, doctors, family, the world, or even ourselves. (9) Thoughts such as "If only I had…" or "How can others just go on with their lives?" occupy our minds. (10) During traumas such as divorce, we often become angry with our ex-mate. (11) During the fourth phase, known as bargaining, we negotiate with God to cure the problem in exchange for our good behavior. (12) The fifth phase, usually the longest lasting, is grieving. (13) We often labor in mourning for months or years. (14) Chipping away at depression, guilt, physical illness, loneliness, panic, and abrupt mood changes employs all our energies. (15) The final phase of grief occurs as acceptance. (16) Often, for those of us facing our own death, acceptance brings the wage of peace. (17) As survivors of loss, such as divorce, we usually find ourselves working to re-build our lives and move on.

L5 Use Effective Expression: Vivid Images

Show, don't tell! Create vivid word pictures that deepen your reader's understanding of your point. Two figures of speech create vivid images: simile and metaphor.

A **simile** is an indirect comparison between two different ideas or things that uses *like, as, as if,* or *as though*.

Example

As Robin crossed the finish line, his legs pumped like pistons.

A **metaphor** is a direct comparison between two different ideas or things that does *not* use *like, as, as if,* or *as though*. Often a metaphor uses words such as *is, are,* or *were* to make the direct comparison between the two ideas.

Example

As Robin crossed the finish line, his legs were pumping pistons.

Practice 6

USE VIVID IMAGES

Revise each of the following sentences to create vivid images by using similes and metaphors suggested by the photos. Discuss your work with your class or in a small group of your peers.

1. To ensure a healthful serving size, limit meat portions to 3 ounces.

2. Adolescence is a stage of human development made up of great change leading to adulthood.

Use Process in Your Academic Courses

Many college courses in subjects such as biology, ecology, history, political science, psychology, and composition use process in their discussions. As you study these subjects, you will learn about processes involving the physical world, mental health, government, and writing. In addition, you will record processes to learn or demonstrate what you have learned. For example, a science lab may require you to conduct an experiment, record the steps you took, and evaluate the process. Some college writing assignments ask you to reflect upon your personal writing process so you can strengthen your writing skills.

USE PROCESS IN A COMPOSITION ASSIGNMENT

During a composition class, a student wrote the following paragraph in her writer's journal to reflect upon the effectiveness of her writing process. Assume you are her peer editor, and, based on what you have learned in this chapter about writing a process paragraph and in Chapter 2, offer her some advice.

Kristen Elizabeth Spengler

Writing 101

September 27, 2015

My Writer's Journal: My Writing Process

(1) I start my writing process by mapping. (2) I make what is like a spider web with one basic idea in the middle of the page and supporting ideas branching off all around it. (3) After brainstorming for a while, I go on the computer and put the ideas I came up with into sentences. (4) Usually, I like to lay it all out on the computer and print it out because it is easier for me to see it while I'm typing my draft. (5) After I type up all the ideas I brainstormed, I print it out and turn it in.

# Workshop: Writing a Process Paragraph Step by Step

Prewrite Your Paragraph

The activities below will walk you through the steps of the prewriting stage of the writing process: choosing a topic, focusing your point, and generating and organizing relevant details.

Choose Your Topic

The following activities are designed to help you choose a topic.

1. Create a bank of topics. Use the suggested headings and brainstorm or list as many processes about each topic as you possibly can. Don't criticize your thoughts; just get as many relevant processes written down as quickly as possible. Compare your bank of topics with those of your classmates.

   - Recycling Trash
   - Auditioning
   - Studying
   - Training an Animal

2. Generate ideas with a freewrite. Choose one of the topics from your topic bank and think of the steps necessary to complete the process. Write about the process for ten minutes without stopping.

3. Select a photograph or series of photographs that illustrates a process. Write captions; brainstorm steps, directions, or phases; and freewrite about the photograph(s). Remember to ask "What is happening?" and "What's the point?" as you generate ideas.

Focus Your Point

Read a freewrite you have generated for a process. Underline words that suggest your values, opinions, or attitudes about the process. Use a thesaurus and choose several vivid words to express your thoughts. Think about why the steps are important. Identify your audience and purpose. Create a list of concrete details and vivid images that show the actions that occur during the process. State in one sentence the point of the process.

AUDIENCE:

PURPOSE:

LIST OF CONCRETE DETAILS:

WHAT'S THE POINT?

Generate and Organize Relevant Details

Using ideas you have recorded so far and the process flowchart, generate and organize details that support your point.

What's the point?

TOPIC SENTENCE: ....

....

....

What is happening?

First Step

Second Step

Third Step

Fourth Step

Write a Draft of Your Paragraph

Using the ideas you generated during the prewriting phase, compose a draft of your process paragraph. Return to the prewriting process at any time to generate additional details as needed. Use your own paper.

Revise Your Draft

Once you have created a draft of a process, read the draft to answer the questions in the "Questions for Revising a Process Paragraph" box that follows. Indicate your answers by annotating your paper. If you answer "yes" to a question, underline, check, or circle examples. If you answer "no" to a question, write needed information in margins and draw lines to indicate placement of additional details. Revise your paragraph based on your reflection. (*Hint:* Experienced writers create several drafts as they focus on one or two questions per draft.)

Questions for Revising a Process Paragraph:

- [ ] Have I stated or implied a focused main idea? Have I created a strong impression? Can I state my point in one sentence?
- [ ] Is the order of the steps, directions, or phases within the process clear? Have I used strong transitions?
- [ ] Have I made my point with adequate details?
- [ ] Have I included only the details that are relevant to my topic sentence?
- [ ] Have I used vivid images to make the process clear to my readers?
- [ ] Have I used concrete details to make my point?

Proofread Your Draft

Once you have made any revisions to your paragraph that may be needed, proofread your paragraph to eliminate careless errors such as fused sentences.

> For more information on fused sentences see pages 420–437.

Grammar in Action: Eliminating Fused Sentences

A **fused sentence** occurs when two or more independent clauses are punctuated as one sentence. Correct a fused sentence by applying any of the following four edits: (1) separate independent clauses with a period and capital letter; (2) insert a coordinating conjunction (*for, and, nor, but, or, yet,* or *so*) and a comma between independent clauses; (3) insert a semicolon between the independent clauses; or (4) insert a semicolon with an appropriate transition between independent clauses.

- **A fused sentence**

    Plants take in water through their roots they take in the gas carbon dioxide through their foliage plants use sunlight to turn water and carbon dioxide into food through the process of photosynthesis.

- **Two ways to correct the above fused sentence**

    ADDED COMMA AND COORDINATING CONJUNCTION "AND" TO SEPARATE INDEPENDENT CLAUSES

    1. Plants take in water through their roots, **and** they take in the gas carbon dioxide through their foliage**;** plants use sunlight to turn water and carbon dioxide into food through the process of photosynthesis.

    ADDED SEMICOLON TO SEPARATE INDEPENDENT CLAUSES

    ADDED PERIOD   CAPITALIZED FIRST LETTER
    ADDED TRANSITION

    2. Plants take in water through their roots**.** **In addition,** they take in the gas carbon dioxide through their foliage**; then,** plants use sunlight to turn water and carbon dioxide into food through the process of photosynthesis.

    ADDED SEMICOLON AND TRANSITION WORD "THEN" TO SEPARATE INDEPENDENT CLAUSES

Practice 8

ELIMINATE FUSED SENTENCES

Edit to eliminate fused sentences.

1. Using anabolic steroids is a fast way to increase body size some athletes are willing to cheat at a sport they take these steroids to increase body mass beyond what hard work alone could produce.

2. Effective questioning occurs in an order that draws out the exact information needed questions should focus on easy-to-answer factual information that puts the person at ease then the interviewer can move to ideas that can't be stated as a fact.

Writing Assignments

MyWritingLab™ Complete this Exercise on mywritinglab.com

Considering Audience and Purpose

Study the sequence of photographs about the set of Pilates exercises at the beginning of the chapter. Draft a process paragraph based on one of the following two writing situations:

Assume you are keeping a personal exercise journal. Write a paragraph in which you describe the steps in your exercise sequence. Include the challenges you might face in each phase of the process.

Assume you are an instructor of an exercise class for a group of senior citizens. Think about specific movements in each step of the exercise that might have to be adapted due to poor balance or stiffness of joints. Write a paragraph for the Senior Citizens' Health Club Newsletter that describes these adapted exercises.

Writing for Everyday Life

Assume that a friend or family member has asked you for advice about how to open a bank account; write a paragraph that explains how to do so. Be sure to include information about necessary personal identification and available banking services. Choose words that reflect one of the following: (1) endorsement of the banking services or (2) warning against possible problems.

Writing for College Life

Assume you are in a college course called Student Success, and you have been assigned to write a brief oral report about how to study. Write a paragraph that records the text for your speech in which you describe the most effective way to take notes during class.

Writing for Working Life

Assume you are the director of the Human Resources department for a corporation, and you are volunteering your services at a job fair designed to help unemployed citizens secure jobs. You have agreed to teach participants how to handle the interviewing process. Write a paragraph as part of your handout that describes the steps necessary to prepare for an interview.

MyWritingLab™

Complete the Post-test for Chapter 6 in MyWritingLab.

7 The Example Paragraph

PART 2 USING PATTERNS OF ORGANIZATION TO DEVELOP PARAGRAPHS

LEARNING OUTCOMES

After studying this chapter you will be able to:

1. Answer the question "What's the Point of Examples?"
2. Compose a Topic Sentence
3. Use Logical Order
4. Develop Relevant Details
5. Use Effective Expression: Parallel Language
6. Use Examples in Your Academic Courses
7. Write an Example Paragraph Step by Step

An example, also called an exemplification, is a specific illustration of a more general idea.

When we communicate—with family members, employers, teachers, or friends—we often use examples to clarify a point we want to make. Think of a situation you were in recently where you used examples to make a point. What makes an example effective?

In everyday life, we illustrate our decorating ideas with paint chips and swatches of fabric. In working life, we offer examples of our hard work and successes when we apply for jobs and promotions. In college life, professors and textbook authors use examples to teach concepts in every discipline.

To create an example paragraph, a writer moves from a general idea to specific examples that support and clarify the main point. Sometimes, as in a science lab report, a writer may present the specific examples first and then come to a general conclusion based on the examples. An effective example paragraph also relies heavily on concrete details, the logical order of importance, and, often, parallel expression.

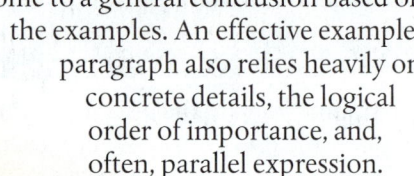

What's the Point of Examples?

Generating and organizing examples help a writer to discover his or her point about a particular topic. The following photographs offer two examples of a soldier's memories of his time in Iraq. Study each photograph. Write a caption that briefly describes each example. Then, answer the question, "What's the point?" with a one-sentence statement of the overall main idea.

PHOTOGRAPHIC ORGANIZER: EXAMPLES

EXAMPLES OF A SOLDIER'S MEMORY OF IRAQ

Example 1:

What is this?

Example 2:

What is this?

What's the point?

My First Thoughts: A Prewriting Activity

Set a time limit, perhaps five minutes, and write in your notebook about the images you just studied. Do not let your pen or pencil stop. Even if you must repeat ideas, keep writing until the time limit is up. Let the ideas flow freely. Getting your first thoughts about a topic on paper is one excellent way to kick start your writing process.

One Student Writer's Response

The following paragraph offers one writer's point about his memories of Iraq during his tour there as a soldier. Read the exemplification and the explanations; complete the activities in **bold type** in the annotations. Then, read the writer's journal entry that records decisions made during the writing process.

Main Idea:
The main idea is the point Joshua is making about the topic Iraq. **Underline Joshua's point about Iraq.**

Listing Order:
The transitional phrase "For example" signals that the paragraph is developed by examples. **Circle one more transitional phrase that signals an example.**

Effective Expression:
Parallelism refers to the way ideas of equal importance are worded. To achieve parallelism, Joshua used the same form of words such as "relax*ing* and attend*ing*." **Double underline two more ideas with -*ing* phrasing.**

Relevant Details:
Concrete details list specific minor details that illustrate Joshua's good memories. **Draw boxes around two more concrete minor details.**

Good Memories Can Be Found Everywhere We Go
Joshua Hartzell

(1) There were a lot of good memories made in Iraq despite why I was there. (2) For example, I have many good memories of good friends; I developed close friendships, much like a family, while I was in the Army. (3) Anthony, my best friend since sixth grade, was among us. (4) By the time we had been sent to Iraq we had both been promoted to Specialist. (5) My friends and I enjoyed relaxing and attending the USO shows in Kuwait, though we disliked having to wear our full desert uniforms in the heat of day. (6) The long sleeves were like wearing a blanket in the summer. (7) Though Iraq was much more dangerous, sitting in a makeshift position we had built in our short sleeves was often pleasant. (8) The sand bag walls, and the cover made of rain ponchos and camouflage netting, provided a surprising relief from the unforgiving sun. (9) Another great memory was when I found a new little friend. (10) On one of the many hot afternoons as I watched the area I was responsible for guarding, wishing for the night to come and make heat waves coming from the ground disappear, my temporary pet puppy wandered up to me in search of food. (11) It was a nice reprieve from sitting alone to watch the endless golden sand. (12) It was nice to find something to remind me of my normal civilian life. (13) Sitting under the green camouflage netting, which gave me way too much time to wonder why it was not in desert camouflage, we shared my tasteless military rations and warm water. (14) The puppy had sandy colored fur helping it blend into the sandy surroundings. (15) For the short time I was able to keep him, I enjoyed the company. (16) I simply called him dog, and he would look at me with his dark snout and big brown eyes as he sat lazily on my lap. (17) At night he would curl up on my lap as I sat in my army green issued sleeping bag to stay warm. (18) It was the good memories like hanging out with my friends and that puppy that kept me positive. (19) I will carry those memories for as long as I live.

The Writer's Journal

PEER EDITING

Student writer Joshua Hartzell completed the following reflection to record some of his thinking about his writing process. Read his writer's journal that describes a few key choices he made as he wrote. Then, in the given space, answer his questions about his use of details in his paragraph. Work with a peer or a small group of classmates.

MAIN IDEA: *While writing this paragraph I wanted to make a point that no matter where you are there are good memories that you can bring back with you. My biggest challenge is always picking what to write about. In this case it seemed relatively easy since I simply picked the couple of memories that I think about more than the rest. My favorite thing about this paragraph is that it shows what the news doesn't. As soldiers, we all strived for some sense of home. The sensitive side that we all have is what keeps us human in inhuman conditions. I don't think that I could revise this paragraph if I had to. It expresses exactly what I wanted it to.*

But what do you think? Did I get my point across? Why or why not?

An exemplification illustrates a main point with one or more examples. To exemplify a point, a writer lists the examples, often according to the order of importance; explains each example with relevant concrete details; and often uses parallel expression.

L2 Compose a Topic Sentence

When you write an exemplification, you limit your topic to a set of specific examples, instances, or cases. Most likely, you also have an opinion or point of view about the examples, and this opinion or attitude is your point or main idea. You may reveal your opinion by listing the examples in a particular order of importance. A topic sentence states the point or purpose of the examples.

For example, the following topic sentence contains (1) the topic, (2) the writer's opinion about the topic, and (3) the pattern of organization used to organize details.

The topic is "body art." The pattern of organization is established with the phrase "such as tattooing and piercing" and the verb "exemplifies." The writer's opinion is stated with the phrase "self-expression."

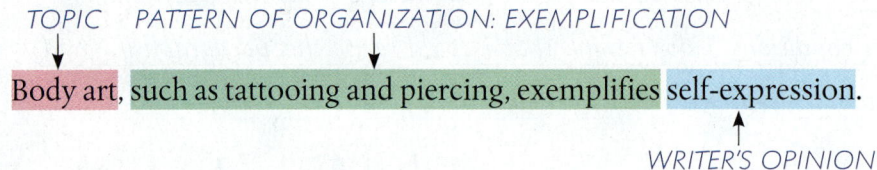

Sometimes in an example paragraph, a topic sentence only implies the pattern of organization, as in the following version.

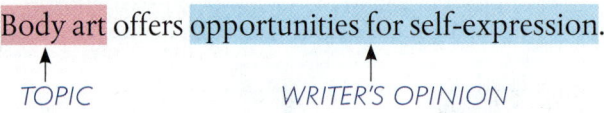

When the example pattern of organization is only implied by the topic sentence, then transitions that signal and list examples establish the pattern of organization within the body of the paragraph. Notice in the following example that the two major detail sentences state the topic, pattern of organization, and writer's opinion.

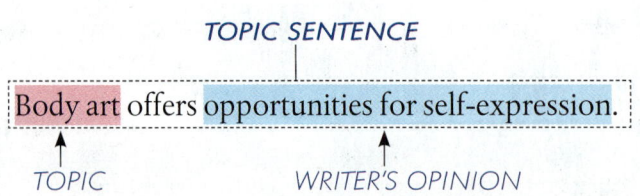

MAJOR DETAIL SENTENCE #1

Tattooing is one example of body art as self-expression.
↑ ↑ ↑
TOPIC PATTERN OF ORGANIZATION: WRITER'S OPINION
       EXEMPLIFICATION

MAJOR DETAIL SENTENCE #2

Piercing is another example of artistic self-expression.
↑ ↑ ↑
TOPIC PATTERN OF ORGANIZATION: WRITER'S OPINION
       EXEMPLIFICATION

Practice 2

COMPOSE TOPIC SENTENCES

The items below present a topic, an opinion, and example signal word(s). Combine the ideas in each group to create a topic sentence for an example paragraph.

1. TOPIC: Foods   OPINION: inflame the condition diverticulitis

   EXAMPLE (OR LISTING) SIGNAL WORDS: Certain

   TOPIC SENTENCE: _____

2. TOPIC: A good friend   OPINION: compassion and honesty

   EXAMPLE (OR LISTING) SIGNAL WORDS: illustrates

   TOPIC SENTENCE: _____

3. TOPIC: Solar energy   OPINION: is versatile and cheap

   EXAMPLE (OR LISTING) SIGNAL WORDS: not included; only implied

   TOPIC SENTENCE: _____

4. TOPIC: SUV drivers   OPINION: rugged, aggressive

   EXAMPLE (OR LISTING) SIGNAL WORDS: _____

   TOPIC SENTENCE: _____

7 THE EXAMPLE PARAGRAPH

121

L3 Use Logical Order

Once you have selected your topic and focused on a main idea, you are ready to generate additional details and list your ideas based on their order of importance. To use examples to illustrate a main point, a writer moves from a general idea to a major support to a minor support. To show the movement between these levels of ideas, a writer uses transitions to signal or list examples. Strong transitions establish coherence, a clear and understandable flow of ideas.

Transitions Used to Signal Examples

an example	for instance	once	to illustrate	
an illustration	for example	including	such as	typically

Transitions Used to List Examples

also	final	for one thing	last of all	second
and	finally	furthermore	moreover	third
another	first	in addition	next	
besides	first of all	last	one	

Practice 3

USE LOGICAL ORDER

◀ Injury from overuse

Fill in the blank with appropriate transitions to signal or list examples.

In the drive to become physically fit, many risk injury by overtraining. Overuse injuries develop through the daily stresses placed on various parts of the body (1)_____ tendons, muscles, (2)_____ joints. Plantar Fasciitis is (3)_____ of an overuse injury from walking, jogging, (4)_____ running. This injury is an inflammation of the band of tissue that stretches across the sole of the foot. (5)_____, the foot is tender from the ball to the heel, making it painful to walk.

USE LISTING ORDER

The following information was published on a government website for consumer protection. Determine the logical order of the sentences. Complete the exercise by answering the question "What's the point?" Discuss your answers with your class or with a small group of peers.

Consumer Beware!

_____ The third and most common example of fraud is phishing.

_____ Phishing is an e-mail message that lures a consumer to a phony website.

_____ The e-mail sender pretends to be from a legitimate government organization, bank, or retailer.

_____ The phishy e-mail stated, "We recently reviewed your account, and we need more information to help us provide you with secure service."

_____ The message also directed the receiver "to visit the Resolution Center and complete the 'Steps to Remove Limitations.'"

_____ A recent instance of phishing came from a phony PayPal site.

_____ A second example of fraud is the phone scam; a caller pretends to represent a trusted organization or company.

_____ In one instance, a caller claims to work for the court and says the listener has been called for jury duty.

_____ The caller then demands personal information such as a social security number, birth date, and credit card numbers.

_____ The first and least common example of fraud is the handyman sting.

_____ The handyman offers to fix the problem, such as replacing a roof or removing a fallen tree, for a cash fee lower than any reputable company could offer.

_____ The handyman shows up on the doorstep of a home in obvious need of repair, usually after severe weather such as a tornado or hurricane.

_____ Most often, the money is paid upfront, and the work is never completed.

What's the point?

_____

_____

_____

L4 Develop Relevant Details

As a writer narrows a topic into a focused main idea, the thinking process brings to mind many details that answer the questions *who*, *what*, *when*, *where*, *why*, and *how*. A writer evaluates the relevance of each detail and uses only those that exemplify the main idea. Some relevant details express major examples of the main point; minor details may further illustrate major examples. Some major and minor details may explain the author's opinion about the examples. During the prewriting phase, a list can help a writer organize ideas as they are generated. Study the following list generated about the topic "America Has a Problem with Gun Violence."

TOPIC:
America Has a Problem with Gun Violence

Shootings Are a Daily Occurrence in America

DETAILS:

One in three people in the U.S. know someone who has been shot.

On average, every day:

32 Americans are murdered with guns.

140 are treated for a gun assault in an emergency room.

51 people kill themselves with a firearm.

45 people are shot or killed in a gun accident.

Gun Violence Takes a Massive Toll on American Children

DETAILS:

One in five U.S. teenagers report having witnessed a shooting.

Eight children and teens under the age of 20 are killed by guns every day.

American children die by guns 11 times as often as children in other high-income countries.

Youth in rural U.S. counties are as likely to die from a gunshot as those living in the most urban counties.

Gun Violence Is a Drain on U.S. Taxpayers

DETAILS:

Medical treatment, criminal justice proceedings, new security precautions, and reductions in quality of life are estimated to cost U.S. citizens $100 billion annually.

The lifetime medical cost for all gun violence victims in the United States is estimated at $2.3 billion, with almost half the costs borne by taxpayers.

During the prewriting phase, a writer naturally generates irrelevant details. In fact, an effective writer often produces far more details than can be used to make a specific point. Irrelevant details do not exemplify, explain, or support the focused point of the paragraph. A careful writer uses the revision process to double check details for relevance and to eliminate irrelevant ones.

Practice 5

7 THE EXAMPLE PARAGRAPH

DEVELOP RELEVANT DETAILS

The following paragraph, adapted from Brady Campaign website, develops the ideas recorded in the brainstorming list about gun violence in America. Circle the main idea. Underline three concrete major examples. Cross out the two details that are not relevant to the main point.

Gun Violence in America

(1) America has a problem with gun violence. (2) Shootings are a daily occurrence in America. (3) For example, one in three people in the United States know someone who has been shot. (4) On average every day, 32 Americans are murdered with guns, 140 are treated for a gun assault in an emergency room, 51 people kill themselves with a firearm, and 45 people are shot or killed in an accident with a gun. (5) Nine out of 10 Americans agree that we should have universal background checks, including three out of four NRA members. (6) Unfortunately, our current background check system only applies to about 60 percent of gun sales, leaving 40 percent (online sales, purchases at gun shows, etc.) without a background check. (7) In addition, gun violence takes a massive toll on American children. (8) More than one in five U.S. teenagers (ages 14 to 17) report having witnessed a shooting. (9) An average of eight children and teens under the age of 20 are killed by guns every day. (10) American children die by guns 11 times as often as children in other high-income countries. (11) Youth (ages 0 to 19) in the most rural U.S. counties are as likely to die from a gunshot as those living in the most urban counties. (12) Furthermore, gun violence is a drain on U.S. taxpayers. (13) Medical treatment, criminal justice proceedings, new security precautions, and reductions in quality of life are estimated to cost U.S. citizens $100 billion annually. (14) The lifetime medical cost for all gun violence victims in the United States is estimated at $2.3 billion, with almost half the costs borne by taxpayers.

—© 2015 Brady Campaign to Prevent Gun Violence. Reprinted with permission.

L5 Use Effective Expression: Parallel Language

Parallel language is the use of similar and balanced expressions in a pair or series of words, phrases, or clauses. Parallelism makes a piece of writing more enjoyable, more powerful, and more readable. Study the following examples from a student's first thoughts about the seasons of the year.

Non-Parallel Words:

Summertime is ideal for swimming, boating, and a picnic.

Revised Words for Parallelism:

Summertime is ideal for swimming, boating, and picnicking.

THIS SERIES OF WORDS (NOUNS) ALL END IN –ING.

Non-Parallel Phrases:

The seasons can go from the fire of summer to the freezing winter.

Revised Phrases for the Parallelism:

The seasons can go from the fire of summer, to the chill of fall, to the freeze of winter, to the breeze of spring.

THIS SERIES OF IDEAS REPEATS A PATTERN OF PREPOSITIONAL PHRASES

Non-Parallel Clauses:

I love the fall because the leaves turn colors, and it's football season.

Revised Clauses for Parallelism:

I love the fall because the leaves turn colors, and television programming turns to football.

THESE CLAUSES ARE NOW BOTH DEPENDENT CLAUSES THAT BEGIN WITH THE SAME SUBORDINATING CONJUNCTION ("BECAUSE") AND USE THE SAME VERB ("TO TURN").

Practice 6

USE PARALLEL EXPRESSION

Revise the following sentences so ideas are expressed in parallel language. Discuss your work with your class or with a small group of your peers.

1. Examples of activities that strengthen the heart include jogging, swimming, and jump rope.

2. A healthy heart lifestyle includes the following: getting plenty of sleep, eating a balanced diet, and regular exercise.

Use Examples in Your Academic Courses

Every college course uses examples to clarify ideas. As you study, you will learn about examples of governments, important historical figures, psychological concepts, scientific principles, effective speeches, and so on. In addition, you will prove what you have learned by providing examples of the concepts and skills you have studied.

USE EXAMPLES IN A SHORT-ANSWER COMMUNICATION ESSAY EXAM

Assume you are taking a college class in communication. Your professor has given your class a set of study questions to help you prepare for an upcoming exam. A peer in your study group started the following prewrite to one of the study questions. Study her notes; then, fill in the blank with a one-sentence answer to the study question. Finally, on your own paper, write a draft of a paragraph. Include appropriate example transition words. Work with a peer or in a small group.

Study Question: What is the purpose of listening?

Answer to Study Question

Example	Example	Example
We learn from others.	We relate to others.	We influence others.
We learn from parents, teachers, and others.	We develop long-lasting relationships.	We respect others.
We learn about others, the world, and ourselves.	We increase understanding.	We earn the respect and trust of others.
	We avoid conflict.	

L7 Workshop: Writing an Example Paragraph Step by Step

Prewrite Your Paragraph

The activities below will walk you through the steps of the prewriting stage of the writing process: choosing a topic, focusing your point, and generating and organizing relevant details.

Choose Your Topic

The following activities are designed to help you choose a topic.

1. Create a bank of topics. Use the suggested headings to brainstorm or list as many examples about each topic as you possibly can. Don't criticize your thoughts; just get as many relevant examples written down as quickly as possible. Add more topics and examples as they occur to you. Compare your bank of topics with those of your classmates.

    - Pollution
    - Job Skills
    - Effective Teachers
    - Alternative Energy Supplies

2. Generate ideas with a freewrite. Choose one of the topics from your topic bank and think of examples that illustrate the topic. Write about the topic and examples for ten minutes without stopping.

3. Select a photograph or series of photographs that illustrates a topic. Write captions, brainstorm examples, and freewrite about the photograph(s). Remember to ask "What do(es) the picture(s) illustrate?" and "What's the point?"

Focus Your Point

Read a prewrite you have generated for an exemplification. Underline words that suggest your values, opinions, or attitudes about the topic and the examples. Think about why the details are important. Identify your audience and purpose. Write a list of additional concrete examples that illustrate your point. State in one sentence the point of the examples.

AUDIENCE: _____

PURPOSE: _____

LIST OF CONCRETE DETAILS: _____

_____

WHAT'S THE POINT? _____

Generate and Organize Relevant Details

Using ideas you have recorded so far and the following idea map, generate and organize details that support your point.

Example: Illustrations of an Idea

What's the point?

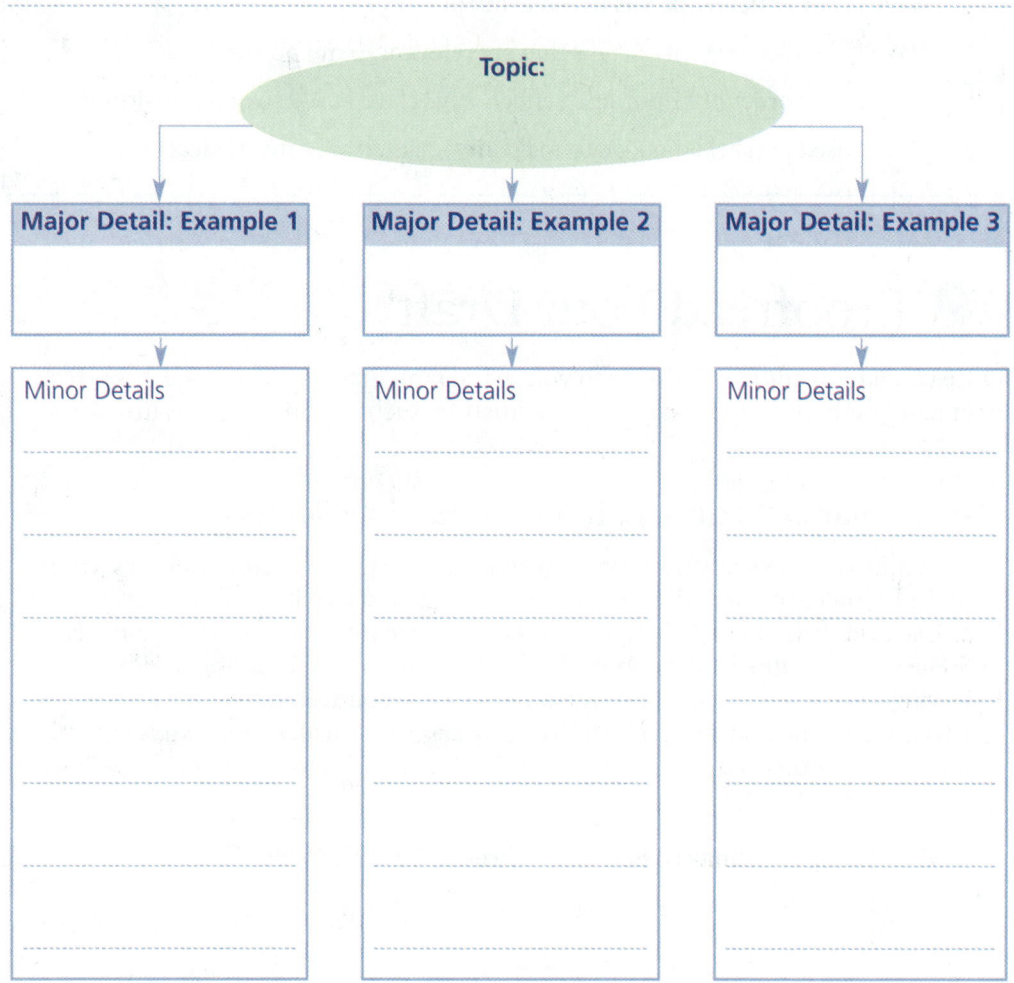

 ## Write a Draft of Your Paragraph

Using the ideas you generated during the prewriting phase, compose a draft of your example paragraph. Return to the prewriting process at any time to generate additional details as needed. Use your own paper.

 ## Revise Your Draft

Once you have created a draft of an example paragraph, read the draft and answer the questions in the "Questions for Revising an Example Paragraph" box that follows. Indicate your answers by annotating your paper. If you answer "yes" to a question, underline, check, or circle examples. If you answer "no" to a question, write the additional details in the margin and draw lines to indicate their placement. Revise your paragraph based on your reflection. (*Hint:* Experienced writers create several drafts as they focus on one or two questions per draft.)

Questions for Revising an Example Paragraph:

- [ ] Have I stated or implied a main idea? Have I made my point? Can I state my point in one sentence?
- [ ] Have I used concrete details to make my point?
- [ ] Have I included only the details that are relevant to my point?
- [ ] Have I used order of importance effectively? Have I used strong transitions?
- [ ] Have I used parallel language to make my ideas clear to my readers?

Proofread Your Draft

Once you have made any revisions to your paragraph that may be needed, proofread your paragraph for proper usage and punctuation, such as using commas in a series.

For more information on using commas in a series, see pages 554–563.

Grammar in Action: Using Commas in a Series

Use commas to separate three or more words, phrases, or clauses in a series. One of the following conjunctions is used between the last two items of a series: *for, and, nor, but, or, yet,* or *so*; for example, sending, receiving, *and* forwarding e-mails. Some experts state that the comma before the conjunction is optional. However, leaving the last comma of the series out may cause confusion, so many experts advise including it. In writing for college, we suggest you include it. Study the following examples:

- **Using Commas to Separate Three or More Words:**

  Jimmy Fallon is candid, creative, and comical.

  COORDINATING CONJUNCTION

- **Using Commas to Separate Three or More Phrases:**

  Texas offers vacation experiences that are enjoyable and educational: exploring Big Ben National Park, visiting the Alamo, and touring the NASA Space Center.

  COORDINATING CONJUNCTION

- **Using Commas to Separate Three or More Clauses:**

  Our company is looking for employees who can find solutions, who can work as a team, and who can excel in their roles.

  COORDINATING CONJUNCTION

USE COMMAS IN A SERIES

Edit these sentences for proper use of commas in a series. Rewrite them on the lines below.

1. I only need three pairs of shoes—running shoes low-heeled pumps and sandals.

2. Snoring can be caused by a variety of factors such as alcohol consumption nasal problems sleep apnea and the structure of your mouth.

Writing Assignments

MyWritingLab™ Complete this Exercise on mywritinglab.com

Considering Audience and Purpose

Study the set of photographs of a soldier's time in Iraq at the beginning of the chapter. Assume you are a volunteer working with Operation Gratitude, a non-profit group that sends care packages to individual U.S. military members stationed in hostile regions. You are sending this soldier a care package. Write a letter expressing your gratitude for his service. Be sure to give examples of your gratitude.

Writing for Everyday Life

Assume that you are keeping a personal journal and you want to capture the essence of your daily life so your children and grandchildren will know about the customs, fashions, or nature of this time in your life and our society. Use examples to make your point. Choose words that reflect one of the following attitudes: (1) realistic, (2) idealistic.

Writing for College Life

Assume you are a member of the Student Government Association, and you are helping with freshman orientation. Identify two or three aspects of college life about which new students should be aware. Use examples to make your point.

Writing for Working Life

Assume a peer is applying for a job as a supervisor of a sales team at Best Buy or the Apple Store (or some other job that requires leadership and commitment) and has asked you for a recommendation. Interview the peer; then, write a one-paragraph recommendation in which you use examples to support your recommendation.

MyWritingLab™
Complete the Post-test for Chapter 7 in MyWritingLab.

8 The Classification Paragraph

LEARNING OUTCOMES

After studying this chapter you will be able to:

- **L1** Answer the question "What's the Point of Classification?"
- **L2** Compose a Topic Sentence
- **L3** Use Logical Order
- **L4** Develop Relevant Details
- **L5** Use Effective Expression: Controlled Sentence Structure
- **L6** Use Classification in Your Academic Courses
- **L7** Write a Classification Paragraph Step by Step

A classification is a division of a topic into one or more subgroups.

Whether we are grocery shopping, studying, job hunting, or searching for that special someone, we often gather and group information based on types. For example, most of us have experienced or observed the social cliques that form in high schools, neighborhoods, and on the job.

A writer uses classification to sort, group, and label items and ideas based on shared traits or types. In everyday life, we fulfill various social roles such as life-partner, parent, sibling, friend, employee, or student. In working life, we promote people to higher levels of responsibility and pay based on particular types of skills and attitudes. In college life, each of us probably prefers certain kinds of courses, likes certain types of teachers, and does better on certain types of tests.

To create a classification paragraph, a writer divides a topic into subgroups based on shared traits or qualities. The writer lists and often labels each subgroup, describes its traits, and offers examples that best represent the group. Because groups and subgroups are listed, transitions are often used to signal logical order and ensure coherence. An effective classification paragraph uses details of description and examples, logical order, and (as in any effective paragraph) sentence variety.

What's the Point of Classification?

Identifying and labeling groups or types helps a writer to discover his or her point about a particular topic. Study the following set of photographs. In the space provided, (1) identify the types of music represented by the three photographs; (2) list the traits of each subgroup; (3) describe specific examples based on the photographs; and (4) answer the question "What's the point?" with a one-sentence statement of the overall main idea.

PHOTOGRAPHIC ORGANIZER: CLASSIFICATION

TOPIC: TYPES OF MUSIC

| 1ST TYPE | 2ND TYPE | 3RD TYPE |

▲ Garth Brooks   ▲ Ludacris and Queen Latifah   ▲ Marc Anthony

WRITING FROM LIFE

1. What type of music does each artist in the photographs represent?

2. Traits: Traits: Traits:

3. Examples: Examples: Examples:

What's the point?

My First Thoughts: A Prewriting Activity

Brainstorm about the images you just studied. Set a time limit, such as five minutes, and write in your notebook about the images and the details you generated. Write as quickly as you can without stopping. Let the ideas flow freely. Getting your first thoughts about a topic on paper is one excellent way to overcome writer's block and set your mind to thinking.

One Student Writer's Response

The following paragraph offers one writer's point about the types of music illustrated by the photographs. Read the classification paragraph below and the explanations; complete the activities in **bold type** given in the annotations. Then, read the writer's journal that records decisions made during the writing process.

Effective Expression: Parallelism refers to the similarity in the way ideas are worded. To achieve parallelism in this sentence, the writer repeats the subject "music" and uses the same form to express each verb. **Double underline three other expressions that repeat a pattern of wording.**

Main Idea: The main idea is the point the author is making about the topic. The topic is "popular music." **Underline the author's point about this topic.**

Listing Order: The transitional phrase "first major type" signals that the paragraph is developed based on classification. **Circle two more phrases that signal a list of types.**

Relevant Details: Relevant details use descriptive details of traits and examples. Descriptive details include sensory details such as "fast, energetic tempo stirs the urge to dance." **Draw a box around two more details that appeal to the senses.**

Music's Variety Is Music's Power

(1) Music expresses our individuality; music connects us to one another; music carries our culture. (2) The power of music comes from the variety of the lives it expresses. (3) Three major types of popular music illustrate the powerful variety of music. (4) The first major type of music is country music. (5) From honky-tonk to rockabilly country music is based on the traditional folk music of the rural South and the cowboy music of the West. (6) Country songs express strong personal emotions about topics such as mother, home, love, hard work, prison, the rambling man, and religion. (7) Country musicians like Garth Brooks typically play such instruments as the guitar and fiddle. (8) The second major type of music that reveals the diversity of music is Hip Hop or rap music. (9) Rap music is a form of music that came about in African American urban communities. (10) Rap is characterized by beat-driven rhymes spoken over instruments or mixed recordings. (11) Rappers like Queen Latifah and Ludacris often express strong political and social views. (12) A third major type that illustrates the powerful variety in music is Salsa music. (13) Salsa, with its origin in Cuba, is a popular form of Latin-American dance music. (14) Salsa is characterized by Afro-Caribbean rhythms; its fast, energetic tempo stirs the urge to dance. (15) Performers like Marc Anthony use percussion instruments such as claves, congas, and cowbells.

The Writer's Journal

PEER EDITING

The student writer of "Music's Variety Is Music's Power" completed the following reflection to record her thinking through the writing process. Read her writer's journal that describes a few key choices she made as she wrote. Then, in the given space, answer her questions about the main idea for her paragraph. Work with a peer or a small group of classmates.

MAIN IDEA: Getting started was really hard for me. I spent a lot of time staring at a blank page, unable to come up with a way to get started. I knew what to say about each type of music, I just couldn't figure out how to word the beginning. Finally, I gave up and just started writing the body of the paragraph, so I think the title and introduction are weak, and there isn't a conclusion.

Could you suggest a better title? What would you do to make the opening more interesting? And is the conclusion okay as it is? Or do I need to add something? If so, what?

A classification makes a main point by grouping or sorting ideas. To support a point through classification, a writer divides a topic into subgroups based on common traits or principles. Writers offer relevant concrete details of descriptions and examples, and (as in every piece of writing) control sentence structure.

L2 Compose a Topic Sentence

When you write a classification, you limit your topic to a set of ideas or groups based on types, shared traits, and common principles. Most likely, you also have an opinion or point of view about the groups, traits, or common principles. This opinion or attitude is your point or main idea. You also reveal your opinion by discussing the groups or traits in a particular order of importance. A topic sentence states the point or purpose of the groups, types, or traits.

For example, the following topic sentence contains (1) the topic, (2) the writer's opinion about the topic, and (3) the pattern of organization used to organize details.

The topic is "friendship." The pattern of organization is established with the phrase "three types of." The writer's opinion is stated with the phrase "equally important interpersonal relationships."

TOPIC   PATTERN OF ORGANIZATION: CLASSIFICATION SIGNAL WORDS

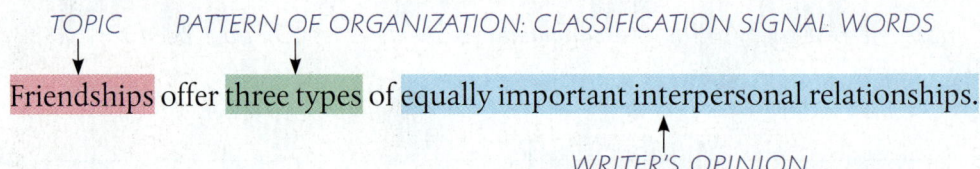

WRITER'S OPINION

The example above illustrates the relationships of the topic, the writer's opinion, and the pattern of organization in this particular topic sentence.

Practice 2

COMPOSE TOPIC SENTENCES

Practice creating topic sentences. The following items present a topic, an opinion, and classification signal word(s). Combine the ideas in each group to create a topic sentence for a classification.

1. TOPIC: *leisure activities*   OPINION: *relaxing and inexpensive, strengthen family ties*

   CLASSIFICATION SIGNAL WORDS: *two types of*

   TOPIC SENTENCE: _____

2. TOPIC: *diet*   OPINION: *healthful*

   CLASSIFICATION SIGNAL WORDS: *several traits*

   TOPIC SENTENCE: _____

Use Logical Order

Once you have divided a topic into groups, types, or traits and focused on a main idea, you are ready to generate additional details and list your ideas in their order of importance. To make a point using classification, a writer moves from a general idea (the group) to a major support (a particular trait of the group) to a minor support (an example of the trait). To signal the movement between these levels of ideas, a writer uses transitions to signal or list groups, types, or traits. Strong transitions establish coherence, a clear and understandable flow of ideas.

Words That Are Used to Signal Groups, Types, or Traits

aspect	classify	group	quality	style
attribute	classification	ideal	rank	trait
branch	collection	kind	section	type
brand	division	level	set	typical
categories	element	order	sort	variety
characteristic	feature	part	status	
class	form	principle	stratum	

Transitions That Combine with Signal Words to List Groups, Types, or Traits

also	final	for one thing	last of all	second
and	finally	furthermore	moreover	third
another	first	in addition	next	
besides	first of all	last	one	

USE LOGICAL ORDER

Based on the logical order of ideas, fill in the blanks with the appropriate classification signal words. Compare and discuss your answers with a peer or in a small group of your classmates.

I write in support of Henry William's promotion in _____ and pay. Mr. William has several _____ that will make him an effective manager. _____ of these _____ are his communication _____ and his _____ of commitment. He is the _____ who listens and learns. He is the _____ who works for the success of his whole _____.

L4 Develop Relevant Details

As a writer narrows a topic into a focused main idea, his or her thinking process brings to mind many details that answer questions such as *who, what, when, where, why,* and *how*. A writer evaluates the relevance of each detail and uses only those that clarify or support the main idea based on classification. Some relevant details identify subgroups, types, or traits of the main point. Minor details may offer examples of subgroups, types, or traits. Some major and minor details may explain the writer's opinion about the topic and how it is being classified. During the prewriting phase, a list can help a writer organize ideas as they are generated. Study the following concept map that was used to generate ideas about the topic "Two types of comedy that dominate television."

Concept Map

Topic:	Two types of comedy that dominate television	
Traits	Type 1: Sketch comedy	Type 2: Situation comedy
Length:	Short scenes or sketches (1-10 mins.)	30 min. story line
Material:	Actors improvise/write scripts Avoids violence, uses bad language	Writers create scripts Avoids violence and bad language
Focus:	Politics, current events, issues, ensemble acting	Social relationships at home and at work, ensemble acting
Examples:	SNL, Mad TV, Key and Peele, The Upright Citizens Brigade, In Living Color, and Ed Sullivan (best show of all)	Modern Family, Brooklyn Nine-Nine, The Big Bang Theory, Meet the Browns

During the prewriting phase, a writer naturally generates irrelevant details. In fact, an effective writer often produces far more details than can be used to make a specific point. Irrelevant details do not explain or support the focused point of the paragraph. A careful writer uses the revision process to double check details for relevance and to eliminate irrelevant ones.

DEVELOP RELEVANT DETAILS

The following paragraph develops the ideas recorded in the brainstorming list about comedy. Circle the main idea. Underline a trait for each group. Cross out the two details that are not relevant to the main point.

Television Comedy: Sketches and Sitcoms

(1) Two types of comedy have long dominated television. (2) One type is sketch comedy. (3) Sketch comedy is a series of short comedy scenes that typically range from one to ten minutes. (4) Often the actors improvise the sketch, making it up as they go; then they write the script based on their improvisation. (5) This kind of humor avoids violence, often uses offensive language, and focuses on politics, issues, and current events. (6) Well-known examples of sketch comedy include *Saturday Night Live, Key and Peele, Mad TV, The Upright Citizens Brigade,* and *In Living Color.* (7) However, *The Ed Sullivan Show* remains the all time best variety show to have appeared on television. (8) A second type of comedy dominating television is the sitcom or situation comedy, also an ensemble routine. (9) Sitcoms are usually set in a specific location such as a home or office, and they present amusing story lines about a group of characters such as a family, friends, or co-workers in an office. (10) Often episodes are self-contained stories that are resolved in less than 30 minutes; some sitcoms do use ongoing story lines based on developing relationships between characters. (11) This type of humor avoids violence, rarely uses offensive language, and focuses on social relationships. (12) Well-known examples of situation comedy include *Modern Family, Brooklyn Nine-Nine, The Big Bang Theory,* and *Meet the Browns.* (13) Overall, sitcoms are more appropriate for family viewing than sketch comedy.

L5 Use Effective Expression: Controlled Sentence Structure

Control of sentence structure enhances effective expression. You can express ideas through the use of four sentence types: simple, compound, complex, and compound-complex. Study the following definitions and examples of these four types of sentences.

1. A **simple sentence** contains one independent clause.

   INDEPENDENT CLAUSE
   MyPlate classifies food into five groups.

2. A **compound sentence** contains two or more independent clauses. These clauses can be joined with:

   a. A comma and a coordinating conjunction (*for, and, nor, but, or, yet, so*: FANBOYS),

   INDEPENDENT CLAUSES
   We must eat healthfully, and we must exercise regularly.

   b. A semicolon,

   INDEPENDENT CLAUSES
   MyPlate has one main role; it is to remind people to eat healthfully.

   OR

   c. A semicolon with a conjunctive adverb.

   INDEPENDENT CLAUSES
   MyPlate.gov is helpful; for example, experts explain calorie values.

3. A **complex sentence** contains one independent clause and one or more dependent clauses. A dependent clause begins with a subordinating conjunction (such as *although, because, when, who, which,* and *that*) placed immediately before a subject and a verb. Sometimes, the subordinating conjunction also serves as the subject of the verb in the dependent clause.

   INDEPENDENT CLAUSE   DEPENDENT CLAUSE
   Physical activity means movement of the body that uses energy.

4. A **compound-complex** sentence contains two or more independent clauses and one or more dependent clauses. This sentence type combines the traits of the compound and complex sentences.

   DEPENDENT CLAUSE   INDEPENDENT CLAUSES
   When we eat well and move often, we feel better, and we do more.

USE SENTENCE VARIETY

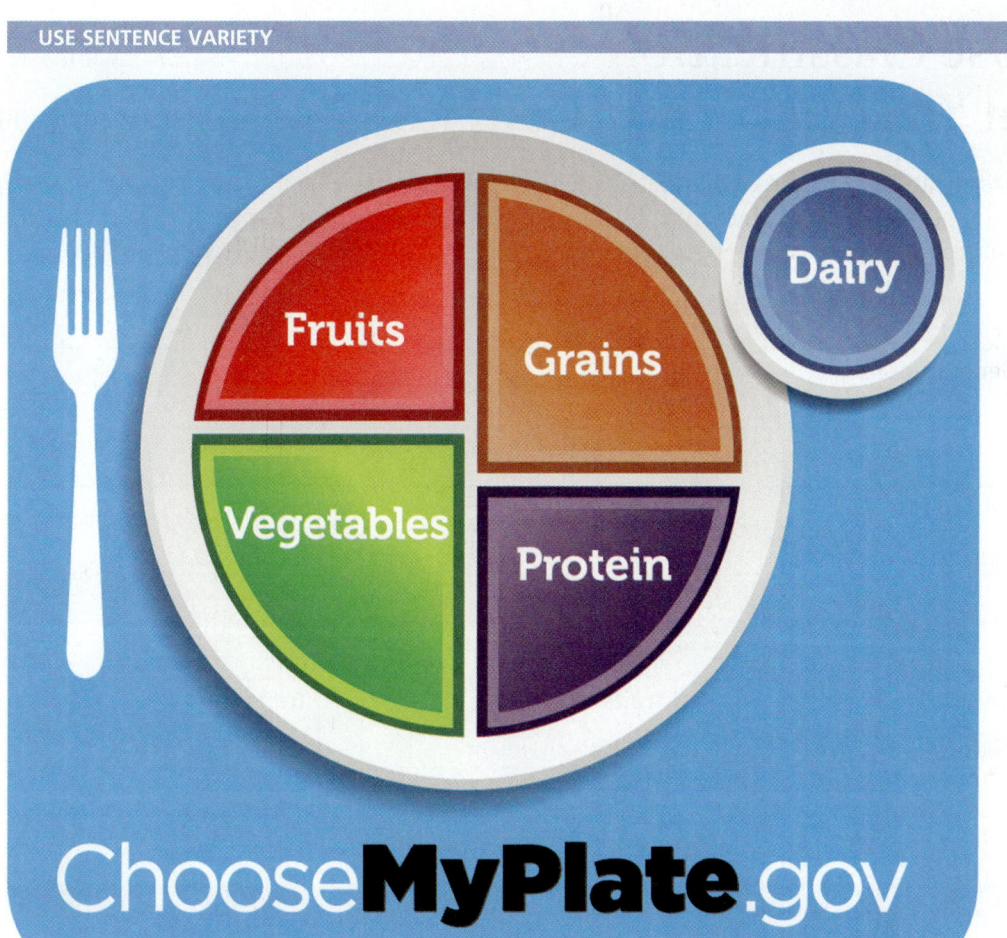

▲ MyPlate Pyramid poster to promote healthy eating

Label each of the following sentences as a simple, compound, complex, or compound-complex sentence. Revise each sentence into the new type of sentence indicated. Discuss your work with your class or with a small group of your peers.

_____ **1.** Foods from wheat, rice, oats, cornmeal, barley, or another cereal grain are grain products. Bread, pasta, oatmeal, breakfast cereals, tortillas, and grits are examples of grain products.

REVISE INTO A COMPOUND SENTENCE: _____

_____ **2.** Oils are fats that are liquid at room temperature, like canola, olive, and other vegetable oils used in cooking.

REVISE INTO A COMPOUND-COMPLEX SENTENCE: _____

L6 Use Classification in Your Academic Courses

Classification plays a role in most academic courses: to narrow a topic. Any academic topic can be narrowed by breaking a larger topic into subgroups. For example, the following concept map was created for a paper about leadership in a sociology class.

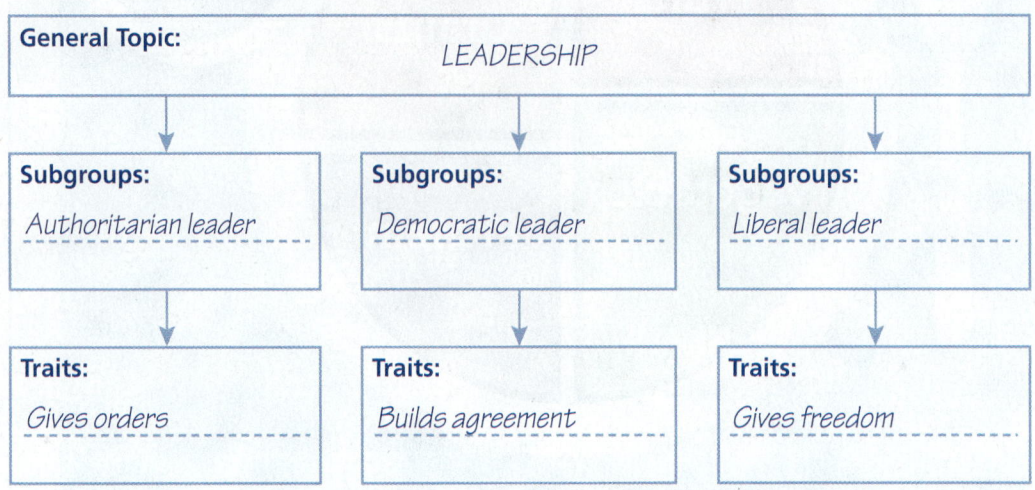

Practice 6

USE CLASSIFICATION TO NARROW AN ACADEMIC TOPIC

Use the following classification concept map to narrow a topic for a history class. Work with a peer or small group of classmates.

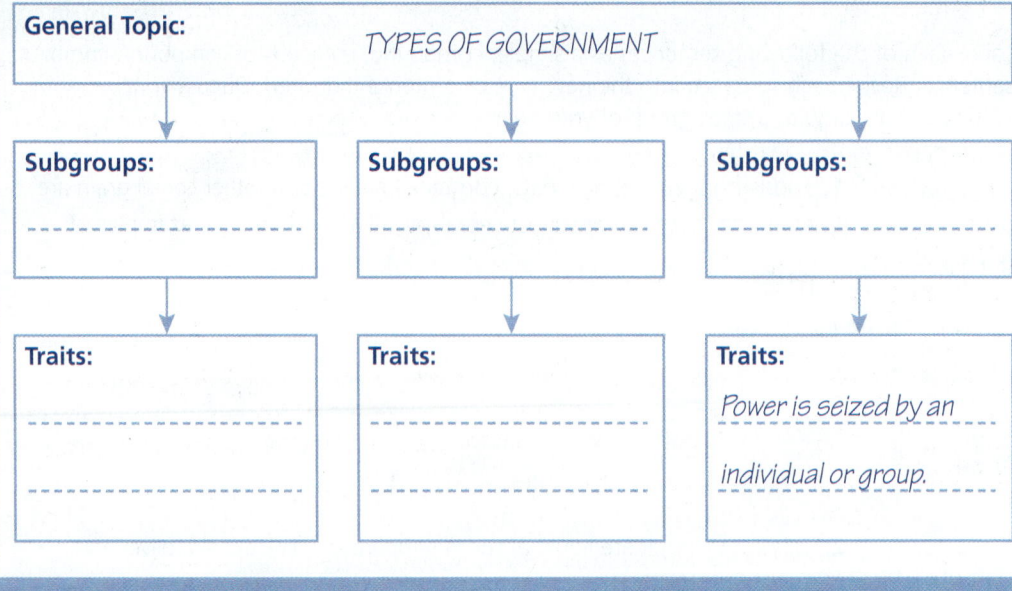

Workshop: Writing a Classification Paragraph Step by Step

Prewrite Your Paragraph

The activities below will walk you through the steps of the prewriting stage of the writing process: choosing a topic, focusing your point, and generating and organizing relevant details.

Choose Your Topic

The following activities are designed to help you choose a topic.

1. Create a bank of topics. Use the suggested headings to brainstorm or list as many categories and subgroups about each topic as you possibly can. Don't analyze your thoughts; just get as many relevant categories written down as quickly as possible. Add more topics and categories as they occur to you. Compare your bank of topics with those of your classmates.

   - Birth Order (traits of oldest, middle, youngest, only child)
   - Music
   - Technology
   - Vehicles
   - Life Roles

2. Generate ideas with a freewrite. Choose one of the topics from your topic bank and think of the traits that set a group or subgroup apart. Write about the traits of the group and subgroups for ten minutes without stopping.

   OR

   Select a photograph or series of photographs that illustrates a group or subgroup. Write captions, brainstorm traits, and freewrite about the photograph(s). Remember to ask "What is the group or subgroup represented by this picture(s)?" and "What's the point?"

Focus Your Point

Read a freewrite you have generated for a classification. Underline words that suggest your values, opinions, or attitudes about the topic and its subgroups or categories. Think about why the traits are important. Think about what examples best represent the group, categories, or subgroups. Identify your audience and purpose. Write a list of additional concrete traits and examples that explain your point. State in one sentence the point of the groups, traits, and examples.

AUDIENCE: ....

PURPOSE: ....

LIST OF TRAITS: ....

WHAT'S THE POINT? ....

Generate and Organize Relevant Details

Use the graphic organizer below to either organize the ideas you have already created or to generate details to support your point.

Types (groups) of		
1st Type/group	2nd Type/group	3rd Type/group
Traits:	Traits:	Traits:
Examples:	Examples:	Examples:

What's the point?

Write a Draft of Your Paragraph

Using the ideas you generated during the prewriting phase, compose a draft of your classification paragraph. Return to the prewriting process at any time to generate additional details as needed. Use your own paper.

Revise Your Draft

Read your draft and answer the questions in the "Questions for Revising a Classification Paragraph" box. Indicate your answers by annotating your paper. If you answer "yes" to a question, underline, check, or circle examples. If you answer "no" to a question, write the additional details in the margin and draw lines to indicate their placement. Revise your paragraph based on your reflection.

> # Questions for Revising a Classification Paragraph:
>
> - [ ] Have I made my point? Can I state my point in one sentence?
> - [ ] Have I divided my topic into groups or categories? Have I clearly labeled each group? Have I discussed the common traits and examples of each group?
> - [ ] Have I used strong transitions of classification?
> - [ ] Have I used concrete details to make my point?
> - [ ] Have I included only the details that are relevant to my topic sentence?
> - [ ] Have I used the following to make my ideas clear to my readers: vivid verbs and images, parallel language, controlled sentence structure?

 ## Proofread Your Draft

Once you have made any revisions to your paragraph that may be needed, proofread your paper to eliminate distracting errors such as comma splices.

> ### Grammar in Action: Eliminating Comma Splices
>
> A **comma splice** occurs when a writer uses *only a comma* to join two or more independent clauses.
>
> COMMA SPLICE ↓
>
> Americans enjoy many vacation options, some choose theme parks, others choose activities such as spring break in Cancun.
>
> ← COMMA SPLICE

For more information on eliminating comma splices, see pages 420–437.

Workshop Practice 7

A **comma splice** can be corrected in three different ways.

> **Three Rules for Properly Joining Two or More Independent Clauses**
>
> 1. Use a comma AND a coordinating conjunction (*for, and, nor, but, or, yet, so*: FANBOYS).
> 2. Use a semicolon.
> 3. Use a semicolon with a transition (*for example, in addition, however, therefore, thus,* etc.).

Study the following examples:

1. Americans enjoy many vacation options; some choose theme parks, but others choose activities such as spring break in Cancun.
2. Americans enjoy many vacation options; for example, some choose trips to theme parks.

ELIMINATE COMMA SPLICES

Edit these sentences to eliminate comma splices. *Hint:* Underline subjects once and verbs twice to identify independent clauses.

1. "Muscle car" is a type of high-speed automobile, it is American made with powerful engines.

2. A muscle car has several distinct traits, it has a V8 engine, two doors, and rear wheel drive.

3. The American public wanted speed and power, in 1949, Oldsmobile created the Rocket V-8.

Writing Assignments

MyWritingLab™ Complete this Exercise on mywritinglab.com

Considering Audience and Purpose

Study the photographs about the types of music at the beginning of the chapter. Assume you have decided to start a collection of music for your younger cousin, who is just becoming interested in music. First, identify the type(s) of music you want to include. Create a list of specific artists and songs for the type or types of music you have chosen. Then, write a one-paragraph note to go with the gift that explains the type(s) of music in the collection.

Writing for Everyday Life

Assume you have just experienced an event as an invited guest. Write a one-paragraph thank you note in which you include the following information: the type of event, the quality of your experience, the most vivid aspects of the event, and the traits of your host that you appreciate. Choose words that reflect one of the following: (1) polite and reserved or (2) warm and enthusiastic.

Writing for College Life

Assume you are in a college psychology class. Your teacher has assigned a chapter on "The Six Basic Emotions and Their Combinations." You have decided to record in your learning log what you currently know about these ideas before you begin your reading assignment. Write one paragraph in which you identify, describe, and classify six basic types of emotions you have observed or experienced.

Writing for Working Life

Assume you are compiling information for a résumé for a position as manager trainee at a business such as Lowe's, Safeway, or The Cheesecake Factory. Use the following categories to create your résumé.

Personal Information: Name, address, phone number, and e-mail address

Objective: Manager Trainee position with <u>name of business</u>

Education:

Work Experience:

Activities:

Complete the Post-test for Chapter 8 in MyWritingLab.

9 The Comparison and Contrast Paragraph

LEARNING OUTCOMES

After studying this chapter you will be able to:

1. Answer the question "What's the Point of Comparison and Contrast?"
2. Compose a Topic Sentence
3. Use Logical Order
4. Develop Relevant Details
5. Use Effective Expression: Use of Coordination and Subordination
6. Use Comparison and Contrast in Your Academic Courses
7. Write a Comparison and Contrast Paragraph Step by Step

A comparison examines how two or more things are similar. A contrast looks at how two or more things are different.

Comparing and contrasting ideas is an essential part of critical thinking. When we choose between Subway and McDonald's or Apple and Dell computers, we are weighing the similarities or differences of products and services and making a choice by comparison shopping. What are some basic comparable points for any consumer to consider when shopping? What are some other situations in which we use comparable points as the basis of our thinking or actions?

In everyday life, we compare or contrast the neighborhoods we want to live in and the prices of homes we want to buy, or the honesty and policies of political candidates as we decide for whom we will vote. In working life, we compare or contrast the salaries, benefits, and working conditions among several career opportunities. In college life, we compare and contrast leaders, governments, cultures, literature, technology, writers, or philosophies in a wide range of courses.

To write a comparison or a contrast paragraph, identify the comparable points between two (or more) topics. Once you identify the points of comparison, brainstorm a list of similarities and differences for each one. Then, list and explain examples of each similarity or difference.

What's the Point of Comparison and Contrast?

Often ideas become clearer when they are analyzed based on how they relate to one another. The comparison and contrast patterns of organization allow a writer to explore the ways in which ideas are related. The following set of photographs documents some similarities and differences between electric and gas vehicles. Study the sets of images. Answer the following questions about each comparable point. Then, answer the question "What's the point?" with a one-sentence statement of the overall main idea.

PHOTOGRAPHIC ORGANIZER: COMPARE AND CONTRAST

SIMILAR TO OR DIFFERENT FROM

GAS VEHICLES
(Audi RS5)

ELECTRIC VEHICLES
(Tesla Model S)

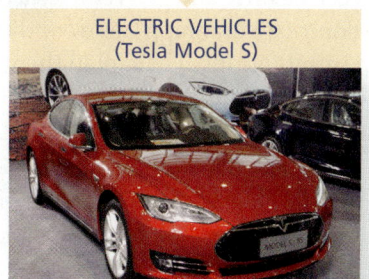

What is the **1st** comparable point?

_____

SIMILAR TO OR DIFFERENT FROM

What is the **2nd** comparable point?

_____

SIMILAR TO OR DIFFERENT FROM

What is the **3rd** comparable point?

_____

What's the point? _____

PREWRITING

My First Thoughts

Brainstorm about the images you just studied. Set a time limit, such as five minutes, and write in your notebook about the images and the details you generated. Write as quickly as you can without stopping. Let the ideas flow freely. Getting your first thoughts about a topic on paper is one excellent way to kick-start your writing process.

One Student Writer's Response

The following paragraph offers one writer's point about the similarities and differences between electric and gas vehicles as illustrated by the photographs. Read the comparison and contrast paragraph below and the explanations; complete the activities in **bold type** in the annotations. Then, read the writer's journal entry that records decisions made during the writing process.

LOGICAL ORDER: Words of comparison or contrast signal similarities or differences. **Circle two more signal words or phrases for comparison or contrast.**

MAIN IDEA: The main idea is the point the author is making about the topic. **Underline the two topics being compared and contrasted and underline the author's point about the two topics.**

RELEVANT DETAILS: Relevant details include descriptive details about similarities or differences between comparable points. **Draw a box around two more details of similarities or differences.**

EFFECTIVE EXPRESSION: This sentence gives equal weight to both types of vehicles. **Double underline another sentence that expresses equal ideas with the use of semicolon.**

Electric or Gas Vehicles?

(1) Pollution, global warming, and the price of fuel pose real problems for an auto industry churning out gas vehicles. (2) However, electric vehicles offer hope for the future. (3) A comparison between electric vehicles and gas vehicles shows pleasing similarities and differences. (4) Most electric vehicles look just like a gas vehicle. (5) For example, the electric-powered Tesla Model S resembles the gas-powered Audi RS5. (6) Both sport the bold look of a sports car, and both have all the standard features. (7) They even perform similarly; both go from 0 to 60 mph in about 5 seconds. (8) Although these similarities promise to please, many drivers will really like the differences between electric and gas vehicles. (9) For example, the lithium-ion battery of the Tesla uses far less energy than the gas guzzling V8 engine used by the RS5. (10) The Tesla can go 265 to 310 miles between charges and costs about $10 to $20 a week in electricity; in contrast, the RS5 averages 20 miles per gallon in the city and 29 on the highway. (11) Plus, based on the price of oil, gasoline can cost as much as $5 a gallon, and those dollars add up with the miles. (12) The final difference is convenience. (13) Many people and much energy must be used to refuel a gas vehicle. (14) Oil has to be refined into gasoline, stored, transported, and pumped. (15) However, to recharge an electric vehicle, all one has to do is plug it into a standard household outlet or a socket on a charging station.

The Writer's Journal

PEER EDITING

The student writer of "Electric or Gas Vehicles?" completed the following reflection to record his thinking through the writing process. Read his writer's journal that describes a few key choices he made as he wrote. Then, in the given space, answer his questions about his use of effective expression in his paragraph. Work with a peer or a small group of classmates.

EFFECTIVE EXPRESSION: *I used coordination to state most of my ideas because I wanted to be sure to cover each point equally, like in sentences 6, 7, and 10. Does the repeated use of signal words for comparison and contrast make my paragraph boring or interesting? Why? I also had trouble with some of my word choices. I really support electric vehicles, but I couldn't find the right words to get my support across. For example, I am not really satisfied with the word "pleasing" in sentence 3.*

Should I leave it out, or could you suggest another word? Is it important to give my opinion, or should I stick with just the facts?

A **comparison** makes a point by discussing the *similarities* between two or more topics. A **contrast** makes a point by discussing the *differences* between two or more topics. To support a point through comparison or contrast, a writer identifies the comparable points of the topic, offers relevant and concrete descriptions and examples for each comparable point, and effectively uses coordination and subordination of ideas.

L2 Compose a Topic Sentence

When you write a comparison or a contrast piece, you limit your thoughts to a set of topics based on their relationship to each other. Most likely you have an opinion or belief about the two topics and their comparable points. Your opinion is your point or main idea. In a comparison or contrast paragraph, you also reveal your opinion by discussing the topics and their points of similarity or difference in the order of your own choosing. A topic sentence states the overall point of the comparison or the contrast between the two topics.

For example, the following topic sentence contains (1) the comparable topics, (2) the writer's opinion about the topic, and (3) the pattern of organization used to organize details.

The comparable topics are "celebrity chefs," and "Giada De Laurentiis and Rachael Ray." The pattern of organization is established with words "even though" and "differ." The writer's opinion is stated with the clause "styles differ greatly."

PATTERN OF ORGANIZATION: TRANSITION WORDS THAT SIGNAL CONTRAST — TOPIC

Even though Giada De Laurentiis and Rachael Ray are both celebrity chefs, their styles differ greatly. ← WRITER'S OPINION

Practice 2

COMPOSE TOPIC SENTENCES

The items present a topic, an opinion, and comparison or contrast signal word(s). Combine the ideas in each group to create a topic sentence for comparison or contrast.

1. TOPIC: the communication styles of men and women

   OPINION: significant

   COMPARISON OR CONTRAST SIGNAL WORDS: differ three ways

   TOPIC SENTENCE: _____

2. TOPIC: Football, Baseball

   OPINION: violent

   COMPARISON OR CONTRAST SIGNAL WORDS: more

   TOPIC SENTENCE: _____

Use Logical Order

Once you have identified the comparable points between your topics and have focused on a main idea, you are ready to generate and organize additional details. To make a point using comparison or contrast, a writer moves from a general idea (the comparison or contrast of two or more topics) to a major support (a comparable point about the topics) to minor supports (details or examples of the comparable point about the topics). To signal the movement among these levels of ideas, a writer uses transitions to signal similarities or differences and examples. Strong transitions establish coherence, a clear and understandable flow of ideas.

Words That Signal Comparison

alike	equally	in the same way	likewise	similarity
as	in a similar fashion	just as	resemble	similarly
as well as	in a similar way	just like	same	
equal	in like manner	like	similar	

Words That Signal Contrast

although	conversely	differently	more	on the other hand
as opposed to	despite	even though	most	still
at the same time	difference	in contrast	nevertheless	to the contrary
but	different	in spite of	on the contrary	unlike
by contrast	different from	instead	on the one hand	yet

USE LOGICAL ORDER

Based on the logical order of ideas, fill in the blanks with the appropriate comparison or contrast signal words. Compare and discuss your answers with a peer or in a small group of your classmates.

If you could build your ideal mate, he or she would probably look, act, and think very much _____ you. By being attracted to people _____ yourself, you validate yourself. You tell yourself that you're worthy of being liked. _____ there are exceptions, the _____ factor probably means that you will be attracted to your own mirror image. You will be attracted to people who are _____ to you in nationality, race, ability, physical traits, intelligence, attitudes, and so on. If you were to ask a group of friends, "To whom are you _____ attracted?" they would probably name the _____ attractive people they know. _____ if you were to watch these friends, you would find that they have relationships with people who are about _____ in attractiveness.

—Adapted from DeVito, Joseph A. *The Interpersonal Communication Book*, 10th ed., Allyn and Bacon, 2004, p. 182.

L4 Develop Relevant Details

As a writer narrows a topic into a focused main idea, the thinking process brings to mind many details that answer the questions *who, what, when, where, why,* and *how*. A writer evaluates the relevance of each detail and uses only those that clarify or support the main idea. In a comparison or contrast paragraph, some relevant major details include those that identify comparable topics or points. Relevant minor details offer examples and explanations of the similarities or differences between comparable points. Relevant details include descriptions, explanations, and examples of similarities or differences between two or more topics. Details are logically ordered to best support the point.

Comparable Topics in a Venn Diagram

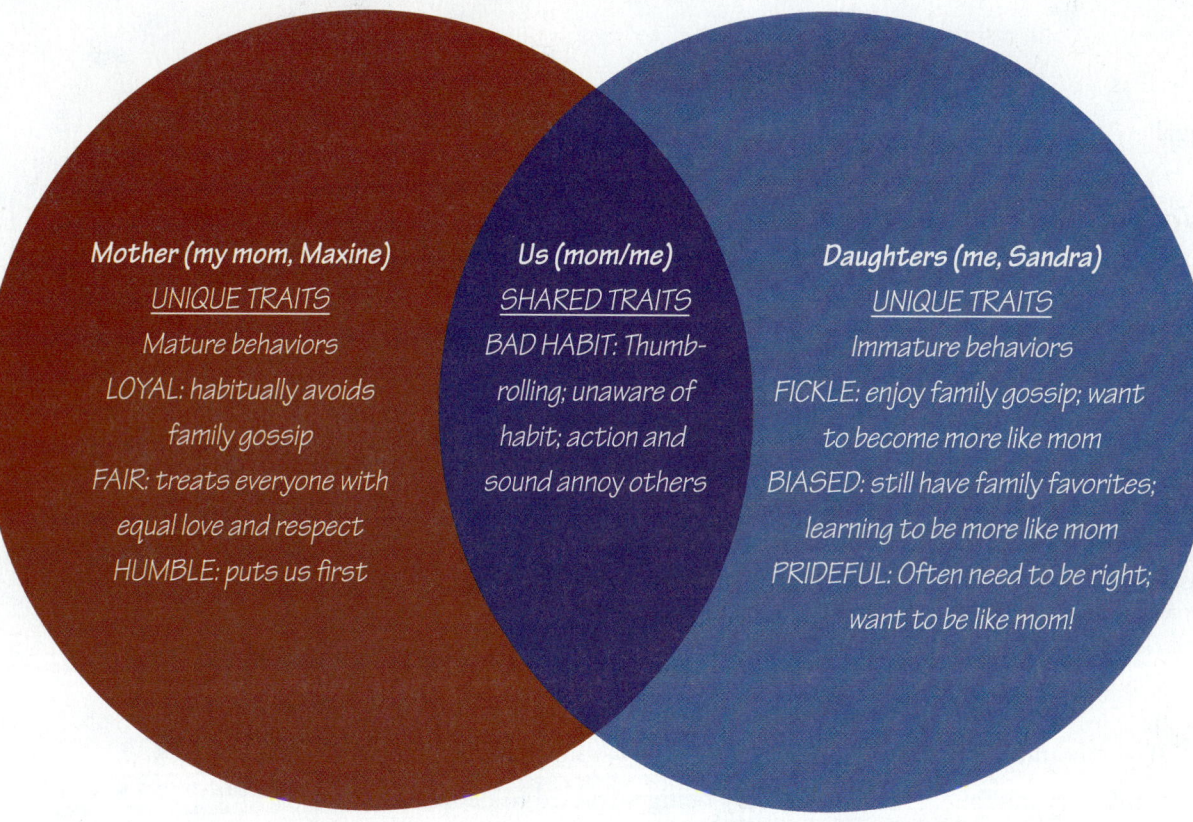

During the prewriting phase, a writer naturally generates irrelevant details. In fact, an effective writer often produces far more details than can be used to make a specific point. Irrelevant details do not explain or support the focused point of the paragraph. A careful writer uses the revision process to double check details for relevance and to eliminate irrelevant ones.

DEVELOP RELEVANT DETAILS

The following paragraph explains and illustrates the ideas generated using the Venn diagram. Circle the main idea. Underline the words that signal similarities or differences and double underline three supporting points of similarities discussed in the paragraph. Cross out two details that are not relevant to the main point.

Bonds of Habits Tie Us Together

(1) I never realized how similar parents and their children can be. (2) My mother, Maxine, has a habit of rolling her thumbs. (3) She sits with her hands clasped, fingers laced, and thumbs rolling. (4) The action creates a soft rhythmic swish as the pad of one thumb brushes the top of her other thumb. (5) I don't know why, but the sight and sound of mother's thumb-rolling drives me to distraction. (6) Sometimes, I can hardly concentrate on my thoughts. (7) She remains completely unaware of the habit or how much it bothers me. (8) The one time I mentioned the behavior, she was embarrassed, and she tried for a while to break herself of the habit. (9) Although I vowed never to develop any such quirk, I recently caught myself in the middle of my own mother-like thumb roll. (10) As my husband described his golf swing, his eyes kept darting to my hands in the same way my own eyes react to Mom's thumb roll. (11) Suddenly he fell silent mid-sentence. (12) We heard a sound just like the one made by mother's thumb roll. (13) Just like my mother, I sat with my hands clasped, fingers laced, and thumbs rolling. (14) My husband asked, "Maxine," (he called me by mother's name instead of my name!) "Maxine, are you aware that you are a thumb-roller? (15) And that, for some reason, it gets on my nerves?" (16) My habit of leaving lids loose on containers also drives my husband nuts. (17) Now I know just how maddeningly similar parents and their children can be.

L5 Use Effective Expression: Use of Coordination and Subordination

Effective expression reflects a writer's thoughtful match of ideas to words and structure. Two types of sentence structures enable effective expression of comparison or contrast: coordination and subordination.

Coordination expresses an **equal** relationship between **similarities** with words such as *and, likewise, similarly, also*. Coordination expresses an **equal** relationship between **differences** with words such as *but, yet, or, however, in contrast*.

A **compound sentence** is an example of **coordination**.

Example

An athlete trains the body for competitions; likewise, a student trains the mind for final exams.

Subordination expresses an **unequal** relationship between **similarities** with words such as *as, just as, just like, like*. **Subordination** expresses an **unequal** relationship between **differences** with words such as *although, even though, while*.

A **complex sentence** is an example of **subordination**.

Example

Just as an athlete trains the body for competitions, a student trains the mind for final exams.

For more information on coordination and subordination, see pages 402–419.

Practice 5

USE COORDINATION AND SUBORDINATION

Label each of the following sentences as a compound or a complex sentence. Identify the pattern of organization expressed by each sentence as comparison, contrast, or both.

1. Although the pessimist and the optimist face many of the same challenges in life, they differ greatly in their actions, words, and thoughts.

SENTENCE TYPE: _____

PATTERN OF ORGANIZATION: _____

2. Just as the pessimist faces rejection and disappointments, the optimist endures those same hardships common to all humans.

SENTENCE TYPE: _____

PATTERN OF ORGANIZATION: _____

3. The pessimist focuses on problems and remains passive; in contrast, the optimist focuses on solutions and takes action.

SENTENCE TYPE: _____

PATTERN OF ORGANIZATION: _____

Use Comparison and Contrast in Your Academic Courses

College writing assignments are often based on information gathered through class lectures, textbook reading assignments, and research. For example, essay exams often test students on material given in class or assigned in readings. Note-taking is an excellent pretest and prewriting activity. When you take or revise notes, set up a graphic organizer into which you can plug information from your class notes or reading assignments. A popular note-taking graphic divides an 11-inch by 8.5-inch page into three sections: a 8-inch by 3-inch left margin for key terms; a 8-inch by 5-inch right margin for notes; and a 3-inch by 8.5-inch wide bottom margin for a summary. This format allows you to write, reflect, and write for understanding as you study.

USE COMPARISON AND CONTRAST IN AN ART APPRECIATION COURSE: TAKING NOTES

Study the following set of notes taken during a lecture in a college art appreciation class. In the bottom margin, write a short paragraph that states and supports the main idea of the notes.

Key terms	Notes
Tragic hero	Virtuous, admirable, rich, powerful, and male, but flawed; inner conflict and guilt; accepts responsibility for suffering; loses all.
Example	5th Century BCE: In *Oedipus the King*, Oedipus loses power, wealth, family, and independence due to his limited wisdom and great pride.
Melodramatic hero	A symbol of good, male or female, a stereotype of courage and honesty, etc. No flaws; no inner conflict or guilt; fights against and defeats evil; all ends well.
Example	Pauline, the heroine of *Perils of Pauline*, is a "damsel in distress" who escapes many life-threatening, thrilling perils (dangers) due to her courage and ingenuity.

Summary: What are the differences between a tragic hero and a melodramatic hero?

....
....
....
....
....

L7 Workshop: Writing a Comparison and Contrast Paragraph Step by Step

Prewrite Your Paragraph

The activities below will walk you through the steps of the prewriting stage of the writing process: choosing a topic, focusing your point, and generating and organizing relevant details.

Choose Your Topic

The following activities are designed to help you choose a topic.

1. Create a bank of topics. Use the suggested headings to brainstorm or list as many similarities or differences about sets of topics as you possibly can. Don't criticize your thoughts. Add more topics, similarities, or differences as they occur to you. Revisit topic banks created during your study of previous chapters and identify comparable topics. Compare your bank of topics with those of your classmates.

   - Family Members
   - Natural Disasters
   - Neighborhoods
   - Movies

2. Generate ideas with a freewrite. Choose one of the topics from your topic bank and think about the points of similarities or differences. Write about the similarities or differences for ten minutes without stopping.

   OR

   Select a set of photographs that illustrates the similarities or differences between two topics. Write a caption, brainstorm comparable points, and freewrite about the photograph(s). Remember to ask, "What are the similarities or differences represented by these images?" and "What's the point?"

Focus Your Point

Read a prewrite you have generated for a comparison or contrast paragraph. Identify your audience and purpose. Annotate the text: Underline or insert words that suggest your values, opinions, or attitudes about the topics and their points of similarity or difference. State in a sentence or two the importance of each similarity or difference between the comparable topics. Generate one or more concrete examples for each comparable point. Finally, state the point of the comparison or contrast paragraph in one sentence.

AUDIENCE: ....

PURPOSE: ....

LIST OF CONCRETE EXAMPLES: ....

....

WHAT'S THE POINT? ....

Generate and Organize Relevant Details

Using ideas you have recorded so far and the concept chart below, generate and organize details that support your point.

Concept Chart: Comparison/Contrast			
COMPARABLE TOPICS:	TOPIC A	LIKE OR UNLIKE	TOPIC B
1st attribute, point, basis of comparison		Like or unlike	
2nd attribute, point, basis of comparison		Like or unlike	
3rd attribute, point, basis of comparison		Like or unlike	

What's the point?

 ## Write a Draft of Your Paragraph

Using the ideas you generated during the prewriting phase, compose a draft of your comparison or contrast paragraph. Return to the prewriting process at any time to generate additional details as needed. Use your own paper.

Revise Your Draft

Once you have created a draft of your comparison or contrast paragraph, read the draft and answer the questions in the "Questions for Revising a Comparison and Contrast Paragraph." box that follows. Indicate your answers by annotating your paper. If you answer "yes" to a question, underline, check, or circle examples. If you answer "no" to a question, write the additional details in the margins and draw lines to indicate their placement. Revise your paragraph based on your reflection.

> ## Questions for Revising a Comparison and Contrast Paragraph:
>
> ☐ Have I chosen appropriately comparable topics? Have I clearly labeled each comparable point as a similarity or a difference?
>
> ☐ Have I made my point? Can I state my point in one sentence?
>
> ☐ Are my ideas logically and clearly ordered? Have I used strong transitions of comparison or contrast?
>
> ☐ Have I used concrete details to make my point?
>
> ☐ Have I included only the details that are relevant to my topic sentence?
>
> ☐ Have I used the following to make my ideas clear and interesting to my readers: vivid verbs and images, parallel language, controlled sentence structure, coordination, or subordination?

Proofread Your Draft

Once you have revised your paragraph, proofread to ensure precise usage and grammar, such as editing for proper use of a comma after introductory elements.

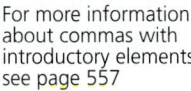

For more information about commas with introductory elements see page 557.

Grammar in Action: Commas after Introductory Elements

Commas are used after introductory elements: a word, phrase, or dependent clause that comes before an independent clause.

A dependent clause—an incomplete thought containing a subject and a verb—is signaled by a subordinating conjunction (*although, because, while…*) or a relative pronoun (*who, which, that…*).

An independent clause is a complete thought containing a subject and a verb.

- Introductory word used with independent clause

  Similarly, Sandra twiddles her thumbs.

- Introductory phrase used with independent clause

  In contrast, comedy's main purpose is to entertain.

- Introductory dependent clause used with independent clause

  Although Bob and Tom are both baby boomers, they differ greatly in values and lifestyles.

COMMAS AND INTRODUCTORY ELEMENTS

Edit the following sentences for proper use of a comma after an introductory element. Identify the type of introductory element used in each sentence. (Hint: first underline subjects and verbs.)

_____ 1. Unlike those who are habitually late Consuelo has received three merit raises for prompt, efficient work.

_____ 2. Like a fire hydrant opened full force Deborah poured out her grief.

_____ 3. However the traveling nurse program offers better pay and greater mobility.

Writing Assignments

MyWritingLab™
Complete this Exercise on mywritinglab.com

Considering Audience and Purpose

Study the set of photographs that show the similarities and differences between electric and gas vehicles. Write a letter to your senator that calls for support for either the electric or the gas vehicle. Explain the points of comparison that prove one is better than the other.

Writing for Everyday Life

Assume that you have just experienced a life-altering event, such as a graduation, a marriage, the birth of a child, a severe loss, or the breaking of a bad habit. You have been asked to talk about "Change" to a specific audience such as the Rotary Club, a civic group. Identify your audience and write a short speech in which you discuss three before-and-after comparable points. Allow your tone through word choice to reflect either sadness and regret or pride and encouragement.

Writing for College Life

Assume you are in a biology class and you read the following question on the final exam:

> In what ways did the human skeleton change as upright posture and bipedalism evolved? Describe the changes by comparing the human skeleton and the skeleton of a quadruped such as a baboon. — Campbell, Mitchell, and Reece. *Biology: Concepts and Connections*, 5th ed. 2005 Longman. p. 620.

Test what you already know about the subject by writing a paragraph. Identify the comparable points of similarities and/or differences between the two topics. Look up words in your dictionary as needed.

Writing for Working Life

Assume that you are applying for a management position at a local business. You have the following experiences, which are listed on your résumé: Treasurer, Student Government Association; Certified in various computer programs; Member of Toastmasters, a public-speaking organization. Write a paragraph in which you compare your skills with those needed at the job for which you are applying.

Complete the Post-test for Chapter 9 in MyWritingLab.

10 The Definition Paragraph

A definition explains what a word or concept means.

PART 2 USING PATTERNS OF ORGANIZATION TO DEVELOP PARAGRAPHS

LEARNING OUTCOMES

After studying this chapter you will be able to:

- **L1** Answer the question "What's the Point of Definition?"
- **L2** Compose a Topic Sentence
- **L3** Use Logical Order
- **L4** Develop Relevant Details
- **L5** Use Effective Expression: Sound Structure and Vivid Images
- **L6** Use Definition in Your Academic Courses
- **L7** Write a Definition Paragraph Step by Step

We are all familiar with the word *definition*. In fact, we apply or create definitions in every aspect of life. Call to mind what you already know about a definition. Answer the following questions: How would you define "a good life"? What are the traits and examples of "a good life"? What information should be included in a definition?

The definition pattern of organization is helpful in all areas of life. In personal life, you rely upon a doctor's definition of your symptoms when you seek medical treatment. In working life, you define your job duties to ensure your best performance. In college life, you will define the specialized meanings and examples of words in each content area.

To create a definition paragraph, the writer names a concept, explains its traits, describes the concept using similar terms, and offers examples of the concept. Often a contrast clarifies meaning; thus, a writer may also include an example and explanation of what the term or concept is *not*.

What's the Point of Definition?

The following definition concept chart shows three visual examples of a concept and one visual example of what the concept is not. Study the chart and the visual examples. Then, write answers to the questions asked in the chart. Consider these questions as you write your answers: What is the concept being defined? What are some examples? What traits does each example represent? Then, answer the question "What's the point?" with a one-sentence statement of the overall main idea.

PHOTOGRAPHIC ORGANIZER: DEFINITION

Definition Concept Chart

What are the traits or characteristics of the concept?

What are some examples?

What is it NOT?

Concept?

What is the concept similar to?

What's the point?

WRITING FROM LIFE

Concept map adapted from following sources:

Frayer, D., Frederick, W. C., and Klausmeier, H. J. (1969). *A Schema for Testing the Level of Cognitive Mastery*. Madison, WI: Wisconsin Center for Education Research.

Schwartz, R., & Raphael, T. (1985). "Concept of definition: A Key to Improving Student's Vocabulary." *The Reading Teacher*, 39, 198–205.

My First Thoughts: A Prewriting Activity

Brainstorm about the images you just studied. Set a time limit, such as five minutes, and write in your notebook about the images and the details you generated. Write as quickly as you can without stopping. Let the ideas flow freely. Getting your first thoughts about a topic on paper is one excellent way to overcome writer's block and set your mind to thinking.

One Student Writer's Response

The following paragraph offers student writer Kuei-Ti Lu's point about the concept depicted in the photographs. Read the definition and the explanations; complete the activities in **bold type** in the annotations. Then, read the writer's journal entry that records decisions made during the writing process.

Relevant Details:
Relevant details include descriptions of traits and examples. **Draw boxes around two additional traits of the Chinese New Year.**

Logical Order:
The transitional phrase "on the first day" indicates a list of some of the days of the celebration. **Circle two other transitions that introduce supporting details.**

Effective Expression:
Vivid images make the point interesting and memorable. This phrase paints a vivid image in the reader's mind. **Double underline two more vivid images.**

Main Idea:
The main idea states Kuei-Ti Lu's point about her topic the Chinese New Year. **Underline her point about the topic.**

Chinese New Year

(1) Chinese New Year is a series of traditional Chinese holidays when people welcome the coming of the year and reunite with families. (2) It begins on the first day and ends on the fifteenth day of a year in the traditional Chinese calendar, and its various festivities are thought to affect the luck and fortune for that year. (3) Regardless of the different activities for different days, Chinese New Year is not a collection of unrelated holidays as of Halloween and Thanksgiving; instead, each day shares a similar anticipation as Christmas Eve and Christmas do. (4) For example, several practices symbolize reunion with families and the expectation for a good year. (5) Specifically, on the first day, people worship ancestors in heaven to thank them for protection, wishing for their continuous protection during the year. (6) On the second day, married people who do not live with their parents visit their parents to celebrate New Year together. (7) On the fifth day, as it is said one of the gods for prosperity visits the humans' world, people display fireworks in hopes of the god's bringing them fortune. (8) And at the night of the fifteenth day, when the first full moon of the year comes, families sit together and view the full moon, which symbolizes reunion. (9) Moreover, throughout Chinese New Year, the Lion Dance, of which the dancing lions are believed to be able to scare away bad things such as accidents and diseases, is performed on the streets. (10) These elements all define the central spirit of Chinese New Year — the anticipation for a good year.

The Writer's Journal

PEER EDITING

The student writer of "Chinese New Year" completed the following reflection to record her thinking through the writing process. Read her writer's journal that describes a few key choices she made as she wrote. Then, in the given space, answer her questions about her use of main idea, relevant details, and effective expression in her paragraph. Work with a peer or a small group of classmates.

EFFECTIVE EXPRESSION: *For the second draft, in which some sentences were too long or not cohesive, I followed the advice of my teacher and divided the sentences or changed their positions in the paragraph. The first sentence now only has the noun defining Chinese New Year and an adjective clause providing the meaning of Chinese New Year. The other details in the original first sentence were placed in separate sentences. Therefore, the definition is clearer than it was.*

LOGICAL ORDER: *As for cohesion, because I found the common meaning among the four days mentioned and Lion Dance, I made the order in which the days appeared in the paragraph chronological and, after that, added Lion Dance followed by the ending sentence, which refers to the central idea of Chinese New Year. The ending sentence does not repeat the first sentence but moves to a deeper meaning of Chinese New Year. In addition to the changes mentioned above, some prepositions and conjunctions were changed to enhance the flow of the paragraph. Does my paragraph flow smoothly? Do you have any suggestions to improve the flow of ideas or my wording?*

A definition clarifies the meaning of a concept. A definition makes a point by classifying a concept, describing its traits, describing what it is *like*, describing what it is *not like*, and illustrating it with examples. To support a point by definition, a writer may also use figurative language.

L2 Compose a Topic Sentence

When you write a definition paragraph, most likely, you have an opinion or belief about the concept, characteristics, or examples. Your opinion is your point or main idea. A topic sentence states the overall point of the definition. Often a definition topic sentence emphasizes one aspect of the definition: its class, its traits, what it is like, or what it is not like.

For example, each of the following two topic sentences contains (1) a concept, (2) the writer's attitude about the concept, and (3) the pattern of organization used to organize details.

Definition by Classification: Group or Traits

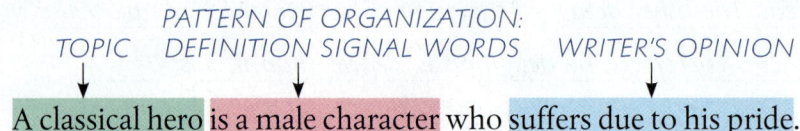

A classical hero is a male character who suffers due to his pride.

Definition by Comparison: Synonyms or Analogies

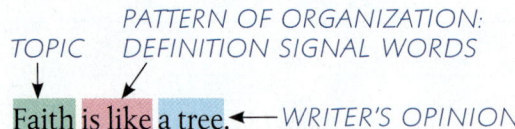

Faith is like a tree. ← WRITER'S OPINION

COMPOSE TOPIC SENTENCES

The items present a topic, an opinion, and definition signal words. Combine the ideas in each group to create a topic sentence for a definition.

1. TOPIC: depression

   OPINION: treatable illness that affects the body and mind

   DEFINITION SIGNAL WORDS: is a

   TOPIC SENTENCE: _____

2. TOPIC: a hypocrite

   OPINION: a spy or a traitor

   DEFINITION SIGNAL WORDS: is

   TOPIC SENTENCE: _____

Use Logical Order

Once you have narrowed your topic into a focused subject, you are ready to generate and organize additional details. To make a point using definition, a writer moves from a general idea (the concept to be defined) to major and minor supporting details. These include traits and examples of *what it is, what it is like,* or *what it is not like.* To signal the relationship between these levels of ideas, a writer often uses the following pattern of wording: "A concept is…"; "A term means…"; "for example." Strong signal words establish coherence, a clear and understandable flow of ideas.

Key Words and Transition Words That Signal Definition

also	constitutes	in particular	means
another trait	defined as	indicates	one trait
are	denotes	is	specifically
connotes	for example	is not	such as
consists of	in addition	like	suggests

USE LOGICAL ORDER: RECOGNIZE RELATIONSHIP OF DETAILS

Fill in the blanks with the appropriate transition or signal words for definition. Work with a peer or in a small group of your classmates.

Sexual Harassment

Sexual harassment _____ a form of sex discrimination. _____, unwelcome sexual advances, requests for sexual favors, and other verbal or physical conduct of a sexual nature is sexual harassment when submission to or rejection of this conduct affects an individual's employment, interferes with an individual's work performance, or creates a hostile or offensive work environment. Sexual harassment can occur in a variety of situations. _____, the victim as well as the harasser may be a woman or a man. The victim _____ always of the opposite sex. The harasser can be the victim's supervisor, an agent of the employer, a supervisor in another area, a coworker, or a non-employee. _____, the victim does not have to be the person harassed but could be anyone affected by the offensive conduct. _____, unlawful sexual harassment may occur without economic injury to or discharge of the victim. The harasser's conduct must be unwelcome, such as a coworker who regularly tells sexually explicit jokes and makes demeaning comments about male coworkers and clients.

—Adapted from United States Equal Employment Opportunity Commission.
"Facts about Sexual Harassment" 15 April 2009

L4 Develop Relevant Details

As a writer narrows a topic into a focused main idea, the thinking process brings to mind many details that answer questions such as *who, what, when, where, why,* and *how*. A writer evaluates the relevance of each detail and uses only those that clarify or support the main idea. In a definition paragraph, some relevant major details include those that classify and describe the traits of a term or concept. Relevant minor details offer examples and illustrations of the term or concept as defined. Some major and minor details may explain the writer's opinion about the concept. Relevant details include types, traits, descriptions, and examples of the concept being defined.

During the prewriting phase, a concept chart can help a writer organize ideas. Study the following Definition Concept Chart about the topic "graffiti."

Definition Concept Chart

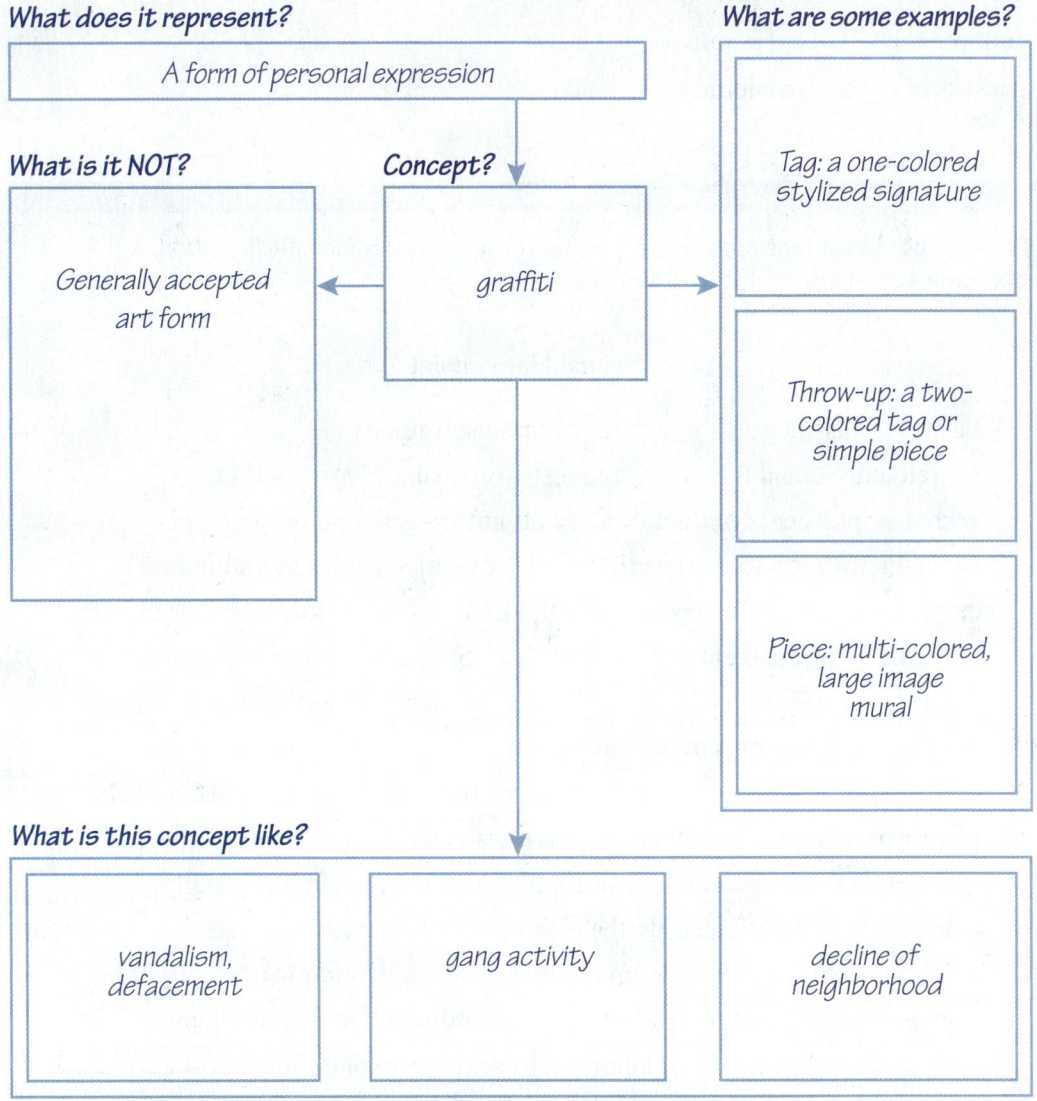

During the prewriting phase, a writer naturally generates irrelevant details. In fact, an effective writer often produces far more details than can be used to make a specific point. Irrelevant details do not explain or support the focused point of the paragraph. A careful writer uses the revision process to double check details for relevance and to eliminate irrelevant ones.

DEVELOP RELEVANT DETAILS

The following paragraph develops the ideas generated about graffiti during the brainstorming and prewriting phases. Circle the main idea. Underline the three major details. Cross out two details that are not relevant to the main point.

Graffiti

(1) Although graffiti is a common sight, many do not understand its true nature: vandalism. (2) Graffiti, a form of personal expression, is the unlawful markings of an individual or group on private and public surfaces. (3) One type of graffiti is known as a tag, a stylized signature of a tagger or writer. (4) A tag is quickly created with one color that starkly contrasts with the background upon which it is written. (5) Tags can be written with spray paint, fat-tipped markers, etching tools, or pre-tagged stickers. (6) Another kind of graffiti is the throw-up, a two-dimensional image made with large bubble letters that are outlined in black or white and filled in with another color. (7) A writer often uses throw-ups to bomb an area in a short amount of time. (8) A third type of graffiti, similar to a mural, is the piece, short for masterpiece. (9) Time-consuming to create, a piece is a large, colorful, and complex image that usually reflects a political or social issue. (10) Piecing demonstrates a high level of aerosol paint control. (11) Unlike more widely accepted forms of art, graffiti is not generally regarded as aesthetically pleasing, nor is it thought of as a means to explore or enhance the appreciation of beauty. (12) Graffiti is much more likely to be labeled as vandalism and defacement, and seen as evidence of a gang or a neighborhood in decline. (13) Instances of graffiti are evident in both urban and suburban public areas such as parks, restrooms, buildings, and trains. (14) Graffiti can be removed by scraping, power washing, chemically treating, or painting the affected surface. (15) Many communities fight graffiti by offering legal walls as concrete canvases for graffiti writers.

▲ An example of tagging

▲ An example of "throw-up" graffiti

▲ Mural-style graffiti

L5 Use Effective Expression: Sound Structure and Vivid Images

Effective expression reflects a writer's thoughtful match of ideas to words and structure. Writers rely heavily on the various forms of the *to be* verb (such as *is*) to write a definition. Often the use of *is* leads to nonstandard phrasing or bland expressions. To add interest and maintain clarity, consider the following hints.

Hint 1: Avoid *is when* and *is where* to construct your definition. One way to eliminate *is when* and *is where* is to follow the verb with a synonym that renames the subject of the sentence.

Nonstandard

Addiction is when a person has a compulsive need for a habit-forming substance such as alcohol.

Revised

Addiction is a compulsive need for a habit-forming substance such as alcohol.

Hint 2: Use *is* to create a vivid image. A vivid image often allows the writer to express a point about the concept being defined.

Addiction is a self-made prison of compulsive need.

Hint 3: Replace *is* with an action verb. An action verb often allows the writer to express a point about the concept being defined.

Addiction imprisons a person in the compulsive need for habit-forming substances such as alcohol.

Practice 5

USE EFFECTIVE EXPRESSION: SOUND STRUCTURE AND VIVID IMAGES

Revise the following sentences to avoid nonstandard phrasing or bland expressions. Discuss your work with your class or with a small group of your peers.

1. An input device is where a machine feeds data into a computer, such as a keyboard.

   REVISED: ....

   ....

▲ Input device

2. A character is when any symbol requires a byte of memory or storage in computer software.

   REVISED: ....

   ....

Use Definition in Your Academic Courses

The definition paragraph serves as an excellent way to write for understanding. By defining key concepts and specialized vocabulary in your content courses, you will deepen your learning.

USE DEFINITION IN A COMMUNICATIONS ASSIGNMENT: DEFINING SPECIALIZED VOCABULARY

The following definition concept chart is based on information taken from a college communications textbook. Demonstrate your understanding of the concept and the relationship among the details in the definition. Using your own words, write a definition of the concept in the space below.

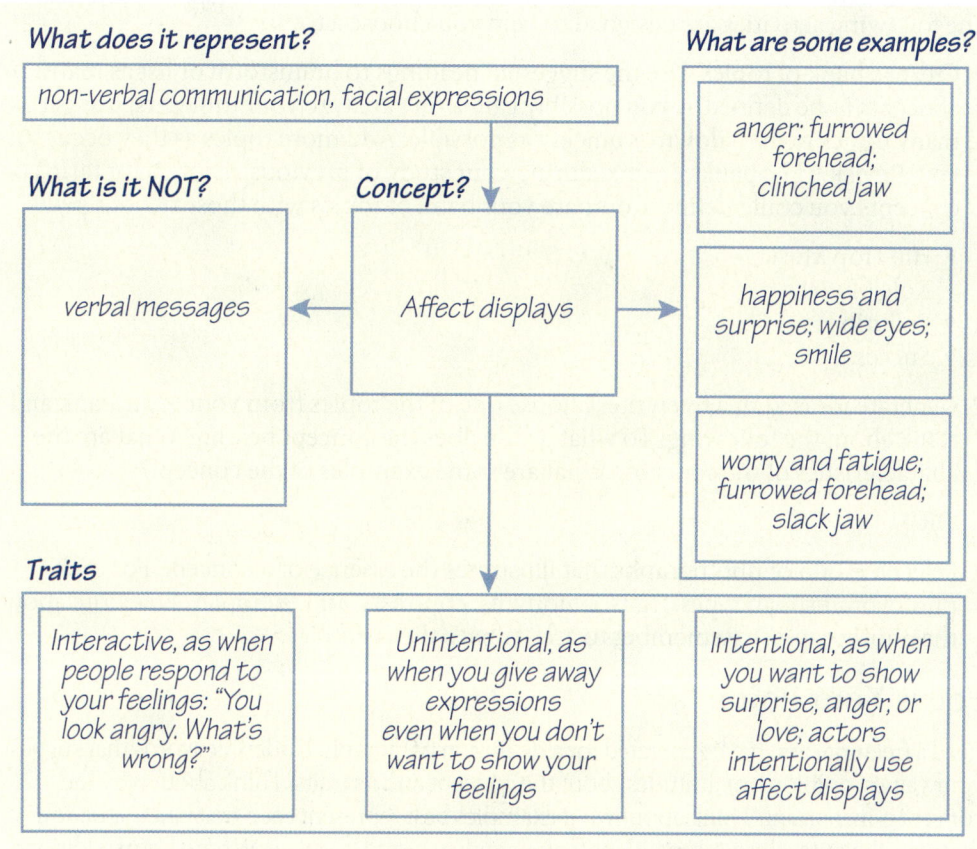

—DeVito, Joseph A. *The Interpersonal Communication Book*, 10th ed. Allyn & Bacon, 2004, p. 182.

L7 Workshop: Writing a Definition Paragraph Step by Step

Prewrite Your Paragraph

The activities below will walk you through the steps of the prewriting stage of the writing process: choosing a topic, focusing your point, and generating and organizing relevant details.

Choose Your Topic

The following activities are designed to help you choose a topic.

1. Create a bank of topics. Use the suggested headings to brainstorm or list as many concepts to be defined as you possibly can. Don't analyze your thoughts; just get as many topics written down as quickly as possible. Add more topics as they occur to you. Revisit topic banks created during your study of previous chapters for terms or concepts you could define. Compare your bank of topics with those of your peers.

   - Hip Hop Music
   - Role Models
   - Pollution
   - Success

2. Generate ideas with a freewrite. Choose one of the topics from your topic bank and think about the following: To what group does the concept belong? What are the characteristics of the concept? What are some examples of the concept?

   OR

   Select a group of photographs that illustrates the essence of a concept. For each photo: brainstorm types, traits, synonyms, contrasts, and examples. Freewrite about the photograph(s). Remember to ask "What's the point?"

Focus Your Point

Read a freewrite you have generated for a definition paragraph. Underline words that suggest your values, opinions, or attitudes about the concept and its traits. Think about why the concept is important. Think about what examples best represent each trait and a situation that best illustrates the concept. Identify your audience and purpose. Write a list of additional concrete examples that explain your point. State in one sentence the point of the definition.

AUDIENCE: _____

PURPOSE: _____

LIST OF DETAILS AND EXAMPLES: _____

WHAT'S THE POINT? _____

Generate and Organize Relevant Details

Using ideas you have recorded so far and the following definition concept chart, generate and organize details that support your point.

Definition Concept Chart

What does the concept represent?

What are some examples?

What is it NOT?   **Concept?**

What is the concept similar to?

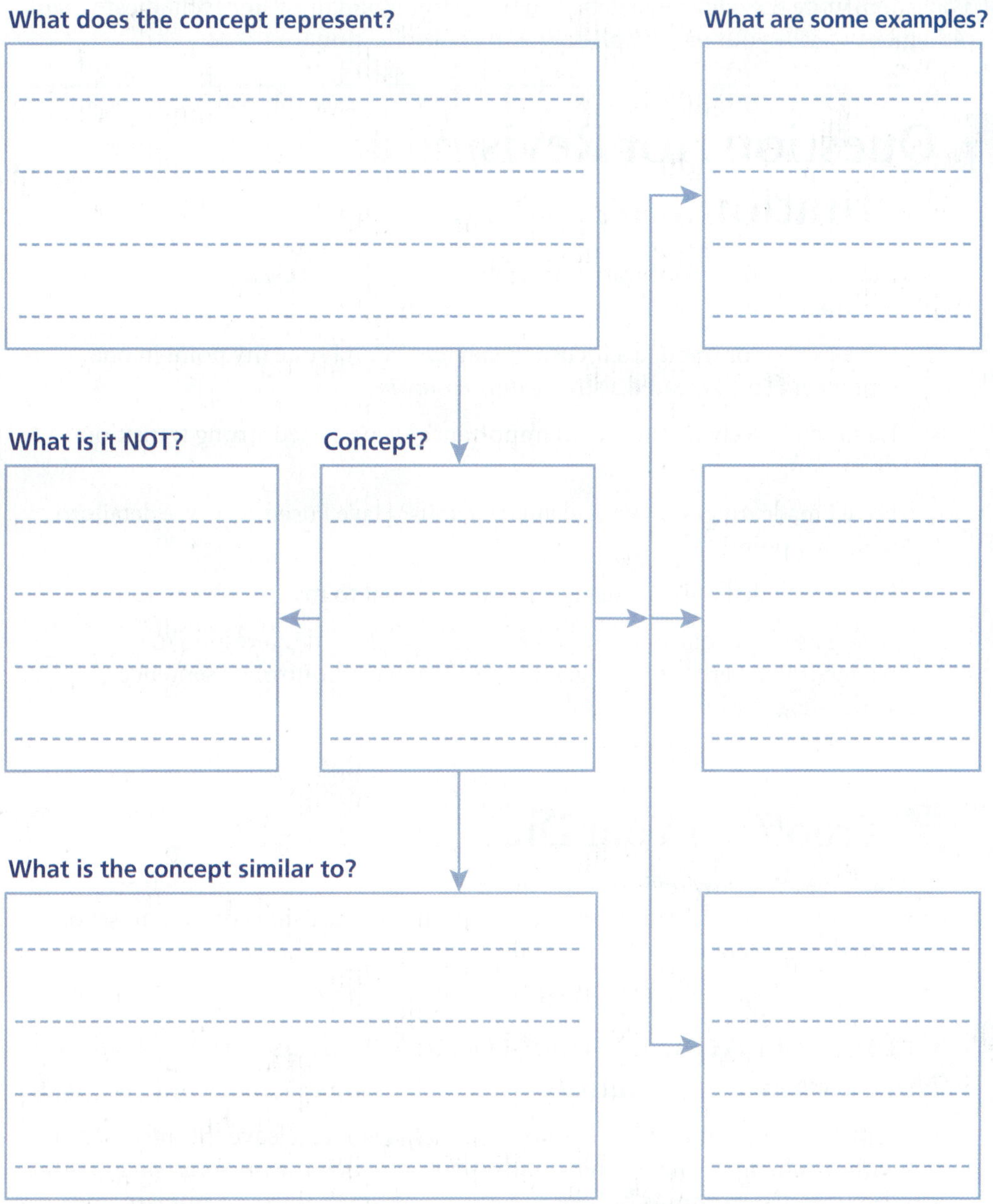

What's the Point? _____

Write a Draft of Your Paragraph

Using the ideas you generated during the prewriting phase, compose a draft of your definition paragraph. Return to the prewriting process at any time to generate additional details as needed. Use your own paper.

Revise Your Draft

Read your draft and answer the questions in the "Questions for Revising a Definition Paragraph" box that follows. Indicate your answers by annotating your paper. If you answer "yes" to a question, underline, check, or circle examples. If you answer "no" to a question, write the additional details in the margins and draw lines to indicate their placement. Revise your paragraph based on your reflection.

Questions for Revising a Definition Paragraph:

- [ ] Have I chosen an important concept to define? Have I clearly classified and illustrated the concept?
- [ ] Have I stated or implied a focused main idea? Can I state my point in one sentence? Have I created a strong impression?
- [ ] Have I effectively used order of importance? Have I used strong transitions of definition?
- [ ] Have I made my point with adequate details? Have I used concrete details to make my point?
- [ ] Have I included only the details that are relevant to my topic sentence?
- [ ] Have I used the following to make my ideas clear and interesting to my readers: vivid verbs and images, parallel language, controlled sentence structure, coordination, or subordination?

Proofread Your Draft

Once you have made any revisions to your paragraph that may be needed, proofread your paragraph for proper usage and punctuation, such as using commas to set off nonessential information.

> For more information on using commas with nonessential information, see pages 558–559.

Grammar in Action: Proper Use of Commas with Nonessential Information

In a sentence, some information is nonessential. If you can leave the information out without changing the meaning of the sentence, then the information is nonessential. Use **commas before** and **after** nonessential words, phrases, and clauses within a sentence. If nonessential words, phrases, and clauses introduce a sentence, use a comma after them.

- **Nonessential Word:**
  My husband, Bob, runs six miles every other day.
- **Nonessential Phrase:**
  Janine, eating a healthful diet and exercising, has lost 25 pounds.
- **Nonessential Clause:**
  My great-grandmother, who is nearly 90 years old, goes bowling every week.

Practice 7

PROPER COMMA USE WITH NONESSENTIAL INFORMATION

Edit these sentences for proper use of commas before and after nonessential words, phrases, or clauses. Underline the nonessential information and insert the commas as needed.

1. Patience, however, is not tolerance of harmful wrongdoing.

2. Jerome, who has been my friend since childhood, does not tolerate gossip.

3. Wanting to stand on his principles, Jerome broke up with a girl who was a gossip.

4. Patience is, on the other hand, acceptance based on forgiveness.

5. Once Iva, who was a gossip until Jerome broke up with her, changed her ways, Jerome asked her out again.

Writing Assignments

MyWritingLab™ Complete this Exercise on mywritinglab.com

Considering Audience and Purpose
Review the photographs about Chinese New Year at the beginning of the chapter. Write a letter to Kuei-Ti Lu, a student from China, in which you invite her and explain the meaning of a special holiday or tradition that she will experience as a guest in your home.

Writing for Everyday Life
Assume that you are seeking counseling to improve a relationship with a family member or coworker. The counselor has asked you to define your role in the relationship. Identify the type of relationship you have, the major traits of the relationship, and examples or incidents that illustrate the nature of your relationship. Allow your tone—through your word choice—to reflect one of the following: (1) concern or (2) resentment.

Writing for College Life
Assume you are a first-semester college student who is enrolled in a study skills class, and you have been assigned to write a paragraph that defines student success. Based on your experience and observations, write a definition of student success that addresses attitudes, behaviors, and skills.

Writing for Working Life
Assume that you work in a retail store that sells clothes, electronics, or some other merchandise. Also assume that sales and morale are down. Write a one-paragraph memo to your supervisor in which you define the morale problem.

MyWritingLab™
Complete the Post-test for Chapter 10 in MyWritingLab.

11 The Cause and Effect Paragraph

LEARNING OUTCOMES

After studying this chapter you will be able to:

L1 Answer the question "What's the Point of Cause and Effect?"

L2 Compose a Topic Sentence

L3 Use Logical Order

L4 Develop Relevant Details

L5 Use Effective Expression: Correct Use of Words

L6 Use Cause and Effect in Your Academic Courses

L7 Write a Cause and Effect Paragraph Step by Step

A cause is the reason an event took place. An effect is the result of an event. Cause leads to effect.

Understanding the relationship between cause and effect is a vital critical thinking skill used in all aspects of life. For example, when an illness strikes us, our physician must correctly identify the cause of our symptoms in order to treat us. In addition, the side effects of any medication to treat the illness must be taken into account. What are some other instances in which we consider causes and effects?

Thinking about cause and effect points out the relationship between events based on reasons and results. For example, in your personal life, you may have identified that stress causes you to eat for comfort. In working life, you may have identified the need to master certain software programs to be competitive in the job market. In college life, you may have identified how logical causes and effects play a role in the study of history, science, or economics. To write a cause and effect paragraph, identify a set of related events, objects, or factors. Then, label each event, object, or factor within the group as either a cause or an effect. Be sure to test each event as a true cause. Events that occur at or near the same time may be coincidental and unrelated. Then, present your details in a logical order that explains why each cause leads to a specific effect.

What's the Point of Cause and Effect?

Often ideas become clearer when they are analyzed based on how they relate to one another. The cause and effect pattern of organization allows a writer to explore the ways in which ideas are related based on reasons and results. The following set of photographs documents a set of causes and effects. Study the images and write captions that identify the appropriate causes and effects illustrated. Answer the following questions: What is this? Why did it happen? What is this further effect? Answer the question "What's the point?" with a one-sentence statement of the overall main idea.

PHOTOGRAPHIC ORGANIZER: CAUSE AND EFFECT

What is this effect?

What is this effect?

▲ Daily exercise

What is this effect?

What is this effect?

WRITING FROM LIFE

What's the point?

My First Thoughts: A Prewriting Activity

Brainstorm about the images you just studied. Set a time limit, such as five minutes, and write in your notebook about the images and the details you generated. Write as quickly as you can without stopping. Let the ideas flow freely. Getting your first thoughts about a topic on paper is one excellent way to kick-start your writing process.

One Student Writer's Response

The following paragraph offers student writer Martin Amezcua's point about the causes and effects illustrated by the photographs. Read the cause and effect paragraph and the explanations; complete the activities in **bold type** in the annotations. Then, read Martin's journal entry that records decisions made during the writing process.

Strong Transitions: The transitional word "because" signals that health and fitness are the result of daily exercise. **Circle two more transitional words or phrases that signal cause and effect.**

Relevant Details: Relevant details include examples or descriptions of causes and effects. **Draw boxes around two more relevant details that give examples or describe a cause or effect.**

Effective Expression: Precise word choice makes a point credible. Writers often confuse the word "affect," a verb that means to influence, with "effect," a noun that means result. **Double underline a verb that can be replaced with "affect(s)." Double underline a noun that can be replaced with "effect."**

Main Idea: The main idea is the point Martin is making about the topic exercise. **Underline his point about this topic.**

The Benefits of Exercise

(1) What can a person do to improve his or her life and live a long and healthy life? (2) It's not something that's a big secret or is in certain people's genes; it's regular exercise. (3) Studies have shown that people live long, healthy, and fit lives because of daily exercise. (4) It doesn't have to be some killer workout routine; it can be as simple as walking, playing sports, dancing, jogging, swimming, or walking the dog on a regular basis. (5) The most important benefit of exercise is that people who live active lives are less likely to get ill and generally live longer. (6) For example, lifting weights builds strong bones and muscles. (7) Walking, jogging, and swimming strengthens the heart and lungs. (8) Since illness occurs less frequently to active people, there is a possibility of avoiding some huge medical bills. (9) Aside from keeping one physically fit, another benefit is exercise helps improve mental health and general sense of well-being. (10) For example, one of the most commonly known benefits of exercise is the reduction of stress. (11) With less stress, a person is better able to focus on what's at hand. (12) On the other hand, exercise can cause a boost in self-esteem and confidence, one of the most overlooked benefits. (13) A positive mind set affects the way a person feels about self, others, and life. (14) One of the least obvious benefits of exercise is that it can help a person get a good sleep. (15) Many suffer from sleeping disorders or don't get a good night's rest because they still have a lot on their mind. (16) Exercising exhausts a person's body and mind, helping to reduce anxious thoughts, and in return help with sleep. (17) Regular exercise promotes health and well-being.

The Writer's Journal

PEER EDITING

Student writer Martin Amezcua completed the following reflection to record his thinking through the writing process. Read his writer's journal that describes a few key choices he made as he wrote. Then, in the given space, answer his questions about his use of relevant details and effective expression in his paragraph. Work with a peer or a small group of classmates.

EFFECTIVE EXPRESSION: *When I got my first draft back, the feedback showed that I had a bad habit of using a plural pronoun with a singular noun. For example, I kept writing things like "a person can walk their dog." I really didn't want to use singular pronouns "he" or "she" because it sounded weird to keep saying things like "a person can walk his or her dog." I think the phrases "he or she" and "his or hers" sound odd, especially when it's repeated in the paragraph. I didn't want to use just "he" or just "she" because I wanted to get both men and women interested in exercise. Do you see any disagreements between my nouns and pronouns? Did I catch them all? What advice could you give me about making nouns and pronouns agree?*

A cause and effect paragraph makes a point by discussing the reasons for and results of a set of events, objects, or factors. To support a point through cause and effect, a writer identifies a set of events, objects, or factors. A writer then identifies the specific details of cause and effect between each of the events, objects, or factors. The writer tests each reason and result to weed out true causes and effects from coincidences. The writer discusses the specific details in the order that reflects the logical relationship among causes and effects. In addition, the writer uses precise word choice for effective expression.

L2 Compose a Topic Sentence

When you write a cause and effect paragraph, you limit your thoughts to a set of topics based on their relationship to each other. Most likely you have an opinion or belief about the topics and their causes and effects; your opinion is your point or main idea. A topic sentence states the overall point of the causes and effects.

For example, the following topic sentence contains (1) the topic, (2) the writer's opinion about the topic, and (3) the pattern of organization used to organize details.

TOPIC → WRITER'S OPINION →

Addiction to television has **led to several** **negative** **effects** on **American students.**

↑ PATTERN OF ORGANIZATION: CAUSE AND EFFECT SIGNAL WORDS

The topic is the "addiction to television [of] American students." The pattern of organization is established with the signal words "led to several effects." The writer's opinion is stated with the modifier "negative."

Practice 2

COMPOSE TOPIC SENTENCES

The items present a topic, an opinion, and cause or effect signal word(s). Combine the ideas in each group to create a topic sentence for a cause and effect paragraph.

1. TOPIC: *smoking cigarettes* OPINION: *adverse*

   CAUSE OR EFFECT SIGNAL WORDS: *leads to physical effects*

   TOPIC SENTENCE: _____

2. TOPIC: *bullying* OPINION: *low self-esteem and anger*

   CAUSE OR EFFECT SIGNAL WORDS: *stems from*

   TOPIC SENTENCE: _____

Use Logical Order

Once you have identified a topic, a set of factors, and their relationships based on cause and effect, and you have focused on a main idea, you are ready to generate and organize additional details. To make a point using cause or effect, a writer moves from a general idea (the overall causal relationship) to a major support (a specific cause or effect of the topic) to minor supports (details or examples of a specific cause or effect). To signal the movement among these levels of ideas, a writer uses transitions to signal causes, effects, and examples. Strong transitions establish coherence, a clear and understandable flow of ideas.

Transitions That Signal Cause and Effect

accordingly	consequently	hence	on account of	so
as a result	due to	if…then	results in	therefore
because of	for that reason	leads to	since	thus

Verbs That Signal Cause and Effect (sample list)

affect	constitute	create	force	institute	restrain
cause	construct	determine	induce	preclude	stop
compose	contribute	facilitate	initiate	prevent	

Nouns That Signal Cause and Effect (sample list)

actor	consequence	end	influence	product
agent	creation	event	issue	result
author	creator	grounds	outcome	source
condition	effect	impact	outgrowth	

USE LOGICAL ORDER: CAUSE AND EFFECT

Fill in the blanks with the appropriate transition or signal words for cause and effect. Work with a peer or in a small group of your classmates.

How Is Stroke Prevented?

A stroke is the _____ of a disease of the blood vessels in the brain, and underlying health conditions can _____ a stroke. For example, heart disease, high blood pressure, high cholesterol, and diabetes can _____ to a stroke. _____ you have any of these conditions, _____ take your medication as prescribed by your health care provider. Second, a healthful diet lowers your risk for a stroke. _____, eat a diet low in saturated fat and rich in fruits, vegetables, and whole grains. For example, eating too much meat and whole milk dairy products can _____ in high cholesterol, which raises your risk for a stroke.

Practice 3

L4 Develop Relevant Details

As a writer narrows a topic into a focused main idea, the thinking process brings to mind many details that answer questions such as *who, what, when, where, why,* and *how*. A writer evaluates the relevance of each detail and uses only those that clarify or support the main idea. In a cause and effect paragraph, some relevant major details include those that identify a specific cause or effect. Relevant minor details offer examples and explanations of the cause or effect. Relevant details include descriptions, examples, and explanations of the causal relationship between a set of events, situations, objects, or factors.

One writer generated these ideas while brainstorming using a fishbone cause and effect concept map.

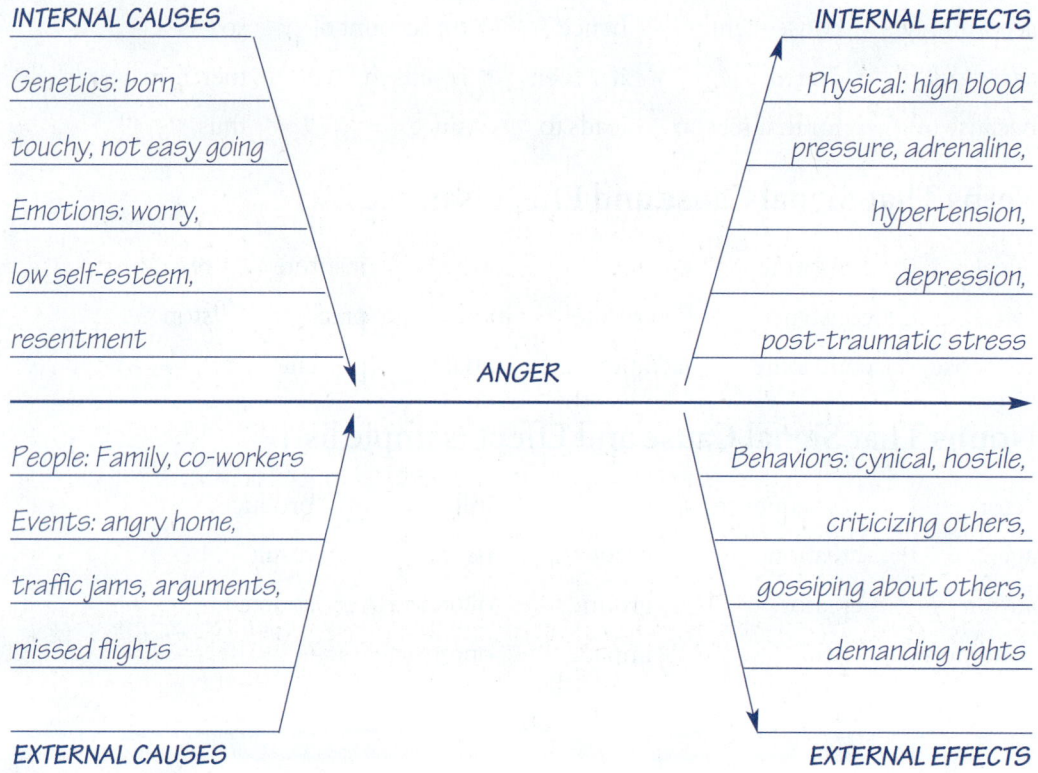

During the prewriting phase, a writer naturally generates irrelevant details. In fact, an effective writer often produces far more details than can be used to make a specific point. Irrelevant details do not explain or support the focused point of the paragraph. A careful writer uses the revision process to double check details for relevance and to eliminate irrelevant ones.

Baseball manager argues with home plate umpire ▶

DEVELOP RELEVANT DETAILS

The following paragraph develops the ideas generated about anger during the brainstorming phase using the fishbone cause and effect concept map shown on page 182. Circle the main idea. In this paragraph, the main idea is stated twice. Underline two causes and two effects. Cross out two details that are not relevant to the main point.

Anger Inside and Out

(1) Anger can be a normal, healthy emotion, yet anger can also spiral out of our control and lead to problems that affect our work, our families, and our lives. (2) To control anger, we need to understand its causes and effects. (3) Basically, anger is the result of both internal and external forces. (4) Genetics and emotions are two internal forces that give rise to anger. (5) According to experts, some people are born innately touchy and easily angered. (6) Others of us are born with mild, easy-going tendencies. (7) Another internal force is the complex mixture of our emotions. (8) Worry, low self-esteem, anxiety, or resentment can cause anger to flare. (9) In addition, external forces such as people and events can trigger anger. (10) For example, if we have been raised in an environment of anger without learning how to cope with negative feelings, we are much more likely to be easily angered. (11) As a result, a disagreement with a family member or coworker, a traffic jam, or a canceled airline flight ignites angry feelings. (12) Not only does our anger arise from internal and external forces, but also our anger has internal and external effects. (13) Anger has immediate physical effects: it causes our heart rate, blood pressure, and adrenaline to rise. (14) Ultimately, chronic anger can lead to hypertension or depression. (15) Post-traumatic stress syndrome also leads to depression. (16) Chronic anger also may result in cynical and hostile behavior toward others. (17) When we feel angry, we may act out our hostility by criticizing others, gossiping about them, or rudely demanding our rights. (18) Ultimately, uncontrolled anger damages our relationships with others and diminishes our quality of life.
(19) We need to understand the reasons and results of our anger before we can hope to control this volatile emotion.

L5 Use Effective Expression: Correct Use of Words

Effective expression reflects a writer's thoughtful choice of words for impact on the reader. Some words, such as *affect* and *effect*, seem closely related because they are similar in their sounds and spellings. These similarities often cause confusion and lead to the misuse of the words. However, their meanings are clearly distinct, so careful writers use the correct word for effective expression.

Affect is a verb that means **to influence.**

Video games **affect** learning by improving concentration and visual skills.

Effect is a noun that means **result.**

Video games have a positive **effect** on learning by improving concentration and visual skills.

Effect is a verb that means **to bring about.**

The new law will **effect** a change in the sentencing of sex offenders.

Practice 5

USE EFFECTIVE EXPRESSION: AFFECT AND EFFECT

Complete the following sentences with the correct use of the words *affect* and *effect*. (Hint: Substitute the words *influence* or *result* as a test for exact meaning in the context of the sentence.)

1. The lack of bright light during winter months produces an _____ known as Seasonal Affective Disorder (SAD), a form of depression.

2. The long, dark hours of winter _____ as much as 6 percent of the population.

3. The _____ of SAD include loss of energy, social withdrawal, overeating, weight gain, and difficulty concentrating.

4. Researchers believe that reduced sunlight _____ the biological rhythms that control the body's internal clock.

5. Researchers also believe that heredity, age, and the body's chemical balance _____ the onset of SAD.

6. Exposure to sun and sun lamps for one to three hours a day _____ a positive change in the mood of one who suffers from SAD.

Use Cause and Effect in Your Academic Courses

Often college writing assignments require that you combine information you learn from your textbooks with your observations about how that information applies to real-world situations. Textbooks may provide graphic organizers to emphasize key concepts and make them easy to understand. Use these graphic organizers to learn and apply the concept. A good way to review your textbook notes is to add examples you have observed in life to the concept you are studying.

USE CAUSE AND EFFECT IN A SOCIOLOGY ASSIGNMENT

Study the following graphic taken from a college sociology textbook. In a small group or with a classmate, add examples of each concept that you and your classmate(s) have observed. Then, write a paragraph in answer to the question at the end of the practice. Use a dictionary as necessary.

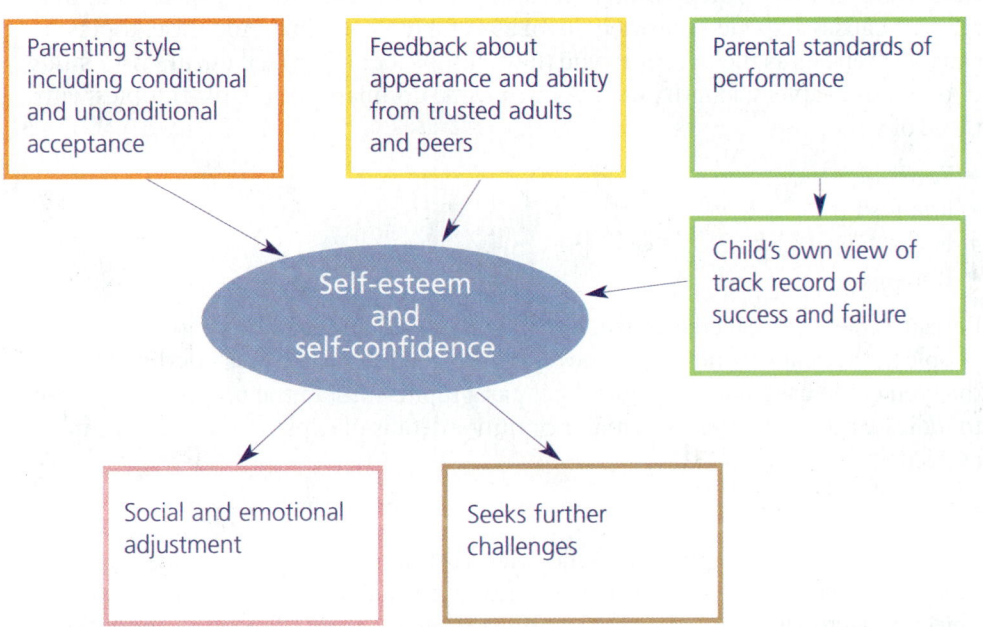

—Jaffe, Michael L. *Understanding Parenting*, 2nd ed. Allyn & Bacon. 1997 p. 241.

EXAMPLE OF PARENTING STYLE: _____

EXAMPLE OF FEEDBACK: _____

EXAMPLE OF PARENTAL STANDARD: _____

EXAMPLE OF CHILD'S VIEW OF SUCCESS AND FAILURE: _____

EXAMPLE OF FURTHER CHALLENGE: _____

EXAMPLE OF ADJUSTMENT: _____

On a separate sheet of paper, answer the following question:
What factors influence children's self-esteem and self-confidence?

L7 Workshop: Writing a Cause and Effect Paragraph Step by Step

Prewrite Your Paragraph

The activities below will walk you through the steps of the prewriting stage of the writing process: choosing a topic, focusing your point, and generating and organizing relevant details.

Choose Your Topic

The following activities are designed to help you choose a topic.

1. Create a bank of topics: Use the suggested headings to brainstorm or list as many causes and effects as you possibly can. Don't criticize your thoughts; just get as many relevant causes and effects written down as quickly as possible. Add more topics, causes, or effects as they occur to you. Revisit topic banks created during your study of previous chapters; identify causes and effects. Compare your bank of topics with those of your peers.

   - YouTube
   - Friendship
   - Fuel-efficient Cars
   - Romance

2. Reread a freewrite you created (such as the one based on the photographs of the people in the chapter opening or the one generated in Practice 6). Underline ideas that you could use for a cause and effect paragraph. Number the points you recorded to indicate a logical order. Add major or minor details of explanation and examples as needed.

   OR

   Select a group of photographs that illustrate a set of related events, situations, objects, or factors. Generate a list that identifies the details of each event, situation, object, or factor as either a cause (reason) or an effect (result). Freewrite about the photograph(s). Remember to ask "What's the point?"

Clarify Your Point

Read a prewrite you have generated for a cause and effect paragraph. Underline words that suggest your values, opinions, or attitudes about the events. Think about why the information is important. Think about what examples best represent each cause or effect. Think about a situation that best illustrates the concept. Identify your audience and purpose. Write a list of additional concrete examples that explain your point. In one sentence, state the point of the cause and effect paragraph.

AUDIENCE: _____

PURPOSE: _____

LIST OF CONCRETE DETAILS: _____

WHAT'S THE POINT? _____

Generate and Organize Relevant Details

Use the graphic organizer below to either organize the ideas you have already created or to generate details to support your point.

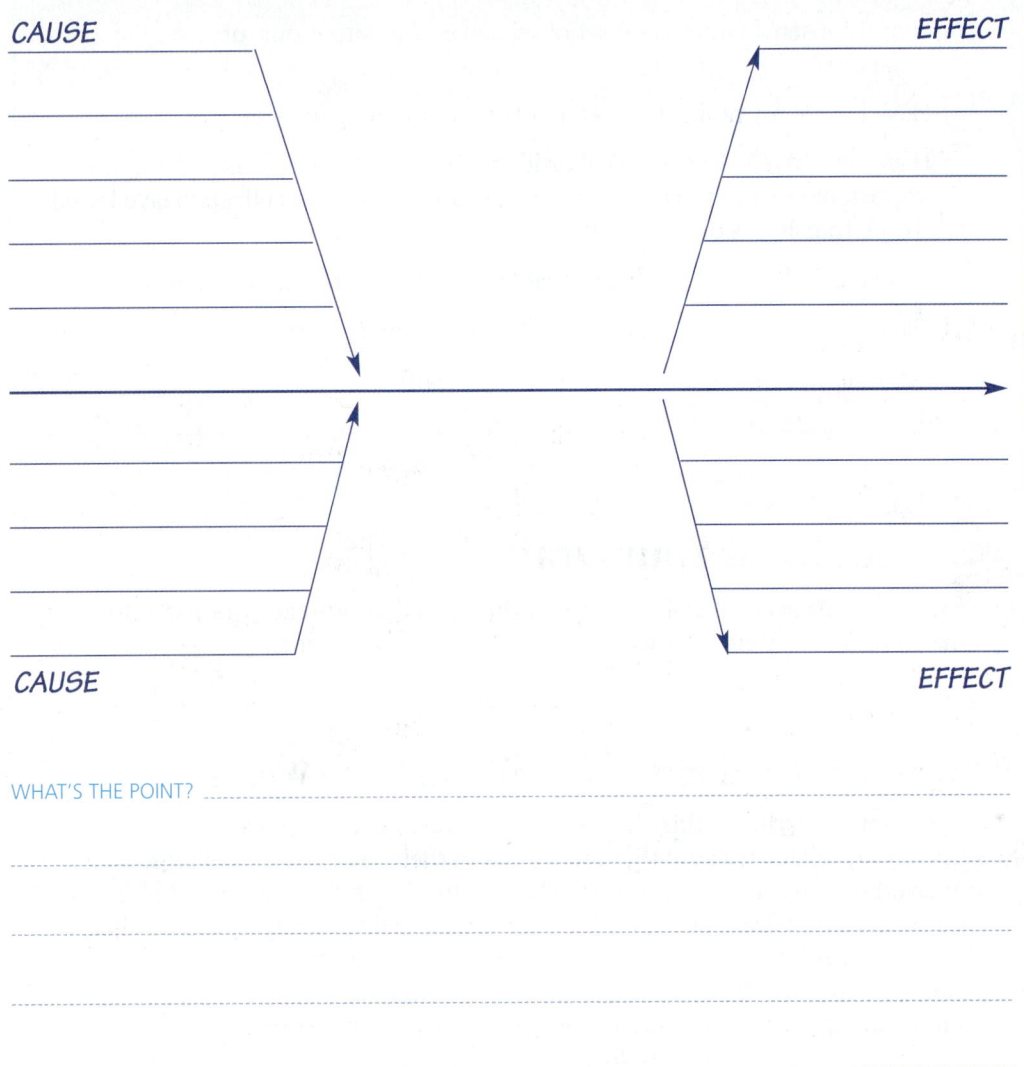

WHAT'S THE POINT? ....

Write a Draft of Your Paragraph

Using the ideas you generated during the prewriting phase, compose a draft of your cause and effect paragraph. Return to the prewriting process at any time to generate additional details as needed. Use your own paper.

Revise Your Draft

Read the draft and answer the questions in the "Questions for Revising a Cause and Effect Paragraph" box that follows. Indicate your answers by annotating your paper. If you answer "yes" to a question, underline, check, or circle examples. If you answer "no" to a question, write the additional details in the margins and draw lines to indicate their placement. Revise your paragraph based on your reflection.

Questions for Revising a Cause and Effect Paragraph:

☐ Have I chosen an important set of related events, situations, objects, or factors?

☐ Have I made my point? Can I state my point in one sentence?

☐ Have I effectively used a logical order based on short-term, long-term, most important, least important, obvious, or subtle causes and effects? Have I used strong transitions of cause and effect?

☐ Have I included only the details that are relevant to my topic sentence?

☐ Have I made my ideas clear and interesting to my readers?

☐ Have I used concrete details to make my point?

Proofread Your Draft

Once you have made any revisions that may be needed, proofread your paper to eliminate unnecessary errors, such as commonly confused words.

For more information on commonly confused words, see pages 607.

Grammar in Action: Commonly Confused Words

As you learned earlier in this chapter, some words, such as *affect* and *effect*, seem closely related because they are similar in their sounds and spellings. The similarities often cause these words to be confused with one another and lead to their misuse. However, their meanings are clearly distinct, so thoughtful writers choose the precise word for effective expression. The following list presents a group of words that are commonly confused. Memorize this list of words and their meanings so you can use each one precisely in your writing.

its, it's	**its** (possessive form of *it*); **it's** (contraction of *it is* or *it has*)
their, they're, there	**their** (possessive of *they*); **they're** (contraction of *they are*); **there** (points to a place)
to, two, too	**to** (suggests movement or direction); **two** (a number); **too** (also)
whose, who's	**whose** (possessive form of *who*); **who's** (contraction of *who is* or *who has*)
your, you're	**your** (possessive form of *you*); **you're** (contraction of *you are*)

PRECISE USE OF COMMONLY CONFUSED WORDS

Edit the following rough draft of a paragraph written by student Seiko Kaneyama about the effects of stress due to a language barrier. Cross out the words used incorrectly and insert the correct word.

The Main Cause of My Stress: The Language Barrier

(1) For me, the language barrier is the biggest source of stress. (2) When I lost my husband to heart failure, I could not express myself in English; no one at the hospital could understand me. (3) The stress reached too the point that I collapsed in tears. (4) Its still one of the most frustrating memories of my life. (5) Today, my stress is from language problems at work. (6) For example, when a mistake is made, someone always blames me. (7) They say, "Your two hard too understand." (8) Or they say that I do not understand what there saying. (9) Its very difficult their. (10) I speak and write Chinese, Japanese, and Korean. (11) English is very difficult; its a very frustrating language.

Writing Assignments

MyWritingLab™ Complete this Exercise on mywritinglab.com

Considering Audience and Purpose

Study the photographs about exercise at the beginning of the chapter. Assume Martin Amezcua is a personal trainer with whom you have been working. Write him a letter thanking him for his help as a coach and explaining the effects that exercise has had on you physically, mentally, and emotionally.

Writing for Everyday Life

Assume that you are the mentor of a young person. Write a one-paragraph letter that explains the dangers of the wrong choices or the benefits of mature choices. Choose your words to reflect one of the following: (1) stern warning or (2) warm encouragement.

Writing for College Life

Assume you are applying for a scholarship for which you must write a one-paragraph essay on the topic "Education Matters." Write a paragraph that explains the impact education has had on you.

Writing for Working Life

Assume that you are applying for a job. Write a one-paragraph cover letter. Explain the impact you can have on the job due to your skills, work ethic, and character.

MyWritingLab™

Complete the Post-test for Chapter 11 in MyWritingLab.

12 The Persuasive Paragraph

LEARNING OUTCOMES

After studying this chapter you will be able to:

L1 Answer the question "What's the Point of Persuasion?"

L2 Compose a Topic Sentence

L3 Use Logical Order

L4 Develop Relevant Details

L5 Use Effective Expression: Use Subjective Words to Persuade

L6 Use Persuasion in Your Academic Courses

L7 Write a Persuasive Paragraph Step by Step

A persuasive claim is a strong stand on a debatable topic supported by facts, examples, and opinions.

In almost every area of our lives, we engage in some form of persuasion. Whether convincing a friend to see a particular movie or proving we are the right candidate for a particular job, we use reasons, logic, and emotion to get others to agree with our views. What are some other situations that use persuasion to influence our beliefs and behaviors? Why are certain arguments or points of view so persuasive?

To be persuasive, a writer asserts a strong stand on one side of a debatable issue. Then, the writer supports that stand by offering convincing evidence such as reasons, facts, examples, and expert opinions. In everyday life, our court system is based on proving claims of guilt or innocence. In working life, we use reasons to resolve workplace disputes. In college life, we encounter debatable claims in every discipline. In addition to asserting a claim and supporting it with evidence, a persuasive writer acknowledges and rebuts (disproves, challenges) the opposition.

What's the Point of Persuasion?

The purpose of persuasion is to convince the reader to agree with a particular claim about a debatable topic. Persuasion is a call to action or a call to a change of mind. The following photos represent several arguments against building a Target store in the location of a popular neighborhood park. Study the photographs. In the space provided, identify the claim, reasons, and an opposing point of view about removing the park to build a Target store. Answer the question "What's the point?" with a one-sentence statement of the overall main idea.

PHOTOGRAPHIC ORGANIZER: PERSUASION

What is the issue?

SUPPORTING POINTS | OPPOSING POINT

What is this reason? | What is this point?

What is this reason?

SUPPORT THAT REFUTES OPPOSING POINT

What is this reason?

What is this reason?

What's the point?

WRITING FROM LIFE

Practice 1

My First Thoughts: A Prewriting Activity

Brainstorm about the images you just studied. Set a time limit, such as five minutes, and write in your notebook about the images and the details you generated. Write as quickly as you can without stopping. Let the ideas flow freely. Getting your first thoughts about a topic on paper is one excellent way to overcome writer's block and set your mind to thinking.

One Student Writer's Response

The following paragraph offers one writer's point that argues against building a new Target store in her neighborhood, as illustrated by the photographs. Read the persuasive paragraph and the explanations; complete the activities in **bold type** in the annotations. Then, read the writer's journal entry that records decisions made during the writing process.

Main Idea: The main idea is the point the author is claiming about the topic. **Underline the topic and circle the writer's claim about this topic.**

Effective Expression: To persuade a reader, an author uses subjective words that express opinions, attitudes, and values. **Double underline at least three more subjective words or phrases.**

Strong Transition: The transition phrase "First of all" signals that the author is offering a reason in support of her claim. **Circle three more transitional words or phrases that signal a reason of support.**

Relevant Details: In persuasion, relevant details not only include facts and consequences, but also refute opposing points. Here, the writer offers another location better suited to a retail store. **Draw a box around one other opposing point and the writer's counter point.**

Let the Children Play: No Target

Dear Mayor and Commissioners:

(1) I strongly oppose relocating our community's invaluable recreational center at the corner of Nova Road and Main Trail to make space for a Target store. (2) I am outraged and shocked that you even think moving our playground so it sits on top of a landfill behind a new Target is an option. (3) Most likely, you think a Target will stimulate the economy, but a Target in this location is not worth the money it would generate. (4) First of all, the intersection will not be able to sustain the kind of traffic that a Target will draw. (5) This type of traffic will create added dangers for the children commuting to their "relocated" park. (6) Secondly, the development will destroy one of the few remaining ecological parks; Nova Park is not only a natural habitat, but also a shady oasis for the many families that live nearby. (7) Why pave over this natural refuge when there is so much bare land out Williamson and US 1? (8) Those roads can better bear the added traffic. (9) Thirdly, a park at the edge of the neighborhood adds more value to the neighborhood than a Target. (10) I am an expectant mother and have planned on walking my child to this park just as my parents did with me. (11) I grew up playing on those monkey bars and swinging under the beautiful canopy of oaks that you now threaten to destroy with a lame, hot parking lot and an unattractive, square building. (12) I do not wish to take my child to the back of a Target store to play. (13) Finally, this type of mega-retail store often increases crime in the surrounding area.
(14) This nearsightedness is not the kind of leadership I will vote for.
Respectfully, A Concerned Citizen

The Writer's Journal

PEER EDITING

The student writer of "Let the Children Play: No Target" completed the following reflection to record her thinking through the writing process. Read her writer's journal that describes a few key choices she made as she wrote. Then, in the given space, answer her questions about her use of logical order and effective expression in her paragraph. Work with a peer or a small group of classmates.

LOGICAL ORDER: I wanted to use an order that would make my argument sound, strong, and smart. So rather than just telling them I was angry about the issue, I also included three examples of why their consideration of this development made me upset. Once I had recorded my three major ideas that began with "First of all," Secondly, "and" Thirdly," I saw that each of those ideas needed support to be more effective. So I added an additional sentence after each major idea to help explain how I felt. Do you agree with the order of my ideas? Why or why not? How could I improve on the order of my ideas?

EFFECTIVE EXPRESSION: When I first sat down to write my city officials about why a Target store should not relocate my neighborhood park, I was angry. I just wanted them to know I was disappointed with them. But as I wrote, I became anxious. The longer I thought about the issue, more and more points against the development flooded my mind. I wanted to address them all without sounding boring. Is my tone okay? Do I come across too strong or angry? How could I improve my tone to not alienate the reader?

A persuasive paragraph makes a point by supporting one side of a debatable topic and refuting the opposing side. The details that support and refute the point include reasons based on facts, examples, effects, and expert opinions on the topic. In addition, a writer uses effective expression to qualify ideas and control the point of view.

L2 Compose a Topic Sentence

A persuasive paragraph gives your opinion or stand on an issue. A topic sentence states the debatable topic, the writer's persuasive opinion, and, possibly, a pattern of organization. Because persuasion is a purpose, the writer may choose any particular pattern of organization to support a claim. In addition, the writer's persuasive opinion is often signaled by the following types of subjective words or phrases: *all, always, only, must, must not, should, should not,* or *too*.

For example, the following topic sentence contains (1) the debatable topic, (2) the writer's persuasive opinion, and (3) a pattern of organization used to organize details.

DEBATABLE TOPIC   WRITER'S OPINION   DEBATABLE TOPIC

Colleges and universities should provide substance free housing for students for several reasons.

PATTERN OF ORGANIZATION: PERSUASION SIGNAL WORDS

Practice 2

COMPOSE TOPIC SENTENCES

The items present a debatable topic, the writer's opinion, and a pattern of organization. Combine the ideas in each group to create a topic sentence for a persuasive paragraph.

1. TOPIC: *education about crystal meth*

   OPINION: *is our best hope to end this plague*

   PATTERN OF ORGANIZATION: *the consequences of*

   TOPIC SENTENCE: _____

2. TOPIC: *procrastination by students, academic failure*

   OPINION: *is the leading*

   PATTERN OF ORGANIZATION: *cause of*

   TOPIC SENTENCE: _____

Use Logical Order

Once you have identified a debatable topic, you are ready to generate and organize the details. To make a persuasive point, a writer moves from a general idea (the claim) to a major support (a reason, fact, example, expert opinion, or reason against the opposing view) to a minor support (also a reason, fact, example, expert opinion, or argument against the opposing view). Transitions and signal words indicate the importance and movement among details. Strong transitions and signal words establish coherence, a clear and understandable flow of ideas.

Transitions That Signal Persuasion

accordingly	even so	however	nonetheless	therefore
admittedly	finally	in conclusion	obviously	thus
although	first (second,	indeed	of course	to be sure
because	third, etc.)	in fact, in truth	on the one hand	truly
but	for	in summary	on the other hand	undoubtedly
certainly	furthermore	last	since	
consequently	granted	meanwhile	some believe	
despite	hence	nevertheless	some may say	

Signal Words That Qualify an Idea as Persuasive (sample list)

all	every	may	often	probably, probable	think
always	has/have to	might	only	seem	too
believe	it is believed	must	ought to	should	usually
could	likely	never	possibly, possible	sometimes	

USE LOGICAL ORDER

Fill in the blanks with the appropriate transition or signal words for persuasion. Work with a peer or in a small group of your classmates.

For the Sake of the Children

For their safety and well-being, children _____ be removed from homes that house meth labs. According to John W. Gillis, the director of the Office for Victims of Crime, "children who live at or visit home-based meth labs face acute health and safety risks." A few of these risks include fire hazards, chemical explosions, physical and sexual abuse, and medical neglect. _____, because of the hand to mouth behavior of young children, they are _____ to ingest toxic chemicals used to make the drug. _____, removal of a child from his or her home is a traumatic experience. _____, the dangers posed by the "meth" lifestyle _____ outweigh the risks posed by removing the child from these chaotic homes.

—Swetlow, Karen. *Children at Clandestine Methamphetamine Labs: Helping Meth's Youngest Victims.* OVC Bulletin. Office for Victims of Crime. U.S. Department of Justice. June 2003. 3 April 2006.

L4 Develop Relevant Details

As a writer narrows a topic into a focused main idea, he or she generates supporting details that answer the questions such as *who, what, when, where, why,* and *how.* A writer evaluates the relevance of each detail and uses only those that clarify or support the main idea. The supports of a persuasive claim are reasons, facts, examples, effects, expert opinions, and details that refute the opposing view.

Compare the following chart of Persuasive Supporting Details with the ideas in the Persuasive Thinking Map about metal detectors in public schools.

Persuasive Supporting Details	
REASON	A cause of an event or action. An explanation. A basis or foundation of an idea.
FACT	A specific detail that is true based on objective proof. Objective proof can be physical evidence, an eyewitness account, or the result of accepted scientific investigation.
EXAMPLE	An illustration or instance of a general idea.
EFFECT	A result or consequence of an event or action. Consider positive effects of claim and negative effects of opposing views.
EXPERT OPINION	A view based on much training and extensive knowledge in a given field. Be sure to stay with opinions of experts in the field of the topic that is being debated. For example, a physician, an expert in medicine, is not an expert in criminal justice.
SUPPORTS THAT REFUTE THE OPPOSING VIEW	To refute is to disprove or counter an opposing point; supports include reasons, facts, effects, examples, and expert opinions.

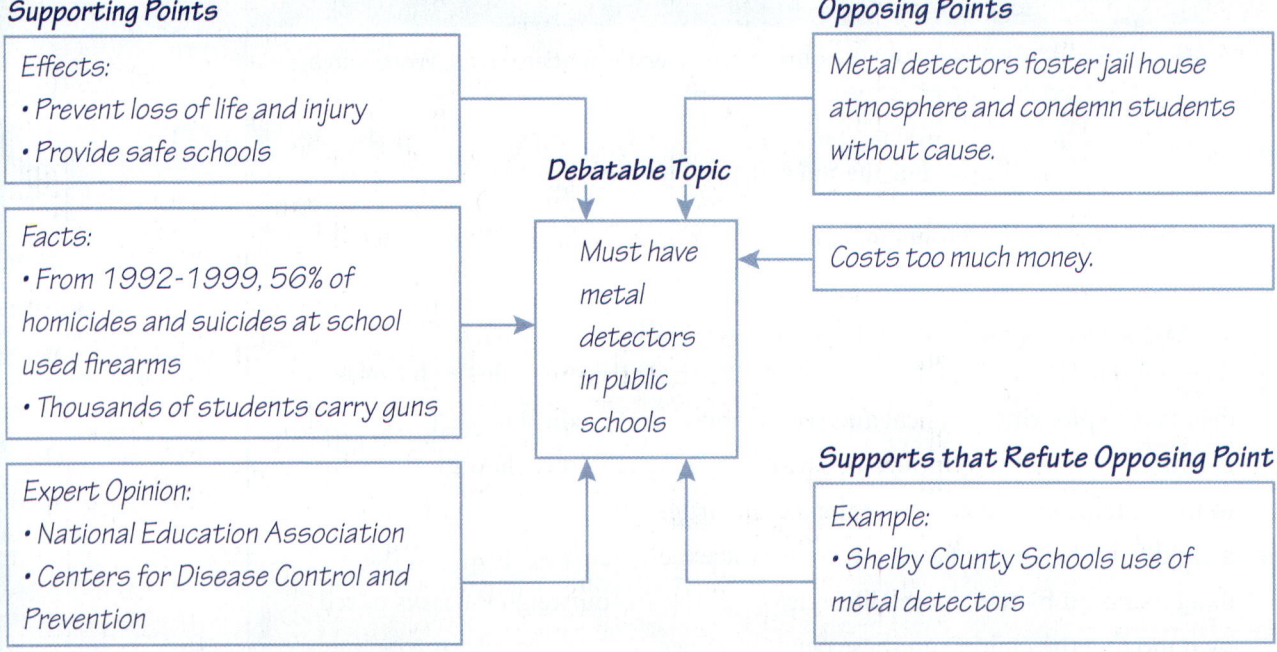

Persuasive Thinking Map

Supporting Points

Effects:
• Prevent loss of life and injury
• Provide safe schools

Facts:
• From 1992-1999, 56% of homicides and suicides at school used firearms
• Thousands of students carry guns

Expert Opinion:
• National Education Association
• Centers for Disease Control and Prevention

Debatable Topic

Must have metal detectors in public schools

Opposing Points

Metal detectors foster jail house atmosphere and condemn students without cause.

Costs too much money.

Supports that Refute Opposing Point

Example:
• Shelby County Schools use of metal detectors

During the prewriting phase, a writer naturally generates irrelevant details. In fact, an effective writer often produces far more details than can be used to make a specific point. Irrelevant details do not explain or support the focused point of the paragraph. A careful writer uses the revision process to double check details for relevance and to eliminate irrelevant ones.

DEVELOP RELEVANT DETAILS

The following paragraph develops the ideas about metal detectors in public schools generated using the persuasive thinking map. Circle the main idea. Underline one example of each of the following: fact, example, effect, and a support that refutes the opposing view. Cross out the detail that is not relevant to the main point.

Pay the Price: Stop the Shootings

(1) Public school officials should use metal detectors to screen students for possession of firearms in order to reduce the numbers of injuries and deaths. (2) The use of metal detectors signals students that safety measures are in place and that violence will not be tolerated. (3) Some oppose the use of metal detectors as a step that fosters a jail house atmosphere and condemns students as guilty without cause. (4) These opponents to metal detectors also decry the economic cost of screening students for possession of firearms. (5) Unfortunately, evidence indicates that the need to provide a safe school and the right to a safe school far outweigh these concerns. (6) According to the Centers for Disease Control and Prevention, from 1992 to 1999, 56% of homicides and suicides occurring at school involved firearms. (7) In addition, the National Education Association estimates that "on a daily basis, 100,000 students carry guns to school, 160,000 miss classes due to fear of physical harm, and 40 are injured or killed by firearms." (8) Tragic school shootings have already occurred and signal that the danger is clear and present. (9) All of these shooters obviously suffered mental health problems. (10) While metal detectors may not halt all violence, their use can be effective. (11) For example, according to news reports, during the 2013–2014 school year, metal detectors identified 11 guns, 8 knives, a blade, a stun gun, an air gun, and box cutters on various school campuses in Shelby County, Tennessee. (12) At one high school, a 15-year-old carried an unloaded .25 caliber RG26 handgun and five live rounds of ammunition. (13) The metal detector kept him from entering the school with the weapon. (14) At another high school, random metal detector sweeps found 2 guns and a fully charged Taser on three different students. (15) All three of these students were arrested, charged, and suspended from school. (16) Though these incidents are extreme, they are not isolated. (17) These incidents show that public schools must screen students for weapons. (18) The cost of not doing so is too high!

Works Cited

Centers for Disease Control and Prevention. "Source of Firearms Used by Students in School-Associated Violent Deaths—United States, 1992–1999." *Morbidity and Mortality Weekly Report* 52(09): 169–72. 7 March 2003. Web. 14 Aug. 2009.

"11 Guns, 8 Knives Found This School Year on SCS Campuses." *WMC Action News 5*. 22 May 2014. Web. 29 Jan. 2015.

"School Violence." National Education Association. Washington, D.C.: 1993.

L5 Use Effective Expression: Use Subjective Words to Persuade

Effective expression is the result of a writer's thoughtful choice of words for impact on the reader. Subjective words reflect a strong stand because they express opinions, emotions, value judgments, and interpretations. Because subjective words express personal opinions, they can bring meanings and stir reactions in the reader not intended by the writer. Therefore, a thoughtful writer carefully chooses subjective words for effective expression. Note the differences between the neutral words and the subjective words in the following list:

Neutral Words	Subjective Words
injury	wound, gash
perpetrator	criminal, delinquent, achiever
shelter	haven, hut

Practice 5

USE EFFECTIVE EXPRESSION: USE SUBJECTIVE WORDS TO PERSUADE

Use your dictionary and thesaurus to find an effective biased word to fill in the blank in each sentence. In the spaces after each sentence, describe the impact you intend to have on your reader through your choice of words. Discuss your work with your class or small group.

1. Spanking is _____

2. Laws that require cyclists to wear helmets are _____

3. Completion of a college education requires _____

4. Burning the United States flag is an act of _____

5. Graffiti is _____

Use Persuasion in Your Academic Courses

Often college textbooks present situations to help you think critically and come to your own conclusions about a debatable topic. An excellent study technique is to write a paragraph in response to the information and questions. Many professors of these courses will also ask you to write an essay in which you explain your understanding of a controversial issue. You may find that you can use the information from the textbook as a resource for your writing assignment.

USE PERSUASION IN A COLLEGE BUSINESS ASSIGNMENT: RESPONDING TO A CONTROVERSIAL ISSUE

Read the following study prompt about an ethical issue based on a college business textbook lesson. Then, follow the directions given in the section "The Dilemma."

Taking a Stance: Ethics in Business

The Situation

A manufacturing facility on a river near your home employs nearly 200 people in your small community. It pays $2 million in taxes to the government each year. Sales tax from purchases made by plant employees and their families contribute an additional $1 million to local government. However, documented evidence reveals that the plant has been discharging large amounts of waste into the river, causing a 25% increase in cancer rates, a 30% reduction in riverfront property values, and a 75% decrease in native fish populations. The plant owner says the facility can stay in business only because there are no regulations mandating expensive treatment of waste from the plant. If such regulations were imposed, he says he would close the plant, lay off its employees, and relocate to a more business-friendly community.

The Dilemma

How would you recommend resolving this situation? How did you come to your recommendation? How did you weigh the costs and benefits associated with each of the plant's impacts? On your own paper, create a persuasive thinking map to support your recommendation. Use the persuasive thinking map on page 196 as a model.

Adapted from Withgott, Jay H.; Laposta, Matthew, *Environment: The Science Behind the Stories*, 5th ed. © 2014, p. 159. Reprinted and Electronically reproduced by permission of Pearson Education, Inc., New York, NY.

L7 Workshop: Writing a Persuasive Paragraph Step by Step

Prewrite Your Paragraph

The activities below will walk you through the prewriting stage of the writing process.

Choose Your Topic

1. Create a bank of topics: Use the suggested debatable topics to brainstorm as many facts, effects, and examples as you possibly can. Get as many ideas written down as quickly as possible. Revisit topic banks created during your study of previous chapters. Compare your bank of topics with those of your peers.

   - Violence in Cartoons
   - Sex Education
   - Teenage Drivers
   - Conserving Energy

2. Choose a topic from Activity 1. Brainstorm points the opposition could use to challenge your ideas. Determine where you could locate relevant expert opinions. For example, can you interview an expert? Locate an expert opinion on the Internet?

   OR

   Select a photograph(s) that illustrate a debatable topic. Generate a list that includes facts, examples, and opposing points. Search for expert opinions to include. Freewrite about the photograph(s). Remember to ask "What's the point?"

Focus Your Point

Read a prewrite you have generated for a persuasive paragraph. Underline words that suggest your values, opinions, or attitudes about the subject. Why is the subject important? Think about the reasons, facts, effects, and examples that best represent your claim. Identify your audience. Think about what specific reaction you want from your audience. Do you want to change minds, raise awareness, or call for a specific action? In one sentence, state the claim of your persuasion.

AUDIENCE: ....

PURPOSE—AUDIENCE REACTION: ....

....

CONCRETE EXAMPLES: ....

....

WHAT'S THE POINT? STATE YOUR CLAIM: ....

....

Generate and Organize Relevant Details

Use the persuasive thinking map below to either organize the ideas you have created or generate details that support your point.

The Debatable Topic: What is the issue? ____________________

____

Supporting Points

Reason 1 ____________________

____

Reason 2 ____________________

____

Reason 3 ____________________

____

Opposing Point

____

____

Support that Refutes Opposing Point

____

____

What's the point?

____

____

PORTFOLIO

Workshop

Write a Draft of Your Paragraph

DRAFTING

Using the ideas you generated during the prewriting phase, compose a draft of your persuasive paragraph. Return to the prewriting process at any time to generate additional details as needed. Use your own paper.

Revise Your Draft

REVISING

Read your draft and answer the questions in the "Questions for Revising a Persuasive Paragraph" box that follows. If you answer "yes" to a question, underline, check, or circle examples. If you answer "no" to a question, write the additional details in the margins and draw lines to indicate their placement. Revise your paragraph based on your reflection.

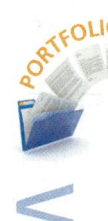

Questions for Revising a Persuasive Paragraph:

- [ ] Have I chosen an important debatable topic?
- [ ] Have I made my point? Can I state my point in one sentence?
- [ ] Have I effectively used reasons, facts, effects, examples? Have I used strong signal words of persuasion?
- [ ] Have I used concrete details to make my point?
- [ ] Have I included only the details that are relevant to my topic sentence? Have I used effective and relevant expert opinions? Have I addressed important opposing points effectively? Have I documented my sources properly?
- [ ] Have I made my ideas clear and interesting to my readers?
- [ ] Have I used subjective words to persuade my reader?

Proofread Your Draft

Once you have made any revisions that may be needed, proofread your paper to ensure appropriate usage and grammar, such as a consistent point of view.

For more information on point of view, see pages 512–514.

Grammar in Action: Consistent Use of Point of View

Point of view is established with the use of personal pronouns. Personal pronouns identify three points of view: first person, second person, and third person.

- **First Person** (informal tone)
  I, me, mine, myself, my
  we, us, ours, our, ourselves

- **Second Person** (informal tone)
  you, your, yours, yourselves

- **Third Person** (formal tone)
  he, him, his, himself   it, its, itself
  she, her, hers, herself   they, them, their, theirs, themselves

Common sense tells us that we cannot shift between several individuals' points of view. However, often, we shift point of view carelessly, as in the following sentence.

> Television addiction contributes to our obesity. When you watch TV all day, you leave no time for exercise.

Consistent use of point of view strengthens coherence or the clear flow of ideas. Therefore, carefully edit your writing to ensure consistent use of point of view, as in the following edited version of the sentence above.

> Television addiction contributes to our obesity. When we watch TV all day, we leave no time for exercise.

Practice 7

CONSISTENT USE OF POINT OF VIEW

Edit these sentences for consistent use of point of view. Cross out the pronoun that causes a shift in point of view and insert a noun or pronoun that establishes consistent use of point of view. Discuss your answers with a small group of peers or with your class.

1. A parent must monitor children's access to the Internet because you are vulnerable to predators in chat rooms and virtual communities like Facebook.

2. Some people believe that abstinence is the only way you can prevent unwanted pregnancies.

3. Getting enough sleep is crucial to a person's long-term health. When you deprive yourself of sleep, you deprive the body of its ability to repair itself through rest.

Writing Assignments

MyWritingLab™
Complete this Exercise on mywritinglab.com

Considering Audience and Purpose

Study the photographs at the beginning of the chapter. Assume you are the mayor who has received this letter from "A Concerned Citizen." Write a one-paragraph response that states your official stand on the issue.

Writing for Everyday Life

Assume that you and your family have decided to take a vacation together. Each of you has a different destination and activity in mind. Write a one-paragraph e-mail to your family in which you try to convince them to travel to your choice of destinations. Be sure to include facts, effects, examples, expert opinions, and reasons that counter any opposition to your choice. Allow your word choice and tone to reflect your enthusiasm.

Writing for College Life

Assume that you disagree with a grade you have received for an assignment. Write a one-paragraph letter to your professor in which you argue for the grade you believe you have earned. Be sure to include facts, examples, and explanations of what you have learned. Allow your word choice and tone to reflect both respect for the professor and self-confidence in your abilities.

Writing for Working Life

Assume that you are a supervisor at a fast food restaurant. You are short of staff, the busy season is approaching, and you need more workers. Write a one-paragraph memo to your district manager, Derwood Kuntz, persuading him to authorize you to hire three additional workers. Be sure to include reasons, facts, examples, effects, and points that will counter any opposition he may pose.

MyWritingLab™

Complete the Post-test for Chapter 12 in MyWritingLab.

13 Understanding the Essay

PART 3 HOW TO WRITE AN ESSAY

LEARNING OUTCOMES

After studying this chapter you will be able to:

L1 Answer the question "What's the Point of an Essay?"

L2 Understand the Five Parts of an Essay

L3 Discuss the Levels of Information in an Essay

L4 Describe the Traits of an Effective Essay

L5 Write an Essay Step by Step

An essay is a series of closely related ideas.

All of us have had some experience studying, writing, or reading essays. What do you already know about essays? Where have you seen essays? What are the traits of an essay?

Perhaps the most common and flexible form of writing, an essay allows powerful personal expression. The essay is used for academic papers, business reports, business letters, newspaper and magazine articles, Web articles, and personal letters, as well as letters to the editor of a newspaper or journal. By mastering the task of writing an essay, you empower your ability to think, reason, and communicate.

What's the Point of an Essay?

L0 1

Like a paragraph, an **essay** is a series of closely related ideas that develop and support the writer's point about a topic. In fact, the paragraph serves as a building block for an essay since an essay is composed of two, three, or more paragraphs. Therefore, the skills you developed to write a paragraph will also help you write an effective essay.

PHOTOGRAPHIC ORGANIZER: THE ESSAY

The following set of pictures depicts several situations in which people are reading different publications. Each of these publications features different types of essays. Study each photograph. Then, predict the topic or purpose for the types of essays written for the audience of each publication (write your predictions in the given spaces). Finally, answer the question: What's the point of an essay?

What's the point of an essay? _____

My First Thoughts: A Prewriting Activity

Set a time limit, such as two to five minutes, and jot down in your notebook your thoughts about the importance or value of the essay as a form of writing. Keep writing without stopping until the time limit is up, even if you have to repeat ideas.

One Student Writer's Response

Read the following student response to the question "What's the point of an essay?"

An essay allows a person to express an idea by using several paragraphs. So an essay lets a person get more details about a topic across to an audience. There are different types of essays. In everyday life, we read essays in newspapers, magazines, and on the Internet. For example, a newspaper has news stories and editorials. These are both essays. A magazine article is an essay. In work life, people write and read business letters and reports. In college life, students write many essays as exams and research papers.

L2 The Five Parts of an Essay

An essay has several basic parts: a **title**; a beginning, made up of an **introductory paragraph** that often includes a stated main idea or **thesis statement**; a middle, made up of **body paragraphs**; and an ending, often made up of a **concluding paragraph**. The following chart shows the general format of an essay.

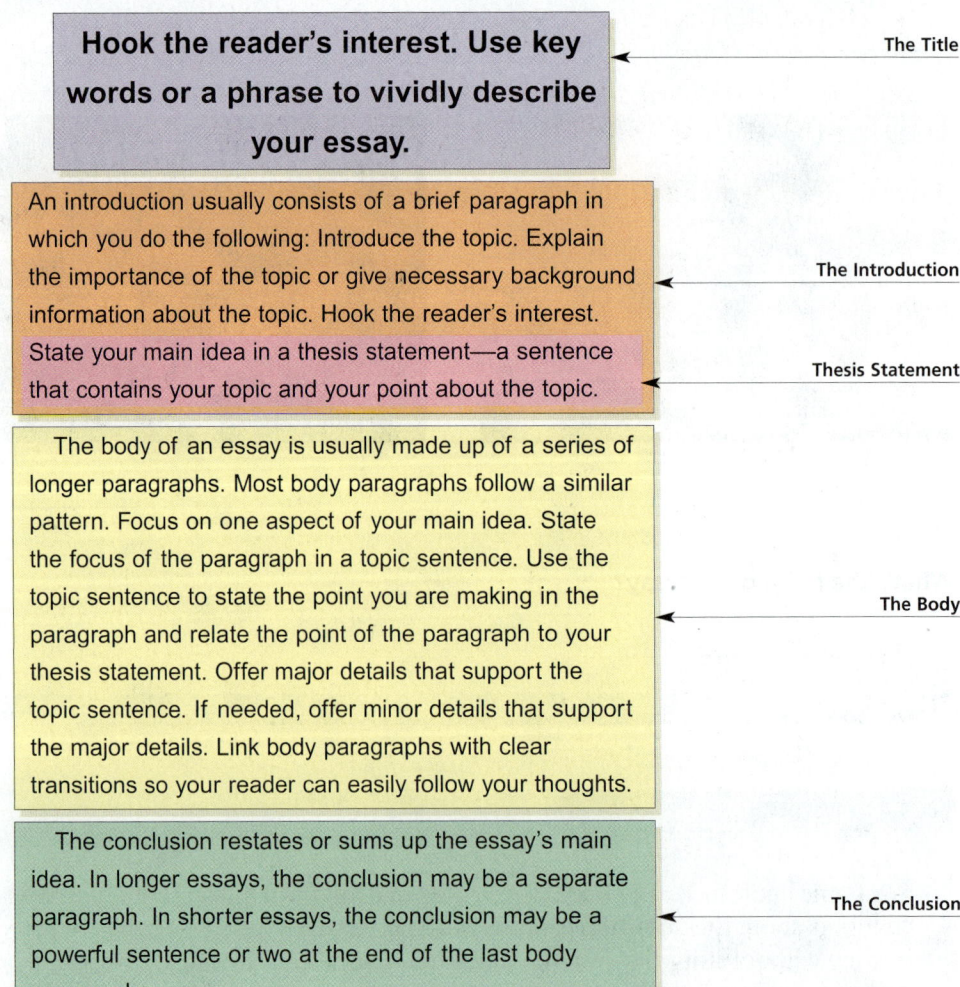

The Title — Hook the reader's interest. Use key words or a phrase to vividly describe your essay.

The Introduction — An introduction usually consists of a brief paragraph in which you do the following: Introduce the topic. Explain the importance of the topic or give necessary background information about the topic. Hook the reader's interest.

Thesis Statement — State your main idea in a thesis statement—a sentence that contains your topic and your point about the topic.

The Body — The body of an essay is usually made up of a series of longer paragraphs. Most body paragraphs follow a similar pattern. Focus on one aspect of your main idea. State the focus of the paragraph in a topic sentence. Use the topic sentence to state the point you are making in the paragraph and relate the point of the paragraph to your thesis statement. Offer major details that support the topic sentence. If needed, offer minor details that support the major details. Link body paragraphs with clear transitions so your reader can easily follow your thoughts.

The Conclusion — The conclusion restates or sums up the essay's main idea. In longer essays, the conclusion may be a separate paragraph. In shorter essays, the conclusion may be a powerful sentence or two at the end of the last body paragraph.

For more on creating effective titles, introductions, and conclusions, see pages 228–237.

UNDERSTAND THE FIVE PARTS OF AN ESSAY

Test your understanding of the structure of an essay. Read the student essay below straight through once or twice. Then, follow the directions in the margin to annotate the essay to identify its five parts.

Lacey Durrance
Professor Ragan
ENC 1101: Section 47
10 October 2015

Traits of a Successful College Student

(1) First-time college students don't realize the reality shock they will receive when they get to college. (2) High school and college atmospheres are extremely different in many ways. (3) College campuses and classes are often larger, college teachers have different expectations, and college students face many new challenges. (4) To get through college successfully, all first-time college students must be dedicated, responsible, and independent. (5) Many won't realize this until it is too late.

(6) Dedication is a primary part of being successful in college. (7) Students must work hard and take action to learn at a college level. (8) Assignments can't be left until the last minute like they might have been in high school. (9) College students must be willing to speak up in class and ask questions when they don't understand. (10) Dedication means setting priorities for success; dedication means putting off going out with friends and caring about producing the best work possible. (11) Dedicated students will do their work and do it well, spending hours reading textbooks, reviewing notes, and revising essays.

(12) For many, being responsible during high school wasn't really necessary. (13) Students might forget to do their homework and the teacher most likely would extend the deadline. (14) In contrast, college students must be responsible for their actions and accept the consequences. (15) Paying attention to what's due and when assignments should be turned in is a prime example. (16) Most college teachers stick to their deadlines and expect students to do so also. (17) Being on time to class is another example of being responsible. (18) Responsibility plays a key role in a successful college career.

(19) However, having dedication and being responsible aren't the only traits college students need to survive. (20) College students must also be independent. (21) Teachers expect students to take notes without assigning them to do so. (22) In high school, teachers often gave out notes to study from or told students where and when to take them. (23) College students must do their work without being reminded every day. (24) However, teachers are there to help their students understand the class material. (25) They will guide their students yet not help complete their work. (26) Being independent is a skill to acquire for college success, as well as life-long success.

(27) College is hard work, and students must have these traits to be successful. (28) Most first-time college students will struggle with the new experience, yet by being dedicated, responsible, and independent, they will thrive in the college world.

WRITING FROM LIFE

1. Draw a circle around the introduction.
2. Underline the thesis statement.
3. Draw a box around the body of the essay.
4. Underline the topic sentence in each body paragraph.
5. Draw a circle around the conclusion.

L3 The Levels of Information in an Essay

In connection with its various parts, an essay offers several levels of information that range from general to specific. Understanding these levels of information helps a writer create and organize ideas throughout the writing process.

▲ Steps to different levels

Titles, Introductions, and Conclusions Express General Ideas

Titles, introductions, and conclusions introduce and summarize ideas. Chapter 14 offers helpful hints about how to effectively use titles, introductions, and conclusions.

Thesis Statement

The thesis statement is a one-sentence summary of the main idea of the essay. All the details in the body paragraphs support the thesis statement.

Types of Supporting Details

Two types of details are often needed to thoroughly explain a main idea: primary and secondary supports. **Primary supports** directly explain the thesis statement. **Secondary supports** indirectly affirm the thesis statement. In an essay, topic sentences of the body paragraphs are the primary supports for the thesis statement. The examples, reasons, and facts within the body of a paragraph reinforce the topic sentence. They serve as secondary supports to the thesis statement.

Levels of Supporting Details

Secondary supports can also be divided into two levels: major details and minor details. A **major detail** supports a topic sentence. A **minor detail** supports a major detail. Thus, a topic sentence supports the thesis statement, and secondary supports explain a topic sentence. The following flow chart illustrates these levels of information in an essay. This chart represents a basic three-paragraph essay. This format is often expanded to include two or more body paragraphs.

The Levels of Information in an Essay

Title

Introduction
Explains the importance of the topic and the writer's point.
Offers background information about the topic.
Hooks the reader's interest.

Thesis Statement
States the main idea in a complete sentence.
Uses specific, effective wording.
Relates to all the details in the essay.

Topic Sentence
States the main idea of the paragraph.
Offers one primary support for the thesis statement.
Relates to all the details in the paragraph.

Major Detail
Supports the topic sentence.
Is a secondary support for the thesis statement.
Is more general than a minor detail.

Minor Detail
Supports a major detail.
Is a secondary support for the thesis statement.
Offers the most specific details in the essay.

Conclusion
Reinforces the importance of the writer's overall point.

Compare this chart to the chart about levels of information in a paragraph on page 51.

A Body Paragraph: Use as many body paragraphs as needed to fully develop the thesis statement.

IDENTIFY THE LEVELS OF DETAIL IN AN ESSAY

Read the following three-paragraph essay. Underline the thesis statement. Next, underline the three major details in the body paragraph.

Street Luging for the Extreme Thrill

(1) Extreme sports take athletic competition to new levels of danger and excitement. (2) They often offer a combination of speed, height, danger, and mind-blowing stunts. (3) Street luging illustrates the allure of extreme sports.

(4) Street luging, like many extreme sports, involves high levels of speed, danger, and adrenaline. (5) First, street luging is all about speed. (6) A pilot lies on his or her back on a luge (a type of skateboard, eight and a half feet long) and flies through a street course at speeds of around 70 miles per hour. (7) As a result, the urethane wheels of the luge may actually flame fire and melt during a run due to the high speeds. (8) Second, street luging courses are known for their rough, hazardous road surfaces and obstacles. (9) For example, very dangerous courses are known as *bacon* while less dangerous ones are labeled *scrambled eggs*. (10) And frequently, luges snag or hook together, wobble, wipe out, or slam into barriers that mark the course. (11) Finally, the dangers of street luging are related to another important attraction of extreme sports—the thrilling rush of an adrenaline high. (12) The adrenaline rush is due to high levels of dopamine, endorphins, and serotonin produced by the body in response to the danger. (13) Adrenaline floods the body with additional surges of energy, power, and well-being so that a person can either fight or flee the danger. (14) Many extreme sports participants are called adrenaline junkies. (15) Luge pilots refer to this feeling as being "amped."

(16) Extreme sports include a wide variety of thrill-seeking sports such as wave surfing, wind surfing, BASE jumping (jumping from buildings, antennas or towers, spans or bridges, or cliffs), parachuting, and drag racing.
(17) Overall, street luging offers athletes all the dangers and thrills that all extreme sports enthusiasts find so attractive.

The Traits of an Effective Essay

The word *essay* means "attempt" or "an effort to accomplish an end." An essay is a writer's attempt to share his or her unique and specific point about a specific subject to a specific audience for a specific purpose. An effective essay supports a **main idea** or **thesis statement** with **relevant details** in **logical order,** using **effective expression.**

A Clear Point: Main Idea or Thesis Statement

What's the point of a focused main idea? To make a clear and powerful point to your reader! An effective essay makes a clear point by focusing on a main idea. A focused main idea is the result of several thinking steps: selecting and narrowing a topic and drafting a **thesis statement**.

> For more on using prewriting techniques and selecting a topic, see pages 30–39.

Select and Narrow a Topic

Many writers break this step into two parts. First, a writer often generates a list of topics. This list serves as a bank of ideas that can be applied to a wide variety of writing situations. Second, a writer considers the writing situation.

Understanding the writing situation helps the writer narrow the topic. For example, the length of an essay often depends on your audience and purpose. A paper for an academic audience such as a history professor may have a required length of 1,000 words. In contrast, a local newspaper may limit the length of letters to the editor to 500 words. The scope of the topic needs to match the required length. For example, the 500-word letter to the editor cannot cover all the reasons one should volunteer at the local soup kitchen for the poor. Instead, you would need to narrow the topic to just two or three reasons. And you would choose only those details that are of interest to your specific audience.

> For more on the writing situation, and topic, purpose, and audience, see pages 20–27.

THE TRAITS OF AN EFFECTIVE ESSAY: SELECT AND NARROW A TOPIC FOR THE WRITING SITUATION

The following pictures present specific writing situations. Each picture represents an audience, and each caption states the purpose for writing to that audience. First, match the audience and purpose to its appropriate topic. Then, write the letter of the topic in the appropriate space. Finally, discuss your answers with your class or in a small group.

Topics: a. What I have learned through research

b. Gratitude for the sacrifice of service

c. How to solve a problem

d. The importance of a healthful diet

_____ Writing Situation 1: To Inform

_____ Writing Situation 2: To Persuade

_____ Writing Situation 3: To Express

_____ Writing Situation 4: To Reflect

Practice 4

Draft a Thesis Statement

After choosing and narrowing a topic, a writer composes a working draft of the thesis statement. A **thesis statement** shares the same traits of a topic sentence for a paragraph. Just as the topic sentence states the main idea of a paragraph, the thesis sentence states the main idea of the essay. Both statements answer the question "What's the point?" This point is the opinion about the topic that you are explaining and supporting in the essay. In fact, your point further narrows your topic. The writer's point or opinion is often referred to as the *controlling idea*.

The controlling idea often includes a pattern of organization as well as the writer's opinion. You learned about patterns of organization as you studied how to develop paragraphs in Chapters 3 to 12. The following graphic illustrates an effective thesis statement.

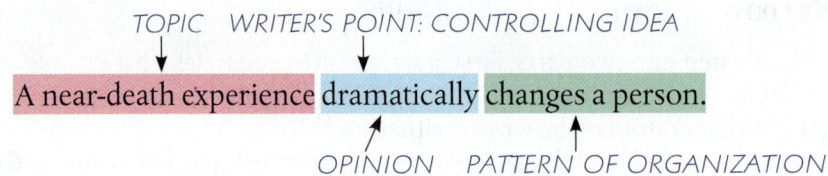

The word "dramatically" is an opinion that must be explained or supported. In addition, the word "changes" suggests a pattern of organization. This word indicates that the writer is going to compare what the person was like before the near-death experience to what he or she is like after the near-death experience. The controlling idea answers the question "What's the point?" of the essay.

Hints for Drafting a Thesis Statement
Use specific statements. Replace vague, general words with vivid, exact words. "Football is a dumb game" is too vague and general. "Football glorifies violence" is specific and vivid.
Always state your thesis statement as a complete sentence.
Avoid announcing your topic. Never say, "I am going to write about football and violence," or "My essay is about football and violence," or "My topic is football violence."
Review and, if necessary, revise your thesis statement after you have written a rough draft. As you think about a topic, the point you want to make often becomes clearer.

Practice 5

THE TRAITS OF AN EFFECTIVE ESSAY: CREATE AND REVISE THESIS STATEMENTS

The following items present a topic and a writer's point about the topic. Combine the ideas in each group to create a thesis statement. Discuss your ideas with your class or in a small group.

1. TOPIC: *workplace aggression*

   WRITER'S POINT: *is on the rise and takes on several forms of behavior*

THESIS STATEMENT: _____

_____

2. TOPIC: cardiovascular disease

WRITER'S POINT: although certain factors are unavoidable, other factors we can influence through our behavior

THESIS STATEMENT: _____

_____

3. TOPIC: major depressive disorder

WRITER'S POINT: a common type of mood disorder with several long-term effects

THESIS STATEMENT: _____

_____

4. TOPIC: use of social networking sites

WRITER'S POINT: five tips for safety

THESIS STATEMENT: _____

5. TOPIC: weight training machines and free weights

WRITER'S POINT: similarities and differences

THESIS STATEMENT: _____

_____

Logical Order

In an effective essay, body paragraphs are arranged in a clear, logical order for a coherent flow of ideas. Likewise, effective writers link each paragraph to the next so that readers can follow their chain of thought.

You can achieve a coherent flow of ideas in several logical ways.

1. *Follow pattern(s) of organization.* At times, a writer follows a particular pattern of organization to make a point. For example, a biography of an important person is based on time order. A description of a significant place follows spatial order. Other times, a writer may need to discuss causes, effects, similarities, or differences to make a point about a topic. Many times, a writer may need to combine several patterns of organization to fully discuss a topic. For example, to logically discuss the significance of an historical event such as 9/11, a writer may need to use time order, spatial order, causes, and effects.

2. *Follow the order of ideas as presented in the thesis statement.* Often the controlling idea of the thesis statement divides the topic into chunks of information.

3. *Present ideas in order of importance.* Often, a writer decides upon and arranges details according to his or her opinion about the importance of the details, known as **climactic order**. Usually, climactic order moves from the least important point in the first body paragraph and builds to the essay's climax, the most important point in the final body paragraph.

Practice 6

THE TRAITS OF AN EFFECTIVE ESSAY: USE LOGICAL ORDER

Complete the exercises, and share your responses with your class or in a small group.

1. **Follow Patterns of Organization.** Use an appropriate combination of time order, spatial order, and contrast order to write three topic sentences (primary supports) suggested by the following thesis statement.

    I. Introduction

    THESIS STATEMENT: *After eleven months of following the diet and exercise training program at CrossFit Fire, Jennie has dramatically changed in several ways.*

    II. _____

    III. _____

    IV. _____

    V. Conclusion

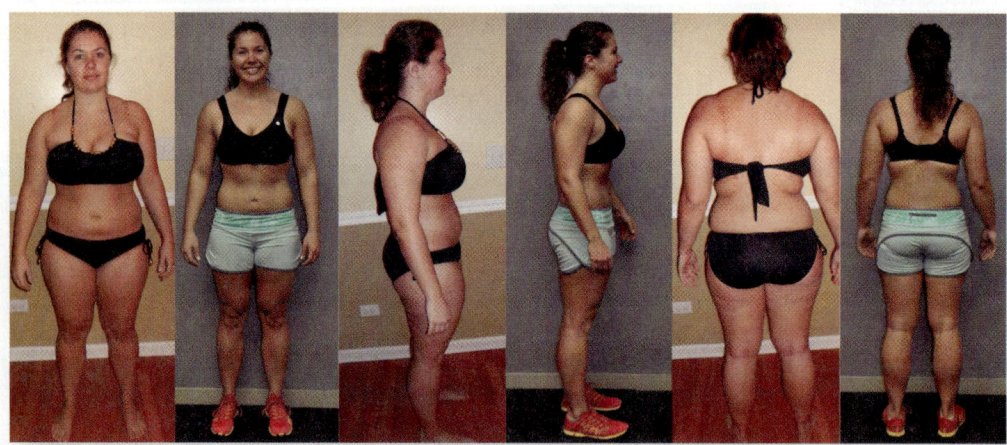

2. **Follow the order of ideas as presented in thesis statement.** Write and arrange in logical order three topic sentences (primary supports) suggested by the following thesis statement.

   I. Introduction

   THESIS STATEMENT: *To ensure your safety during a severe storm, you should stock up on supplies, secure your home, and be prepared to evacuate.*

   II. _____

   _____

   III. _____

   _____

   IV. _____

   _____

   V. Conclusion

   ▲ Stock up on supplies.

   ▲ Secure your home.

   ▲ Be prepared to evacuate.

3. **Present ideas in order of importance.** Write and arrange in climactic order three topic sentences (primary supports) suggested by the following thesis statement.

   I. Introduction

   THESIS STATEMENT: *Stress challenges us in almost every aspect of our lives.*

   II. _____

   _____

   III. _____

   _____

   IV. _____

   _____

   V. Conclusion

Connecting Paragraphs

In addition to ordering paragraphs coherently, writers clearly connect each paragraph to the next so that readers can follow their chain of thought. The following chart lists and illustrates several options to connect paragraphs to each other.

Connecting Paragraphs	
Echo or repeat important words or phrases from the thesis statement in body paragraphs.	
I. Thesis statement:	We can *ease* the *pain* that occurs from illness or injury in several different ways.
II. Topic sentence:	*Pain* can be *eased* by deep breathing.
III. Topic sentence:	Visualization and imagery *ease pain*.
Refer to the main idea of the previous paragraph in the topic sentence of the present paragraph.	
I. Thesis statement:	Applying the principles of computer ergonomics reduces the chances of injury and fatigue.
II. Topic sentence:	The *computer screen* should be *placed properly* to avoid painful injuries to the neck.
III. Topic sentence:	*Proper placement* of the *screen* not only *reduces* the possibility of *neck injury* but also eases eye fatigue.
Use transitional words, phrases, or sentences.	
I. Thesis statement:	Sleep disorders can deprive sufferers of much needed rest and complicate their lives.
II. Topic sentence:	*One type* of sleep disorder is known as night terrors.
III. Topic sentence:	*Another type* of sleep disorder, nightmares, torments many people.
IV. Transition sentence and topic sentence:	*At least the previous two disorders* occur in the privacy of one's home. Narcolepsy, a *third kind* of sleep disorder, can occur suddenly anywhere, and at any time without warning.
Tie the last idea in one paragraph to the opening of the next paragraph.	
I. Thesis statement:	Hurricane activity is on the rise, is likely to increase, and calls for new methods of preparation.
II. Topic sentence and ending idea of paragraph:	Hurricane activity is on the rise because of higher ocean temperatures and lower vertical wind shear. Therefore, these *climate changes* are likely to continue for as many as 10 to 40 years.
III. Topic sentence:	These *shifts in climate* call for new methods of hurricane preparation.

Practice 7

THE TRAITS OF AN EFFECTIVE ESSAY: CONNECT PARAGRAPHS

Read the following essay. Underline the connections between paragraphs. Circle the key ideas that are repeated throughout the essay. Discuss with your class or in a small group the different types of connections the writer used and evaluate their effectiveness.

A Song of Humility

(1) The neighborhood of my youth hummed with the songs of our carefree play. (2) The beat of hammers building forts and the zings of the over-ripe ammunition of our orange wars in Winter Haven, Florida, blended beautifully with the music of the times. (3) The Beatles, and all the other really far-out groups, deafened us to any world but our very own. (4) No one was more deaf than I.

(5) At that time, I was particularly deaf to the family that lived two streets over and halfway down a dusty clay side road. (6) This out of sync family lived poorer than we did. (7) They grew their own food, raised chickens, and loved loud country music. (8) Every time I passed their house, I felt sorry for them, in a smug sort of way. (9) One afternoon the mama of that family labored up the hill to our house. (10) Her son had cut a record, and she "would be obliged if we was to listen to it" and tell her what we thought. (11) I was too busy marveling at her stained clothes and dusty feet to hear how respectfully my mother responded.

(12) Mother treated everyone with respect and tried to teach her children to do so as well. (13) She insisted that the whole family listen to the twangy tune about love and shirttails, but only I took great joy in mocking it. (14) Mother told me to return the record and say she thought it "a fine tune." (15) When I objected, she said, "Consider this an unavoidable duty!" (16) I stood a long time studying the rusty door of that family's dust-covered house, wondering why I hadn't the courage to do my duty.

(17) Finally, my good friend Florence appeared at the end of the alley. (18) "Florence," I cried in great relief, "come here quick." (19) I ran to meet her, and we stood a few feet away with our backs turned from the door I so dreaded. (20) In the loud, exuberant tones of an inconsiderate child, I belted out the details of my dilemma. (21) "You ought to hear this … stupid … only hicks … and I have to … Hey, wait for me," I said to her retreating back. (22) I had hoped to push my obligation into her hands. (23) "Naw," she said without looking back, "I'm already late."

(24) So, I turned to do my hated duty. (25) Then I saw the son, the singer, dart from the door into the shadows of the house. (26) I wheeled about and cried, "Florence, come back." (27) I ran to her, begging, "He heard me. (28) What should I do? (29) He heard everything I said." (30) Florence shrugged and turned away. (31) I pivoted and marched to the steps. (32) The son stepped out to meet me. (33) My words resonated in the silence that loomed between us, and I cursed the supper time desertion of the dusky streets. (34) "Young lady," he said gently. (35) I looked at him. (36) "Thank ya for bringing back my demo."

(37) To this day, the timbre of his voice shames me. (38) I had mocked him, yet he sought to soothe my soul. (39) And, now, when I feel the deafness of prejudice threaten me, I remember the song of humility I learned that day from a fine young singer.

For concept maps of specific patterns of organization, such as narration, classification, and definition, see pages 92, 138, and 168.

Relevant Details

In an effective essay, the writer provides enough relevant details to adequately or thoroughly support the essay's main idea.

Generate Details with a Writing Plan

Most writers generate details during the prewriting stage by listing or freewriting. Once you have generated an adequate amount of details, you need to organize them into a writing plan. Many writers use clustering or outlining to help them create a plan for the essay. Clustering and outlining are excellent ways to see if you have enough details to support the point of your essay.

   Some writers begin the writing process by generating details and then drafting a thesis statement, while other writers draft a working thesis statement first and then generate details. The following two practice exercises offer you an opportunity to work with both approaches. In your own writing, you should experiment to see which approach works best for you.

Often, a writer uses a prewriting technique, such as a concept map, to generate primary and secondary details. Then, the writer drafts a working thesis statement to summarize the point of the details generated with the concept map.

Practice 8

THE TRAITS OF AN EFFECTIVE ESSAY: GENERATE DETAILS, DRAFT A THESIS, CREATE A WRITING PLAN

Study the following list of details. Create a writing plan by filling in the concept map with groups of details from the list. Then, write a one-sentence summary (a thesis statement) of the main point that they support.

respects others	diffuses confrontations	remains professional
builds consensus	states clear expectations	encourages input from others
fosters team work	seeks solutions	

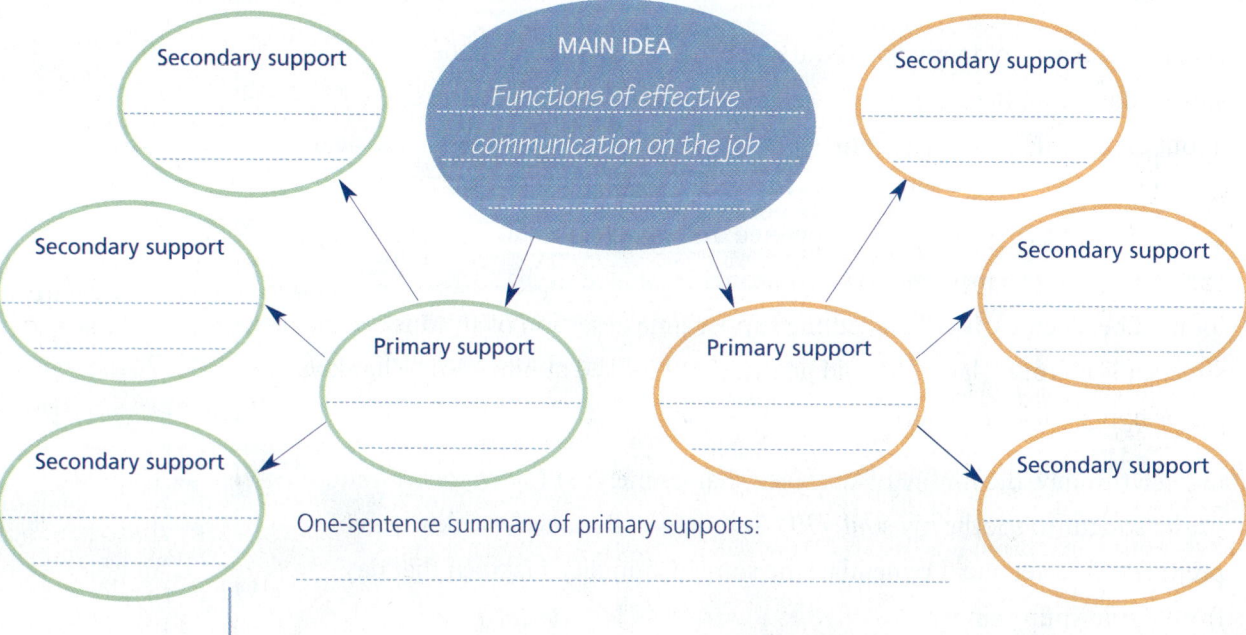

One-sentence summary of primary supports:

218

Evaluate Details

In an effective essay, every detail supports the thesis statement. *All* the details work together as a unit to explain and support the writer's point. During the prewriting process, a writer brainstorms many details, some of which may not be related to the focus of the main idea. Therefore, as you create your writing plan, you should test the details to be sure that each one is relevant to the thesis statement. Drop those details that do not support either the thesis statement or the thesis statement's primary supports. You also may want to check details for relevance once more during the revision stage of the writing process.

THE TRAITS OF AN EFFECTIVE ESSAY: TEST DETAILS FOR RELEVANCE

Study the following writing plan. Cross out details that are not relevant to the thesis statement. The following questions will help you test details for unity. Share your work with your class or in a small group of peers.

- What is the topic and controlling idea of the thesis statement? Circle the topic. Underline the controlling idea.

- Which details are the primary supporting details (the ones that will be used as topic sentences for body paragraphs)? Number the three primary supports A, B, and C.

- What are the secondary details? Number each secondary detail to correspond to a primary point: A1, A2, and so on; B1, B2, and so on; and C1, C2, and so on.

THESIS STATEMENT: *Due to the nature of lightning, you must follow lightning safety guidelines to reduce risk of injury or death.*

_____ Lightning is a complex event.

_____ Lightning is described as having two components: leaders and strokes.

_____ The leader is the probing feeler sent from the cloud.

_____ The return streaks of light are a series of strokes that produce the actual lightning bolt or flash that we see.

_____ Lightning is also common, unpredictable, and dangerous.

_____ At any given moment, there are 1,800 thunderstorms in progress somewhere on the earth. This amounts to 16 million storms each year.

_____ Lightning has been seen in volcanic eruptions, extremely intense forest fires, surface nuclear detonations, heavy snowstorms, and large hurricanes.

_____ No one can predict the location or time of the next stroke of lightning.

_____ Lightning has been the second largest storm killer in the U.S. for the last 40 years, exceeded only by floods.

_____ Following proven lightning safety guidelines can reduce your risk of injury or death.

_____ Count the seconds between the time you see lightning and the time you hear the thunder.

_____ You should already be in a safe location if that time is less than 30 seconds.

_____ The safest location during lightning activity is an enclosed building.

_____ Stay inside until 30 minutes after you last hear thunder.

Effective Expression: Using a Thesaurus

One aspect of effective expression is choosing the precise word to convey your point with power and clarity. Effective writers often refer to a thesaurus to avoid repetition and to find the exact words needed to make their point. A thesaurus is a collection of words, their synonyms (words of similar meaning), and their antonyms (words of opposite meaning). Online thesauruses, such as Merriam-Webster.com, provide a search box so you can search a specific word for its related words. In addition to the common features, many online thesauruses also provide additional information in a single search, such as full entries for related words. In a writer's search for the right words, a thesaurus provides a resource of a wide range of words with varying connotations.

Practice 10

EFFECTIVE EXPRESSION: USING A THESAURUS

Study the two entries adapted from the thesaurus on Merriam-Webster.com.* Then, answer the questions that follow.

Humility

NOUN. The absence of any feelings of being better than others <displaying genuine *humility*, the peace activist accepted the Nobel Prize on behalf of all who have worked to end the violence> **Synonyms:** demureness, down-to-earthness, humbleness, lowliness, meekness, modesty. **Antonyms:** arrogance, assumption, egotism, haughtiness.

Modesty

NOUN. The quality or state of being morally pure <in this day and age, *modesty* in a teenager is very becoming> **Synonyms:** chasteness, immaculacy, innocence, *modesty*, purity. **Antonyms:** immodesty, impurity.

1. What part of speech are these two words? _____

2. *Arrogance* is an _____ for humility. *Innocence* is a _____ for modesty.
   Insert a word from the entries to complete these statements:

3. Charlene dresses with _____ and style.

4. Jerome accepted responsibility for his mistake with _____.

*By permission. From Merriam-Webster's Collegiate® Thesaurus © 2015 by Merriam-Webster Inc. (www.Merriam-Webster.com)

Workshop: Writing an Essay Step by Step

To create an effective essay, use the complete writing process. Begin by prewriting; then, move on to drafting, revising, and editing. Writing rarely develops in a neat and orderly process. Some writers need to generate details before they can compose a working thesis statement. Others have to know exactly what their main point is before they can generate details. The following series of workshops encourages you to follow the prewriting steps in a certain order. Feel free to move between steps or to return to any step in the process as needed.

 ## Prewriting

During the prewriting stage, you figure out what you want to say, why you want to say it, and to whom you want to say it.

Select and Narrow Your Topic

Select a topic on your own, pick a topic from a previous practice or workshop, or choose one of the following topics. Identify your audience and purpose.

- Movie heroes (or villains)
- Violence in sports
- Technology everyone should own
- A great achievement
- A fun activity
- Common fears

Create a Tentative Thesis

Then, draft a tentative thesis statement.

TOPIC: ....

AUDIENCE: ....

PURPOSE: ....

THESIS STATEMENT: ....

For an overview of the writing process, see pages 28–29.

For more on the prewriting stage of the writing process, see pages 30–39.

Generate Supporting Details with a Writing Plan

Generate primary and secondary supporting details by listing a writing plan or use the concept map to create a writing plan. Use the reporter's questions *who? what? when? where? why?* and *how?* to produce details.

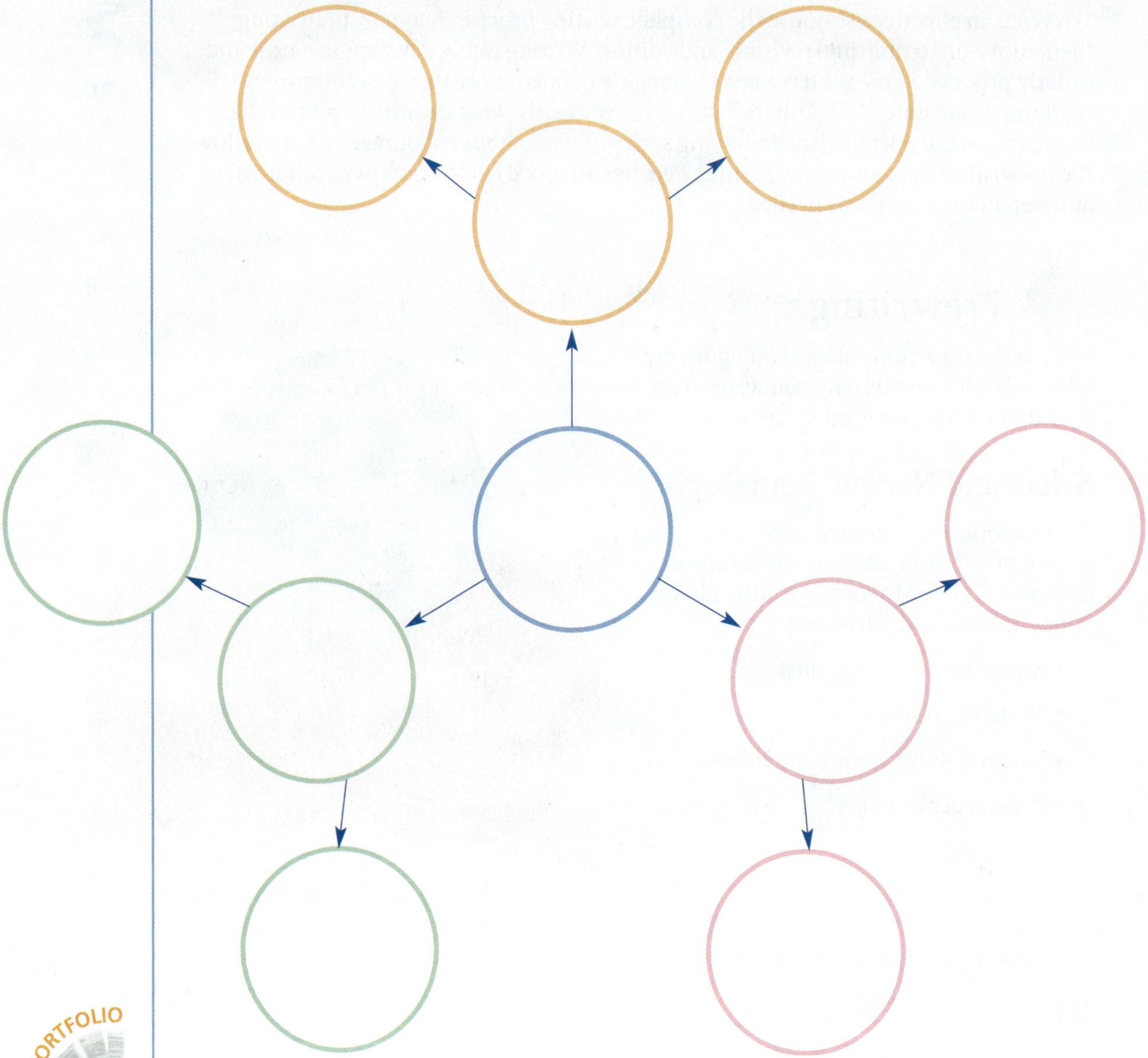

Now that you have generated some details to support your tentative thesis, you probably have a clearer sense of your controlling idea. The following thesis statement has been revised to focus the topic by including the writer's opinion and a pattern of organization.

TOPIC   WRITER'S POINT: CONTROLLING IDEA

Voter turnout remains dismal for several reasons.

OPINION   PATTERN OF ORGANIZATION (CAUSE AND EFFECT)

Revise Your Thesis Statement

Revise your thesis so that it includes the topic, your point about the topic, and, if appropriate, a pattern of organization.

REVISED THESIS STATEMENT:

Evaluate Your Details

Use a writing plan to test your details. Complete the following outline with your revised thesis statement and details from your list or concept map. Make sure you have an adequate amount of details to convince your reader of your point. If you do not have the necessary major and minor details to support each topic sentence, brainstorm additional details. Delete details that are not related to your thesis statement or to the topic sentences (the primary supports for your thesis statement).

I. INTRODUCTION

REVISED THESIS STATEMENT:

II.

    A.

    B.

III.

    A.

    B.

IV. CONCLUSION:

> For more on the drafting stage of the writing process, see pages 42–43.

Write a Draft of Your Essay

Often, a writer pauses during the drafting stage of the writing process to scan what has been written so far, particularly when using a computer to write. Sometimes, while scanning, a writer may begin to make small revisions. Scanning may help a writer stay focused and can help with expression. However, you should resist the urge to spend very much time revising at this point. Your main purpose is to get a rough draft written. You can make effective revisions once you have a working draft.

Using your writing plan, write a rough draft of the body of your essay. Don't worry about the introduction and conclusion for now. Have a dictionary and thesaurus nearby just in case you get stuck trying to think of a word.

Revise Your Essay Draft

Revision is much more than simply recopying the essay so that it is neater. A good revision requires time. So, put your essay aside for an hour or two, or, even better, a day or two. You want to look at your essay with fresh eyes. Then, set aside enough time to revise your essay more than once—that way, you do not have to think of everything in one sitting. During the revising stage of your writing, think about your essay on two different levels: logic and style. The following chart offers you some helpful questions to guide you through your revision.

> For more on the revising stage of the writing process, see pages 44–45.

> For more information about sentence variety, see pages 490–509.

Questions for Revising an Essay:

- ☐ Does the essay have a clearly stated thesis statement?
- ☐ Are my topic sentences clearly stated?
- ☐ Have I provided relevant support?
- ☐ Is each body paragraph fully developed with major and minor details as needed?
- ☐ Which ideas need more support?
- ☐ Is each topic sentence directly related to my thesis statement?
- ☐ Is each detail in each body paragraph related to its topic sentence?
- ☐ Have I used logical order?
- ☐ Have I provided clear connections between paragraphs?
- ☐ Have I provided clear connections between sentences within paragraphs?
- ☐ Have I used effective expression?
- ☐ Do my sentences vary in type and length?

Reread your essay, and as you revise, mark up your rough draft with the changes you intend to make: (1) cross out irrelevant details and vague, weak, or trite expressions, and write stronger words directly above or near them; (2) draw arrows to show where you want to move information; (3) add more details in the margin and draw a line to indicate where you will put them.

One Student Writer's Revision Process

At the beginning of this chapter, you read the essay Lacey Durrance composed for her English class. Take a moment to reread her final draft on page 207. Then, study her revisions of one draft of the essay's first two paragraphs. How does this draft differ from her final draft?

Traits of a Successful College Student

(1) First-time college students don't realize the reality shock they will receive when they get to college. (2) High school and college atmospheres are extremely different in many ways. (3) ~~Schools~~ *College campuses and classes* are larger; ~~there are different~~ *college* teachers ~~with~~ *have* different expectations, and ~~different experiences~~ *college students face many new challenges*. (4) College is a big part of growing up, and with growing up comes certain traits ~~that you need to have~~ *needed* to make it in college. (5) All first-time college students must ~~have dedication, be~~ *be dedicated,* responsible, and ~~be~~ independent, to get through college successfully. (6) Many won't realize this until it is too late, and without these traits, they won't succeed.

(7) Dedication is ~~the biggest~~ *a primary* part of being successful in college. (8) Students must want a good grade, and know what they need to do to achieve it. (9) ~~Among my own personal experiences of being a first time college student, dedication has played a major part of being successful. (10) I had to change my learning process to adapt to college and so have former students.~~ (11) Students must ~~be~~ *work* hard ~~working~~ and take action to learn at a college level. (12) ~~Things~~ *Assignments* can't be left until the last minute like they might have been in high school. (13) College students ~~can't only want a good grade, but must do the~~ *must be willing to speak up in class and ask questions when they don't understand, even if they are afraid they will look foolish.* ~~work to get that grade.~~ (14) ~~Dedication~~ *Dedicated students* will ~~get~~ *do* their work ~~done~~ and do it well. (15) College is very different in the sense that a lot is expected from students, and they won't be walked through anything. Dedication means setting priorities for success; dedication means putting off going out with friends; dedication means caring about producing the best work possible.

Proofreading Your Essay

Once you have revised your essay to your satisfaction, take time to carefully proofread your work. Check for the mistakes that you commonly make such as spelling errors, misplaced or missing commas, shifts in verb tense, or shifts in point of view. Publishing a clean, error-free draft proves you are committed to excellence and that you take pride in your work.

Proofread to correct spelling and grammar errors. Mark the corrections you need to make directly on the most recent draft of your essay. Create a neat, error-free draft of your essay.

> For more on the proofreading stage of the writing process, see pages 46–47.

REVIEW: UNDERSTANDING THE ESSAY

1. What are the four parts of an essay?

   a. _____

   b. _____

   c. _____

   d. _____

2. What are the four levels of information in an essay?

   a. _____

   b. _____

   c. _____

   d. _____

3. What are two types of details in an essay?

   a. _____

   b. _____

Academic Learning Log: Chapter Review

4. What are the two levels of secondary details?

   a. _____

   b. _____

5. An effective essay supports a _____ idea with _____ details in _____ order and _____ expression.

6. What are the four phases of the writing process for composing an essay?

   a. _____

   b. _____

   c. _____

   d. _____

7. How will I use what I have learned about writing an essay? Discuss how you will apply to your own writing what you have learned about writing an essay.

   _____

   _____

   _____

   _____

8. What do I still need to study about writing an essay? Discuss your ongoing study needs by describing what, when, and how you will continue studying about how to write an essay.

   _____

   _____

   _____

MyWritingLab™

Complete the Post-test for Chapter 13 in MyWritingLab.

14 Effective Titles, Introductions, and Conclusions

LEARNING OUTCOMES

After studying this chapter you will be able to:

L1 Answer the question "What's the Point of Effective Titles, Introductions, and Conclusions?"

L2 Compose Effective Titles

L3 Compose Effective Introductions

L4 Compose Effective Conclusions

Titles, introductions, and conclusions work together to emphasize the writer's point.

The importance of effective titles, introductions, and conclusions is obvious in the composition of a movie. Think of a good movie you have seen lately. How did its title hook your interest? How did the title relate to the point of the movie? How effective was the opening of the film? How was the conclusion of the movie related to its beginning?

Just as in a successfully constructed movie, an essay with an effective title, introduction, and conclusion is more likely to have a strong impact on your audience.

What's the Point of Effective Titles, Introductions, and Conclusions?

Effective titles, introductions, and conclusions work together to emphasize the writer's point in an essay.

PHOTOGRAPHIC ORGANIZER: EFFECTIVE TITLES, INTRODUCTIONS, AND CONCLUSIONS

Study the following series of pictures of the World Trade Center in New York City. For each photograph, write a caption that records a point you would like to make in a personal essay. Then, answer the question "What's the point?" to create your thesis statement. Finally, compose a first draft of a title, introduction, and conclusion for your essay.

Title:

Introduction:

BEFORE SEPTEMBER 11, 2001   SEPTEMBER 17, 2001   MAY 2013

▲ Twin Towers

▲ Ruins of World Trade Center

▲ Freedom Tower, New York City

Caption:

Caption:

Caption:

What's the point (thesis statement)?

Conclusion:

Practice 1

WRITING FROM LIFE

My First Thoughts: A Prewriting Activity

Set a time limit, such as five minutes, and write in your notebook about the images you just studied. Do not let your pen or pencil stop. Even if you must repeat ideas, keep writing until the time limit is up. Let the ideas flow freely. Getting your first thoughts about a topic on paper is a great way to start the writing process.

One Student Writer's Response

The following paragraph offers one writer's response to the call to write a title, introduction, and conclusion based on the images of the 9/11 events. Read the text below and the annotations. Complete the activities in **bold type** given in the annotations. Then, read the writer's journal that records decisions she made during the writing process.

Title:
An effective title can be a word or phrase that helps the reader understand the writer's point by stating the topic and suggesting the writer's opinion about the topic.
Underline the topic and circle the writer's opinion.

> We Are Not Defeated
>
> As the sacred scripture "beauty for ashes" implies, out of tragedy comes wisdom. Our reaction as a nation to the events of September 11, 2001, has proven this saying to be true. Our strength, courage, and hope have overcome destruction and fear.
>
> Through the terror and fear of destruction, we as a nation learned the depth of our strength, courage, and hope.

Introduction:
An effective introduction stirs the reader's interest, establishes the relevance of the topic, and often suggests or states the main idea.
Underline the sentence that states the main idea.

Conclusion:
An effective conclusion restates the main idea to reinforce the writer's point in the reader's memory.
Underline the words that restate the topic and the writer's opinion.

THE WRITER'S JOURNAL

The student who wrote "We Are Not Defeated" wrote the following journal entry to record her thoughts about using a title, introduction, and conclusion. Read her writer's journal that describes a few key choices she made as she wrote. Underline any strategies that you might be able to use in your own writing.

> It's very hard to write about September 11, 2001. It's a very emotional topic. More than a decade later, I realize how far we have come. Many people are still suffering, but now we can see how strong we are as a nation. So I focused on the "strength, courage, and hope" I've seen shown by survivors. I like the way the message sounds stronger by repeating those three words in the title, introduction, and conclusion. I also like how a title, intro, and conclusion can sum up an essay.

Thoughtful titles, introductions, and conclusions enhance the effectiveness of an essay. Often these three aspects of the essay are written after the thesis statement and body paragraphs have been drafted. Although titles are the first part of the essay that catches the reader's attention, many writers create them after the introduction and conclusion.

Compose Effective Titles

An **effective title** fulfills the following purposes:

- It hooks the reader's interest.
- It vividly describes the topic of your essay.

You should write your essay, reread your essay for its overall impact, and then create your title. Your title should be brief, and you should not use italics, quotations, or underlining for emphasis. Instead, center the title on the page about an inch above the introductory paragraph. Capitalize the first word and other key words of the title, except for prepositions such as *in, on, for, at* and articles such as *a, an,* and *the*. The following chart describes and illustrates several types of effective titles.

Types of Titles		
The question title: States the main point as a question.	EXAMPLES:	Is Cloning Moral? Why Clone?
The descriptive title: Uses key words to form the thesis statement.	EXAMPLES:	The Arrogance of Cloning Cloning Offers Hope
The recommendation title: Calls for action.	EXAMPLES:	Cloning Must Be Banned Clone On!
The general-specific title: States the general topic, followed by a controlling point.	EXAMPLES:	Cloning: An Unethical Procedure Cloning: The Scientific Method Working for Progress
The pattern(s) of organization title: Uses the words that establish the essay's central pattern(s) of organization.	DESCRIPTION EXAMPLES:	The Town of My Birth The Beauty of the Beach
	NARRATION EXAMPLES:	Sojourner Truth's Journey An Unforgettable Memory
	PROCESS EXAMPLES:	How to Deal with Cranky Customers Starting Your Own Business
	EXAMPLE/ ILLUSTRATION EXAMPLES:	Why Winning Isn't Easy Why Pets Are People Too
	CLASSIFICATION EXAMPLES:	Types of Sexual Harassment Kinds of Camps for Kids

Types of Titles (continued)		
	COMPARISON/ CONTRAST EXAMPLES:	The Differences between Male Talk and Female Talk Why Soccer is the Real Football
	DEFINITION EXAMPLES:	The Forgiving Heart The Meaning of Bravery What It Means to Be Compulsive
	CAUSE/EFFECT EXAMPLES:	Why Parents Send Their Kids to Camp The Reasons Students Cheat The Effects of Binge Drinking
	PERSUASION EXAMPLES:	The Need for Smaller Classes in Public Schools We All Have the Right to Die Commit to Life to the Very End

Practice 2

COMPOSE EFFECTIVE TITLES

Read the following three-paragraph business memo and supply a title in the blank labeled RE (for the topic of the memo).

Memo

To: Sales Associates
From: Shanika Thomas, Store Manager
Date: 3 November 2015
RE: _____

Do you want to win the $200 bonus promised to each employee of the store which best represents our company's ideals: professional, friendly, fast service? Corporate representatives will be popping in unannounced sometime over the next few weeks to rate us as individuals and as a team.

To ensure our win, keep the following tips in mind. Reflect professionalism in your personal attire, the store's appearance (keep shelves stocked and orderly), and in your work ethic. Reflect friendliness in your attitudes to supervisors, coworkers, and, most importantly, to our customers. Finally, be quick to help each other and the customer. Greet the customer promptly and politely. The moment a customer walks in through our door, make that person feel as if he or she is the most important person on earth.

If each and every one of you continues to do the fine job that has put our store in the finals of this competition, we will all be winners!

Compose Effective Introductions

An effective introduction serves the following purposes:

- It introduces the essay topic.
- It explains the importance of the essay topic and/or gives necessary background information about the topic.
- It hooks the reader's interest.
- It presents the essay's main idea in a thesis statement.

Many writers choose to end the introductory paragraph with the thesis statement.

The following chart describes and illustrates several types of introductions you can use to effectively begin your essay. The thesis statement in each introduction is underlined.

Types of Introductions	
An interesting illustration or anecdote	**EXAMPLE:** The Wooten family makes a point of sharing the evening meal as special family time. Every evening, just as the family begins to dine and enjoy each other's company, the phone begins its non-stop ringing with unwanted harassment from telemarketers. Thankfully, the family can now put a stop to the harassment. <u>The National Do Not Call Registry is open for business, putting consumers in charge of the telemarketing calls they get at home.</u>
A surprising fact or statement	**EXAMPLE:** According to recent estimates, as many as 2.4 million to 5.1 million Americans have Alzheimer's disease. Sadly, the number of people with this disease is only going to grow if current trends continue. That's because the risk of Alzheimer's increases with age. And the U.S. population is aging. The number of people age 65 and older is expected to reach 72 million in 2030. And the number of people with Alzheimer's doubles for every 5-year interval beyond age 65. <u>We must fund research to find a cure for this terrible disease.</u> — U.S. National Institute on Health. "Alzheimer's Information." *ADEAR Homepage.* Dec. 2010. 12 Sept. 2011. Web.
A direct quotation	**EXAMPLE:** In 1961 a copy writer named Shirley Polykoff was working for the Foote, Cone & Belding advertising agency on the Clairol hair-dye account when she came up with the line: "If I've only one life to live, let me live it as a blond!" <u>In a single slogan she had summed up what might be described as the secular side of the Me Decade.</u> "If I've only one life to live, let me live it as _____!" (You have only to fill in the blank.) — Tom Wolfe, "The Me Decade and the Third Great Awakening," *New York Magazine,* August 23, 1976.
A definition	**EXAMPLE:** Hope is belief that the impossible is possible. Hope is the future counted in the present. Hope is a light, a map, and a compass. <u>Hope gave me the will to fight and survive cancer.</u>

Types of Introductions (continued)

A contradiction or opposing view	**EXAMPLE:** Many oppose the view that talking on cell phones while driving should be outlawed. Instead many believe that this behavior is no more dangerous than the many other tasks drivers perform while driving, such as lighting a cigarette, putting on makeup, or fiddling with the radio or air conditioner. However, common sense dictates that cell phone use while driving must be banned. — Adapted from "Ban Cell Phones: Save Lives"
A vivid description	**EXAMPLE:** The neighborhood of my youth hummed with the songs of our carefree play. The beat of hammers building forts and the zings of the over-ripe ammunition of our orange wars in Winter Haven, Florida, blended beautifully with the music of the times. The Beatles, and all the other really far-out groups, deafened us to any world but our very own. No one was more deaf than I. — "A Song of Humility"
A general or historical background	**EXAMPLE:** During the many thousands of years of human prehistory, people made their living by collecting food and other necessities from nature. All group members had equal access to life-sustaining resources. Most people throughout the world now live in economies much different from this description. In anthropology (the study of humankind), economic systems include three elements: livelihood, consumption, and exchange. — Miller, Barbara. *Cultural Anthropology*, 6th ed., p. 82.

Practice 3

COMPOSE EFFECTIVE INTRODUCTIONS

Read the following four introductory paragraphs. Underline the thesis statement and identify the type of introduction used in each one. Discuss your answers with your class or in a small group of peers.

- **a.** An interesting illustration or anecdote
- **b.** A surprising statement or fact
- **c.** A direct quotation
- **d.** A definition
- **e.** A contradiction or opposing view
- **f.** A vivid description
- **g.** General or historical background

_____ **1.** Heat kills! In fact, excessive heat is the number one weather-related killer, causing more fatalities per year than floods, lightning, tornadoes, hurricanes, winter storms, and extreme cold, according to the National Weather Service's storm data from 2001 to 2010. Therefore, when you exercise in warm, humid temperatures, protect yourself by taking a few sensible safety measures.

_____ **2.** To Frederick Douglass is credited the plea that, "the Negro be not judged by the heights to which he has risen, but by the depths from which he has climbed." Judged on that basis, the Negro woman embodies one of the modern miracles of the modern World.
– Mary McLeod Bethune, "A Century of Progress of Negro Women" speech, Chicago Women's Federation (30 June 1935).

3. Many are convinced that playing video games is a complete a waste of time. Others believe gaming has harmful, even antisocial effects. However, video games may actually foster critical thinking, problem solving, self-esteem, and social interaction.

4. When we first saw Henry, we knew he had to be ours. He had only been recently rescued from a cruel breeder who supplied greyhounds to local race tracks. We were told that the breeder caged Henry in a metal crate with shredded newspaper for bedding for 18–22 hours each day. He fed Henry cheap 4-D meat for Greyhounds. The 'D' stands for dying, diseased, disabled and dead livestock. Henry had barely survived the E. coli poisoning from this feed. At one time, almost every detail of Henry's skeleton could be seen beneath his thin skin. The fact is that these kinds of abuses are more common than not. Greyhound racing should be outlawed.

Compose Effective Conclusions

An **effective conclusion** fulfills the following purposes:

- It brings the essay to an end.
- It restates the essay's main idea and sums up the major points in the essay.

In longer essays, the conclusion may be a separate paragraph. In shorter essays, the conclusion may be a powerful sentence or two at the end of the last body paragraph. Just remember that a conclusion must stay on point, so don't introduce new information.

The following chart describes and illustrates several types of conclusions you can use to effectively and powerfully end your essay.

Types of Conclusions	
A question	**EXAMPLE:** Don't you want to experience the well-being that results from a healthful diet and regular exercise?
A quotation	**EXAMPLE:** Just as renowned coach of the Green Bay Packers Vince Lombardi said, "The difference between a successful person and others is not a lack of strength, not a lack of knowledge, but rather in a lack of will."
A call to action	**EXAMPLE:** This is not a time for indecision or hesitation. This is a time for commitment and action. Tell your federal, state, and local governments that you demand a coordinated response plan for natural disasters.
A suggestion	**EXAMPLE:** Your best friend is the one who will tell you a hard truth for your own good.
A warning about consequences	**EXAMPLE:** If instruments used for ear and body piercing are not properly cleaned and sterilized between clients, then you could contract HIV, hepatitis B, or hepatitis C.

Types of Conclusions (continued)	
A vivid image	**EXAMPLE:** Down the mountain we shall go and down the passes, and as the valleys open the world will open, Utopia, where men and women are happy and laws are wise, and where all that is tangled and confused in human affairs has been unravelled and made right. —H. G. Wells' "A Modern Utopia," Chapman and Hall, 1905.
A summary	**EXAMPLE:** Therefore, it is especially important to wash your hands before, during, and after you prepare food, before you eat, after you use the bathroom, after handling animals or animal waste, when your hands are dirty, and more frequently when someone in your home is sick. —National Center for Infectious Diseases, "Wash Your Hands Often," Prevention and Control, General Public, Centers for Disease Control and Prevention, U.S. Department of Health & Human Services.

Practice 4

COMPOSE EFFECTIVE CONCLUSIONS

Read the following four conclusions. Identify the type of conclusion for each selection. Discuss your answers with your class or in a small group of peers.

a. A question
b. A quotation
c. A call to action
d. A suggestion
e. A warning about consequences
f. A vivid image
g. A summary

.... **1.** Fellow citizens, we will meet violence with patient justice—assured of the rightness of our cause and confident of the victories to come.
—President George W. Bush, "Address to a Joint Session of Congress and the American People, 2001."

.... **2.** The crew of the space shuttle Challenger honored us by the manner in which they lived their lives. We will never forget them, nor the last time we saw them, this morning, as they prepared for their journey and waved goodbye and "slipped the surly bonds of earth" to "touch the face of God."
—President Ronald Reagan, Eulogy for the Challenger Astronauts, 1986.

.... **3.** The measure of a student's achievement is not in the grade from a teacher, too often these days a symbol of high inflation and low value, but in the wisdom gained from learning. Daniel Pederson stated it best in *Newsweek*, March 3, 1997: "When *A* stands for average, do grades mean anything at all?"

.... **4.** Our life on earth has already reaped many benefits from past and current space exploration. The establishment of a human colony on the moon would further enhance the quality of life on this planet. Products designed for independent life on the moon will someday become part of everyday life on Earth, advancing research in robotics, communications, medicine, computer technologies, food and nutrition, clothing, environmental and architectural design, rocketry, fuel and energy, building materials, and agriculture. We should shoot for the moon!

Academic Learning Log: Chapter Review

CHAPTER REVIEW: EFFECTIVE TITLES, INTRODUCTIONS, AND CONCLUSIONS

Complete the chart by filling in the blanks with information from the chapter:

Types of Titles

- The Question Title
- The Descriptive Title
- _____
- The General-Specific Title

The Patterns of Organization Title:

_____

- Description
- Narration
- Process
- Example/Illustration
- Classification
- Comparison/Contrast
- Definition
- Cause/Effect
- Persuasion

Types of Introductions

- An interesting illustration or anecdote
- A surprising fact or statement
- A direct quotation
- A definition
- A contradiction or opposing view
- _____
- _____

Types of Conclusions

- A question
- _____
- _____
- A suggestion
- A warning about consequences
- A vivid image
- A summary

1. How will I use what I have learned about titles, introductions, and conclusions?

   _____
   _____

2. What do I still need to study about titles, introductions, and conclusions?

   _____
   _____

MyWritingLab™
Complete the Post-test for Chapter 14 in MyWritingLab.

15 Using Patterns of Organization to Develop Essays

LEARNING OUTCOMES

After studying this chapter you will be able to:

- **L1** Answer the question "What's the Point of Using Patterns of Organization to Develop Essays?"
- **L2** Develop Your Point in a Descriptive Essay
- **L3** Develop Your Point in a Narrative Essay
- **L4** Develop Your Point in a Process Essay
- **L5** Develop Your Point in an Illustration Essay
- **L6** Develop Your Point in a Classification Essay
- **L7** Develop Your Point in a Comparison and Contrast Essay
- **L8** Develop Your Point in a Definition Essay
- **L9** Develop Your Point in a Cause and Effect Essay
- **L10** Develop Your Point in a Persuasive Essay
- **L11** Develop Your Point in an Essay That Combines Patterns

Patterns of organization help arrange, present, and develop ideas into an essay.

We use patterns of organization to clearly arrange and present thoughts and ideas as we engage in academic, business, and everyday life. Students who go to RateMyProfessor.com are looking for certain traits in and ratings about a teacher and may compare these qualities with those of another teacher. Factory owners must think about the effects of commonly used chemicals in the manufacturing process and train their employees on safety procedures. To make a particular dish or dessert, cooks must closely follow a recipe's steps and instructions and do those steps in order. Similarly, many writers use patterns of organization to develop their ideas into an essay.

What's the Point of Using Patterns of Organization to Develop Essays?

PHOTOGRAPHIC ORGANIZER: USING PATTERNS OF ORGANIZATION IN ESSAYS

Study the following series of pictures. First, answer the questions below each of the photographs to identify the major details that could be used in an essay about the topic.

DESCRIPTION: _Places to Skateboard_   TOPIC: _Skateboarding_

FIRST PLACE   SECOND PLACE   THIRD PLACE

What's the point of the description?

Now that you have used a pattern of organization to brainstorm about a topic, think about how patterns of organization can help you write an essay. Answer the question:

What's the point of learning about using patterns of organization to write an essay?

My First Thoughts: A Prewriting Activity

Set a time limit, such as five minutes, and jot down in your notebook your thoughts about using patterns of organization. In addition to the examples mentioned above, what are some other situations that require thinking about time sequences, comparisons, contrasts, definitions, or persuasive ideas?

One Student Writer's Response

THE WRITER'S JOURNAL

Read the following student journal entry that records the writer's thoughts about using patterns of organization to develop an essay.

> *Earlier we learned how patterns of organization help us write paragraphs. So I can see how patterns of organization will help us write essays, too. For example, I could write three paragraphs describing the different places to skateboard. The pictures also made me think of other ways to talk about skateboarding, like the types of skateboards, or how to do certain skateboard tricks. So I get how a pattern of organization helps you see a topic in different ways.*

L2 Develop Your Point in a Descriptive Essay

The ability to describe people, places, or things accurately is a useful life skill.

In your personal life, you may need to file a police report or insurance claim about the damage, loss, or theft of your property. You must be able to describe the damaged, lost, or stolen goods.

In your college life, you will rely upon description in many content courses. For example, you may need to describe a natural environment for a science class or a piece of artwork for a humanities class.

In your working life, you may need to describe the physical specifications of office equipment.

To write a **descriptive essay**, a writer describes a person, place, or object based on its location or the way it is arranged in space. Spatial order describes an arrangement of details from top to bottom, from bottom to top, from right to left, from left to right, from near to far, from far to near, from inside out, or outside to inside. The writer also relies upon sensory details such as sight, sound, smell, taste, and touch to create vivid mental images so that the reader can see what is being described. Descriptive transition words signal that the details follow a logical order based on two elements:

1. How the person, place, or object is arranged in space.

2. The starting point from which the writer chooses to begin the description.

For information on writing a descriptive paragraph, see pages 68–85.

Transition Words Used to Signal Description

above	at the side	beneath	close to	here	nearby	there
across	at the top	beside	down	in	next to	under
adjacent	back	beyond	far away	inside	outside	underneath
around	behind	by	farther	left	right	within
at the bottom	below	center	front	middle		

One Student Writer's Response

Read the following descriptive essay written by student Allyson Melton for an English class. Then, read the essay a second time. Finally, complete the activities and answer the questions that follow.

The Brilliance of Nature

1 (1) Too often, the brilliance of nature goes unnoticed. (2) This became very apparent to me, early one morning, on my way to work. (3) As I merged with the flock of procrastinating people, late as usual, I sped along, aware of the neon yellow dashes on the road flashing by as I sped along. (4) The flock of us grudgingly slowed to a stop as we approached a red light. (5) While waiting impatiently for the signal to go green, I diverted my eyes from the glare of the traffic light. (6) The sights and sounds around me revealed a vision of color and movement.

2 (7) The view to my left filled my vision with color and movement. (8) The road was lined with trees, each one proudly standing tall. (9) Dressed in their brightly colored costumes of jade, olive, emerald, and lime, they stood against the heavens as a magnificent tribute to the earth. (10) Their brown trunks, solid and strong-willed, stood unwaveringly in the face of time. (11) A skirt of green grass encircled the weathered tree roots. (12) To my right, a gleaming shopping center towered above the people who milled around its base. (13) Shoppers constantly lined in and out of the mall doors; they reminded me of ants carrying grains of sand or tiny crumbs to and from their anthill. (14) The light gray sidewalk provided a path mostly for bicyclists, spinning their wheels in an effort to gain ground, and joggers, bobbing along with the iPod ear buds plugged in like drooping antennae.

3 (15) The view ahead wavered in a vapor of exhaust fumes and noise. (16) The road, packed with cars of all colors and shapes, stretched before me. (17) Everything from the small, bright red sports car to the gigantic, black Hummer had come to a stop on this stretch of asphalt. (18) I rolled my window down to feel the cool morning air only to be greeted by honking horns and obnoxious music from nearby cars. (19) The bass from the music of the car beside me was so loud I could feel the boom, boom, boom move through my frame and land at the top of my head with an extra "boom" for emphasis. (20) Before quickly rolling my window up again, I caught a whiff of the sharp smell of exhaust fumes.

4 (21) The red light still burned brightly, so I ventured a quick look up at the sky and couldn't look away. (22) It contained every hue imaginable, moving from pink to purple, blue to gray, and orange to yellow. (23) The newly risen sun, so yellow it was nearly white, shimmered in the mist of the new day. (24) Golden sun rays sprayed a flock of birds with a splendid display of light and shadow. (25) Their wings had hypnotic powers in their rhythmic beatings. (26) Hundreds, even thousands formed a fluid ribbon of birds, winding through the topaz sky in a graceful stream, never fraying from its curve. (27) Though I couldn't see even one bird up close, I could imagine their feathers blowing in the cool morning air as they swept through the sky. (28) As I watched, the stream continued to speed across the sky without hesitation, as if they all knew exactly where they were going. (29) When I finally broke my gaze, I looked around again.

5 (30) The people in their cars around me were still staring fixatedly forward at that commanding red light while the glory of nature flew over their heads. (31) As the birds continued to flow across the heavens, the light switched to green. (32) As much as I wanted to linger and watch them, I had to move forward again.

Practice 2

READ AND EVALUATE THE ESSAY

Complete the activities below after you have read the essay a second time.

1. What kind of title does the writer use? _____

2. What type of introduction does the writer use? _____

_____

3. Double underline the thesis statement.

4. For each of the body paragraphs, underline the topic sentence. Circle the descriptive transition words. List two major details for each paragraph below.

Major Details (Paragraph 2): _____

_____

_____

Major Details (Paragraph 3): _____

_____

_____

Major Details (Paragraph 4): _____

_____

_____

5. What type of conclusion does the writer use? _____

6. What is the purpose of the essay? Explain your answer. _____

_____

_____

7. Who is the audience for the essay? Explain your answer. _____

_____

_____

8. What did you like best about the essay? Why? _____

_____

_____

_____

9. What about the essay could be improved? _____

_____

_____

Writing Assignments for a Descriptive Essay

MyWritingLab™ Complete this Exercise on mywritinglab.com

Plan and illustrate your essay with one or more photographs of your own choosing. Write caption(s) for the photograph(s) that reflect your point(s).

Considering Audience and Purpose

Assume you are a witness or victim of an ATM robbery, and authorities have asked you to write a description of the two thieves and the getaway car. Your description will be included in the official police report, will be used by a sketch artist to create a picture of the thieves and their car, and may be distributed to the media to alert the public.

Writing for Everyday Life

Most of us have a favorite spot or place to which we return or that we reminisce about with fondness. Describe your favorite place or the favorite spot of someone you know. Write an essay that describes the site's special qualities for the regional newspaper of this favorite location.

Writing for College Life

Assume you are writing an essay about popular culture for a sociology class. Describe a person or object that represents an aspect of pop culture: a film actor; the costume or instrument of a singing artist; a cartoon character.

Writing for Working Life

Assume you work for a travel agency, and your clients—parents with three children ranging in ages from 3 to 15—ask you for advice about where to go for a one-week vacation. The family has expressed an interest in going someplace that offers natural beauty and outdoor activities. Write a letter to the parents describing the destination you recommend for their vacation.

Additional Descriptive Topics

A scene that provokes strong emotions   A person of interest
A vandalized or dilapidated neighborhood   An exotic animal and its habitat
Ideal gifts for a loved one   The scene after violent weather

L3 Develop Your Point in a Narrative Essay

Narration is a fundamental part of everyday life.

> For information on writing a narrative paragraph, see pages 86–99.

- In your personal life, you may wish to share an important moment or event you experienced with a friend or family member in a letter or e-mail.

- In your college life, you will study biographies and write essays about important figures in subjects such as history, science, and the arts. You will also study and narrate significant events that have occurred in various fields of study, such as wars in history or case studies in psychology.

- In your working life, you may need to narrate an individual or departmental accomplishment in a report, memo, or letter.

In a **narrative essay,** a writer recounts a series of events or actions that occurred during a specific period of time. The writer presents an event and then shows when each of the additional events occurred in relation to it. Thus, narrative details follow a logical order based on time or chronological order. The following transition words establish the flow of ideas or coherence of a narration essay by signaling when actions or events occurred and in what order.

Transition Words Used to Signal Narration

after	currently	first	next	second	ultimately
afterward	during	last	now	since	until
as	eventually	later	often	soon	when
before	finally	meanwhile	previously	then	while

One Student Writer's Response

Read the following narrative essay written by student Daniela Martine. Then, read the essay a second time. Finally, complete the activities and answer the questions that follow.

The Pure, Driving Force of Nature

1 (1) Thump, thump, thump was the only sound we heard as we pulled the economy rental car onto the shoulder of the road. (2) We had somehow managed to get a flat tire. (3) Having been prepared, this caused only a minor setback in our vacation. (4) My boyfriend, John, and I silently cursed ourselves for being too cheap to purchase the upgraded rental model, the one for an additional hundred dollars. (5) We were somewhere in the dried pampas of Argentina. (6) But it didn't matter. (7) We were about to be reminded about the special joy of travel.

2 (8) John arched his back and drew a deep breath, seeming to inhale the moisture from the clouds. (9) They seemed close enough to reach out our hands and touch them. (10) Dried grass and gravel crunched under John's shoes as he walked to the rear of the rental to retrieve the jack, the spare, and the tools necessary to change a tire. (11) He refused my assistance. (12) He just wanted me to look pretty in my bright, long, flowing skirt we purchased from an artisan in Llao Llao the previous day. (13) He's a great traveling companion.

3 (14) "This must be why they call it the Switzerland of South America," said John, who had a deep, solid resonance in his voice that went down like honey. (15) He was referring to the snow-capped mountains lining the horizon. (16) "It's hard to believe this place has *the most happening ski scene come July,*" John quoted the resort's brochure.

4 (17) "I know," I replied, "It's hard to imagine this kind of beauty." (18) Llao Llao is Mapuche Indian, the region's native folk language, and means "*sweet sweet*." (19) After witnessing the "lush ancient forests" and the "pure glacial lakes," it is not hard to understand, exactly, how suitable "*sweet sweet*" really is.

5 (20) The sky was an intense blue backdrop for the clouds rolling low over the horizon, casting shadows as they continued their journey to the mountains. (21) Avenida Bustillo is the 19-mile path that cuts through the tundra between Llao Llao and Bariloche.

6 (22) It was also, where we found ourselves stranded in the middle of nowhere with a flat tire. (23) Technically, we were not stranded. (24) Heaven was, literally, within hand's reach. (25) I stretched out my fingers to brush a strand of John's hair from his sweaty forehead. (26) The sheen of sweat on his arms reflected the afternoon sun perfectly. (27) Each droplet shimmered in the sun's rays. (28) His muscles flexed as he spun the wrench a few, final times. (29) Then he looked up and around. (30) I could see that look in his eyes. (31) He likes to take time to allow his memory to absorb all aspects of nature.

7 (32) I believed John when he said we would make it safely to Bariloche, where we had reservations for a unique, eco-spa experience. (33) I was always a sucker for his voice. (34) He could say anything he wanted, and he usually did. (35) It was his idea to take this vacation in Argentina. (36) His destinations have been fantastic in the past. (37) I thought no place could beat Costa Rica in its immaculate splendor and utter beauty. (38) Not only what we saw , but the smells and tastes we experienced as well, like the beans and rice we had for breakfast or the pineapple we bought at a roadside stand. (39) But this adventure promised to exceed them all. (40) After John finished changing the tire, we took a moment to enjoy the view of lush grasslands rolling towards pristine blue water that melded into the sapphire sky outlined by a horizon of snow-capped mountains. (41) We felt only elated and clean. (42) A flat tire forced us to step away from ourselves and our schedule for a few moments and come face to face with the pure, driving force of nature, giving us a better understanding of who and what we are. (43) We should all take the opportunity to travel as a way of revisiting our planet and ourselves.

READ AND EVALUATE THE ESSAY

Complete the activities below after you have read the essay a second time.

1. What kind of title does the writer use? _____

2. What type of introduction does the writer use? _____

_____

3. Double underline the thesis statement.

4. For each of the body paragraphs, underline the topic sentence. Circle the narrative transition words. List two major details for each paragraph below.

Major Details (Paragraph 2): _____

_____

Major Details (Paragraphs 3–5): _____

_____

Major Details (Paragraph 7): _____

_____

5. What type of conclusion does the writer use? _____

6. What is the purpose of the essay? Explain your answer. _____

_____

7. Who is the audience for the essay? Explain your answer. _____

_____

8. What did you like best about the essay? Why? _____

_____

_____

9. What about the essay could be improved? _____

_____

Writing Assignments for a Narrative Essay

MyWritingLab™ Complete this Exercise on mywritinglab.com

Plan and illustrate your essay with one or more photographs of your own choosing. Write caption(s) for the photograph(s) that reflect your point(s).

Considering Audience and Purpose
Assume you have been asked to speak to a group of teenagers about peer influences on their development. You have decided to use a personal childhood experience to develop your ideas. Your purpose is to explain how one childhood experience with a peer influenced you.

Writing for Everyday Life
Most of us, like the writer of "The Pure, Driving Force of Nature," have a vivid memory of a place we have visited that holds a special memory or reveals a personal value. What does a vivid memory from your life reveal about you, your family, or someone you know? Recount a vivid memory in an essay that you intend to publish in a newsletter for family members or friends who live far away.

Writing for College Life
Narrate an important event such as the terrorist attack on 9/11, the swearing in of the President of the United States, the launching of a space telescope, the civil rights march on Washington and Dr. Martin Luther King, Jr.'s "I Have a Dream" speech, as though you had witnessed it. Write a report for your college history class about the event as you saw it unfold.

Writing for Working Life
Assume you are applying for a management job with a retail store such as Apple, Macy's, or H&M. What life and work experiences can you relate that show your ability to listen, solve problems, manage merchandise, and motivate others? Write an essay sharing an incident or series of events that show you are the best candidate for the job.

Additional Narrative Topics

A clash with authority	An ideal day or a horrible day
An important lesson learned	The story behind a celebrity's rise to fame
A life-changing experience	The time you met someone important to you

L4 Develop Your Point in a Process Essay

The ability to clearly communicate the steps in a process is a basic skill necessary for success in all areas of life.

- In your personal life, you may want to share advice with a friend or relative about how to reduce stress or how to handle a job interview.

- In your college life, many academic disciplines, such as biology, sociology, and psychology, rely on process. For example, you may be required to record the process you used in a science lab activity, or you may choose to write a research paper on the stages of grief for a psychology class.

- In your working life, you may need to write a marketing plan, an action plan, or a company procedure.

A **process essay** shows actions that can be repeated at any time, with similar results. Like narration, a process essay is organized by time order (also called chronological order). A writer uses the process pattern of organization for three reasons:

1. To give steps, directions, or procedures for completing a task.
2. To analyze or study the steps, cycles, or phases of a process.
3. To explain how to complete a task and to analyze the process.

The following transition words establish the flow of ideas or coherence of a process essay.

> For information on writing a process paragraph, see pages 100–115.

Transition Words Used to Signal a Process

after	during	later	previously	ultimately
afterward	eventually	meanwhile	second	until
as	finally	next	since	when
before	first	now	soon	while
currently	last	often	then	

One Student Writer's Response

Read the following process essay written by student Allyson Melton. Then, read the essay a second time. Finally, complete the activities and answer the questions that follow.

How I Write and Learn

1   (1) Everyone has different ways of using the writing process and learning. (2) Understanding the way I write and how I learn has not been easy. (3) It has taken an in-depth exploration of my work and abilities. (4) This semester, I analyzed my writing and study methods and created a plan to help me improve in these two areas. (5) As a result, my writing and study process have improved.

2   (6) First, I carefully looked at the feedback I got on all my essays. (7) When I got feedback on my first few essays, I saw areas that needed work. (8) Parts of my writing process needed to change. (9) For one, my use of the writing process was not very well developed. (10) For example, my prewriting stage didn't exist or consisted of taking a few short, random notes on lined paper. (11) Usually, I jumped right to the drafting stage on the computer to make revisions easier. (12) I tried to think of details in order and find the right words as I went along. (13) Because I was trying to think of what to say and how to say it, this phase took me a long time. (14) It was a real struggle. (15) When I finally felt my draft was finished, I went back over it, made corrections, and printed it to turn it in.

3	(16) After learning about the four phases of the writing process, I made a plan that used the full writing process. (17) First, my prewriting phase became more in depth. (18) When I chose my topic, I also thought about my audience and what they might like to know or need to know about a topic. (19) I decided to list more details and create an outline or concept map to follow before moving on to the drafting phase. (20) Then the next step, writing the rough draft, was quicker and easier. (21) I stopped spending so much time trying to fix every little thing as I went along. (22) I waited to fix those things when I revised and proofread. (23) Third, I planned more time for the revising phase. (24) After printing a copy of my rough draft, I read it carefully, rearranged details, looked for omitted details, and made better word choices. (25) In addition, I asked members of my family to read it and give me feedback. (26) I made notes on the paper and returned to the computer to revise. (27) Then, I reread my paper to make sure the changes didn't cause any new problems. (28) If they did, I corrected them. (29) Finally, I made a plan for the proofreading phase. (30) I focused on the grammar rules that were on-going problems. (31) To help me with this last phase, I made a checklist of things to look for. (32) Finally, I returned to the computer one last time to make corrections and print my finished paper.

4	(33) I changed some of the ways I listen and study. (34) My study process is very simple. (35) During class, which I attend regularly, I do my best to listen to the professor. (36) As she talks, I take notes. (37) But I often miss points while I'm writing. (38) To fix this, I planned to take shorter notes during class. (39) I learned to write down just the key ideas. (40) Then after class I recalled and added details. (41) When out of class, my study process included doing all the required reading and taking notes. (42) My notes were useful but were not always enough to help me to really learn. (43) Therefore, I set aside time to review the reading more than once to make sure I understood the concepts and rules. (44) Reviewing my tests helped me see my strengths and weaknesses. (45) The grammar test showed my problems with run-ons, dangling modifiers, capitalization, subject/verb agreement, and lay/lie usage.

5	(46) I created the following plan of action to improve my grammar skills (with deadlines in parentheses). (47) For each skill, I also completed MyWritingLab lessons by the deadlines:

- Run-on sentences—study Ch. 22, pages 420–437. Do practices 1–9. (2/6/16)
- Dangling modifiers—study Ch. 24, pages 458–467. Do practices 1–5. (2/20/16)
- Capitalization—study Ch. 34, pages 590–597. Do practices 1–5. (3/5/16)

- Subject/verb agreement—study Ch. 25. Do practices 1–16. (3/19/16)
- Lay/lie usage—Do lessons on MyWritingLab (4/2/16)

6   (48) By improving my use of the writing process, my study techniques, and my knowledge of grammar I have become a better writer and a better student in general, which will help me greatly in my future efforts, whatever they may be.

READ AND EVALUATE THE ESSAY

Complete the activities below after you have read the essay a second time.

1. What kind of title does the writer use? _____

2. What type of introduction does the writer use? _____

3. Double underline the thesis statement.

4. For each of the body paragraphs, underline the topic sentence. Circle the process transition words. List two major details for each paragraph below.

Major Details (Paragraph 2): _____

Major Details (Paragraph 3): _____

Major Details (Paragraph 4): _____

Major Details (Paragraph 5): _____

_____

5. What type of conclusion does the writer use? _____

6. What is the purpose of the essay? Explain your answer. _____

7. Who is the audience for the essay? Explain your answer. _____

8. What did you like best about the essay? Why? _____

9. What about the essay could be improved? _____

Writing Assignments for a Process Essay

MyWritingLab™
Complete this Exercise on mywritinglab.com

Plan and illustrate your essay with one or more photographs of your own choosing. Write caption(s) for the photograph(s) that reflect your point(s).

Considering Audience and Purpose

Assume you are a student-worker in the admissions and registration office at your college. You have been asked to create a brochure for students that illustrates and explains the registration process from a student's point of view. Write several paragraphs that take students through the registration process. Consider creating a brochure based on what you write.

Writing for Everyday Life

At some point in our lives, all of us suffer the loss of a loved one or a valued object. Tell how you or someone you know coped with such a loss. Write a letter to a friend in which you share the steps you or someone you know took to overcome the grief of loss.

Writing for College Life

Assume you are enrolled in the college class Introduction to Psychology, and your professor has assigned a chapter about stress. Your professor wants to be aware of what you already know about stress before you read the chapter. Write an essay that explains several steps one can take to reduce stress.

Writing for Working Life

Assume that you are on a committee at work that is looking into ways in which employees can better manage their time and increase productivity. What recommendations would you make for employees whose tasks include phone calling, e-mailing, writing reports, filing paperwork, and attending meetings? Interview a staff assistant (such as in the English, science, or some other department at your college) for timesaving tips on the job. Write a report in which you outline several timesaving steps. Insert the appropriate information into the following MLA citation format to document your source:

```
Last Name of Person Interviewed, First Name of Person Interviewed.
    Personal Interview. Day Month Year.
```

Additional Process Topics

How to win an argument

How to get a promotion or recommendation

How to develop a friendship

How to save money or shop smart

How to make a piece of art, such as a print, a woodcut, or an etching

How to set up a program or piece of technology (such as a cell phone, e-mail, website, or blog)

Develop Your Point in an Illustration Essay

Illustration may be the pattern of organization that you will use most often.

- In your personal life, think about how you often rely on examples and illustrations to make your point, such as when you recommend a restaurant or movie to a friend.
- In your college life, illustrations and examples effectively clarify a main point in all areas of study. For example, for a history class, you may choose to explain the contributions Frederick Douglass made to the civil rights of African Americans by offering several examples or illustrations.
- In your working life, examples and illustrations help you prove that you or an employee under your supervision deserve a raise.

In the illustration essay, a writer offers a focused main idea about a particular topic and then presents a series of examples or illustrations to clarify or support the main idea. Example words signal that a writer is giving an instance of a general idea.

> For information on writing an example paragraph, see pages 116–131.

Transition Words Used to Signal Examples and Illustration

| an illustration | for instance | once | to illustrate |
| for example | including | such as | typically |

One Student Writer's Response

Read the following example and illustration essay written by student Beth Zivistski for an English class. Then, read the essay a second time. Finally, complete the activities and answer the questions that follow.

Fads: POG-Mania

1 (1) In all areas of life, our society is constantly swept up in the latest craze, and with the rise of every new fad comes the depressing downfall of the former fad. (2) Fads make their way into the world as fast as they are shut out. (3) A fad arises out of a particular culture, becomes intensely popular for a brief time, and then loses popularity suddenly and dramatically. (4) Ironically, fad-mania blindly leads to the retirement of great ideas, such as the fabulous milk cap game now known as POGs.

2 (5) Milk cap games were an excellent example of a fad that arose out of a particular culture. (6) Milk cap games originated when milk and juice were sold in glass bottles rather than the current disposable containers. (7) This fad-game first got its name from a brand of a tropical fruit drink made up of passion fruit, orange, and guava juice called POG. (8) Kids collected the round wax coated cardboard disks that sealed the

bottles and invented simple games that everyone could play. (9) Nearly every household, rich or poor, had access to milk caps, which made the game very inclusive. (10) Children enjoyed this popular form of entertainment until the establishment of screw-on lids and disposable containers virtually put an end to milk caps and these engaging games.

3 (11) Most fads, such as milk games, began as a simple, fun idea. (12) For example, the standard rules for POG playing were simple. (13) Two or more players placed an equal number of POGs into a common stack. (14) The milk caps would be piled artwork side up on a level surface. (15) To determine who would go first, players flipped a POG or played Ro-Sham-Bo (Paper, Scissors, Rock). (16) The first player threw his or her "kini" or slammer, an object used to hit the stack of POGs. (17) Usually a slammer was bigger, thicker, and heavier than a POG, often made of plastic or different types of metal. (18) All of the milk caps that landed face down went to that player. (19) The milk caps left over were restacked for the next player's turn. (20) The players exchanged turns until every milk cap had been won, and the player with the most milk caps was the winner. (21) Like all fads, the POG craze started simply, in this instance, with children using the milk caps for inexpensive fun.

4 (22) POGs were also an illustration of the intense popularity to which a fad could rise. (23) As the fad grew in popularity, companies flooded the market with POG products. (24) In the early 1990s, a number of companies started their own series of game pieces to compete in the new craze. (25) For example, the company Tilt, Poison, and Kapz offered POGs decorated with skulls, crossbones, and eight balls. (26) Even fast food restaurants illustrated POG mania as they latched onto the new fad and included POGs in their kid's meals. (27) POGs were not just a source of entertainment through game play. (28) They became available in sets of original artwork, sports and team logos, or even pictures of the latest Saturday morning cartoons. (29) Purchasing POGs became an obsession. (30) For example, people began collecting POGs, and some felt the need to own every single POG in a series. (31) These factors made POGs collectable as well as tradable. (32) The popularity of POGs was also evident in its international following, as illustrated by the World Pog Federation (WPF), created by players who loved POGs so much that they wanted an official body to direct the craze. (33) The WPF created its own official brand that was printed with the POG logo on the back. (34) The front artwork carried a variety of designs including cartoons, POG history, and POG incentives.

5   (35) POGs also illustrated the criticism and blame most fads face for fostering undesirable consequences and behaviors. (36) For example, many criticized POGs for fostering overspending. (37) When so many companies offered such a wide range of POG series available for purchase, expenses for a POG devotee quickly mounted up. (38) Children used their allowances to buy POGs; adults spent exorbitant amounts of money ensuring they had complete sets of brand name POGs for sports teams, athletes, or other popular cultural icons. (39) Another example of the criticism against POGs was the belief that the game was a form of gambling. (40) People would play for keeps in the hopes of enlarging their POG holdings. (41) Oftentimes, players would lose their own POGs in the process; then they would have to purchase more. (42) Many critics opposed POGs as an illustration of the antisocial behaviors that a fad can generate. (43) For example, fights sometimes broke out over POGs. (44) This game, for some children, was much more than entertainment; therefore, if these children lost a certain favored POG, they would react as children often do with tears, insults or even fists. (45) POGs, and especially slammers, were often stolen. (46) In addition, many educators complained that POG playing served as a distraction to school work. (47) Eventually, these negative aspects led to the banning of POGs by many public schools in North America.

6   (48) Like all fads, POGs decreased suddenly and dramatically in popularity. (49) Today, instead of lining the shelves in major retail markets, POGs may possibly be found on eBay or in specialty game and card shops. (50) Like fads, POG playing rose out of its culture, began as a way to have fun, reached intense heights of popularity, garnered criticism, and then faded away as just another one of those crazy trends that swept across the nation and over international borders. (51) Even so, POG playing is still fondly remembered by those who still love them to this day. (52) POGs illustrate the irony of fad-mania: the short-lived devotion to a really good idea.

Practice 5

READ AND EVALUATE THE ESSAY

Complete the activities below after you have read the essay a second time.

1. What kind of title does the writer use? _____

2. What type of introduction does the writer use? _____

3. Double underline the thesis statement.

4. For each of the body paragraphs, underline the topic sentence. Circle the example or illustration transition words. List two major details for each paragraph below.

Major Details (Paragraph 2): _____

_____

Major Details (Paragraph 3): _____

_____

Major Details (Paragraph 4): _____

Major Details (Paragraph 5): _____

_____

5. What type of conclusion does the writer use? _____

6. What is the purpose of the essay? Explain your answer. _____

_____

7. Who is the audience for the essay? Explain your answer. _____

_____

8. What did you like best about the essay? Why? _____

_____

_____

9. What about the essay could be improved? _____

_____

Writing Assignments for an Illustration Essay

MyWritingLab™
Complete this Exercise on mywritinglab.com

Plan and illustrate your essay with one or more photographs of your own choosing. Write caption(s) for the photograph(s) that reflect your point(s).

Considering Audience and Purpose

Assume you serve as a member of the Parent-Student-Teacher Association (PSTA), and you have been asked to write a report to be submitted to the principal. The purpose of the report is to explain the improvements your group wants to be funded. Identify and illustrate the need for three improvements at the school.

Writing for Everyday Life

Think about the creativity and cleverness of the human mind as seen through various inventions. Which invention best represents human achievement in our generation? Write an essay for your local newspaper that illustrates the most helpful invention of our time.

Writing for College Life

Think about the importance of integrity, reliability, or candor in our culture. What three people in the news illustrate these concepts? Write an essay for a college course in ethics that gives three illustrations of people who epitomize integrity, reliability, or candor.

Writing for Working Life

Assume that you are a local businessperson and you have been asked to share with a youth group your thoughts on the value of an education. What examples or illustrations would you choose to convince students to make education a top priority? What knowledge or skills did you gain through your education that helped you succeed in your business? Write a speech to be given to the youth and their parents in which you illustrate the importance of an education.

Additional Illustration Topics

Lack of morality on television

A healthful diet or an outlandish diet

The best or worst commercials

Good gifts that don't cost much money

Annoying or dangerous driving behaviors

Acts of kindness

L6 Develop Your Point in a Classification Essay

Classification allows you to order or group your thoughts based on traits of a category.

- In your personal life, you may want to warn a young person in your family or social group about types of peer pressure or dangerous behaviors to avoid.
- In your college life, you will use classification in the sciences to write about classes of species or habitats; in the humanities, to write about styles of artists, artistic movements, modes of architecture, literature, and branches of philosophies; in business and history classes, to write about different kinds of economic systems and governments.
- In your working life, you may need to write reports that identify types of markets for your products, job descriptions based on the nature of the position you need to fill, or a cover letter that describes the set of skills you bring to the workplace.

> For information on writing a classification paragraph, see pages 132–147.

Writers use the **classification essay** to sort or divide ideas into smaller groups and then describe the common traits of each subgroup. The writer lists each subgroup, describes its characteristics, and offers examples that represent the group. Because groups and subgroups are listed, transitions that suggest additional categories are often used to ensure coherence.

Transitions Used to Signal Classification

another (group, kind, type)	first (group, categories, kind, type, order)
characteristics	second (group, class, kind, type, traits)

One Student Writer's Response

Read the following classification essay written by student Josiah Cobb for a music appreciation class. Then, read the essay a second time. Finally, complete the activities and answer the questions that follow.

Types of Guitars

1   (1) When people think of guitars, they most likely think of an oldies band such as the Beatles and their guitars, or an iconic performer like B.B. King and his guitar "Lucille" or, more currently, Mark Tremonti and his signature Paul Reed Smith guitar. (2) However, most people are unaware of the differences among guitars. (3) Not all guitars are alike. (4) True, guitars share fundamental traits: they are stringed instruments with a neck, a flat back, incurving sides, and a flat peg disc with rear tuning pegs. (5) However, apart from these shared traits, a range of guitars from acoustic to electric have evolved that enable musicians to create an array of distinct sounds. (6) Currently, four types of guitars allow musicians to produce a variety of sounds in today's music.

2 (7) The acoustic guitar is a favored instrument used in most types of current music. (8) Bands today rely on the bright sound of the acoustic guitar to fill in the gaps with the guitar's unique, deep, full sound. (9) The acoustic guitar is simply a hollow body that has a neck and a set of thick bronze strings which together produce a bigger sound than the other types of guitars. (10) Because most acoustic guitars are not amplified by an external device, their sound is not loud and often cannot compete with other instruments in a band or orchestra. (11) However, one of the secrets to a good sounding acoustic guitar is the pick-up, which detects the mechanical reverberations of the strings and acts as a microphone. (12) A pick-up is mounted on the body of the guitar close to the strings. (13) The Simon & Garfunkel folk song "Fifty-Ninth Street Bridge" offers an excellent example of the rhythmic, strumming sound created with the acoustic guitar.

▲ Acoustic guitar

3 (14) The classical or nylon guitar is a kind of acoustic guitar designed especially for finger picking, which is the art of plucking the string with the fingers instead of using a pick to strum over the strings. (15) The classical guitar has nylon strings instead of bronze strings, and the body of the classical guitar is larger than the other types of guitars. (16) This design produces a reverberation as if it were in a large room. (17) In addition, the neck of the guitar is broader than the ones on steel string guitars, allowing for more complex finger work. (18) Classical guitars do have acoustic pick-ups in them most of the time. (19) One of the most popular examples of the classical guitar's crisp, nimble tones can be heard in "Classical Gas" by Mason Williams.

▲ Electric guitar

4 (20) A third kind of guitar is the electric guitar. (21) The unique design of the electric guitar makes it a versatile instrument. (22) The body of the electric guitar is solid, small, and can be any shape. (23) Most electric guitars today have two pick-ups. (24) The modern day pick-ups are usually small rectangular pieces of plastic with six small magnets. (25) These pick-ups use the magnets to feel the vibrating string and then transfer the sound through an amplifier so the player can hear the pitch of the strings. (26) Many guitarists love the electric guitar because they can get any sound out of it they want. (27) For instance, by using the neck pick-up, the guitarist can get the really low end sound of a hardcore band, or by using the bridge pick-up, he or she can get the bright high end sound of ska music. (28) The electric guitar also lets the musician mimic the sounds of other types of guitars such as the acoustic, Dobro, or the classical. (29) One illustration of a well-known song performed on the electric guitar is U2's blazing, bone-rattling song "Vertigo."

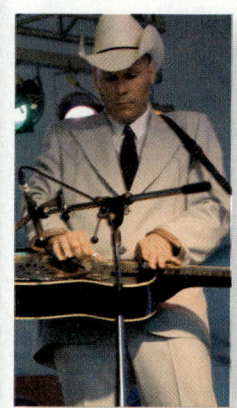

▲ Dobro guitar

5   (30) A fourth type of guitar is the Dobro. (31) Though not many people know about the Dobro or think of it as a guitar, it is one of the hardest forms of guitar to learn. (32) The Dobro is an instrument that is very small and is placed on a table so the strings are parallel to the ground. (33) The player then takes a guitar pick and plucks the strings as if finger picking but with a pick. (34) In addition, instead of using fingers to produce certain pitches from the guitar, the player uses a slide. (35) A slide is usually either a small piece of wood with metal, or a glass tube into which a finger is inserted. (36) The Dobro uses an electric guitar pick-up, which gives it a country guitar sound. (37) A prime example of the Dobro twang can be heard in the classic country song "An Old Cowboy's Dream" by Don Edwards.

6   (38) Although guitars come in various shapes and styles and produce a wide range of sounds, each one has the same basic idea: a set of strings pulled to a certain tension to combine different pitches and create something that everyone enjoys—music.

Practice 6

READ AND EVALUATE THE ESSAY

Complete the activities below after you have read the essay a second time.

1. What kind of title does the writer use? _____

2. What type of introduction does the writer use? _____

3. Double underline the thesis statement.

4. For each of the body paragraphs, underline the topic sentence. Circle the classification transition words. List two major details for each paragraph below.

Major Details (Paragraph 2): _____

Major Details (Paragraph 3): _____

Major Details (Paragraph 4): _____

_____

_____

_____

Major Details (Paragraph 5): _____

_____

_____

_____

5. What type of conclusion does the writer use? _____

6. What is the purpose of the essay? Explain your answer. _____

_____

_____

7. Who is the audience for the essay? Explain your answer. _____

_____

_____

8. What did you like best about the essay? Why? _____

_____

_____

_____

9. What about the essay could be improved? _____

_____

_____

_____

Writing Assignments for a Classification Essay

MyWritingLab™ Complete this Exercise on mywritinglab.com

Plan and illustrate your essay with one or more photographs of your own choosing. Write caption(s) for the photograph(s) that reflect your point(s).

Considering Audience and Purpose

Assume you are a member of Students Against Destructive Decisions (SADD). The original mission of this group focused on preventing drunk driving. However, SADD has expanded its role to include several types of destructive decisions such as underage drinking, other drug use, violence, depression, and suicide. Many people do not know about this expanded focus. To get the word out about SADD, your local chairperson has asked you to write an essay to accompany short video clips (acted out by other local members) that will be posted on YouTube. Your purpose is to describe the different types of destructive decisions for which SADD offers help.

Writing for Everyday Life

Many of us have an ideal in mind when we think about a person who fulfills a particular role in our lives: a mate, a boss, a teacher, a friend, and so on. What are the traits of any one of these ideals? Write a tribute to a boss, company, friend, teacher, or family member in which you describe the ideal traits of a boss, job, friend, mate, or child.

Writing for College Life

Assume that you are a student in a college music appreciation course, and your class is discussing how types of music reveal cultural values. What types of music best reflect American culture? Write an essay that identifies three or four types of American music. (Feel free to change the term "American" to reflect any culture of your choice.)

Writing for Working Life

Assume you are an employee at a grocery store that has been receiving a record number of complaints such as the following examples: empty shelves, rude or slow cashiers, sticky floors, no one to answer questions, and so on. Write a letter for the employee suggestion box in which you classify typical customer complaints and discuss types of employee attitudes that could reduce complaints.

Additional Classification Topics

Kinds of vacations people take

Types of technology that record or play music

The basic food groups in a balanced diet

The market for a particular product, celebrity, or experience: *Hunger Games* novels, Kanye West, or white water rafting

Styles of personal expression: fashion, hobby, or interior design

Categories of movies, television shows, or books

Develop Your Point in a Comparison and Contrast Essay

Many ideas become clearer when you evaluate them in relation to one another.

- In your personal life, comparing and contrasting products before a purchase makes you a wise shopper.
- In your college life, you will be asked to compare and contrast leaders, governments, cultures, literature, writers, and philosophies in a wide range of subject areas such as history, humanities, English, science, and economics.
- In your working life, you may compare and contrast bids on a job, phone or Internet services for your office, or prospective employees during an interview process.

For information on writing a comparison and contrast paragraph, see pages 148–161.

The **comparison and contrast essay** shows the similarities and differences between or among topics based on comparable points. The following transition words signal comparison and contrast.

Transition Words That Signal Comparison

alike	in a similar fashion	just as	resemble	similarly
as	in a similar way	just like	same	
as well as	in like manner	like	similar	
equally	in the same way	likewise	similarity	

Transition Words That Signal Contrast

although	conversely	differently	nevertheless
as opposed to	despite	even though	on the contrary
at the same time	difference	in contrast	on the one hand
but	different	in spite of	on the other hand
by contrast	different from	instead	still

One Student Writer's Response

Read the following comparison and contrast essay written by student J. R. Hill for an English class. Then, read the essay a second time. Finally, complete the activities and answer the questions that follow.

Reading the Waves

1   (1) Along the edges of Florida's East coast lie miles and miles of inviting blue-green ocean water and alluring sun-bleached beaches to which thousands of bronzed surfers flock on any given day. (2) Each of these beaches varies in its sand composition, reef formations, and surfing conditions. (3) Although the East coast of Florida is made mainly of soft, sandy beaches and a hard ocean bottom, no beach along the Atlantic coast remains the same as the specific conditions change that cause

waves to form and break. (4) Two main surf spots, the Ponce Inlet Jetty and the Sun Glow Pier, only a few miles apart, represent the distinctly different surfing experiences available on Florida's East coast.

2 (5) The first difference between the Ponce Inlet Jetty and the Sun Glow Pier is the shape of the beaches. (6) Many expert surfers looking for a challenge choose the Ponce Inlet Jetty because of its rocky beach formation off which waves form. (7) The Inlet has a long stretch of rocks jutting up from the beach and reaching hundreds of feet out into the ocean, creating a cove. (8) In contrast, the Sun Glow Pier does not have an inlet off which waves can form. (9) Instead this coast stretches out as an unbroken, barrier-free contour of beach, ideal for beginner surfers.

3 (10) The floor of the ocean and thus the depth of the water just off the coast of the Ponce Inlet Jetty and the Sun Glow Pier also differ significantly. (11) On the one hand, because of the protective jetty at Ponce Inlet, the sand on the ocean floor there does not dramatically shift so the depth of the ocean floor near the jetty remains fairly consistent and uniform. (12) On the other hand, since Sun Glow Pier does not have a rock jetty, the sand there constantly shifts and redistributes the depth of the ocean floor near the coast. (13) The few Pier pilings add to the unevenness of the water's depth. (14) Sand gathers around the pilings and leaves holes where sand is swept away between pilings.

4 (15) Not only do the beaches, ocean floor, and water depth differ, but also the formation of waves at the two locations varies greatly. (16) At the Ponce Inlet Jetty, the waves form off the rock jetty and shape into a solid, organized wave. (17) When a wave comes to shore, the jetty pushes it into an A shape, also called an A-frame wave or peak. (18) The A-frame gains size in a matter of seconds to form a clean, structured, and powerful wave. (19) The wave then breaks on the fairly flat or uniform ocean bottom on top of two or three feet of water. (20) Unlike the well-formed, powerful waves of Ponce Inlet, the waves at Sun Glow have no

▼ *Sun Glow Pier beach*

solid objects (such as the rock jetty and the even ocean floor) off which to push. (21) Without solid objects and consistent water depth to help form it, the wave remains in its natural form. (22) In its natural form, the wave breaks in unorganized sections because the uneven depth of the ocean floor does not push the wave to break evenly. (23) The wave may look as if it is crumbling from the top to the bottom.

5   (24) The variations in the waves at these two beaches offer two very different surfing experiences. (25) The duration and flexibility of the surfer's ride differ at each location. (26) The consistent depth of water at the Ponce Inlet Jetty makes the wave break harder and faster, which enables the surfer to gain fast speeds. (27) At these fast speeds, the surfer is able to execute a great number of technical maneuvers. (28) After completing one maneuver, the surfer still has enough wave power to push through into the next maneuver. (29) Many surfers enjoy this long ride with clean conditions, making the Ponce Inlet Jetty a popular surf spot for expert surfers, as well as those who are learning to master more intricate moves. (30) In contrast, due to the uneven bottom and the unorganized, quickly crumbling waves, the waves at the Sun Glow Pier lose a great amount of power. (31) Unlike the longer ride at the Ponce Inlet Jetty, this weaker wave at the Sun Glow Pier leaves the surfer a short amount of time to complete maneuvers. (32) Generally, a surfer can only complete one or two maneuvers, and once a maneuver is completed, the surfer is left to fight for speed to continue on the wave to shore. (33) The wave at the Sun Glow Pier is great for the beginner surfer who needs to learn the basics and understand waves.

6   (34) The Ponce Inlet Jetty and the Sun Glow Pier, though only a few short miles apart, are two entirely different beaches. (35) These two spots are prime examples of the different surfing experiences available to surfers along Florida's East coast. (36) So before surfers grab their boards, they should carefully read their wave!

Ponce Inlet Jetty

Practice 7

READ AND EVALUATE THE ESSAY

Complete the activities below after you have read the essay a second time.

1. What kind of title does the writer use? _____

2. What type of introduction does the writer use? _____

3. Double underline the thesis statement.

4. For each of the body paragraphs, underline the topic sentence. Circle the comparison and contrast transition words. List two major details for each paragraph below.

Major Details (Paragraph 2): _____
_____

Major Details (Paragraph 3): _____
_____

Major Details (Paragraph 4): _____
_____

Major Details (Paragraph 5): _____
_____

5. What type of conclusion does the writer use? _____

6. What is the purpose of the essay? Explain your answer. _____
_____

7. Who is the audience for the essay? Explain your answer. _____
_____

8. What did you like best about the essay? Why? _____
_____

9. What about the essay could be improved? _____
_____

Writing Assignments for a Comparison and Contrast Essay

MyWritingLab™ Complete this Exercise on mywritinglab.com

Plan and illustrate your essay with one or more photographs of your own choosing. Write caption(s) for the photograph(s) that reflect your point(s).

Considering Audience and Purpose

Assume you have just moved from a large city to a small town, and other members of your family or friends are considering making the same move. Write a letter that discusses the differences (or similarities) between living in a particular large city (such as Chicago, New York, or Atlanta) and living in a small town of your choice.

Writing for Everyday Life

Assume you have an account on a social networking website, such as Facebook or LinkedIn, and you compose and post your thoughts on a regular basis. Recently, you have noticed that many of us experience a tremendous change in our circumstances, attitudes, or beliefs. This week you are writing about the specific ways that you or someone you know has changed over time or due to a specific event. Contrast what you or someone you know were like earlier in life with what you or that person are like now.

Writing for College Life

Assume you have been working with two of your peers on a required group project and the two students differed greatly in their performance. What were the differences in their attitudes, work habits, and products? Use the goals stated on a course syllabus as the context for your evaluation of their performances. Write the required report to your teacher in which you contrast your peers' performance.

Writing for Working Life

Assume you are a realtor, and a client of yours is moving into the area from across the country. Your client has asked you to identify a couple of homes in a specific price range. You have found two homes in which your client may be interested. How do the two homes compare in terms of location, price, square footage, and special features? Write a letter to your client that compares and contrasts the two homes.

Additional Comparison and Contrast Topics

Two pieces of music, art, or books

A scene before and after a terrible storm

Comparable products: various e-book readers

Communication habits of men and women

Dating customs of different cultures or generations

Disciplining children as opposed to punishing them

An original and a remade movie, or a book and a movie based on it

L8 Develop Your Point in a Definition Essay

You may encounter definitions most often in academic settings. However, the definition pattern of organization is helpful in all areas of life.

- In your personal life, knowing the definition of "whole grains" and being able to identify examples that fit the definition will protect you against false advertising and enable you to make healthful choices.
- In your college life, you will be expected to know the specialized meanings and examples of many terms in each content area.
- In your working life, you need to understand the terms of your company's insurance policy and examples of what is covered so you can make a claim when needed or offer reasonable coverage to your employees.

For information on writing a definition paragraph, see pages 162–175.

In the **definition essay,** the writer explains the meaning of a new, difficult, or special term or concept. A definition may include traits, comparisons, causes, or effects. In addition, a writer may include an explanation of what the term or concept is *not*. Examples are used to illustrate the various components or elements of the term being defined. The following key words and transition words signal the definition pattern of organization.

Key Words and Transition Words That Signal Definition

Key Words:	are	denotes	is	means
	connotes	indicates	is not	suggests
Transition Words:	also	in addition	one trait	
	another trait	in particular	specifically	
	for example	like	such as	

One Student Writer's Response

Read the following definition essay written by student Rodnique Stókes. Then, read the essay a second time. Finally, complete the activities and answer the questions that follow.

What is Effective Leadership?

1   (1) Dr. Martin Luther King has earned a place in history as one of the most effective leaders of all time. (2) He once said, "I am not interested in power for power's sake, but I'm interested in power that is moral, that is right and that is good." (3) Effective leadership is vital in all walks of life. (4) We need leadership in business, in politics, in education, in religion. (5) We need female leadership, male leadership, Asian leadership, Hispanic leadership, Black leadership. (6) Any and all groups benefit from effective leadership.

(7) Since leadership is so vital, we need a clear understanding of what leadership really means. (8) Any definition of effective leadership rests on understanding the traits one must have to be able to guide, direct, or influence others. (9) Effective leadership is based on the respect and power a person has earned.

2   (10) To clearly define effective leadership, it is helpful to think about examples of poor leadership. (11) Sometimes, poor leadership is just weak or ineffective. (12) For example, a weak boss doesn't recognize problems, search for solutions, or take responsibility for decisions. (13) Poor leadership may also be dangerous and dark. (14) For example, Hitler was a brilliant man. (15) Hitler was skilled at inspiring and directing his followers. (16) Yet his leadership was based on racism and hatred, led to a world war, and caused millions to die horrible deaths. (17) His dark leadership affected the twentieth-century to a degree that few other humans have affected any other time in history. (18) We tend to follow those who behave badly or think wrongly because of our need for simplicity and stability. (19) Even poor leadership can provide a false sense of order and certainty in a disordered and uncertain world.

3   (20) For effective leadership to exist, a foundation of respect must be built in order for that particular person to be given the honor to lead. (21) Black leadership throughout the history of the United States has given us powerful examples of effective leadership. (22) Fredrick Douglass, born a slave, taught himself to read. (23) He wrote his autobiography. (24) He became a free man and an activist for freedom. (25) He influenced many for the good, including President Lincoln. (26) Madame C. J. Walker started her own company. (27) By 1919, The Madame C. J. Walker Manufacturing Company occupied an entire city block in downtown Indianapolis and employed over

▲ Madame C. J. Walker.

▲ Frederick Douglass

▲ Mary McLeod Bethune

▲ Martin Luther King Jr.

3,000 people. (28) In the first half of the twentieth-century, W. E. B. DuBois became an intellectual leader in the United States as a sociologist, historian, civil rights activist, author, and editor. (29) Mary McLeod Bethune, an educator and civil rights activist, started a college for African Americans in Daytona Beach, Florida, which is still in existence today. (30) She also served as an advisor to President Franklin D. Roosevelt. (31) And the leadership of Dr. Martin Luther King, Jr. has reached beyond his lifetime to inspire generations to come.

4   (32) Effective leadership earns respect. (33) But effective leadership also respects the position of power. (34) Effective leadership uses its power to transform the lives of others. (35) Transformational leadership involves the process where leaders develop followers into leaders. (36) Transformational leaders do more with colleagues and followers than set simple rules or guidelines. (37) They behave in ways that result in their being a positive role model, which is the direct opposite of a poor leader.

5   (38) Several tasks, or functions, define leadership. (39) These consist of suggesting new ideas, asking for suggestions, requesting additional information or facts, being friendly, warm and responsive to others. (40) Effective leadership increases the well-being of a group, organization, or community. (41) Effective leadership is respect and trust hard earned and power well used.

READ AND EVALUATE THE ESSAY

Complete the activities below after you have read the essay a second time.

1. What kind of title does the writer use? _____

2. What type of introduction does the writer use? _____

3. Double underline the thesis statement.

4. For each of the body paragraphs, underline the topic sentence. Circle the definition signal words. List two major details for each paragraph below.

Major Details (Paragraph 2): _____
_____

Major Details (Paragraph 3): _____
_____

Major Details (Paragraph 4): _____
_____

Major Details (Paragraph 5): _____
_____

5. What type of conclusion does the writer use? _____

6. What is the purpose of the essay? Explain your answer. _____
_____

7. Who is the audience for the essay? Explain your answer. _____
_____

8. What did you like best about the essay? Why? _____
_____

9. What about the essay could be improved? _____
_____

Writing Assignments for a Definition Essay

MyWritingLab™
Complete this Exercise on mywritinglab.com

Plan and illustrate your essay with one or more photographs of your own choosing. Write caption(s) for the photograph(s) that reflect your point(s).

Considering Audience and Purpose

Assume you are in need of financial aid to continue your education, and you have found several available scholarships from a particular organization such as the following: The Hispanic Scholarship Fund, The United Negro Scholarship Fund, The Organization of Chinese Americans, or the Truman Scholarship. All of these scholarships require essays. Most of these essays ask candidates to define some aspect of themselves. Adapt one of the following topics to the organization of your choice, and write an essay to compete for a scholarship:

1. Define your heritage based on its significance.
2. Define yourself as a leader.
3. Define the kind of contribution you hope to make.

Writing for Everyday Life

Assume a couple in your family or the family of someone you know is going to celebrate their fiftieth anniversary and their union has served as a model of a strong and loving relationship. What would you say has made their partnership so successful? Write the text for a speech you will deliver at their anniversary celebration in which you define *partnership* and honor their life together.

Writing for College Life

Assume that in a college health class you have been studying about the connection between mind and body and how important self-understanding is to a healthful lifestyle. How well do you know yourself? What brings you joy? What is your idea of a fulfilling, purposeful life? What is your mission? How do you want to be remembered? Write an essay that expresses a mission statement for your life in which you define your ideals and goals.

Writing for Working Life

Assume you are starting a small business, such as a restaurant, a fitness club, a toy store, or some kind of specialty shop. To receive financial backing from investors, you have been asked to write a mission statement for your business. Write an essay that defines your small business. What service or commodity are you selling? Who are your potential customers? Why is this service or commodity needed? Where is the best location for your business? How will your product or service be superior to other similar products or services?

Additional Definition Topics

A computer term such as blog, RSS, tweet

A disorder such as insomnia, anorexia, Type 2 Diabetes, or Seasonal Affective Disorder

A natural phenomenon such as a sinkhole, tropical depression, fault line, or coral reef

Develop Your Point in a Cause and Effect Essay

Understanding the relationship between cause and effect is a vital critical thinking skill that enhances all areas of life.

- In your personal life, understanding the cause of a misunderstanding, or recognizing the effect of an over-the-counter or prescription drug can protect your relationships or your health.

- In your college life, you will be asked to analyze the causes and effects of wars, inventions, discoveries, natural disasters, economic recessions, or mental and physical diseases. An analysis of causes and effects deepens your understanding of information in every content area.

- In your working life, to ensure success you need to understand why a product sells, reasons for poor performance, or the effects of decisions on employee morale or the company's budget.

A writer uses the **cause and effect essay** to explore why something happened or what results came from an event. A cause explores the reason something happens, and an effect examines the result or outcome. The following transition words signal cause and effect.

> For information on writing a cause and effect paragraph, see pages 176–189.

Transitions That Signal Cause and Effect

accordingly	because of	due to	leads to	since	therefore
as a result	consequently	if…then	results in	so	thus

One Writer's Response

Read the following cause and effect essay from the National Institute on Alcohol Abuse and Alcoholism. Then, read the essay a second time. Finally, complete the activities and answer the questions that follow.

Alcoholism: Getting the Facts

1   (1) For most people who drink, alcohol is a pleasant accompaniment to social activities. (2) Moderate alcohol use—up to two drinks per day for men and one drink per day for women and older people—is not harmful for most adults. (3) (A standard drink is one 12-ounce bottle or can of either beer or wine cooler, one 5-ounce glass of wine, or 1.5 ounces of 80-proof distilled spirits.) (4) Nonetheless, a large number of people get into serious trouble because of their drinking. (5) Currently, nearly 17.6 million adult Americans abuse alcohol or are alcoholic. (6) Several million more adults engage in risky drinking that could lead to alcohol problems. (7) These patterns include binge drinking and heavy drinking on a regular basis. (8) In addition, 53 percent of men and women in the United States report that one or more of their close relatives has a drinking problem. (9) Due to the scope of this problem, it is important to understand the effects of alcoholism and alcohol abuse, as well as identify their causes.

2 (10) Alcoholism, also known as "alcohol dependence," is a disease with at least four recognizable effects or symptoms. (11) One impact of alcoholic dependence is a strong craving for alcohol. (12) An alcoholic feels a strong need, or compulsion, to drink. (13) Another impact is a loss of control: alcoholics cannot limit their drinking on any given occasion. (14) People who are not alcoholic sometimes do not understand why an alcoholic can't just "use a little willpower" to stop drinking. (15) However, alcoholism has little to do with willpower. (16) Alcoholics are in the grip of a powerful craving that can be as strong as the need for food or water. (17) Third, alcohol dependence eventually results in physical dependence: withdrawal symptoms, such as nausea, sweating, shakiness, and anxiety, occur when an alcoholic stops drinking. (18) Finally, a tolerance for alcohol develops. (19) Thus the need to drink greater amounts of alcohol in order to "get high" occurs.

3 (20) Alcohol abuse differs from alcoholism in that it does not result in an extremely strong craving for alcohol, loss of control over drinking, or physical dependence. (21) Alcohol abuse, a pattern of drinking, leads to one or more of the following four situations within a 12-month period. (22) Alcohol abuse often leads to failure to fulfill major work, school, or home responsibilities. (23) Drinking occurs in situations that are physically dangerous, such as while driving a car or operating machinery. (24) Alcohol-related legal problems are recurring, such as being arrested for driving under the influence of alcohol or for physically hurting someone while drunk. (25) Finally, drinking continues despite ongoing relationship problems that are caused or worsened by the drinking. (26) Although alcohol abuse is basically different from alcoholism, many effects of alcohol abuse are also experienced by alcoholics.

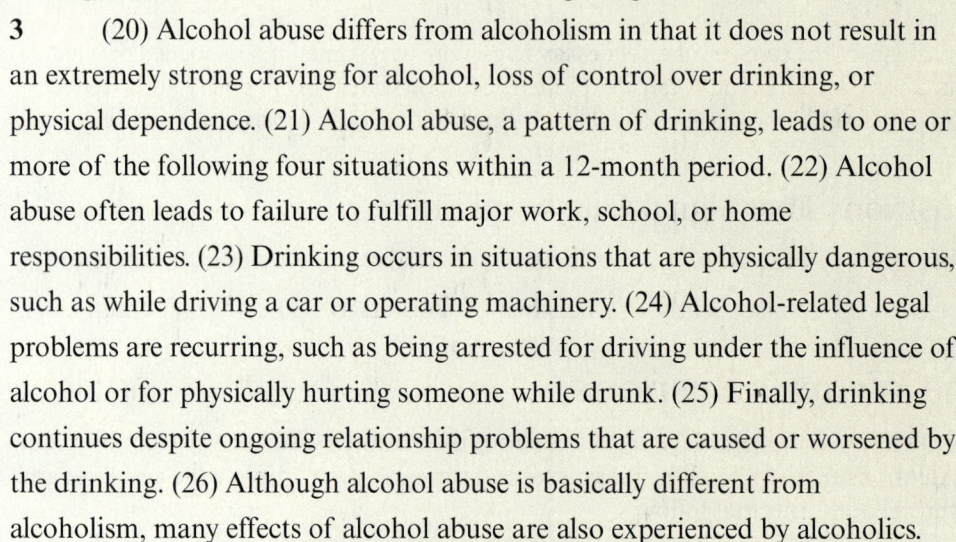

4	(27) The long-term consequences of alcohol misuse are serious—in many cases, life threatening. (28) Heavy drinking can increase the risk for certain cancers, especially those of the liver, esophagus, throat, and larynx (voice box). (29) Heavy drinking can also cause liver cirrhosis, immune system problems, brain damage, and harm to the fetus during pregnancy. (30) In addition, drinking increases the risk of death from automobile crashes as well as recreational and on-the-job injuries. (31) Furthermore, both homicides and suicides are more likely to be committed by persons who have been drinking. (32) In purely economic terms, alcohol-related problems cost society approximately $185 billion per year. (33) In human terms, the costs cannot be calculated.

5	(34) Many people wonder why some individuals can use alcohol without problems but others cannot. (35) Alcohol misuse occurs for several reasons. (36) One important reason has to do with genetics. (37) Scientists have found that having an alcoholic family member makes it more likely that if a person chooses to drink he or she too may develop alcoholism. (38) Genes, however, are not the whole story. (39) In fact, scientists now believe that certain factors in a person's environment influence whether a person with a genetic risk for alcoholism ever develops the disease. (40) A person's risk for developing alcoholism can increase based on the person's environment, including where and how he or she lives; family, friends, and culture; peer pressure; and even how easy it is to get alcohol.

6	(41) Those who choose to ignore these facts about alcoholism and alcohol abuse may be the very ones who will suffer the devastating effects associated with drinking-related problems.

—Adapted from "Getting the Facts," National Institute on Alcohol Abuse and Alcoholism (2001)

ROCK BOTTOM

Practice 9

READ AND EVALUATE THE ESSAY

Complete the activities below after you have read the essay a second time.

1. What kind of title does the writer use? _____

2. What type of introduction does the writer use? _____
_____

3. Double underline the thesis statement.

4. For each of the body paragraphs, underline the topic sentence. Circle the cause and effect transition words. List two major details for each paragraph below.

Major Details (Paragraph 2): _____
_____

Major Details (Paragraph 3): _____
_____

Major Details (Paragraph 4): _____
_____

Major Details (Paragraph 5): _____

5. What type of conclusion does the writer use? _____

6. What is the purpose of the essay? Explain your answer. _____
_____
_____

7. Who is the audience for the essay? Explain your answer. _____
_____
_____

8. What did you like best about the essay? Why? _____
_____
_____

9. What about the essay could be improved? _____
_____

Writing Assignments for a Cause and Effect Essay

MyWritingLab™ Complete this Exercise on mywritinglab.com

Plan and illustrate your essay with one or more photographs of your own choosing. Write caption(s) for the photograph(s) that reflect your point(s).

Considering Audience and Purpose

Assume you are a volunteer with an organization such as Meals on Wheels, Habitat for Humanity, or Scouts, or that you volunteer at a particular place such as a school, hospital, or animal shelter. You have been asked to give a speech to an audience of college students to raise awareness about volunteering. Write a speech that discusses the need for and benefits of volunteering.

Writing for Everyday Life

Many of us have rebelled against our parents (or another authority figure) or know someone who has. What are some of the things against which youth rebel? Why? Is most youthful rebellion harmless or are serious long-term effects more likely? Why? Write an encouraging letter to a young person who is in conflict with authority that explains some of the causes and possible effects of youthful rebellion.

Writing for College Life

Assume you are enrolled in a sociology class, discussing the ways in which technology has changed society during your lifetime or over the lifetime of your grandparents. What are some of the intended benefits or unexpected outcomes of having automobiles, dishwashers, GPS, smart phones, tablets, the Internet, or other pieces of technology? Write an essay for this class explaining the effects of a specific piece of technology on modern culture.

Writing for Working Life

Assume your company has asked you to speak about the "elements of success" during an employee training day. Think of highly successful people such as Jennifer Lopez, Bill Gates, Larry Page, Hillary Clinton, Mark Zuckerberg, Rihanna, and Pope Francis. What motivates or drives people to such high levels of success? Write a speech to motivate a group of work colleagues by explaining the reasons for success.

Additional Cause and Effect Topics

Excessive mood swings or compulsive behavior

Low or high self-esteem

Benefits of a particular exercise: walking, jogging, and so on

Benefits of humor

A natural disaster such as a hurricane, tornado, or tsunami

Benefits of team sports

Addiction to or withdrawal from a drug such as nicotine or caffeine

10 Develop Your Point in a Persuasive Essay

Persuasion is used in every aspect of life.

- In your personal life, you come across attempts to persuade you in magazine, radio, and television advertisements. As a parent, you may persuade your children to eat healthful foods and get lots of exercise. Or you may persuade your partner to go on a much needed vacation.

- In your college life, you will be asked to take a stand on issues in all the areas you study. For example, in a social science class, you may want to argue for or against gun control, or in a science class, you may take a stand for or against cloning.

- In your working life, you use persuasion when you try to convince a prospective employer that you are the best candidate for the job. Or you may need to write your own advertisement to get people to come to your store or restaurant.

> For information on writing a persuasive paragraph, see pages 190–203.

In a **persuasive essay,** a writer takes a strong stand on a debatable issue and offers thoughtful, convincing reasons in its support. To create a credible argument, a writer uses facts and examples, offers expert and informed opinions, considers consequences, and answers the opposition. The following transitions signal persuasion.

Transition Words Used to Signal Persuasion

accordingly	even so	in conclusion	nonetheless	therefore
admittedly	finally	indeed	obviously	thus
although	first (second, third, etc.)		of course	to be sure
because	for	in fact	on the one hand	truly
but	furthermore	in summary	on the other hand	undoubtedly
certainly	granted	last	since	
consequently	hence	meanwhile	some believe	
despite	however	nevertheless	some may say	

One Writer's Response

Read the following persuasive essay. Then, read the essay a second time. Finally, complete the activities and answer the questions that follow.

Ban Cell Phones: Save Lives

1   (1) No one understands the dangers of using a cell phone while driving better than Rob and Patti Pena. (2) On November 3, 1999, their 2-year-old daughter Morgan Lee died as a result of injuries sustained in a car crash the previous day. (3) As she sat securely strapped into her car seat in the back seat of her mother's car, a driver who ran a stop sign while using his cellular phone broadsided their car. (4) The only legal penalty the driver faced was a $50 fine and two traffic tickets.

(5) Regrettably, the tragic loss of Morgan Lee is not an isolated case. (6) According to a study by the Harvard Center for Risk Analysis, researchers estimated that the use of cell phones by drivers caused approximately 2,600 deaths. (7) Cell phone use while driving should be banned.

2   (8) Of course, not everyone agrees that talking on a cell phone while driving should be outlawed. (9) In fact, many believe that this behavior is no more dangerous than the many other tasks drivers perform while driving. (10) Obviously, drivers constantly multitask as they eat, fiddle with the radio or air conditioner, light a cigarette, apply makeup, read a map, and converse with their passengers. (11) Obviously, common sense dictates that these tasks should be kept to a minimum. (12) Certainly, any activity that absorbs a driver's attention has the potential to adversely affect the driver's control of the vehicle and reaction to hazards and traffic signals. (13) However, to suggest that one set of careless behaviors excuses another reckless behavior defies common sense. (14) Common sense also suggests that the dangers posed by these distractions do not compare to the dangers posed by using a cell phone while driving.

3   (15) Human Factors experts study the relationship between human limitations and the design of technology. (16) These experts note that drivers face visual, auditory, mechanical, and cognitive distractions. (17) Using a cell phone while driving incorporates every one of these distractions. (18) Darla Burton offers an excellent example of how using a cell phone while driving combines all four.

4   (19) The cell phone in Darla's purse rings as she speeds down the Interstate. (20) Immediately, she becomes visually distracted as she takes her eyes off the road and leans across the front seat to grab her purse. (21) The insistent ringing serves as an auditory alarm that urges her to hurry her movements. (22) As she rummages for the phone in her purse and fumbles with the mechanics of sliding open and pressing the button to answer the phone, she swerves out of her lane. (23) A passing motorist blares his car's horn in warning; Darla jerks her car back into her own lane. (24) The caller is her boyfriend, and with an angry voice, he continues an argument that began days ago. (25) Darla, distracted cognitively as she argues with her boyfriend, becomes lost in the conversation and unaware of her bearings. (26) Suddenly, she notices that her exit is looming quickly. (27) Without thinking or looking in her rear view and side mirrors, she veers across three lanes to make the exit. (28) Luckily, she narrowly avoids sideswiping another vehicle. (29) Darla's behavior is typical of many people who use a cell phone while driving.

5 (30) Those who oppose banning cell phone use while driving argue that hands-free cell phones reduce these risks, and they do, but not enough. (31) Hands-free cell phones may limit visual and mechanical distractions, but auditory and cognitive distractions are still issues of concern. (32) Some believe that these distractions are no different than the distraction of talking with a passenger in the car. (33) However, talking on a cell phone is significantly different than talking with a passenger in a car. (34) First, a passenger in a vehicle often contributes to the safety of the driving situation by providing an additional set of eyes and ears to warn against road hazards. (35) When a driving situation demands the focused attention of the driver, a passenger in the car helps control the flow of conversation so that the driver can safely attend to the task of driving. (36) In addition, most people are conditioned to immediately respond to a ringing phone. (37) This need to answer often overrides convenience or safety issues and drags attention away from the challenges of the road.

6 (38) The sheer number of cell phone users also adds to the seriousness of the problem. (39) There are currently over 327.5 million cell phone users in this country alone. (40) According to Distraction.gov, in the month of June 2011, more than 196 billion text messages were sent or received in the United States, up nearly 50% from June 2009. (41) According to the 2011 U.S. government "National Phone Survey on Distracted Driving Attitudes and Behaviors," 77% of cell phone owners drive while using their cell phones. (42) If that trend has continued, then about 171 million drivers currently talk on their phones while driving, at least some of the time. (43) In addition, current in-car communication services allow users to check e-mail and calendars and surf the web while driving. (44) The wireless industry offers a range of mobile options such as digital streaming, which has the potential to further distract drivers.

7 (45) Remember Morgan Lee Pena and the thousands of other possible victims of someone's need to stay plugged in. (46) Join the fight to ban cell phone use while driving. (47) Write to your politicians, and tell them to support cellular phone legislation. (48) Urge them to ban cell phone use while driving and to enact strong penalties against violators. (49) Write to your cellular provider and ask the company to support laws that restrict cellular phone use while driving. (50) Finally, if you take a cell phone with you in your car, set a good example; pull over and stop before you make or take a call. (51) Tell your friends and family to do the same for their safety and the safety of others. (52) Stay safe! (53) Save lives! (54) Don't talk; just drive!

READ AND EVALUATE THE ESSAY

Complete the activities below after you have read the essay a second time.

1. What kind of title does the writer use? _____

2. What type of introduction does the writer use? _____

3. Double underline the thesis statement.

4. For each of the body paragraphs, underline the topic sentence. Circle the persuasion signal words. List two major details for each paragraph below.

Major Details (Paragraph 2): _____

Major Details (Paragraph 3): _____

Major Details (Paragraph 4): _____

Major Details (Paragraph 5): _____

Major Details (Paragraph 6): _____

5. What type of conclusion does the writer use? _____

6. What is the purpose of the essay? Explain your answer. _____

7. Who is the audience for the essay? Explain your answer. _____

8. On your own paper, write what you liked best about the essay and why.

9. On your own paper, suggest what about the essay could be improved.

Writing Assignments for a Persuasive Essay

MyWritingLab™ Complete this Exercise on mywritinglab.com

Plan and illustrate your essay with one or more photographs of your own choosing. Write caption(s) for the photograph(s) that reflect your point(s).

Considering Audience and Purpose

Assume you are a reporter for your college's newspaper. Identify a problem that affects many people on your campus, such as poor lighting in the parking lot, inadequate parking, or poor food service. Write a column calling for administrative action to correct the problem. Your purpose is to offer compelling evidence that action must be taken.

Writing for Everyday Life

Think about the amount of graphic violence and sexual content on television shows and the numbers of hours people spend watching these images. Should sponsors such as Kellogg, Nike, McDonald's, and Wal-Mart support shows that contain graphic violent and sexual content? Write a letter to a company that sponsors a particularly graphic television show to persuade the company to withdraw its sponsorship.

Writing for College Life

Assume you are taking a sociology course, and you have been studying about the impact of clothes (or fashion) on human behavior. Your professor directs your attention to Northwest High School, where school uniforms will soon be required. What are some of the reasons administrators and parents might have for supporting school uniforms, and what are some of the reasons students have for opposing them? Write a letter to the principal of the school taking a strong stand for or against school uniforms for students attending Northwest High School.

Writing for Working Life

Assume you are the manager of a retail store in a local mall, and one of your employees has consistently performed at a high level. Write a letter to your supervisor in which you recommend a promotion and raise for your employee.

Additional Persuasive Topics

Animal testing for cosmetic or medical research

Manned space flights

Abstinence-only sex education courses

Stricter gun laws

Surveillance cameras installed in all public places

Decriminalization of marijuana

Develop Your Point in an Essay That Combines Patterns

Often, writers find that the most effective way to express their view about a particular topic is to layer several patterns of organization into one essay.

- In your personal life, you may find it necessary to write an apology for a misunderstanding with a family member or friend. In your letter, you may find it helpful to discuss the *types* of stresses you have been facing, the *effects* such stresses have had upon you, and the *reasons* you value that individual.
- In your college life, you will combine patterns of organization as you study topics in greater depth. For example, in humanities courses you may choose to write about the *origin*, *types*, and *impact* of art or artifacts produced by a particular culture.
- In your working life, you may need to write a report that *defines* a problem, *compares* several solutions, and *recommends* a course of action.

In an **essay that combines patterns of organization**, a writer divides the topic into subsections based on a series of patterns of organization best suited for each paragraph that develops the main point. For example, "alcoholism," discussed in an earlier essay by using causes and effects, could also be discussed by combining several patterns of organization. As a disease, alcoholism has recognizable stages or cycles that could be discussed using process. In addition, several types of treatment are available and could be discussed using classification. Or perhaps sharing personal testimonies or case histories of recovering alcoholics in the form of narratives could convince someone to seek help. Many other topics also can be developed in greater depth by combining patterns.

Transition words used within each paragraph signal the type of pattern of organization used to develop that particular paragraph. Therefore, draw from the lists of transitions given throughout this chapter for each of the specific patterns of organization as needed.

One Student Writer's Response

Study the following combined pattern essay written by student Doug Frazier. Then, read the essay a second time. Finally, complete the activities and answer the questions that follow.

The Games People Play

1	(1) Games have always been a part of human culture. (2) Archeologists have uncovered the use of board games as far back as 4000 B.C.E. in ancient Babylonia. (3) While board games apparently appeared as the first type of game, other forms such as card games and tiled games evolved as people began to understand, enjoy, and develop the concept of games. (4) The variety and enjoyment of games expanded as technology advanced through the millennia. (5) Most recently, over the past 30 years, the newest and perhaps most radical change to games has occurred with the invention of the computer video game. (6) The advent of computer video games enabled a significant jump in gaming evolution. (7) While video games share many of the same traits as traditional games, the distinct qualities of computer games intensify both the dangers and the pleasures of gaming.

2 (8) To appreciate the impact of video games on the gaming experience, a general understanding of a few types and features of traditional games is necessary. (9) Overall, traditional games often reflect three types of intense, real-life experiences: physical combat or skill, intellectual strategy, and chance. (10) The group of games based on physical skills is made up of a wide range of activities such as races, archery, and darts; the outcome of these games relies upon the physical abilities of the players. (11) Another group of games are based on strategy, such as chess, and rely upon the player's ability to make rational decisions. (12) Many games combine the first two types of games so that players need both physical skill and strategy to win such as in organized sports like soccer, baseball, and football. (13) The third type of game utilizes chance and often uses dice or some kind of random number selection that dictates the outcome; examples of these games include bingo and lotteries. (14) Often games of chance also combine with strategy, so that knowledge or skill helps determine the outcome. (15) For example, through a series of plays, Monopoly and poker combine chance and strategy to determine a winner.

3 (16) All of these traditional games share a few basic traits. (17) First, games usually offer an avatar or icon that represents the player; in Monopoly the original avatars were metal tokens based on objects found in households across America (the flat iron, purse, lantern, car, thimble, shoe, top hat, and the rocking horse); in sports the avatars are the team's name and mascot like the Eagle for the Philadelphia Eagles in the National Football League. (18) Traditional games also present an environment that challenges the players or allows the players to challenge each other, and traditional games keep track of the player's success or scores. (19) In addition, traditional games foster social interaction; part of the fun of playing is experiencing the game with someone else.

4 (20) A comparison of traditional games to video games finds many similarities. (21) Just like traditional games, video games offer avatars. (22) For example, in the video game King Kong based on director Peter Jackson's version of the classic story, players can choose the adventurer Jack Driscoll as the avatar, or choose Kong, thus playing the game through the eyes of the ape. (23) Both traditional and video games present environments in which challenges are posed by the game player and opponent; in addition, both traditional and video games keep track of a player's success or score and reward the players when they overcome challenges or challengers. (24) Moreover, video games actually combine physical skill, strategy, and chance. (25) Physical skill is needed to rapidly figure out and adapt to the immense amount of visual information provided on the video screen. (26) In addition, the player must make rational decisions based on this information and make moves in a logical sequence. (27) Thus video games, like many traditional games, require strategy. (28) Finally, many video games are programmed to allow apparently random events to occur, so they are similar to games of chance as well.

5   (29) Although traditional and video games are similar, they do indeed differ in drastic ways. (30) Traditional games are much more unpredictable than video games. (31) Traditional board and card games require other players to enrich the environment and to create the uncertainty which generates the fun. (32) Video games, on the other hand, are a form of artificial intelligence (A.I.) programmed into the computer. (33) While A.I. is impressive, it is ultimately limited and lacks the unpredictable flexibility of human thought; therefore, the outcomes of the challenges are ultimately much more predictable. (34) Traditional games and video games differ in the social experiences they offer. (35) A.I. fosters an antisocial experience. (36) Often, video players do not need other players. (37) Traditionally, games have been seen as such an enjoyable activity partly because of the time spent making and enjoying friends. (38) During this time, players learn how to win and lose with dignity and to respect the integrity of others. (39) In contrast, many video games absorb individual players in countless hours of isolated play. (40) The great majority of these games also demand that players engage in simulated antisocial acts of murder and mayhem. (41) For example, "Carmageddon" is described on the package as "The racing game for the chemically imbalanced." (42) The goal of this gory video game is to "waste contestants, pedestrians, and farmyard animals for points and credit." (43) Some critics of video games consider these differences from traditional games alarming and dangerous.

6   (44) Experts warn that violent video games can have a negative impact. (45) These types of video games may increase aggressive thoughts, feelings, and behaviors; arouse hostility; and decrease helping behaviors. (46) Because video game players must make active decisions to choose violent strategies to win, players may learn that violence is fun and rewarding. (47) Another negative effect may be that players become numbed or blunted emotionally to violence and come to accept violence as a normal part of life. (48) Because players view violence as inevitable, they may not develop the skills needed to make nonviolent choices when they are faced with real life challenges.

7   (49) The ways in which video games differ from traditional games may present some reasons for caution; still the distinctive nature of video games offers some positive pleasures. (50) A video game player often learns how to play the game through trial and error. (51) So video games are fun to explore. (52) As the player explores the world of the video game, he or she must rethink choices and come up with strategies based on new information. (53) In addition, to achieve ultimate victory, a player must think about the short-term and long-term effects of each decision or move in the game. (54) Finally, many players enjoy figuring out the limits of the game. (55) The fun lies in figuring how the game's program works and if there are any flaws in the program. (56) Thus, video games make critical thinking enjoyable.

8   (57) Traditional and computer games share many traits. (58) Both require physical skill, chance, and strategy to win. (59) However, video games offer a different kind of gaming experience. (60) Video games are often violent and antisocial by nature, yet they make problem solving a fun activity. (61) Some critics consider video games far more dangerous than traditional games.

READ AND EVALUATE THE ESSAY

Complete the activities below after you have read the essay a second time.

1. What kind of title does the writer use? _____

2. What type of introduction does the writer use? _____

3. Double underline the thesis statement.

4. For each of the body paragraphs, underline the topic sentence. Circle the signal words for the various patterns. List two major details for each paragraph below. Name the pattern of organization.

Major Details (Paragraph 2): _____
_____

Major Details (Paragraph 3): _____
_____

Major Details (Paragraph 4): _____
_____

Major Details (Paragraph 5): _____
_____

Major Details (Paragraph 6): _____

Major Details (Paragraph 7): _____
_____

5. What type of conclusion does the writer use? _____

6. What is the purpose of the essay? Explain your answer. _____
_____

7. Who is the audience for the essay? Explain your answer. _____
_____

8. On your own paper, write what you liked best about the essay and why.

9. On your own paper, suggest what about the essay could be improved.

Writing Assignments for a Combined Pattern Essay

MyWritingLab™ Complete this Exercise on mywritinglab.com

Plan and illustrate your essay with one or more photographs of your own choosing. Write caption(s) for the photograph(s) that reflect your point(s).

Considering Audience and Purpose

Assume you are a dissatisfied customer with several complaint issues, and you are writing a formal complaint to the manager. Identify the types of complaints you have; discuss the causes of your dissatisfaction, and list the steps you expect the manager to take to rectify the situation.

Writing for Everyday Life

Technological advances are rapidly accelerating. How important is it to stay abreast of the new technologies? Why? What are the types of new technologies, such as podcasting or multimedia cell phones? Which ones are most accessible, easy to use, affordable, or important? Why? Write a consumer report for an online posting in which you analyze the importance of keeping up with technology.

Writing for College Life

Assume you are taking a college humanities course, and you have been studying the concept of cultural traditions. Many of us have favorite traditions or rituals that have been handed down to us by our families or cultures. How does a tradition or ritual reflect a particular family, culture, heritage, or value? Write an essay in which you analyze the significance of a particular ritual or tradition.

Writing for Working Life

Assume you work in an environment full of conflict, and you have learned effective conflict resolution skills. Identify some typical conflicts that occur on a particular job: Between a team supervisor and a team member at a car dealership. Between a waiter and a diner. Between colleagues at a walk-in health clinic. What causes these conflicts? What are the steps to effective conflict resolution? Write a report for a supervisor that documents a conflict, evaluates the causes of the conflict, and recommends steps to resolve the conflict.

Additional Combined Pattern Topics

Minimum wage	Inspiring or effective teachers
National identity cards	A popular public figure
A living will	Internet fraud

Academic Learning Log: Chapter Review

REVIEW: MAKE YOUR POINT USING PATTERNS OF ORGANIZATION

Complete the chart by filling in the blanks with information from the chapter:

A **descriptive essay** describes a person, place, or object based on its location or the way it is arranged in _____; relies upon _____ details such as sight, sound, smell, taste, and touch to create vivid mental images so that the reader can see what is being described.

A **narrative essay** recounts a series of _____ or actions that occur during a specific period of _____.

A **process essay** shows actions in time order (also called chronological order) that can be repeated at any time, with similar results for three reasons:

1. To give steps, _____, or procedures for completing a task.
2. To analyze or study the steps, _____, or phases of a process.
3. To explain how to complete a task and to analyze the process.

An **illustration essay** offers a focused main idea about a particular topic and then presents a series of _____ or _____ to clarify or support the main idea.

A **classification essay** sorts or divides ideas into smaller groups and then describes the common _____ of each subgroup. The writer lists each _____, describes its characteristics, and offers examples that represent the group. Because groups and subgroups are listed, transitions that suggest additional categories are often used to ensure coherence.

A **comparison and contrast essay** shows the _____ and _____ between or among two topics based on comparable points.

A **definition essay** explains the meaning of a new, difficult, or special _____ or concept. A definition may include traits, comparisons, causes, or effects. In addition, a writer may include an explanation of what the term or concept is _____. Examples are used to illustrate the various components or elements of the term being defined.

A **cause and effect essay** discusses why something happened or what results came from an event. A cause explores the _____ something happens, and an effect examines the _____ or outcome.

A **persuasive essay** takes a strong stand on a debatable issue and offers thoughtful, convincing reasons in its support. To create a credible argument, a writer uses _____ and _____, offers expert and informed _____, considers consequences, and answers the _____.

An **essay that combines patterns** divides the topic into subsections based on a _____ of _____ of organization best suited for each paragraph that develops the main point.

MyWritingLab™
Complete the Post-test for Chapter 15 in MyWritingLab.

16 Research Strategies and Resources

LEARNING OUTCOMES

After studying this chapter, you will be able to:

- **LO1** Answer the question "What's the Point of Research?"
- **LO2** Find and Evaluate Sources
- **LO3** Avoid Plagiarism
- **LO4** Develop Your Reading/Writing Strategy for Research
- **LO5** Master the Basics of MLA

> "In much of society, research means to investigate something you do not know or understand."
> —Neil Armstrong, American Astronaut

Research is the process of gathering, evaluating, and combining information for a specific purpose. Through research, we learn a new concept, clarify an idea, support a viewpoint, or make a sound decision. College life, work life, and everyday life all benefit from research.

What's the Point of Research?

The following photographs illustrate several research situations in college life, work life, and everyday life. Study each photograph and its caption. In the spaces provided, state the need for research in each situation. Then, state the overall point of research.

PHOTOGRAPHIC ORGANIZER: THE PURPOSE OF RESEARCH

College Life:
Female student selecting library books as resources for a term paper

Work Life:
A detective with evidence from a crime scene

Everyday Life:
Woman checking food labeling

Work Life:
Reporter interviewing a man for a news story

What's the Point of Research?

WRITING FROM LIFE

My First Thoughts: A Prewriting Activity

Set a time limit, such as two to three minutes, and quickly write down in your notebook your thoughts about the importance of research or your prior experience with research. Do not stop writing, even if you must repeat ideas. Keep writing until the time limit is up.

One Student Writer's Response

The following freewrite is one writer's response to the question "What's the point of research?"

> When you don't know very much about a topic, you can learn more about it by researching. Most of the time, I use the Internet to get information. Like, when I was shopping for a car, I went online and googled Kelley's Blue Book so I would know how much my old car was worth when I went to trade it in. I also visited several websites of auto dealers to compare cars and prices. Research is also important in college. Many teachers assign a research paper or project to make us learn more about a topic in the course. Research is a way to learn on your own.

Research gives power to your decisions, studies, and viewpoints. Knowing the best research strategies and resources will help you find and use the information you need in your college life, work life, and everyday life.

L2 Find and Evaluate Sources

One of the most basic and early steps in the research process is finding useful and trustworthy information. A good way to begin your research is to ask the following three questions:

- What kind of information do I need?
- Where can I find the information I need?
- How can I know the information I find is reliable or trustworthy?

The rest of this section offers you strategies and resources to answer these basic research questions.

What Kind of Information Do I Need?

Basically, two types of information inform our thinking and writing: facts and opinions.

- A **fact** is something that can be shown to be true, to exist, or to have happened based on evidence. The following statistic is an example of a fact: "About one-third of U.S. adults (34.9%) are obese." The source of this fact is the government agency the Centers for Disease Control and Prevention (CDC).

- An **opinion** is a personal view somebody takes about an issue. Our thinking and writing is most powerful when it is based on expert opinions. An expert opinion is a personal view based on training, education, and experience in a particular field. For example, a doctor offers you an expert opinion about your health. The following statement is an example of an expert opinion given by Dr. Oz, a heart surgeon and author—a medical expert. "You can control your health destiny." This quote is his expert opinion as stated in page 2 of his best-selling book about health, *You: The Owner's Manual*.

An undeniable fact or an expert opinion is a convincing supporting detail for any point you need or want to make.

FIND AND EVALUATE SOURCES: IDENTIFYING FACTS AND OPINIONS

Assume you are beginning a research project for one of your college classes. You are evaluating a few general sources to locate key facts and expert opinions. Identify each of the following sources as **F** for a source of facts or **EO** as a source for an expert opinion.

_____ 1. *World Book Encyclopedia*   _____ 4. *Merriam's Webster Collegiate Dictionary*

_____ 2. A medical reference book   _____ 5. A trained grief counselor

_____ 3. The U.S. Census Bureau   _____ 6. A published professor with Ph.D. in the field

Practice 2

Where Can I Find the Information I Need?

Identifying the type of information you need helps you know where to look for it. The two main storehouses of information are the library and the Internet. Both offer a variety of resources for help in locating information as well as sources of information.

Library Resources and Sources:

- Seek out the reference librarian. **Reference librarians** are trained to teach you how to use the library and its resources. They answer queries about specific information. They also can recommend good sources for specific topics. Reference librarians have to stay up to date with technology and customer needs; thus they are able to assist your use of all types of research resources.

- Search the library's online catalogue. The **library's online catalogue** is an index of materials held by the library. Easily reached from the Internet, it is used mainly to locate books and other material physically located at a library. You can search for a source by author, title, subject, or keywords. As you find a source you think you may use, write down the title, author, and call number (or other reference information) so you can locate the item on its library shelf.

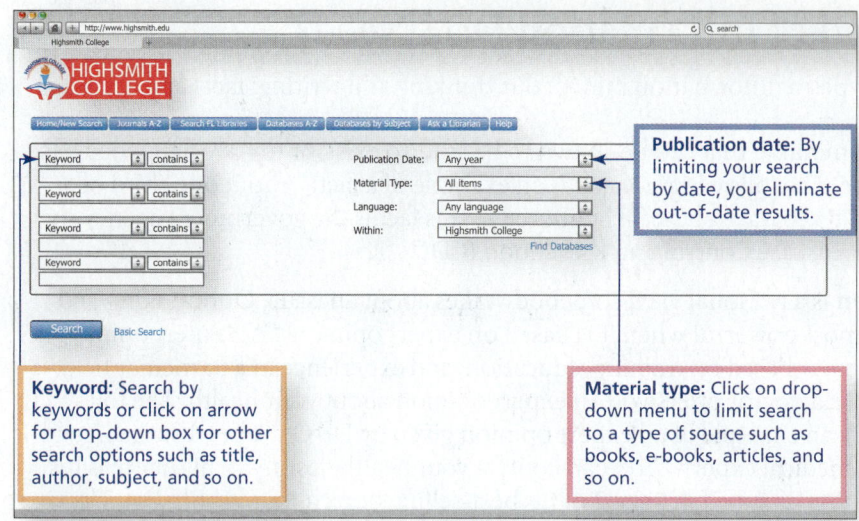

- Search the library's electronic database collection. The **library's electronic database collection** is a computer-based collection of records or listings of a wide variety of information. This information is organized with searchable fields, such as author, title, subject, or keywords. A library's electronic database collection gives you access to thousands of sources such as magazine, journal, and newspaper articles and essays, and e-books.

— Screen shot General OneFile. © Gale, a part of Cengage Learning, Inc. Reproduced by permission.
www.cengage.com/permissions

FIND AND EVALUATE SOURCES: LOCATING INFORMATION IN A LIBRARY

Practice using your college's library as a resource for research. Choose one of the following research topics or a topic of your own choice: The Causes or Effects of Stress; How to Start a Small Business; Types of Sleep Disorders. Then, complete the following activities. Ask a reference librarian for assistance as needed.

1. Identify a research topic: ....

2. Find a book on your research topic using your college's online catalogue. Record the following information about the book:

   Title ....

   Author(s) or Editor(s) ....

   City of publication .... Publisher .... Year published ....

   Call # .... Available or checked out? .... Print or e-book ....

3. Find a magazine or journal article using your college library's electronic database collection. Record the following information about the article:

   Title of article ....

   Author(s) if given ....

   Magazine/journal title (Source) ....

   Date published .... Page # ....

   Name of database ....

Practice 3

Internet Resources and Sources

A **search engine** is a service that indexes, searches, and retrieves information from millions of sites on the Internet. A search engine records each word within a document on the Internet. When you conduct a search, it matches your key words to the records it has in its databases and retrieves a list of links that match your request. Examples of search engines are *Yahoo*, *Google*, *Ask.com*, and *Bing*.

- Search by keywords. A **keyword** is a word used as a query or point of reference for seeking more information about a topic. If a keyword is too broad, then too many results are returned. If a keyword is too narrow, then too few results are returned.
  - Use quotation marks or Boolean (NOT, OR) operators to group words together. Enclosing words in quotation marks tells the search engine to search for the complete phrase, not the individual words. Searches that use the Boolean operator "NOT" tell the search engine to search for sites that mention the first item, but not the second. Finally, searches that use the Boolean operator "OR" tell the search engine to search for one term or the other. For example, a search for *"green energy" NOT nuclear* will find sites on green energy that do not mention nuclear power. Searches for *"green energy" OR nuclear* will find sources that discuss either green energy or nuclear power. Spell your keywords carefully, and consider alternate spellings.
  - Investigate your search engine's Advanced Search options. Most sites allow you to limit results by date, type of site, or many other options.
- Search by website domains. To search by domains, you need to understand a website's URL. A URL is a site's universal resource locator, also referred to as the website's address. Basically, a URL has three main parts:

PROTOCOL   SERVER OR HOST NAME   RESOURCE INFORMATION

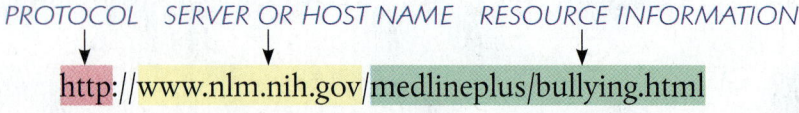

http://www.nlm.nih.gov/medlineplus/bullying.html

Notice the three letters at the end of the host name; these letters identify the type of organization that hosts the information. To search a topic by a domain, think about which domain is most likely to host the type of information you need. Then, include the domain in your query by leaving a space after the last word and typing a period and the three letters of the domain.

Types of Domains That Host Websites with Examples		
.com	companies and commercial sites	msnbc.com
.edu	educational institutions	http://owl.english.purdue.edu
.gov	government organizations	http://www.usa.gov
.org	nonprofit organizations	http://redcross.org

- Use an Internet bookmark. An **Internet bookmark** acts as a marker for a website. Once you find a website as a source of information, you can save it for easy and quick access. Look in the toolbar of your web browser for the Favorites or Bookmark option.

FIND AND EVALUATE SOURCES: LOCATING INFORMATION ON THE INTERNET

Practice using the Internet as a resource for research. Use the same topic you chose for Practice 3. Find an Internet site on your research topic using a search engine such as google.com, yahoo.com, or bing.com. Record the following information about the article.

Website name _____

Website address (URL) _____

Website author(s) if given _____

Website sponsor _____

Date of last update _____ Date of your access _____

Practice 4

Track Your Sources

When you find a source you think you may use, take the following steps.

- Write in a log or cut and paste into a Word file the information about the source's publication. (See pages 307–315 for more details about citing the publication information.)
- Send to your e-mail account the record of or the link to the source.
- Download the document, or create a copy of the document by cutting and pasting it into a Word file.

Find and record the following information:

- Author's full name
- Title of article
- Title of book, periodical, or site
- Publisher of book, periodical, or site
- Date of publication, or for websites, the date of latest update

- For books and articles, page numbers of sections where you located information
- For websites, date you accessed the information
- For websites, the URL, also called the website's address

In some websites, you may not find all the usual publication information. For example, some organizations do not identify a specific person as an author. In addition, you may need to click around in the site to find all the information.

How Can I Know the Information I Find Is Reliable or Trustworthy?

Before publishing material in books, newspapers, magazines, and scholarly journals, editors and peers carefully evaluate sources and review information to ensure they are reliable and accurate. But even then, print materials may reveal a bias or share incomplete or misleading information. The Internet, on the other hand, allows anyone to publish information without any screening of the information for reliability or accuracy. Thus, more than ever before, we must carefully evaluate information to determine how reliable and accurate it is. The following chart offers a guide for evaluating sources from the library and the Internet. If a source qualifies as usable based on this guide, then use that source as **PAART** of your research.

PAART: A Guide to Evaluating Sources	
Purpose Why did the author write?	Identify the purpose of the information: to inform, to persuade, to entertain. Identify the type of information: fact, opinion, expert opinion. Identify any specific bias: cultural, personal, political, religious viewpoints.
Authority Who is the author or host?	Identify the author, publisher, source, or sponsor. Identify contact information: e-mail or street address. Identify the qualifications of the author: education, experience. For a website: Identify the type of domain that hosts the site.
Accuracy How correct is the information?	Note errors: grammar, spelling, typographical (typos). Verify the information in another source. Identify the source of the information. Look for reviewers or editors of the publication.
Relevance How does the information relate to the topic of the research?	Identify the intended audience for the publication. Evaluate how the information relates to your topic of research. Review a variety of sources before making a final choice to use a particular source.
Timeliness When was the information written?	Evaluate the need for current or historical information. Note the date of the publication. Note if the information has been updated or revised. For a website: Test the hyperlinks to make sure they still work.

The PAART guide can be used to quickly evaluate a source for research in college, work, and everyday life. We need to test information before we accept it as useful to our thinking or decision-making process.

Practice 5

FIND AND EVALUATE SOURCES: EVALUATING INFORMATION USING PAART

Practice using PAART to evaluate a source. Assume you are researching a topic for a college class. Answer each question with a score from 5 to 1. A score of 5 means excellent, and a score of 1 means unacceptable. Then, add up the total score and circle the score range for the source you evaluated. Discuss your experience with a peer or a small group of classmates. What makes a source excellent?

PAART: A Guide to Evaluating Sources			
Title of Source:			
Criteria	Questions to Evaluate Source	Rating of Source	
Purpose What?	Is the purpose of the publication made clear?	5 4 3 2 1	
	Is the type of information appropriate for the research topic?	5 4 3 2 1	
	Does a specific bias influence the information?	5 4 3 2 1	
Authority Who?	Is the author, publisher, source, or sponsor of the publication stated?	5 4 3 2 1	
	Is contact information available?	5 4 3 2 1	
	Is the author qualified to address the topic?	5 4 3 2 1	
	For a website: Is the domain that hosts the site appropriate for the topic?	5 4 3 2 1	
Accuracy How?	Are there errors: grammar, spelling, typographical (typos)?	5 4 3 2 1	
	Can the information be verified in another source?	5 4 3 2 1	
	Is the source of the information reliable?	5 4 3 2 1	
	Has the information been reviewed by peers or editors in the field?	5 4 3 2 1	
Relevance How?	Is the intended audience for the publication made clear?	5 4 3 2 1	
	Does the information relate to the topic of research?	5 4 3 2 1	
	Is the information at the appropriate level?	5 4 3 2 1	
	Have a variety of sources been reviewed before making a final choice to use a particular source?	5 4 3 2 1	
Timeliness When?	Does the topic of research call for current or historical information?	5 4 3 2 1	
	Is the date of the publication given?	5 4 3 2 1	
	Is the date of publication appropriate for the need of current or historical information?	5 4 3 2 1	
	Has the information been updated or revised?	5 4 3 2 1	
	For a website: Do the hyperlinks still work?	5 4 3 2 1	
	Total score		

Score Range	Excellent 100–81	→ 80–61	→ 60–41	→ 40–21	Unacceptable 20–0

L3 Avoid Plagiarism

Plagiarism is the act of presenting the words or ideas of another author as one's own or using information without giving credit to its original source. Plagiarism is a form of stealing that leads to serious consequences in both the classroom and the workplace. The penalties for plagiarism in the classroom may range from failing the assignment to expulsion. Likewise, plagiarism in the workplace may result in demotion, lack of opportunity for promotion, or job loss. Plagiarism is not only unethical, it is also illegal. Original work is protected by copyright law. Thus, plagiarism can result in legal action. Many times, plagiarism is not a deliberate act. Instead, plagiarism may occur from a lack of knowledge about how to use the work of others or how to give them proper credit for their work. You can avoid plagiarism by properly paraphrasing, summarizing, quoting, and citing the words and ideas of other people.

Paraphrasing a text is accurately restating an idea using your own words. The following chart outlines five steps for paraphrasing.

The Five R's of Paraphrasing: Read, Restate, Revise, Revisit, Repeat	
Read	Read the text to understand the author's meaning. Highlight key ideas. Look up words you don't know.
Restate	Put the original text out of sight. Recall in writing the author's ideas using your own words.
Revise	Wait for a space of time (from a few minutes to a few days) to create an opportunity to see your paraphrase with fresh eyes. Then, revise your paraphrase for clear wording and smooth flow of ideas.
Revisit	After drafting your paraphrase, revisit the original text. Compare your paraphrase to the author's wording. Change any wording that is too close to the author's words. Double check to make sure your paraphrase correctly restates the author's message.
Repeat	Complete the preceding steps as many times as needed to draft a sound paraphrase.

With a peer or small group of classmates, study the following example of a paraphrase. Read the original text and the paraphrase. Then, discuss how the paraphrase differs from the original text. Finally, discuss how the paraphrase is similar to the original text.

Original Text:

Health and safety procedures for body artists may be regulated by city, county, or state agencies. Reputable shops and tattoo parlors govern themselves and follow strict safety procedures to protect their clients—and their body artists.

Source of Text:

"Body Art: Tattoos and Piercings." Centers for Disease Control and Prevention (CDC) 29 Aug. 2011. Web.

Paraphrase:

Trustworthy tattooists and body piercers are rigorous in hygiene. They are also faithful to the laws set in place by different levels of government. Responsible "body artists" take steps to ensure the physical well-being of their customer and themselves ("Body Art: Tattoos and Piercings").

Notice that the paraphrase is about the same length as the original text. Also notice that in the paraphrase, any exact words taken from the original text are placed in quotation marks. Finally, the source of the paraphrase is cited in the text to avoid plagiarism. Since the source does not have an author, the title is used in the citation. Also, since this information is from the Internet, no page number is given. However, the page numbers where information appears in a print source are included in the citation. The complete publication information will also be provided in the Works Cited Page. You will learn more about in-text citations and the Works Cited page later in this chapter (see pages 307–315).

AVOID PLAGIARISM: PARAPHRASING

Assume you work as a manager of several departments at a local retail store. You have a job opening for a supervisor of one of your departments. You have asked applicants to respond in writing to the following question: "How would you describe your style of leadership?" Several of your applicants have paraphrased a passage from a textbook you suggested they read as part of their training for management. Read the original text. Then, evaluate each applicant's paraphrase. Mark each one **A** for acceptable or **U** for unacceptable. Finally, discuss your answers and reasoning with a peer or a small group of classmates.

Original text:
Democratic leaders work with employees to find the best way to complete the job while maintaining final authority. Being a democratic leader means you value the opinions of the others in your group. That's why democratic leaders surround themselves with skillful employees. Democratic leaders empower others, and their decisions are better informed because of the input of their fellow employees.

Source of text:
Van Syckle, Barbara and Brian Tietje. *Anybody's Business*. Upper Saddle River, NJ: Prentice Hall, 2010. 136. Print.

_____ **Applicant 1's Paraphrase:** A "democratic" manager creates a team approach by hiring qualified and dedicated workers and seeking their views about how best to solve a problem or carry out a task before coming to a final decision. This type of manager makes thoughtful decisions. This type of manager taps into and releases the power of each worker.

_____ **Applicant 2's Paraphrase:** A "democratic" manager creates a team approach by hiring qualified and dedicated workers and seeking their views about how best to solve a problem or carry out a task before coming to a final decision. This type of manager makes thoughtful decisions. This type of manager taps into and releases the power of each worker (Van Syckle and Tietje 136).

_____ **Applicant 3's Paraphrase:** Democratic leaders work with workers to find the best way to complete the job. Democratic leaders maintain final authority. A democratic leader values the views of the others in your group. That's why democratic leaders surround themselves with skillful employees. Democratic leaders empower others. Their decisions are better informed because of the input of coworkers.

_____ **Applicant 4's Paraphrase:** Democratic leaders work with workers to find the best way to complete the job. Democratic leaders maintain final authority. A democratic leader values the views of the others in your group. That's why democratic leaders surround themselves with skillful employees. Democratic leaders empower others. Their decisions are better informed because of the input of coworkers (Van Syckle and Tietje 136).

Summarizing a text entails reducing a section of text to its main points. A summary is much shorter than the length of the original text as it only includes the most important ideas. The following chart outlines a three-step process for summarizing. If the author states the main idea in a topic sentence, follow through to step 3a. If an author does not state the main idea in a topic sentence, then skip step 3a and follow step 3b. An acceptable summary also paraphrases the author's ideas.

The Three-Step Process for Writing a Summary	
1. Delete	Cross out unnecessary material. Cross out repetitive material.
2. Condense	Use a word to replace a list. Use a word to replace individual parts of an action.
3.a. State	Underline and then rephrase the topic sentence or thesis statement,
	OR
3.b. Create	Compose a topic sentence or thesis statement if not stated.

Since you paraphrase ideas in a summary, any exact words taken from the original text are placed in quotation marks. Just as with a paraphrase, the source of the summary is cited in the text and Works Cited page to avoid plagiarism (see pages 300–301). Many experts suggest that you begin a summary with the title of the original text and the author's name.

With a peer or small group of classmates, study the following example of a summary. The original text has been annotated to illustrate the Three-Step Process for Writing a Summary. Read the original text, the annotations, and the summary. Then, discuss how the summary differs from the original text. Finally, discuss how the summary is similar to the original text.

Original Text:

What is Bullying?

Step 1. Delete unnecessary material.

Step 3. Underline, rephrase main idea.

Both kids who are bullied and who bully others may have serious, lasting problems. Therefore, parents, educators, and children need to know what bullying is and take steps to stop bullying from occurring. Bullying is the unwanted, aggressive behavior among school-aged children that involves a real or perceived power imbalance and is repeated over time. Kids who bully use their power—such as physical strength, access to embarrassing information, or popularity—to control or harm others. Power imbalances can change over time and in different situations, even if they involve the same people. Bullying behaviors happen more than once or have the potential to happen more than once. Bullying includes actions such as making threats, spreading rumors, attacking someone physically or verbally, and excluding someone from a group on purpose.

Step 1. Delete repetitive material.

Step 2. Condense this section to list "verbal, social, and physical bullying."

There are three types of bullying. One type, verbal bullying, is saying or writing mean things. Verbal bullying includes teasing, name-calling, inappropriate sexual comments, taunting, or threatening to cause harm. Another type, social bullying, involves hurting someone's reputation or relationships. Social bullying includes leaving someone out on purpose, telling other children not to be friends with someone, spreading rumors about someone, or embarrassing someone in public. A third type, physical bullying, involves hurting a person's body or possessions. Physical bullying includes hitting/kicking/pinching, spitting, tripping/pushing, taking or breaking someone's things, or making mean or rude hand gestures.

—Adapted from "Bullying Definition." Stopbullying.gov 13 July 2015.

Summary: According to "What is Bullying?" by Stopbullying.gov, bullying is the repeated harassment of an individual of lesser physical strength or social standing by one or more persons in a position of power. Three types of bullying are verbal, social, and physical.

AVOID PLAGIARISM: SUMMARIZING

Assume you are a tutor working with a small group of peers in your college's writing center. Today, you are looking over a set of practice summaries they have submitted for your input. Read the original text and each summary. Then, evaluate each summary as **A** for acceptable or **U** for unacceptable. Finally, discuss your answers and reasoning with a peer or small group of classmates.

Original Text:

Which Traits Fit You Best?

To introduce my clients to birth order, I often give them a little quiz: Which of the following sets of personality traits fits you best? (Anyone taking this quiz must understand that he or she doesn't have to be everything in a certain list of traits. Just pick the list that has the most items that seem to describe you and your way of operating in life.)

A. perfectionist, reliable, conscientious, list maker, well organized, hard driving, natural leader, critical, serious, scholarly, logical, doesn't like surprises, loves computers.

B. mediator, compromising, diplomatic, avoids conflict, independent, loyal to peers, many friends, a maverick, secretive, unspoiled

C. manipulative, charming, blames others, attention seeker, tenacious, people person, natural salesperson, precocious, engaging, affectionate, loves surprises

D. little adult by age seven; very thorough; deliberate; high achiever; self-motivated; fearful; cautious; voracious reader; black and white thinker; uses "very," "extremely," "exactly," a lot; can't bear to fail; has very high expectations for self; more comfortable with people who are older or younger.

If you noted that this test seemed rather easy because A, B, and C listed traits of the oldest right down to the youngest in the family, you're right. If you picked list A, it's a very good bet you are a first born in your family. If you chose list B, chances are you are a middle child (second born of three children, or possibly third born of four). If list C seemed to relate best to who you are, it's likely you are the baby of the family and are not all that happy that this book has no pictures. (Just kidding—I like to have a little fun with last borns because I'm one myself, but more on that much later.)

But what about list D? It describes the only child, and I threw it in because in recent years I have been getting more and more questions from children who know they are "first borns" but want to know how they are different from people who have siblings.

Source of Text: Leman, Kevin. *The Birth Order Book*. Grand Rapids, MI: Revell, 2008. 14–15. Copyright © 2008 Revell, a division of Baker Publishing Group. Used by permission.

_____ **Summary 1:** In his book *The Birth Order Book*, Kevin Leman describes possible personality traits based on birth order. First borns are most likely demanding leaders; middle children are apt to be tactful referees or go-betweens. Last borns are prone to be intelligent show-offs. Finally, only children are often mature and competitive (14–15).

_____ **Summary 2:** Personality traits are likely influenced by one's birth order. Some of the traits of first borns are perfectionist, reliable, and conscientious. The traits of middle children include being mediators, compromising, and diplomatic. Last born children are manipulative, charming, and seek attention. Only children are little adults by age seven, very thorough, and high achievers. (Leman 14–15).

Practice 7

_____ **Summary 3:** Personality traits are likely influenced by one's birth order. First borns are most likely demanding leaders; middle children are apt to be tactful referees or go-betweens. Last borns are prone to be intelligent show-offs. Finally, only children are often mature and competitive.

_____ **Summary 4:** Personality traits are likely influenced by one's birth order. First borns are most likely demanding leaders; middle children are apt to be tactful referees or go-betweens. Last borns are prone to be intelligent show-offs. Finally, only children are often mature and competitive (Leman 14–15).

Quoting a text entails repeating the exact words of the author. When you use the exact words of another person, you enclose that exact wording within a pair of quotation marks. You should use quotes rarely and purposefully in your writing. A well-placed quote adds interest, emphasis, and authority to an important point. Too many quotes make it look like you didn't take time to understand the text well enough to offer a fresh view of the topic. The following chart presents **PAC,** a few tips for quoting text.

	PAC: Tips for Quoting
Put the quote in context.	Introduce the quote with information about when, where, and why the quote was first stated. Explain the significance of the quote.
Attribute the quote to its source.	Identify the speaker or writer of the quote. Use various verbs other than "he says" or "she says" to give attribution, such as the following: argues notes states thinks claims points out suggests writes comments remarks
Cite correctly the publication information of the source.	In their book _Anybody's Business_, Barbara Van Syckle and Brian Tietje claim, "Democratic leaders empower others" (136).

With a peer or a small group of classmates, study the following use of a quote in a piece of writing. Annotate the writing to identify the PAC tips for using a quote. Underline the information that gives the context of the quote. Circle the attribution of the quote. Circle the publication information. Underline the quote with a squiggly line.

Example of Quoting:

> On a cold, snowy day, January 21, 1961, John F. Kennedy at the age of 43 took the oath of office as the youngest man elected to office. Kennedy exclaimed, "And so, my fellow Americans, ask not what your country can do for you; ask what you can do for your country" (_American Rhetoric: Top 100 Speeches_). Kennedy effectively beckoned an entire generation into public service with this moving call to action.

—John F. Kennedy, Inaugural Address, January 20, 1961.

Notice several aspects of this example of proper quoting that apply as general rules for quoting text. First, a comma follows the attribution verb "exclaimed" to introduce the quote. Second, a pair of quotation marks enclose the exact words of President Kennedy. Third, the source or publication information is placed inside a pair of parentheses and immediately follows the quote. Finally, the end sentence punctuation is placed outside the closing parenthesis.

Practice 8

AVOID PLAGIARISM: QUOTING

Evaluate the effectiveness of the following quotes. In the given spaces, give suggestions, if needed, for improvement of each quote based on PAC: Tips for Quoting.

Quote 1: In January 2009, Captain Sullenberger landed a crippled US Airways plane on the Hudson River, saving the lives of all onboard. In his book *Highest Duty*, he states   We need to try to do the right thing every time, to perform at our best, because we never know which moment in our lives we'll be judged on   (314).

Suggestions for improvement: _____

Quote 2: "Never eat more than you can lift," Miss Piggy.

Suggestions for improvement: _____

Practice 9

AVOID PLAGIARISM: PARAPHRASING, SUMMARIZING, AND QUOTING

Assume you are writing a column about alcohol use for your college newspaper. You plan to use the following source for information. On your own paper compose three types of notes from the original text: a paraphrase, a summary, and a quote.

Original Text:

> Alcohol use is very common in our society. Drinking alcohol has immediate effects that can increase the risk of many harmful health conditions. **Excessive alcohol use**, either in the form of *heavy drinking* (drinking more than two drinks per day on average for men or more than one drink per day on average for women), or *binge drinking* (drinking five or more drinks during a single occasion for men or four or more drinks during a single occasion for women), can lead to increased risk of health problems such as liver disease or unintentional injuries.
>
> **Source of Text:** "Alcohol & Public Health." Centers for Disease Control and Prevention. *CDC.gov*, n.d., Web. 29 Aug. 2011.

PREREAD: SURVEY/QUESTION

READ: QUESTION/ANNOTATE

PREWRITE: RECITE/REVIEW/BRAINSTORM

Preread:

- Choose a topic to research.
- Create questions based on titles, headings, bold/italic terms, and visuals.
- What is my prior knowledge?
- What is my purpose for researching?
- Who is the intended audience for my research?
- Is this information relevant to my research?
- What kind of information is needed? Where can I find information? Is the information reliable?
- Find and evaluate sources.

Read:

- Ask/record questions.
- Annotate text.
- Underline main ideas.
- Circle new/key words.
- Highlight key details.
- Restate ideas out loud.
- Take notes. Record attribution of sources.

Prewrite:

- Organize notes taken.
- List, cluster, outline topics based on survey; leave room to fill in details during reading.
- Take notes. Restate ideas.
- Record quotes.
- Narrow writing topic based on reading/notes.
- Generate details based on narrowed topic, audience, and purpose for research.
- Freewrite a first response.
- Outline or map out details.

L4 Develop Your Reading/Writing Strategy for Research

Effective research is based on combining reading and writing into a strategy to locate and use information to compose and support a thesis about a topic. You have learned how to survey information to question and annotate text. You have learned to comprehend the writer's point by reciting and reviewing main ideas and supporting details. You have learned to brainstorm and organize details in response to what you have read. You have thought carefully about the use of effective expression to make your point clear to your own readers. All of these steps are vital to the research process.

Developing your own reading/writing strategy for research enables you to find and use the information you need in your everyday life, college life, and work life. A reading/writing strategy integrates the steps of reading and writing in order for a researcher to investigate a topic, comprehend information, and compose a written report of the findings of the research. Just as it is with any reading/writing situation, the strategy for research is recursive; the steps are repeated as needed.

Draft
- Refer to notes.
- Write a thesis statement.
- Write the body, introduction, and conclusion of your research.
- Include quotes, paraphrases of expert opinions.
- Include facts from reliable sources.
- Avoid plagiarism.

Review/Revise
- Refine ideas.
- Review draft for clear use of wording, details, and organization.
- Annotate draft with needed revisions.
- Rewrite draft based on review and annotations.
- Apply proper documentation style: MLA or APA.
- Avoid plagiarism.

Proofread:
- Polish ideas.
- Reread draft to identify/correct errors in grammar, spelling, usage, style of documentation.

THINKING THROUGH THE RESEARCH WRITING PROCESS

Reflect on your research and writing process. On your own paper, in your journal or portfolio, record your prior experiences with research and writing. First, describe the steps you usually take when you research information to include in your writing. Then, describe the steps you usually take when you compose a piece of writing based on your research. Finally, discuss how you plan to use the information you learned in this chapter about research and writing. How will your research and writing processes change?

Practice 10

Master the Basics of MLA

Each academic content area has its own style for citing and documenting sources. The most commonly used are the American Psychological Association (APA), Chicago Manual of Style (CMS), and the Modern Language Association (MLA). When you receive a research assignment, ask your teacher to clarify which style you are required to follow. Most students begin their college studies with an English course. Thus, MLA is usually the first style learned and is the focus of this chapter. This section is designed to give you an overview of and practice with the basics of MLA in-text citations in the body of your essay and the Works Cited page, a list of all sources used in your research.

In-Text Citations

Each paraphrase, summary, or quote of an original source you include in your writing must be noted in the body of your essay where it appears. This notation is called an "in-text citation" or "parenthetical notation." The following annotated examples show the basic forms of in-text citations for non-Web and Web sources. Note the use of commas, italics, quotation marks, parentheses, and periods.

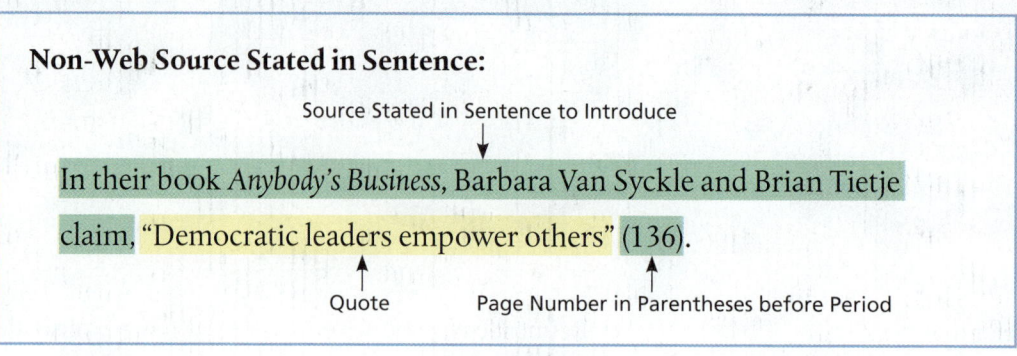

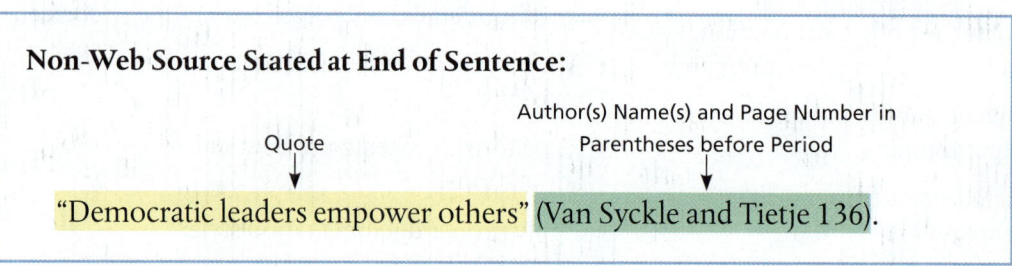

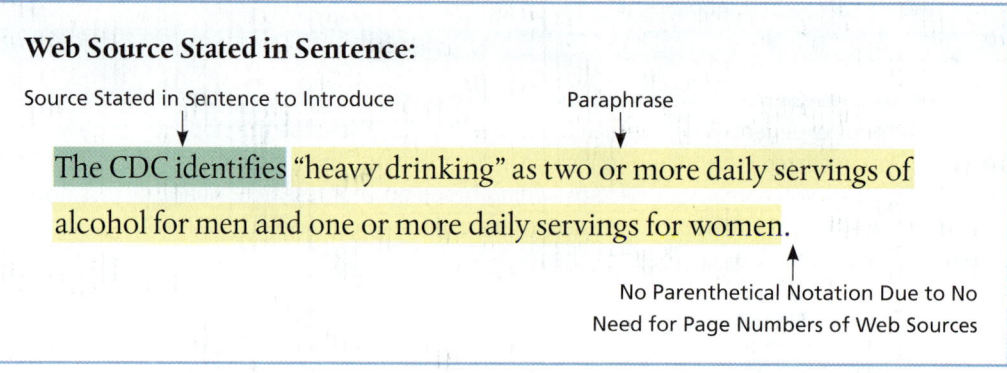

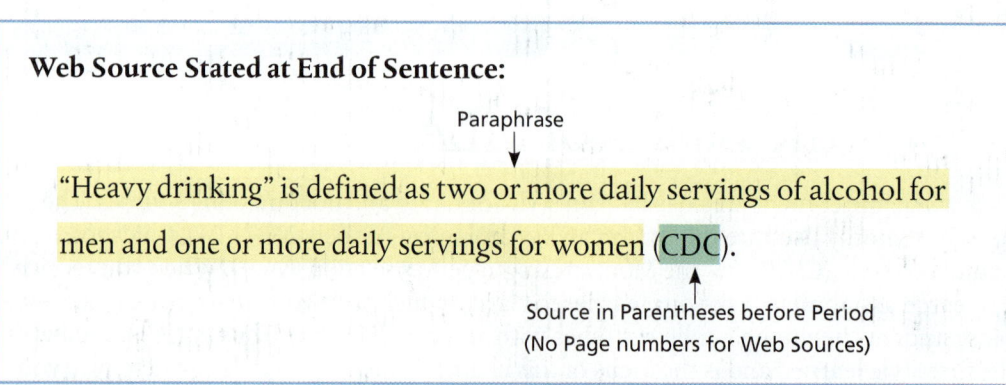

Works Cited Page

A Works Cited page is a complete listing of all the sources you used in your writing, including paraphrases, summaries, and quotes. The following section offers you an overview of the general guidelines for formatting a Works Cited page and a few basic models of common types of entries.

Tips for Formatting Works Cited Page: MLA Style	
General Format	Start the Works Cited page as a separate page at the end of your research paper.
	Continue using the format of the entire paper: one-inch margins, last name heading, and page numbering.
	Center the words Works Cited at the top of the page. Do not italicize the words Works Cited or place them in quotation marks.
	Double space the entire page. Do not skip spaces between entries.
	Create a hanging indent by indenting by five spaces the second and subsequent lines of each citation.
	Identify the medium of publication for each entry such as Print, Web, Film, CD-Rom, DVD, or Personal Interview.
	URLs are no longer required by MLA, but if requested by a teacher or employer, place URLs in <angle brackets> at the end of the entry before the period. For long URLs, break lines before the slashes.
Order of Listing for Entries	List entries alphabetically by the authors' last name. Authors' names are given in the following order: last name first, then middle names or initials, followed by the first name. If there are multiple authors, list only the first author's name in this order; list the later authors in standard (first, middle, last) order.
	Do not include titles such as Dr., Sir, Mr., or Ph.D.
	Do include identifiers such as Jr. or II. **Example**: King, Martin Luther, Jr.
	When no author is given, begin entry with and alphabetize by title of article, book, or website.
Grammar Rules	Use italics for titles of longer works such as books and magazines, and quotation marks for short works such as poems and articles.
	Capitalize each word in the titles of articles, books, magazines except for articles (*a, an, the*), prepositions (*of, for, in*) or conjunctions (*and, but*) unless one appears as the first word in the title. **Example**: *Death of a Salesman*.

Compare these tips to the format of the Works Cited page in the student research essay on page 319. Now that you have an idea about the general format of a Works Cited page, the following sections offer annotated examples to model common types of entries. These models show how to format non-Web and Web sources as entries in a Works Cited page.

Basic MLA Format for Works Cited entries call for four broad categories of information that are presented in the citation in the following order.

Name of author(s): The name of whoever wrote the information: Last name, First name. For an anthology, name of editor(s) are also given.

Title of Source: The name of the book, article, or website you are citing. Use quotes for smaller works such as poems and articles. Use italics for larger works such as books and magazines. Include both when you are citing a small part of something larger like an article in a newspaper.

Publication Information: Any information about where and when the source was created. Information may include the city of publication, the publishing company, the year published, issue number, volume number, edition, and page numbers.

Medium: The format of the source such as Print, Web, Video, DVD, CD-Rom, etc.

For each of the following models for non-Web and Web sources, the type of entry is given, along with the specific pattern of information required for the type of entry, and is followed by an annotated illustration. Note the use of commas, italics, quotation marks, parentheses, and periods.

MLA Formats for Non-Web Sources

Book:

Author. *Title of Book.* City of Publication: Publisher, Year. Medium.

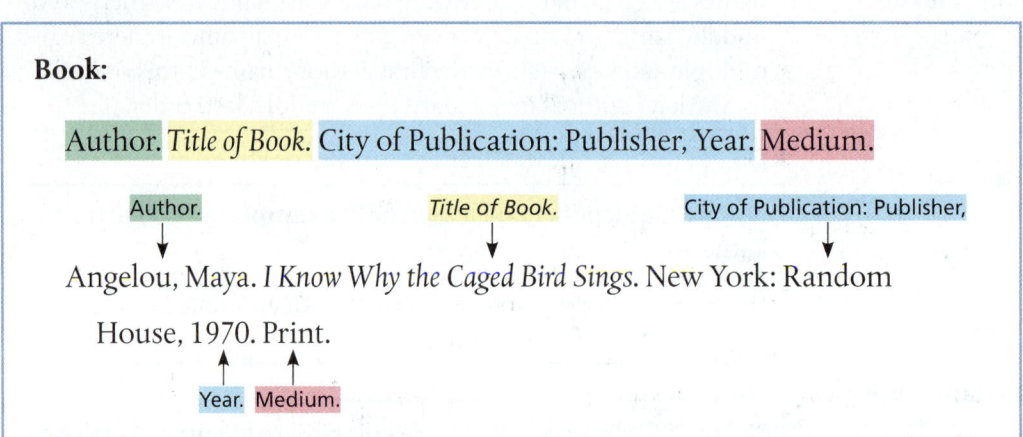

Book by two or three authors: Format is the same as a book with one author except for treatment of the second author's name. List authors in the order that they appear on the title page of publication. Use natural order for the name of the second author. Note the hanging indent of second line of entry.

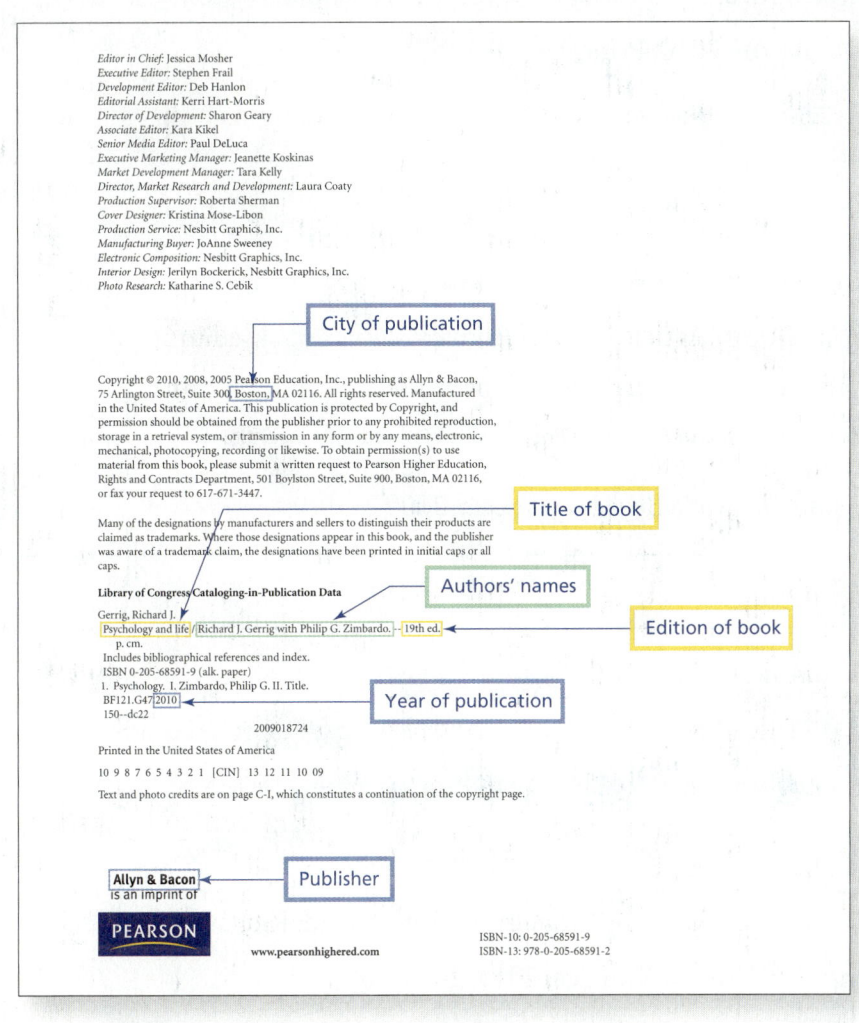

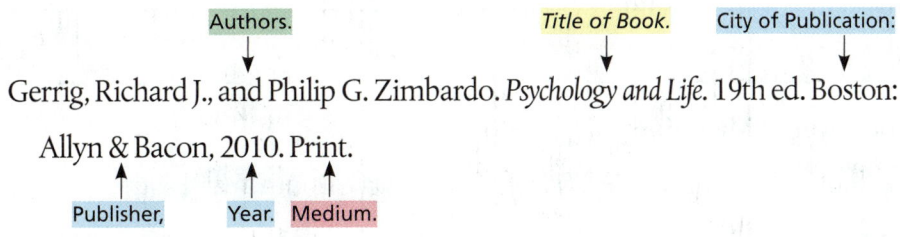

Book by more than four or more authors: Format is the same as for other books except only the name of the first author listed on title page is used followed by "et al." which means "and others."

Carlson, Neil R., et al. *Psychology: The Science of Behavior*. Boston: Allyn & Bacon, 2010. Print.

Article from reference book:

Author(s). "Title of Article." *Title of Reference Book*. Year. Medium.

If no author is listed, start with the title of the article.

"Terrorism." *The World Book Encyclopedia*. 2009 ed. Print.

Selection from an Anthology:

Author(s). "Title of Selection." *Title of Anthology*. Ed. Editor(s) name(s). City of Publication: Publisher, Year. Page numbers. Medium.

Sheehan, George. "Running." *Runners on Running*. Ed. Richard Elliot. Champaign: Human Kinetics, 2011. 2-8. Print.

Article from a Magazine:

Author(s). "Title of Article." *Title of Magazine* Day Month Year: Page numbers. Medium.

Ferreira, Briella M. "Key to Paradise." *Coastal Living* June 2014: 20-24. Print.

Article from a Newspaper:

Author(s). "Title of Article." *Title of Newspaper* Day Month Year: Section Page numbers. Medium.

Haug, Jim. "March of Dimes Raises Flag on Disparities in Birthrate." *The Daytona Beach News-Journal* 2 March. 2015: D2. Print.

DVD:

Title. Dir. Director's Name. Company, Release year. DVD.

Birdman. Dir. Alejandro González Iñárritu. Regency Enterprises, 2014. DVD.

Sound Recording:

Name of Performer(s). "Title of Song." *Title of Album.* Name of Recording Company, Year of release. File Type.

Taylor Swift. "Shake It Off." *1989.* Big Machine Records, 2014. MP3.

Television or Radio Program:

"Title of Episode." *Title of Program.* Network or Station. Date of broadcast. Medium.

"That's Me Without You." *Nashville.* ABC. 24 Sept. 2014. Television.

Personal Interview:

Interviewee. Personal Interview. Day Month Year.

White, Frank. Personal Interview. 8 Nov. 2015.

MLA Formats for Web Sources

Article or Page within a Website:

Author(s). "Article/Page Title." *Site Name.* Publisher or Sponsor of Site, Date of last update or copyright. Medium. Date of Access.

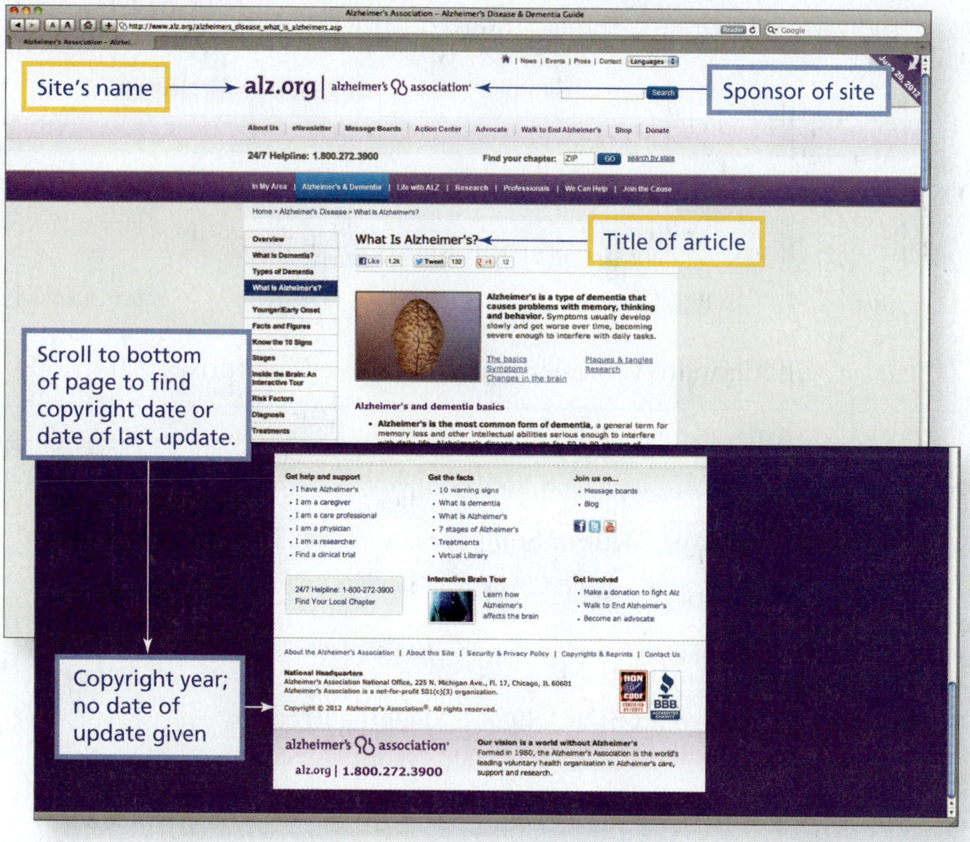

"Title." — Site *Name.* — Sponsor of Site, — Date of last update.

"What is Alzheimer's?" *Alz.org.* The Alzheimer's Association, 2 March 2015. Web. 2 March 2015.

Medium. — Date of Access.

Picture from the Web:

Name(s) of Artist(s). Title. Date of Composition. Medium. Host Institution, City. Site Name. Date of Access.

Creator. — *Title.* — Medium. — Date of Access.

NASA. *Night Flight.* 1983. JPEG Image. *Nasa.gov.* 2 March 2015.

Date of Composition. — Site Name.

Magazine Article from a Library Database:

Author(s). "Article Title." *Magazine Title* Day Month Year: Page numbers. *Name of Database*. Medium. Date of Access.

Begley, Sharon. "A Climate Whodunit." *Newsweek* 6 Dec. 2010: 23. *General OneFile*. Web. 2 March 2015.

Newspaper Article from a Library Database:

Author(s). "Article Title." *Newspaper Title* Day Month Year, Edition. *Name of Database*. Medium. Date of Access.

Hellmich, Nanci. "Outlook on Obesity is Pretty Grim—U. S. Could Hit 50% by 2030." *USA Today*. 30 Aug. 2011, Final. *NewsBank*. Web. 2 March 2015.

MASTER THE BASICS OF MLA

Assume you are writing a research essay about an important current issue for a sociology class. You have chosen to investigate the dangers of using cell phones while driving. You have found and recorded the following publication information about your sources. Create a Works Cited entry in correct MLA format for each source. (Refer to the MLA formats on pages 307–315.)

Source 1: **Article title:** Resisting the Call

Author(s): Tom Guerriero and Dave Yetman

Magazine title: Automobile Magazine

Date of publication: Oct. 2011

Page numbers: 39+

Database: General OneFile

Date of Access: Aug. 31, 2016

Source 2: **Article title:** Driver Electronic Use in 2008.

Website name: National Center for Statistics and Analysis (NCSA) Data Resource Website: Traffic Safety Facts

Publisher/sponsor of site: National Highway Safety Administration (NHSA)

URL: <http://www-nrd.nhtsa.dot.gov/Pubs/811184.PDF>.

Date of last update: Sept. 2009.

Date of access: Aug. 20, 2016

Source 3: **Article title:** Cellphone Use, Texting in 28 Percent of Crashes—Traffic Study Results Inspire Group to Fight Distracted Driving

Author: Ashley Halsey III

Newspaper title: Washington Post

Date of publication: Jan. 13, 2010

Section: A

Page: 6

Sample Student Research Essay

The following student essay serves as a model of the use of the MLA style for citing and documenting sources in a research essay. The annotations point out and explain the student's application of MLA style.

General Format:
1-inch margins. Double spaced. Each page has header of writer's last name and page number.

Stewart 1

Adam Stewart

Professor Henry

English 101

10 September 2015

Flush with left margin, list writer's name, professor's name, course number, and date.

Sleeping Disorders

Center title without use of quotation marks, bold font, or italicized font.

    Sleeping disorders cause adults all around the world to suffer by being deprived of the comfort and rest of sleep. One common sleep disorder is sleep apnea. The American Sleep Apnea Association claims that 4% of the population suffers from sleep apnea. Sleep apnea is a "temporary absence of breathing while sleeping" (Wilson 60). During sleep, people with this disorder may stop breathing a couple hundred times and for up to a minute every night. A person suffering from this disorder may not realize he or she is waking up to continue breathing. In most cases, a member of the household detects the problem before the victim does. Understanding the types and treatment of sleep apnea increases the chances of finding relief from the disorder.

Note this example of a quotation correctly punctuated and cited in-text.

State the main idea of the essay in a thesis statement at the end of the introductory paragraph.

    There are three types of sleep apnea: obstructive, central, and mixed (Robinson and Frey). Obstructive sleep apnea is caused by a blockage of the airways in the throat, mostly from enlarged tonsils. Central sleep apnea is caused by a failure on the part of the brain to control breathing; no physical blockage is the cause. Usually central sleep apnea occurs in people who also struggle with other health problems ("Sleep Apnea"). Mixed sleep apnea is caused by a combination of blockage and lack of a signal from the brain (Robinson and Frey). Obstructive sleep apnea, referred to as OSA, is the most common type. This disorder is very common with people who snore obsessively and men and women over

Note this example of a paraphrase correctly cited in-text.

Stewart 2

the age of 40 who are obese. Studies by the National Institute of Health (NIH) show that all males who are 20% or more overweight suffer with OSA. When the apnea occurs, the airway collapses, breathing ceases, and the brain loses oxygen. This loss of oxygen affects the heart, blood pressure, and can lead to damage in the cardiovascular system (Wilson 140). These periods of irregular breathing cause a person to go into a lighter stage of sleep. Because the brain has to awaken to breathe, the apnea keeps a person from entering a deep sleep, which leads to a loss of alertness, a possible change in personality, tiredness, and trouble functioning the following day (Wilson 293). There are several conditions associated with a sleep apnea such as ulcers, severe headaches, arthritis, and diabetes (Albert 82).

Sleep apnea is treated depending on the severity of the disorder. In mild cases, losing weight and sleeping on one's side are recommended. Ingestion of sedatives and avoiding alcoholic beverages before bed is also a remedy ("Sleep Apnea"). There are oral mouth devices that keep the airway open and help to reduce snoring. Moderate to severe cases are usually treated with a Continuous Positive Airway Pressure Machine, referred to as C-PAP. The C-PAP is a mask worn while sleeping that blows air into the nose keeping the airway open and unobstructed (Robinson and Frey). In the most severe cases a person may have to get a tracheotomy, a surgical incision in the throat that allows the sleeper to breathe directly through the wind pipe, in order to keep breathing properly. If the apnea is left untreated or undetected, long term effects such as muscle spasms, stroke and heart attack, impotence, and headaches could haunt the person for the rest of their life (Albert 36).

> Note this example of a summary correctly cited in-text.

Stewart 3

Works Cited

Albert, Katherine A. *Get a Good Night's Sleep.* New York: Simon & Schuster, 1996. Print.

"Sleep Apnea." *MedlinePlus.* U.S. National Library of Medicine National Institutes of Health, 29 Aug. 2011. Web. 31 Aug. 2015.

Robinson, Richard, and Rebecca J. Frey. "Sleep Apnea." *The Gale Encyclopedia of Medicine.* Ed. Jacqueline L. Longe. 3rd ed. Detroit: Gale, 2007. 5 vols. July 2010. Web. 31 Aug. 2015.

Wilson, Virginia N. *Sleep Thief.* Orange Park: Galaxy Books Inc., 1996. Print.

"What is Sleep Apnea?" *SleepApnea.org.* American Sleep Apnea Association, Sept. 2007. Web. 28 Aug. 2015.

Writing Assignments

MyWritingLab™ Complete this Exercise on mywritinglab.com

Considering Audience and Purpose

Review the photographs in Practice 1 about the purpose of research. Assume you volunteer at the local library and you have been asked to give a speech about the value of research in everyday life, college life, and work life. Write a draft of your speech to post on the library's website after you give your presentation. Use information you have learned from this chapter. Also, interview your professor for tips and advice. Document the information from these sources by using in-text citations and a Works Cited page.

Writing for Everyday Life

Assume you are a member of a local consumer group. The purpose of your group is to share information that will help members wisely manage or save money. Your group publishes a newsletter online once a month. This month, you have been asked to write a column about ways to save money at the grocery store. Find two to three sources of information for your column. Document the information by using in-text citations and a Works Cited page.

Writing for College Life

Assume that you are taking a college course in health, and you are interested in the health benefits of organic food. Find two or three sources about organic food. In addition to the benefits of organic food, you may want to include in your essay information about the traits, the expense, and the use of organic food. Document the information from sources by using in-text citations and a Works Cited page.

Writing for Working Life

Assume that you are preparing to enter the workforce in a profession of your choice (such as a nurse, a manager at a local retail store, a real estate salesperson, etc.). You have decided to draft a general cover letter that you can adapt to fit possible job applications. In your cover letter, you plan to discuss how well suited you are for the responsibilities of the job. Find two or three sources that describe the tasks, responsibilities, and qualifications of the type of job you are seeking. Include information from these sources in your cover letter. Document the information from sources by using in-text citations and a Works Cited page.

Academic Learning Log: Chapter Review

WHAT HAVE I LEARNED ABOUT RESEARCH STRATEGIES AND RESOURCES?

1. What are two kinds of information that inform our thinking and writing? _____

2. What are two main storehouses of information? _____

3. What is PAART? _____

4. What is plagiarism? _____

5. What are four ways to avoid plagiarism? _____

6. What are the five R's of paraphrasing? _____

7. What is the three-step process for writing a summary? _____

8. What are the tips for quoting? _____

9. What is MLA? _____

10. What are in-text citations? _____

11. What is a Works Cited page? _____

12. I still need to learn or practice the following concepts and skills: _____

13. The most helpful information I learned by studying this chapter is _____

Complete the Post-test for Chapter 16 in MyWritingLab.

17 Nouns and Pronouns

PART 4 THE BASIC SENTENCE

LEARNING OUTCOMES

After studying this chapter you will be able to:

- **L1** Answer the question "What's the Point of Nouns and Pronouns?"
- **L2** Recognize Types and Uses of Nouns
- **L3** Identify Count and Noncount Nouns
- **L4** Identify Articles and Nouns
- **L5** Identify Pronouns and Antecedents
- **L6** Make Clear Pronoun References
- **L7** Make Pronouns and Antecedents Agree
- **L8** Clearly Use Pronoun Case

A noun names a person, animal, place, or thing. A pronoun stands in the place of a noun that has been clearly identified earlier in the text.

Thinking about a real-life situation helps us to understand the purpose of nouns and pronouns in our communication. The following photograph captures the essence of a controversial tourist attraction. Study the picture, complete the activity, and answer the question "What's the point of learning about nouns and pronouns?"

What's the Point of Nouns and Pronouns?

PHOTOGRAPHIC ORGANIZER: NOUNS AND PRONOUNS

The following passage is adapted from a news story about the Skywalk bridge over the Grand Canyon that was built as a tourist attraction by the Hualapai tribe. All of the nouns and pronouns have been omitted from the passage. Work with a small group of your peers. Use the picture to help fill in the blanks with nouns and pronouns that make the passage sensible. Answer the question "What's the point of learning about nouns and pronouns?"

Skywalk

A Native American _____ fastened a massive glass-bottomed _____ to the _____ of the _____. The ambitious tourist _____ has angered _____ and some tribal _____. The _____ (pronounced WALL-uh-pie) are an impoverished _____ of about 2,200 _____. _____ live at the _____ remote western _____. A private _____ constructed the $30 million _____ to lure _____ to the _____.

What's the point of learning about nouns and pronouns?

_____

_____

One Student Writer's Response

The following paragraph offers one writer's reaction to the activity based on "Skywalk."

> I couldn't believe how hard this activity was! It was like trying to solve a riddle or a mystery. At least we had the picture to give us some clues. I was glad to be able to work with a group, too. Together we came up with more ideas, but we still couldn't figure out what all the words should be. This activity taught me that nouns and pronouns give really important information. You can't say what you want to say without using nouns and pronouns. I also learned that the words around pronouns and nouns can act like clues. Several times we chose a word that matched the word in front of it, like "the edge" and "an impoverished tribe."

L2 Recognize Types and Uses of Nouns

Often, nouns are the first words we learn to speak as we hear the names of people. The word "noun" comes from the Latin word *nomen*, which means "name." A **noun** names a person, animal, place, object, element, action, or concept.

What a Noun Names	
Person:	Chris Rivers; a sales clerk
Animal:	Kitty; the cat
Place:	Lake Tahoe; a state park
Object:	Kleenex; tissue paper
Element:	water; air; gas
Action:	running
Concept:	Islam; a religion

One type of noun is the proper noun. A **proper noun** names an individual person, place, or thing. Proper nouns are always capitalized. The second type of noun is the common noun. A **common noun** is a general name for any member of a group or class. Common nouns are not capitalized.

Two Types of Nouns	
Proper Noun	**Common Noun**
Barnes & Noble	bookstore
Outback Steak House	restaurant
Diesel	blue jeans
Batman	action hero
Polk County	county

RECOGNIZE TYPES AND USES OF NOUNS

Identify the following words as proper nouns or common nouns. Edit to capitalize the proper nouns.

1. museum
2. smithsonian museum
3. basketball team
4. news anchor
5. lester holt
6. alcohol
7. development
8. Miami heat
9. adolescents
10. restaurant
11. henry
12. toddler
13. frank's diner
14. tylenol
15. macy's
16. department store
17. bud light
18. tissue
19. eggo waffle
20. aspirin

A proper or common noun can function in a sentence as a subject, an object of a verb, an object of a preposition, or an appositive (which describes another noun).

Uses of a Noun

Function in Sentence   **Example**

- Subject

  PROPER NOUN, SUBJECT

  Roberto finished first.

- Object of a verb

  VERB   *COMMON NOUN, OBJECT OF VERB "DRANK"*

  Maria **drank** **coffee**.

- Object of a preposition

  PREPOSITION   *PROPER NOUN, OBJECT OF PREPOSITION "TO"*

  Justin went **to** **AutoZone**.

- Appositive (describes another noun)

  COMMON NOUN, APPOSITIVE DESCRIBING "SIMON"

  Simon, the **manager**, has arrived.

Practice 3

RECOGNIZE TYPES AND USES OF A NOUN

Identify the 20 nouns used in the following sentences. Analyze the functions of each noun. Then, complete the chart, listing each noun based on its function.

1. The Surgeon General reports the following information.

2. In the U.S., 11 million underage youths drink alcohol.

3. Of the 11 million, 7.2 million do binge drinking.

4. Binge drinkers consume four or more alcoholic drinks within two hours.

5. Joel, a 17-year-old binge drinker, has suffered alcohol poisoning.

6. Alcohol, the most commonly abused drug among youth, outranks underage use of tobacco or illicit drugs.

Practice 3

Sentence	Subject		Object of Verb		Object of Preposition		Appositive	
	Proper Noun	Common Noun	Proper Noun	Common Noun	Proper Noun	Common Noun	Proper Noun	Common Noun
1								
2								
3								
4								
5								
6								

Identify Count and Noncount Nouns

Count nouns name distinct individual units of a group or category. Count nouns usually refer to what we can see, hear, or touch. Count nouns are typically common nouns and can be singular or plural. Most plural count nouns are formed by adding –s or –es. However, many singular count nouns use irregular spellings in their plural form.

For more information on irregular spellings, see pages 598–609, "Improving Your Spelling."

Examples of Count Nouns		
	Singular	**Plural**
Regular	age baby dress garden	ages babies dresses gardens
Irregular	calf deer man person	calves deer men people

Noncount nouns name a nonspecific member of a group or category. Noncount nouns, which are typically common nouns, do not have plural forms. Noncount nouns name things that cannot be divided into smaller parts. Often, noncount nouns represent a group of count nouns. The following chart illustrates the differences between count and noncount nouns.

Examples of Noncount Nouns and Corresponding Count Nouns			
Noncount Noun		**Count Noun**	
air, oxygen, steam anger, happiness, grief	English, Spanish, Latin beauty, honesty, truth	gases emotions	languages concepts

Practice 4

IDENTIFY COUNT AND NONCOUNT NOUNS

Read the following sentences. Annotate the **boldfaced** nouns as a count (C) or noncount noun (NC).

1. A video **game** for **kids** offers the same sort of **humor** as watching a **cartoon**.

2. For example, **nose-picking** is a favorite **type** of **animation** found in both.

3. In addition, both offer **acts** of **violence** involving bad **guys** and **guns** as **entertainment**.

4. In the **game** "Secret Rings," the **player** tries to win **rings** of **gold** floating in the **air**.

5. The **game** gets off to a slow **start**, but the **pace** picks up quickly.

L4 Identify Articles and Nouns

An **article** is a type of adjective that describes a noun as being general or specific.

Indefinite articles: *A* and *an* are used before a singular noun that refers to any member of a larger group: *a cat*, *an umbrella*. These articles are often used to introduce a noun for the first time in the discussion. Use *a* before a noun that begins with a consonant: *a cat*. Use *an* before a noun that begins with a vowel: *an umbrella*.

Definite article: *The* is used before a singular or plural noun that refers to a specific member of the larger group: *the cat*, *the hat*. The article *the* is often used to indicate a noun that has already been introduced into the discussion. "A cat is at the front door; the cat looks hungry." *The* is the most commonly used word in the English language.

Zero article: No article is used before the noun. An example: *Time is money*. Use zero article to refer to general ideas.

- *A Chinese woman moves to a different country.*
- *The Chinese woman has a difficult time communicating.*
- *English is a foreign language to her.*

Deciding which article to use with a noun can be a challenge. You must determine if the article refers to a count noun or a noncount noun, and you must determine if the noun is singular or plural. The following chart illustrates the proper combinations.

Nouns and Their Articles		
	Count Nouns	**Noncount Nouns**
Singular	A, An	The
Plural	The	—

IDENTIFY ARTICLES AND NOUNS

Read the sentences below. Insert the correct article (*a*, *an*, or *the*) in the blanks provided.

(1) Dry, irritated skin is _____ threat to _____ person's well-being. (2) To understand _____ threat, you need to understand skin. (3) Well-moisturized skin offers _____ barrier against bacteria and viruses. (4) As _____ individual ages, _____ body's cell turnover slows down, and damage occurs. (5) _____ damage comes from weather, from chilly temperatures and dry indoor heat. (6) Long, hot baths and showers also damage _____ skin. (7) _____ natural protective layer of oil is stripped away by too much washing. (8) _____ lotion treatment can restore _____ protective barrier of moisture. (9) Many of _____ lotion treatments contain petrolatum, glycerin, or shea butter, _____ oil that prevents water loss.

Identify Pronouns and Antecedents

Pronouns and antecedents work closely together to communicate an idea. A pronoun refers to or stands in the place of a noun that has been clearly identified earlier in the discussion. An **antecedent** is the noun to which a pronoun refers. Every pronoun should refer clearly and specifically to one particular antecedent.

ANTECEDENT OF PRONOUN "IT"   PRONOUN "IT" REFERS TO ANTECEDENT "PACKAGE"

When the FedEx **package** arrived, the receptionist put **it** on the front counter.

In the preceding example, the pronoun "it" clearly refers to the antecedent "package."

Make Clear Pronoun References

Because a pronoun takes the place of a noun, careful writers make the relationship between a pronoun and its antecedent obvious and clear. Remembering a few guidelines can help you make clear pronoun references.

Guidelines for Clear Pronoun Reference
• A pronoun refers clearly and unmistakably to one antecedent.
• The antecedent of a pronoun is clearly stated.
• A pronoun appears near its antecedent.
• A pronoun does not make a broad or sweeping reference to an entire group of words.

For more information on using precision in drafting sentences, see pages 510–523, "Sentence Clarity: Point of View, Number, and Tense."

Faulty pronoun references usually occur when the guidelines for clear reference are ignored. Once you understand why faulty pronoun references occur and how they can be corrected, you can avoid them in your writing; then you can make clear pronoun references.

Correct Faulty Pronoun References

Faulty Pronoun Reference to More Than One Antecedent

PROBLEM: The pronoun does not clearly and unmistakably refer to one specific antecedent.

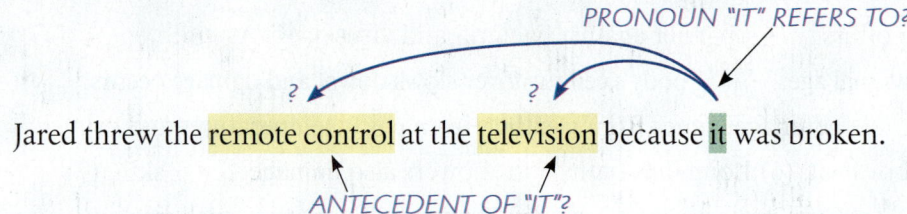

Jared threw the remote control at the television because it was broken.

CORRECTION: Correct by replacing the pronoun with a noun.

Jared threw the remote control at the television because the remote control was broken.

ADDED NOUN REPLACES PRONOUN WITH NO CLEAR ANTECEDENT

Faulty Pronoun Reference to Implied or Missing Antecedent

PROBLEM: The antecedent is not stated or is missing.

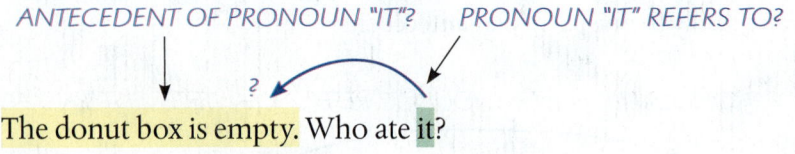

The donut box is empty. Who ate it?

CORRECTION #1: Correct by replacing the pronoun with a noun.

ADDED NOUN REPLACES PRONOUN WITH NO CLEAR ANTECEDENT

The donut box is empty. Who ate the last donut?

CORRECTION #2: Correct by rewording to include a clear antecedent for the pronoun.

ANTECEDENT OF PRONOUN "IT"

The last donut is gone. Who ate it?

Faulty Pronoun Reference due to Distant Pronoun Reference

PROBLEM: The pronoun does not appear near its antecedent.

ACTUAL ANTECEDENT OF PRONOUN "WHICH"

Saleem found the **key** on the back **seat** of his **car**, **which** opens the basement door.

ANTECEDENT OF "WHICH"?   DISTANT RELATIVE PRONOUN

CORRECTION: Correct by rewording to place the pronoun closer to its antecedent.

ANTECEDENT OF PRONOUN "WHICH"   PRONOUN "WHICH" REFERS TO ANTECEDENT "KEY"

Saleem found the **key**, **which** opens the basement door, on the back seat of his car.

Faulty Pronoun Reference due to Broad Pronoun References

PROBLEM: The pronoun refers to a group of words, such as an entire sentence.

ANTECEDENT OF PRONOUN "WHICH"?   PRONOUN "WHICH" REFERS TO?

Mick told Megan about his date with Kanesha, **which** annoyed Megan.

CORRECTION: Correct by rewording to eliminate the pronoun.

Megan was annoyed because Mick told her about his date with Kanesha.

MAKE CLEAR PRONOUN REFERENCE

Revise the following sentences for clear pronoun reference.

1. Maxine spewed coffee into her food because it tasted terrible.

2. Colleen told Samantha that her dress was torn.

3. Employees must check with their managers who need sick-leave forms.

4. As Henry approached the baby's high chair, it screamed.

Practice 6

5. That guy is walking a big shaggy dog who was Carlos's roommate in college.

6. Wikipedia is a free online encyclopedia, and it offers almost 4 million articles; that's why I like it.

7. Cats offer friendship and hunt vermin which are the best pets in the world.

8. Angelo fell on his arm as he tripped over the toy and broke it.

9. We planted the rose bush next to the back porch that Simon gave us.

10. Inhale deeply through your nose, hold it for five seconds, and then slowly exhale.

L7 Make Pronouns and Antecedents Agree

A pronoun and its antecedent must agree with each other in three ways: person, number, and gender. The following chart presents pronouns based on these traits.

Pronouns: Person, Number, and Gender		
	Singular	**Plural**
First Person	I, me, my, mine	we, us, our, ours
Second Person	you, your, yours	you, your, yours
Third Person	he, him, his (**masculine**) she, her, hers (**feminine**) it, its (**neutral**)	they, them, their, theirs (**neutral**)

Pronoun agreement makes the relationship between a pronoun and its antecedent obvious and clear. **Faulty pronoun agreement** reflects vague wording and results in reader confusion. Remembering a few guidelines can help you establish pronoun agreement.

> **Guidelines for Clear Pronoun Agreement**
>
> - Pronoun choice establishes consistent use of the person of pronouns.
> - Singular pronouns refer to or replace singular nouns.
> - Plural pronouns refer to or replace plural nouns.
> - Feminine pronouns refer to or replace feminine nouns.
> - Masculine pronouns refer to or replace masculine nouns.
> - Use gender-neutral plural pronouns and antecedents in statements that could apply to either women or men.

Faulty pronoun agreement usually occurs when the guidelines for clear agreement are ignored. Once you understand why faulty pronoun agreement occurs and how it can be corrected, you can avoid vague agreements in your writing; then you can create agreement based on person, number, and gender.

Correct Faulty Pronoun Agreement

Faulty Pronoun Agreement Due to Shift in Person

PROBLEM: When the person of the pronoun differs from the person of the antecedent, it is called a faulty **shift in person**. In the example below, the faulty shift is from third person to second person.

ANTECEDENT, A THIRD-PERSON NOUN

While a **contestant** sings, the judges evaluate **your** performance.

SECOND-PERSON PRONOUN "YOUR" DOES NOT AGREE

CORRECTION #1: Change the antecedent to agree with the pronoun.

ADDED SECOND-PERSON ANTECEDENT AGREES WITH SECOND-PERSON PRONOUN

After **you** finish a song, the judges evaluate **your** performance.

CORRECTION #2: Change the pronoun to agree with the antecedent.

THIRD-PERSON ANTECEDENT AGREES WITH ADDED THIRD-PERSON PRONOUN

After a **contestant** finishes a song, the judges evaluate **her** performance.

Faulty Pronoun Agreement Due to Shift in Number

PROBLEM: In a sentence with a faulty **shift in number,** the pronoun is a different number than the number of the antecedent. In the two examples below, the faulty shift is from singular to plural; the revised sentences show two different ways to correct the same problem.

SINGULAR ANTECEDENT

PLURAL PRONOUN DOES NOT AGREE WITH SINGULAR ANTECEDENT "ATHLETE"

A college athlete must keep their grades at a B average to be eligible to play.

SINGULAR ANTECEDENT

PLURAL PRONOUN DOES NOT AGREE WITH SINGULAR ANTECEDENT "EVERYONE"

Everyone on the women's soccer team has their gear loaded on the bus.

CORRECTION: Make the antecedent the same number as the pronoun.

PLURAL ANTECEDENT AGREES WITH PLURAL PRONOUN

College athletes must keep their grades at a B average to be eligible to play.

SINGULAR ANTECEDENT AGREES WITH SINGULAR PRONOUN

Everyone on the women's soccer team has her gear loaded on the bus.

Faulty Pronoun Agreement Due to Shift in Gender

PROBLEM: In a sentence with a faulty **shift in gender**, the pronoun is a different gender than the gender of the antecedent. Most often, gender agreement problems are due to using the masculine pronoun to refer to antecedents that could apply to either men or women.

SINGULAR ANTECEDENT IS NEUTRAL ("STUDENT" COULD BE EITHER MASCULINE OR FEMININE)

A student can buy his books online.

MASCULINE, SINGULAR PRONOUN "HIS" DOES NOT AGREE WITH NEUTRAL ANTECEDENT "STUDENT"

CORRECTION #1: Reword to make the pronoun the same gender as the antecedent.

NEUTRAL, SINGULAR ANTECEDENT AGREES WITH NEUTRAL, SINGULAR PRONOUN "HIS OR HER"

A student can buy his or her books online.

If you reword the sentence by making the pronoun and its antecedent (neutral and) plural, make sure all other parts of the sentence are plural as necessary.

NEUTRAL, PLURAL ANTECEDENT AGREES WITH NEUTRAL, PLURAL PRONOUN

Students can buy their books online.

CORRECTION #2: Reword to make the antecedent the same gender as the pronoun. In the instance below, this requires adding a masculine proper noun ("John") to match the masculine pronoun.

ADDED MASCULINE, SINGULAR ANTECEDENT   MASCULINE, SINGULAR PRONOUN "HIS" REFERS TO MASCULINE, SINGULAR ANTECEDENT "JOHN"

John, a student, can buy his books online.

ADDED COMMAS SET OFF NEW APPOSITIVE PHRASE

CORRECT FAULTY PRONOUN AGREEMENT

Edit the following sentences to create pronoun agreement. Cross out the faulty pronoun and insert the appropriate pronoun.

1. People should check their credit reports to find out if you have been victimized by identity theft.

2. A person can have his credit report sent to him for free.

3. A victim of identity theft loses more than money; they lose peace of mind.

4. A consumer should be diligent about paying bills; your payment history counts for 35 percent of your credit score.

5. A household budget allows you to control a person's finances.

6. Many families have difficulty meeting its monthly bills when faced with unexpected expenses.

7. When you impulsively buy fast food and coffee to go, you spend more than people realize.

8. A person needs to create and stick to a written budget so he can monitor his cash flow.

9. Every person who budgets can avoid relying on their credit cards to make ends meet.

10. Write a sentence that requires subject-verb agreement. Suggested topic: Household expenses.

L8 Clearly Use Pronoun Case

Pronoun case identifies the function of a pronoun in a sentence. The definitions and examples of the three cases of pronouns are shown in the following chart.

	Pronoun Case					
	Subjective Case		**Objective Case**		**Possessive Case**	
	Singular	Plural	Singular	Plural	Singular	Plural
1st Person	I	we	me	us	my, mine	our, ours
2nd Person	you	you	you	you	your, yours	your, yours
3rd Person	he, she, it	they	him, her, it	them	his, his her, hers its	their, theirs
	who whoever		whom whomever		whose	

Subjective case pronouns act as subjects or predicate nouns. A **predicate noun** restates the subject, usually by completing a linking verb such as *is*.

SUBJECTIVE CASE PRONOUN

We are going to audition for a gig at the Comedy Club.

SUBJECT   SUBJECTIVE CASE PRONOUN RENAMES THE SUBJECT "COMEDIAN"

The funniest comedian is she.

Objective case pronouns act as an object of a verb or preposition. The **object** of a verb is the noun or pronoun to which the action of a verb is directed or to which the verb's action is done.

VERB   OBJECT OF THE VERB "CAPTIVATED"

The comedian captivated them.

PREPOSITION   OBJECT OF THE PREPOSITION "TO"

To whom are you speaking?

Possessive case pronouns show ownership.

INDICATES THAT THE GLASSES BELONG TO "TOM"

Tom put his glasses on the bookshelf.

INDICATES THAT THE CAR BELONGS TO "JASON AND CINDY"

By the time Jason and Cindy parked their car, the baseball game was over.

IDENTIFY PRONOUN CASE

Underline the pronouns in each sentence. Then, identify the case of each pronoun.

1. The Library of Congress has added a popular Rolling Stones song to its archives.

2. The song "(I Can't Get No) Satisfaction" was first recorded in 1965; it was an instant hit.

3. The Library of Congress wants to preserve significant recordings because many of them have disappeared over the years.

4. The panel who choose the recording is made up of members of the public and a panel of music, sound, and preservation experts.

5. The Rolling Stones are an English rock band that built its success on blues and rock and roll.

6. Two other popular songs of 1965 were "I Got You Babe" by Sonny and Cher and "The Times They Are a Changing," by Bob Dylan.

7. The song "Satisfaction" is different; it expressed "dis-satisfaction" with the status quo, the way it was.

8. The lyrics of "Satisfaction" rail against society for its materialism and shallowness.

9. The singer in the song is a man who is frustrated by the hype of useless advertisements for a better life and his own failing love life.

10. Write a sentence that requires the use of a subjective case pronoun. Suggested topic: Favorite musical group.

▲ Mick Jagger and Charlie Watts of the Rolling Stones

Correct use of pronoun cases relies on having an understanding of the function of the pronoun in the context of its use. Remembering a few guidelines can help you choose the appropriate case of a pronoun.

> **Guidelines for Use of Pronoun Cases**
>
> - Choose the appropriate pronoun case in comparisons using *as* or *than* based on the meaning of the sentence.
> - Use the appropriate pronoun case in compound constructions, such as compound subjects, compound objects of verbs, or compound objects of prepositions.

Misuse of pronoun case usually occurs when the function of the pronoun is ignored or misunderstood. Once you understand why misuse of pronoun case occurs and how it can be corrected, you can choose the appropriate pronoun case based on the context of its use.

Correct Faulty Use of Pronoun Case in Comparisons Using "as" or "than"

Pronouns in comparisons using "as" or "than" can be in the subjective, objective, or possessive case. Most writers have no difficulty using the possessive case correctly: *Sam's car is prettier than **mine***. However, writers often confuse the subjective and objective cases (for example, incorrectly substituting "I" for "me," "he" for "him," "she" for "her," or "who" for "whom" because they think it sounds more formal).

PROBLEM: The objective case pronoun is being used as the subject of a clause.

DEPENDENT CLAUSE WITH UNSTATED VERB "IS"

Jerome is as concerned as her.

INCORRECT USE OF OBJECTIVE CASE PRONOUN

CORRECTION: If the pronoun is a subject, correct by replacing the pronoun with a subjective case pronoun. To identify whether a pronoun in a comparison is a subject or an object, mentally complete the comparison by filling in the implied words and then choose the pronoun that matches it logically.

SUBJECTIVE CASE PRONOUN ACTS AS SUBJECT OF IMPLIED VERB "IS"

Jerome is as concerned as she [is].

IMPLIED VERB

PROBLEM: The subjective case pronoun is being used as the object of a verb.

INCORRECT USE OF SUBJECTIVE CASE PRONOUN

The transit strike affected Marion as much as I.

CORRECTION: If the pronoun is an object, correct by replacing the pronoun with an objective case pronoun. To identify whether a pronoun in a comparison is a subject or an object, mentally complete the comparison by filling in the implied words and then choose the pronoun that matches it logically.

OBJECT OF IMPLIED VERB "AFFECTED"

The transit strike affected Marion as much as [it affected] me.

In some cases, the pronoun in a comparison could function as either a subject or an object and still make sense either way, but it would change the sentence's meaning. Both examples below are correct, but the first sentence means that Miguel respects Carlotta more than you respect her and the second sentence means that Miguel respects Carlotta more than he respects you.

SUBJECTIVE CASE PRONOUN "I" ACTS AS THE SUBJECT OF THE IMPLIED VERB "RESPECT"

Miguel respects Carlotta more than I [respect Carlotta].

OBJECTIVE CASE PRONOUN "ME" IS THE OBJECT OF THE IMPLIED VERB "RESPECTS"

Miguel respects Carlotta more than [he respects] me.

Correct Faulty Use of Case in Compound Constructions

In some instances, a pronoun is joined with a noun or another pronoun to form a **compound.**

- **Joseph and I** went to a concert together.
- The mailman delivered the letter to **Joseph and me**.

To decide whether the subjective or objective case should be used for a pronoun in a compound, use the same rules that apply for a pronoun that is not in a compound. Use the subjective case for pronouns that function as subjects and the objective case for pronouns that function as objects.

PROBLEM: The objective case pronoun is being used in a compound subject.

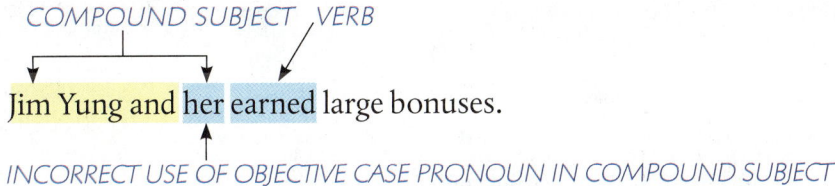

INCORRECT USE OF OBJECTIVE CASE PRONOUN IN COMPOUND SUBJECT

CORRECTION: If the pronoun is a subject, correct by replacing the pronoun with the subjective case pronoun. To identify a pronoun as part of a compound subject, delete the other part of the compound so the pronoun stands alone, and see whether the sentence still makes sense. In the example here, you would delete "Jim Yung." The revised sentence, "Her earned large bonuses," does not make sense, which indicates that the pronoun used is part of a compound subject and should be subjective, not objective.

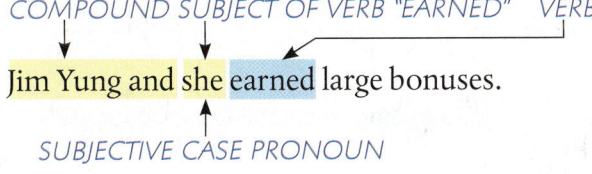

PROBLEM: The subjective case pronoun is being used in a compound object.

VERB   COMPOUND OBJECTS

The supervisor told Bob and I the news.

MISUSED SUBJECTIVE CASE PRONOUN

CORRECTION: If the pronoun is an object of either a verb or a preposition, correct by replacing the pronoun with the objective case pronoun. To identify a pronoun as part of a compound object, delete the other part of the compound so the pronoun stands alone, and see whether the sentence still makes sense. In the example, you would delete "Bob." The revised sentence, "The supervisor told I the news," does not make sense, which indicates that the pronoun used is part of a compound object and should be objective, not subjective.

VERB   COMPOUND OBJECTS OF THE VERB "TOLD"

The supervisor told Bob and me the news.

Practice 9

PRONOUN CASE: USE COMPARISONS AND COMPOUND CONSTRUCTIONS

Edit (as needed) the following sentences to ensure proper use of pronoun cases.

1. Michael, a highly skilled massage therapist, says that John is as effective as him.

2. In fact, many customers like John better than he.

3. Michael and him charge the same rates for a deep tissue massage.

4. Daniella strongly recommends both Michael and he as massage therapists.

5. Who would you and him recommend as a massage therapist?

6. John is the one whom is the best and the one who I recommend.

7. Margaret, whom is also a massage therapist, treated Jerome and I to a massage.

8. Him and Chantal need a massage more than any of us.

9. However, Chantal is not one whom will enjoy a massage more than you and me.

10. Write a sentence that requires the proper use of pronoun case. Suggested topic: A good friend.

Reflexive and intensive pronouns include all the pronouns ending in *-self* or *-selves*. Often, in everyday, informal speech, the irregular forms of reflexive or intensive pronouns can be heard: *hisself*, *theirself*, and *theirselves*. However, these forms are to be avoided in standard, written English. The following chart lists the standard forms and uses of reflexive and intensive pronouns.

Reflexive and Intensive Pronouns		
Person	Singular	Plural
First Person	myself	ourselves
Second Person	yourself	yourselves
Third Person	himself, herself, itself	themselves

Reflexive pronouns refer back to the subject.

REFLEXIVE PRONOUN "HERSELF" REFERS TO SUBJECT "JEANNIE"

Jeannie rewarded herself with a two-week cruise to the Bahamas.

Intensive pronouns add emphasis to another noun or pronoun.

INTENSIVE PRONOUN EMPHASIZES "DR. GILLON"

Dr. Gillon himself made a surprise appearance.

PROBLEM: Because reflexive and intensive pronouns always refer to other nouns or pronouns, reflexive and intensive pronouns are never used on their own as the subject of a sentence.

REFLEXIVE PRONOUN MISUSED AS SUBJECT

My wife and myself went to the movies last night.

CORRECTION: Replace the reflexive pronoun with a subjective pronoun.

ADDED SUBJECTIVE PRONOUN

My wife and I went to the movies last night.

Practice 10

PRONOUN CASE: USE REFLEXIVE AND INTENSIVE PRONOUNS

Complete each sentence by filling in the blank with the appropriate reflexive or intensive pronoun.

1. I do not need assistance; I can lift the weight by _____.

2. Gil _____ heard the diagnosis from the doctor.

3. Charlene gives _____ a daily shot of her medicine for diabetes.

4. The President and the Vice President _____ appeared at the rally.

5. You need to tell _____ that success is possible.

6. If you arrive at the house first, let _____ in please.

7. Julia is a two year old who loves to read to _____.

8. Dan and I treated _____ to dinner and a movie.

9. Angelina Jolie _____ wrote and directed the film.

10. I _____ bought the house.

Practice 11

NOUN AND PRONOUN REVIEW

Test your understanding of nouns and pronouns by filling the blanks with the nouns, articles, and pronouns that best complete each idea.

Cheating is often (1) _____ key to success for video gamers. At some point in (2) _____ game, (3) _____ has gotten stuck. Today's gamers use cheat sites to get unstuck and to learn how to master difficult games. When (4) _____ pay $60 for a game, (5) _____ want to get (6) _____ money's worth. While (7) _____ can get (8) _____ gamer blackballed in competitive video game play, solo cheating is widely practiced. Still, few gamers want to admit that they (9) _____ cheat. Most gamers want to believe that (10) _____ are better players than (11) _____. For example, Jessie is always arguing with (12) _____ about (13) _____ is the best gamer—(14) _____ or I. The (15) _____ for cheating has given rise to dozens of Web (16) _____ dedicated to game cheating. Importantly, (17) _____ gamer (18) _____ cheats cannot say (19) "_____ (20) _____ won this game!"

Editing Assignments

MyWritingLab™ Complete this Exercise on mywritinglab.com

Editing for Everyday Life

Assume you got into a fight last night with your significant other, and you are writing a note of apology. Edit the following apology to ensure proper use of nouns, articles, and pronouns. Use your own paper or complete the exercise on MyWritingLab.com.

Dear Jess,

Too often disagreement come between you and I. Yesterday, our arguing seemed to upset others more than it upset ourselves. As you know, the quick tempers run in my family. And your family is just as fiery as us. Yesterday, however a fault was all me. I can't blame anyone but me. I should not have embarrassed you by arguing with your brother Jonathan, whose also full of the remorse. You and me have been together an long time. One hopes you can find within yourself to forgive Jonathan and me.

Regretfully, Pat

Editing for College Life

Assume you are taking a test for a unit in Interpersonal Communication 101. On the written portion of the test, you are asked to explain some of the differences between individualistic cultures and collective cultures. You have ten minutes left to proofread your response. Edit to ensure proper use of nouns, articles, and pronouns. Use your own paper or complete the exercise on MyWritingLab.com.

Exam question: What are the major contrasting traits between individualistic and collective cultures?

Individualistic and collective cultures differ in several aspect. Individualist cultures focus on the goales of an individual. You're responsible for yourself, and perhaps your immediate family. Your values are guided by your own consciences. A person's success is measured by surpassing other members of his group. Members of individualist culture are competitive, individualistic, and direct. Individualist cultures include American, Swedish, and German. In contrast, collective cultures focus on the goales of the group. Members of collective cultures are cooperative, submissive, and polite. You're responsible for a entire group and to group's values and rules. Collective cultures include Japaneses, Arabic, and Mexican.

Editing for Working Life

Assume you are a hairstylist who has recently opened a new salon. You have composed a letter to send to your customers to inform them about your move. Edit the letter to ensure proper use of nouns, articles, and pronouns. Use your own paper or complete the exercise on MyWritingLab.com.

Dear Friends,

    I would like to invite you to share in me new venture. I will now be at a following location: Waves & Day Spa, The Renaissance Center, 453 S. Oleander Street. We will offer your the same services at the same prices and also the addition of massage, facials, spa pedicures and manicures. There is also an selection of spa packages and escapes available. I will be working your same days Tuesday through Saturday with same flexible hours to accommodate yours schedule. I welcome you to join my new team and I at my new location and assure you that there will be same comfortable jovial atmosphere of a small salon with the offer of Day Spa services I appreciate your loyalty over the years and hope you will come see me at the new salon for a fresh new start to this new year.

Sincerely,

Denise Cossaboon

Academic Learning Log: Chapter Review

WHAT HAVE I LEARNED ABOUT NOUNS AND PRONOUNS?

To test and track your understanding, answer the following questions.

1. A noun names a _____, animal, place, object, or concept.

2. A _____ noun names an individual person, place, or thing; a _____ noun is a general name for any member of a group or class.

3. A noun can function as a _____, object of a verb, object of a _____, or appositive.

4. _____ nouns name distinct individual units of a group or category;

   _____ nouns name a nonspecific member of a group or category.

5. An _____ article is used before a singular noun that refers to any member of a larger group.

6. The definite article _____ is used before a singular or plural noun that refers to a specific member of a larger group.

7. A pronoun refers clearly and specifically to _____ antecedent.

8. An antecedent is the _____ to which a pronoun refers.

9. A pronoun and its antecedent must agree with each other in three ways: _____,

   _____, and _____.

10. The three pronoun cases are _____ case, _____ case, and _____ case.

11. A reflexive pronoun refers to the _____.

12. An intensive pronoun adds _____ to another noun or pronoun.

13. **How will I use what I have learned about nouns and pronouns?**
    In your notebook, discuss how you will apply to your own writing what you have learned about nouns and pronouns.

14. **What do I still need to study about nouns and pronouns?**
    In your notebook, discuss your ongoing study needs by describing what, when, and how you will continue studying pronouns and nouns.

MyWritingLab™

Complete the Post-test for Chapter 17 in MyWritingLab.

18 Adjectives and Adverbs

LEARNING OUTCOMES

After studying this chapter you will be able to:

L1 Answer the question "What's the Point of Adjectives and Adverbs?"

L2 Understand the General Functions and Purposes of Adjectives and Adverbs

L3 Use Adjectives: Forms, Placement, and Order

L4 Use Adverbs

L5 Use the Degrees of Adjectives and Adverbs: Absolute, Comparative, and Superlative

L6 Master *Good* and *Well*

An adjective describes a noun or a pronoun. An adverb describes a verb, an adjective, or another adverb.

Thinking about a real-life situation helps us to understand the purpose of adjectives and adverbs in our communication. The following photograph captures the action of a highly skilled basketball player, LeBron James. Study the picture, complete the activity, and answer the question "What's the point of learning about adjectives and adverbs?"

What's the Point of Adjectives and Adverbs?

PHOTOGRAPHIC ORGANIZER: ADJECTIVES AND ADVERBS

Assume you are a sports reporter for your college newspaper and you are writing a series of articles on great NBA basketball players. This week your column features LeBron James. Work with a small group of your peers. Use the picture to help you fill in the blanks with adjectives and adverbs that best describe the action in the photo.

The Amazing LeBron James

LeBron James is an _____ basketball player. His vertical leap is usually the _____ of all the players on the court. Other players' attempts to block James' shots are _____, because James' moves to the basket are _____ and _____ than his opponents could cope with. His _____ arms let him release the ball _____ to the basket while his body is _____ feet _____ from the basket. LeBron James is one of the _____ players in the NBA.

What's the point of adjectives and adverbs?

One Student Writer's Response

The following paragraph offers one writer's reaction to the paragraph about LeBron James.

> This activity taught me how important adjectives and adverbs are. They paint a vivid picture so the reader can see the point of a topic or issue. I also noticed that each member of our group chose different words to describe LeBron James and the action in the photograph. For example, one person in our group described James as an "unbelievable basketball player" while another person said he is "an aggressive basketball player." So my choice of adjectives and adverbs helps me to get my own point across. I also noticed that adjectives describe people and things; while adverbs describe actions.

L2 Understand the General Functions and Purposes of Adjectives and Adverbs

Adjectives and adverbs are descriptive words that illustrate, modify, or limit the meaning of other words. Adjectives and adverbs have specific functions in a sentence and thus express precise meanings. Understanding the function and purpose of adjectives and adverbs allows a writer a thoughtful and effective expression of ideas.

An **adjective** modifies—in other words, it describes or limits—a noun or a pronoun. It answers one or more of the following questions:

- What kind?
- Which one?
- How many?

Maya has a loud voice.

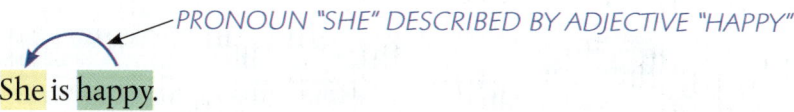

She is happy.

An **adverb** modifies, or describes, a verb, an adjective, or another adverb. It answers one or more of the following questions:

- How?
- Why?
- When?
- Where?
- To what extent?

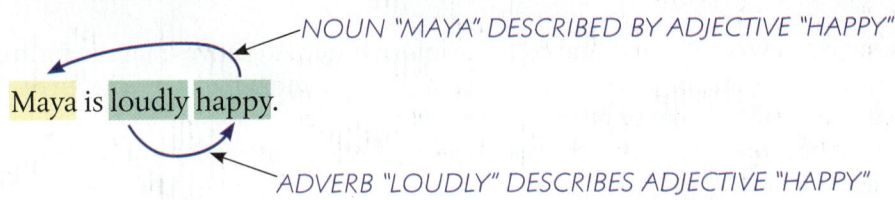

VERB "TALKS" DESCRIBED BY ADVERB "LOUDLY"

Maya talks loudly.

NOUN "MAYA" DESCRIBED BY ADJECTIVE "HAPPY"

Maya is loudly happy.

ADVERB "LOUDLY" DESCRIBES ADJECTIVE "HAPPY"

Practice 2

UNDERSTAND THE FUNCTION AND PURPOSE OF ADJECTIVES AND ADVERBS

Identify the **boldfaced** words in each sentence as adjectives (ADJ) or as adverbs (ADV).

1. Camping has **persistently** remained one of life's **greatest** bargains.

2. A couple can camp **inexpensively**.

3. An **entire** set of **high-quality** equipment can cost **less** than $500.

4. Nights in **many** areas can get **very** cold.

5. Sleeping bags are **widely** available in **various** weights at **reasonable** prices.

6. There are **three different** types of camping: **primitive** camping, **recreational** camping, and **wilderness** camping.

7. Recreational campgrounds **typically** cost $20 to $30 a night and offer **clean** toilets, **hot** showers, laundry facilities, and **convenience** stores.

8. Primitive campsites cost $5 to $10 a night and **normally** supply **picnic** tables, toilets, and **drinking** water.

9. Wilderness camping is **often** permitted in **many** national and state parks for a **small** fee.

10. Since **no** facilities exist in the wild, wilderness campers **simply** must supply **all** their own food, water, and shelter.

L3 Use Adjectives: Forms, Placement, and Order

Writers use adjectives to relay vivid and concrete information. Adjectives range in forms. Thus, they offer multitudes of descriptive words. In addition, more than one adjective may be used to describe a noun or pronoun. However, for effective expression of an idea, adjectives must be properly placed. Likewise, a series of adjectives appear in a certain order within a sentence.

Participles Used as Adjectives

Many adjectives are formed by adding *-ed* or *-ing* to verbs. These **participle adjectives** serve two purposes: The *-ed* form describes a person's reaction or feeling; the *-ing* form describes the person or thing that causes the reaction.

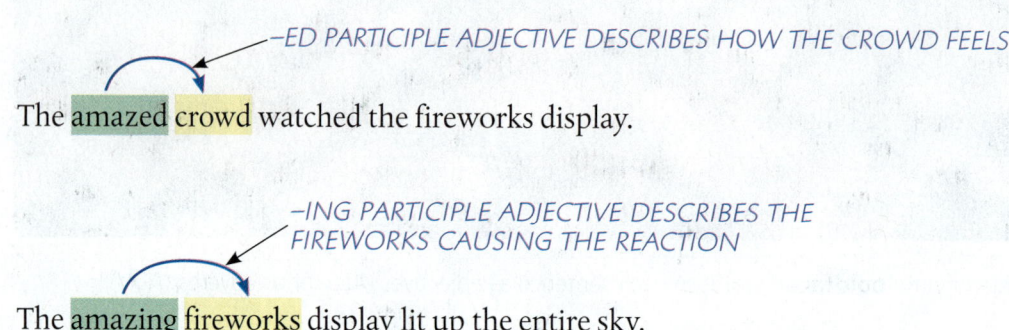

—ED PARTICIPLE ADJECTIVE DESCRIBES HOW THE CROWD FEELS

The amazed crowd watched the fireworks display.

—ING PARTICIPLE ADJECTIVE DESCRIBES THE FIREWORKS CAUSING THE REACTION

The amazing fireworks display lit up the entire sky.

The following chart lists some of the most common participles used as adjectives.

Common Participles Used as Adjectives			
alarmed	alarming	exhausted	exhausting
amused	amusing	fascinated	fascinating
annoyed	annoying	frightened	frightening
bored	boring	horrified	horrifying
concerned	concerning	irritated	irritating
confused	confusing	pleased	pleasing
depressed	depressing	satisfied	satisfying
discouraged	discouraging	shocked	shocking
encouraged	encouraging	stimulated	stimulating
engaged	engaging	terrified	terrifying
excited	exciting	worried	worrying

Practice 3

PARTICIPLES AS ADJECTIVES

Complete the following ideas by filling in the blanks with the proper participle adjective. Create the participle adjectives from the following words: *amaze, amuse, bore, dare, fascinate, shock, terrify, thrill,* and *watch*.

1. Last night, we saw a truly _____ spectacle, Cirque du Soleil's show "O."

2. Cirque du Soleil's shows will be seen by almost 100 million people in over 200 cities around the world, and I'm willing to bet that not a person will feel _____.

3. "O" was *riveting* from beginning to end—there wasn't a _____ moment.

4. The _____ crowd gasped as they watched the gymnastic and trapeze feats pulled off by incredibly brave performers.

5. Cirque du Soleil's shows range from serious to _____.

6. Cirque du Soleil's artists accomplish _____ feats as they juggle objects and leap in the air.

7. These performers dive from _____ heights and thrill _____ audiences with their acrobatics.

8. *Michael Jackson One* is a _____ show full of _____ choreography.

9. Criss Angel, the most _____ magician in television history, is the star of a Cirque du Soleil show in Las Vegas.

10. Write a sentence using a participle as an adjective. Suggested topic: Your favorite movie or video game. _____

Nouns and Verbs Formed as Adjectives

In addition to the *-ed* and *-ing* word endings, many adjectives are formed by other types of word endings. Just as a suffix transforms a verb into a specific type of adjective or adverb, a suffix also can create adjectives out of nouns. Adjectives come in so many forms that using a few carefully chosen adjectives can add power and interest to your writing. For your reference, the following chart lists a few frequently used adjectives by some of their word endings.

Common Adjectives

Word Endings	-able -ible	-ful	-ic	-ish	-ive	-less	-ly -y	-ous
Examples	acceptable	bashful	alcoholic	boorish	abusive	cheerless	antsy	ambiguous
	accessible	cheerful	aquatic	oafish	combative	jobless	cagy	auspicious
	doable	forgetful	dramatic	devilish	decisive	mindless	daffy	courageous
	honorable	graceful	erratic	elfish	instinctive	needless	earthy	glamorous
	laughable	joyful	gigantic	lavish	receptive	noiseless	lively	industrious
	obtainable	merciful	majestic	skittish	reflective	pointless	manly	malicious
	plausible	peaceful	melodic	snobbish	secretive	senseless	seemly	nervous
	tangible	rightful	organic	squeamish	selective	useless	smelly	righteous

Practice 4

FORMS OF ADJECTIVES: NOUN AND VERBS USED AS ADJECTIVES

Complete the following ideas by filling in the blanks with the proper form of an adjective. Create adjectives from the following nouns and verbs: *accept, combat, decide, drama, earth, forget, job, nerve, right,* and *use.*

1. Mandy's work is _____.

2. This can opener is broken and _____.

3. Mother has become _____.

4. Many workers are currently _____.

5. A _____ person tells the truth.

6. Toddlers can be so _____.

7. The flowers have a sweet _____ scent.

8. Effective leaders are _____.

9. Public speaking makes many people _____.

10. Josh expresses his anger in his _____ tone.

Placement of Adjectives

A careful writer not only chooses the precise word for impact, but also arranges words in the most effective order for the greatest impact on the reader. As you work with adjectives, be aware that the placement of adjectives varies based on their relationship to other words.

Adjectives can appear before a noun.

ADJECTIVE "NERVOUS" DESCRIBES NOUN "SUSPECT"

The nervous suspect offered an alibi.

Adjectives can appear after **linking verbs** such as *is, are, were, seems,* and *appears.*

LINKING VERB "SEEMED" JOINS ADJECTIVE "PLAUSIBLE" TO NOUN "ALIBI"

The alibi seemed plausible.

Adjectives can appear after **sensory verbs**—those that describe physical senses—such as *look, smell, feel, taste,* and *sound*.

SENSORY VERB "LOOKED" JOINS ADJECTIVE "FRIGHTENED" TO NOUN "SUSPECT"

The suspect looked frightened.

PLACEMENT OF ADJECTIVES

Create 10 sentences that demonstrate proper placement of adjectives. Use the adjectives and nouns in the following chart to create your sentences.

Nouns				Adjectives			
benefit	home	protest	teenager	alarmed	honorable	lavish	tangible
customer	judge	race		bashful	horrifying	peaceful	
garbage	mother	wreck		exhausting	irritated	smelly	

1.
2.
3.
4.
5.
6.
7.
8.
9.
10.

Order of Adjectives

Adjectives that appear before a noun follow a particular order. Effective writers use adjectives sparingly. Rarely are more than two or three used in one sequence. The chart below outlines the preferred order of adjectives in English arranged by common types and includes three examples of expressions that follow that order. Notice that the order moves from the subjective description of *opinion* to objective descriptions such as *material* and *purpose*.

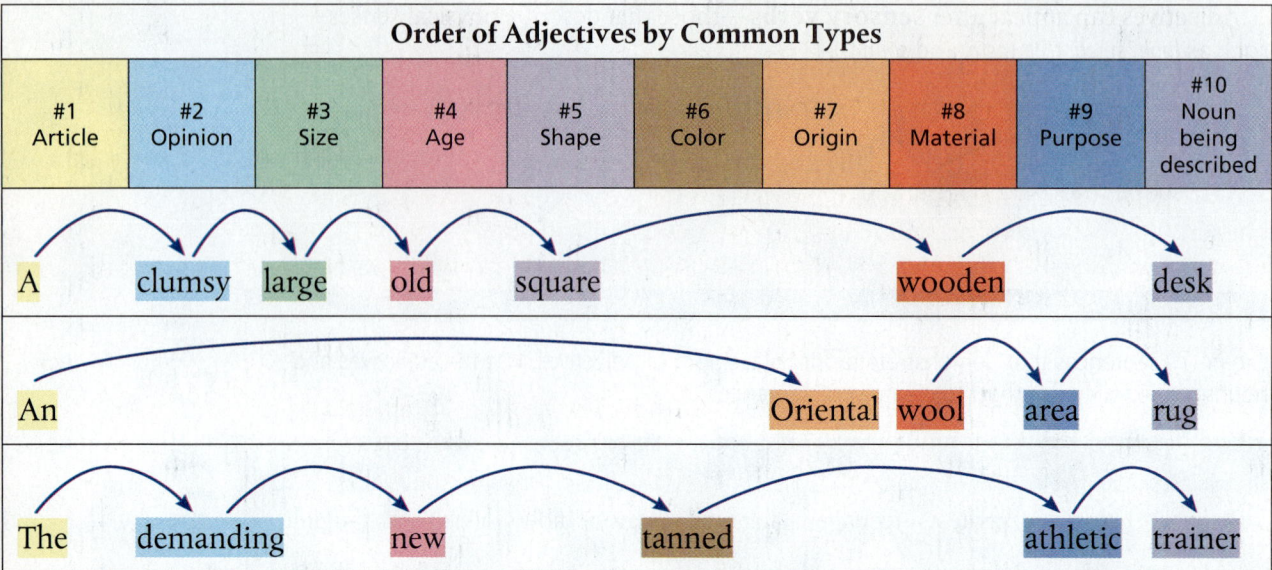

Practice 6

ORDER OF ADJECTIVES

A. Choose the option that best completes the idea by listing adjectives in appropriate order.

1. A _____ bird hopped on the birdfeeder.
   a. small, brown, skittery   b. brown, small, skittery   c. skittery, small, brown

2. A _____ cat bounded into the backyard.
   a. Siamese, young, silver   b. young, silver Siamese   c. young, Siamese, silver

3. The _____ creature sounded the alarm.
   a. tiny, feathered   b. feathered, tiny

4. As the bird chattered and hopped in alarm, it tipped the birdfeeder and spilled the _____ birdseed.
   a. ample, fresh, organic   b. fresh, ample, organic   c. organic, ample, fresh

5. The scene remains a _____ memory.
   a. fond, vivid childhood   b. vivid, fond childhood   c. childhood vivid, fond

B. Describe each noun with a set of two or more adjectives. List adjectives in proper order.

1. _____ iPhone

2. _____ website

3. _____ mother

4. _____ Will Smith

5. _____ *American Idol*

Use Adverbs

The most common use of adverbs is to describe verbs. In addition, adverbs modify other types of words such as adjectives and other adverbs. In purpose, adverbs answer the reporter's questions *When? Where?* and *How?*

Many adverbs are derived from adjectives, many adverbs end in *-ly*, and many adverbs are gradeable based on degree or quantity. In fact, adverbs provide very specific types of information. The following chart lists some of the most frequently used adverbs based on the type of information they provide.

Common Adverbs				
Time, Frequency, or Sequence	**Place**	**Manner**	**Certainty or Negation**	**Degree or Quantity**
When?	**Where?**	**How?**	**How?**	**How much?**
after	everywhere	automatically	actually	absolutely
			certainly	
already	here	badly	clearly	almost
always	inside	beautifully	perhaps	a lot
at first	outside	cheerfully	probably	completely
consequently	somewhere	fast	maybe	enough
during	there	happily	obviously	entirely
early		hard	surely	extremely
every		quickly		fully
finally		seriously	not	hardly
often		slowly	never	least
once		well		less
never				little
next				more
now				most
rarely				much
recently				not
regularly				partly
seldom				rather
sometimes				really
soon				too
then				too little
thus				too much
tomorrow				totally
usually				very
when				
while				
yesterday				

Practice 7

ADVERBS

Add three adverbs to each sentence pair, so that the sentences give more information.

1. Beat the eggs. Add sugar.

2. Watch the ball. Be prepared to hit it and run.

3. When I was a child, we went to the beach. My father drove the car.

4. I've studied for the science test. I find that class difficult.

5. Leigh completed her degree. She applied for a job and found an apartment.

6. Mickey takes notes and misses class. He earns high grades.

7. Susan broke her toe climbing up a steep ravine. She limped back to camp.

8. I sleep late. However, I'm going to wake up.

9. Jamal is considering two job opportunities. He will accept the job that pays.

10. Write your own pair of sentences using three adverbs. Suggested topic: A childhood memory.

_____

_____

_____

L5 Use the Degrees of Adjectives and Adverbs: Absolute, Comparative, and Superlative

A common error in using adjectives and adverbs occurs when a writer uses the wrong form to make degrees of comparisons between two things or among three things. Adjectives and adverbs take the form of three degrees: **absolute**, **comparative**, and **superlative**. The degrees of adverbs are formed by adding the suffixes *-er* or *-est* or by using *more* or *most*. For example, *more* or *most* establishes a degree of comparison with adverbs that end in *-ly*.

Absolute

The absolute degree makes no comparison, or makes a one-to-one comparison (in which the adjective or adverb describes both things equally).

ABSOLUTE ADJECTIVE "SWEET" DESCRIBES COMPOUND SUBJECT "RAISINS AND PRUNES"

Raisins and prunes are sweet.

ABSOLUTE ADJECTIVE "SWEET" DESCRIBES "RAISINS" AND "PRUNES" EQUALLY

Raisins are as sweet as prunes.

Comparative

The comparative degree compares and makes distinctions between two people or things, usually by using the adverb *more* or *less* or by adding the suffix *-er*. Sentences often include *than*.

COMPARATIVE ADJECTIVE "SWEETER" COMPARES "RAISINS" TO "PRUNES"

Raisins are sweeter than prunes.

COMPARATIVE ADVERB "MORE GENEROUSLY" DESCRIBES VERB "ACTED" AND COMPARES HOW RIANA ACTED TO HOW JAY ACTED

Riana acted more generously than Jay [acted].

IMPLIED VERB

Superlative

The superlative degree makes distinctions among three or more people or things, usually by using the adverb *most* or *least* or by adding the suffix *-est*.

SUPERLATIVE ADJECTIVE "SWEETEST" COMPARES "PRUNE" TO ALL THE OTHER PRUNES

This is the sweetest prune I have ever eaten.

SUPERLATIVE ADVERB "MOST GENEROUSLY" DESCRIBES VERB "ACTED" AND COMPARES HOW RIANA ACTED TO HOW ALL THE STUDENTS ACTED

Riana acted the most generously of all the students.

Degrees of Adjectives and Adverbs

Degree of Comparison	Absolute: One as _____ as	Comparative: Two -er _____ than	Superlative: Three or More -est the _____
Adjectives	good	better	best
	bad	worse	worst
	large	larger	largest
	little	less	least
	much	more	most
	far	further/farther	furthest/farthest
Adverbs	busy	busier	busiest
	early	earlier	earliest
	carefully	more carefully	most carefully
	slowly	more slowly	most slowly
	well	better	best

Practice 8

DEGREES OF ADJECTIVES AND ADVERBS: USING ABSOLUTES, COMPARATIVES, AND SUPERLATIVES

Complete each of the following sentences with the appropriate absolute, comparative, or superlative adjectives or adverbs.

1. If the choice is between a diet and exercise to lose weight, exercise is the _____ choice.

    a. good   **b.** better   **c.** best

2. Lifting weights is a _____ way to burn calories.

    a. good   **b.** better   **c.** best

3. Working out instead of just dieting is a _____ healthier way to control weight.

    a. good   **b.** more   **c.** much

4. Dieters lose _____ muscle mass than exercisers.

    a. much   **b.** more   **c.** most

5. Cassie _____ changed her diet and exercise habits.

    a. slowly   **b.** more slowly   **c.** most slowly

6. At her _____, she weighed 250 pounds.

    a. heavy   **b.** heavier   **c.** heaviest

7. As _____ as she was, she stayed active and focused on changing her lifestyle choices.

    a. large   **b.** larger   **c.** largest

8. She now feels the _____ she has ever felt.

   a. well   **b.** better   **c.** best

9. Now she can walk _____ than 5 miles at a time.

   a. far   **b.** farther   **c.** farthest

10. Write a sentence using a comparative or superlative. Suggested topic: A day in life.

_____

_____

Spelling Guidelines
Comparative and Superlative Adjectives and Adverbs

Number of Syllables	Word Ending	Comparative	Superlative
One-syllable adjectives or adverbs	any kind	add -er	add -est
Examples	fast hard young	faster harder younger	fastest hardest youngest
One-syllable adjectives	consonant-vowel-consonant	double last consonant add -er	double last consonant add -est
Examples	big sad wet	bigger sadder wetter	biggest saddest wettest
Two-syllable adjectives and adverbs	ending in -y	change -y to -i; add -er	change -y to -i; add -est
Examples	busy pretty silly	busier prettier sillier	busiest prettiest silliest
Two- or more-syllable adjectives or adverbs	not ending in -y	no change in spelling; use *more*	no change in spelling; use *most*
Examples	exciting dangerous difficult	more exciting more dangerous more difficult	most exciting most dangerous most difficult

Practice 9

SPELLING COMPARATIVES AND SUPERLATIVES

Fill in the following chart with the correct spellings of each form of the comparatives and superlatives. Use *more* and *most* as needed.

Absolute	Comparative	Superlative	Absolute	Comparative	Superlative
1. afraid			11. jolly		
2. amused			12. kind		
3. chilly			13. old		
4. classy			14. quick		
5. creepy			15. quiet		
6. cute			16. recently		
7. efficient			17. red		
8. fat			18. small		
9. foamy			19. tan		
10. hard			20. wide		

L6 Master *Good* and *Well*

Two of the most often-confused words in the English language are *good* and *well*. One reason these two words are so often confused is that *well* can be used as either an adverb or an adjective to discuss health issues.

- **Good** is an adjective that describes a noun or pronoun.

    ADJECTIVE "GOOD" DESCRIBES NOUN "VOICE"

    Sally's singing voice sounds good.

    ADJECTIVE "GOOD" DESCRIBES NOUN "JOB"

    You did a good job.

- **Well** is an **adverb** that usually describes a **verb**.

    ADVERB "WELL" DESCRIBES VERB "DID"

    I did well on my test.

    ADVERB "WELL" DESCRIBES VERB "HEAR"

    You hear well with your hearing aid.

- Exception **Well** is an **adjective** when used to describe a person's health issues.

    PRONOUN "I" IS DESCRIBED BY ADJECTIVE "WELL"

    I feel well.

    PRONOUN "HE" IS DESCRIBED BY ADJECTIVE "WELL"

    He was sick, but he seems well now.

Practice 10

GOOD AND WELL

Fill in each blank with *good* or *well*.

1. Your new office looks _____.
2. Jeremiah is not feeling _____.
3. Michael dances _____.
4. Apple makes _____ computers.
5. I have a _____ feeling about this.
6. The asparagus tastes _____.
7. The steak is _____ done.
8. Most celebrities live _____.
9. Simon is a _____ judge of talent.
10. Write a sentence that appropriately uses *good* or *well*. Suggested topic: The condition of a person or thing.

    _____

    _____

Practice 11

ADJECTIVES AND ADVERBS CHAPTER REVIEW

Prove your mastery of the chapter learning outcomes by choosing the adjective or adverb that best completes the sentence.

1. (Amused/Amusing), Maria laughs (soft/softly).
2. The (graceful/gracious) dancer leapt into the air.
3. They bought a (new large/large new) couch.
4. Robert talks (quick/quickly) and has (already/ready) finished his speech.
5. Billie is (serious/seriously) ill and is (now/never) waiting to see the doctor.
6. (Once/Then) she takes her medicine, her health will (sure/surely) improve.
7. November and December are the two (busier/busiest) months in the year.
8. Vacation days seem to pass (more quickly/most quickly) than other days.
9. Many professional athletes seem to perform (good/well) under pressure.
10. Many believe that Peyton Manning is a (good/well) quarterback.

Editing Assignments

Editing for Everyday Life

Assume you own a parrot whose behavior has been highly amusing. You want to share his antics with a friend so you have composed the following e-mail. Edit the e-mail to ensure proper use of adjectives and adverbs.

Dear Jim,

You won't believe what Charlie, my African Grey large parrot, did to our family during this past month. For weeks, our doorbell rang every night in the middle of the night. I first angry blamed the neighbors. They repeatedly reassured me that they knew nothing about the situation. After several nights, we became frightened, so we called the police. The police seemed most skeptical than our neighbors about our story, yet they diligent watched our house every night. Derrick, finally my son, noticed Charlie. The whole time, Charlie had been mimicking the sound of our doorbell. That bird had never seemed happiest.

LOL, Jen

Editing for College Life

Assume you are taking a study skills course, and you have been asked by your professor to reflect upon your progress as a learner as part of your midterm assessment. You are to describe what and how you have learned. Edit to ensure appropriate use of adjectives and adverbs.

Self-Assessment Reflection:

Even though I have learned muchly this semester, I feel as if I have more to learn. One of the best important things I learned is that I am an auditory learner. I do my better when something is explained to me. So I now read out loud important information that I want to remember, or I pair up with a study buddy and talk about what we are studying. I need to hear information, so attendance is much important for me than it is for someone who isn't an auditory learner. Time management is another vital important skill that I am trying to apply. I then always have a study schedule. I want to do good in college. I have become a well student.

Editing for Working Life

Assume you have written the following letter resigning from a job you really enjoy. Edit to ensure appropriate use of adjectives and adverbs.

> Dear Ms. Brown:
>
> It is with great regret that I must submit my resignation due to my family's relocation to Texas. I have thorough enjoyed working as a team leader for the area's region. This area is the larger in the state, and our team has had the higher ratings for customer service and productivity. I remember as an exciting new employee how much I looked forward to all the wonderfully opportunities available under your leadership. I have not been disappointed in the least. My success is due to your encouraged mentorship. I thank you for your support, and I wish you and the company all the best.
>
> Sincerely,
>
> Sam Yoo

WHAT HAVE I LEARNED ABOUT ADJECTIVES AND ADVERBS?

To test and track your understanding, answer the following questions.

1. An adjective modifies a _____ or _____.
2. An adverb modifies a _____, an _____, or another _____.
3. Participle adjectives are formed by adding _____ or _____ to verbs.
4. Adjectives often appear in the following order: _____, opinion, size, age, shape, _____, origin, material, purpose.
5. Adverbs answer the questions _____, where, and _____.
6. Adjectives and adverbs take the form of three degrees: _____, _____, and _____.
7. The _____ degree makes distinctions between two things, usually by using the adverb *more* or *less* or by adding the suffix *-er*.
8. The _____ degree makes distinctions among three or more things, usually by using the adverb *most* or *least* or by adding the suffix *-est*.
9. *Good* is an _____.
10. Most often, *well* is an _____.
11. **How will I use what I have learned about adjectives and adverbs?**
    In your notebook, discuss how you will apply to your own writing what you have learned about adjectives and adverbs.
12. **What do I still need to study about adjectives and adverbs?**
    In your notebook, discuss your ongoing study needs by describing what, when, and how you will continue studying adjectives and adverbs.

MyWritingLab™

Complete the Post-test for Chapter 18 in MyWritingLab.

19 Verbs

LEARNING OUTCOMES

After studying this chapter you will be able to:

- **1** Answer the question "What's the Point of Verbs?"
- **2** Identify the Three Basic Tenses of Verbs
- **3** Identify Regular and Irregular Verbs in the Past Tense
- **4** Differentiate Key Verbs in the Past Tense: *To Have, To Do, To Be*
- **5** Identify the Purpose of the Past Participle
- **6** Use the Present Perfect Tense
- **7** Use the Past Perfect Tense
- **8** Use the Passive Voice
- **9** Distinguish among Three Commonly Confused Helping Verbs: *Can, Could, Would*

Verbs describe actions or events that occur in time.

Thinking about a real-life situation helps us to understand the need for verbs as we communicate. The following photograph illustrates the challenges of mountain climbing. Study the picture, complete the activity, and answer the question "What's the point of verbs?"

PART 4 THE BASIC SENTENCE

What's the Point of Verbs?

PHOTOGRAPHIC ORGANIZER: VERBS

Assume your friend has survived a dangerous situation and has been asked to share his experience with others. He asks you to read what he has written so far. What do you notice about his use of time order? How does his use of time order (verb tense) affect his message?

Surviving a Fall Off the Mountain

Our 7,400-foot climb up the winter slopes of Mt. Hood challenges and exhilarated us. Thankfully, we decide to take Mountain Locator Units, small beacons that could send out radio signals to rescuers. When a storm moved in, we start our descent in blowing snow. We had no visual reference around us, so we couldn't know if we were going up or down. Then the three of us who were roped together with Champion, a black Labrador mix, disappear over an icy ledge. Champion provided warmth for us as we huddled under sleeping bags and a tarp. She takes turns lying on each one of us during the night. The activation of an emergency radio beacon bringed rescuers to us. We survived because we were prepared, we didn't panic, and Champion keeps us warm.

What's the point of verbs?

One Student Writer's Response

The following paragraph offers one writer's reaction to the paragraph "Surviving a Fall Off the Mountain"

> *When I read the paragraph about falling off the mountain, I couldn't tell when it happened. Did it happen in the past? Sometimes, it seemed like things were happening right now. The time flow kind of jumped around. Also some of the verbs didn't sound right, like "bringed." I don't think I've ever heard that word before. Isn't it supposed to be "brought"? Verbs help a writer tell about events and when things happen in time. Verbs also help describe people or things.*

A **verb** expresses an action, event, or state of being. **Verb tense** expresses the different times at which an action, event, or state of being occurs. The three basic tenses are past, present, and future. However, verb forms such as the past participle combine with helping verbs to form the perfect tenses and the passive voice.

L2 Identify the Three Basic Tenses of Verbs

The **simple present tense** of a verb expresses action (*run*) or a state of being (*am, are, is*) in current time, habitual actions (*He runs daily.*), general truths, or scientific knowledge (*Truth is beauty.*). The present tense is also used to discuss works of art and literature (*Romeo courts Juliet.*).

The **simple past tense** is used to describe a completed action or event. The action or event might have taken place long ago or it might have happened recently, but either way, the past tense is used to indicate that it has already occurred. The simple past tense is also often used to tell a story. Frequently, the use of the past tense is also signaled by particular expressions of time: *yesterday, last night, last week, last year, three years ago*, and so on.

The **simple future tense** expresses an action (*will run*) or state of being (*will be*) that has not yet occurred. The simple future tense is formed by using the helping verb *will*.

The following time line illustrates the sequence of tenses.

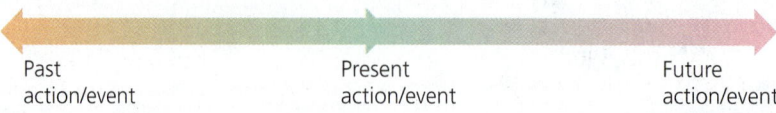

Past action/event — Present action/event — Future action/event

Practice 2

IDENTIFY THE THREE BASIC TENSES OF VERBS

Underline the verbs in each sentence. Then, above each verb, write **P** for past tense, **PR** for present tense, or **F** for future tense.

1. Raul will be home soon.
2. He is on his way now.
3. He worked later than usual.
4. The traffic is backed up on the highway.
5. Raul listens to audio books during traffic jams.
6. In his favorite book, the hero is brutal.
7. Raul always dreaded the drive to work.
8. Now he looks forward to the daily drive.
9. Raul and I will watch a movie later.
10. We watched *The Avengers* last night.

Identify Regular and Irregular Verbs in the Past Tense

The past tense is one of the most commonly used verb tenses in English. The past tense takes on different forms for regular and irregular verbs.

Regular Verbs in the Past Tense

The following chart shows the general rule for forming the past tense of regular verbs, the spelling rules for exceptions, and examples of each rule.

Rules for Forming Past Tense of Regular Verbs		
	Base Form	**Past Tense**
General Rule:		
Regular verbs form the past tense by adding **-ed** to the base form of the verb.	walk	walk**ed**
Spelling Exceptions:		
There are several exceptions to the way in which regular verbs form the past tense:		
1. When the base form of the verb ends in **-e**, only add **-d**.	live save	live**d** save**d**
2. When the base form of the verb ends with a consonant and **-y**, delete the **-y** and add **-ied** in its place.	cry try	cr**ied** tr**ied**
3. When the base form of the verb ends with **-p** or **-it**, double the last letter before adding the **-ed.**	stop permit	stop**ped** permit**ted**

Practice 3

IDENTIFY REGULAR VERBS IN THE PAST TENSE

Fill in each blank with the past tense form of the regular verb in parentheses.

1. Chimpanzees possibly _____ (use) "hammers" at least 4,300 years ago.

2. Researchers _____ (discover) the hammers in the West African country, Ivory Coast.

3. The chimpanzees _____ (crack) nuts with the hammers.

4. A "chimpanzee stone age" _____ (start) in ancient times.

5. Chimps _____ (hunt) for termites using straw and blades of grass.

6. A recent video _____ (show) a chimp using tools.

7. In the video, the chimp _____ (probe) termite mounds using a short stick like a fishing probe.

8. One chimp _____ (pull) the fishing probe between his teeth to fray it.

9. When the chimp _____ (fray) the stick, it _____ (collect) the termites better.

10. Write a sentence with a regular verb in the past tense. Suggested topic: An important invention.

_____

_____

Irregular Verbs in the Past Tense

Unlike regular verbs, irregular verbs do not use *-ed* to form the past tense. Nor does the past tense of irregular verbs conform to uniform spelling rules with clear exceptions. In fact, some of the most commonly used verbs are irregular, and most writers commit these words to memory so their proper use is automatic. The chart lists the base form and past tense form of some commonly used irregular verbs. When in doubt about the correct form of a verb, consult a dictionary to check the spelling of the past tense of an irregular verb.

Some Common Irregular Verbs in the Past Tense

Base Form	Past Tense	Base Form	Past Tense
be	was, were	light	lit
become	became	lose	lost
break	broke	make	made
bring	brought	mean	meant
buy	bought	meet	met
choose	chose	pay	paid
come	came	put	put
cut	cut	quit	quit
deal	dealt	read	read
dig	dug	ride	rode
drink	drank	ring	rang
drive	drove	rise	rose
eat	ate	run	ran
fall	fell	say	said
feed	fed	see	saw
feel	felt	sell	sold
fly	flew	send	sent
forget	forgot	shake	shook
forgive	forgave	shine	shone (shined)
freeze	froze	sing	sang
get	got	sit	sat
give	gave	sleep	slept
go	went	speak	spoke
grow	grew	spend	spent
hang	hung	swim	swam
have	had	take	took
hear	heard	teach	taught
hide	hid	tear	tore
hold	held	tell	told
hurt	hurt	think	thought
keep	kept	throw	threw
know	knew	understand	understood
lay (to place)	laid	wake	woke (waked)
lead	led	wear	wore
leave	left	win	won
let	let	write	wrote
lie (to recline)	lay		

Practice 4

IDENTIFY IRREGULAR VERBS IN THE PAST TENSE

Fill in the blanks with the past tense form of the irregular verbs in the parentheses.

1. A slave named James Armistead _____ (make) history as the most important Revolutionary War spy.

2. Armistead _____ (take) on the role of an escaped slave to enter the camp of the traitor Benedict Arnold.

3. As an orderly and a guide, Armistead _____ (go) North with Arnold to learn about British war plans without being detected.

4. As a double agent, he also _____ (give) incorrect information to the British troops.

5. General Arnold _____ (bring) Armistead with him to guide his troops through local roads.

6. British officers _____ (speak) openly about their military plans in front of Armistead.

7. Armistead _____ (write) reports containing this information.

8. He then _____ (meet) with other American spies to deliver his reports.

9. After the war, Armistead _____ (become) a farmer.

10. Write a sentence using the past tense of an irregular verb. Suggested topic: Heroic actions.

_____

_____

_____

LO 4 Differentiate Key Verbs in the Past Tense: *To Have, To Do, To Be*

Three key verbs are used both as main verbs and as helping verbs to express a wide variety of meanings: *to have, to do,* and *to be*. These three verbs are irregular verbs, so it's essential to memorize their correct forms in the past tense.

To Have	**To Do**	**To Be**
had	did	was (singular)
		were (plural)

IDENTIFY IRREGULAR VERBS IN THE PAST TENSE

Fill in the blanks with the past tense form of the verbs *to have, to do,* or *to be*.

1. Researchers recently _____ a large study that indicates midday napping reduces coronary mortality by more than a third.

2. The most effective nappers _____ those who took 30 minute naps at least three times per week.

3. These men and women _____ a 37 percent lower coronary mortality risk than those who took no naps.

4. The protective effect of napping _____ especially strong among working men.

5. Like many others, Jordan _____ many long-lasting headaches before finding relief through short naps.

6. Jordan _____ trouble taking naps; he _____ not fall asleep easily and _____ easily awakened.

7. For years, Jordon avoided naps because he thought napping _____ a sign of laziness or weakness.

8. When he _____ nap, his naps _____ at least an hour long, leaving him groggy and disoriented.

9. One day, he napped for just 20 minutes and _____ alert, refreshed, and pain free when he woke up.

10. Write a sentence using the past tense of *to have, to do,* or *to be*. Suggested topic: Sleep problems.

....

....

....

Identify the Purpose of the Past Participle

A **participle** is a verb form that can be used to establish tenses or voices, or it can be used as a modifier, which describes, restricts, or limits other words in a sentence. The **past participle** of a verb joins with helping verbs to form the present perfect and past perfect tenses and the passive voice. In addition, the past participle can act as an adjective that describes another word. Just as with the simple past tense, the past participle takes on different forms for regular and irregular verbs.

Past Participles of Regular Verbs

In general, regular verbs form the past participle by adding -ed to the base form of the verb. Just as with the simple past tense, there are several spelling exceptions for the past participle of regular verbs.

Base Form	Past Tense	Past Participle
live	lived	lived
cry	cried	cried
permit	permitted	permitted

For more about past tense forms, see pages 366–371.

Practice 6

IDENTIFY THE PAST PARTICIPLE OF REGULAR VERBS

Complete the following chart with the proper forms of the past tense and the past participle of each verb.

Base	Past Tense	Past Participle
1. accept		
2. agree		
3. bang		
4. bat		
5. cheat		
6. clip		
7. hurry		
8. relax		
9. supply		
10. whine		

Past Participles of Irregular Verbs

As with the simple past tense, irregular verbs do not use *-ed* to form the past participle. Nor does the past participle of irregular verbs conform to uniform spelling rules with clear exceptions. In addition, the past participle forms of many irregular verbs vary from their past tense forms. Practice 7 and the chart that follows list the base form, past tense form, and past participle of some commonly used irregular verbs. It is not a comprehensive list, however. As with the simple past forms of irregular verbs, when in doubt, careful writers consult a dictionary to find the form and spelling of the past participle of an irregular verb. Throughout the rest of this chapter, the activities dealing with irregular verbs focus on those that, based on research, occur most frequently in English.

Practice 7

IDENTIFY THE PAST PARTICIPLE OF IRREGULAR VERBS

The following chart contains the top ten irregular verbs listed by frequency of use. Supply the proper forms of the past tense and the past participle of each verb. Consult pages 366–375 or a dictionary as necessary.

Base	Past Tense	Past Participle
1. say		
2. make		
3. go		
4. take		
5. come		
6. see		
7. know		
8. get		
9. give		
10. find		

Some Common Irregular Past Participles

Base Form	Past Tense	Past Participle
be	was, were	been
become	became	become
break	broke	broken
bring	brought	brought
buy	bought	bought
choose	chose	chosen
come	came	come
cut	cut	cut
deal	dealt	dealt
dig	dug	dug
drink	drank	drunk
drive	drove	driven
eat	ate	eaten
fall	fell	fallen
feed	fed	fed
feel	felt	felt
find	found	found
fly	flew	flown
forget	forgot	forgotten
forgive	forgave	forgiven
freeze	froze	frozen
get	got	gotten
give	gave	given
go	went	gone
grow	grew	grown
hang	hung	hung
have	had	had
hear	heard	heard
hide	hid	hidden
hold	held	held
hurt	hurt	hurt
keep	kept	kept
know	knew	known
lay *(to place)*	laid	laid
lead	led	led
leave	left	left
let	let	let
lie *(to recline)*	lay	lain
light	lit	lit
lose	lost	lost
make	made	made
mean	meant	meant
meet	met	met
pay	paid	paid
put	put	put

Some Common Irregular Past Participles (continued)		
Base Form	**Past Tense**	**Past Participle**
quit	quit	quit
read	read	read
ride	rode	ridden
ring	rang	rung
rise	rose	risen
run	ran	run
say	said	said
see	saw	seen
sell	sold	sold
send	sent	sent
shake	shook	shaken
shine	shone (shined)	shone (shined)
sing	sang	sung
sit	sat	sat
sleep	slept	slept
speak	spoke	spoken
spend	spent	spent
swim	swam	swum
take	took	taken
teach	taught	taught
tear	tore	torn
tell	told	told
think	thought	thought
throw	threw	thrown
understand	understood	understood
wake	woke (waked)	woken (waked)
wear	wore	worn
win	won	won
write	wrote	written

IDENTIFY THE PAST PARTICIPLE

You already have experience using part participles in everyday speech. Complete the following well-known phrases. Fill in the blanks with the past participle form of the **irregular** verb in parentheses. Consult a dictionary or the chart on pages 374–375 as needed.

1. a _____ heart (break)
2. a _____ few (choose)
3. _____ a rotten hand (deal)
4. _____ up (feed)
5. _____ and _____ (lose)/(find)
6. _____ in full (pay)
7. a _____ for your money (run)
8. _____ out (wear)
9. well _____ (read)
10. hand _____ (write)

Practice 8

L6 Use the Present Perfect Tense (*Has* or *Have* and the Past Participle)

The **present perfect tense** connects the past to the present. The present perfect tense states the relationship of a past action or situation to a current, ongoing action or situation. The present perfect tense is formed by joining the helping verbs **has** or **have** with the past participle.

The purposes of the present perfect tense are:

- to express change from the past to the present.

PAST ACTION — PRESENT PERFECT "HAS IMPROVED" EXPRESSES CHANGE FROM THE PAST ACTION TO A PRESENT ONE

Jamel was sick for three weeks, but he has improved.

- to express a situation or action that started in the past and continues to the present.

PRESENT PERFECT "HAVE RACED" EXPRESSES AN ONGOING ACTION, WHICH STARTED IN THE PAST AND IS CONTINUING NOW

Carmen and Michelle have raced stock cars for several years.

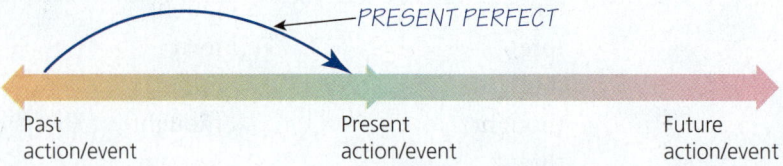

Past action/event — Present action/event — Future action/event

Practice 9

USE PRESENT PERFECT TENSE

Fill in the blanks with the present perfect tense of the **regular** verbs in the parentheses in order to complete each sentence. Use the helping verbs *has* or *have* to form the present perfect tense.

1. David and Julia _____ (create) a loving home for their children.

2. Julia _____ (plant) a vegetable garden to feed her family.

3. David _____ (create) an obstacle course for his children to enjoy.

4. They _____ (start) a home library to help their children learn to read.

5. Write a sentence using the present perfect tense of a regular verb. Suggested topic: Something thoughtful that I've done. _____

USE THE PRESENT PERFECT TENSE: REGULAR AND IRREGULAR VERBS

A. Fill in the blanks with the present perfect tense of the **irregular** verbs in parentheses. Use the helping verbs *has* or *have* to form the present perfect tense.

1. As a photojournalist, I _____ (go) to many parts of the world, looking for stories to tell.

2. I _____ (take) photos of some amazing people—from children to old people, and everyone in between.

3. My editor _____ (tell) me that he doesn't know how I manage to keep going.

4. I keep going because I _____ (get) so many thrills from my work!

5. Write a sentence using the present perfect tense of an irregular verb. Suggested topic: Photos I've taken. _____

B. Fill in the blanks with the present perfect tense of the verbs in parentheses. The verbs may be either **regular** or **irregular** verbs. Use the helping verbs *has* or *have* to form the present perfect tense.

1. Fashion week _____ (come) to be the fashion industry event.

2. Fashion week _____ (bring) designers and buyers together to showcase the latest fashion trends.

3. Milan, London, and Paris _____ (influence) the fashion scene throughout the years.

4. New York _____ (dominate) fashion since World War II.

5. Write a sentence using the present perfect tense of either a regular or an irregular verb. Suggested topic: Your favorite piece of clothing. _____

L7 Use the Past Perfect Tense (*Had* and the Past Participle)

The **past perfect** connects two past actions or situations. The past perfect is formed by joining the helping verb *had* with a past participle.

The purposes of the past perfect tense are:

- to connect a previous action or event with a later action or event.

PAST ACTION #1 THE PAST PERFECT "HAD LEFT" SHOWS THAT THIS ACTION OCCURRED BEFORE THE OTHER PAST ACTION "SAMUEL WENT..."

PAST ACTION #2

Samuel went to Starbucks, but everyone had left. ← PAST ACTION #1

- to express an action or event that happened before a certain past time.

A PAST TIME

THE PAST PERFECT "HAD STUDIED" SHOWS THAT THIS ACTION OCCURRED BEFORE THE PAST TIME "DINNERTIME"

By dinnertime, Suzanne had studied for hours and hours.

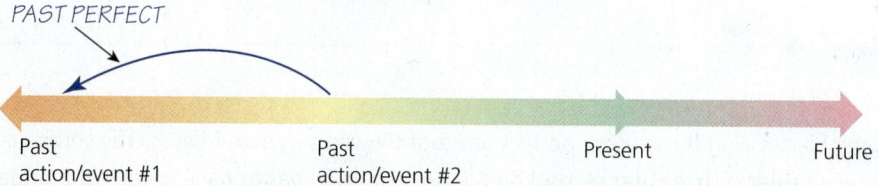

Practice 11

USE THE PAST PERFECT TENSE: REGULAR VERBS

Fill in the blanks with the past perfect tense of the **regular** verbs in the parentheses. Use the helping verb *had* to form the past perfect tense.

1. Although Juneteenth was made a Texas state holiday in 1980, African Americans _____ (celebrate) Juneteenth for many decades before that.

2. Juneteenth was established to commemorate June 19, 1865, the day word of the end of the Civil War reached Galveston, Texas, months after General Lee _____ (surrender).

3. More than two years before that, on January 1, 1863, Abraham Lincoln _____ (issue) the Emancipation Proclamation, declaring an end to slavery in the slave states.

4. Nonetheless, slavery _____ (continue) in Texas until June 19, 1865, when Union troops brought the news to Galveston.

5. Write a sentence using the past perfect tense of a regular verb. Suggested topic: A national holiday. _____

USE THE PAST PERFECT TENSE: REGULAR AND IRREGULAR VERBS

A. Fill in the blanks with the past perfect tense of the **irregular** verbs in the parentheses. Use the helping verb *had* to form the past perfect tense.

1. During my annual checkup, I discovered that my previous physician, Dr. Griffin, _____ (hold) on to my records instead of sending them to my current physician, Dr. Doughney.

2. Six months before, I _____ (write) Dr. Griffin to request that he forward my records to Dr. Doughney.

3. By the time I filled out all the required forms for a new patient and another form requesting my records, I _____ (stand) at the receptionist's window for 30 minutes.

4. I _____ (hear) from several friends that Dr. Doughney was an excellent doctor.

5. Write a sentence using the past perfect tense of an irregular verb. Suggested topic: An annoying event. _____

B. Fill in the blanks with past perfect tense of the verbs in parentheses. The verbs may be either regular or irregular verbs. Use the helping verbs **has** or **have** to form the perfect past tense.

1. By 2005, electronic medical records (EMRs) _____ (evolve) as a way to store and retrieve a patient's medical history.

2. However, by 2011, most doctors _____ not _____ (begin) to use EMRs.

3. Doctors in the Midwest _____ (be) more likely to use EMRs than those in the Northeast.

4. Of those doctors using EMRs, very few _____ (use) all four functions to report test results, orders for prescriptions, orders for tests, and physician notes.

5. Write a sentence using the past perfect tense of a regular or an irregular verb. Suggested topic: A useful tool. _____

L8 Use the Passive Voice (*To Be* and the Past Participle)

In English, verbs establish two types of voices: the active voice and the passive voice. So far, you have only worked with the active voice. Expressing what the subject of a sentence does, action verbs establish the **active voice.** When the subject of a sentence receives the action (or is acted upon), the sentence is in the **passive voice.** The passive voice is formed by joining *to be* with a past participle. In addition the passive voice can be expressed in every tense.

The purpose of the passive voice is to tell the reader what is done to a subject.

Active Voice

SUBJECT "CONSTANCE" PERFORMS THE ACTION

Constance took her daughter to the hospital.

Passive Voice

SUBJECT "CONSTANCE" RECEIVES THE ACTION

Constance was taken to the hospital by her neighbor.

Examples of the tenses of the passive voice

Present Tense

SUBJECT   PRESENT TENSE OF "TO BE"   PAST PARTICIPLE OF "PACK"

The clothes are packed.

Past Tense

SUBJECT   PAST TENSE OF "TO BE"   PAST PARTICIPLE OF "STORE"

The furniture was stored.

Present Perfect Tense

SUBJECT   PRESENT PERFECT TENSE OF "TO BE"   PAST PARTICIPLE OF "WRAP"

The china has been wrapped in bubble pack.

Past Perfect Tense

SUBJECT   PAST PERFECT TENSE OF "TO BE"   PAST PARTICIPLE OF "TAKE"

Their possessions had been taken to a storage facility.

USE THE PASSIVE VOICE WITH REGULAR AND IRREGULAR VERBS

A. Fill in the blanks with the passive voice of the **regular** verbs in the parentheses. Use the proper form of *to be* as a helping verb to form the passive voice.

1. The restaurant .... (open) in 2015.

2. Before the restaurant opened, the market for Italian food .... (analyze).

3. After the owners had argued for months over the name for the restaurant, finally, the name *Pantheon* .... (agree) upon.

4. To ensure high-quality customer service, the wait staff .... (train) by experts in hospitality management.

5. Write a sentence using the passive voice of a regular verb. Suggested topic: A new neighborhood business. ....

B. Fill in the blanks with the passive voice of the **irregular** verbs in parentheses. Use the proper form of *to be* with the past participle to form the passive voice.

1. We've been waiting almost an hour—maybe our order .... (lose) somewhere in the recesses of the kitchen.

2. From the looks of it, your spinach soufflé probably .... (sit) on.

3. From the taste of it, my crabmeat casserole probably .... (throw) into the microwave.

4. Customers .... not .... (make) to feel very welcome here!

5. Write a sentence using the passive voice of an irregular verb. Suggested topic: A customer complaint. ....

LO9 Distinguish among Three Commonly Confused Helping Verbs: *Can, Could, Would*

Helping verbs are auxiliary verbs that team up with main verbs for precise expression of an action or state of being. Three helping verbs are often confused in usage: *can*, *could*, and *would*. These auxiliary verbs help express the meaning of ability, opportunity, possibility, permission, and intention. The following provides definitions and examples for each of these three helping verbs.

- *Can* expresses physical or mental ability in the present tense.

    "CAN" EXPRESSES A PHYSICAL ABILITY

    I can run a marathon.

    "CAN" EXPRESSES A MENTAL ABILITY

    I can solve mathematical equations.

- *Could* expresses physical or mental ability, opportunity, possibility, or permission.

    "COULD" EXPRESSES A PHYSICAL OR MENTAL ABILITY

    She could run a marathon.

    "COULD" EXPRESSES A LOST OPPORTUNITY

    You could have tried harder than you did.

    "COULD" EXPRESSES POSSIBILITY

    He could have been the culprit.

    "COULD" EXPRESSES PERMISSION

    He said that we could begin the driving test.

- *Would* expresses past routine or intention in the past tense.

    "WOULD" EXPRESSES PAST ROUTINE

    He would win every race.

    He would have won every race, but he lost the last one.

    "WOULD" EXPRESSES PAST INTENTION

    She said she would do the dishes.

USE CAN, COULD, AND WOULD

Complete each sentence with the helping verb that best completes the idea: *can*, *could*, or *would*.

1. In the early 19th century, communication technology was very limited and news _____ travel between Europe and the United States only at the speed of ships.

2. Later, thanks to the development of the telegraph and then of radio, news _____ travel almost instantaneously between Europe and the United States.

3. In the early 20th century, radio became enormously popular, and every night families _____ stop what they were doing and gather around the radio to listen to news and other programs.

4. Today, we _____ instantly access information, regardless of time or location.

5. Our ancestors _____ not believe the speed and ease of today's communication tools.

6. Information we _____ send with the click of a button _____ have taken weeks or months to share.

7. Information technology _____ provide isolated communities with the latest news and events.

8. Smart cards _____ function like an electronic passbook to manage personal or business bank accounts.

9. John says he _____ have gotten a smart card, but he probably _____ not use it.

10. Write a sentence about the past using *would* or *could*. Suggested topic: Changes in society.

_____

_____

_____

Practice 15

VERBS: CHAPTER REVIEW

Demonstrate your mastery of the chapter's learning outcomes by filling the blanks with verbs from the box that best complete the meaning of each sentence. Some verbs may be used more than once.

are	could	had	is	remains	spins	varied	will
be	did	happened	left	seen	stocked	was	would
clatter	disappeared	have	occurred	speculated	turns	were	

1. It _____ a story that _____ into a legend.

2. A ship _____ sighted at sea and boarded; its sails _____ full, its wheel _____ aimlessly, cabin doors _____ in the wind, and no one _____ onboard.

3. In 1872, the crew of the Mary Celeste _____ without a trace of a struggle.

4. What _____ a mystery.

5. The ship _____ fully _____ with provisions, and the sailor's pipes and tobacco _____ where they _____ them.

6. The belongings of Captain Briggs, his wife, and infant daughter _____ untouched as if they _____ returned.

7. The impression of the infant girl _____ on a bed.

8. Explanations _____ from alien abductions to poison by cargo fumes.

9. We _____ probably never know what happened in 1872, but many _____ about what _____.

10. In 1885, the same ship wrecked on a reef, _____ not sink, but _____ never leave the reef.

Editing Assignments

MyWritingLab™ — Complete this Exercise on mywritinglab.com

Editing for Everyday Life

Read the following blog. Edit the paragraph to ensure proper usage of verbs. Use your own paper or complete the exercise on MyWritingLab.com.

> Here at last is the long promised summary of what I have be up to lately. Guess what? I have good news. I find my dream job! I had gave up hope. I had even think about signing up as a temporary worker with an agency in the city. Then I ranned into Caitlyn Myers who graduate a year ahead of me. Delight to help a classmate, she tells me about an opening in an art gallery near Central Park. I was hire last week as the director of the gallery. This is the very kind of job I hope to get. Well, my cell phone has rang the whole time I have sit here typing, so I am going to post my good news and sign off for now. — Ciao, Danni

Editing for College Life

The following lab report was written by a student for a science class. The professor required the use of the passive voice. Edit to ensure proper usage of verbs. Use your own paper or complete the exercise on MyWritingLab.com.

LAB REPORT

	Cheri Jackson	May 15/24
Lab 7: Responses to Abiotic Factors	(Name)	(Date/ Lab Section)

Overview

This lab was design to understand the responses to abiotic factors by tracking transpiration by plants. Abiotic factors are made up of air, water, or temperature. Transpiration is known as the loss of water from a plant through evaporation. The behavior and structure of an organism are affect by the loss of water through evaporation.

Procedure and Results

A long branch with healthy leaves was select. Next, a clean cut at the base was made, and the cut end was immediately transfer to a pan of water. The leaves were keep dry. A second cut was made a cm or so above the first. The cut end was not exposed to the air since an air bubble could form in plant's tissue. The cut end was kept under water, and the stem was carry through a rubber stopper. Petroleum jelly was spread at the top and bottom of the cork to seal and hold the stem in the stopper attached to a length of tubing. A bubble was introduced into the tubing. As water was took up by the plant, the bubble move. Water uptake was measured by marking regular gradations on the tube. Next, the prepared plant leaf was placed under a lamp, and the movement of the air bubble were measured at one-minute intervals for five minutes. The light was turn off, and a small fan was move next to plant. This effect of wind was measured at one-minute intervals for five minutes. The results indicate that light and wind speed up transpiration of plants.

Editing for Working Life

Read the following report written by a manager to be submitted at a meeting. Edit to ensure proper usage of the past participle and related forms. Use your own paper or complete the exercise on MyWritingLab.com.

BASIC WEB DESIGN

Prepared and Submitted by Diane Lipari

As requested, I have analyze our website for its appeal and usability. The information I have gathers indicates a need for the application of basic Web design principles. Through a survey, our users send us two messages. They don't care about new features. They just want easy usability. Before 2015, our website follow the basic guidelines of Web design. However, since our company's reorganization, we have not designate a person responsible for updating the Web. Two actions have recommended. The first recommendation has already been implemented. Qualify and experience, Raul Mendez take responsibility for our company's Web design. He has promises to carry out the second recommendation, which is to follow these guidelines:

- Provide text they read.
- Answer their questions with detailed information.
- Provide easy-to-use navigation and search options.
- Eliminate bugs, typos, corrupted data, dead links, and outdated content.

WHAT HAVE I LEARNED ABOUT VERBS?

To test and track your understanding, answer the following questions.

1. What is the general rule for forming the past tense of regular verbs? Give an example.

2. What are three exceptions to the way in which regular verbs form the past tense? Give examples.

   a.

   b.

   c.

3. What can be said about the past tense forms of irregular verbs? ....

....

4. List the past tense forms of the irregular verbs *to be*, *to have*, and *to do*: ....

....

5. List three often-confused helping verbs: ....

6. The present perfect tense is formed by joining the helping verbs _____ or _____ with the past participle.

7. What are two purposes of the present perfect tense? ....

....

....

8. The past perfect tense is formed by joining the helping verb _____ with the past participle.

9. What are two purposes of the past perfect tense? ....

....

....

10. The passive voice is formed by the combination of _____ with a past participle; can be expressed in every _____; and has two purposes: ....

....

11. **How will I use what I have learned about verbs?**
    In your notebook, discuss how you will apply to your own writing what you have learned about regular and irregular verbs.

12. **What do I still need to study about the verbs?**
    In your notebook, discuss your ongoing study needs by describing what, when, and how you will continue studying regular and irregular verbs.

Academic Learning Log: Chapter Review

Complete the Post-test for Chapter 19 in MyWritingLab.

20 Subjects, Verbs, and Simple Sentences

PART 4 THE BASIC SENTENCE

LEARNING OUTCOMES

After studying this chapter you will be able to:

L1 Answer the question "What's the Point of Subjects, Verbs, and Simple Sentences?"

L2 Identify Types of Subjects

L3 Identify Types of Verbs

L4 Compose the Simple Sentence

L5 Locate Subjects and Verbs to Identify Complete Thoughts

A simple sentence, also called an *independent clause*, includes a subject and a verb and expresses a complete thought.

Communicating about a real-life situation helps us to understand the purpose of subjects, verbs, and simple sentences. The photograph on the facing page illustrates one immediate effect of strenuous exercise. Read the statements given in Practice 1 about Venus Williams, and answer the question "What's the point of subjects, verbs, and simple sentences?"

What's the Point of Subjects, Verbs, and Simple Sentences?

PHOTOGRAPHIC ORGANIZER: SUBJECTS, VERBS, AND SIMPLE SENTENCES

Read the following set of statements. Circle the one that makes the most sense. Discuss why the statement you chose makes sense and why the other two do not.

Swigs a bottle of water in one long gulp.

Venus Williams, preparing for the French Open.

Venus Williams, preparing for the French Open, swigs a bottle of water in one long gulp.

What's the point of subjects, verbs, and simple sentences?

_____

_____

One Student Writer's Response

The following paragraph offers one writer's reaction to the statements about Venus Williams and the importance of subjects, verbs, and simple sentences.

> The first statement "swigs a bottle of water in one long gulp" doesn't make any sense by itself. Who's doing this? "Venus Williams, preparing for the French Open" doesn't make any sense by itself either. I need more information! The ideas do make sense when they are put together. Venus Williams takes a drink because she is preparing for the French Open. It's hard to figure out what someone is saying when a subject or a verb is missing. I think both must be needed to say something.

Subjects, Verbs, and Simple Sentences

A subject and a verb unite to state a focused and complete thought in a sentence. You already have a great deal of experience using subjects, verbs, and simple sentences. As we think silently, we use subjects and verbs to frame most of our thoughts. Most often, we converse with each other by using subjects and verbs, and much of what we read in newspapers, magazines, and books and on the Internet is expressed by using subjects and verbs.

L2 Identify Types of Subjects

A **subject** is the person, place, object, or topic about which a writer expresses a focused thought or makes an assertion. To identify a subject, ask: Who or what did this? Alternatively, ask: Who or what is this?

A subject is expressed in a variety of ways based on the focus of the writer's thought or point. Four common types of subjects include the **simple subject**, the **gerund subject**, the **action/being subject**, and the **compound subject**.

Simple Subjects: Four Types

- **Simple Subject, Type 1:** A single person, place, or topic is the focus of thought.

    SUBJECT
    ↓
    Thunder frightens Henry.

- **Simple Subject, Type 2:** A gerund, a word ending with *-ing*, is the point.

    Laughing reduces stress.
    ACTION SUBJECT

- **Simple Subject, Type 3:** A phrase expresses the focus of thought.

    SUBJECT

    <u>What one does</u> speaks louder than what one says.

- **Simple Subject, Type 4:** A suggestion or command is the focus of thought.

    ↑Make a difference by voting.

    "YOU" IS IMPLIED, AS THE SUBJECT OF THE SENTENCE, WHICH IS A COMMAND.

Compound Subject

- **Compound Subject:** Two or more people, places, objects, or topics are the subjects of a focused thought.

    COMPOUND SUBJECT

    <u>Florida</u>, <u>Texas</u>, and <u>California</u> produce over 11 million tons of citrus per year.

    COMPOUND SUBJECTS ARE OFTEN JOINED BY THE COORDINATING CONJUNCTION "AND."

IDENTIFY TYPES OF SUBJECTS

Underline the subject once in each of the following sentences. Then, identify each subject by type by writing *simple*, *compound*, or *gerund* in the blanks. Share and discuss your answers with a peer or group of classmates.

_____ 1. Nurses perform five basic tasks.

_____ 2. Assessment and assistance in the diagnosis are two tasks of nurses.

_____ 3. The three remaining tasks include planning, implementing, and evaluating patient care.

_____ 4. What nurses observe daily about their patients influences treatment.

_____ 5. Nursing offers flexible work schedules in 4-, 8-,10-, or 12-hour shifts.

_____ 6. Hospitals, clinics, and hospices are just three of many places of employment for nurses.

_____ 7. Remember that nurses often must lift, carry, push, and pull heavy loads.

Practice 2

_____ 8. Meeting the demands of nursing requires physical and emotional strength.

_____ 9. Consider nursing as a rewarding career path.

10. Write a sentence using a specific type of subject. Suggested topic: A rewarding career.

_____

_____

L3 Identify Types of Verbs

A **verb** makes an assertion about a subject. A verb states an occurrence (*occur, happen*), a state of being (*is, seems*), or an action (*run, talk*) of the subject. Various verb forms express different kinds of information about the subject of a sentence. Three basic types of verbs include **linking verbs, action verbs,** and **helping verbs**.

Linking Verbs

A **linking verb** connects the subject to a word that renames, describes, or defines the subject. Linking verbs often describe a state of being. The following chart lists common linking verbs and a few examples of their uses in sentences.

Commonly Used Linking Verbs

am, is, are, was, were, being, been…	SUBJECT LINKING VERB The ice cream is cold and sweet.
appear, become, look, seem, turn	SUBJECT LINKING VERB The cheese turned moldy.
feel, smell, sound, taste	SUBJECT LINKING VERB The burrito tasted spicy.

IDENTIFY LINKING VERBS

Fill in each blank with a linking verb that best completes the meaning of the sentence. Discuss your responses in a small group or with your class.

1. Flooding .... the most common of all natural disasters.

2. A flood can quickly .... a serious, life-threatening event.

3. A flash flood .... the result of torrential rainfall within a short time and .... to .... out of nowhere.

4. Flash floods quickly .... dry creek beds and canyons into raging and deep rivers.

5. Another type of flood .... a tsunami.

6. Tsunamis .... the product of the forceful movement of the seabed due to underwater events such earthquakes or volcanic eruptions.

7. A tsunami .... in a series of waves that drive seawater inland with a .... flood.

8. A tsunami wave .... like a massive, sky-high wall of water carrying rocks, mud, and debris.

9. Flood waters often .... of gasoline and raw sewage.

10. Write a sentence using a linking verb. Suggested topic: Flood damage to a home or community. ....

Action Verbs

An **action verb** shows the behavior of the subject.

SUBJECT   ACTION VERB
Justin and Mia prepared for the upcoming storm.

SUBJECT   ACTION VERB
Justin and Mia waterproofed their home.

IDENTIFY ACTION VERBS

Underline the action verb twice in each of the following sentences.

1. Officials alerted the public to the flash flood threat.

2. Justin and Mia raised furniture, appliances, and valuables off the floors.

3. They gathered supplies such as battery-powered flashlights and radios, rain gear, several days of canned goods and bottled water, medicine and first-aid goods.

4. Mia identified an evacuation route as well as nearby shelters.

5. Mia filled the car's gas tank with fuel and the car's trunk with several days of clothing for the family.

6. Justin installed check valves in the home's sewer traps to stop any backup of floodwaters into the house.

7. Justin mounted storm shutters on the windows.

8. Justin and Mia constructed barriers of sandbags for all outside doors.

9. They also sealed basement walls against seepage with a waterproof compound.

10. Write a sentence using an action verb. Suggested topic: A severe storm.

_____

_____

Helping Verbs

A **helping verb** is used with a main verb to create a verb phrase. Helping verbs are also used to form questions. The verbs *be, do,* and *have* can be used alone or as helping verbs.

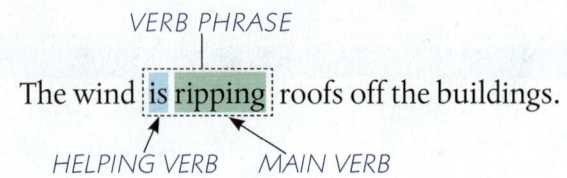

The wind **is ripping** roofs off the buildings.

HELPING VERB   MAIN VERB

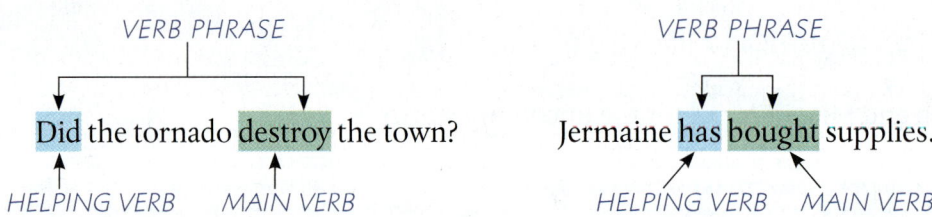

Did the tornado destroy the town?   Jermaine has bought supplies.

HELPING VERB   MAIN VERB   HELPING VERB   MAIN VERB

Common Helping Verbs						
be	do	have	may	should	shall	have to
being	does	had	might	could	can	have got to
been	did	has	must	would	will	ought to
am						supposed to
are						used to
is						
was						
were						

Practice 5

IDENTIFY HELPING VERBS

Underline the verb phrase twice in each of the following sentences.

1. Natural disasters have become life-altering events for survivors.
2. A natural disaster, such as a hurricane or tornado, can inflict great emotional and financial damage.
3. Destroyed property, lost resources, and physical injury do occur unfortunately.
4. Many survivors may experience severe post-traumatic stress disorders.
5. Some could even withdraw into states of depression.
6. Natural disasters also have revealed the better side of human nature.
7. Neighbors do come together to share food, shelter, and other resources in the aftermath of a disaster.
8. We all should be prepared for a natural disaster.
9. Have you lived through a natural disaster?
10. Write a sentence using a helping verb. Suggested topic: Being a good neighbor.

Compose the Simple Sentence

A **simple sentence** is a group of related words that includes a subject and a verb and expresses a complete thought. A simple sentence is also known as an **independent clause**. An idea that is missing a subject or verb is a fragment or incomplete thought.

For more information on correcting fragments, see pages 438–457.

Distinguishing between a Fragment and the Simple Sentence

Fragment with Missing Subject

VERB ⟶ Uses her fame to help refugees around the world.

Fragment with Missing Verb

SUBJECT ⟶ Angelina Jolie using her fame to help refugees around the world.

Simple Sentence

                              VERB

SUBJECT ⟶ Angelina Jolie uses her fame to help refugees around the world.

Practice 6

COMPOSE SIMPLE SENTENCES

Create a simple sentence from each of the following fragments. From the box below, fill in the blank with a subject or verb that best completes each thought.

Verbs	Subjects
makes	Volunteers
is	Volunteering
provide	Volunteer
donate	
serve	

1. Volunteering _____ serving others without reward.

2. Each year countless ordinary Americans _____ assistance to others through volunteer work.

3. _____ improve their job skills, build their resumes, and enhance their experience.

4. Some people _____ to help solve a problem in society.

5. These _____ may give time to an organization that feeds and clothes the poor.

6. Others _____ to help people they know.

7. They may _____ blood for a sick friend, relative, or acquaintance.

8. Some _____ enjoy participating in civic life.

9. They _____ as workers at voting polls or on clean-up crews for public lands.

10. Write a simple sentence. Suggested topic: The benefits of volunteering.

_____

Locate Subjects and Verbs to Identify Complete Thoughts

To avoid fragments and to state ideas as complete thoughts, proofread to identify the subjects and verbs of each sentence. Identifying prepositional phrases as you proofread will help you locate the subject of the sentence.

Understand the Prepositional Phrase

A **preposition** is a word that has a noun or pronoun as its object and states a relationship between its object and another word. A prepositional phrase begins with a preposition and ends with the object of the preposition.

PREPOSITIONAL PHRASE

PREPOSITION → as the first female chief ← OBJECT OF THE PREPOSITION

The following chart lists a few common prepositions and examples of their objects.

Common Prepositions with Possible Objects			
Preposition	**Object**	**Preposition**	**Object**
about	the house	from	the past
along	the street	in	my wallet
after	the movie	like	him
around	the room	of	the boys
as	the parent	on	the chair
below	the surface	over	the others
by	evening	to	the college
during	the storm	while	sleeping
for	Texas	with	patience

Find the Prepositional Phrases

The object of the preposition can never be the subject or the verb of a sentence. Since subjects and verbs are often surrounded by prepositional phrases, you need to identify these phrases. Identifying prepositional phrases keeps you from confusing them with the subject of the sentence. And often, once these phrases are identified, the subject and the verb—or lack of either—becomes easier to recognize.

Practice 7

IDENTIFY PREPOSITIONAL PHRASES

Place parentheses around all (prepositional phrases) in the following simple sentences.

1. One of the best nuts to eat for good health is the walnut.
2. The walnut over all other nuts offers twice the antioxidants for lowering of cholesterol.
3. Getting plenty of potassium can cut your risk of stroke by 20%.
4. A diet of fatty fish like salmon and sardines reduces risk of heart disease.
5. Forty-seven percent of adults report nodding off or falling asleep while driving during any given month.
6. The sponges in our kitchens used for dishwashing can have more germs than a toilet bowl.
7. Germs from cold viruses linger on remote controls, water faucets, refrigerator handles and doorknobs as long as 24 hours.
8. Touch spots around public places such as ATM keypads and grocery cart handles are hotbeds for germs.
9. All of us need to wash our hands frequently during the day and always before eating.
10. Write a sentence using prepositional phrases. Suggested topic: Healthful lifestyle.

_____

The FIL Process

To identify subjects and verbs, follow these three simple steps:

1. **F**ind Prepositional Phrases: Place parentheses around (prepositional phrases).
2. **I**dentify the Verb: Underline the verb (action or linking) twice.
3. **L**ocate the Subject: Ask: Who or what did this or who or what is this? The answer is the subject. Underline the subject once.

SUBJECT   PREPOSITIONAL PHRASES   VERB

<u>All</u> (of the applicants) (for the job) <u><u>must pass</u></u> an exam.

Practice 8

IDENTIFY SUBJECTS AND VERBS

Identify the subjects and verbs in the following simple sentences. Annotate each sentence: Place parentheses around (prepositional phrases), underline the verb twice, and underline the subject once.

1. The world of work is changing.
2. The rise of smart machines and automatic systems) is replacing human workers' performance of repetitive tasks.
3. Places and methods of work continue to reflect the impact of social media, game design, and happiness psychology.

4. The innovations of technology demand the development of high-level skills by workers.

5. Skill in oral communication has become a key element of success in management and customer service.

6. Much of an effective manager's time is spent listening to others, working out problems, and providing feedback for improvement.

7. Mastery of mathematical computation skills is increasingly vital in the workforce.

8. Errors in calculations produce inaccurate reports, inferior products, and loss of profits.

9. The ability of knowing how to learn empowers a worker to master new skills on the job.

10. The changes in the world of work should not be feared by employees but embraced as opportunities for personal and professional growth.

SUBJECTS, VERBS, AND SIMPLE SENTENCES REVIEW

Read the following paragraph written by a student. Annotate each sentence by underlining subjects once, underlining verbs twice, and placing parentheses around (prepositional phrases). *Hint:* Some sentences use the understood subject *you*. Then, write three simple sentences of your own.

(1) Can you improve your job prospects for the future? (2) Sure, you can! (3) Volunteer work is one good way of getting useful experience. (4) Your college may offer advice through its career services. (5) In every job, you can impress your supervisor by your hard work and can gain glowing references for future jobs. (6) Bosses, teachers, and counselors all could be sources of references in the future. (7) Working hard at your job will help you with your job skills. (8) Research your interests through books, on the Internet, and by talking to people. (9) At all times, keep yourself open to different possibilities. (10) It is not always easy! (11) So avoiding discouragement and staying positive are both important! (12) We do not know now about our future. (13) The job of your dreams, with some effort on your part, will become clear to you.

Write three simple sentences. Suggested topic: The ideal job.

1. ....

2. ....

3. ....

Editing Assignments

MyWritingLab™ Complete this Exercise on mywritinglab.com

Editing for Everyday Life

Read the following thank-you note for a surprise birthday party. In each sentence, underline the subject once, underline the verb twice, and place parentheses around the (prepositional phrase). Use your own paper.

Dear Dave and Jennifer:

Please accept my thanks for such a wonderful surprise birthday party. I really was surprised. I was able to visit with so many people. I haven't seen most of them in a long time! Everyone loved the spicy food and cold drinks. The theme of "Mexican Nights" was perfect. Thanks, too, for the great gift. Bob, along with the children, also sends you a big thank you. We owe you one!

Thanks, again,

Beverly

Editing for College Life

Read the following paragraph written for a psychology class. In each sentence, underline the subject once, underline the verb twice, and place parentheses around the (prepositional phrase). Use your own paper.

Natural disasters, such as tsunamis and hurricanes, are stressors. These stressors can affect the mental well-being of victims. Survivors of a disaster often deal with shock, fear, grief, anger, resentment, guilt, shame, helplessness, and hopelessness. They may feel emotionally numb, lose interest in daily activities, have trouble concentrating, and experience memory loss. In addition, physical symptoms such as tension, fatigue, sleeplessness, and bodily aches or pain are common. Victims may also suffer with nightmares or images from the disaster. These reactions are normal and expected.

Editing for Working Life

Read the following e-mail exchanged between professionals at a bank. Identify subjects, verbs, and prepositional phrases. Insert missing subjects or verbs as needed. *Hint:* Some sentences use the understood subject *you*. Use your own paper.

> TO: Dwayne <Dwayne@ITsolutions.com>
> FROM: Kendis Moore Kendis@ITsolutions.com
> SUBJECT: Promotion
>
> Dear Dwayne,
>
> Please accept my congratulations for your promotion to Manager of Information Systems. You and your team will handle activities like installation and upgrading of hardware and software. In addition, you will manage programming and systems design, development of computer networks, and implementation of Internet and intranet sites. By the end of the month, please analyze the computer needs of the organization. Once again, congratulations, and feel free to call on me for assistance.
>
> Best regards,
>
> Kendis Moore

Academic Learning Log: Chapter Review

WHAT HAVE I LEARNED?

To test and track your understanding, complete the following ideas. Use several sentences as needed for each response.

1. A subject is _____

2. The four types of subjects are _____

3. A verb _____

The three basic types of verbs are _____

4. A simple sentence is _____

5. **How will I use what I have learned?**
   In your notebook, discuss how you will apply what you have learned about subjects and verbs to your own writing.

6. **What do I still need to study about subjects and verbs?**
   In your notebook, describe your ongoing study needs by describing what, when, and how you will continue studying subjects and verbs.

Complete the Post-test for Chapter 20 in MyWritingLab.

21 Compound and Complex Sentences

PART 4 THE BASIC SENTENCE

LEARNING OUTCOMES

After studying this chapter you will be able to:

L1 Answer the Question "What's the Point of Compound and Complex Sentences?"

L2 Recognize Types of Clauses: Independent and Dependent

L3 Compose a Compound Sentence

L4 Compose a Complex Sentence

L5 Compose a Compound-Complex Sentence

A compound sentence joins together two or more independent clauses. A complex sentence combines one independent or main clause and one or more dependent clauses.

Communicating about a real-life situation helps us to understand the purpose of compound and complex sentences. The photograph on the facing page illustrates some of the benefits of computer games. Read the statements given in Practice 1, complete the activities, and answer the question "What's the point of compound and complex sentences?"

What's the Point of Compound and Complex Sentences?

PHOTOGRAPHIC ORGANIZER: COMPOUND AND COMPLEX SENTENCES

▲ A child using educational software

The following ideas are stated using four types of sentences: (1) simple; (2) compound; (3) complex; and (4) compound-complex. Discuss with a small group of peers in what ways these sentences differ from each other.

1. Children can benefit from computer games.
2. Computer games are a lot of fun, and they can promote skill development.
3. Some innovative after-school programs, which have grown in recent decades, use computer games in just this way.
4. Fun games are motivating, and motivation leads to better learning; therefore, after-school programs that use computer games have had success.

What's the point of compound and complex sentences?

WRITING FROM LIFE

One Student Writer's Response

The following paragraph offers one writer's thoughts about the differences among sentence types.

> To study the list of sentences, I underlined the subjects and verbs in each one. The first sentence was the only one that focused on one topic. It had only one subject and verb. The rest of the sentences had two or more ideas. Also, some sentences joined ideas with words like "and," "which," and "therefore." Another way the sentences differed was the use of punctuation. Some used commas, and one used a semicolon. I always struggle with commas and semicolons. Overall, I would say using different types of sentences will give me more ways to say what I want to say.

L2 Recognize Types of Clauses: Independent and Dependent

A **clause** is a group of related words that includes a subject and a verb. Two types of clauses provide the basis of all sentences: (1) the **independent clause** and (2) the **dependent clause**.

1. The Independent Clause

A focused and complete thought expressed with a subject and a verb; also known as a *main clause* or **simple sentence**.

> For more on simple sentences, see pages 388–401.

INDEPENDENT CLAUSE
(COMPLETE THOUGHT)

Severe **dehydration** *may result* in shock and death.

SUBJECT VERB

2. The Dependent Clause

(1) An incomplete thought expressed with a subject and a verb marked by a subordinating conjunction such as *after*, *before*, or *when*.

DEPENDENT CLAUSE
(INCOMPLETE THOUGHT)

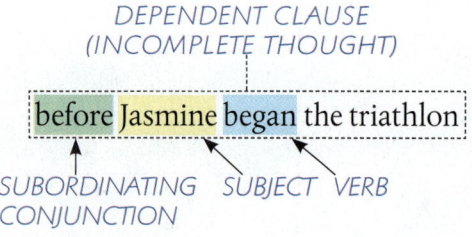

before Jasmine began the triathlon

SUBORDINATING SUBJECT VERB
CONJUNCTION

(2) An incomplete thought marked by a relative pronoun, such as *who* or *which*, acting as the subject of the verb.

RELATIVE PRONOUN
(ACTING AS SUBJECT)   VERB   DEPENDENT CLAUSE (INCOMPLETE THOUGHT)

which included running, swimming, and bike riding

RECOGNIZE TYPES OF CLAUSES

Identify each of the following clauses as **I** for independent or **D** for dependent. *Hint:* Circle subordinating conjunctions and relative pronouns.

1. Dehydration can occur from extreme exertion such as participating in a triathlon.

2. Because people sweat a lot when exerting themselves.

3. Paying attention to signs of dehydration is important.

4. Which may include dizziness and dry mouth.

5. Although dehydration can occur even without great exertion, especially in the summertime.

6. When someone loses more fluids than he or she takes in.

7. The human body which is about two thirds water.

8. Shedding water weight as a quick way to lose weight can cause dehydration.

9. Because some illnesses cause dehydration through vomiting and diarrhea.

10. Create an independent clause. Suggested topic: How to avoid dehydration.

Compose a Compound Sentence

A compound sentence is made up of two or more independent clauses. A **compound sentence** links independent clauses together as **equally important** ideas through one of three methods.

Three Ways to Combine Independent Clauses into a Compound Sentence

1. **A comma and a coordinating conjunction:** The coordinating conjunction serves as a transition that shows the equal relationship of ideas within the sentence. Use the acronym FANBOYS to help you remember the seven coordinating conjunctions—*for, and, nor, but, or, yet,* or *so.*

[Independent clause,] coordinating conjunction [independent clause.]

Coordinating Conjunctions (FANBOYS) and Meanings						
Coordinating Conjunction	For	And	Nor	But	Or	Yet	So
Meaning	Result	Addition	Negation	Contrast	Choice	Contrast	Result

2. A semicolon, conjunctive adverb, and a comma: The conjunction shows the relationship of ideas within the sentence. In addition, the conjunctive adverb introduces the next clause. A comma follows the conjunctive adverb since it is an introductory element of the next clause.

[Independent clause;] conjunctive adverb, [independent clause.]

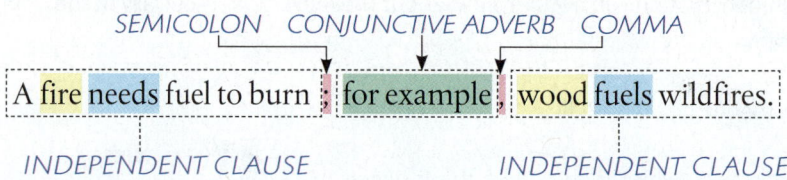

Common Conjunctive Adverbs and the Relationships They Express					
Addition	**Cause or Effect**	**Comparison or Contrast**	**Example**	**Emphasis**	**Time**
also	accordingly	however	for example	certainly	finally
besides	as a result	in comparison	for instance	indeed	meanwhile
further	consequently	in contrast		in fact	next
furthermore	hence	instead		still	then
in addition	therefore	likewise		undoubtedly	thereafter
incidentally	thus	nevertheless			
moreover		nonetheless			
		otherwise			
		similarly			

3. A semicolon: A semicolon joins two closely related independent clauses.

[Independent clause;] [independent clause.]

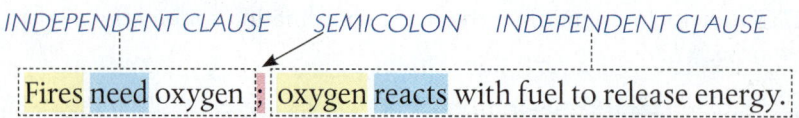

COMPOSE COMPOUND SENTENCES

Insert the proper punctuation in each of the following compound sentences. *Hint:* Identify the subjects and verbs. Place parentheses around (prepositional phrases); underline the subject once; underline the verb twice.

1. A wildfire differs from other fires it is larger, faster, and much more unpredictable.

2. A wildfire spreads in surprising ways for example a wildfire can jump roads and rivers.

3. The origin of the word wildfire comes from the ancient term "Greek fire" for fire bombs used in naval warfare, but today, the term means uncontrolled burning.

4. Four causes of wildfires occur naturally natural causes include spontaneous combustion, sparks from falling rocks, volcano eruptions, and lightning.

5. Human activity also ignites wildfires for instance arson, campfires, and discarded cigarette butts trigger numerous wildfires.

6. The amount of flammable material around a fire is its fuel load, so a small fuel load generates a small fire and a large fuel load creates an intense, fast spreading fire.

7. Three traits of fuel affect a fire they are moisture size and shape and arrangement.

8. In ground fires, the fuel is mainly on the ground in contrast in ladder fires, the fuel reaches above ground in levels from tall shrubs, to tree trunks, hanging vines, and canopies.

9. The temperature, wind, and moisture of weather greatly affect a fire however wind with its supply of oxygen may have the greatest impact.

10. Write a compound sentence. Suggested topic: Wildfire prevention.

For more information on how to identify subjects, verbs, and prepositional phrases, 397–398.

Practice 4

COMPOSE COMPOUND SENTENCES

Create compound sentences by combining the following sets of simple sentences. Vary the ways in which you join ideas. Use appropriate conjunctions and punctuation to show the relationship between the ideas within each new sentence.

1. A fire extinguisher is a necessary safety tool. Most people do not know how to use one.

2. Different types of fires need different types of extinguishers. Different substances are used on electrical fires and grease fires.

3. Five different substances are used to put out fires. Most fire extinguishers carry labels matching their substance to a type of fire.

4. Class A extinguishers put out fires in ordinary combustibles. They put out fires in flammable materials such as cloth, wood, paper, rubber, and many plastics.

5. Class B extinguishers stop fires involving flammable liquids. Grease, gasoline, oil, and oil-based paints require this type of extinguisher.

6. Class C extinguishers are equipped to put out a fire caused by an appliance. This device snuffs fires caused by any electrical equipment.

7. Class D extinguishers are used on flammable metals. Factories mainly use these extinguishers.

8. Restaurants usually use class K extinguishers. These devices are intended for fires caused by oils and fats used in cooking appliances.

9. Portable fire extinguishers are intended for quick use on small fires. Large or quickly spreading fires require professional firefighters.

_____

_____

10. Write a compound sentence. Suggested topic: Fire dangers in the home.

_____

Practice 4

Compose a Complex Sentence

A **complex sentence** contains one independent or main clause and one or more dependent clauses. A **dependent clause** expresses a **subordinate** or minor detail about the idea in the independent clause. A complex sentence joins independent and dependent clauses by placing a subordinating conjunction at the beginning of the dependent clause. **Subordinating conjunctions** state the unequal relationship between the main clause and the subordinate clause.

Subordinating Conjunctions and the Relationships They Express				
Cause	**Contrast**	**Time**	**Place**	**Condition**
as	although	after	where	even if
because	as if	as	wherever	if
in order that	even though	as long as		only if
now that	though	before		unless
since	whereas	once		when
so	while	since		whether or not
		until		
		when		
		whenever		
		while		

A subordinating conjunction signals the beginning of a dependent clause.

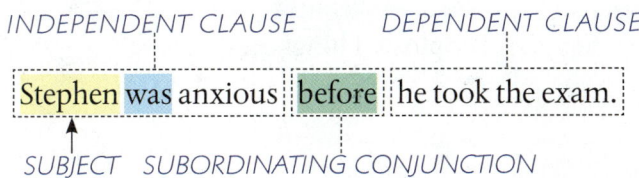

INDEPENDENT CLAUSE   DEPENDENT CLAUSE

Stephen was anxious before he took the exam.

SUBJECT   SUBORDINATING CONJUNCTION

Practice 5

COMPOSE COMPLEX SENTENCES

Underline the dependent clauses in each sentence. In the blank after each sentence, state the relationship between the dependent clause and the main clause.

1. Since he was an elementary school student years ago, Stephen has always struggled with test anxiety. _____

2. He feels anxious even if he memorizes all the material. _____

3. Stephen found a tutoring center where students can get tips about dealing with test anxiety. _____

4. Because he learned tips to use during a test, he now approaches tests with a calm attitude. _____

5. Studying for a test should begin on the first day of class because cramming at the last minute doesn't work. _____

6. When you pace your studies over days or weeks, you don't have to try to learn everything the night before an exam. _____

7. Before you begin a test, read all the directions and skim over all the questions. _____

8. First, write down key facts and ideas so that you don't worry about forgetting them. _____

9. If you don't know an answer, skip it and come back if you have time. _____

10. Write a complex sentence using a subordinating conjunction. State the relationship between your dependent and main clauses. Suggested topic: How to deal with anxiety.

    ....

    ....

A special kind of subordinating conjunction is the relative pronoun. A **relative pronoun** connects the dependent clause to a noun in the main clause. The choice of a relative pronoun indicates whether the dependent clause is describing a person or a thing.

Relative Pronouns and What They Indicate		
People	**Things**	**People or Things**
who	which	that
whom		
whose		

MAIN CLAUSE NOUN   RELATIVE PRONOUN

The number of **people** **who** struggle with weight problems is growing.

DEPENDENT CLAUSE

COMPOSE COMPLEX SENTENCES

Insert the relative pronoun that best completes each sentence. Circle the nouns described by the relative pronoun.

1. Mindfulness refers to an attitude .... blends thought and action.

2. Connor, ... lost 40 pounds, wanted to change bad habits.

3. Therefore, he mindfully avoided hamburgers, French fries, and Coca-Cola, ... were his favorite foods.

4. Instead, he ate a wide variety of foods .... were high in vitamins and low in calories.

5. Mindfulness is being aware of our senses and experiences, ... may include physical sensations and emotional feelings.

6. For example, people .... are mindful consider the causes and effects of their cravings for food.

7. Cravings .... are based on emotional needs may lead to poor food choices.

8. Those .... crave empty carbohydrates, like potato chips, may be seeking relief from stress.

9. The best advice for those of you .... stress most affects is "focus on the present moment and quiet your thoughts."

10. Write a complex sentence using a relative pronoun. Suggested topic: An important decision.

....

....

Placement and Punctuation of a Dependent Clause within a Complex Sentence

1. **Before the main clause:** A dependent clause at the beginning of a sentence acts as an introductory element and must be set off with a comma.

Subordinating conjunction dependent clause, main clause.

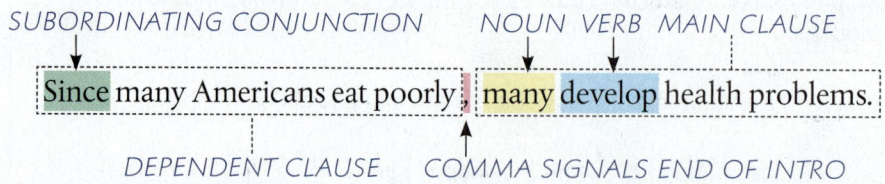

2. **In the middle of the main clause:** The context of the clause controls the use of commas. Many dependent clauses in the middle of a sentence are **relative clauses**. Relative clauses are either essential or nonessential.

   (a) If the dependent clause adds information **essential** to the meaning of a sentence, no commas are needed. Most often essential information limits or restricts the meaning of a common noun such as *man* or *woman*.

Main relative pronoun dependent clause clause.

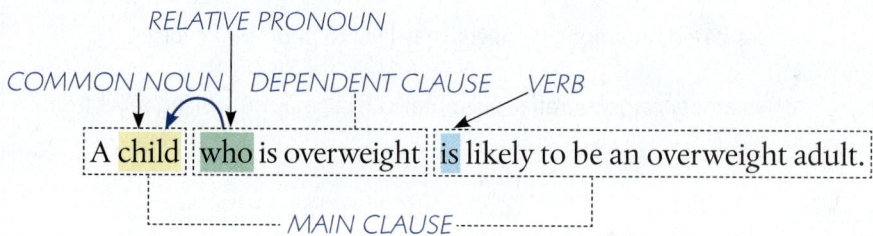

   (b) If the dependent clause adds information that is **nonessential** to the meaning of the main clause, insert **commas** before and after the dependent clause. Usually a nonessential clause describes a proper noun.

Main, relative pronoun dependent clause, clause.

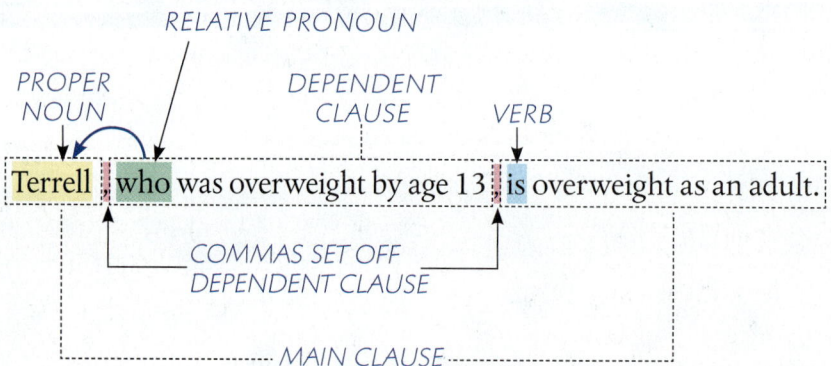

3. After the main clause: The context of the clause controls the use of commas in these instances:

(a) If the dependent clause begins with a **subordinating conjunction**, no comma is needed.

Main clause *subordinating conjunction dependent clause.*

MAIN CLAUSE   SUBORDINATING CONJUNCTION   DEPENDENT CLAUSE

Fast foods are poor dietary choices because they are high in calories and fat.

(b) If the dependent clause begins with a relative pronoun, determine if the information is essential or nonessential. An **essential** dependent clause does not need a comma.

Main clause *dependent clause.*

MAIN CLAUSE   RELATIVE PRONOUN   ESSENTIAL DEPENDENT CLAUSE

We should also avoid certain dietary options that have high levels of sodium.

(c) Insert a comma before a dependent clause that is **nonessential**.

Main clause *relative pronoun dependent clause.*

MAIN CLAUSE   COMMA   RELATIVE PRONOUN   NONESSENTIAL DEPENDENT CLAUSE

I no longer eat Whoppers, which are high in calories, fat, and sodium.

COMPOSE COMPLEX SENTENCES

A. Edit each of the following complex sentences for proper punctuation. *Hint:* One sentence is already correctly punctuated.

1. Organic meat, poultry, eggs, and dairy products come from animals that are given no antibiotics or growth hormones.

2. Organic food differs from other foods because it is produced without pesticides, sewage sludge, or radiation.

3. Organic food is produced by farmers who work to enhance environmental quality for future generations.

4. Before a product can be labeled organic the farmer must meet USDA organic standards.

B. Create five complex sentences by combining the following sets of simple sentences. Use appropriate subordinating conjunctions, relative pronouns, and punctuation to show the relationship between ideas within each new sentence.

5. Organic food has long been available for people. In recent years it has been available for pets.

6. People want their pets to be healthy and happy. They buy their pets organic food.

7. It's not clear that organic food is better for pets. There hasn't been much research on this yet.

8. One reason many people don't buy organic food for their pets is the price. The price is often higher than the price of other pet food.

9. My cat tried a pricey new organic cat food. She would no longer eat anything else.

10. Write a complex sentence. Suggested topic: A reason to eat organic food.

Adapted from U.S. Department of Agriculture. "Organic Food Standards and Labels: The Facts." April 2002.

L5 Compose a Compound-Complex Sentence

For more on coordinate and subordinate ideas, see pages 404–413.

A **compound-complex sentence** contains two or more independent clauses and one or more dependent clauses. A compound-complex sentence joins coordinate and subordinate ideas into a single sentence. All the punctuation rules for both compound and complex sentences apply to the compound-complex sentence.

DEPENDENT CLAUSE   MAIN CLAUSE   MAIN CLAUSE

Before she earned her driver's license, Kit studied the rules, and she practiced driving.

SUBORDINATING CONJUNCTION   COMMA   COMMA   COORDINATING CONJUNCTION

COMPOSE COMPOUND-COMPLEX SENTENCES

Create and properly punctuate compound-complex sentences by combining the following simple sentences. Discuss your work with a classmate or a small group of peers.

1. Shelly is a defensive driver. She keeps her eyes moving. She avoids a fixed stare.

2. Shelly was first learning to drive. Another driver ran a stop sign. Shelly's car was wrecked beyond repair.

3. Shelly didn't cause the accident. The accident left her with three broken ribs. She might have been able to avoid the collision.

4. Shelly wasn't watching the road. She was thinking about her upcoming graduation. She never saw the other car coming.

5. Shelly now assumes other drivers will make mistakes. She scans the road ahead, to the side, and in the rear. She is able to react safely to the actions of another driver.

6. She assumes other drivers will not see her. She avoids maneuvering into their path. She scans the road thoroughly before changing speed or direction.

Practice 8

7. Shelly approaches an intersection cautiously. Other drivers may not obey traffic signals. She anticipates the need to avoid a traffic hazard.

   _____

   _____

8. Shelly always follows another car at a safe distance. The driver in front slams on brakes. She can avoid a collision, stay in her lane, and not be hit by the car behind her.

   _____

   _____

9. Shelly is grateful to be alive. She was a distracted driver once. Now, she drives safely. It's a matter of life or death.

   _____

   _____

10. Write a compound-complex sentence. Suggested topic: Dangerous driving habits.

    _____

    _____

Practice 9

FOUR SENTENCE TYPES REVIEW

Write and properly punctuate four different types of sentences. Suggested topic: A favorite holiday.

1. Simple _____

   _____

2. Compound _____

   _____

3. Complex _____

   _____

4. Compound-Complex _____

   _____

Editing Assignments

MyWritingLab™ Complete this Exercise on mywritinglab.com

Editing for Everyday Life

The following journal entry is from the personal diary of a person who wants to lose weight and get healthy. Edit the paragraph for correct punctuation of sentence types. Use your own paper or complete the exercise on MyWritingLab.com.

Dear Diary:

Today, I am starting a new lifestyle that will include a healthful diet and regular exercise so I need to identify my current exercising and eating habits. The first is easy because I don't exercise. I will drive around a parking lot for 30 minutes looking for a close parking space and I spend way too much time in front of the television. I watch TV every night from 4:00 p.m. until bedtime which is usually 11:00 p.m. My diet consists mostly of diet sodas and fast food! I sure do have my work cut out for me.

Editing for College Life

Read the following paragraph, written for a humanities course, about the impact of art on the viewer. The assignment asked students to react to a piece of art of their own choosing, such as a sculpture, photograph, or painting. Edit the paragraph for correct punctuation of sentence types.

The powerful impact of art on a person is evident in my own response to Michelangelo's statue of David. Although I have seen only photographs of this remarkable sculpture, its beauty and balance are striking. Michelangelo who is perhaps the most gifted artist of all times captured the physical strength and grace of this Jewish hero from the Old Testament. Muscles of perfect proportion reveal David's strength a stance of action reveals his agility and a steady gaze reveals his confidence. Michelangelo's David looks like the hero who could kill a lion with his bare hands, fell a giant with one well placed stone from his sling, and establish a kingdom. I appreciate this piece of art because it captures the essence of the beauty of humanity; David seems strong yet gentle.

Editing for Working Life

Read the following memo written from an employee to a supervisor. Edit the paragraph for correct punctuation of sentence types.

To: April Gulleme, Manager
From: Ricardo Menendez
RE: Customer Complaints

As you requested, I am submitting a report that includes customer complaints and recommendations gathered from the suggestion box. Some customers complained about slow service in contrast others complained about being interrupted too often by servers while a few servers received rave reviews. Some customers complained during the week about the noisy atmosphere yet others complimented the lively entertainment on the weekends.

I recommend two actions. First, the servers who are efficient and appreciated by customers can mentor the other servers these server-trainers will be paid for their efforts. Second, we can offer and advertise different types of entertainment on different days of the week; for example, on weekends we can offer lively entertainment; on weeknights we can offer toned-down, easy-listening music.

Academic Learning Log: Chapter Review

WHAT HAVE I LEARNED?

To test and track your understanding, answer the following questions.

1. What is a clause, and what are the two types of clauses?

2. What is a simple sentence?
3. What is a compound sentence?
4. What is a complex sentence?
5. What is a complex-compound sentence?

6. **How will I use what I have learned?**
   In your notebook, discuss how you will apply to your own writing what you have learned about sentence types. When will you apply this knowledge during the writing process?

7. **What do I still need to study about sentence types?**
   In your notebook, discuss your ongoing study needs by describing what, when, and how you will continue studying sentence types.

MyWritingLab™

Complete the Post-test for Chapter 21 in MyWritingLab.

22

Editing Run-ons: Comma Splices and Fused Sentences

LEARNING OUTCOMES

After studying this chapter you will be able to:

L0 1 Answer the Question "What's the Point of Editing Comma Splices and Fused Sentences?"

L0 2 Identify Comma Splices and Fused Sentences

L0 3 Identify Five Ways to Edit Comma Splices and Fused Sentences

- Use a Period and a Capital Letter
- Use a Comma Followed by a Coordinating Conjunction
- Use a Semicolon
- Use a Semicolon Followed by a Conjunctive Adverb
- Use a Subordinating Conjunction

A comma splice is an error that occurs when a comma is used by itself to join two sentences. A fused sentence is an error that occurs when two sentences are joined without any punctuation.

According to research, comma splices and fused sentences are two of the most common errors made by student writers. The photograph on these pages shows a natural phenomenon that stirs human emotions and imagination. Read about this special place and then answer the question "What's the point of learning about editing comma splices and fused sentences?"

What's the Point of Editing Comma Splices and Fused Sentences?

PHOTOGRAPHIC ORGANIZER: COMMA SPLICES AND FUSED SENTENCES

Read the following short description of Niagara Falls, adapted from a 1913 essay written by Rupert Brooke for the *Westminster Gazette*. This version contains one comma splice and three fused sentences. How do these errors affect the reading of the passage?

Niagara Falls

Half a mile or so above the Falls, on either side, the water of the great stream begins to run more swiftly in confusion it descends with ever-growing speed it begins chattering and leaping, breaking into a thousand ripples, throwing up joyful fingers of spray, sometimes it is divided by islands and rocks sometimes the eye can see nothing but a waste of laughing, springing, foamy waves.

Adapted from Rupert Brooke, "Niagara Falls," Westminster Gazette, 1913.

What's the point of learning about editing comma splices and fused sentences?

WRITING FROM LIFE

One Student Writer's Response

The following paragraph offers one writer's response to the opening paragraph about Niagara Falls.

> I had to read the paragraph several times to figure out what the author was saying. I couldn't tell when one sentence ended and another one started. I guess a comma splice or fused sentence occurs because a writer joins sentences without the proper punctuation. Without proper punctuation that signals the end of one thought and the beginning of another, ideas become confusing as they run on. Proper punctuation signals the beginning or end of each sentence. Proper punctuation makes ideas clear and easy to follow.

Comma splices and fused sentences are punctuation errors that occur when independent clauses are improperly joined to form a compound sentence. To properly combine clauses into a compound sentence, the end of each independent clause must be signaled by appropriate punctuation, such as a semicolon, a comma followed by a coordinating conjunction, or a period at the end of the sentence.

L2 Identify Comma Splices and Fused Sentences

A **comma splice** occurs when a comma is used by itself (without a coordinating conjunction) to join two independent clauses.

COMMA SPLICE

Gambling may be fun, it also can be addicting.

INDEPENDENT CLAUSE   INDEPENDENT CLAUSE

A **fused sentence** occurs when two independent clauses are joined without any punctuation.

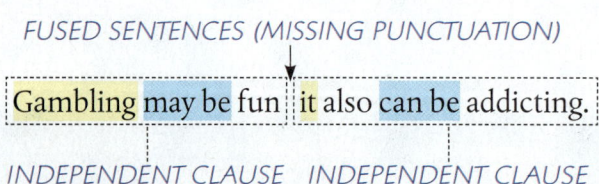

FUSED SENTENCES (MISSING PUNCTUATION)

Gambling may be fun it also can be addicting.

INDEPENDENT CLAUSE   INDEPENDENT CLAUSE

IDENTIFY COMMA SPLICES AND FUSED SENTENCES

Test your ability to identify comma splices, fused sentences, and properly combined clauses. Write **CS** for comma splice, **FS** for fused sentence, or **C** for correctly punctuated.

_____ 1. Out-of-control gambling has harmful effects a chronic gambler puts at risk her relationships with others and her finances.

_____ 2. Certain forms of gambling are legal, for example, many states operate lotteries.

_____ 3. Other types of gambling are legal in specific places casinos are legal in Nevada.

_____ 4. Gambling is an adult-only activity laws declare gambling illegal for underage children.

_____ 5. In some states, patrons must be 21 years old to gamble, other states require minimum ages as low as 17 years old.

_____ 6. The first time Sam gambled he was 19 years old and had $40 in his pocket he ended up with $3000.

_____ 7. Two years later, Sam was $15,000 in debt, he had stolen thousands of dollars from his job to gamble, he was addicted to gambling.

_____ 8. According to experts, more than half of America's adolescents gamble in some form, about one third gamble on a weekly basis.

_____ 9. Many children learn to gamble from parents some parents give children lottery tickets as gifts or they encourage their children to bet a few dollars on a favorite sports team.

_____ 10. Gambling early in life is likely to lead to an addiction to gambling later in life.

L3 Identify Five Ways to Edit Comma Splices and Fused Sentences

As a writer, you have the choice of several ways to edit or avoid comma splices and fused sentences. Each method creates a specific effect. Most experts recommend varying your use of these methods, rather than always relying on the same one.

1. Separate sentences using a period and capital letter.

Punctuating the independent clauses as separate sentences is a method often used to edit comma splices and fused sentences.

Comma Splice:

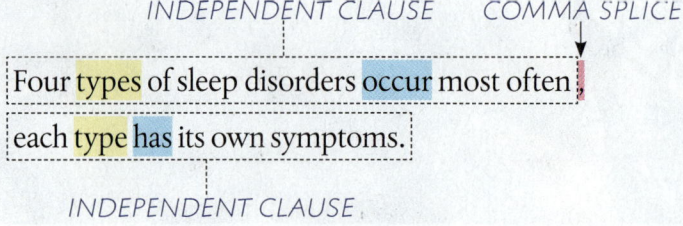

Fused Sentences (without punctuation):

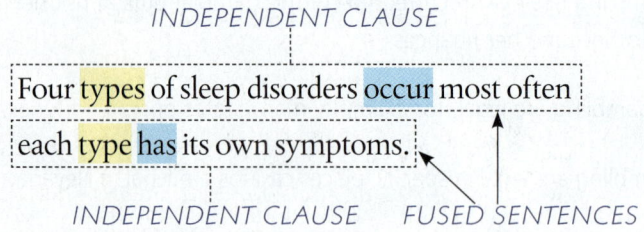

Edited to Correct:

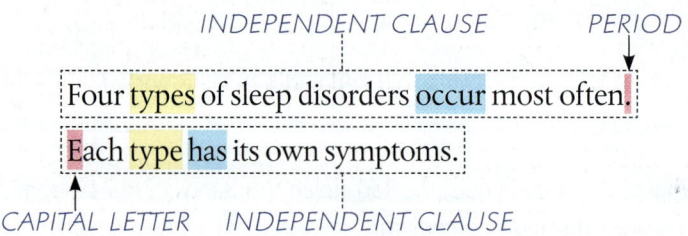

EDIT TO CORRECT COMMA SPLICES AND FUSED SENTENCES: USE A PERIOD AND CAPITAL LETTER

Edit the following sentences to eliminate comma splices and fused sentences. Separate clauses by inserting a period and a capital letter as needed.

1. The most common sleep disorder is insomnia, symptoms include the inability to fall asleep or stay asleep.

2. Sleep apnea is also a common sleep problem snoring, snorting, and gasping sounds during sleep indicate sleep apnea.

3. Kicking or twitching leg movements during sleep are warning signs of restless leg syndrome this sleep disorder affects many people.

4. Restless leg syndrome can also seem like a creepy-crawly feeling in feet, calves, and thighs walking around or rubbing the leg usually helps.

5. Sleep disorders have serious effects, for example, narcolepsy seriously disrupts a sufferer's day.

6. A person with narcolepsy is likely to become drowsy or to fall asleep, often at inappropriate times and places, daytime sleep may occur with or without warning and may be irresistible.

7. Drowsiness may persist for prolonged periods of time nighttime sleep may be fragmented with frequent awakenings.

8. There is strong evidence that narcolepsy may run in families, eight to twelve percent of people with narcolepsy have a close relative with the disease.

9. Narcolepsy can occur in both men and women at any age, its symptoms are usually first noticed in teenagers or young adults.

10. Write a compound sentence. Suggested topic: Sleep problems.

2. Join sentences with a comma followed by a coordinating conjunction.

Sentences can be properly joined by inserting a comma followed by a coordinating conjunction between the independent clauses. The acronym FANBOYS stands for each of the coordinating conjunctions: *for, and, nor, but, or, yet, so.* This method of combining sentences states the relationship between ideas of equal importance.

Comma Splice:

Fused Sentences (without punctuation):

Edited to Correct:

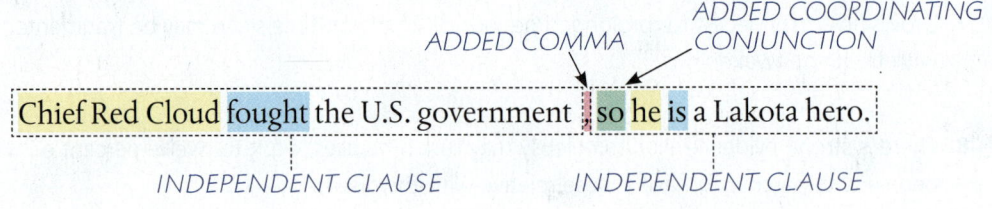

Practice 4

EDIT TO CORRECT COMMA SPLICES AND FUSED SENTENCES: USE A COMMA FOLLOWED BY A COORDINATING CONJUNCTION

Edit the following sentences to eliminate comma splices and fused sentences. Join independent clauses with a comma and a coordinating conjunction.

1. Red Cloud lived from 1822 to 1909 he was head Chief of the Oglala Lakota from 1868 to 1909.

2. Red Cloud was born near North Platte, Nebraska, he became a skilled hunter, horseman, and warrior at a young age.

3. He was Chief at a tragic time in his people's history their way of life was being destroyed by white settlers.

4. Chief Red Cloud waged war against the United States the army had constructed forts along the Bozeman Trail.

5. The Bozeman Trail served as a route to the Montana gold fields for miners and settlers, the trail cut through the heart of Indian Territory.

6. Red Cloud remembered the removal of the Eastern Lakota from Minnesota in 1862 and 1863, he launched a series of assaults on the forts.

7. Chief Red Cloud's successful strategies forced the United States to close the Bozeman Trail he negotiated a treaty resulting in the United States abandoning its forts along the trail.

8. His war against the United States was called Red Cloud's war it was a two-year ordeal.

9. Red Cloud's war was the most successful war waged by an Indian nation against the United States even Red Cloud finally ended up living on an Indian Reservation.

10. Write a compound sentence using a comma and a coordinating conjunction. Suggested topic: A heroic action.

3. Join sentences with a semicolon.

Use a semicolon to join independent clauses when no conjunction is present. A semicolon indicates that the two sentences of equal importance are so closely related that they can be stated as one sentence; however, a semicolon alone does not state the relationship between the two clauses. The relationship between clauses may be one of the following: *time, space, order of importance, general to specific, addition, cause, effect, comparison,* or *contrast.*

Comma Splice:

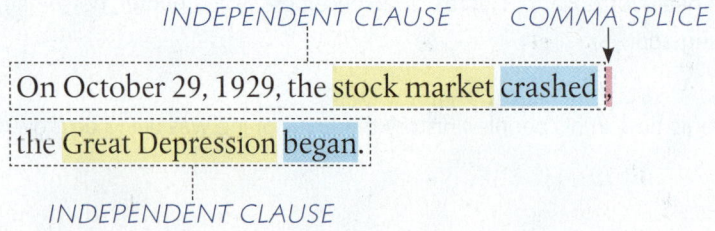

Fused Sentences:

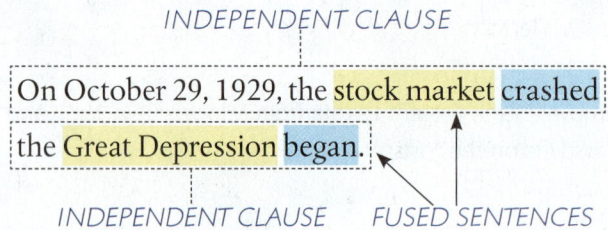

Edited to Correct:

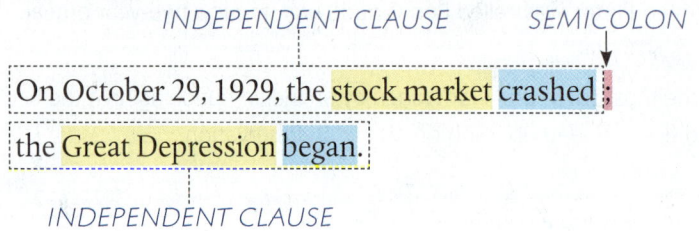

EDIT TO CORRECT COMMA SPLICES AND FUSED SENTENCES: USE A SEMICOLON

Edit the following sentences by inserting semicolons as needed to correct comma splices and fused sentences.

1. The Great Depression lasted from 1929 to 1941 it stands as a historical calamity.

2. The Stock Market crashed in 1929, it took nearly 30 years to regain pre-crash levels.

3. Experts still argue about the causes of the Great Depression, its effects were obvious.

4. Thousands of banks failed and closed, less money was available retailers dropped prices employers cut their work force.

5. Unemployment skyrocketed a quarter of the workforce was without jobs by 1933, and many people became homeless.

6. President Herbert Hoover attempted to handle the crisis, he was unable to improve the situation.

7. Hoovervilles cropped up across the country they were shanty towns that consisted of tents and scrap materials and were made by the homeless.

8. In 1932, President Franklin Delano Roosevelt promised a "New Deal" for the American people Congress created the Works Progress Administration (WPA), which offered work relief for thousands of people.

9. In 1941, America entered into World War II, the Great Depression ended.

10. Write a compound sentence using a semicolon. Suggested topic: The homeless.

4. Join sentences with a semicolon followed by a conjunctive adverb.

Use a semicolon with a conjunctive adverb to join independent clauses. Conjunctive adverbs are transition words that state the relationships between ideas of equal importance. A few common examples include *also, for example, hence, however, indeed, then, therefore,* and *thus*.

> For more information about joining ideas of equal importance, see pages 405–408, "Compound and Complex Sentences."

Comma Splice:

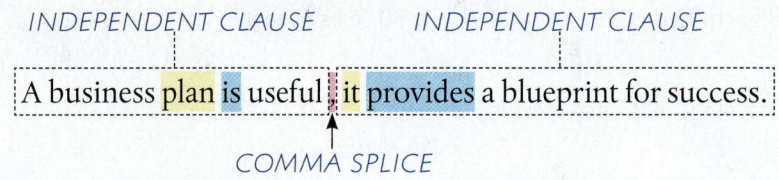

Fused Sentences:

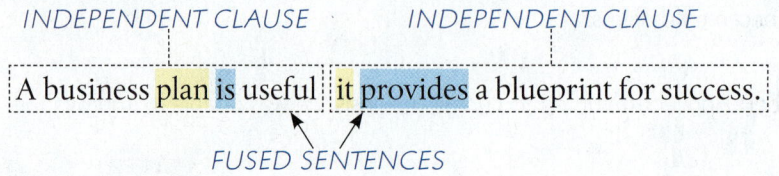

Edited to Correct:

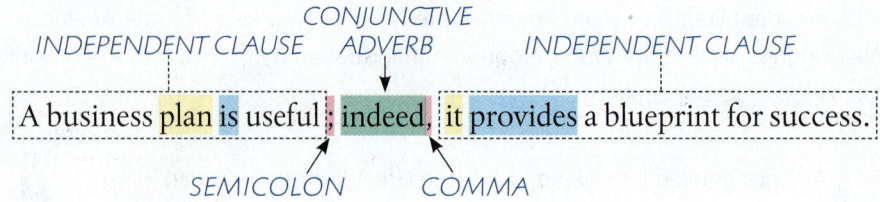

Not only do these transitions state the relationship between ideas, but they also introduce an independent clause and must be set off with a comma.

Practice 6

EDIT TO CORRECT COMMA SPLICES AND FUSED SENTENCES: USE A SEMICOLON FOLLOWED BY A CONJUNCTIVE ADVERB

Edit the following sentences to correct comma splices and fused sentences. Join independent clauses with a semicolon and one of the following transitions: *also, for example, hence, however, therefore*.

1. A business plan is like a calling card, a plan announces the presence and purpose of your business.

2. One type of business plan is a concept plan another type is a money plan.

3. A concept plan describes your product and target market, this plan explains the organization of management.

4. A money plan explains expected costs and profits of your business a money plan is needed to persuade investors to lend you money.

5. The main reason small businesses fail is lack of planning, a business plan is a step to success.

6. You can start a new business of your own, many people would rather buy an existing business or a franchise.

7. A business plan will help you to get organized it's almost impossible to get financing for your business unless you have a plan.

8. Business plans actually consist of various different plans the marketing plan lays out the strategies that help you catch the attention of prospective customers.

9. Friends, family, and other individuals are not likely to be able to loan what you need, you will probably decide to apply for a bank loan.

10. Write a compound sentence using a semicolon and a conjunctive adverb. Suggested topic: Why I would (wouldn't) want to start my own business.

5. Join sentences using a subordinating conjunction.

> For more information on complex sentences, see pages 409–414, "Compound and Complex Sentences."

Not all ideas are of equal importance. Frequently, writers choose to join ideas in a complex sentence made up of an independent clause and one or more dependent clauses. A subordinating conjunction signals the beginning of a dependent clause and states its subordinate relationship to the independent clause. Some examples of subordinating conjunctions include *although, as, because, if, when,* and *while*. Relative pronouns also connect a dependent clause to an independent clause. Examples of relative pronouns include *that, which,* and *who*.

Comma Splice:

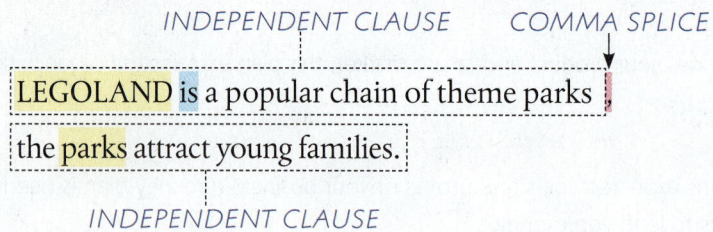

Fused Sentences:

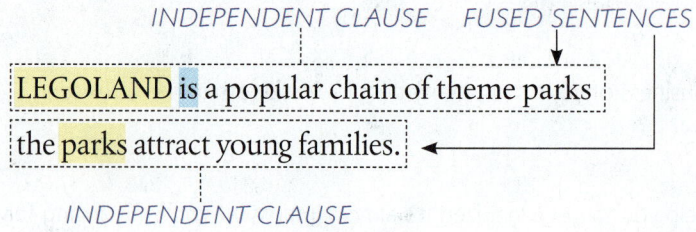

Edited to Correct with Subordinating Conjunction:

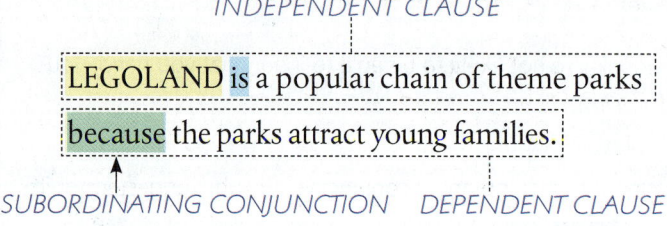

Edited to Correct with Relative Pronoun:

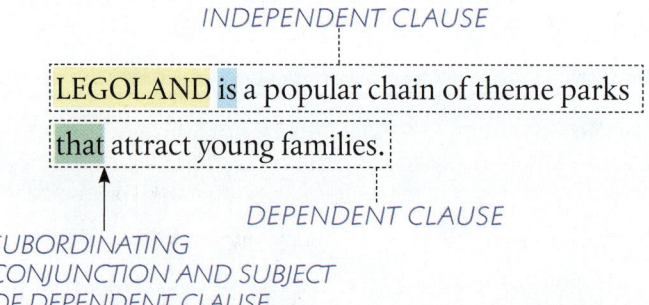

EDIT TO CORRECT COMMA SPLICES AND FUSED SENTENCES: USE A SUBORDINATING CONJUNCTION

Revise the following sentences into complex sentences to correct comma splices and fused sentences. Use the following subordinating conjunctions: *although, because, that, where, which, while, who*.

1. The LEGO Group and Merlin Entertainment co-own LEGOLAND. LEGOLAND has parks in Denmark, England, Germany, and the United States.

2. LEGOLAND is divided into specific areas these areas are mostly the same in all the parks.

3. All the parks include DUPLO Village, toddlers can fly a plane, drive a car, or explore a whole town.

4. LEGOLAND has roller coasters they are not very scary.

5. The roller coasters are tame, they are designed for younger children.

6. Children drive slow, one-seat toy cars or boats, their parents watch on the sidelines.

7. These "pink-knuckle" rides are ideal for children 2- to 12-year-olds want a thrill ride without white knuckles gripping a safety bar.

8. Trained service animals are permitted in LEGOLAND, other pets are not allowed.

9. The tickets run from $65 to $75 per person, the park is worth the cost.

10. Write a complex sentence using any subordinating conjunction. Suggested topic: Your favorite theme park.

Practice 8

COMMA SPLICES AND FUSED SENTENCES CHAPTER REVIEW

Revise the following sentences to correct fused sentences and comma splices.

1. Sleepwalking is a disorder characterized by walking or other activity while seemingly asleep, Lady Macbeth, in Shakespeare's play, is perhaps the most famous sleepwalker.

2. Sleepwalking is associated with deep sleep, sometimes it occurs during lighter sleep.

3. A sleepwalker may just sit up and seem awake, he may walk around, he may perform complicated activities such as moving furniture and even driving a car.

4. A common misconception is that sleepwalkers should not be awakened, experts say that there's no harm in awakening a sleepwalker.

5. Sleepwalking usually doesn't require consultation and treatment by a physician a visit to a physician is appropriate if sleepwalking occurs frequently or in combination with other symptoms.

FUSED SENTENCES AND COMMA SPLICES: CHAPTER REVIEW

Edit and revise the paragraph below, adapted from the article "Sleep Health," from the U.S. government website *Healthy People 2020* to correct fused sentences and comma splices.

Sleep Health

Poor sleep health is a common problem for example, 25 percent of U.S. adults report insufficient sleep or rest at least 15 out of every 30 days. Sleep is a critical factor in health and well-being it is a basic need for infant, child, and adolescent health and development. Sleep loss and untreated sleep disorders affect basic patterns of behavior they negatively affect family health and interpersonal relationships. Fatigue from sleepiness can reduce productivity it increases the chance for mishaps such as medical errors and motor vehicle or industrial accidents. Adequate sleep is vital to fight off infection, prevent diabetes, perform well in school, and work effectively and safely. Sleep timing and duration affect a number of bodily functions that are critical to individual health, if left untreated, sleep disorders and chronic short sleep are associated with many health risks. These risks include heart disease, high blood pressure, obesity, diabetes, and all-cause mortality. Sleep health is a particular concern for individuals with chronic disabilities and disorders such as arthritis, kidney disease, epilepsy, Parkinson's disease, and depression. Among older adults, the results of untreated sleep disorders decrease health-related quality of life also for the elderly, sleep loss can lead to functional limitations and loss of independence, and is associated with an increased risk of death from any cause.

Adapted from "Sleep Health." *Healthy People 2020*. https://www.healthypeople.gov/2020/topics-objectives/topic/sleep-health

Editing Assignments

MyWritingLab™
Complete this Exercise on mywritinglab.com

Editing for Everyday Life

Read the following letter of protest written to a county council. Edit to correct comma splices and fused sentences. Use your own paper or complete this exercise on MyWritingLab.com.

Dear Roberta Clancy, Chairperson of the County Council:

Recent news articles published the council's intention to allow WC Homes, Inc. to cut down a pair of century-old oak trees on the Marsh Loop these trees evidently stand in the way of progress. WC Homes, Inc. plans to develop a neighborhood of 1,000 single homes, the trees will block access to the entrance of the neighborhood. Marsh Loop has long been known for its unique beauty and importance as a wildlife refuge. Developers are rapidly changing this rare and important natural environment into an over-built urban area. Many voters agree with me you cut down these trees you will be out of office.

Sincerely,

Jane Watts

Editing for College Life

The following paragraph was written during an essay exam for a health class. The exam question asked the student to explain the need for proper technique in weight training. Edit to correct comma splices and fused sentences. Use your own paper or complete this exercise on MyWritingLab.com

> Weight training is an excellent exercise you can improve your strength, increase muscle tone, lose fat, gain muscle mass, and improve bone density. You use a sloppy technique, you stand a good chance of doing more harm than good. Common injuries can occur during weight training these include sprains, strains, tendonitis, fractures, and dislocations. The Mayo Clinic offers several suggestions on proper technique. First, remember to breathe holding your breath during weightlifting can increase your blood pressure to dangerous levels. Second, don't overdo it. The amount of weight you lift should make your muscles feel tired after 10 to 15 repetitions. A weight that causes fatigue at 12 repetitions creates muscle strength and toning. Finally, don't rush. And don't jerk the weights up, lift and lower the weights in a slow, fluid movement.

Editing for Working Life

Read the following letter written as a follow-up to a job interview. Edit to correct comma splices and fused sentences. Use your own paper or complete this exercise on MyWritingLab.com.

> Dear Ms. Tucker:
>
> Thank you very much for taking time to talk with me about the position of department manager. I enjoyed meeting you and the members of the department, I am excited about the chance to work with such a dynamic team. I, too, am a self-starter yet a team player. I like to encourage individuals to take ownership of projects but to still involve team members. Based on our meeting, I believe this is the job for me my qualifications are an excellent fit, particularly my training in technology and communication. The position is exactly what I'm looking for I'm confident that I can be a significant contributor to the success of the graphics department. I sincerely hope you agree. Thank you, again, for giving so much of your time I look forward to hearing from you.
>
> Sincerely,
>
> Justin M. Agler

WHAT HAVE I LEARNED ABOUT CORRECTING COMMA SPLICES AND FUSED SENTENCES?

To test and track your understanding, complete the following ideas. Use several sentences as needed for each response.

1. A comma splice occurs when

2. A fused sentence is

3. What are the five ways to eliminate comma splices and fused sentences?

4. **How will I use what I have learned about correcting comma splices and fused sentences?**
   In your notebook, discuss how you will apply to your own writing what you have learned about comma splices and fused sentences.

5. **What do I still need to study about correcting comma splices and fused sentences?**
   In your notebook, discuss your ongoing study needs by describing what, when, and how you will continue studying comma splices and fused sentences.

MyWritingLab™

Complete the Post-test for Chapter 22 in MyWritingLab.

23 Editing Fragments into Sentences

PART 5 EDITING THE BASIC SENTENCE

LEARNING OUTCOMES

After studying this chapter you will be able to:

LO 1 Answer the Question "What's the Point of Editing Fragments?"

LO 2 Recognize the Difference Between a Sentence and a Fragment

LO 3 Edit or Revise to Correct Seven Types of Fragments

- Prepositional Phrase Fragments
- Appositive Phrase Fragments
- Infinitive Phrase Fragments
- Gerund Phrase Fragments
- Participle Phrase Fragments
- Dependent Clause Fragments
- Relative Clause Fragments

A fragment is an incomplete thought.

Thinking about a real-life situation helps us to understand the impact of fragments on our ability to communicate. The photo illustrates a couple in search of a place to live. Read about the situation and answer the question "What's the point of learning about fragments?"

What's the Point of Editing Fragments?

PHOTOGRAPHIC ORGANIZER: FRAGMENTS

▲ Apartment for rent

Suppose you are looking for a new apartment. You ask two landlords the same questions. Below are the two replies.

Landlord A:
"If it's a little messy, well … sometimes partial refunds … for damages … not leaving behind personal belongings…"

Landlord B:
"You will get your security deposit back if you leave the apartment in the same or better condition than it is in right now, if you don't leave any of your belongings behind, and if you pay your last month's rent. We can go around the apartment right now and make a list of the condition of each room so we'll have a reference point when you're ready to move out."

With which landlord will you be able to communicate easily and clearly if you move in?

What's the point of learning about fragments?

WRITING FROM LIFE

One Student Writer's Response

The following paragraph offers one writer's reaction to the statements about the security deposit given by the landlords.

> *Landlord A never finishes a thought, so I have no idea what he means. His answers are vague, and he doesn't seem to care about being understood. Maybe he thinks I should just know what he means. In contrast, Landlord B spoke clearly using complete sentences. I know exactly what is expected.*
>
> *Landlord B is going to be easier to talk to and understand. The difference between the two responses makes me realize how important it is to use complete sentences if you want to be understood. When others can understand your thoughts, you can connect with them and even change how they think about things or how they act. That's real power.*

L2 Recognize the Difference Between a Sentence and a Fragment

The ability to write ideas in complete thoughts, or sentences, is an important tool in building coherent paragraphs and essays. A sentence has two traits.

SENTENCE: Complete Thought—Complete Information

TRAIT ONE: A sentence states a complete and independent thought.

TRAIT TWO: A sentence contains a subject and a verb.

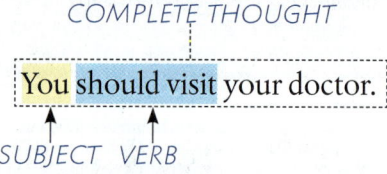

A **sentence** contains all the information needed to clearly express a complete thought. In contrast, a fragment can often be recognized by what is missing from the thought. A **fragment** is an incomplete thought.

FRAGMENT: Incomplete Thought—Missing Information

A **fragment** is missing a subject, a verb, or both a subject and a verb.

Missing Subject:	Does not disqualify you from exercising
Missing Verb:	Edward taking a physical exam
Missing Subject and Verb:	To safely participate and to reduce risk of injury

Even when a group of words includes both a subject and a verb, it still can be a fragment. A subordinating conjunction signals a fragment that has both a subject and a verb. These types of fragments are missing an independent clause.

Fragment (Missing an Independent Clause):

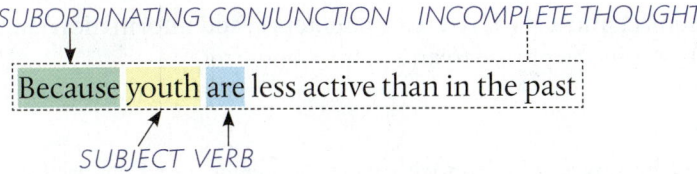

To identify a fragment, ask the following questions:

- Does the idea have a verb?
- What is the subject of the verb?
- Does the idea express a complete thought?

IDENTIFY FRAGMENTS

Identify fragments and sentences. Write **F** for *fragment* next to the incomplete thoughts. Write **S** for *sentence* next to the complete thoughts.

_____ 1. Regular physical activity, fitness, and exercise are critically important.

_____ 2. For the health and well-being of people of all ages.

_____ 3. Research has proven that all individuals can benefit from regular physical activity.

_____ 4. Whether they engage in vigorous exercise or some type of moderate physical activity.

_____ 5. Might enjoy exercising on a regular basis.

L3 Edit or Revise to Correct Seven Types of Fragments

This section discusses seven common types of fragments: (1) prepositional phrase, (2) appositive phrase, (3) infinitive phrase, (4) gerund phrase, (5) participle phrase, (6) dependent clause, and (7) relative clause. This section also discusses techniques you can use to revise these fragments into a sentence. Fragments are either phrases or dependent clauses punctuated as if they are sentences. A writer may use two techniques to edit or revise fragments into sentences.

- Combine existing ideas.
- Add missing ideas.

Phrase Fragments

A **phrase** is a group of words that acts as a single unit. A phrase is a fragment because it does not contain both a subject and a verb. To create a sentence, add information (such as a subject, a verb, or both), or join the phrase to an existing sentence.

1. Prepositional Phrase

A **prepositional phrase** begins with a preposition (such as *at, on, in, to, toward, for, since,* and *of*) and ends with the object of the preposition. A prepositional phrase adds information about direction, manner, space, and time, such as *in the house* or *after the game*.

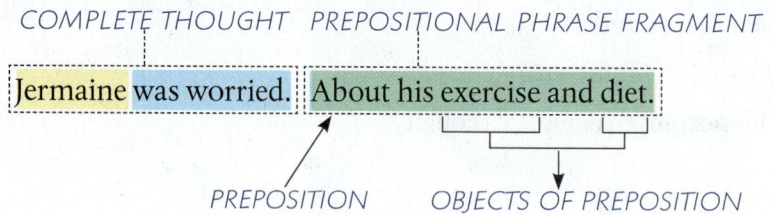

Revised to Combine Ideas:

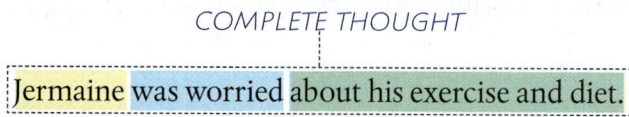

Revised to Add Ideas:

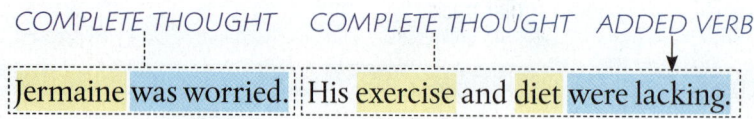

Practice 3

EDIT PREPOSITIONAL PHRASE FRAGMENTS INTO SENTENCES

Edit the fragments in the following items into sentences by joining ideas or adding ideas.

1. Excess body fat is harmful. To your organs' abilities to function.

2. With properly functioning organs. Your body can better digest food, circulate blood, and ward off diseases.

3. Your diet should be well balanced. With fats, proteins, and carbohydrates.

4. In the interest of saving time. Don't skip breakfast.

5. Eating a healthful breakfast. As a daily habit. For successful weight loss.

6. Through physical activity and exercise. You can burn more calories than you eat.

7. Since regular exercise strengthens muscles. Heart disease and back pain can be reduced.

8. Exercise and diet can also improve the way you feel. About how you look and perform your daily activities.

9. Over the past few years. There are some weight loss programs. With a quick-fix promise. People have been misled.

10. Write a sentence correctly using one or more prepositional phrases. Suggested topic: Diet and exercise.

23 EDITING FRAGMENTS INTO SENTENCES

443

2. Appositive Phrase

An **appositive phrase** contains a noun that renames or describes another noun in the same sentence. An appositive phrase combines with a complete thought to add detail. Place an appositive phrase next to the noun it renames.

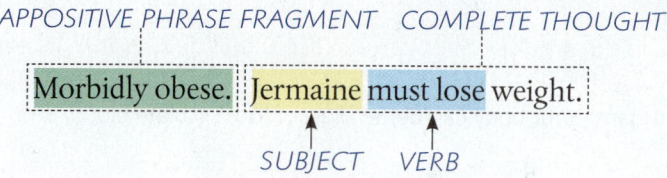

Revised to Combine Ideas:

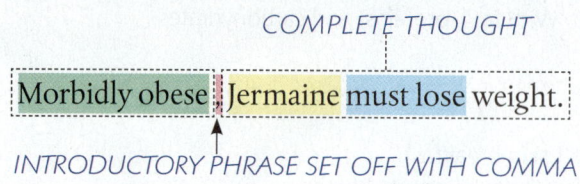

Revised to Add Ideas:

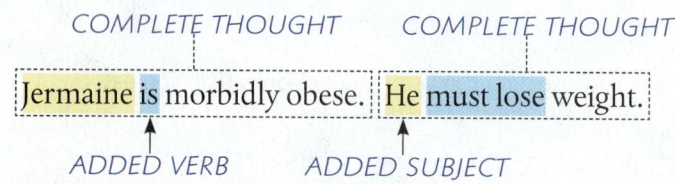

EDIT APPOSITIVE PHRASE FRAGMENTS INTO SENTENCES

Practice 4

Edit the fragments in the following items into sentences by joining ideas or adding ideas.

1. A weight at least twice one's ideal weight. Morbid obesity is life threatening.

2. The relationship between one's weight and height is known as BMI. Or Body Mass Index.

3. An index of obesity. BMI measures the percentage of fat and muscle mass in the body.

4. A healthful lifestyle should promote a normal BMI. An average of 22 on the index.

5. Overweight is a BMI that ranges from 25 to 29. Based on the index.

6. Jermaine's wife. Sue has a BMI of 32. A number indicating obesity.

7. Jermaine's BMI ranks him as morbidly obese. 280 pounds and 6 feet tall and 40 BMI.

8. Addicts of junk food and television. They put their health at risk.

9. Jermaine and Sue can reduce their health risks with a wiser lifestyle. One of regular exercise and healthful eating.

10. Write a sentence using an appositive. Suggested topic: Causes of weight gain.

3. Infinitive Phrase

An infinitive is a form of a verb, but it is not a verb. Combining *to* with a verb forms an **infinitive**, as in *to go*, *to talk*, and *to think*. An **infinitive phrase** is made up of an infinitive and the object of the infinitive, such as *to quit smoking* or *to run a mile*. An infinitive phrase can act as a noun, an adjective, or an adverb.

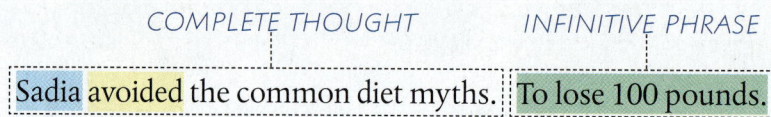

Revised to Combine Ideas:

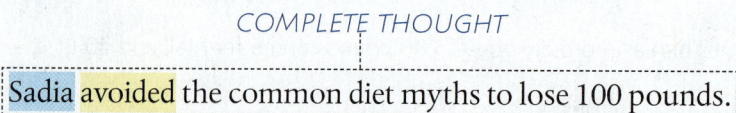

Revised to Add Ideas:

EDIT INFINITIVE PHRASE FRAGMENTS INTO SENTENCES

Edit the fragments in the following items into sentences by joining ideas or adding ideas.

1. To lose weight. One must adopt a lifestyle of eating that promotes normal weight.

2. Fad diets and diet myths confuse people. To believe in quick fixes. To try unhealthy solutions.

3. Diet fads and myths do not help. To shed excess weight long term.

4. To eat less. That is the number one diet fad and myth.

5. The body needs fuel. To survive.

6. One should take in fewer calories than the body burns. To drop excess pounds.

7. Skipping meals is not healthy. To cut calories. To lose weight.

8. Many dieters believe that eating fats makes them fat, so all fats are feared. To be avoided.

9. Some fats, like those in fish, nuts, and olive oil, help the body. To absorb nutrients. And to feel full longer.

10. Write a sentence that uses an infinitive phrase. Suggested topic: A diet fad or myth.

-ing Phrases: Gerunds and Participles

An *-ing* phrase can function as either a noun or an adjective. An *-ing* phrase used as a noun is called a **gerund**. An *-ing* phrase used as an adjective is called a **participle**.

4. Gerund Phrase

A **gerund** is a form of a verb, but it is not a verb. A gerund is a noun that ends in *-ing*, such as *going*, *talking*, and *thinking*. A **gerund phrase** is made up of a gerund and the object of the gerund, such as *quitting smoking* or *running three miles*. A gerund phrase functions as a noun. For example, a gerund phrase can be the subject of a sentence or an object of a verb or preposition.

```
      COMPLETE THOUGHT              -ING PHRASE FRAGMENT (GERUND)
   Jermaine exercises regularly.   Running three miles several times a week.
```

Revised to Combine Ideas:

```
            ADDED PREPOSITION    ACTS AS AN OBJECT OF THE PREPOSITION "BY"
   Jermaine exercises regularly by running three miles several times a week.
```

Revised to Add Ideas:

```
      COMPLETE THOUGHT    ACTS AS AN OBJECT OF THE ADDED VERB "ENJOYS"
   Jermaine enjoys running three miles several times a week.
```

EDIT GERUND PHRASE FRAGMENTS INTO SENTENCES

Edit the fragments in the following items into sentences by joining ideas or adding ideas.

1. Sharika stays strong and flexible. Keeping fit through yoga.

2. Yoga often includes dynamic stretches. Moving the body in a sequence of poses.

3. Improving flexibility. Yoga is a beneficial exercise.

4. Flexibility is the range of a joint's motion. Preventing injuries through all stages of life.

5. Many trainers recommend both dynamic and static stretches. Improving flexibility.

6. Performing a static stretch. Stretch a muscle to its farthest point and then hold the position.

7. Holding a yoga pose. That is a static stretch. Moving between yoga poses. That requires dynamic stretches.

8. Dynamic stretching unlike static stretching. Actively moving a joint through a range of motion.

9. Yoga offers several benefits in addition to flexibility. Reducing stress, controlling weight, and improving breathing.

10. Write a sentence using a gerund phrase. Suggested topic: A beneficial exercise.

_____

_____

Practice 6

5. Participle Phrase

A participle is a form of a verb, but it is not a verb. A **participle** is an adjective that ends in *-ing*, such as *going*, *talking*, and *thinking*. A **participle phrase** is made up of a participle and the object of the participle such as *quitting gambling* or *swimming a mile*. A participle phrase functions as an adjective; it describes nouns and other adjectives.

-ING PHRASE FRAGMENT (PARTICIPLE)   COMPLETE THOUGHT

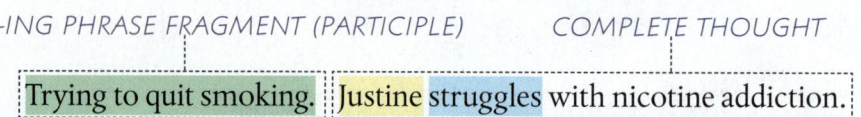

Revised to Combine Ideas:

COMPLETE THOUGHT

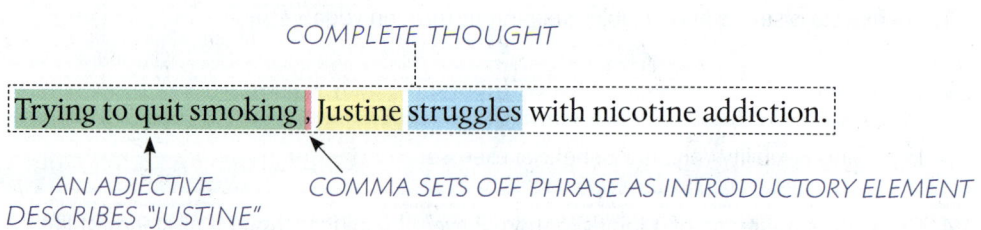

AN ADJECTIVE DESCRIBES "JUSTINE"   COMMA SETS OFF PHRASE AS INTRODUCTORY ELEMENT

Revised to Add Ideas:

COMPLETE THOUGHT

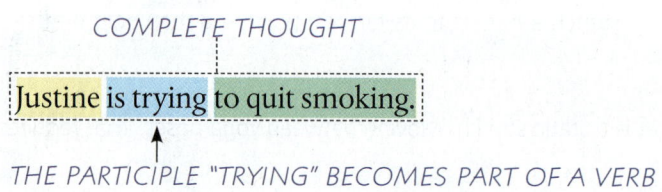

THE PARTICIPLE "TRYING" BECOMES PART OF A VERB

EDIT PARTICIPLE PHRASE FRAGMENTS INTO SENTENCES

Edit the fragments in the following items into sentences by joining ideas or adding ideas.

1. Causing physical and mental dependence. Nicotine is as addictive as heroin or cocaine.

2. Developing a tolerance for nicotine. Smokers increase the number of cigarettes they smoke.

3. Inhaling smoke deep into the lungs. A smoker quickly absorbs the nicotine and the bloodstream carries it throughout the body.

4. Nicotine is a powerful drug. Affecting the brain, the metabolism, the heart, blood vessels, and all other parts of the body.

5. Many smokers don't quit because of nicotine withdrawal symptoms. Including dizziness, depression, anxiety, irritability, headaches, and weight gain.

6. There are more than five hundred chemical compounds added to cigarettes. Making them even more addictive.

7. Adding ammonia to cigarettes. Tobacco companies increased the nicotine kick felt by the smoker.

8. Irritating to skin, eyes, and the respiratory system. Ammonia in cigarettes increases the harm of second-hand smoke.

9. Marketing menthol cigarettes as "safer" and "healthier." The tobacco industry added the natural substance menthol. Having a cooling sensation and the ability to relieve minor pain and prevent infection.

10. Write a sentence that uses a participle phrase. Suggested topic: Drug addiction.

Clause Fragments

A **clause** is a set of words that contains a subject and a verb. An **independent clause** states a complete thought in a sentence that begins with a capital letter and ends with punctuation such as a period or semicolon. In contrast, a **dependent clause** expresses an incomplete thought or fragment.

> For more on dependent and subordinate clauses, see page 409–414.

6. Dependent Clause

A **dependent clause**, also known as a **subordinate clause**, does not make sense on its own. A dependent clause is formed by placing a subordinating conjunction in front of a subject and a verb.

A **subordinating conjunction** states the relationship between a dependent clause and an independent clause.

The following chart lists common subordinating conjunctions.

Subordinating Conjunctions and the Relationships They Express				
Cause	**Contrast**	**Time**	**Place**	**Condition**
as	although	after	where	even if
because	as if	as	wherever	if
in order that	even though	as long as		only if
now that	though	before		unless
since	whereas	once		when
so	while	since		whether or not
		until		
		when		
		whenever		
		while		

To create a sentence, combine the dependent clause with an independent clause. Or revise the dependent clause into an independent clause by dropping the subordinating conjunction.

DEPENDENT CLAUSE   INDEPENDENT CLAUSE

When Jada turned eighteen.   She moved into her own apartment.

Revised to Combine Ideas:

When Jada turned eighteen, she moved into her own apartment.

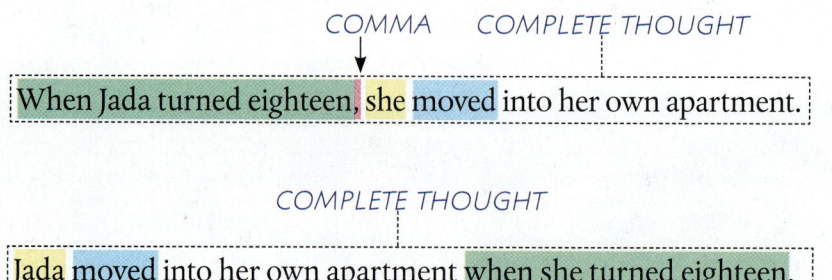

Jada moved into her own apartment when she turned eighteen.

Revised to Add Ideas:

COMPLETE THOUGHT PERIOD   COMPLETE THOUGHT
Jada turned eighteen. Then, she moved into her own apartment.

EDIT DEPENDENT CLAUSE FRAGMENTS INTO SENTENCES

Edit the fragments in the following items into sentences by joining ideas or adding ideas.

1. Jada rented her first apartment. Because she moved from her hometown to attend college.

2. Before she rented her apartment. Jada had saved and planned for the move.

3. She had worked as a waitress and saved money. While she attended high school.

4. She even put off college. Until she had saved enough money for move-in costs.

5. Because she had done her research, Jada knew about the costs of application fees and rental deposits.

6. Once she had paid move-in fees. She had enough funds to pay for several months of rent.

7. Jada's aunt co-signed on the lease. Since Jada was a first-time renter.

8. After deciding on the perfect apartment. Jada carefully read the lease agreement.

9. Jada checked the faucets, toilets, lights, and all appliances. Before she signed the lease.

10. Write a sentence using a dependent clause. Suggested topic: Living expenses.

Practice 8

7. Relative Clause

One type of dependent clause is the **relative clause**, which describes a noun or pronoun in an independent clause. A **relative pronoun** introduces the relative clause and relates it to the noun or pronoun it describes.

Relative Pronouns				
who	whom	whose	which	that

Join the relative clause to the independent clause that contains the word it describes. Or revise the relative clause into an independent clause by replacing the relative pronoun with a noun.

INDEPENDENT CLAUSE   RELATIVE CLAUSE FRAGMENT

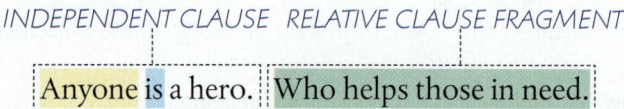

Anyone is a hero. Who helps those in need.

Revised to Combine Ideas:

COMPLETE THOUGHT

Anyone who helps those in need is a hero.

Revised to Add Ideas:

COMPLETE THOUGHT   COMPLETE THOUGHT

Anyone can be a hero. A hero helps those in need.

EDIT DEPENDENT RELATIVE CLAUSE FRAGMENTS INTO SENTENCES

Edit the fragments in the following items into sentences by joining ideas or adding ideas.

Practice 9

1. Timmy Tyrell is a hero. Who raises money to help children battle cancer.

2. Timmy watched two of his friends battle cancer. Which inspired him to take action.

3. Timmy who is nicknamed "Mini" and is only seven years old. He races Go-Karts.

4. He has raced Go-Karts since he was 3 years old at the Old Dominion Speedway. Which is located in Virginia.

5. He now races to raise money for families. Whose children have been struck by cancer.

6. The money that is raised. Mini donates to the Jeffrey Virostek Foundation.

7. Fans pledge donations for every lap. That Mini completes.

8. So far, Mini has raised $7,000. Which was matched by NASCAR driver Jeff Gordon.

9. Families for whom cancer is a reality. They receive services and help with expenses.

10. Write a sentence using a relative clause. Suggested topic: A local hero.

EDIT PHRASE AND CLAUSE FRAGMENTS INTO SENTENCES: CHAPTER REVIEW

A. Read the following sets of ideas. Identify the type of phrase fragment. Then, revise the ideas to eliminate fragments by combining or adding ideas.

1. Bones play many roles in the body. Providing structure, protecting organs, anchoring muscles, and storing calcium.

   TYPE OF FRAGMENT: _____

   REVISED SENTENCE: _____

2. Adequate calcium consumption and weight-bearing physical activity are necessary. To build strong bones and optimize bone mass.

   TYPE OF FRAGMENT: _____

   REVISED SENTENCE: _____

3. The body cannot produce calcium. A mineral needed to produce bone.

TYPE OF FRAGMENT: _____

REVISED SENTENCE: _____

_____

4. By the age of 20. The average woman has acquired most of her skeletal mass.

TYPE OF FRAGMENT: _____

REVISED SENTENCE: _____

_____

5. Consuming foods and drinks that contain calcium during childhood. Builds strong bones.

TYPE OF FRAGMENT: _____

REVISED SENTENCE: _____

_____

6. Children should eat calcium rich greens. To build their bones.

TYPE OF FRAGMENT: _____

REVISED SENTENCE: _____

_____

B. Edit the ideas to eliminate fragments by combining or adding ideas.

7. Sleep apnea is a common disorder. That can be very serious.

8. Sleep apnea episodes. Pauses that typically last 10–20 seconds or more, can occur 20 to 30 times or more an hour.

9. One who moves from deep to light sleep throughout the night. That person suffers from lack of sleep.

10. Sleep apnea stops the flow of air from the lungs to the mouth and nose. Which makes it difficult to gasp a breath.

FRAGMENTS: CHAPTER REVIEW

Proofread the following paragraph for fragments. Revise to eliminate fragments by combining or adding ideas.

How to Maintain Your Weight

(1) In order to stay at the same body weight, people must balance the amount of calories in the foods and drinks they consume. (2) With the amount of calories the body uses. (3) Physical activity is one important way to use food energy. (4) Most Americans spend much of their working day in activities that require little energy. (5) In addition, many Americans of all ages now spend a lot of leisure time each day being inactive. (6) For example, watching television or working at a computer. (7) To burn calories. (8) Devote less time to sedentary activities. (9) Spend more time in activities like walking to the store or around the block. (10) Use stairs rather than elevators. (11) Less sedentary activity and more vigorous activity may help you reduce body fat and disease risk. (12) Try to do 30 minutes or more of moderate physical activity on most—preferably all—days of the week. (13) The kinds and amounts of foods people eat. (14) Affect their ability to maintain weight. (15) High-fat foods contain more calories per serving than other foods. (16) Which may increase the likelihood of weight gain. (17) However, even when people eat less high-fat food. (18) They still can gain weight from eating too many foods high in starch, sugars, or protein. (19) Eat a variety of foods. (20) Emphasizing pasta, rice, bread, and other whole-grain foods as well as fruits and vegetables. (21) These foods are filling, but lower in calories than foods rich in fats or oils. (22) The pattern of eating may also be important. (23) Snacks provide a large percentage of daily calories for many Americans. (24) Unless nutritious snacks are part of the daily meal plan. (25) Snacking may lead to weight gain. (26) A pattern of frequent binge eating, with or without alternating periods of food restriction, may also contribute to weight problems.

—Adapted from "Balance the Food You Eat with Physical Activity—Maintain or Improve Your Weight." Nutrition and Your Health: Dietary Guidelines for Americans. U.S. Department of Agriculture. Dec. 1995.

Editing Assignments

Editing for Everyday Life

Read the following letter to a doctor requesting information. Edit to eliminate fragments. Use your own paper or complete this exercise on MyWritingLab.com.

> Dear Dr. Alito:
>
> Please send my records to the office of Dr. Alice Godbey. Who is currently treating me for a stress fracture in my right shin. Because your office ordered the x-rays of the injury. You must approve their release. Since you are my primary physician, Dr. Godbey's office will return the x-rays to your office. After my surgery.
>
> Sincerely,
>
> Sandra Acuri

Editing for College Life

Read the following paragraph written for a history class. Edit to eliminate fragments. Use your own paper or complete this exercise on MyWritingLab.com.

> Sojourner Truth who was first known as Isabella Baumfree. Born a slave somewhere around 1797. While in slavery. She had five children with the man she married, Thomas Jeffery Harvey. Fleeing slavery around 1827. She left the country and lived in Canada. Isabella returned to New York. When the state abolished slavery in 1829. She worked with Elijah Pierson preaching on street corners for more than a decade. Later, she became a well-known speaker against slavery and for women's rights. She is still noted today. For her famous speech, "Ain't I a Woman?"

Editing for Working Life

Read the following request for supplies in a department of a retail business. Edit to eliminate fragments. Use your own paper or complete this exercise on MyWritingLab.com.

> To: Office Supply Department
> From: Customer Service Department
> Re: Order # 3214
>
> According to our records. Our order for three computer desks, three computer chairs, and three filing cabinets was placed three weeks ago. At that time, you assured us that you would deliver this order promptly. Since our need was urgent. To meet the needs of our customers. We have added three new employees. Employees who began reporting to work two weeks ago. If these items are not delivered by the end of the week, I will refer this matter to your supervisor.

WHAT HAVE I LEARNED ABOUT CORRECTING FRAGMENTS?

To test and track your understanding of correcting fragments, complete the following ideas. Use several sentences as needed for each response.

1. What are the two traits of a sentence?

2. A fragment is

3. A phrase is

4. A clause is

5. Two types of clauses are _____ and _____ clauses.

6. The five types of phrases discussed in this chapter include _____, _____, _____, _____, and _____.

7. Two ways to eliminate fragments are _____ ideas and _____ ideas.

8. **How will I use what I have learned?**
   In your notebook, discuss how you will apply to your own writing what you have learned about correcting fragments.

9. **What do I still need to study about fragments?**
   In your notebook, discuss your ongoing study needs by describing what, when, and how you will continue studying fragments.

Academic Learning Log: Chapter Review

23 EDITING FRAGMENTS INTO SENTENCES

MyWritingLab™
Complete the Post-test for Chapter 23 in MyWritingLab.

24 Editing Misplaced and Dangling Modifiers

LEARNING OUTCOMES

After studying this chapter you will be able to:

L1 Answer the Question "What's the Point of Editing Misplaced and Dangling Modifiers?"

L2 Edit Misplaced Modifiers

L3 Edit Dangling Modifiers

A modifier is a word or phrase that describes, clarifies, or gives more information about another word in a sentence.

A misplaced modifier is a word or phrase illogically separated from the word it describes. A dangling modifier is a word or phrase intended to modify a word not stated in the sentence.

Modifiers are words that describe, restrict, or limit other words in a sentence. For example, modifiers help us communicate what we see or how we feel. The photo on the next page illustrates a person experiencing intense feelings.

What's the Point of Editing Misplaced and Dangling Modifiers?

PHOTOGRAPHIC ORGANIZER: MISPLACED AND DANGLING MODIFIERS

Read the sentence that describes the marathon runner and answer the question.

> Running the marathon, her legs cried out in pain.

What is the point of correcting misplaced and dangling modifiers?

_____

_____

_____

WRITING FROM LIFE

One Student Writer's Response

When I first read the sentence, I kind of laughed because it created such a funny image in my mind of "legs crying." I know the author didn't mean to be funny. But the way the idea is worded takes away from the serious nature of the situation. And as a reader, I don't know who ran the marathon. Information is either jumbled or missing from this sentence. I suggested the following revision: "While running the marathon, Lynda cried out in pain from leg cramps."

Sentence clarity can be achieved through appropriately placed and clearly expressed modifiers. A **modifier** is a word or phrase that describes, clarifies, or gives more information about another word in a sentence. Confusion in meaning occurs when a modifier is misplaced in the sentence or when the word being modified is not stated in the sentence. To avoid confusion, place modifiers next to the word that is being described.

L2 Edit Misplaced Modifiers

A **misplaced modifier** is a word or phrase illogically separated from the word it describes. The result is a lack of clarity. The following section offers a few examples and revisions of common types of misplaced modifiers.

MISPLACED WORD A misplaced word is separated from the word it limits or modifies.

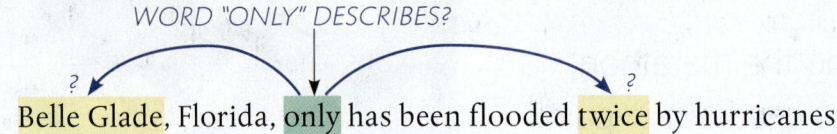

Belle Glade, Florida, only has been flooded twice by hurricanes.

Edit #1

Belle Glade, Florida, has been flooded only twice by hurricanes.

Edit #2

Only Belle Glade, Florida, has been flooded twice by hurricanes.

MISPLACED PHRASE A phrase that describes a noun is placed next to the wrong noun and separated from the word it modifies.

Jammed into his backpack, Sean hunted through the papers.

PHRASE "JAMMED INTO HIS BACKPACK" DESCRIBES?   ADDED COMMA SETS OFF INTRODUCTORY PHRASE

Edit

Sean hunted through the papers jammed into his backpack.

MISPLACED CLAUSE A dependent clause that describes a particular word is placed next to the wrong word and is separated from the word the clause describes.

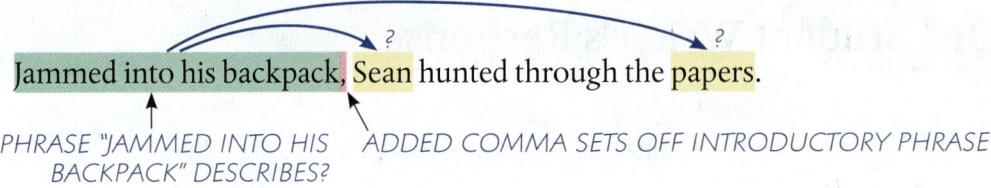

The 60-year-old woman was hounded by the reporter who gave birth to twins.

Edit

The 60-year-old woman who gave birth to twins was hounded by the reporter.

EDITING MISPLACED MODIFIERS

Edit the following student sentences to correct misplaced modifiers.

1. The groom dropped the wedding ring, trembling with nervousness.

2. Topped with onions and mushrooms, the guests enjoyed filet mignon.

3. Only Fran drinks wine on the weekends.

4. Tired and sweaty, the sun beat down on the runners.

5. Jennifer Hudson had joined Weight Watchers, who has lost around 80 pounds.

6. The meteorologist predicted rain on the television.

7. For Halloween, Derrick gave out homemade cookies to children wrapped in plastic-wrap.

8. Charlene almost studied six hours for the exam.

9. The youth was sentenced to community service by the judge who was arrested for shoplifting.

10. Write a sentence using a modifier. Suggested topic: A special event.

L3 Edit Dangling Modifiers: Two Revision Tips

A **dangling modifier** is a word, phrase, or clause intended to modify a word not stated in the sentence. Therefore, the dangling modifier seems to describe the nearest word, yet it doesn't make sense. To revise dangling modifiers, you may need to add or rephrase ideas.

Sentence #1

While cleaning the house, a fifty dollar bill turned up.

Sentence #2

Running in second place, the finish line came into view.

EDITING TIP #1 Change the dangling modifier into a logical clause with a subject and a verb.

Edited Sentence #1

ADDED SUBJECT AND VERB TO CREATE DEPENDENT CLAUSE

While I was cleaning the house, a fifty dollar bill turned up.

Edited Sentence #2

ADDED SUBJECT AND VERB TO CREATE INDEPENDENT CLAUSE

I was running in second place; the finish line came into view.

ADDED SEMICOLON JOINS TWO INDEPENDENT CLAUSES

EDITING TIP #2 Revise the main clause to include the word being modified.

Edited Sentence #1

PHRASE DESCRIBES ADDED SUBJECT AND VERB

While cleaning the house, I found a fifty dollar bill.

Edited Sentence #2

PHRASE DESCRIBES ADDED SUBJECT AND VERB

Running in second place, I saw the finish line come into view.

EDITING DANGLING MODIFIERS

Edit the following student sentences to eliminate dangling modifiers.

1. Having a job, holidays are really appreciated!

2. Walking down Fifth Avenue, the Empire State Building looked awesome.

3. Voted out of office, their policies were quickly reversed.

4. Thinking about it later, the house seemed too large and expensive.

5. Having scored 19 touchdowns, the game was definitely out of reach.

6. The sunset was beautiful relaxing on the beach.

7. Late for work, his briefcase dropped and broke while running for the bus.

8. Once entering the office work room, the donuts tempt me.

9. As I approached the crib, it giggled.

10. Write a sentence using a modifier. Suggested topic: An everyday event.

Practice 4

EDITING MISPLACED AND DANGLING MODIFIERS

Revise to correct misplaced and dangling modifiers. Move or add ideas as needed.

1. As a kid, my parents had pretty strict rules.

2. Jupiter Jones is the heroine in the movie *Jupiter Ascending* played by Mila Kunis.

3. Joanna gave a dog to her daughter named Spot.

4. Jamal was referred to a specialist suffering from a rare infection.

5. After saying good-bye, the train pulled away.

6. While only halfway over, we left the movie due to its graphic violence.

7. We almost ate the whole cake.

8. Surprised by the honor, the award went to Jerome.

9. Screaming in pain, the big toe was broken.

10. The door frightens the cat that loudly creaks on its hinges.

EDITING MISPLACED AND DANGLING MODIFIERS

In the space provided below, revise the following paragraph to eliminate misplaced and dangling modifiers.

Who says that the rich only can go on European vacations? You may be an impoverished student, but European travel is well within your reach if you plan carefully. By having some flexibility, plane tickets to Europe can be cheap. For example, prices for tickets in the off-season are far lower than those for tickets during the summer tourist season. And once you are traveling within Europe, tickets are available from budget carriers like Ryanair that don't cost much money. Traveling by train or bus can also be a low-cost option. Restaurants may be expensive, but grocery stores aren't. Tucked into your picnic basket, you can bring sandwiches, fruit, and delicacies and have a feast on a park bench. And you don't have to stay in hotels. One alternative is hostels, found across Europe. And looking on a website, other possibilities emerge, including people who will take you into their home as a guest.

Editing Assignments

Editing for Everyday Life

Edit the following posting for a blog on a social networking site such as Facebook. Eliminate misplaced or dangling modifiers.

> Thursday, January 26, 2016
>
> We had the best weekend ever! Only our friends come to visit a couple of times a year. We decided to swim with the dolphins eager to have fun. Surprised by their sleek and smooth skin, our hands gently caressed the dolphins. The dolphins loved swimming with us. They actually made eye contact with us. It was an awesome experience.

Editing for College Life

Edit the following part of a report, written for a psychology class. Eliminate misplaced or dangling modifiers. The student was asked to illustrate a personal trait.

> I go to unfamiliar places by myself. Swimming in shark-infested waters, my parents worry about me. I walk alone through dark areas to get to my car without pepper spray. I make friends with weird people, making poor choices about what is safe and what is threatening. I am too trusting.
>
> As a very young child, my parents had to keep an extra close eye on me. As the story goes, I had a tendency to wander off in search of new companions. At the age of four, my parents, brother, and sister lost track of me on a day trip to Wet N' Wild. Unconcerned, I skipped through the masses, tugging on the shorts of giants, asking "Do you know my Dad? Have you seen my Mom?" Eventually, I spotted a woman who must have been a lifeguard in a red bathing suit. She wasn't, but when I asked her for help to find my family, she obliged, returning me to my panic-stricken mother and father.

Editing for Working Life

Edit the following performance evaluation of an employee. Eliminate misplaced or dangling modifiers.

> To: Human Resources
> From: Anna Shrimali, Manager
> RE: Evaluation of Joanna Santiago
>
> Joanna Santiago has been employed for three months. As an employee, her work is completed to a level above and beyond expectations. She is well able to deal with any type customer prone to listen carefully and act quickly. In addition, her efforts have saved our diligent company several thousands dollars. Only Ms. Santiago thinks of the good of the team, accepting the hardest assignments without complaint. I fully recommend Ms. Santiago for both a promotion and a raise.

WHAT HAVE I LEARNED ABOUT MISPLACED AND DANGLING MODIFIERS?

To test and track your understanding, answer the following questions.

1. What is a misplaced modifier? _____

2. How is a misplaced modifier corrected? _____

3. What is a dangling modifier? _____

4. What are two ways to correct a dangling modifier? _____

5. How will I use what I have learned about misplaced and dangling modifiers?
   In your notebook, discuss how you will apply to your own writing what you have learned about misplaced and dangling modifiers. When during the writing process will you apply this knowledge?

6. What do I still need to study about misplaced and dangling modifiers?
   In your notebook, discuss your ongoing study needs by describing what, when, and how you will continue to study about misplaced and dangling modifiers.

Complete the Post-test for Chapter 24 in MyWritingLab.

25 Editing for Subject-Verb Agreement: Present Tense

PART 5 EDITING THE BASIC SENTENCE

LEARNING OUTCOMES

After studying this chapter you will be able to:

L1 Answer the Question "What's the Point of Editing for Subject-Verb Agreement?"

L2 Understand the Basics of Subject-Verb Agreement

L3 Create Subject-Verb Agreement Using *To Have, To Do, To Be*

L4 Create Subject-Verb Agreement Using Subjects Separated from Verbs

L5 Create Subject-Verb Agreement Using Singular or Plural Subjects

- Create Subject-Verb Agreement Using Indefinite Pronouns
- Create Subject-Verb Agreement Using Collective Nouns
- Create Subject-Verb Agreement Using *Either-Or/Neither-Nor*
- Create Subject-Verb Agreement Using Fractions, Titles, and Words Ending in *-s*
- Create Subject-Verb Agreement Using Subjects after Verbs
- Create Subject-Verb Agreement Using Relative Pronouns

In the present tense, subjects and verbs must agree in person and in number. Singular subjects must take singular verbs; plural subjects must take plural verbs.

Subject-verb agreement in the present tense ranks as one of the most common errors in written and spoken English. Rules for subject-verb agreement in regional dialects may differ from those of standard English. It is important to understand the difference between regional speech and standard English and to be able to use the standard English rules. Look at the picture and statements on the following page, and answer the question, "What's the point of subject-verb agreement?"

What's the Point of Editing for Subject-Verb Agreement?

PHOTOGRAPHIC ORGANIZER: SUBJECT-VERB AGREEMENT

Complete the following activity and answer the question "What's the point of subject-verb agreement?"

Assume you are a manager, and you are interviewing possible candidates for a job opening in your department. Which candidate's response to your question sounds more professional? Why?

Manager's question:
What is a current example of your greatest strength as an employee?

Candidate 1:
My greatest strengths is listening, following directions, and problem solving. For example, procedures comes to us from the home office, and I listens carefully to understand them. Confusion occur with deliveries, and I been working to prevent the problem.

Candidate 2:
My greatest strengths are listening, following directions, and problem solving. For example, procedures come to us from the home office, and I listen carefully to understand them. Confusion often occurs with deliveries, and I've been working to prevent the problem.

What's the point of subject-verb agreement?

....

....

Practice 1

WRITING FROM LIFE

One Student Writer's Response

The following paragraph records one writer's thoughts about the point of subject-verb agreement in the job interview example.

> I think candidate 2 sounds better than candidate 1. Candidate 1 comes across like she is talking to a friend instead of trying to get a job. When trying to get a job, you want to come across the best you can when you write and when you talk. So you should use good grammar and make your subjects agree with your verbs in your application and during your interview. It shows you know the rules and care about how you come across.

L2 Understand the Basics of Subject-Verb Agreement

In the present tense, subjects and verbs must agree in person and in number. So a singular subject must have a singular verb, and a plural subject must have a plural verb. The following chart uses the sample verb "sit" to illustrate present tense agreement in number.

Present Tense Agreement		
	Singular **Subject** and **Verb**	Plural **Subject** and **Verb**
First Person	I sit	We sit
Second Person	You sit	You sit
Third Person	He / She / It — sits	They sit

For standard verbs, only the third person singular verb is formed by adding *-s* or *-es*.

Third person singular subject	→	present tense verb ends with *-s* or *-es*
He	→	apologizes
She	→	accepts
It	→	catches

UNDERSTANDING THE BASICS OF SUBJECT-VERB AGREEMENT

Fill in the following charts with the correct form of each subject and verb. A few blanks are completed as examples.

1. To Listen	Subject	Verb
First person singular	I	listen
Second person singular/plural		
Third person singular		

2. To Hear	Subject	Verb
First person plural		
Second person singular/plural		
Third person plural	They	hear

3. To Watch	Subject	Verb
First person singular		
Second person singular/plural		
Third person singular		

4. To Hope	Subject	Verb
First person singular		
Second person singular/plural		
Third person singular		

5. To Fax	Subject	Verb
First person plural		
Second person singular/plural		
Third person singular	He	

Practice 3

EDIT FOR BASIC SUBJECT-VERB AGREEMENT

Circle the verb form that agrees with the subject of each of the following sentences.

1. Drugs (contributes contribute) to careless driving because a drug (affects affect) a driver both mentally and physically.

2. For example, Samuel (takes take) a new headache medicine, and the side effects (includes include) drowsiness.

3. Then, he (decides decide) to drive even though he (realizes realize) he shouldn't because of this new medicine.

4. The medication (makes make) him drowsy, and it (becomes become) difficult for him to stay alert.

5. The medication (slows slow) Samuel's reflexes considerably, so they (causes cause) a delay in his reactions to driving conditions.

6. Samuel (falls fall) asleep behind the wheel. His car (veers veer) into oncoming traffic.

7. Other drivers (honks honk) their horns. Many (swerves swerve) to get out of Samuel's way.

8. Samuel (tries try) to regain control of his car, but three other cars (slams slam) into him one after another.

9. Many drugs (impairs impair) a person's motor skills and reaction time. Also, they (impedes impede) judgment.

10. Many prescription drugs (comes come) without warnings against operating machinery. Samuel's medicine (carries carry) a warning against driving and operating machinery.

L3 Create Subject-Verb Agreement Using *To Have, To Do, To Be*

Three key verbs are used both as main verbs and as helping verbs to express a wide variety of meanings: *to have, to do,* and *to be*. Memorize their present tense singular and plural forms to ensure subject-verb agreement.

To Have: Present Tense		
	Singular **Subject** and **Verb**	Plural **Subject** and **Verb**
First Person	I have	We have
Second Person	You have	You have
Third Person	He / She / It has	They have

Practice 4

CREATE SUBJECT-VERB AGREEMENT: *TO HAVE*

Write the form of the verb *to have* that agrees with the subject in each of the following sentences.

1. My younger brother _____ problems with asthma.

2. As a result, he _____ to use an inhaler.

3. Researchers _____ developed fun inhalers for children.

4. With these inhalers, children _____ fewer complaints about taking their medication.

5. Research _____ proven that positive emotions increase well-being and the effectiveness of treatment.

6. For example, one company _____ designed dolls and toys to fit inhalers in form and size.

7. Called Medidolls, these inhalers _____ the look of a toy, so a Medidoll protects the inhaler, makes it easy to carry, and is fun to use.

8. New nebulizers _____ cool designs like a fire truck or panda bear.

9. Using fun inhalers and nebulizers, children with asthma _____ a better attitude about taking their medicine.

10. Write a sentence using *has* or *have* as a verb. Suggested topic: A useful product.

    _____

    _____

    _____

To Do: Present Tense

	Singular **Subject** and **Verb**	Plural **Subject** and **Verb**
First Person	I do	We do
Second Person	You do	You do
Third Person	He / She / It does	They do

Practice 5

CREATE SUBJECT-VERB AGREEMENT: *TO DO*

Write the form of the verb *to do* that agrees with the subject in each of the following sentences.

1. A robot called Probo has been developed; he _____ many things to comfort sick young children in hospitals.

2. Probo's outside feels soft and cuddly; its inside parts _____ the hard work of understanding children's emotions and communicating with them.

3. Probo can't give hugs yet, but it _____ purr when hugged.

4. The words Probo says aren't words in a real language, but they _____ provide comfort because of their warm, sympathetic tone.

5. Since the color green _____ evoke positive responses like relaxation and comfort, Probo is green.

6. Children _____ respond to Probo's seven facial expressions, which are angry, disgusted, scared, happy, sad, surprised, and tired.

7. Probo and other similar robots _____ a variety of helpful tasks.

8. For example, they _____ serve as a way to inform children of medical routines, therapy, and operations.

9. Researchers _____ believe that robots can have a positive impact on seriously ill children.

10. Write a sentence using *do* or *does* as the verb. Suggested topic: The ideal robot.

_____

_____

The verb **to do** is often used with the adverb *not* to express a negative thought. Frequently this negative is stated in the form of the contractions *doesn't* and *don't*, which combine the verb and adverb into shorter words. The verb part of the contraction must still agree with its subject.

To Do and Not: Contraction Form		
	Singular **Subject** and **Verb**	Plural **Subject** and **Verb**
First Person	I don't agree	We don't agree
Second Person	You don't seem well	You don't seem well
Third Person	He / She / It — doesn't care	They don't care

CREATE SUBJECT-VERB AGREEMENT: *TO DO* AND *NOT*

Fill in the blank with the form of the verb *to do* that agrees with the subject of each of the following sentences. Use the contractions *doesn't* and *don't* as needed.

1. He _____ have to study to earn high grades, but I have to study for hours.

2. It _____ hurt your reputation to admit that you are wrong.

3. Even when we ask politely, they _____ turn down the music.

4. You still _____ understand why I am so angry.

5. As a vegan, she _____ eat meat or eggs.

6. The government _____ have the right to limit our freedom of speech.

7. We _____ have the legal right to speak or write slander against another.

8. You _____ want to go to the concert on Friday?

9. Write a sentence using *do, does, doesn't,* or *don't*. Suggested topic: A helpful piece of advice.

    ....

    ....

The *to be* verb is unusual because it uses three forms in the present tense: *am, is,* and *are*.

	To Be: Present Tense	
	Singular **Subject** and **Verb**	Plural **Subject** and **Verb**
First Person	I am	We are
Second Person	You are	You are
Third Person	He / She / It — is	They are

Practice 7

CREATE SUBJECT-VERB AGREEMENT: TO BE

Write the form of the verb *to be* that agrees with the subject of each of the following sentences.

1. A smart phone .... a multi-purpose device.

2. Smart phones .... able to take pictures, download music, and access the Internet.

3. We .... delighted with the innovations in smart phones.

4. Siri, Apple's voice interaction software for smart phones, ... able to use voice commands to send messages, place calls, and schedule meetings.

5. Bluetooth .... a technology that enables wireless headsets and hands-free phone systems.

6. A smart phone's camera .... able to take sharp, high-resolution pictures.

7. All current smart phones .... equipped with GPS navigation for directions and maps.

8. Clearly, cell phones .... evolving.

9. Write a sentence using a form of the verb *to be*. Suggested topic: A useful tool.

_____

_____

L4 Create Subject-Verb Agreement Using Subjects Separated from Verbs

Subjects are often separated from their verbs by prepositional phrases. A **preposition** is a word that has a noun or pronoun as its object and states a relationship between its object and another word. A **prepositional phrase** begins with a preposition and ends with the object of the preposition. The object of the preposition can never be the subject of a sentence. Identifying prepositional phrases keeps you from confusing them with the subject of the sentence. The verb of a sentence agrees with the subject, not the object of the preposition.

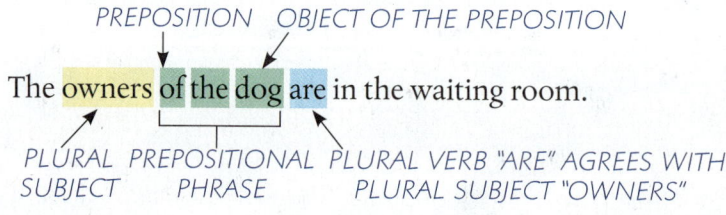

PREPOSITION   OBJECT OF THE PREPOSITION

The owners of the dog are in the waiting room.

PLURAL SUBJECT   PREPOSITIONAL PHRASE   PLURAL VERB "ARE" AGREES WITH PLURAL SUBJECT "OWNERS"

The following chart of prepositional phrases lists a few common prepositions and sample objects.

Common Prepositional Phrases			
Preposition	**Object**	**Preposition**	**Object**
at	work	of	concern
from	home	on	the desk
in	the office	with	experience

CREATE SUBJECT-VERB AGREEMENT: SUBJECTS SEPARATED FROM VERBS

Choose the verb form that agrees with the subject of each of the following sentences. Cross out prepositional phrases. Underline the subject. Circle the appropriate verb.

1. Counselors at a college career center (assists assist) students and alumni in various ways.

2. A student with a well-crafted resume and good references (has have) an advantage in a tight job market.

3. Many employers in the area (lists list) jobs at the college career center.

4. Students at a large college (benefits benefit) from school-sponsored job fairs with employers from a range of companies.

5. Often, an inventory of interests and strengths (suggests suggest) some possible careers.

6. Other types of needs (is are) also met by college counseling services.

7. Often, students with mental or emotional issues (seeks seek) the help of a college counselor.

8. The length of counseling (depends depend) on the student's problems or goals.

9. Most recent graduates of college (claims claim) to have used a college counseling service.

Practice 8

Create Subject-Verb Agreement Using Singular or Plural Subjects

To establish subject-verb agreement, first identify a subject as plural or singular. Some subjects may seem singular or plural when actually they are not. The following section identifies and discusses several of these types of subjects and the rules of their agreement with verbs.

Create Subject-Verb Agreement Using Indefinite Pronouns

Indefinite pronouns do not refer to specific nouns. Most indefinite pronouns are singular; a few are plural, and some can be either singular or plural. Consider the context of the indefinite pronoun to achieve subject-verb agreement.

- Singular indefinite pronouns agree with singular verbs.

  Everyone has a computer.

  SINGULAR INDEFINITE PRONOUN   SINGULAR VERB "HAS" AGREES WITH SINGULAR INDEFINITE PRONOUN "EVERYONE"

Singular Indefinite Pronouns					
anybody	each	everyone	neither	no one	somebody
anyone	either	everything	nobody	nothing	someone
anything	everybody	much	none	one	something

- Plural indefinite pronouns agree with plural verbs.

  Few have a computer.

  PLURAL INDEFINITE PRONOUN   PLURAL VERB "HAVE" AGREES WITH PLURAL INDEFINITE PRONOUN "FEW"

Plural Indefinite Pronouns			
both	few	many	several

- Some indefinite pronouns are singular or plural based on context and meaning. The context determines agreement with singular or plural verbs.

Example of Indefinite Pronoun That Is Singular Based on Context

INDEFINITE PRONOUN IS SINGULAR BASED ON CONTEXT

All has ended well.

SINGULAR VERB "HAS" AGREES WITH SINGULAR INDEFINITE PRONOUN "ALL"

Example of Indefinite Pronoun That Is Plural Based on Context

INDEFINITE PRONOUN IS PLURAL BASED ON CONTEXT

All of the students have left.

PLURAL VERB "HAVE" AGREES WITH PLURAL INDEFINITE PRONOUN "ALL"

Singular or Plural Indefinite Pronouns Based on Context				
all	any	more	most	some

Practice 9

CREATE SUBJECT-VERB AGREEMENT: INDEFINITE PRONOUNS

Choose the verb form that agrees with the subject of each of the following sentences. Underline the subject. Circle the appropriate verb.

1. Everyone (is are) shaped by genes and the environment.

2. Both (plays play) important roles in our development.

3. Few of our characteristics (is are) purely genetic; most (shows show) significant environmental influences.

4. At one time, some experts believed that all (was were) born as blank slates.

5. Now, most (believes believe) the "blank slate" theory is naïve or too simple to be true.

6. In the view of the nativist, all of our traits and behaviors (is are) inherited.

7. Many (speculates speculate) that our personalities and mental abilities are "wired in" before birth.

8. According to the nativist view, all of the human species (is are) a product of evolution.

9. Few of today's scientists (accepts accept) nature over nurture; rather most (agrees agree) it's a mix of both.

10. Write a sentence using an indefinite pronoun. Suggested topic: A common human characteristic. _____

Create Subject-Verb Agreement Using Collective Nouns

Collective nouns are singular forms of names of groups. They name a collection of people, animals, or items as a unit. The agreement between a collective noun and a verb depends on the context of the sentence.

- **When a collective noun acts as one unit, a singular verb is needed to achieve agreement.**

   The **flock** of birds **is** about to take flight.

   COLLECTIVE NOUN   SINGULAR VERB

- **When a collective noun represents the individuals in a group, a plural verb is needed to achieve agreement.**

   PLURAL VERB

   The **faculty are** disagreeing about the curriculum.

   COLLECTIVE NOUN REFERS TO THE INDIVIDUALS ON THE FACULTY

Common Collective Nouns				
assembly	class	crowd	gang	staff
audience	clergy	enemy	group	team
band	committee	faculty	herd	tribe
cast	company	family	jury	troop
choir	crew	flock	pride	unit

Practice 10

CREATE SUBJECT-VERB AGREEMENT: COLLECTIVE NOUNS

Choose the verb form that agrees with the subject of each of the following sentences. Underline the subject. Circle the appropriate verb.

1. As curtain time approaches, the audience (fills fill) the auditorium and (takes take) their seats.
2. The committee (considers consider) all petitions and in most cases (gives give) its approval.
3. The faculty (has have) many advanced degrees, including some PhDs.
4. The company (manufactures manufacture) a wide range of bolts, screws, nails, and other fasteners, all in its Pittsburgh plant.
5. The Monday night class (takes take) its final exam three weeks from tonight.
6. The class (turns turn) in their assignments today.
7. The family (travels travel) on a three-week vacation to a different location every year.
8. The cast (volunteers volunteer) some of their free time to charity work.
9. The jury (is are) in disagreement about the defendant's guilt.
10. Write a sentence using a collective noun. Suggested topic: Going to a concert.

_____

_____

Create Subject-Verb Agreement Using *Either-Or/ Neither-Nor*

Either or ***neither*** often signals a singular subject that requires a singular verb.

- **To ensure subject-verb agreement, identify and cross out prepositional phrases.**

SINGULAR SUBJECT   SINGULAR VERB

Either is eligible for employment.

Either-or and ***neither-nor*** join parts of a subject; the verb agrees with the nearer part of the subject.

- When all parts of the subject are singular, the verb is singular.

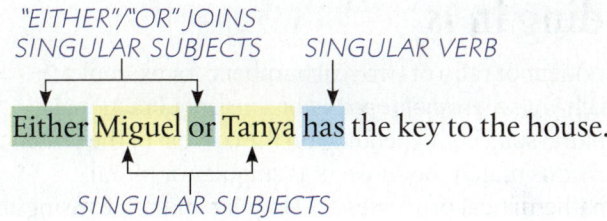

- When all parts of the subject are plural, the verb is plural.

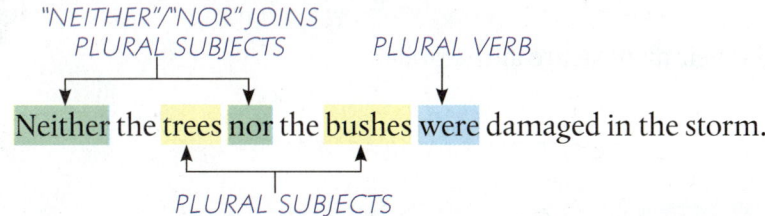

- When one part of the subject is singular and the other part is plural, the verb agrees with the nearer part. For smooth expression, place the plural part of the subject closer to the verb.

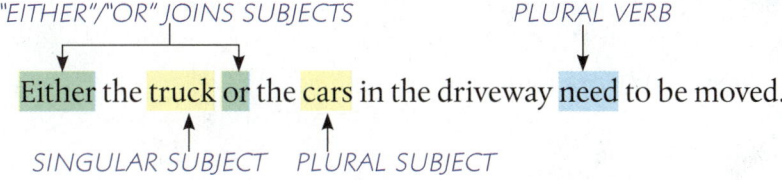

CREATE SUBJECT-VERB AGREEMENT: *EITHER-OR/NEITHER-NOR*

Choose the verb form that agrees with the subject of each of the following sentences. Cross out prepositional phrases. Underline the subject. Circle the appropriate verb.

1. Neither of the men (has have) applied for a student loan.
2. For many students, either student loans or scholarships (is are) necessary to pay for higher education.
3. Either the counselors or your faculty advisor (has have) information about financial aid.
4. Neither the President of the Student Government Association nor the campus representatives (does do) the will of the student body.
5. Either of your two current professors (is are) an excellent source for a recommendation.
6. Neither Jamie nor most of her classmates (knows know) how to apply for financial aid.
7. Joe plans well so that neither his two jobs nor his girlfriend (keeps keep) him from studying.
8. Neither the members of the club nor the advisor (remembers remember) last month's meeting.
9. Neither of those two students (has have) earned any grade lower than an "A."
10. Write a sentence using *either* or *neither*. Suggested topic: College life. _____

Create Subject-Verb Agreement Using Fractions, Titles, and Words Ending in -s

A **fractional expression** states the quotient or ratio of two real numbers; for example, the fraction ¾ expresses a 3 to 4 ratio, which is also *seventy-five percent* or a *majority*. Fractional expressions can be either singular or plural subjects, depending on the context of the sentence.

Thus, the verbs in fractional expressions match the subjects as singular or plural accordingly. Sums and products of mathematical processes are singular and require singular verbs. To ensure subject-verb agreement, identify and cross out prepositional phrases.

PLURAL SUBJECT (BASED ON CONTEXT)   PLURAL VERB

A majority express their displeasure at the polls.

SINGULAR SUBJECT (BASED ON CONTEXT)   SINGULAR VERB

Fifty percent was destroyed in the fire.

PLURAL SUBJECT (BASED ON CONTEXT)   PLURAL VERB

Two-thirds have rotted on the trees.

SINGULAR SUBJECT   SINGULAR VERB

Two and four is six.

- **Titles** are singular subjects and require a singular verb.

SINGULAR SUBJECT   SINGULAR VERB

Into the Woods with Meryl Streep was a great movie.

SINGULAR SUBJECT   SINGULAR VERB

"Rules of Change" by Neil Young was recorded for the album *The Monsanto Years*.

Some **words that end in -s** (for example, *thanks, assets, glasses*) seem to refer to a single idea or item but are plural and require a plural verb. Others (for example, *mathematics, economics*) are singular and require a singular verb.

PLURAL SUBJECT   PLURAL VERB

My assets have increased over the past ten years.

Economics is my favorite subject.

SINGULAR SUBJECT   SINGULAR VERB

Practice 12

CREATE SUBJECT-VERB AGREEMENT: FRACTIONS, TITLES, AND WORDS ENDING IN -S

Choose the verb form that agrees with the subject in each of the following sentences. Cross out the prepositional phrases. Underline the subject. Circle the appropriate verb.

1. My glasses (is are) broken.
2. Thirty percent of my life earnings (is are) paid in taxes.
3. Eighty percent of students (turns turn) their work in on time.
4. "Yellow Flicker Beat" (is are) the first single released from the soundtrack for the movie *The Hunger Games: Mockingjay Part 1*.
5. *Morning Phase* by Beck (was were) the winner of the Grammy for Best Rock Album in 2015.
6. Written by Lee Child, the novel *61 Hours* (is are) about a rugged investigator, Jack Reacher.
7. Three hundred and forty-two divided by six (equals equal) fifty-seven.
8. Today's news (reports report) a fatal crash on the interstate.
9. One hundred thousand dollars (is are) a significant amount of money.
10. Write a sentence using a fraction, title, or plural word that seems singular. Suggested topic: A favorite DVD.

Create Subject-Verb Agreement Using Subjects after Verbs

In some instances, a writer may choose to place the subject after the verb. To ensure subject-verb agreement, identify the verb, identify (and cross out) prepositional phrases, and ask who or what completes the action or state of being stated by the verb.

There and **Here** are never the subject of a sentence. Both of these words signal that the subject comes after the verb.

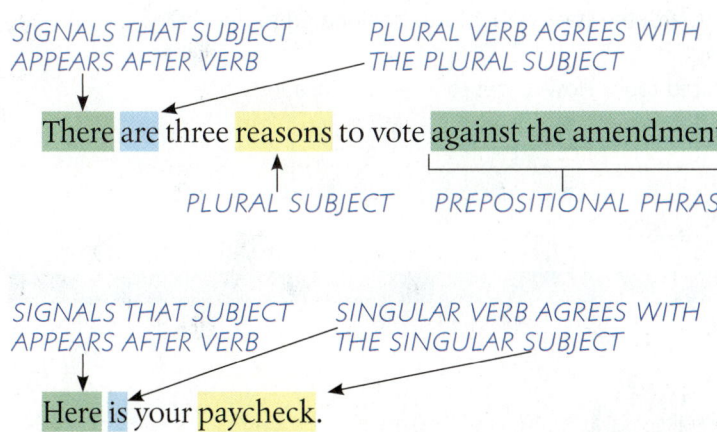

Agreement in Questions relies on understanding that the subject comes after the verb or between parts of the verb.

SINGULAR VERB   *SINGULAR SUBJECT*

Where is the closest fast-food restaurant?

PLURAL VERB "DO" AGREES WITH THE PLURAL SUBJECT "LIGHTS"

How do city lights harm the turtles' nesting season?

PLURAL SUBJECT

Writers having difficulty determining the subject in a question can identify it by reversing the word order into a statement—in the examples above, "The closest fast-food restaurant is…" and "City lights do harm…."

Practice 13

CREATE SUBJECT-VERB AGREEMENT: SUBJECTS AFTER VERBS

Choose the verb form that agrees with the subject of each of the following sentences. Cross out prepositional phrases. Underline the subject. Circle the appropriate verb.

1. There (is are) four reports due by the end of the month.

2. Here (is are) the pliers, hammer, and screwdriver that have been missing.

3. (Do Does) the chicken in the refrigerator need to be cooked tonight?

4. Where (is are) the first aid station?

5. Why (does do) you need to borrow the car?

6. Here on the counter (is are) the keys Sonja misplaced.

7. How (does do) the car perform after its 6,000 mile tune-up?

8. There (is are) four more hours before the start of the next work shift.

9. There by the front door (is are) the stack of books to be donated to the library.

10. Write a question. Suggested topic: How to get to a specific location.

Create Subject-Verb Agreement Using Relative Pronouns

Agreement with relative pronouns relies on identifying the relationships among a **relative pronoun** (a pronoun such as *that, which, who,* and *whom* that introduces a dependent clause), its **antecedent** (the word the pronoun refers to), and its verb. When a relative pronoun refers to a plural antecedent, it requires a plural verb. When a relative pronoun refers to a singular antecedent, it requires a singular verb. Note that relative pronouns signal a dependent clause. The antecedent for the relative pronoun is often found in the independent clause.

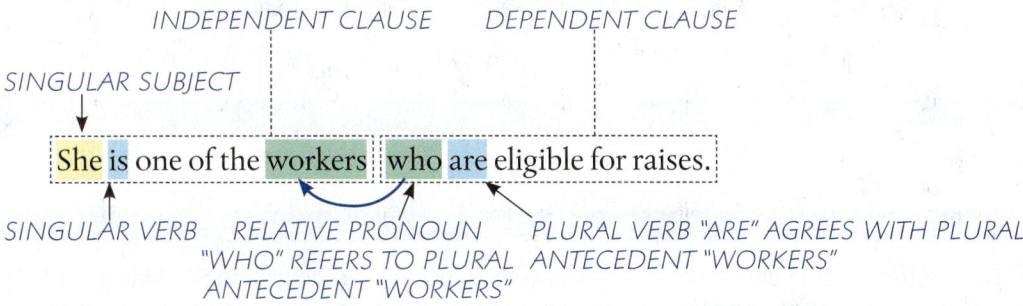

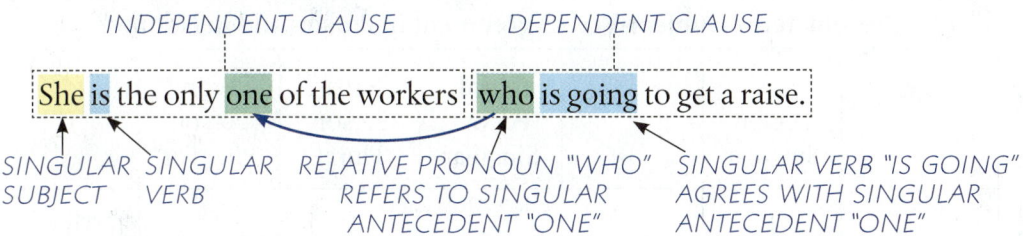

Relative Pronouns		
who	which	that

CREATE SUBJECT-VERB AGREEMENT: RELATIVE PRONOUNS

Choose the verb form that agrees with the subject of each of the following sentences. Underline the antecedent of the relative pronoun once. Underline the relative pronoun twice. Circle the appropriate verb.

1. Robert, who (has have) an impressive résumé, will apply for the management position.

2. The sandwiches that (is are) in the brown paper bag belong to me.

3. The buildings are on a block that (overlooks overlook) the park.

4. The computer virus that (has have) affected your computer also caused my system to crash.

5. The people who (is are) on the committee have the final vote.

6. Saul, who (leads lead) the committee, does not influence the vote.

7. The chairs that (was were) broken have been sent to the shop for repair.

8. The only chair remaining was an antique rocker, which (belongs belong) to Sue.

9. Ask the people who (has have) received a notice for jury duty to take a seat in the jury box.

10. Write a sentence using a relative pronoun. Suggested topic: A necessary item.

CREATE SUBJECT-VERB AGREEMENT: CHAPTER REVIEW

Demonstrate your understanding of subject-verb agreement by completing 50 blank items in the following chart of verbs used in preceding chapter practices. Then, answer the question: *What is the pattern or rule for subject-verb agreement in person and number?*

Present Tense Subject-Verb Agreement in Person and in Number					
	First Person Singular		Third Person Singular	First Person Plural	Second Person Singular
	I			We		They
To Have	have					
To Be				are		
To Do						do
To Agree		agree				
To Benefit					benefit	
To Decide	decide					
To Express						express
To Make			makes			
To Show						show

Practice 16

SUBJECT-VERB AGREEMENT REVIEW

Read the following short paragraph. Edit to ensure subject-verb agreement in the present tense.

We is about to walk through the security scanner at the airport when we is asked by the airport personnel to step aside into a special area. They asks us to sit quietly and wait for the security supervisor. My mother becomes impatient and begin demanding an explanation. She wants to know why we is being stopped from boarding our plane. She worry that we will miss our flight. My sister and her husband is having their first baby, so we wants to be sure we get there in time for the birth. My mother whisper under her breath to me, "This is a situation that are meant to test one's patience!"

Editing Assignments

MyWritingLab™
Complete this Exercise on mywritinglab.com

Editing for Everyday Life

Read the following testimonial written as an endorsement by a member of a local gym. Edit the paragraph to ensure subject-verb agreement.

If you is looking to make a dramatic change in how you looks and feels, then you need to hire **Ryan Belcher** with **Gold's Gym** as your personal trainer. My progress is the result of his training. He creates routines that is based on your specific needs. For example, my friend and I has been out of shape and overweight for years. Every training session, Ryan do his best to push us to work harder than we believes we can. We lift weights for strength; we does aerobics for endurance, and we stretch for flexibility. "I now has more lean muscle than fat."

One hundred percent of Ryan's clients reaches their goals.

Editing for College Life

The following paragraph was written by a student to earn five points on a math exam. The student had to explain the steps he took to correctly solve the math problem. Edit to ensure subject-verb agreement.

I has repaired my answer to the question I missed on this week's quiz. To correctly solve this equation, I use the distributive law. The test question is "What is the value of x in the problem: $2(x + 3) + 4(x - 5) = 10$?" These is my steps to solve this problem.

Step 1: I multiplies each of the terms in the first expression in parentheses by two. 2 times x are 2x, and 2 times 3 are 6. The equation now is $2x + 6 + 4(x - 5) = 10$.

Step 2: I multiply each of the terms in the second expression in parentheses by four. 4 times x equal 4x, and 4 times -5 equal -20. The equation is now $2x + 6 + 4x - 20 = 10$.

Step 3: Now I add and subtracts like terms, so the equation is now $6x - 14 = 10$.

Step 4: I add 14 to both sides of the equation: $6x = 24$.

Step 5: Finally I divides each side by six. Six go into six one times, and six go into 24 four times. $x = 24 \div 6$. x is 4.

Editing for Working Life

Read the following flyer written by an entrepreneur who is starting up a landscaping and lawn maintenance business. Edit to ensure subject-verb agreement.

Does your garden beds need weeding or replanting?
Does your grass need mowing?
Are you one of those people who needs help selecting the right plant for the right location?
Lush Lawns are the company to meet your needs. **Lush Lawns** employ experts who knows how to create and maintain beautiful landscapes. **Lush Lawns** plant, weed, mulch, edge, and mow for a low monthly price. It don't pay to wait.
Call now and begin enjoying a lush lawn of your own.

Academic Learning Log: Chapter Review

WHAT HAVE I LEARNED ABOUT SUBJECT-VERB AGREEMENT?

To test and track your understanding, answer the following questions.

1. What is the rule for subject-verb agreement? _____

2. How is the third person singular verb formed? _____

3. What are the three forms of the present tense of the verb *to be*? _____

4. _____ sometimes separate subjects from their verbs.

5. Indefinite and collective pronouns are singular or plural based on the _____ of the sentence.

6. When _____ joins part of a subject, the verb agrees with the _____ part of the subject.

7. Sums and products of mathematical expressions require _____ verbs.

8. The words _____ and _____ are never the subject of a sentence; rather, they signal that the subject follows the verb.

9. In a _____, the subject comes after the verb or between parts of the verb.

10. Agreement with relative pronouns relies on identifying the relationship among a relative pronoun, its _____, and its verb.

11. **How will I use what I have learned about subject-verb agreement?**
    In your notebook, discuss how you will apply to your own writing what you have learned about subject-verb agreement.

12. **What do I still need to study about subject-verb agreement?**
    In your notebook, discuss your ongoing study needs by describing what, when, and how you will continue studying subject-verb agreement.

MyWritingLab™

Complete the Post-test for Chapter 25 in MyWritingLab.

26 Revising for Sentence Variety

PART 6 REVISING TO IMPROVE EXPRESSION

LEARNING OUTCOMES

After studying this chapter you will be able to:

L1 Answer the Question "What's the Point of Sentence Variety?"

L2 Vary Sentence Purpose

L3 Vary Sentence Types by Combining Ideas

L4 Vary Sentence Openings

L5 Vary Sentence Length

Sentence variety is the use of sentences of different lengths, types, and purposes.

Communicating about a real-life situation helps us to understand the purpose of sentence variety. The photograph on the facing page illustrates a woman who deals with stress on a daily basis. Read the accompanying short paragraph about the woman in Practice 1, complete the activities, and answer the question "What's the point of sentence variety?"

What's the Point of Sentence Variety?

PHOTOGRAPHIC ORGANIZER: SENTENCE VARIETY

Read the following short paragraph. What do all the sentences have in common? Describe the overall effect of the paragraph.

Marla has a high-stress lifestyle. She is a single mother of a preschool child. She works as a receptionist for a dentist's office. She is going to school full time. She is training to be a dental hygienist. She is always on the go. She is learning to cope with stress.

What is the point of sentence variety?

_____

_____

_____

_____

Practice 1

WRITING FROM LIFE

One Student Writer's Response

The following paragraph records one writer's thoughts about the point of sentence variety in the paragraph about Marla in Practice 1.

> *In the paragraph about Marla and her stress, every sentence begins the same way, with her name or the pronoun "she," and five of the seven sentences use the verb "is." In addition, the sentences are all about the same length, using six to nine words, and they are all simple sentences. The paragraph seems boring and bland.*

Sentence variety adds interest and power to your writing. You can achieve sentence variety by varying the purposes, types, openings, and length of your sentences.

L2 Vary Sentence Purpose

Every sentence expresses a purpose.

Four Purposes for Sentences

1. **Declarative sentences** make a statement to share information and are punctuated with a period. Declarative sentences are often used to state a main idea and supporting details.

   Half of college undergraduates have four or more credit cards.

2. **Interrogative sentences** ask a question and are punctuated with a question mark. Usually, the writer also provides an answer to the question. An interrogative sentence may be used to introduce a topic and lead into a topic sentence.

   How can you protect yourself from credit card debt?

3. **Imperative sentences** give a command that demands an action and are punctuated with a period. Imperative sentences are often used to give directions to complete a process or to persuade a reader to take action.

   Avoid reckless spending. Follow these steps.

4. **Exclamatory sentences** express a strong emotion and are punctuated with an exclamation point. Exclamatory sentences emphasize a significant point.

   Credit cards will never make you rich!

Most often, you will rely upon the declarative sentence to share information with your reader. However, thoughtful use of a question, command, or exclamation gives your writing variety and adds interest to your ideas.

Practice 2

VARY SENTENCE PURPOSE

Read the following paragraph, adapted from "Choosing a Credit Card: The Deal is in the Disclosures," a June 2008 article on the U.S. Federal Trade Commission website. Identify the purpose of each sentence.

Credit Card Tips

(1) Did you know some credit card plans let the issuer change the APR (Annual Percentage Rate)? (2) This rate change can raise or lower the finance charge on your account. (3) The issuer must tell you that the rate may change and how the rate is determined. (4) In addition, many credit cards charge membership fees. (5) Issuers have a variety of names for these fees, including "annual," "activation," and "monthly maintenance" fees. (6) These fees may appear monthly, periodically, or as one-time charges. (7) When you are choosing a credit card, there are many features to consider. (8) Don't commit to a credit card until you understand how you will be billed. (9) To avoid reckless spending, think about how you plan to use your credit. (10) Using a credit card is a form of borrowing: you have to pay the money back!

Sentence 1. _____   Sentence 6. _____

Sentence 2. _____   Sentence 7. _____

Sentence 3. _____   Sentence 8. _____

Sentence 4. _____   Sentence 9. _____

Sentence 5. _____   Sentence 10. _____

Vary Sentence Types by Combining Ideas

You learned in Chapters 20 and 21 about the four types of sentences: simple, compound, complex, and compound-complex. When writers rely on one type of sentence more than the others, their work becomes dull and flat, like a speaker delivering a speech in a monotone. As writers combine sentences, they must decide if the combined ideas are equal in importance, or if one idea is more important than another.

Coordinating ideas makes each idea equal in importance. To combine coordinate ideas, use a comma and a coordinating conjunction (FANBOYS: *for, and, nor, but, or, yet,* or *so*).

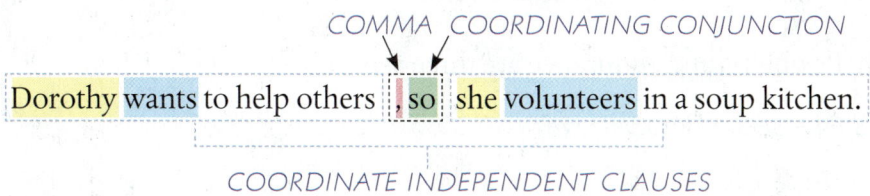

Subordinating ideas makes one idea dependent on (and less important than) another idea. To make an idea subordinate, use a subordinating conjunction (*after, although, as, because, before, since, unless,* etc.). If the new subordinate clause begins the sentence as an introductory element, include a comma at the end of that clause to set it off from the main independent clause.

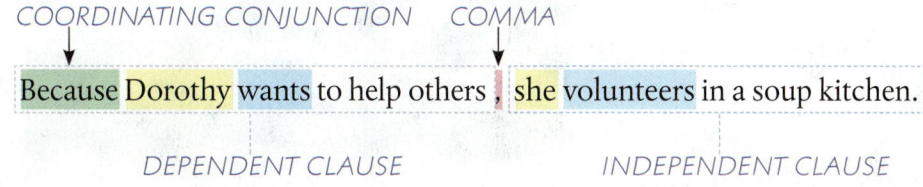

As you study methods of combining sentences, you will learn how to coordinate or subordinate ideas. To add interest and emphasis to your writing, vary the types of your sentences. Many writers use the revision process to combine sentences to achieve variety and interest.

Combine Two or More Simple Sentences into One Simple Sentence

A series of short simple sentences often creates a choppy flow of ideas. Combining closely related short simple sentences into one simple sentence creates a smooth flow of ideas. Short simple sentences can be combined in several ways.

Combine Sentences with a Compound Subject

When two separate simple sentences possess the same verb, they can become one sentence with a compound subject; a **compound subject** is two or more nouns or pronouns joined by the coordinating conjunction *and*. Note that the verb form of a compound subject must be plural. This method of coordinating ideas places equal emphasis on each subject.

For more about subject-verb agreement, see pages 468–489.

Original Sentences:

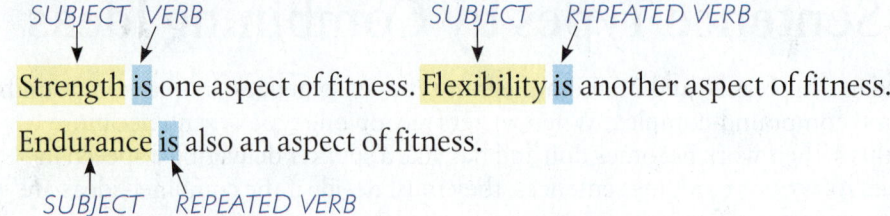

Strength is one aspect of fitness. Flexibility is another aspect of fitness. Endurance is also an aspect of fitness.

Sentences Combined with a Compound Subject:

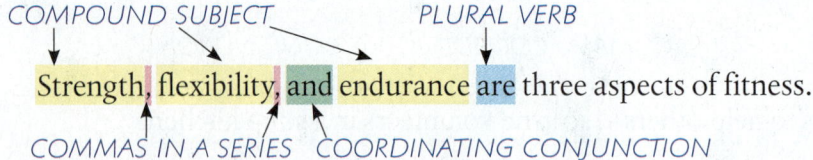

Strength, flexibility, and endurance are three aspects of fitness.

Practice 3

VARY SENTENCE TYPES: COMBINE SENTENCES WITH A COMPOUND SUBJECT

Combine the following simple sentences into a new simple sentence using compound subjects. *Hint:* Delete words or reword ideas as needed to create a smooth flow of ideas.

1. Balance improves through strength training. Bone density increases through strength training. Muscle mass increases. Energy levels increase. Overall quality of life improves.

2. Dynamic stretching is a type of flexibility training. Static active stretching is another type of flexibility training. Static passive stretching is a third type of flexibility training.

3. Risk of injury decreases with flexibility training. Muscle soreness decreases with flexibility training.

4. Stair climbing is an endurance training activity. Rowing also builds endurance. Jumping rope is another way to increase endurance.

5. Write a simple sentence with a compound subject. Suggested topic: Forms of exercise.

Combine Sentences with a Compound Verb

When two separate simple sentences possess the same subject, they can become one sentence with a **compound verb**, two or more verbs joined by a coordinating conjunction of addition or contrast: *and, or, but,* or *yet*. When only two verbs are joined, no comma is needed before the conjunction. This method of coordinating ideas places equal emphasis on each verb.

Original Sentences:

                          SUBJECT   VERB

Face-recognition **software** **takes** images of human faces.

The **software** **analyzes** facial images. The **software** **identifies** the images.
     SUBJECT   VERB   *SUBJECT   VERB*

Sentences Combined with a Compound Verb:

                    SUBJECT   COMPOUND VERB

Face-recognition **software** **takes, analyzes, and identifies** images of human faces.

                    COORDINATING CONJUNCTION

Practice 4

VARY SENTENCE TYPES: COMBINE SENTENCES WITH A COMPOUND VERB

Combine the following simple sentences into a new simple sentence using compound verbs.

1. Face-blindness can be an inherited disorder. Alternatively, it may occur as the result of a head injury.

2. A person with face-blindness can recognize the faces of very familiar people. However, he or she is unable to recognize the faces of others.

3. Face-blind people have difficulties in social situations. But they can use strategies to minimize these difficulties.

4. To identify another person, face-blind people can look at visual characteristics such as hair. They can listen for voice cues. They also can pay close attention to other people's reactions and responses.

5. Write a simple sentence with a compound verb. Suggested topic: Overcoming a difficulty.

Combine Sentences with a Participle Phrase

Participle phrases are used as adjectives to describe a noun or a pronoun. A participle phrase is placed directly in front of the noun or pronoun it describes and is set off with a comma. This sentence combination subordinates an idea; it places less emphasis on the idea in the participle phrase.

The **present participle** is the *-ing* form of a verb, such as *causing* or *biting*. A **present participle phrase** begins with a present participle; ends with an object, a noun, or a pronoun; and indicates two actions occurring at the same time.

> For more about participles, see pages 371–381.

Original Sentences:

West Nile virus can cause severe or fatal illness. The virus spreads through mosquito bites.

Sentences Combined with a Present Participle Phrase:

COMMA SETS OFF INTRODUCTORY ELEMENT   SUBJECT   VERB

Causing severe or fatal illness, West Nile virus spreads through mosquito bites.

PRESENT PARTICIPLE PHRASE DESCRIBES SUBJECT "WEST NILE VIRUS"   INDEPENDENT CLAUSE

VARY SENTENCE TYPES: COMBINE SENTENCES WITH A PRESENT PARTICIPLE PHRASE

In each of the items below, combine the two given sentences into one new sentence using a present participle phrase as an introductory element. Use appropriate punctuation.

1. The West Nile virus is a seasonal epidemic in North America. It flares up in the summer and continues into the fall.

2. West Nile virus causes symptoms such as fever, body aches, headache, and sometimes swollen lymph glands and rash. West Nile virus lasts only a few days in most cases.

3. West Nile encephalitis can develop from West Nile virus. West Nile encephalitis includes symptoms such as headache, high fever, neck stiffness, stupor, coma, and convulsions.

4. Kadeem wore long sleeves, long pants, and socks when outdoors. Kadeem attempted to reduce the risk of contracting West Nile virus.

_____
_____
_____

5. Write a sentence using the present participle phrase as an introductory element. Suggested topic: Flu medicines.

_____
_____
_____
_____

A **past participle** is the *-ed* or *-en* form of a verb, such as *talked* or *bitten*. A **past participle phrase** begins with a past participle; ends with an object, a noun, or a pronoun; and is often created by revising a sentence with a *to be* verb and a past participle into a past participle phrase.

Original Sentences:

SUBJECT   VERB   SUBJECT   VERB

Carlota was bitten by mosquitoes. She feared contracting the West Nile virus.

Sentences Combined with a Past Participle Phrase:

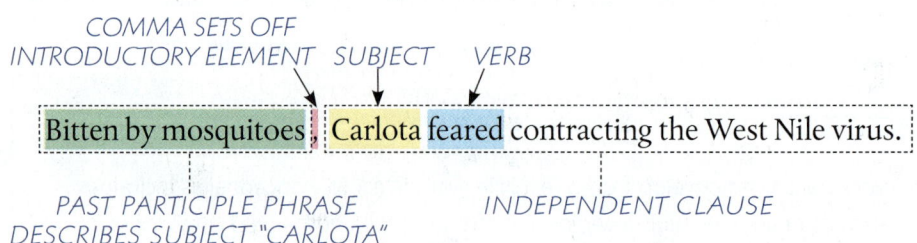

COMMA SETS OFF
INTRODUCTORY ELEMENT   SUBJECT   VERB

Bitten by mosquitoes, Carlota feared contracting the West Nile virus.

PAST PARTICIPLE PHRASE   INDEPENDENT CLAUSE
DESCRIBES SUBJECT "CARLOTA"

VARY SENTENCE TYPES: COMBINE SENTENCES WITH A PAST PARTICIPLE PHRASE

In each of the items below, combine the two given sentences into one new sentence using a past participle phrase as an introductory element. Use appropriate punctuation.

1. DEET is intended to be applied to the skin or to clothing. It primarily protects against insect bites.

2. DEET was developed by the United States Army in response to the Army's experience of jungle warfare during World War II. DEET protects against tick and mosquito bites.

3. Laboratory rats were exposed to frequent and long-term use of DEET. The rats experienced serious brain cell death and behavior changes.

4. DEET has not proven to be of significant harm to human health. DEET is the most common active ingredient in insect repellents.

5. Write a sentence using a past participle phrase. Suggested topic: Annoying or dangerous insects.

Combine Sentences with an Appositive

An **appositive phrase** renames or restates a noun or pronoun. This sentence combination subordinates an idea: it places less emphasis on the idea expressed by an appositive. An appositive can appear at the beginning, middle, or end of a sentence since it appears next to the noun or pronoun it renames. The use of commas depends upon where the appositive appears.

PLACEMENT OF APPOSITIVES AND COMMAS

Beginning of sentence: An appositive at the beginning of a sentence is an introductory element. Use a comma to set off an appositive at the beginning of the sentence.

Original Sentences:

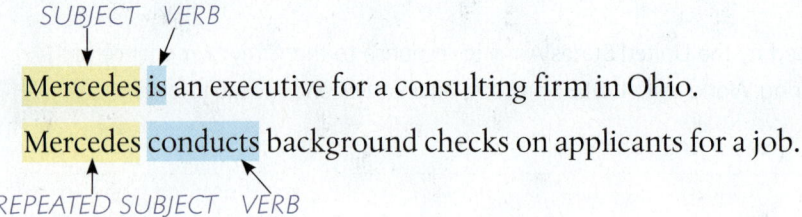

Sentences Combined with an Appositive:

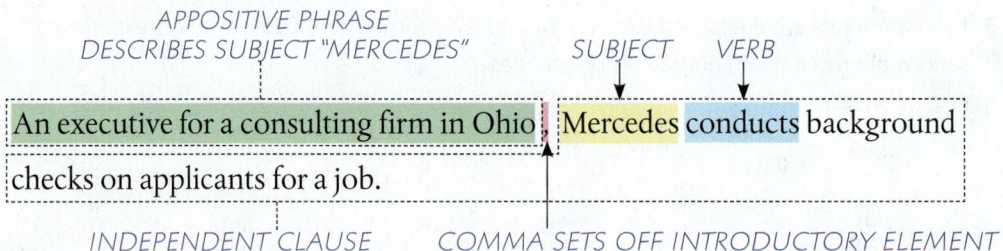

Middle of sentence: Use a pair of commas to set off an appositive phrase that interrupts an independent clause.

Original Sentences:

Business managers use Google and Yahoo! to conduct background checks on job applicants. Google and Yahoo! are powerful search engines for the Web.

Sentences Combined with an Appositive:

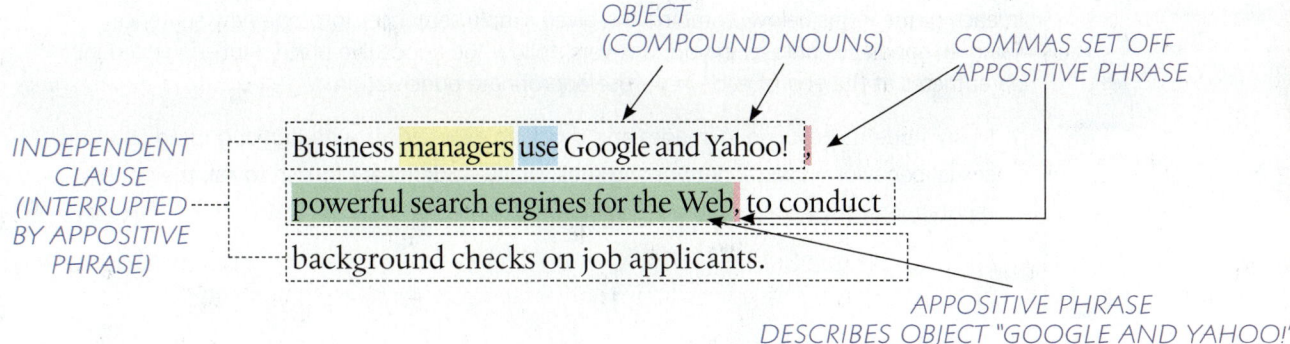

End of sentence: Use a comma to set off an appositive phrase at the end of a sentence.

Original Sentences:

Students should be wary of posting personal information on Facebook.

Facebook is a popular social networking site.

Sentences Combined with an Appositive:

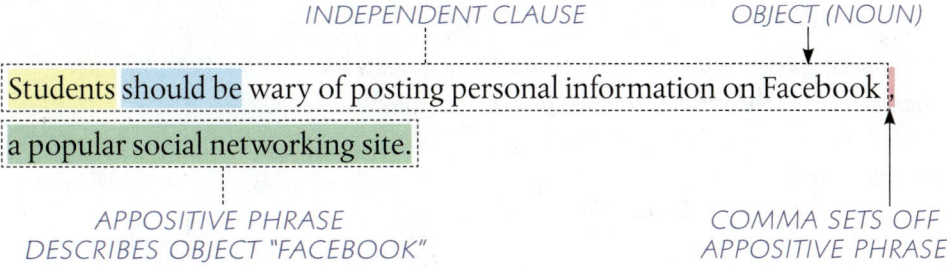

Practice 7

VARY SENTENCE TYPES: COMBINE SENTENCES WITH AN APPOSITIVE

In each of the items below, combine the given simple sentences into one new sentence using an appositive phrase. In your answers, follow the appositive placement suggested in parentheses at the end of each item. Use appropriate punctuation.

1. Many students post risqué images and shocking experiences with drinking, drug use, and sexual behavior on social networking sites. Many students are foolish to risk their public reputations with these postings. *(beginning of sentence)*

2. Some students experiment with a wide range of personal behaviors. They are eager to explore their new freedom away from home. *(beginning of sentence)*

3. Personal behavior is a reflection of a person's judgment. The personal behavior of an employee may concern an employer. *(middle of sentence)*

4. An employer should not have the legal right to consider personal behavior. Personal behavior is a matter covered by the right to privacy. *(end of sentence)*

5. Write a sentence with an appositive phrase. Suggested topic: The dangers of a social networking site such as Facebook.

Combine Ideas Using Compound and Complex Sentence Types

Combine ideas of equal importance using **coordination**, joining independent clauses into a **compound sentence**. Combine ideas of unequal importance—a main idea and a subordinate, or minor, idea—using **subordination**, joining an independent clause with a dependent clause into a **complex sentence**.

> For information on how to create compound and complex sentences, see pages 402–419.

VARY SENTENCE TYPES: COMBINE IDEAS USING COMPOUND AND COMPLEX SENTENCES

Use subordination and coordination to logically combine the ideas in the ten sentences below into five sentences. Punctuate properly. (*Note:* For more help on how to create compound and complex sentences and punctuate them correctly, see Chapter 21.)

(1) As a departing employee, keep in mind you may want to return to the organization. (2) You should strive to be remembered as professional. (3) To leave a good impression, emphasize the positive experiences. (4) Don't criticize colleagues or supervisors. (5) Leaving a poor impression can lead to a poor recommendation and a series of shut doors. (6) Leaving a positive impression can result in an excellent recommendation and open options for the future. (7) Resist the urge to leave a nasty note to a boss or coworker. (8) Act as professionally on the last day as on the first. (9) For example, Randall left the firm with an excellent last impression. (10) His boss and coworkers have agreed to act as references for future jobs.

LO 4 Vary Sentence Openings

Most often, we begin our sentences with the subject followed by the verb. To add interest and to shift the emphasis of an idea, you can vary the ways in which you begin a sentence. You have already worked with several types of sentence openings: participle phrases, appositives, and dependent clauses. Two additional ways to begin a sentence include using adverbs and prepositional phrases. As introductory elements in a sentence, both an adverb and a prepositional phrase are set off with a comma.

Adverb

- Describes or modifies another adverb, a verb, or an adjective.
- Answers the questions: *How? How often? How much? When? Where?* and *Why?*
- Usually ends in *-ly: angrily, beautifully, frequently.*

ADVERB   COMMA SETS OFF INTRODUCTORY ELEMENT

Eagerly, Emilo shops for an engagement ring.

Prepositional Phrase

- Begins with a preposition and ends with a noun or pronoun, the object of the preposition.
- Object of the preposition describes or modifies another word in the sentence.
- Common prepositions and objects: *about the yard, at the store, by the door, in the house, on the way, to the corner, with you.*

PREPOSITIONAL PHRASE

At the store, Emilo finds the perfect diamond ring.

COMMA SETS OFF INTRODUCTORY ELEMENT

VARY SENTENCE OPENINGS: ADVERBS AND PREPOSITIONAL PHRASES

Revise the openings of the sentences to vary emphasis and expression. Move the adverb or prepositional phrase to the beginning of the sentence as appropriate.

1. We, as consumers, should be aware of the tricks used by advertisers to sell their products.

2. Advertisers frequently use sex and sexuality to sell products.

3. An annoying jingle in many ads fixes a product in our memory.

4. Advertisers habitually rely on a celebrity testimonial to convince us to buy a product.

5. Write a sentence that begins with an adverb or a prepositional phrase. Suggested topic: An ad I find effective.

Vary Sentence Length

To add interest to your writing, vary the length of your sentences. When a writer relies too heavily on one sentence length, the work will be dull, flat, or uninteresting. Too many long sentences make a piece boring or confusing. Too many short sentences can seem choppy and immature. The sentence-combining techniques you have learned throughout this chapter will also help you create sentences of varying lengths.

Practice 10

VARY SENTENCE LENGTH

Revise the following paragraph written for a college humanities course. Vary the length of the sentences by combining the thirteen sentences into six new sentences.

> (1) Conversation is a five-step process. (2) The first step is the greeting. (3) The greeting can be either verbal or nonverbal. (4) The second step is feedforward. (5) Feedforward gives the other person a general idea about the topic of conversation. (6) The third step is business. (7) Business is the conversation's focus and details. (8) The fourth step is feedback. (9) Feedback is verbal and nonverbal responses from the other person. (10) Step five is the closing. (11) The closing is the goodbye. (12) The closing ends the conversation. (13) The closing can be verbal and nonverbal signals.
>
> Adapted from Joseph A. DeVito, *Interpersonal Messages: Communication and Relationship Skills,* 2nd ed.

Practice 11

REVISING FOR SENTENCE VARIETY: CHAPTER REVIEW

Assume you have written the following draft for an assigned essay in a college writing class. Revise the paragraph to demonstrate your understanding of sentence variety based on purpose, types, openings, and length of sentences.

> (1) Many people need to lose weight. (2) The Centers for Disease Control and Prevention (CDC) is a government agency. (3) The CDC studies obesity trends in the United States. (4) In 2011, the CDC reported that 12.5 million people were obese. (5) These 12.5 million were just children and adolescents. (6) About one-third of U.S. adults were obese. (7) Overweight is a label for ranges of weight that are greater than what is healthy for a given height. (8) Obesity is the same kind of label. (9) An adult, generally, who is 5'9" is overweight at 169 pounds. (10) This same person is obese at 203 pounds. (11) Healthy weight isn't about a diet. (12) It's about a lifestyle. (13) A healthful lifestyle of exercise and wise food choices.

Practice 11

Editing Assignments

MyWritingLab™
Complete this Exercise on mywritinglab.com

Editing for Everyday Life

The following letter to the editor of a local newspaper was written to protest a city's decision to install video cameras and a face-recognition program to reduce crime. Revise the letter to create a variety of purposes, types, patterns, openings, and sentence lengths. Use your own paper or complete this exercise on MyWritingLab.com.

Dear Editor:

A serious violation of our rights has come to my attention. Our city has installed a face-recognition program. They say the program is to reduce crime. The cameras are an invasion of our privacy. These cameras are installed at every major intersection. The government has no right to do this. This will record our actions without our knowledge or consent. I wonder how many rights we will lose in the fight against crime and terror. City and county commissioners voted for this program. We must vote them out of office.

—Julie Q. Public

Editing for College Life

Your humanities teacher has assigned a short response paper about the significance of landmarks such as the Golden Gate Bridge. Assume you have composed the following piece of writing. Revise the draft to create a variety of purposes, types, patterns, openings, and sentence lengths. Use your own paper or complete this exercise on MyWritingLab.com.

The Golden Gate Bridge stands as a symbol of human ingenuity. It was completed in 1937. It cost $35 million. The bridge spans the The Golden Gate. The Golden Gate is the strait connecting the San Francisco Bay to the Pacific Ocean. The bridge was once the longest suspension bridge in the world. It is now the second longest one. The bridge is 1.7 miles long. It is 90 feet wide. It has six lanes. The bridge is known for its beauty. Its color is an orange vermilion called International orange. The color was chosen for two reasons. It blends well with the natural environment. It is visible in fog. Lighting outlines the bridge's cables and towers. The lighting enhances the beauty of the bridge. The lights attract many visitors. This bridge is a remarkable engineering feat.

Editing for Working Life

Jerome Offiah, a recent graduate looking for employment, knows that many employers surf the Web for information about potential employees. Jerome Offiah maintains a blog on a social networking service such as MySpace and has drafted the following posting to make a positive impression on potential employers. Revise his draft to create a variety of purposes, types, patterns, openings, and sentence lengths. Use your own paper or complete this exercise on MyWritingLab.com.

I wonder if you are looking for a solid, reliable employee. I am your man. I am a recent college graduate. I majored in business and graduated with a 3.5 GPA. I can identify problems and research solutions. I collaborate with others. I bring these abilities to the workforce. I value hard work. I value being on time. I appreciate constructive criticism. I have several goals. I want to work with a large corporation. I hope to advance into management. I look forward to the opportunity to travel. I am a hard worker and a quick learner. You can count on me.

Academic Learning Log: Chapter Review

WHAT HAVE I LEARNED ABOUT USING SENTENCE VARIETY?

To test and track your understanding of sentence variety, answer the following questions.

1. What are the four purposes for sentences?

   (a) _____

   (b) _____

   (c) _____

   (d) _____

2. What are the six ways to combine simple sentences?

   (a) _____

   (b) _____

   (c) _____

   (d) _____

   (e) _____

   (f) _____

3. What are five ways to vary sentence openings?

   (a) _____

   (b) _____

   (c) _____

   (d) _____

   (e) _____

4. Why is it important to vary sentence length?

   _____

5. **How will I use what I have learned?**
   In your notebook, discuss how you will apply to your own writing what you have learned about sentence variety. When will you apply this knowledge during the writing process?

6. **What do I still need to study about sentence variety?**
   In your notebook, discuss your ongoing study needs by describing what, when, and how you will continue studying and using sentence variety.

MyWritingLab™

Complete the Post-test for Chapter 26 in MyWritingLab.

27 Revising for Sentence Clarity: Person, Point of View, Number, and Tense

PART 6 REVISING TO IMPROVE EXPRESSION

LEARNING OUTCOMES

After studying this chapter you will be able to:

1. Answer the Question "What's the Point of Sentence Clarity?"
2. Use Consistent Person and Point of View
3. Use Consistent Number
4. Use Consistent Tense

Sentence clarity creates a logical flow of ideas through consistency in person, point of view, number, and tense.

Communicating about a real-life situation helps us to understand the purpose of sentence clarity. The photograph on the facing page illustrates a particular situation. Read the accompanying original and revised sentences about the situation in Practice 1, complete the activities, and answer the question "What's the point of sentence clarity?"

What's the Point of Sentence Clarity?

PHOTOGRAPHIC ORGANIZER: SENTENCE CLARITY

What do you think the following sentence means? How could the sentence seem confusing to some readers?

Original Sentence: Jonathan and his son often walked on the beach and talk about his ups and downs in everyday life.

Is the above sentence describing current or past events? Whose everyday life is being discussed—Jonathan's or his son's, or do they share about both their lives?

Read the revised sentence below for clarity. How is the revised sentence different from the original? Which revised words clarify the meaning of the sentence?

Revised Sentence: Jonathan and his son often walk on the beach and talk about the ups and downs of their everyday lives.

What is the point of sentence clarity?

One Student Writer's Response

The following paragraph offers one writer's reaction to the clarity of the sentence about the walk on the beach.

> The first sentence doesn't make much sense because of the way the verbs and pronouns are used. The verb "talk" is in the present tense, yet the verb "walked" is in the past tense. An event can't take place in the present and past at the same time. Also, the use of the pronoun "his" is very confusing. Do they only talk about one person? Then which one? In the revised sentence, the verbs match in time, and the pronoun "their" refers to both people. The revised sentence also changed "life" to "lives" to match "their."

Sentence clarity is the precise choice of the form and arrangement of words and groups of words within a sentence. A clearly stated sentence is consistent in person, point of view, number, and tense. As a result, sentence clarity helps create a coherent flow of ideas within and among sentences. Often, writers work on sentence and paragraph clarity during the revision process. As you study the sentence clarity techniques in this chapter, revise pieces of your own writing and peer edit for a classmate. Apply and track what you are learning as you go.

L2 Use Consistent Person and Point of View

The term **person** refers to the use of pronouns to identify the difference between the writer or speaker, the one being written or spoken to, and the one being written about or spoken of. **Point of view** is the position from which something is considered, evaluated, or discussed; point of view is identified as first person, second person, or third person. Person and point of view also communicate tone.

Three Points of View

Person	Traits	Pronouns
First Person	The writer or speaker; informal, conversational tone	singular: *I, me* plural: *we, our*
Second Person	The one being written or spoken to; can remain unstated; informal, conversational tone	singular: *you* plural: *you*
Third Person	The one being written about or spoken of; formal, academic tone	singular: *he, she, it, one* plural: *they*

Illogical Shift in Person

An abrupt or **unnecessary shift in person or point of view** causes a break in the logical flow of ideas. The key is to use the same phrasing throughout a paragraph.

Illogical Shift in Person:

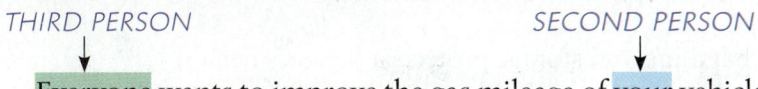

Everyone wants to improve the gas mileage of your vehicle.

Revisions:

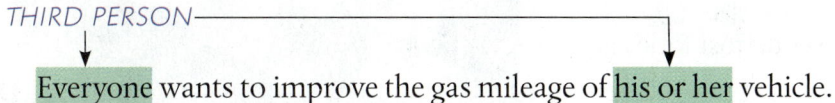

Everyone wants to improve the gas mileage of his or her vehicle.

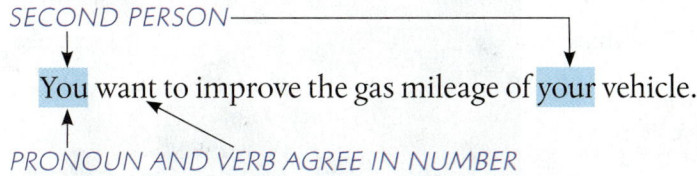

You want to improve the gas mileage of your vehicle.

PRONOUN AND VERB AGREE IN NUMBER

USE CONSISTENT PERSON AND POINT OF VIEW

Edit the following statements to ensure consistent use of person in each sentence. Revise verbs as necessary to agree with their subjects.

1. More people are choosing hybrid cars to reduce your gas expenses.
2. If a person is concerned about the environment, you may drive a hybrid car.
3. When you drive a hybrid, one will produce less harmful emissions.
4. We all will benefit from breathing less air pollution in their daily commute.
5. If you buy a hybrid vehicle, one will be making a responsible decision.
6. I've been thinking about buying a hybrid because you have to drive so many miles to work.
7. Charlie Ellison said he wouldn't buy a hybrid because you wouldn't save that much money.
8. If one's driving is mostly stop and go in the city, then you might save enough money in gas to pay for the high sticker price of a hybrid.
9. Our family loves our hybrid Prius because you get such great gas mileage.
10. If pollution worries you, then one can choose to walk, ride a bike, join a car pool, or use public transportation.

USE CONSISTENT PERSON AND POINT OF VIEW

Edit the following paragraph to ensure consistent use of person and point of view.

Proper Storage for Food Safety

(1) Proper food handling and storage protects a person's health; therefore, a cook must wisely defrost, store, and dispose of food. (2) First, we must properly defrost frozen foods. (3) You should never defrost foods at room temperature, which can allow bacteria a better chance to grow. (4) Instead, you must thaw foods in the refrigerator, microwave, or bowl of cold water that is changed every 30 minutes. (5) In addition, you should set the refrigerator below 40°F. (6) A wise cook doesn't rely on the refrigerator's built-in dial but rather uses a separate thermometer to judge the temperature, as advised by the U.S. Department of Agriculture. (7) Finally, I must put cooked food in the refrigerator or freezer within 2 hours of purchase or preparation. (8) Since harmful bacteria and microorganisms grow between 40°F and 140°F, leaving your food at room temperature for long can increase your chance of contracting a food-borne illness. (9) You should keep refrigerated leftovers for only four days; then You should throw them away. (10) A wise cook protects the health of those your consumers.

For more information on point of view, see the "Grammar in Action" section on page 202.

Use Consistent Number

The term *number* refers to the difference between a singular noun or pronoun and plural nouns and pronouns. Once you choose a point of view, carefully edit your writing to ensure **consistent use of number**: singular pronouns refer to singular nouns, and plural pronouns refer to plural nouns.

	Singular	**Plural**
First Person	I, me, my, mine myself	we, our, ours ourselves
Second Person	you, yours, yourself	you, yours, yourselves
Third Person	he, she, it him, her, his, hers, himself, herself, itself one, everyone, none	they them theirs themselves

Illogical Shift in Number

Pronouns refer to nouns. Pronouns must agree in number with the nouns they reference. When pronouns act as the subject of a verb, they, too, must agree in number. An abrupt or **unnecessary shift in number** causes a break in the logical flow of ideas.

Illogical Shift in Number:

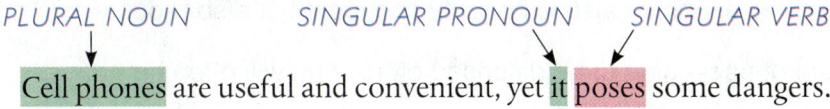

Cell phones are useful and convenient, yet it poses some dangers.

Revision:

Cell phones are useful and convenient, yet they pose some dangers.

USE CONSISTENT NUMBER

Edit the following statements to ensure consistency in number within each sentence.

1. A typical teen spends much time texting their friends.

2. Those who text and drive put his life at risk.

3. Sexting is using a cell phone to send private sexual messages or revealing photos to another person. However, they may forward these private messages to others or post it online.

4. Cell phones allow much more privacy than ever before. It has silent or vibrating ringtones.

5. A student can secretly get an answer in a text message for their test while they take them.

6. A drug dealer can easily, quickly, and secretly connect with their buyers.

Practice 4

7. Some experts fear that cell phones pose health problems for those who use it.

8. A headset may reduce risk of radiation from a cell phone by putting distance between them and the body.

9. The harder a phone has to work to get reception, the more radiation they emit.

10. When people use cell phones, he or she should consider their safety and well-being.

Practice 5

USE CONSISTENT NUMBER, PERSON, AND POINT OF VIEW

Revise the following paragraph for consistency of number as well as of person and point of view within and across sentences. Change nouns, pronouns, and verbs as needed. Different changes are possible.

Recycling for the Greater Good

(1) Consumers can recycle much of what they get. (2) One just needs to take several simple steps. (3) A product usually comes in several sizes. (4) Their economy size is not only cheapest but also reduces the amount of packaging to be disposed of. (5) You will often be able to reuse a container, rather than throwing them away. (6) For example, if it is cleaned, jam jars can be used as a juice glass. (7) Old clothes in good shape should be given to people who can use it. (8) Electronic equipment can also be donated, and many communities have centers for donating them. (9) Children should be encouraged to help recycle, as habits one acquires in their early life will stay with them in one's later life. (10) Every day, consumers who recycle make a difference to his or her environment.

L4 Use Consistent Tense

Consistent tense expresses the logical sequence of events or existence. Verb tense expresses the time or duration of an action or state of being. Primary tenses include three time frames: The **past** *was*; the **present** *is*; the **future** *will be*. The following chart outlines several hints to achieve sentence clarity through consistent tense.

For Consistent Tense
1. Use the same verb tense for each action or state occurring within the same timeframe. **Past Tense**:   Monica graduated from college and began searching for a job. **Present Tense**:   Monica graduates from college and begins searching for a job. **Future Tense**:   Monica will graduate from college and begin searching for a job.
2. Change tense to indicate a logical movement in timeframe from one action or state to another. **Past to Present Tense**:   Stephen, who changed careers, currently works as an insurance adjuster for Allstate. **Present to Future Tense**:   Although Stephen currently holds an entry level position, he will advance into a management position.
3. Choose and remain in one primary tense to express your points. **Past tense expresses completed action**: Monica sat attentively, made direct eye contact, and spoke with confidence. She understood the importance of making a good first impression, so she listened carefully to each question and offered thoughtful responses. **Present tense expresses the immediacy of a current event**: Monica sits attentively, makes direct eye contact, and speaks with confidence. She understands the importance of making a good first impression. So she listens carefully to each question and offers thoughtful responses.

Illogical Shift in Tense

An abrupt change from one verb tense to another without a logical reason, also called an **illogical shift in tense,** breaks the logical flow of ideas and causes confusion.

Illogical Shift in Tense:

                PAST TENSE   *PRESENT TENSE*
                   ↓   ↓
To find a job, Yuniko used job search engines and posts her résumé online.

Revisions:

                PAST TENSE   *PAST TENSE*
                   ↓   ↓
To find a job, Yuniko used job search engines and posted her résumé online.

              PRESENT TENSE   *PRESENT TENSE*
                   ↓   ↓
To find a job, Yuniko uses job search engines and posts her résumé online.

Practice 6

USE CONSISTENT TENSE

Edit the following essay to ensure consistency in tense.

The Winning Interview

(1) The best jobs often go to the candidates with the best interviewing skills. (2) Preparing for a job interview is essential to a successful interview. (3) If you were facing a job interview, consider the following tips. (4) Before the interview, study yourself and the job. (5) First, study your own strengths and weaknesses; be prepared to address both. (6) Second, study the job description and list five reasons you were best qualified for the job. (7) Third, study the company, its products, and its services. (8) During the interview, look and act like you were interested. (9) First, dress professionally. (10) Second, be positive so you showed enthusiasm for the job. (11) Finally, at the end of the interview, ask questions focused on the job and its responsibilities.

Practice 7

USE CONSISTENT TENSE

To give this paragraph more immediacy, edit it by revising all past tense verbs to make them present tense verbs.

Boomer grasped the bar above his head, swung, and pulled himself into the first set of the workout. His chin cleared the bar 10, 15, 20 times. He didn't stop; the crowd watched and counted each pull, "30 . . . 40 . . . 50." Boomer dropped to the ground. The crowd chanted the count as he rapidly completed 50 repetitions. Boomer stood, turned, and jumped 50 times on top of the 28 inch box. He completed the workout in 4 minutes.

USE CONSISTENT TENSE

Many pieces of writing move logically and effectively from past to present tense. Edit the following essay to ensure consistency in tense based on the logical movement of time.

One Successful Man!

(1) Bill Gates was considered by many to be one of the most successful and generous businessmen alive. (2) Co-founder of Microsoft, this billionaire sees the widening gap between the rich and the poor as a moral challenge, so he and his wife were dedicating their lives and fortune to helping others. (3) Bill Gates' generosity equaled his business success. (4) In 2000, Gates and his wife Melinda establishes the Bill & Melinda Gates Foundation. (5) Their foundation has the purpose of reducing "extreme poverty and poor health in developing countries, and the failures of America's education system," according to the foundation's website. (6) Thus, the foundation's $42.3 billion assets were used to improve the quality of technology, education, and health across the globe. (7) Their generosity found a kindred spirit in billionaire investor Warren Buffett. (8) In 2006, Buffett donates $31 billion to the Gates Foundation to be paid in annual installments. (9) Bill Gates was indeed a most successful and generous man.

Practice 9

SENTENCE CLARITY: CHAPTER REVIEW

Revise the following student paragraph for consistent use of point of view, number, and tense.

(1) It is 5:00 p.m. on a Friday, and the commuters in town are in his car driving home from work. (2) As always, someone is driving carelessly, and they is likely endangering other drivers. (3) Careless drivers rarely think about why he or she drives so recklessly. (4) One major cause of careless driving are the driver's emotions. (5) Any kind of emotion can take your mind off the road. (6) For example, last Saturday, a teenage boy was so excited and happy about winning a football game that he races home at high speeds, nearly sideswiping another car on the way. (7) Another emotion that caused careless driving is anger. (8) When people have heated arguments while driving, for example, sometimes you release the adrenaline running through your body by driving aggressively. (9) You rode the bumpers of other cars and swerved in and out of lanes to pass slower drivers. (10) Emotions, whether positive or negative, is a major cause of careless driving.

Editing Assignments

> **MyWritingLab™**
> Complete this Exercise on mywritinglab.com

Editing for Everyday Life

Revise the following short article, written for a neighborhood newsletter, for sentence clarity. Use your own paper or complete this exercise on MyWritingLab.com.

> *Attention All Residents: We are going green!*
>
> *As a community, we have taken several steps to help the environment. First, last week, the neighborhood begins a recycling program. Everyone receives three blue plastic storage bins for their plastic, aluminum, and glass garbage. On Tuesday of each week, put your recycling bins at their curbs for the 9:00 a.m. pick up. Second, watering restrictions will begin next week. Residents can water your yards or wash their cars only on Tuesday, Thursday, and Sunday after 5:00 p.m. or before 8:00 a.m. Finally, to save gas, car pooling for around town errands are available every morning between 9:00 a.m. and noon. Everyone can make a difference! Go green!*

Editing for College Life

Edit the following paragraphs, written in response to a short essay question on a history exam, for sentence clarity. Use your own paper or complete this exercise on MyWritingLab.com.

> **Test Question:** What were the differences between Native American and European combat styles?
>
> **Student Answer:** Native Americans conducted warfare very differently from Europeans. Your weapons included bows and arrows, knives, tomahawks, spears, and clubs. War parties do not attack in battle formations but use the forest as their cover and ambushed enemies in guerrilla-like raids. The tactic made it impossible to shoot you. In addition, a skilled Native American archer easily fires off "three or four arrows" with great accuracy by the time musketeers prepared his awkward weapon for firing.
>
> In contrast, Europeans were trained to fight on open fields, during fair weather, and in the daylight hours. Strictly disciplined, European soldiers marched in step and fight in formation. Officers march at the head of the column. At first they used matchlock muskets, which proved to be awkward, inaccurate, and unreliable.

Editing for Working Life

Edit the following cover letter for a job to ensure sentence clarity. Use your own paper or complete this exercise on MyWritingLab.com.

Pete Kramer
200 North Gravel Lane
Murphyville, Georgia 32345
204-573-2345
pkramer@aol.com

March 30, 2015

Ms. Sara Livermore
Director of Human Resources
Livermore Construction
43231 Hightower Road, Suite 300
Jacksonville, Florida 54323

Dear Ms. Livermore:

My teacher, Mr. Connors, told me that you were looking for an electrician's apprentice at your firm, Livermore Construction. I have just finished an intensive 16-week training program. I learn all the parts of the electrician's trade and also pass the test for the Electrical Workers Union Apprentice Certificate.

I noticed in your advertisements that you includes CAT 5 wiring in all the houses you builds. During the last five weeks of my training, I help install CAT 5 wiring in a local school.

I will be attending a vocational competition in Jacksonville with my teacher Mr. Connors from April 15 to April 19. If it was convenient I would like to visit Livermore Construction and talks with you about the possibility of employment. I will call you next week to schedule a time. My resume is enclosed. If you have any questions, please call me.

With confidence,
Pete Kramer
enc.

—Adapted from the Job Corps Wheel of Career Opportunity Website at <JCStudent.org>, U.S. Department of Labor

Academic Learning Log: Chapter Review

WHAT HAVE I LEARNED ABOUT SENTENCE CLARITY?

To test and track your understanding of sentence clarity, answer the following questions.

1. What is sentence clarity? _____
_____
_____

2. What are three techniques used to achieve sentence clarity?

   (a) _____,

   (b) _____, and

   (c) _____.

3. **How will I use what I have learned?**
   In your notebook, discuss how you will apply to your own writing what you have learned about sentence clarity. When will you apply this knowledge during the writing process?

4. **What do I still need to study about sentence clarity?**
   In your notebook, discuss your ongoing study needs by describing what, when, and how you will continue studying and using sentence clarity.

MyWritingLab™

Complete the Post-test for Chapter 27 in MyWritingLab.

PART 6 REVISING TO IMPROVE EXPRESSION

28 Revising for Parallelism

LEARNING OUTCOMES

After studying this chapter you be able to:

- **L1** Answer the Question "What's the Point of Parallelism?"
- **L2** Use Parallel Words
- **L3** Use Parallel Phrases
- **L4** Use Parallel Clauses
- **L5** Punctuate for Parallelism

Parallelism is the expression of equal ideas using similar words, phrases, or clauses in matching grammatical form.

Memorable quotations can help us to understand the purpose of parallelism. The photographs on the next page represent well-known public figures who made powerful statements. Read the quotations, complete the activities, and answer the question "What's the point of parallelism?"

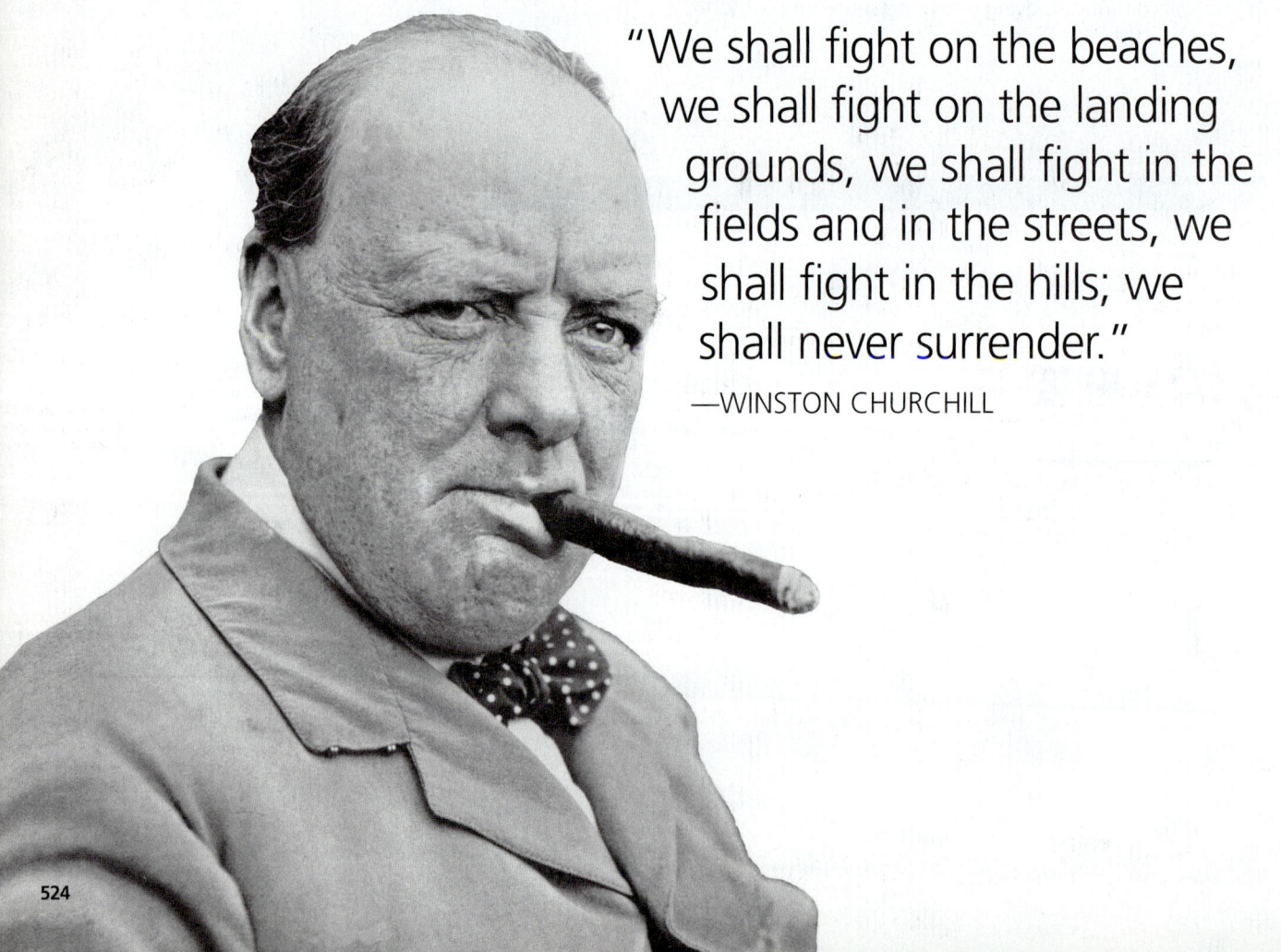

"We shall fight on the beaches, we shall fight on the landing grounds, we shall fight in the fields and in the streets, we shall fight in the hills; we shall never surrender."

—WINSTON CHURCHILL

What's the Point of Parallelism?

PHOTOGRAPHIC ORGANIZER: PARALLELISM

Each of the following well-known quotations uses parallelism to make an idea memorable and powerful. What do these statements have in common?

"I came; I saw; I conquered."
—JULIUS CAESAR

"We have nothing to fear but fear itself."
—FRANKLIN D. ROOSEVELT

"Scratch a lover; find a foe."
—DOROTHY PARKER

What is the point of parallelism?

_____

_____

_____

One Student Writer's Response

The following paragraph records one writer's definition of parallelism based on the traits of the example quotations.

> *The sentences have a few things in common. Each one repeats words or similar types of words. For example, the quote "I came; I saw; I conquered" uses three short simple sentences; they repeat the subject "I" and use the same kind of verb. This quote shows a chain of actions. "Scratch a lover; find a foe" has two short sentences, and both begin with a verb. "Nothing to fear but fear itself" repeats a word. So I think parallelism repeats the same kind of words, phrases, and sentences. Parallelism is kind of musical. It's got rhythm.*

Parallelism refers to the balance of equal ideas expressed in the same grammatical form. Parallel expressions bring clarity, interest, and power to a piece of writing. You can achieve parallelism by emphasizing equal ideas using similar structures and patterns of words, phrases, or clauses. You can also use certain types of conjunctions and punctuation to signal parallel structures.

L2 Use Parallel Words

Parallel structure uses a pair or series of closely related compound words to emphasize a point. Parallel words often, but not always, use similar **suffixes** (word endings).

Nonparallel:

ADJECTIVE OR VERB   *NOUN*

Prehistoric Paleo-Indians were wandering and hunters.

Revised for Parallelism:

PARALLEL NOUNS

Prehistoric Paleo-Indians were wanderers and hunters.

Nonparallel:

ADVERB   *PREPOSITIONAL PHRASE*

Paleo-Indians skillfully hunted game and with diligence gathered berries.

Revised for Parallelism:

PARALLEL ADVERBS

Paleo-Indians skillfully hunted game and diligently gathered berries.

Nonparallel:

NONPARALLEL VERBS

They flaked and crafting flint into spears.

Revised for Parallelism:

PARALLEL VERBS

They flaked and crafted flint into spears.

USE PARALLEL WORDS

Edit the following sentences to achieve parallelism with parallel words.

1. Ancestors of today's Pueblo Indians, the Anasazi were farming and craftsmen.

2. The Anasazi men wove baskets, and the Anasazi women were making pottery.

3. Their clothing was scanty, consisting of woven G-strings for men and short skirts of fiber for women.

4. They hunted small game with spear throwers and using nets and snares.

5. They cultivated poorly crops of squash and maize and living in simple shelters.

6. The Anasazi became known as Basket Makers; they wove beautifully and useful baskets.

7. Baskets were skillfully woven of coiled fabrics and pottery was elaborate decorated with geometrically designs.

8. The Pueblo culture rose out of the Anasazi Basket Makers and continuing the same mode of life.

9. Cleverly and in a gradual way, the Anasazi developed an irrigation system to survive in an arid environment.

10. Write a sentence that uses parallel words. Suggested topic: A good way to make something.

L3 Use Parallel Phrases

Parallel structure uses a pair or series of closely related compound phrases to emphasize a point. Parallel phrases repeat similar word patterns or groups.

Nonparallel:

　　　　　　　　　　　　　　　　　　　　INFINITIVE PHRASE　　NOUN PHRASE

Around 300 C.E., the Mayas learned to build cities, jewelry crafting, and to develop trade.

　　　　　　↑
　　INFINITIVE PHRASE

Revised for Parallelism:

Around 300 C.E., the Mayas learned to build cities, to craft jewelry, and to develop trade.

　　　　　　　　　　　PARALLEL INFINITIVE PHRASES

Nonparallel:

　　　　　　　　　　　PRESENT PARTICIPLE PHRASE

Maya women worked hard, planting the seeds, weeded the crops, and reaped the harvest.

　　　　　　　PAST PARTICIPLE PHRASES

Revised for Parallelism:

Maya women worked hard, planting the seeds, weeding the crops, and reaping the harvest.

　　　　　PARALLEL PRESENT PARTICIPLE PHRASES

Nonparallel:

WORD (NOUN)　　PHRASE (NOUN)

Architecture and building a system of roads were two major accomplishments of the Inca.

Revised for Parallelism:

　　　　　　　PARALLEL NOUN PHRASES

Developing a style of architecture and building a system of roads were two major accomplishments of the Inca.

Practice 3

USE PARALLEL PHRASES

Edit the following sentences to achieve emphasis through parallel phrases.

1. The Inca empire began in 1200 in Peru and its ending in 1535 with its conquest by the Spanish.

2. To see their enemies and in self defense, they built fortresses on top of steep mountains.

3. By developing an irrigation system and they used llamas for meat and transportation, the Inca provided resources for their population.

4. The Inca were the rulers of the largest native empire in the Americas and controlling 12 million people.

5. The state religion centered on worship of the Sun. The Inca believed their emperors descended from the Sun god and worshipping them as divine beings.

6. To distinguish social status or suggesting class membership, the Inca nobility altered the shape of their heads into a cone-like form.

7. Shaping the head was accomplished by wrapping tight cloth straps around the heads of their newborns or application of some type of force on the child's soft skull.

8. The Incas considered the coca plant to be sacred and having magical qualities.

9. They chewed the coca leaves for lessening hunger and for relieving pain during work.

10. Write a sentence that uses parallel phrases. Suggested topic: An interesting fact about American culture.

Use Parallel Clauses

Parallel structure uses a set of closely related clauses to emphasize a point. Parallel structure begins with a clause and continues with clauses to create a balanced, logical statement to express closely related ideas. Use parallel words and phrases within clauses.

Nonparallel:

INDEPENDENT CLAUSE

About 50 million people inhabited the Americas by 1490, and roughly 75 million people who were living in Europe.

DEPENDENT CLAUSE (ILLOGICAL MIXED STRUCTURE)

For more information on sentence types and sentence elements, see pages 388–401, "Subjects, Verbs, and Simple Sentences," and pages 402–419, "Compound and Complex Sentences."

Revised for Parallelism:

PARALLEL INDEPENDENT CLAUSES

About 50 million people inhabited the Americas by 1490, and roughly 75 million people lived in Europe.

Nonparallel:

DEPENDENT CLAUSE

Myth teaches that Europeans discovered an uninhabited America; in history, Native peoples inhabited a cultivated, civilized America.

INDEPENDENT CLAUSES

Revised for Parallelism:

PARALLEL DEPENDENT CLAUSES

Myth teaches that Europeans discovered an uninhabited America; history teaches that Native peoples inhabited a cultivated, civilized America.

PARALLEL INDEPENDENT CLAUSES

Practice 4

USE PARALLEL CLAUSES

Revise the following sentences to achieve emphasis through parallel clauses.

1. Native Americans believed that humans were merely a part of the natural world and in the need for humans to revere nature.

2. Europeans saw the land as something to own and control, in contrast with Native Americans seeing the land as something to have a place in and sustain.

3. Before a hunt Native Americans prepared themselves spiritually, and during a hunt showing great humility.

4. The terms "American Indians," "Native Americans," and "First Nations" are synonyms, and all which refer to the same people.

5. "Indigenous people" refers to any group who lived in a place first; for example, native African people living in Africa first are also indigenous.

6. Most indigenous people in Canada call themselves "First Nations," yet most indigenous people in the United States who are calling themselves "American Indians."

7. In search of a new route to Asia, Christopher Columbus called the natives of America "Indian" because he was thinking he had landed in the East Indies.

8. Nearly 95% of Native Americans died in the years after Columbus's landing; diseases that Europeans bringing to the Americas were killing millions of natives.

9. Epidemic diseases like smallpox, measles, and typhus had never occurred in the Americas, so Native Americans who had no resistance.

10. Write a sentence that uses parallel clauses. Suggested topic: My beliefs about the environment.

L5 Punctuate for Parallelism

The comma (sometimes along with coordinating conjunctions) and the semicolon signal equal ideas. In addition, numbered, lettered, or bulleted items in a list signal ideas of equal importance. Ideas marked by these pieces of punctuation are best expressed with parallelism.

Coordinating conjunctions always signal an equal relationship among words, phrases, and clauses. Use **commas** between parallel items in a series. Use a comma with a coordinating conjunction to join independent clauses.

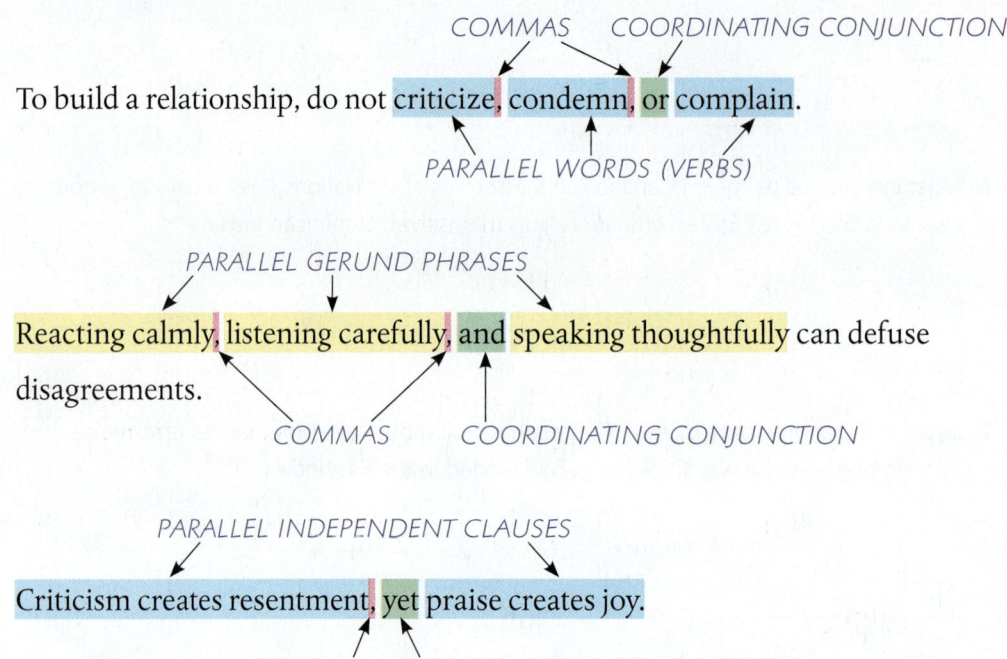

Semicolons signal two or more closely related independent clauses.

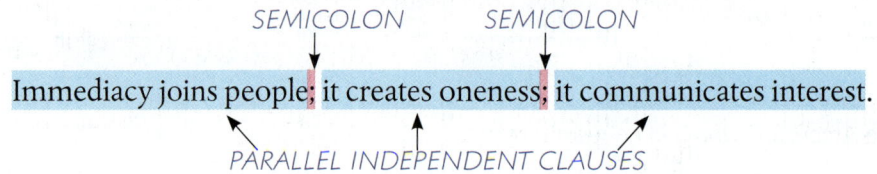

Numbers, letters, or bullets signal items in a list. Lists are often used in résumés, business letters, and presentations. Note that colons can introduce a list, and semicolons can separate items.

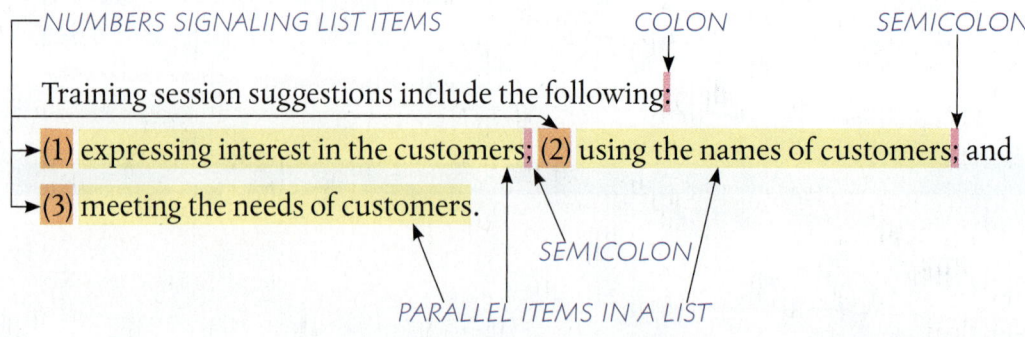

PUNCTUATE FOR PARALLELISM

Edit the following sentences for proper use of punctuation for parallel expression.

1. Space is an important factor in communication; for example four types of distances are intimate personal social and public distances.

2. Intimate space ranges from 0 to 18 inches personal distance ranges from 18 inches to about 4 feet social distance ranges from 4 to 12 feet public distance ranges from 12 to more than 25 feet.

3. People interact in three types of territories: (1) primary territories like a bedroom or office; secondary territories like the cafeteria or a classroom seat (3) public territories like a restaurant or shopping mall.

4. The specific distance you maintain between yourself and others depends on several factors gender age and personality.

5. Animals mark their primary and secondary territories likewise humans mark their territories to show ownership.

6. Humans use three types of markers central markers boundary markers and earmarkers.

7. Central markers are items you place in a space to reserve it for you for example a drink at a bar books on your desk or a sweater on a library chair are central markers.

8. Boundary markers divide your space from others fences around a yard armrests on a plane and contours of molded plastic seats on a bus are boundary markers.

9. Earmarks are identifying marks that indicate your possession of a space or object examples include the following trademarks nameplates and initials on a shirt or attaché case.

10. Write a sentence using parallelism. Suggested topic: The media and personal space.

Adapted from DeVito, Joseph A., *Interpersonal Messages: Communication and Relationship,* 2nd Ed. © 2011. Reprinted and Electronically reproduced by permission of Pearson Education, Inc., New York, NY.

Practice 6

REVISING FOR PARALLELISM: CHAPTER REVIEW

Each of following items is a nonparallel version of a famous quote in which the author or speaker originally used parallelism. Revise each statement for parallel use of words, phrases, clauses, and correct punctuation. Compare your responses to the original quotes provided by your teacher.

1. You can fool all the people sometimes, and some of the people all the time, but you cannot fool everybody always.

   —Abraham Lincoln

2. Ask not what your country can do for you ask what am I doing for my country.

   —Cicero, 1st-century, B.C.E., and President Kennedy, "Inaugural Speech," 1961

3. It was the best of times it was a time of the worst events.

   —Charles Dickens, *A Tale of Two Cities*

4. To strive to seek to find and not yielding.

   — Alfred, Lord Tennyson, "Ulysses"

5. It is by logic we prove but by intuition we find things out.

   —Leonardo da Vinci (1452–1519), artist, inventor, "Renaissance Man"

6. Give me liberty or you can kill me.

   —Patrick Henry, Speech to the Virginia Convention, 1775

7. We hold these truths to be self-evident, that all men created equal, that they are endowed by their Creator with certain unalienable Rights, that among these are Life Liberty and being happy.

—The Declaration of Independence, 1776

8. Early to bed rising early makes a man healthy worth much and wise.

—Benjamin Franklin, *Poor Richard's Almanack*, 1735

9. Do unto others as you would have others treat you.

—*The Bible*, Luke 6:31

10. If talk is made of silver then silence is golden.

—Arabic proverb

Editing Assignments

MyWritingLab™
Complete this Exercise on mywritinglab.com

Editing for Everyday Life

Assume you are putting together a cookbook of your grandmother's favorite recipes to reproduce and give as gifts to family members. Edit the following portion of a recipe for parallel expression. Use your own paper or complete this exercise on MyWritingLab.com.

Chocolate Fudge Square Cake

Beat margarine and cocoa. Adding unbeaten eggs one at a time. Add sugar, flour, and salt. Stir in nuts. Poured into greased 7 x 11 inch pan. Bake at 350° for 25 to 30 minutes. Removing from oven. Cover with scant layer of marshmallows and returning to oven until marshmallows are puffy and soft. Remove from oven. Poured and spread icing over marshmallows for marbled effect.

Editing for College Life

Assume you are giving a PowerPoint presentation in your Communication class. Edit the following outline of your PowerPoint slides so that each element is parallel. Use your own paper or complete this exercise on MyWritingLab.com.

Title Slide:

The Self in Interpersonal Communication

Slide Two:

Self-Disclosure
Influences on Self-Disclosure
Rewarding Self-Disclosure
Dangers of Self-Disclosure

Slide One:

Dimensions of the Self
Self-Concept
Being Aware of Self
Self-Esteem

Slide Three:

Communication Apprehension
The Nature of Communication Apprehension
Theories of Communication Apprehension Management

—From Joseph A. DeVito, *The Interpersonal Communication Book*, 10th ed., Longman 2004, p. viii.

Editing for Everyday Life

Edit the following portion of a résumé to ensure parallel expression.

CAREER OBJECTIVE

- To secure a Management position
- I want to contribute to the success of the organization.

SUMMARY OF QUALIFICATIONS

- Experienced in retail management.
- I am skilled in the following areas: analytical thinking, creative thinker, decision-making, problem solver, and time management.

Academic Learning Log: Chapter Review

WHAT HAVE I LEARNED ABOUT PARALLELISM?

To test and track your understanding, answer the following questions. Use several sentences as needed for each response.

1. What is parallelism? _____
   _____

2. Parallel _____ often, but not always, use similar suffixes (word endings).

3. Parallel phrases repeat similar _____.

4. Repeat parallel patterns of _____ to pace ideas through the thoughtful arrangement and sequence of sentence types.

5. What types of punctuation signal parallelism? (a) _____; (b) _____;
   and (c) _____.

6. Commas are used with _____ to join independent clauses.

7. Semicolons signal two or more closely related _____.

8. **How will I use what I have learned?**
   Discuss how you will apply to your own writing what you have learned about parallelism. When will you apply this knowledge during the writing process?

9. **What do I still need to study about parallelism?**
   Discuss your ongoing study needs by describing what, when, and how you will continue studying and using parallelism.

MyWritingLab™
Complete the Post-test for Chapter 28 in MyWritingLab.

29 Revising for Effective Expression

PART 6 REVISING TO IMPROVE EXPRESSION

LEARNING OUTCOMES

After studying this chapter you will be able to:

- **LO1** Answer the Question "What's the Point of Effective Expression?"
- **LO2** Use Concise Language
- **LO3** Use Active and Positive Language
- **LO4** Use Concrete Language
- **LO5** Use Creative Language: Similes and Metaphors
- **LO6** Use Fresh Language

Effective expression makes language clear and interesting.

Thinking about a real-life situation helps us understand the purpose and need for effective expression in our communication with others. Complete the following activity and answer the question "What's the point of effective expression?"

What's the Point of Effective Expression?

PHOTOGRAPHIC ORGANIZER: EFFECTIVE EXPRESSION

Assume you received the following e-mail from a coworker. What is your impression of the person based on the language used in the e-mail?

FROM: Kendis Moore Kendis@ITsolutions.com
Date: January 15, 2016
TO: Dwayne <Dwayne@ITsolutions.com>
SUBJECT: FW: A Good Cause

FYI

--------Forwarded Message

From: "Douglas Whitten"
Date: January 15, 2016
To: All Employees of Clarke Photography & Printing
Subject: A Good Cause!

I know everyone is busy as a bee, so I am not going to beat around the bush. It's time to get the United Way Campaign under way. Last year, we let it fall through the cracks, but this year, we are going to hit the nail on the head and raise a boat load of money. You may think this is not important, but you're dead wrong. Now don't drop the ball. Be sure to give to the United Way.

What's the point of effective expression?

One Student Writer's Response

The following paragraph offers one writer's reaction to the e-mail from the coworker.

> *I am not impressed with the coworker based on the sound of the memo. It's too informal; it doesn't sound professional at all. And it's boring and uninspiring. I would hit delete after the first sentence. It doesn't sound like the writer takes the campaign very seriously.*

Effective expression is a result of thoughtful word choice. Mark Twain once said, "The difference between the almost right word and the right word is really a large matter—it's the difference between the lightning bug and the lightning." * During early drafts, writers often relate thoughts and ideas without concern for word choice. Words or phrases are needlessly repeated, and clichés—overused expressions or ideas—are sometimes included in the draft. This rush to record ideas as they occur makes good use of the writing process *if* we take time to revise for effective expression after we have completed a draft. Effective expression involves concise, active, positive, concrete, creative, and fresh writing. Use the revision process to achieve effective expression.

L2 Use Concise Language

The most effective writing is concise and to the point. Concise language avoids wordiness—the use of unnecessary or redundant words and phrases that add nothing to the writer's meaning. The following example illustrates the difference between wordiness and concise writing.

Wordy

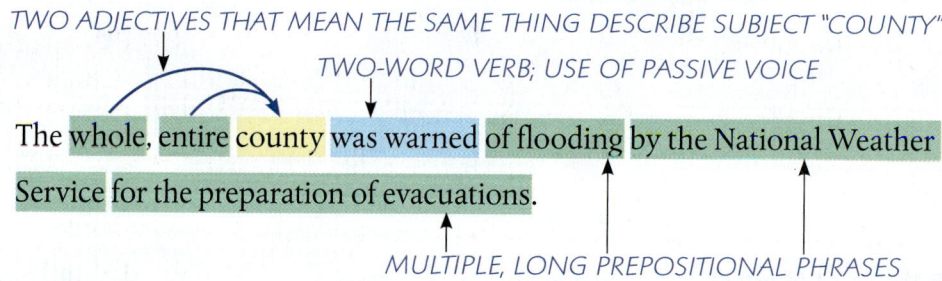

Concise

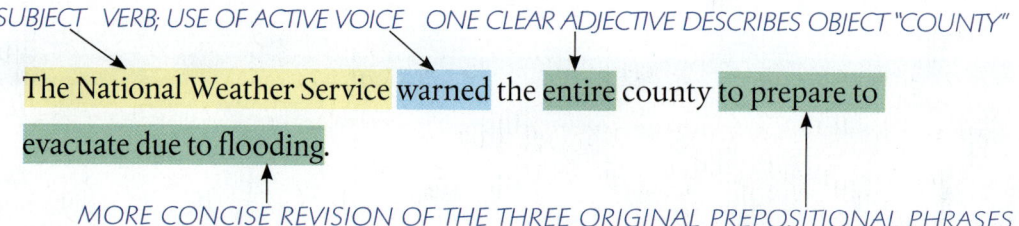

*Mark Twain (Samuel L. Clemens). George Bainton, *The Art of Authorship*, pp. 87–88 (1890).

Wordy Expressions with Revisions for Conciseness

Wordy	Concise
absolutely certain	certain
advanced notice	notice
has the ability	can
he is a man who; she is a woman who	he; she
disappear from view	disappear
during the same time that	when
given the fact that	because
in an impatient manner	impatiently
in order to	to
in spite of the fact	although, though
in this day and age	today
in today's world	today, currently
personal opinion	opinion
personally, I think	I think
reason why is that	because
red in color	red
refer back	refer
repeat again	repeat
small in size	small
summarize briefly	summarize
there is no doubt but that	no doubt, doubtless
the fact that she had not succeeded	her failure
this is a topic which	this topic
very unique	unique
whole entire	whole; entire

USE CONCISE LANGUAGE

Read each sentence and revise it using concise language.

1. A lake in southern Chile mysteriously disappeared from view.

2. The disappearance of a lake five acres in size is a situation that is puzzling in nature.

3. In March, the lake was exactly the same level as it had always been; by May the whole entire lake had vanished.

4. A river that flowed out of the lake was reduced to a trickle during the same time the lake vanished.

5. The lake probably disappeared due to the fact that an earth tremor opened a crack in the ground that acted like a drain.

6. There is no doubt but that amazing natural occurrences exist in today's world.

7. The organization The Seven Natural Wonders polled the personal opinions of experts to identify the most unique natural wonders in the whole entire world.

8. Personally, I think the most amazing natural event is the aurora borealis, also known as the Northern Lights.

9. The Grand Canyon has the ability to amaze visitors with its large in size scope and range of reds and browns in color.

10. This is a topic, The Natural Wonders of the World, which should demand our attention in this day and age in order to protect these wonders from disappearing from view.

Use Active and Positive Language

The most effective writing uses active, positive language to state ideas. The **active voice** states what somebody or something did. The **passive voice** states what was done to someone or something. Sentences written in the active voice are more concise because the active voice uses fewer words to state an action, and it clearly states the relationship between the subject and the action. In contrast, the passive voice uses more words to state an action, and the relationship between the subject and the action is less clear. The active voice is more direct and more powerful than the passive voice.

Passive Voice

THE SUBJECT "ANNA" RECEIVES THE ACTION PERFORMED BY SOMEONE ELSE.

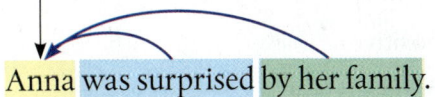

Anna was surprised by her family.

Active Voice

THE SUBJECT "FAMILY" PERFORMS THE ACTION.

Anna's family surprised her.

Effective writing also involves stating ideas in a positive voice, which is more powerful than stating them in a negative voice. Too often, the use of a negative expression makes language seem unclear. The following chart offers some tips and examples for creating positive language.

Tips for Creating a Positive Voice
• Say what something **is** instead of what it **is not**. *Negative:* The diet does not allow you to eat as much as you want of such favorites as sweets, chips, and fried foods. *Positive:* The diet allows you to eat your favorite foods in moderate amounts.
• Say what **can** be done instead of what **cannot** or **should not** be done. *Negative:* Bridget should not consider auditioning for the singing competition because she has never sung in front of an audience. *Positive:* Bridget can practice singing in front of friends and family to get used to singing in front of an audience; she will then be better prepared for the audition.
• Propose an **action** in addition to offering an **apology** or **explanation**. *Negative:* I'm sorry I didn't call last night, but what do you expect? I worked all day and had school until 9:00 p.m. *Positive:* I'm sorry I didn't call last night, but I was feeling overwhelmed with school and work. Perhaps we can meet for coffee when my schedule is less hectic.

The following chart lists a few examples of negative expressions in one column and positive revisions to those expressions in the other column.

Examples of Negative Expressions with Revisions to the Positive	
Negative Expression	**Positive Expression**
cannot lie	must tell the truth
cannot reconnect without	reconnect by
cannot waste resources	value resources
do not forget	remember
do not be late	be on time
do not be negative	be positive
never delay a response	respond quickly
never be rude	be polite
sorry, we cannot respond until	we will respond by
you misunderstood	let me clarify

Practice 3

USE ACTIVE AND POSITIVE LANGUAGE

Revise these sentences from passive voice to active voice or from negative statements to positive statements. Share and discuss your answers with a peer or your class.

1. Severe weather warnings must not be taken lightly by the public.

2. Severe weather alerts are issued by the National Weather Service (NWS), yet many do not pay attention to these official warnings.

3. No one in the warning zone of a weather alert is free from danger.

4. Minor flooding, moderate flooding, and major flooding are used by the NWS as flood severity categories.

5. Latrelle should not go out in the boat today because of the storm warnings.

6. The speed limit for boats on the Tomoka River does not allow boaters to go faster than 25 miles per hour.

7. Latrelle does not forget to equip his boat with life vests as required by law.

8. Many boaters are ticketed and fined by boat patrols for speeding, intoxication, and lack of safety gear.

9. Weather is unpredictable; lives are saved by life vests, so weather alerts and safety rules must be respected.

10. Write a sentence that uses active, positive language. Suggested topic: An alert or warning.

Use Concrete Language

Another key to effective writing is using **concrete language**. When writers use concrete language, they give readers vivid descriptions that can be visualized. Concrete language is the result of the thoughtful choice of nouns, verbs, adjectives, and adverbs. Your choice of words can mean the difference between writing that is **abstract** (vague, nonspecific writing) and writing that is concrete. Let's look at the difference between abstract and concrete nouns, verbs, adjectives, and adverbs.

An **abstract noun** names an emotion, feeling, idea, or trait detached from the five senses. A **concrete noun** names an animal, person, place, or object that the reader can see, touch, taste, hear, or smell (sensory details). The following chart illustrates the difference between concrete and abstract nouns.

Abstract Noun	Concrete Noun
beauty	rainbow
love	kiss
strength	steel
work	sweaty

An **abstract verb** or verb phrase tells about a state of being or describes a general or nonspecific action. A **concrete verb** or verb phrase shows a specific action or creates a clear picture for the reader. The following chart illustrates the difference between abstract and concrete verbs and verb phrases.

Abstract Verb	Concrete Verb
He is angry.	He spews curses.
I got an "A" on the exam.	I earned an "A" on the exam.
Jerome went in the room.	Jerome walked into the room.
Jerome went, "Hey."	Jerome said, "Hi."

An **abstract adjective** is a broad and general description that is open to interpretation based on opinion. A **concrete adjective** shows a specific trait or sensory detail and is not open to interpretation. The best writing relies on the strength of concrete nouns and verbs, so use adverbs only when necessary.

Abstract Adjective	Concrete Adjective
awesome sound	echoing canyon
good taste	salty ocean
weird behavior	quiet disposition
loud music	heavy-metal concert

An **abstract adverb** is a broad and general description that is open to interpretation based on opinion. A **concrete adverb** shows a specific trait or sensory detail and is not open to interpretation. The best writing relies on the strength of concrete nouns and verbs, so use adverbs only when necessary.

Abstract Adverb	Concrete Adverb
a lot	daily
kind of	quietly
sort of	gently
pretty much	most
really	intensely
very	extremely

USE CONCRETE LANGUAGE

Revise these sentences from abstract language to concrete language. Share and discuss your answers with a peer or your class.

▲ Lake Tahoe

1. Pretty much all of us go to Lake Tahoe a lot.

2. Lake Tahoe is a beautiful place that we really enjoy visiting.

3. The children have a wonderful time and a lot of fun in the water.

4. It feels really good to get some rest on the beach.

5. We worked hard to get up the North Canyon, but the beautiful view was worth the work.

6. We went on sort of long horseback rides around some trails with guides pretty much every day.

7. We saw a lot of wildlife and enjoyed the fantastic sounds of nature.

8. Our whole family really wants to go back.

Practice 4

9. Sandy went, "I love the beauty of Lake Tahoe."

_____
_____

10. Write a sentence that uses concrete language. Suggested topic: A favorite vacation spot.

_____
_____

L5 Use Creative Expressions: Similes and Metaphors

Creative expressions deepen the reader's understanding of a writer's meaning. Similes and metaphors are two ways you can include creative expression in your writing. Similes and metaphors are figures of speech that compare two unrelated ideas.

A **simile** is a comparison between two ideas that uses *like, as, as if,* or *as though.*

"LIKE" CREATES A COMPARISON OF TWO NOUNS/IDEAS

"I put my hands in the pockets and flapped the jacket like a bird's wings."

—Gary Soto, "The Jacket"

A **metaphor** is a comparison between two ideas that does **not** use *like, as, as if,* or *as though.*

"OF" CREATES A COMPARISON OF TWO NOUNS/IDEAS

"I returned to the sea of necessity."

—E. B. White, "The Sea and the Wind that Blows"

HELPING VERB "IS" CREATES A COMPARISON OF TWO NOUNS/IDEAS

"Poverty is an acid that drips on pride until all pride is worn away."

—Jo Goodwin Parker, "What is Poverty?"

Note: In the last two examples, the writers clarified or deepened the meaning of an abstract noun by connecting it to a concrete noun. To create similes and metaphors, make a logical connection between an abstract noun and a concrete noun.

Practice 5

USE CREATIVE EXPRESSIONS

The following list features metaphors and similes created by famous authors. Identify each as **M** for metaphor or **S** for Simile.

1. _____ "Shall I compare thee to a summer's day? Thou art more lovely and more temperate."
—William Shakespeare, *Sonnet 18*.

2. _____ "I am the Good Shepherd . . . I lay down my life for the sheep." —Jesus, *The Bible*, John 10: 14–15.

3. _____ "He was like a cock who thought the sun had risen to hear him crow."
—George Eliot, *Adam Bede*, 1859.

4. _____ "Curley was flopping like a fish on a line." —John Steinbeck, *Of Mice and Men*, 1937.

5. _____ "Dying is a wild night and a new road." —Emily Dickinson, 1830–1886.

6. _____ "A good conscience is a continual Christmas." —Benjamin Franklin, 1706–1790.

7. _____ "Conscience is a man's compass." —Vincent Van Gogh, 1853–1890.

8. _____ "Oh my love is like a red, red rose." —Robert Burns, 1794.

9. _____ "Advertising is the rattling of a stick inside a swill bucket." —George Orwell, 1903–1950.

10. Write a sentence that uses a simile or metaphor. Suggested topic: A lifelong goal.

_____

_____

Use Fresh Language

Effective writing also relies on using fresh language as opposed to clichés. Clichés are weak statements because they have lost their originality and forcefulness. See the example below.

Cliché:

OVERUSED NOUN PHRASE TO REPRESENT NATURE   OVERUSED PHRASE TO DESCRIBE SNOWY WEATHER

Mother Nature covered the ground with a snowy white blanket.

Fresh Language:

STRONG, ORIGINAL NOUNS AND ADJECTIVES DESCRIBE SNOWY WEATHER IN VIVID DETAIL

"On top of this ice were as many feet of snow. It was all pure white, rolling in gentle undulations where the ice-jams of the freeze-up had formed."

—Jack London, "To Build a Fire"

The following chart lists popular clichés and their meanings.

Clichés and Their Meanings	
Cliché	**Meaning**
a needle in a haystack	hard to find
all thumbs	clumsy
as easy as pie	easy
beat around the bush	to speak indirectly about something
backstabber	an untrustworthy or deceitful person
busy as a bee	always working, very busy
drop the ball	to fail at a task
fall between the cracks	overlooked, not attended to
fit to be tied	angry
hidden agenda	sneaky
hit the nail on the head	to be correct about something
like a bull in china shop	tactless, clumsy
like a chicken with its head cut off	inefficient, erratic
never a dull moment	exciting
off your rocker	crazy, poor judgment
one foot in the grave	terminally ill
one in a million	rare; well-liked
splitting hairs	focusing on unimportant details
wishy-washy	lack of conviction, unclear
water over the dam	a past event that cannot be changed

Instead of relying on clichés such as the ones presented here, use fresh language as you revise your writing. When logical, create your own similes and metaphors to express your meaning.

Practice 6

USE FRESH LANGUAGE

Revise the following sentences by eliminating clichés and replacing them with fresh, creative language. Share and discuss your answers with a peer or your class.

1. The money Nyeeta won at the Las Vegas casino was burning a hole in her pocket.

2. Although she just lost her job at the factory, Stacey believed there was light at the end of the tunnel.

Practice 6

3. When Tony turned 50, he felt over the hill.

4. Rochelle's new position at the hospital kept her busy as a bee.

5. Risa boasted that changing a tire was as easy as pie but she was all thumbs and needed help.

Practice 7

REVISING FOR EFFECTIVE EXPRESSION: CHAPTER REVIEW

Revise the following sentences for effective expression. Remember to use the key ingredients of effective expression—concise, active, positive, concrete, creative, and fresh language.

1. Jamal is absolutely certain that he can afford a new car given the fact that he has a job and money in savings.

2. We must never forget the attacks of September 11, 2001, and the loss of 2,996 lives.

3. Maria is kind of sick with a cold.

4. This winter is something else.

5. Jules hit the nail on the head when he said Justin was a bull in a china shop.

Editing Assignments

MyWritingLab™
Complete this Exercise on mywritinglab.com

Editing for Everyday Life

Assume you are writing a thank-you letter for a graduation gift you received from a relative. Revise this letter using effective expression.

> Dear Grandfather,
>
> Thank you for the wallet and money I got from you. I personally think that you are a man who is very generous and thoughtful. I am as happy as a lark with my new wallet, and the hundred dollars you put inside it made my day. I have always been supported by you. I am filled with gratitude.

Editing for College Life

Assume you are taking a sociology class and you are studying current events. You are required to write a paragraph discussing the impact on society of a new technological invention. Revise this draft for effective expression.

> The "brain-machine interface" has been developed by Hitachi, Inc. This development has the ability to totally change the way we use technology. The device can be controlled by brain activity, so you don't have to lift a finger to make anything happen. Slight changes in the brain's blood flow are analyzed, and the brain motion is converted to electrical signals. To demonstrate, a reporter was given a cap to wear that was also connected with optical fibers to a toy train. When she did simple math in her head, the train moved. A TV remote controller is being developed by Hitachi's scientists. Soon we may be able to turn on any electrical device with a simple thought.

Editing for Working Life

Assume you are working at an entry-level position for a firm that offers opportunities for advancement. You need to schedule a week off for personal reasons. Revise the following memo using effective expression. Use your own paper.

> To: Mr. Gordon
>
> From: Raul Estevez
>
> RE: Request for Personal Leave
>
> I am writing you to request personal leave due to the fact that surgery must be performed on my knee that will require a week's recovery time. I wanted to give you advanced notice given the fact that we are short on staff, but I absolutely must be off on the days of July 1 through July 8.

Academic Learning Log: Chapter Review

WHAT HAVE I LEARNED ABOUT USING EFFECTIVE EXPRESSION?

To test and track your understanding, answer the following questions.

1. The most effective writing is _____ and to the point.

2. _____ avoids wordiness.

3. _____ is the use of unnecessary or redundant words and phrases that add nothing to the writer's meaning.

4. The _____ voice states what somebody or something did.

5. The _____ voice states what was done to somebody or something.

6. Stating ideas in the _____ is much more powerful than stating them in the _____.

7. _____ language is the result of the thoughtful choice of nouns, verbs, adjectives, and adverbs.

8. A _____ is a comparison between two apparently unrelated ideas using *like* or *as*.

9. A _____ is a comparison between two apparently unrelated ideas.

10. A _____ is a trite or overused expression.

11. **How will I use what I have learned about effective expression?**
    In your notebook, discuss how you will apply to your own writing what you have learned about effective expression. When during the writing process will you apply this knowledge?

12. **What do I still need to study about effective expression?**
    In your notebook, discuss your ongoing study needs by describing what, when, and how you will continue studying effective expression.

MyWritingLab™

Complete the Post-test for Chapter 29 in MyWritingLab.

30 The Comma

LEARNING OUTCOMES

After studying this chapter you will be able to:

- **L1** Answer the Question "What's the Point of Commas?"
- **L2** Use Commas with Items in a Series
- **L3** Use Commas with Introductory Elements
- **L4** Use Commas to Join Independent Clauses
- **L5** Use Commas with Parenthetical Ideas
- **L6** Use Commas with Nonessential and Essential Clauses
- **L7** Use Commas with Appositives
- **L8** Use Commas with Dates and Addresses
- **L9** Identify Other Uses of the Comma

A comma is a valuable, useful punctuation device because it separates the structural elements of a sentence into manageable segments.

Misuse of the comma ranks as one of the most common errors in punctuation. Thinking about a real-life situation helps us to understand the purpose of commas in our communication. Complete the following activity and answer the question "What's the point of commas?"

What's the Point of Commas?

PHOTOGRAPHIC ORGANIZER: COMMAS

Assume you are working with a civic group to educate the public about the effects of pollution and the need for clean fuels. You have written the following paragraph to post on the group's Web blog. This draft does not include any commas. As you read the paragraph, think about where and why commas are needed.

Clean Fuel: Energy Crops

(1) To live is to pollute or so it seems. (2) From the Pacific trash vortex to the weekly landfill collection to the fumes that our cars emit daily it seems almost impossible to live without polluting our water land and air. (3) But what if it could be different? (4) What if we as a country became oil independent and plant dependent like energy vegetarians? (5) Energy dependence on oil is crude archaic and best left in the past with the dinosaurs! (6) Energy crops are the future! (7) Energy crops are plants that can be used to make biofuels. (8) These crops can be grown quickly densely and on land unusable for growing other crops. (9) Investing in biofuels also creates jobs. (10) The more we use biofuels the faster we help our country become energy independent.

What's the point of commas?

_____

_____

Adapted from "Ceres: Making Biofuels Bigger and Better," February 15, 2013, U.S. Department of Energy Website, http://energy.gov/articles/ceres-making-biofuels-bigger-and-better September, 18, 2015.

One Student Writer's Response

The following paragraph offers one writer's reaction to the paragraph "Clean Fuel: Energy Crops."

> The paragraph "Clean Fuel: Energy Crops" was confusing. I had to reread several sentences to make sense of what the writer was saying. One sentence that confused me was "To live is to pollute or so it seems." Another confusing sentence was "From the Pacific trash vortex to the weekly landfill collection to the fumes that our cars emit daily it seems almost impossible to live without polluting our water land and air." When I first read this sentence, my mind read "water land" as the name of something. It would help to put a comma between "water" and "land" Now that I think about it, I guess, commas keep a reader from getting confused.

The primary purpose of the **comma** is to make a sentence easy to read by indicating a brief pause between parts of the sentence that need to be separated.

L2 Use Commas with Items in a Series

Use commas to separate a **series of items** in a list. A series of items in a list can be **three** or more words, phrases, or clauses. In addition, a series of items can be made up of subjects, verbs, adjectives, participles, and so on. Items in a series are parallel and equal in importance.

Series of Words

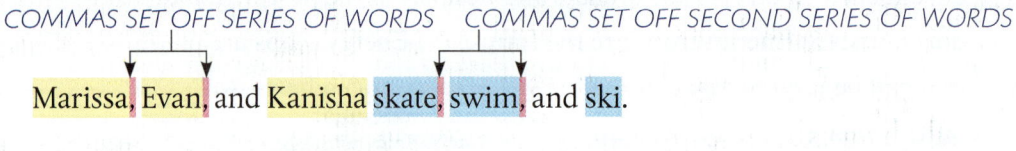

COMMAS SET OFF SERIES OF WORDS   COMMAS SET OFF SECOND SERIES OF WORDS

Marissa, Evan, and Kanisha skate, swim, and ski.

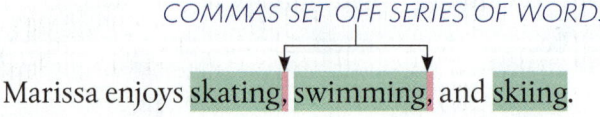

COMMAS SET OFF SERIES OF WORDS

Marissa enjoys skating, swimming, and skiing.

Series of Phrases

COMMAS SET OFF SERIES OF PHRASES

Marissa likes to skate, to swim, and to ski.

> For more information about parallel structure, see pages 524–537, "Parallelism."

Series of Clauses

COMMAS SET OFF SERIES OF CLAUSES

Marissa is one who trains hard, who eats well, and who wins often.

Note: Journalists for newspapers and magazines often omit the comma before the coordinating conjunction that joins the last item in the series; however, in academic writing, this comma, which is called the **serial comma**, is usually included.

Use Commas with Introductory Elements

Use commas to set off the introductory element of a sentence. **Introductory elements** are ideas that appear at the beginning of a sentence. Introductory elements come before a main clause. Introductory elements can be a word, phrase, or clause.

- An introductory element—a word, phrase, or clause—that precedes an independent (or main) clause must be followed by a comma.

Introductory Word

COMMA SETS OFF INTRODUCTORY WORD

Overall, good health is achieved through wise choices.

Introductory Phrase

COMMA SETS OFF INTRODUCTORY PHRASE

To achieve good health, one should exercise on a regular basis.

Introductory Dependent Clause

COMMA SETS OFF INTRODUCTORY DEPENDENT CLAUSE

As Maria increased her physical activity, her sense of well-being improved.

Use Commas to Join Independent Clauses

Use a comma with a coordinating conjunction to join two or more equally important and logically related independent clauses. An **independent clause** is a complete thought or sentence. To join sentences with a coordinating conjunction, place the comma before the conjunction. The acronym **FANBOYS** identifies the seven coordinating conjunctions: *for, and, nor, but, or, yet,* and *so*. The following chart lists these conjunctions and the logical relationships they establish between ideas.

Coordinating Conjunctions and the Relationships They Establish: **FANBOYS**						
For	**A**nd	**N**or	**B**ut	**O**r	**Y**et	**S**o
reason, result	addition	negation	contrast	choice, condition, possibility	contrast	addition, result

- Place a comma *before* the coordinating conjunction that joins independent clauses.

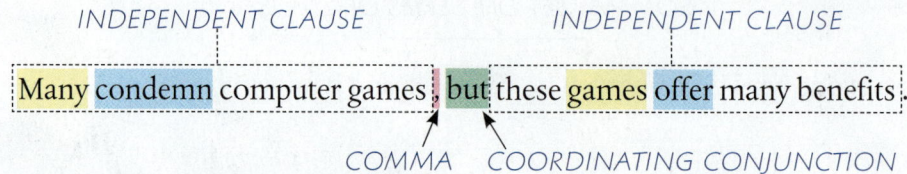

L5 Use Commas with Parenthetical Ideas

A **parenthetical idea** interrupts a sentence with information that is **nonessential** to the meaning of the sentence. Such an idea could be enclosed in parentheses. However, more often, a comma comes before and after such an idea. These interruptions can be words, phrases, or clauses.

- Use commas to set off a parenthetical idea.

Parenthetical Word

COMMAS SET OFF PARENTHETICAL WORD

The demanding customer was, however, a generous tipper.

Parenthetical Phrase

COMMAS SET OFF PARENTHETICAL PHRASE

The polite customer, surprisingly heartless, left no tip.

Parenthetical Clause

COMMAS SET OFF PARENTHETICAL CLAUSE

Jennifer, who had been working a 12-hour shift, smiled at the sight of the generous tip.

Note: Two specific types of parenthetical ideas are the **nonessential clause** and the **nonessential appositive** (word or phrase). The uses and misuses of commas with these specific types of words, phrases, and clauses are discussed in greater detail in the next two sections.

L6 Use Commas with Nonessential and Essential Clauses

A parenthetical idea, the **nonessential clause**, offers additional and unnecessary information that does not change the meaning of the sentence. Often nonessential information appears in a relative clause introduced by the relative pronouns *who* or *which*. A nonessential relative clause gives information about a nearby noun.

- Use commas to set off a nonessential clause. Commas come before and after a nonessential clause that interrupts a sentence. A single comma sets off a nonessential clause at the end of a sentence.

NONESSENTIAL CLAUSE DESCRIBES MISHANDA

Mishanda, who is the mother of three, is a firefighter.

COMMAS SET OFF NONESSENTIAL CLAUSE

NONESSENTIAL CLAUSE DESCRIBES "FIRE STATION 92"

She works at Fire Station 92, which is located on Nova Road.

COMMAS SET OFF NONESSENTIAL CLAUSE

An **essential clause** also offers information about a nearby noun, but by contrast with a nonessential clause, it restricts or limits the meaning of a nearby noun and is necessary to the meaning of the sentence. The following examples illustrate the differences between an essential and a nonessential clause.

- Essential clauses should not be set off with commas.

Essential Clause

ESSENTIAL CLAUSE LIMITS THE MEANING OF SUBJECT "ACTOR" BY IDENTIFYING THE SPECIFIC ACTOR BEING REFERRED TO

The actor who drove drunk at speeds up to 107 mph was arrested.

NO COMMAS NEEDED BEFORE AND AFTER ESSENTIAL CLAUSE

Nonessential Clause

NONESSENTIAL CLAUSE GIVES EXTRA INFORMATION ABOUT SUBJECT "SETH GILLIAM"

Seth Gilliam, who drove drunk at speeds up to 107 mph, was arrested.

COMMAS SET OFF NONESSENTIAL CLAUSE

Use Commas with Appositives

Use commas to set off an appositive. An **appositive** is a word or phrase that renames a nearby noun.

An **essential appositive** restricts or limits the meaning of a nearby noun and is necessary to the meaning of the sentence. Essential appositives should not be set off with commas. The following examples show the differences between an essential and a nonessential appositive.

Essential Appositive

NO COMMAS NEEDED BEFORE AND AFTER ESSENTIAL APPOSITIVE

The actor Chris Evans plays Captain America.

As a parenthetical idea, a **nonessential appositive** offers information that could be left out without changing the meaning of the sentence. A comma comes before and after a nonessential appositive when it interrupts an idea. A single comma sets off a nonessential appositive at the end of a sentence.

Nonessential Appositive

COMMAS SET OFF NONESSENTIAL APPOSITIVE RENAMING NOUN

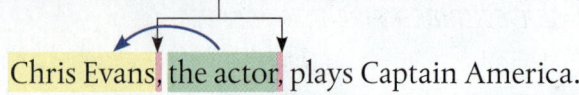

Chris Evans, the actor, plays Captain America.

COMMA SETS OFF NONESSENTIAL APPOSITIVE DESCRIBING NOUN

Justine enjoys dining at Le Hut, a local eatery.

L8 Use Commas with Dates and Addresses

Use commas to set off information in dates and addresses. When a date or address is made up of two or more parts, a comma separates the parts. When the parts of a date are both words or are both numbers, a comma separates the parts. And a comma follows the last item unless it is the final detail of a list or sentence.

- **Place commas after the day and year of a date.**

  Barack H. Obama was born on August 4, 1961, to middle-class parents.

- **When writing the day and the date, place a comma after the day.**

  Obama became the 44th President on Tuesday, November 4, 2008, in Washington.

- **Place commas after the street name, town or city, and state of an address.**

  All presidents reside at 1600 Pennsylvania Avenue, Washington, DC, during their terms.

- **Set off two or more geographical names with a comma.**

  Obama was born in Honolulu, Hawaii, and is a graduate of Harvard Law School.

L9 Identify Other Uses of the Comma

Commas are also used in two additional ways.

1. Use commas to separate consecutive coordinate adjectives of equal importance. **Coordinate adjectives** are a series or two or more adjectives that could be arranged in any order or could be strung together with the word *and*. They each modify the noun directly. By contrast, **cumulative adjectives** are a series of two or more adjectives that accumulate before a noun, with each adjective modifying the adjectives that follow. Cumulative adjectives must follow a certain order to make sense. Commas should not be used with cumulative adjectives.

2. Use commas to set off direct speech.

- **Commas between consecutive coordinate adjectives:** Use two questions to determine whether adjectives are coordinate.
   A. Can the word *and* be smoothly placed between the adjectives?
   B. Can the order of the adjectives be reversed?

If the answer is *yes* to either of these questions, then separate these coordinate adjectives with a comma.

Use Commas with Coordinate Adjectives

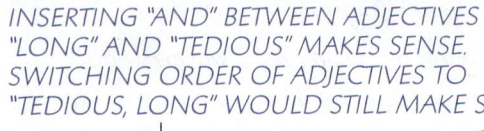

For more information about the proper sequence of cumulative adjectives, see pages 353–354, "Adjectives and Adverbs."

Do Not Use Commas with Cumulative Adjectives

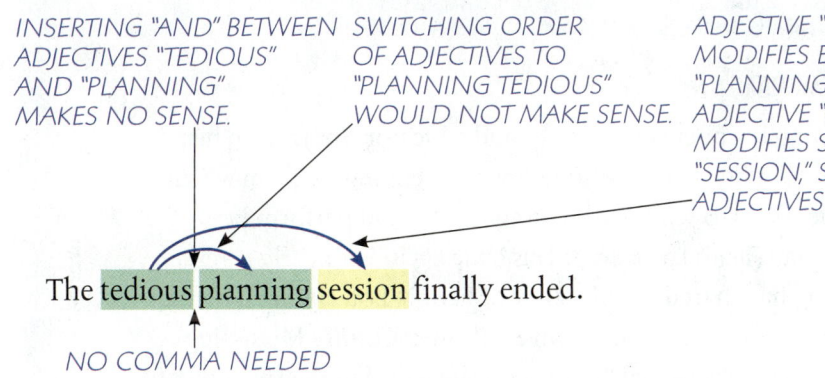

- **Commas after a verb that introduces a quotation:** The comma is used to set off the "said" clause, called the speech tag, and the comma is placed before the quoted information.

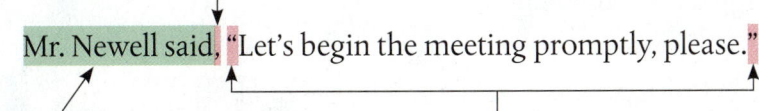

For more information about proper use of quotation marks, see pages 572–581, "Quotation Marks."

Editing Assignments

> MyWritingLab™
> Complete this Exercise on mywritinglab.com

Editing for Everyday Life

Assume you have been struggling with sleep issues, and you have decided to write and post your feelings about your experience on a blog about sleep disorders. Proofread and edit the posting to ensure appropriate use of commas.

Dreams! I have them too. They plague me nightly. They swarm in on me as soon as I fall asleep and relentlessly tear through my mind until I wake. Always they are of pain loss suffering and violence. They often feature those people who are in my life. The cast is an unpredictable rotation through the night or from one night to the next. Because of them there is no rest in my sleep.

Editing for College Life

Assume your government professor has asked you to write a one-paragraph report about a local person who takes an active role in civic life. Proofread and edit the report to ensure appropriate use of commas.

Billie Jean Young

Billie Jean Young is a poet actor activist and educator. She lives in her rural Choctaw County Alabama hometown of Pennington from which she travels the world to work with young people and perform her one-woman play *Fannie Lou Hamer: This Little Light*. For nearly three decades Young has shared the life story of Fannie Lou Hamer a human rights activist and sharecropper from Sunflower County Mississippi. Billie Jean Young seeks to make change in the world in the spirit of Fannie Lou Hamer.

Editing for Working Life

Assume you have written a letter of recommendation. Proofread and edit the letter to ensure appropriate use of commas.

Dear Ms. Brown:

As you requested I am sending you this written recommendation to hire Sophia Larson as a full-time dental hygienist. Ms. Larson who has worked in our office for five years is a highly skilled personable hygienist. In addition you will find her to be an excellent educator advocate and manager. Ms. Larson a licensed clinician has 15 years of experience. I offer my strongest recommendation on behalf of Sophia Larson.

Sincerely,

Winston Ferrell

Academic Learning Log: Chapter Review

WHAT HAVE I LEARNED ABOUT COMMAS?

To test and track your understanding, answer the following questions.

1. Use commas to separate a series of items in a list; a series of items in a list can be _____ or more words, phrases, or clauses.

2. Use commas to set off the _____ elements, ideas that appear at the beginning of a sentence.

3. Use commas in union with a coordinating conjunction to create a _____ sentence, which is a sentence made up of two or more independent clauses.

4. Use a pair of commas to set off a _____ idea, which is an idea that interrupts a sentence.

5. Use commas to set off a nonessential clause; often nonessential information appears in a relative clause introduced by _____ or _____.

6. Use commas for appositives, words or phrases that _____ nouns.

7. When a date or address is made up of _____ parts, use a comma to separate the parts.

8. Use commas between _____ adjectives.

9. Use a comma _____ a verb that introduces a quotation.

10. In your notebook, answer the following questions: How will I use what I have learned about commas? What do I still need to study about commas?

MyWritingLab™

Complete the Post-test for Chapter 30 in MyWritingLab.

31 The Apostrophe

PART 7 PUNCTUATION AND MECHANICS

LEARNING OUTCOMES

After studying this chapter you will be able to

L1 Answer the Question "What's the Point of the Apostrophe?"

L2 Use the Apostrophe to Show Ownership

L3 Use the Apostrophe to Form Contractions

L4 Recognize Common Misuses of the Apostrophe

The apostrophe is used to show ownership and to form contractions by replacing omitted letters or numbers.

Thinking about a real-life situation helps us to understand the purpose of the apostrophe in our writing. Complete the following activity and answer the question "What's the point of the apostrophe?"

What's the Point of the Apostrophe?

PHOTOGRAPHIC ORGANIZER: THE APOSTROPHE

Apostrophes are often used in signs for businesses and in highway billboards. For example, the signs depicted in these photographs illustrate two different uses of the apostrophe. Study the signs shown in the photographs on pages 564–565 and explain why an apostrophe was used in each one.

WRITING FROM LIFE

What's the point of apostrophes?

One Student Writer's Response

The following paragraph offers one writer's reaction to the pictures that use apostrophes.

> The sign for the trading post uses an apostrophe to show that Tanner owns the trading post. The sign about Oklahoma City uses an apostrophe to shorten a word. Some letters are left out of the word "national."

An **apostrophe** is used for two general purposes:

- To show ownership
- To form contractions

The apostrophe is often misused because words with apostrophes sound similar to other words, as in the following sentence:

INCORRECT USE OF APOSTROPHE

The cat loves it's toy mouse.

The use of the word *it's* in this sentence is incorrect because the contraction *it's* means *it is* or *it has*, as in the phrases *it's a shame* or *it's been a long time*. Instead, the correct word to use is the possessive pronoun *its* to state that the toy mouse belongs to the cat. Understanding the purposes of an apostrophe will help you reduce its misuse.

Use the Apostrophe to Show Ownership

The **possessive form** of a noun and some pronouns is created by using an apostrophe followed, at times, by an *-s*. The possessive tells the reader that someone or something owns or possesses the next stated thing.

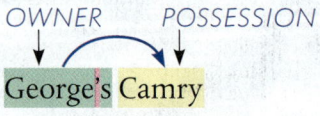
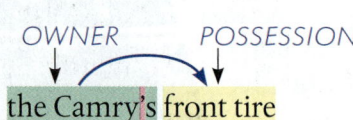

The following chart lists and illustrates the rules for using an apostrophe to show possession.

Using the Apostrophe for Ownership		
To Show Possession for	Correct Use of Apostrophe	Example
A singular noun	add 's	my husband's job Henry's car
A singular noun ending with -s	add 's *add '	the boss's memo James's home James' home
A regular plural noun ending with -s	add '	the writers' colony
An irregular plural noun	add 's	women's clothing
Compound words	add 's	vice president's speech sister-in-law's business (Note: Do not confuse the possessive form with the plural form, as in *sisters-in-law*)
Joint ownership of an item	add 's to the last noun	Abbott and Costello's comedy
Individual ownership	add 's to both nouns	Marco Rubio's and Jeb Bush's approaches to public speaking (Each person has his own approach.)
Indefinite pronouns ending with "one" or "body"	add 's	someone's computer

*It is also acceptable to add just an apostrophe for singular nouns ending with -s.

L3 Use the Apostrophe to Form Contractions

An apostrophe is used to indicate the omission of letters to form a *contraction*. Most often, a **contraction** is formed to join two words to make one shorter word such as *don't* for *do not*. However, sometimes an apostrophe is used to form a one-word contraction such as *ma'am* for *madam* and *gov't* for *government*. An apostrophe (') takes the place of the letter or letters that are dropped to form the contraction.

The use of contractions gives a piece of writing an informal tone that records on paper the way we speak in general conversation. Writing for college courses usually requires a formal, academic tone. Thus, many professors discourage the use of contractions. Check with your professors about the required tone of your writing assignments. To ensure proper use of the apostrophe, the following chart illustrates how contracted verbs are formed.

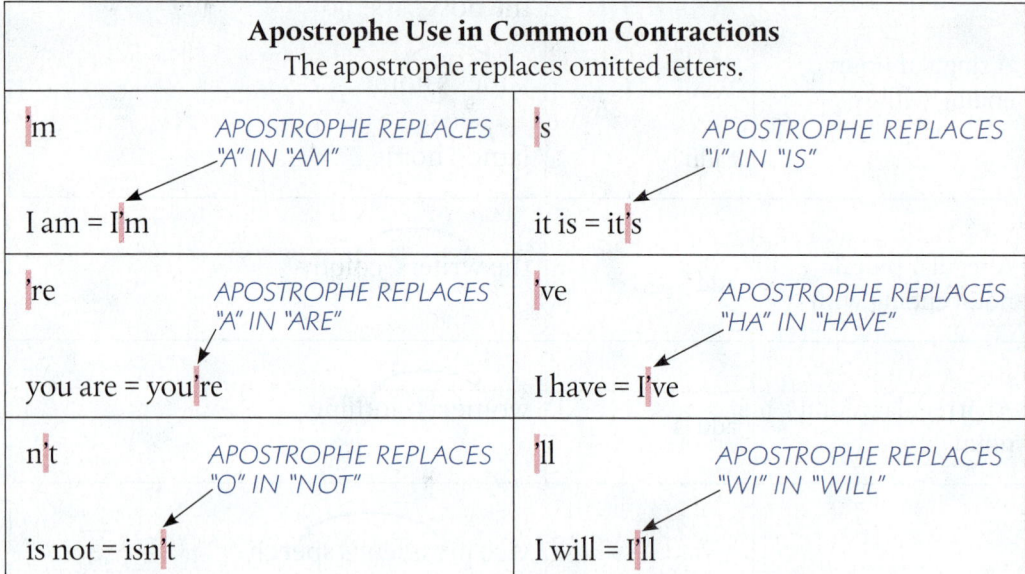

L4 Recognize Common Misuses of the Apostrophe

Quite often, the apostrophe is misused in several specific ways. The following chart lists and illustrates these common misuses of the apostrophe. Always base your use of an apostrophe on a specific rule. Proofread your writing for these common mistakes.

- Do not use an apostrophe to form a plural noun.

Correct Plural	Incorrect Plural
homes	home's
books	book's

- Do not use an apostrophe to form a possessive pronoun.

Correct	Incorrect
ours	our's
hers	her's
theirs	their's

- Do not omit the apostrophe to form the possessive indefinite pronoun.

Correct	Incorrect
one's	ones
everybody's	everybodys

- Do not confuse contractions with similar sounding words.

Contraction	Possessive Pronoun
it's (it is)	its
who's (who is)	whose
they're (they are)	their

Editing Assignments

MyWritingLab™ Complete this Exercise on mywritinglab.com

Editing for Everyday Life

Assume you have been having problems with a cell phone you just bought, and you are writing a letter of complaint to the manufacturer. Proofread and edit the body of the letter to ensure appropriate use of apostrophes.

Recently, I purchased the Diamond Phone your currently advertising. Im writing to express my disappointment with you're product. I no longer use my phone for several reasons. First, the callers voice sounds muffled, or I cant hear someones voice message because of an echo in the phone. Im also disappointed in the quality of pictures taken with this phones camera. Bright colors looked washed out, and the prints didnt look crisp. In addition, the devices video feature isnt working. Overall, its been a disappointing purchase!

Editing for College Life

Assume you have been required to write a one-paragraph summary about stress for your psychology class. Proofread and edit the paragraph to ensure appropriate use of apostrophes.

Human action takes place within a persons' life space. Forces or demands within the life space cause ones movement from activity to activity. An individuals motivation leads to many demands. However, a human beings resources often cant meet those demands, so a person feels the strain to perform. Stress is the normal reaction. Its harmful to well-being and results in negative feelings and behaviors. Examples of stressors range from tolerating a neighbors loud music to losing a loved one. A natural disasters' impact, like a major earthquake, is so vast that it's known as a cataclysmic event. Demands or stressors cause an individual to make adjustments. An individual whose stressed needs to develop coping behaviors.

Editing for Working Life

Assume you have been asked by a colleague to proofread her letter of resignation. Edit the letter to ensure appropriate use of apostrophes and to eliminate contractions.

218 Elm Drive
New Haven, GA 33215

Ms. Anna Rivers
Rivers Advertising Agency
2 Summit Drive
New Haven, GA 33215

July 6, 2015

Dear Ms. Rivers:

Id like to inform you that Im resigning from my position as an office assistant for the Rivers Advertising Agency, effective August 1. Ill be starting as Alcott Companys office manager in September. Thank you for the opportunities that you have provided me during the last five years. Ive enjoyed working for yourre agency and appreciate the support provided me during my time with the company. Even though I will miss my colleagues, Im looking forward to this new challenge and to starting a new phase of my career. If I can be of any help during this transition, please dont hesitate to let me know.

Sincerely,

John Olarte

Academic Learning Log: Chapter Review

WHAT HAVE I LEARNED ABOUT THE APOSTROPHE?

To test and track your understanding, answer the following questions.

1. What are two general purposes of an apostrophe?

    a. To show _____

    b. To form _____

2. What are four common misuses of the apostrophe to avoid?

    a. Using apostrophes to form _____

    b. Using apostrophes to form _____

    c. _____ to form possessive indefinite pronouns

    d. Confusing contractions with _____

3. **How will I use what I have learned about the apostrophe?**
   In your notebook, discuss how you will apply to your own writing what you have learned about the apostrophe.

4. **What do I still need to study about the apostrophe?**
   In your notebook, discuss your ongoing study needs by describing what, when, and how you will continue studying the apostrophe.

MyWritingLab™

Complete the Post-test for Chapter 31 in MyWritingLab.

32 Quotation Marks

PART 7 PUNCTUATION AND MECHANICS

LEARNING OUTCOMES

After studying this chapter you will be able to:

1. Answer the Question "What's the Point of Quotation Marks?"
2. Follow General Guidelines for Using Quotation Marks
3. Format and Punctuate Direct Quotations
4. Format and Punctuate Dialogue
5. Use Direct and Indirect Quotations
6. Punctuate Titles

Quotation marks are used to set off exact words either written or spoken by other people or to set off titles of short works.

Quotation marks help us to record the ideas of other people. Thinking about a real-life situation helps us to understand the purpose of quotation marks in our communication. Complete the following activity and answer the question "What's the point of quotation marks?"

What's the Point of Quotation Marks?

PHOTOGRAPHIC ORGANIZER: QUOTATION MARKS

Assume you are a fan of celebrity fitness trainer Bob Harper. You are researching his approach to physical fitness and weight loss. In your research, you have come across the following ideas. Use these ideas to test your current understanding of the use of quotation marks. Note the various correct ways to use quotation marks. Then, complete the survey about quotation marks that follows.

- Bob Harper is a coach on NBC's hit TV show *The Biggest Loser*.
- Bob Harper is the creator of the "Inside Out" method of weight loss.
- Bob tweets, "Make the commitment to live a healthier lifestyle . . . TODAY!"
- Bob tells his clients to challenge their minds, bodies, and spirits to lose weight.
- "Bob Harper," one of his fans declares, "is an inspiration to millions of people."

WRITING FROM LIFE

Survey about the Use of Quotation Marks: Mark each statement T for True or F for False.

_____ 1. Certain types of titles may be set off in quotation marks.

_____ 2. The exact words of a speaker are set off with a pair of quotation marks.

_____ 3. The end period of a sentence comes after a quotation mark.

_____ 4. A speech tag is a subject and verb that identifies a speaker.

_____ 5. Speech tags only appear in front of a quotation.

_____ 6. Commas appear inside quotation marks.

_____ 7. All ideas of others must be placed in quotation marks.

_____ 8. All titles are surrounded by quotation marks.

_____ 9. A quotation is the use of someone's exact words.

_____ 10. The title of a television show is not punctuated with quotation marks.

What's the point of quotation marks?

_____

_____

One Student Writer's Response

The following paragraph offers one writer's reaction to the survey about the use of quotation marks.

> Taking the survey about the use of quotation marks showed me what I know. For example, I marked #1 as true, but I'm not sure which types of titles use quotation marks. So the survey also shows me what I still need to learn about quotation marks. As another example, I said #7 was true, that all the ideas of other people had to be put in quotes, but it's not true. I want to know when exactly to use quotes and when not to. The survey also taught me some things too. For example, I didn't know what a speech tag was until I took the survey.

Use **quotation marks** (" ") to set off **direct quotes**—the exact words spoken by someone or quoted from another source—and for titles of short works. Always use quotation marks in pairs. The first quotation mark ("), also called the **opening quotation mark**, indicates the beginning of the quoted material. The second quotation mark ("), also called the **closing quotation mark**, indicates the end of the quoted material. Four general rules guide the use of quotation marks with other pieces of punctuation.

L2 Follow General Guidelines for Using Quotation Marks

1. Place commas (,) and periods (.) inside the quotation marks (" ").

   QUOTATION MARKS ENCLOSE EXACT WORDS OF THE JUSTICE DEPARTMENT

   According to a recent article, the Justice Department promised to "combat gangs and guns," lower crime rates, and help local police in crimes involving juveniles.

   COMMA GOES INSIDE QUOTATION MARK

   The article also said gangs contributed to "a nationwide crime spike."

   PERIOD GOES INSIDE QUOTATION MARK

2. Place semicolons (;) and colons (:) outside the quotation marks.

   We must say "no more violence"; we must strengthen gun control laws.

   SEMICOLON GOES OUTSIDE QUOTATION MARK

   There is one sure way we can say "no more violence": we can shut down violent media.

   COLON GOES OUTSIDE QUOTATION MARK

3. Place a question mark (?) inside quotation marks when it is part of the quotation. Place a question mark outside quotation marks when the larger sentence is a question, but the quotation included in it is not.

We should ask, "How does violence in movies and music affect youth?"

QUESTION MARK GOES INSIDE QUOTATION MARK BECAUSE IT IS PART OF THE QUOTATION. (THE QUOTATION IS A QUESTION.)

Did she really say "no more violence"?

QUESTION MARK GOES OUTSIDE QUOTATION MARK BECAUSE THE SENTENCE ITSELF IS A QUESTION, BUT THE QUOTATION INCLUDED IN IT IS NOT.

4. Use single quotation marks for quoted information—or titles of short works—that appear within direct quotation.

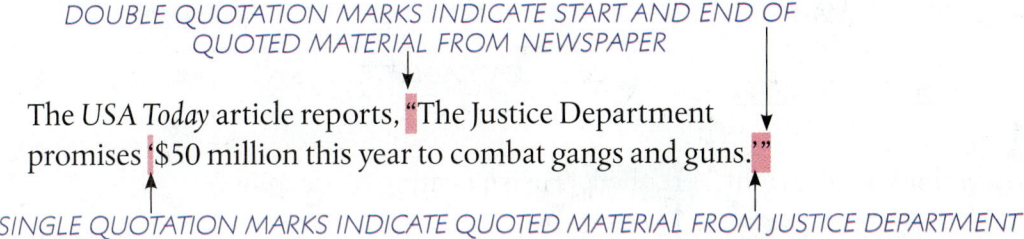

DOUBLE QUOTATION MARKS INDICATE START AND END OF QUOTED MATERIAL FROM NEWSPAPER

The USA Today article reports, "The Justice Department promises '$50 million this year to combat gangs and guns.'"

SINGLE QUOTATION MARKS INDICATE QUOTED MATERIAL FROM JUSTICE DEPARTMENT

Format and Punctuate Direct Quotations

One part of a direct quotation is the **speech tag** or the credit given to the source, the person who spoke or wrote an idea. A speech tag is formed by a subject (the speaker) and a verb that indicates the subject is speaking. The location of the speech tag affects the punctuation of a direct quotation. A speech tag can appear at the beginning, in the middle, or at the end of a quote. The following examples highlight the correct use of commas, periods, capitalization, and quotation marks based on the placement of the speech tag.

Punctuating Direct Quotations

• Speech tag at the beginning of quote

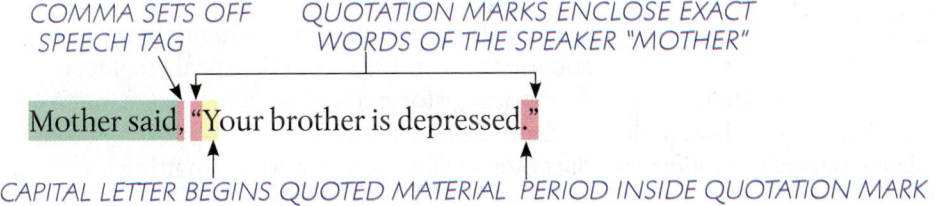

COMMA SETS OFF SPEECH TAG   QUOTATION MARKS ENCLOSE EXACT WORDS OF THE SPEAKER "MOTHER"

Mother said, "Your brother is depressed."

CAPITAL LETTER BEGINS QUOTED MATERIAL   PERIOD INSIDE QUOTATION MARK

- Speech tag in the middle of quote

(1) Quotation is stated in one sentence:

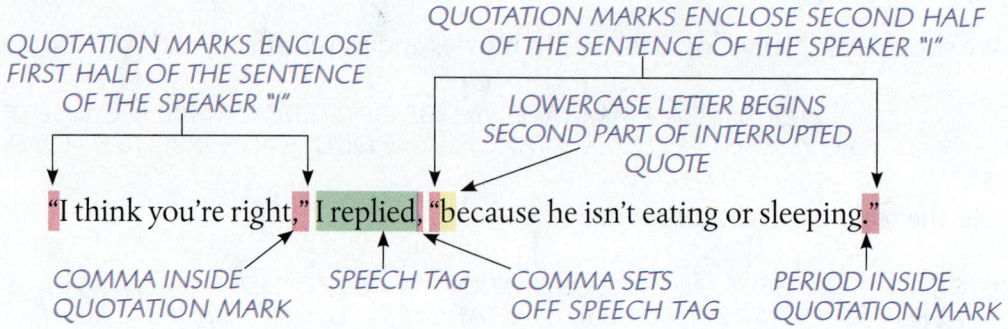

(2) Quotation is stated in two sentences:

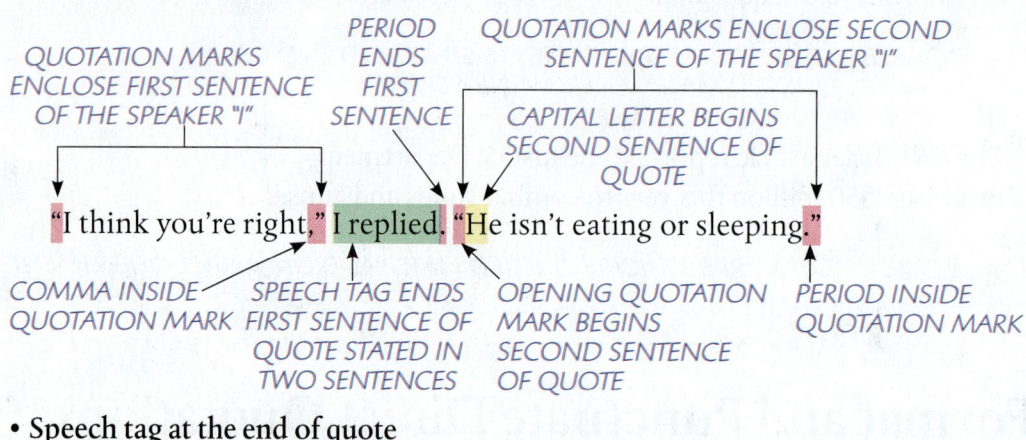

- Speech tag at the end of quote

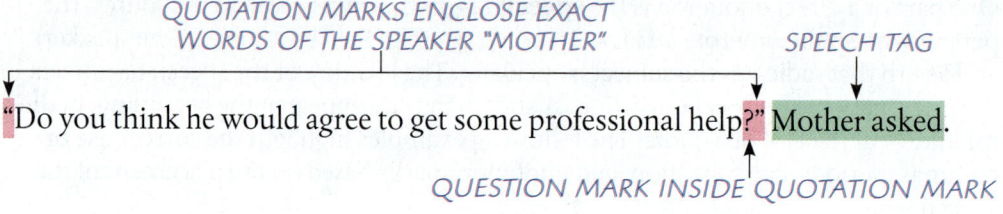

Format and Punctuate Dialogue

Including dialogue in a piece of writing adds interest, details, and authenticity. Dialogue conveys action, time, place, and the traits and values of the speakers. Most often, dialogue is associated with creative writing, storytelling, and journalism, but a well-crafted or carefully chosen piece of dialogue can also effectively support a point in an academic paper. The following chart offers a few basic tips for formatting and punctuating dialogue.

Tips for Formatting and Punctuating Dialogue
• Follow the formatting and punctuation rules for direct quotations.
• Use quotation marks to indicate a speaker's exact words.
• Use speech tags to make sure the reader knows who is speaking.
• Vary the placement of speech tags.
• Begin a new paragraph to change speakers; record each person's turn at speaking, no matter how brief, in a separate paragraph.
• When a speaker's speech is longer than one paragraph:
Begin the speech with a quotation mark.
Do not use a quotation mark at the end of the first paragraph or subsequent paragraphs.
Instead, begin each new paragraph in the speech with a quotation mark.
End the speech with a closing quotation mark at the end of the last paragraph.

Applying Appropriate Formatting

Note the ways in which a student taking a unit exam for a college communication class applies appropriate formatting and punctuation rules for writing dialogue.

Communication Unit Exam Study Question: *Define and illustrate the communication process.*

In his book *Interpersonal Communication*, Joseph DeVito states, "The communication process is made up of five phases: opening, feed-forward, business, feedback, and closing." The opening may be a greeting or a question. Feed-forward sets the tone and indicates the topic of conversation. Business is the core focus or goal of the conversation. Feedback is a summary of what has been said. Finally, closing is the goodbye. The following dialogue illustrates these five stages of communication.

"Hi, Summer, how are you?" Joe asked. ← *New paragraphs signal change in speakers.*

"Hey, Joe. I'm okay. How about you? What's up?" Summer replied. ← *Varied use of speech tag.*

"Well, I was wondering if I could see your notes from yesterday's class." Joe said. "I want to ace this next test."

"Yeah, it was a lot of information. Where were you anyway?" Summer asked.

"I was in a wreck!" Joe exclaimed. "I was driving down Williamson Boulevard and was going through an intersection. I had the green light. And this truck suddenly runs the red light and slams into me on the passenger's side. The impact spun me completely around. ← *No closing quotation mark because this one speech is two paragraphs long.*

"We had to wait about 30 minutes before the police arrived. Then I had to wait another hour before the tow truck showed up. By that time, class was over. My car is totaled, a complete loss. The other driver didn't even have insurance." ← *Quotation mark signals continued speech.* / *Quotation mark signals end of two-paragraph speech.*

"At least you weren't hurt. Here are my notes," Summer grinned.

"Thanks, Summer, I owe you one," Joe replied.

L5 Use Direct and Indirect Quotations

The spoken or printed words of other people are written in two ways: as a direct quotation or as an indirect quotation. So far, you have been learning about the **direct quotation**, which uses a pair of quotation marks to indicate someone else's exact words. In contrast, an **indirect quotation** rephrases or rewords what someone said or wrote. An indirect quotation is a **paraphrase** of someone else's words. Never use quotation marks with indirect quotations. To paraphrase a direct quotation into an indirect quotation, follow these steps:

> **How to Paraphrase a Direct Quote into an Indirect Quote**
>
> 1. Remove quotation marks and internal capital letters.
> 2. Add the word *that* to introduce the paraphrased idea.
> 3. Revise verbs into past tense, except for actions continuing in the present.
> 4. Revise verbs that command into their infinitive form; revise speech tag for sense.
> 5. Revise pronouns and signal words as needed.

Original Direct Quotation:

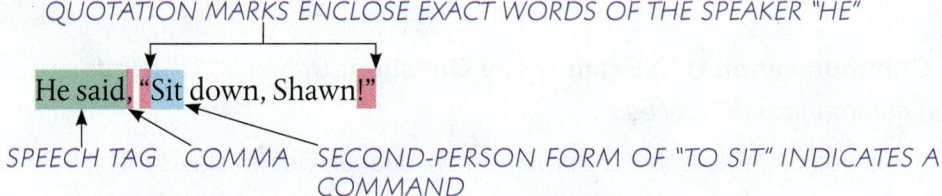

Revised Indirect Quotation:

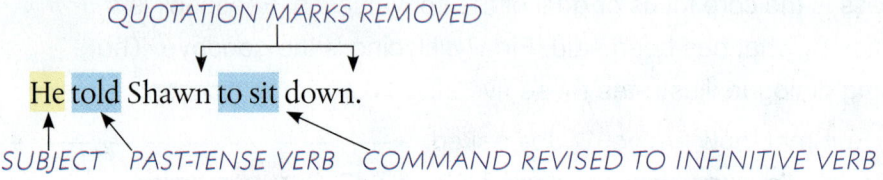

Original Direct Quotation:

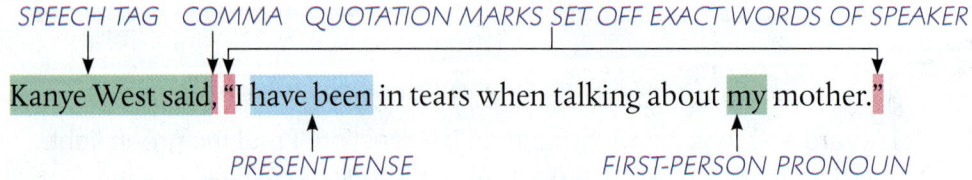

Indirect Quotation:

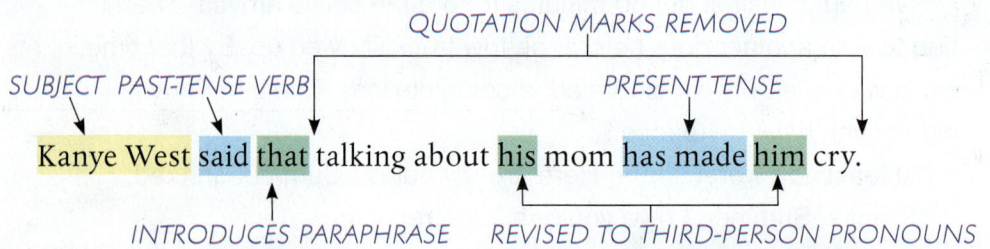

Punctuate Titles

Quotation marks are also used to set off the titles of short works such as essays, short stories, short poems, songs, articles in magazines, TV episodes, and chapter titles in books.

- Follow the general rules for using quotation marks.
- Do not use quotation marks to set off titles of larger publications such as magazines, newspapers, and books. These larger publications are set off with italics or, if you are writing by hand, underlining.

Poems

QUOTATION MARKS SET OFF POEM TITLE

You can go online to hear Sylvia Plath read her poem "Lady Lazarus."

Songs

QUOTATION MARKS SET OFF SONG TITLE

Pharrell Williams scored a big hit with the release of his single "Happy."

Television Shows

TV SHOW TITLE IN ITALICS

My favorite episode of the *Big Bang Theory* sitcom is "The Bakersfield Expedition."

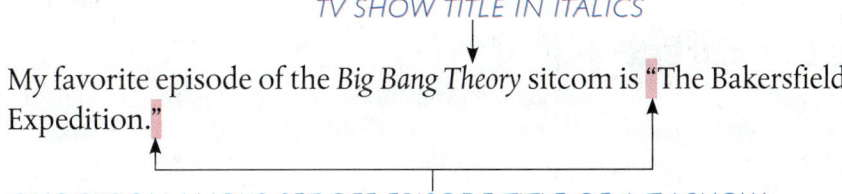

QUOTATION MARKS SET OFF EPISODE TITLE OF A TV SHOW

Editing Assignments

Editing for Everyday Life

Assume you have been in an automobile accident that is not your fault. The person who caused the accident denies that she is responsible. You have decided to make a written record of the event for your insurance company. Edit the following excerpt from the report. Insert quotation marks and other punctuation as needed. Use your own paper or complete this exercise on MyWritingLab.com.

> I was traveling north on Clyde Morris Avenue when I stopped for a red light. Once the light turned green, I began to accelerate and pulled out to cross over Highway 1. Suddenly, a 2006 white Ford pick-up truck slammed into the rear of the passenger's side of my 2011 Maxima. At the same time, my daughter cried out from the seat behind me, She ran a red light! The force of the impact sent me spinning. Before I could get out of my car, Roxanne DeVille, the driver who caused the accident, ran up to me. Are you all right? she asked. I am so sorry, she sobbed, because it's all my fault. I was trying to answer my cell phone and didn't notice the red light. I am so sorry!

Editing College Life

Assume you have written a summary paragraph about an article you read for a psychology course. Edit the paragraph. Insert quotation marks and other punctuation as needed. Use your own paper or complete this exercise on MyWritingLab.com.

> In the *Psychology Today* article How to Be Popular, Hara Estroff Marano talks about the eight traits that make people popular. Marano also argues that popularity is a trait that can be and should be learned. She writes having social contact and friends, even animal ones, improves physical health. Some of the traits of popular people include positive thinking and a good sense of humor.

Editing for Working Life

Assume you are working at the customer service desk of a retail store like Macy's and you need to report a customer's complaint to your supervisor. Edit the paragraph. Insert quotation marks and other punctuation as needed. Use your own paper or complete this exercise on MyWritingLab.com.

> Mr. Saul Richey was upset by the treatment he received from sales associate Martin Hawkins in the jewelry department. According to Richey, Hawkins refused to honor a discount coupon. Mr. Richey pointed out that the coupon was part of a promotion mentioned in the Sunday Times article A Jewelry Buyer's Dream: High Value at Low Cost. Mr. Richey said Your sales clerk was loud and rude; I was very embarrassed. I will never deal with that man again.

Academic Learning Log: Chapter Review

WHAT HAVE I LEARNED ABOUT QUOTATION MARKS?

To test and track your understanding, answer the following questions.

1. Quotation marks are used in pairs to indicate _____ and _____.

2. _____ and _____ go inside the quotation marks.

3. Semicolons and colons go _____ the quotation marks.

4. Use a pair of quotation marks to set off a _____, which records the exact words of another person.

5. A _____ is the credit given to the source of a quotation.

6. A speech tag can be placed _____, _____, or _____.

7. **How will I use what I have learned about quotation marks?**
   In your notebook, discuss how you will apply to your own writing what you have learned about quotation marks.

8. **What do I still need to study about quotation marks?**
   In your notebook, discuss your ongoing study needs by describing what, when, and how you will continue studying quotation marks.

MyWritingLab™
Complete the Post-test for Chapter 32 in MyWritingLab.

PART 7 PUNCTUATION AND MECHANICS

33

LEARNING OUTCOMES

After studying this chapter you will be able to:

L1 Answer the Question "What's the Point of End Punctuation?"

L2 Use the Period

L3 Use the Question Mark

L4 Use the Exclamation Point

End Punctuation: Period, Question Mark, and Exclamation Point

End punctuation marks the end of a complete thought.

Thinking about a real-life situation helps us to understand the purpose of end punctuation in our communication. Complete the following activity and answer the question "What's the point of end punctuation?"

What's the Point of End Punctuation?

PHOTOGRAPHIC ORGANIZER: END PUNCTUATION

Assume you are a writer for your college newspaper. Your assignment this week is to report on a local event. You have composed a rough draft about the county fair. As you read the following rough draft, think about the need for punctuation at the end of complete thoughts. Think about the different types of end punctuation you already know about. Also think about the use of capital letters to mark a sentence. To see how much you already know about end punctuation, edit the draft. Insert end punctuation where you think it is needed.

WRITING FROM LIFE

Evening Excitement

The best time to enjoy the county fair is at night the sun sets the fair lights come on vibrant red and yellow lights outline the Ferris wheels and roller coasters festive signs beckon crowds to eat corn dogs, funnel cakes, and elephant ears everything tastes even better in the cool of the night why not go tonight you'll have a blast

What's the point of end punctuation?

_____

_____

One Student Writer's Response

The following paragraph offers one writer's reaction to the paragraph "Evening Excitement."

> *Without any end punctuation, I had to keep rereading to make sense of the ideas. I had to really stop and think about where one sentence ended and another one started. I am used to seeing capital letters at the beginning of a new idea. If I put a period to end a sentence, then I capitalize the first word of the next sentence. So both end punctuation and capital letters are needed. All sentences end with some kind of punctuation mark.*

A **sentence** is a complete thought that begins with a capital letter and ends with a specific type of end punctuation. The **punctuation marks** that indicate the end of a sentence (called **end punctuation**) are **the period**, **the question mark**, and **the exclamation point**. Each of these end punctuation marks indicates the purpose or type of a sentence. The following sections present a series of charts that show the relationship among end punctuation, the type of sentence, and the purpose of the sentence. Several sections also explain common end punctuation misuses to avoid.

L2 Use the Period

> For more information on types and purposes of sentences, see pages 490–509, "Sentence Variety."

End Punctuation	Type of Sentence	Purpose of Sentence
The Period (.)	Ends a declarative statement	To inform
	Ends an imperative statement	To command without urgency
	Ends an indirect question	To declare uncertainty

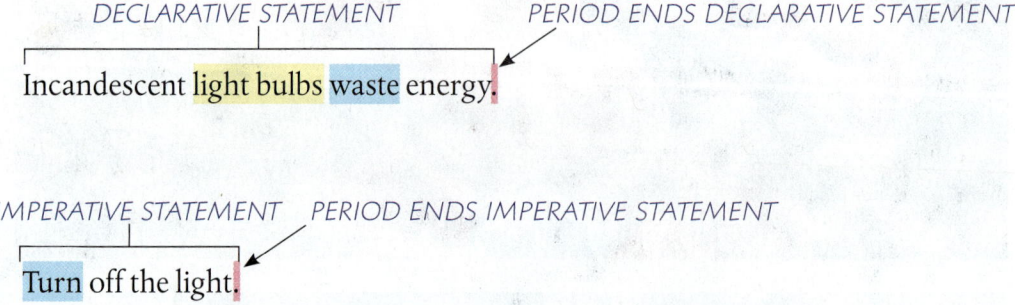

DECLARATIVE STATEMENT — PERIOD ENDS DECLARATIVE STATEMENT

Incandescent light bulbs waste energy.

IMPERATIVE STATEMENT — PERIOD ENDS IMPERATIVE STATEMENT

Turn off the light.

An **indirect question** tells about or reports a question asked by someone by paraphrasing it rather than reporting the exact words used. An indirect question usually begins with phrases like *I wonder if* or *he asked*. Place a period at the end of an indirect question.

PERIOD ENDS INDIRECT QUESTION

I wonder how much a new phone will cost me.

Use the Question Mark

End Punctuation	Type of Sentence	Purpose of Sentence
The Question Mark (?)	Ends an interrogative statement	To question
	May invert order of subject and helping verb	To question
	May begin with *what*, *who*, or *how*	To ask a direct question
	Often uses a helping verb such as *do*, *can*, *will*, or *would*	To make a request
	Records the exact words of a question stated by someone	To record the exact words of a question stated by someone

QUESTION MARK ENDS INTERROGATIVE STATEMENT

Why don't you turn off the lights?

QUESTION MARK ENDS INTERROGATIVE STATEMENT

Is Justine still using incandescent light bulbs?

SPEECH TAG   QUESTION MARK ENDS DIRECT QUESTION

Meghan asked, "Where are you going?

L4 Use the Exclamation Point

End Punctuation	Type of Sentence	Purpose of Sentence
The Exclamation Point (!)	Ends an exclamatory statement	To express strong emotion
	Ends a strong imperative (command)	To express urgency, warning, or a forceful command
	Ends an interjection, a single word or phrase used as an exclamation that stands apart from the rest of a sentence	To cry out, to utter an emotion
	Used with interjections beginning with *how* or *what*	To emphasize an idea

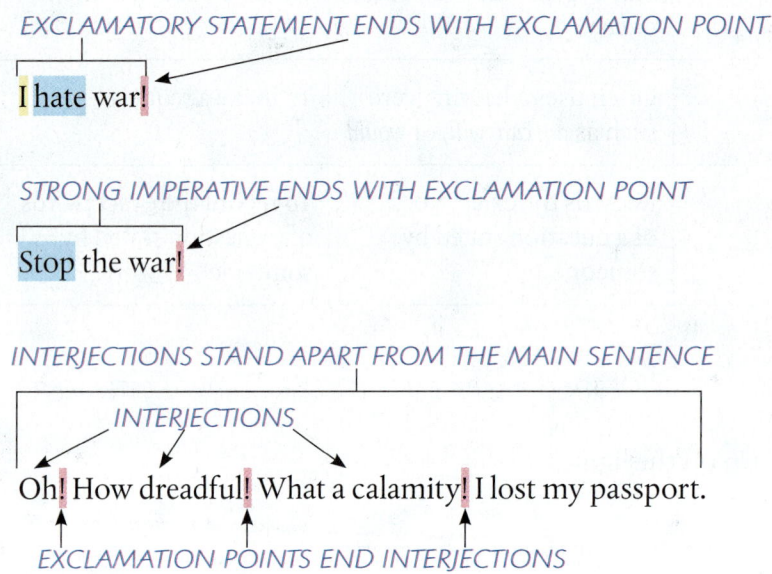

EXCLAMATORY STATEMENT ENDS WITH EXCLAMATION POINT

I hate war!

STRONG IMPERATIVE ENDS WITH EXCLAMATION POINT

Stop the war!

INTERJECTIONS STAND APART FROM THE MAIN SENTENCE

INTERJECTIONS

Oh! How dreadful! What a calamity! I lost my passport.

EXCLAMATION POINTS END INTERJECTIONS

Hints for Use of Exclamation Points

- Use the exclamation point sparingly. Overuse makes the comment less meaningful.
- Use only one exclamation point for a sentence; avoid using several at a time to emphasize an argument.
- **Avoid use of exclamation points in academic writing.**

Editing Assignments

Editing for Everyday Life

Assume you are writing an e-mail to a family member about a travel experience. You write your first draft as a freewrite without concern for punctuation. You take time to proofread before you click the send button, and you see the need to insert end punctuation. Edit the e-mail to insert appropriate end punctuation. Capitalize words as needed. Use your own paper or complete the exercise on MyWritingLab.com.

Hi Aunt Jo,

you wouldn't believe what happened to me at the airport when I tried to check in at the ticket counter, I couldn't find my wallet I had left my new wallet with all my identification at home and had mistakenly picked up my old wallet now, you may be asking how that could have happened I know this was so avoidable an airline representative asked, "Do you have any government issued identification with you" thank goodness I still had a library card in my old wallet she marked my ticket for "special screening" by security how stressful it all was

Editing for College Life

Assume you are working with a study group to prepare for a unit exam in a college biology course. Your group has divided up a list of study questions provided by your professor. You have written the following draft to answer one of the questions assigned to you. Proofread and edit the answer for correct use of end punctuation. Use your own paper or complete the exercise on MyWritingLab.com.

> *what is the cell theory how did this theory develop*
>
> in 1665, the English scientist and inventor Robert Hooke created a primitive microscope and used it to look at an "exceeding thin . . . piece of cork" he went on to report that he saw "a great many little Boxes" hook called these boxes "cells" because he thought they looked like the tiny rooms, or cells, used by monks in 1839, German botanist Matthias Schleiden concluded that cells form the basic structure of plants he also concluded that plant growth occurs by adding new cells in 1855, German physician Rudolf Virchow completed the cell theory by concluding that all cells come from previously existing cells thus, three principles make up the cell theory every living organism is made up of one or more cells the smallest living organisms are single, and cells are the units of multicellular organisms all cells arise from preexisting cells

Editing for Working Life

Assume you are working in a local restaurant to gain experience in the industry. You want to learn about running a small business because your long-term goal is to open your own restaurant. You notice a way to improve customer satisfaction, so on your break, you quickly write down your thoughts. As you read your first draft, you see the need for end punctuation. Edit this draft to insert appropriate end punctuation. Use your own paper or complete the exercise on MyWritingLab.com.

> *My First Thoughts: Ways to Improve Customer Satisfaction*
>
> in what ways can we improve customer satisfaction we need to improve our music and our napkins the early crowd is older and quieter the late evening crowd is younger and more active our music should be customized to meet their different tastes I suggest classical or soft rock music for the early crowds the evening crowds are more likely to enjoy hard rock or pop music the quality of our napkins is another detail that needs improvement I wonder how much we spend on our current small, thin paper napkins they need to be replaced with super-large, high quality paper napkins good napkins are well worth the money!!!!

Academic Learning Log: Chapter Review

WHAT HAVE I LEARNED ABOUT END PUNCTUATION?

To test and track your understanding, answer the following questions.

1. The _____ ends a declarative or a mild _____ statement or an _____.

2. The purpose of a declarative sentence is to _____; the purpose of an imperative sentence is to _____.

3. The question mark ends an _____; the purpose of this sentence type is to _____.

4. A question mark is not used at the end of an _____ question.

5. An exclamation point ends an _____ statement, a strong _____, and an _____.

6. The purpose of an exclamatory sentence is to express _____, urgency, _____, or a forceful _____.

7. **How will I use what I have learned about end punctuation?**
   In your notebook, discuss how you will apply to your own writing what you have learned about end punctuation.

8. **What do I still need to study about end punctuation?**
   In your notebook, discuss your ongoing study needs by describing what, when, and how you will continue studying end punctuation.

MyWritingLab™

Complete the Post-test for Chapter 33 in MyWritingLab.

34 Capitalization

PART 7 PUNCTUATION AND MECHANICS

LEARNING OUTCOMES

After studying this chapter you will be able to:

- **L1** Answer the question "What's the Point of Capitalization?"
- **L2** Apply Capitalization Rule 1: The First Word of Every Sentence
- **L3** Apply Capitalization Rule 2: The Pronoun *I*
- **L4** Apply Capitalization Rule 3: Greetings and Salutations
- **L5** Apply Capitalization Rule 4: Titles of Publications
- **L6** Apply Capitalization Rule 5: Proper Nouns
- **L7** Apply Capitalization Rule 6: The Title of a Person
- **L8** Apply Capitalization Rule 7: Proper Adjectives

Capitalization clearly identifies the beginning of a new idea or the names of specific people, places, and things.

Thinking about a real-life situation helps us to understand the purpose of capitalization in our communication. Complete the following activity and answer the question "What's the point of capitalization?"

What's the Point of Capitalization?

PHOTOGRAPHIC ORGANIZER: CAPITALIZATION

Many experts fear that excessive text messaging harms an individual's ability to write well. Other experts believe text messaging can teach students the appropriate use of language for different situations and audiences. For example, the use of capitalization in text messages differs from standard rules. The person in the photo is about to send a text message to her family about a delay in her travel plans. Read her text message and consult the glossary of text message lingo, common expressions used in text messages. Explain how she uses capitalization in her message. Next, identify standard uses of capitalization you have seen in written language. Do you think text messaging harms an individual's ability to write well?

How r u?

FYI   Flight   L8.

AFAIK   CYA   L8R   2NITE

BFN

Text Message Glossary

AFAIK   (As Far As I Know)

BFN   (Bye for Now)

CYA   (See You)

FYI   (For Your Information)

L8R   (Later)

2NITE   (Tonight)

What's the point of capitalization?

WRITING FROM LIFE

One Student Writer's Response

The following paragraph offers one writer's reaction to the text message.

I do a lot of text messaging, so I know that some people capitalize everything in their messages while others don't capitalize anything. I don't like to use capital letters in my messages because my phone makes it hard to type capital letters. Using capitals helps me see what I am writing. As I think about capitalization rules, I think of the names of people, places, days of the week, days of the month, and the first word of a sentence. I always follow these rules when I write for school or work, but I am not so sure about some capitalization rules, like people's titles. I can see how experts think text messaging hurts written language.

Capitalization refers to writing letters (and sometimes words) in uppercase letters. The most frequent usage of capitalization, however, is writing a word with its first letter in uppercase (and the rest of its letters in lowercase) to indicate the beginning of a sentence.

Following seven basic rules will ensure proper use of capitalization in your writing.

RULE 1: Capitalize the first word of every sentence.

CAPITAL LETTERS INDICATE THE START OF NEW SENTENCES

> Extreme horror films provide thrill rides for loyal fans.
> The core audience of horror films is made up of 18- to 22-year-old males. Many criticize horror films for being too graphic.

RULE 2: Capitalize the pronoun *I*.

ALWAYS CAPITALIZE THE FIRST-PERSON SINGULAR PRONOUN "I"

> I do not enjoy watching horror movies. Because I keep my eyes closed through most of a horror movie, I think they are a waste of my money.

RULE 3: Capitalize the first letter of the first words in written greetings and salutations (for example, *Dear friends,* or *Best regards*).

ALWAYS CAPITALIZE THE FIRST LETTER OF THE FIRST WORDS IN WRITTEN GREETINGS OR CLOSINGS (IN LETTERS, MEMOS, E-MAILS, ETC.)

> Dear Mr. Sanchez:
>
> I am writing to protest your support of horror films. As a sponsor of this type of film, you foster fear and violence in our culture. Until you stop sponsoring horror films, I will no longer buy items from your company.
>
> Sincerely,
>
> Dorothea Simmons

RULE 4: Capitalize principal words in titles of publications.

In titles of publications, such as books, magazines, newspapers, songs, poems, plays, and articles, capitalize the first letter of the first and last words, the principal words, and the first word that comes after a semicolon or colon.

Do not capitalize the first letters of the following in titles, unless they are the first or last word or come after a semicolon or colon: articles (*a, an, the*), prepositions (such as *in, of,* and *with*), and conjunctions (such as *and, but,* and *for*). Keep in mind that capitalization styles for titles differ in certain academic disciplines, so always check with your teacher for style guidelines.

Article	ALWAYS CAPITALIZE THE FIRST LETTER OF THE FIRST WORD IN A PUBLICATION TITLE "Eight Top Jobs for Parents" ALWAYS CAPITALIZE THE FIRST LETTER OF THE PRINCIPAL WORDS IN A PUBLICATION TITLE
Book	ALWAYS CAPITALIZE THE FIRST LETTER OF THE PRINCIPAL WORDS IN A PUBLICATION TITLE *The Grapes of Wrath*
Magazine/Journal	*Sociology: The Journal of the British Sociological Association*
Newspaper	*New York Times*
Play or Movie	UNLESS THEY ARE THE FIRST OR LAST WORD, DO NOT CAPITALIZE THE FIRST LETTER OF MINOR WORDS, ARTICLES, PREPOSITIONS, OR CONJUNCTIONS IN TITLES *The Taming of the Shrew*
Poem	"Death Be Not Proud"
Song	"Dearly Beloved"
Website	Health.gov

Note: Digital terms, such as Internet or the World Wide Web, use initial capitalization.

RULE 5: Capitalize the first letters in all essential words in proper nouns.

Proper nouns name specific people, places, things, and events. Proper nouns include people's names; certain titles of people (see Rule 6 on page 595 for details), places, and regions; organizations and associations; and publications. Each of the examples in the following chart illustrates various rules for capitalizing proper nouns.

Note the capitalization of initials and abbreviations. Do not capitalize common nouns.

ALWAYS CAPITALIZE THE FIRST LETTER IN EACH PART OF A PERSON'S NAME

ALWAYS CAPITALIZE A PERSON'S INITIALS

	Common Nouns	Proper Nouns
People	a woman	Ms. Eileen Long
	a man	Mr. D. O. Nape
	a professor	Professor Walker
	an officer	Captain Rivera or Capt. Rivera
	a relative, an aunt	Aunt Jo
	a father, my mother	Father, Mother
	a believer of a religion	Christian, Catholic, Muslim
	member(s) of an organization	Republican(s), Boy Scout(s)
Places and Regions	a lake	Lake Tahoe
	a country	Mexico
	a street	Main Street
Things	a language	English
	an academic course	Psychology 101
	a history course	World History I
	a ship	*Titanic*
	south (a direction)	the American South (a region)
	a religion	Christianity, Judaism, Islam
	a sacred text	the Koran, the Qur'an, the Bible
	a god	God, Christ, Allah, Buddha, Zeus
	a group/organization	the Rolling Stones, the Kiwanis Club
	a department, office, or institution	the Senate, the Department of Commerce, Daytona State College
	a monument	Lincoln Memorial
	a company	Apple, Inc.
Events, Time Periods	a day	Friday
	a month	January
	an era	the Middle Ages
	a movement	the Civil Rights Movement
	a war	the Vietnam War
	a holiday	Easter, Passover, Thanksgiving, Ramadan

THE FIRST LETTER OF THE TITLES OF FAMILY RELATIVES (PARENTS, AUNTS AND UNCLES, ETC.) REMAIN LOWERCASE AS COMMON NOUNS, BUT BECOME CAPITALIZED WHEN A SPECIFIC RELATIVE (THE SPEAKER'S) IS REFERRED TO

RULE 6: Capitalize the first letter of the title of a person when the title precedes the person's name.

Some writers capitalize the first letter of a title of very high rank even when it follows a proper name. Capitalization of the first letter of a title is also common if it appears at the end of a letter, e-mail, or other correspondence, following the person's name. Do not capitalize those titles when they appear on their own as common nouns (without modifying a particular person's name).

ALWAYS CAPITALIZE THE FIRST LETTER OF A PERSON'S TITLE WHEN IT APPEARS BEFORE THE PERSON'S NAME

Doctor Kit Doughney

Professor Rivers

WHEN A PERSON'S TITLE APPEARS AFTER THE PERSON'S NAME, THE INITIAL LETTER OF THE TITLE REMAINS LOWERCASE

Kit Doughney, a medical doctor

Van Rivers, a professor of science

IN SOME CASES, IF IT'S A HIGH-RANKING TITLE, WRITERS WILL CAPITALIZE A TITLE EVEN IF IT APPEARS AFTER THE NAME

Prime Minister Cameron

David Cameron, Prime Minister of the United Kingdom of Great Britain and Northern Ireland

Secretary of State Kerry

John Kerry, the Secretary of State

RULE 7: Capitalize proper adjectives. Proper adjectives are formed from proper nouns.

Proper Noun	Proper Adjective
Africa	Africans
America	Americans
Florida	Floridian
Japan	Japanese
Spain	Spanish
Shakespeare	Shakespearean

Use and capitalize brand-name trademarks as proper adjectives:

Kleenex tissue

Scotch tape

Editing Assignments

Editing for Everyday Life
Assume you are writing an e-mail to a friend about a horror movie you just saw. Edit the paragraph for proper use of capitalization.

> i did not want to go see this movie. horror movies are not my thing, but I gave in and reluctantly went along to see *the lazarus effect*. i probably won't sleep soundly again for years. the motion picture association Of america gave it a PG-13 rating for "horror, violence, terror, and sexual references." i didn't see a lot of the movie. i kept covering my eyes with my hands. but i heard every blood curdling sound. i would never recommend this movie.

Editing for College Life
Assume you are taking a health course and you have been assigned to write about the importance of sleep. Edit the paragraph for proper use of capitalization.

> according to the national sleep foundation, every person has Individual Sleep Needs, in general, an adult needs seven to eight hours of sleep each night. a constant lack of sleep can lead to several serious consequences. according to dr. dement, lack of sleep increases risk of motor vehicle accidents. lack of sleep may lead to a greater chance of obesity, diabetes, and heart problems. lack of sleep can also lessen a person's ability to pay attention or remember new information. dr. dement is a cofounder of the stanford sleep disorders clinic in stanford, california.

Editing for Working Life
Assume you are a supervisor for a small company, and you must write a letter of complaint. Edit the letter for proper use of capitalization.

> dear mr. rodriguez:
>
> as someone who has used your services for several years, i am very disappointed with the quality of the work performed by your company, best electronic company, on thursday, may 18th of this year. during the repair, your crew damaged carpets, baseboards, and walls. photographs of the damages and an estimate of the repair cost are enclosed.
> yours truly,
>
> anna b. wright, supervisor
> quality print shop

Academic Learning Log: Chapter Review

WHAT HAVE I LEARNED ABOUT CAPITALIZATION?

To test and track your understanding, answer the following questions.

1. Capitalize the _____ of every sentence.

2. Capitalize the pronoun _____.

3. Capitalize the first letter of the first words of _____ and _____.

4. Capitalize the first letter of _____ words in _____.

5. Capitalize the first letter of the _____ of a person when the title _____ the person's name.

6. Capitalize the first letter of _____ nouns. Do not capitalize _____ nouns.

7. Capitalize the first letter of _____ adjectives.

8. **How will I use what I have learned about capitalization?**
   In your notebook, discuss how you will apply to your own writing what you have learned about capitalization.

9. **What do I still need to study about capitalization?**
   In your notebook, discuss your ongoing study needs by describing what, when, and how you will continue studying capitalization.

MyWritingLab™

Complete the Post-test for Chapter 34 in MyWritingLab.

35 Improving Your Spelling

PART 7 PUNCTUATION AND MECHANICS

LEARNING OUTCOMES

After studying this chapter you will be able to:

L1 Answer the Question "What's the Point of Improving Your Spelling?"

L2 Apply Five Steps to Improving Your Spelling

L3 Apply Basic Rules for Improving Your Spelling

a. Recognize Vowel and Consonant Patterns

b. Recognize How Suffixes Are Used

c. Add *-s* or *-es* to Nouns and Verbs

d. Double the Final Consonant

e. Drop or Keep the Final *E*

f. Change or Keep the Final *Y*

g. Recognize How Prefixes Are Used

h. Choose *ie* or *ei*

L4 Recognize and Correct Commonly Misspelled Words

To spell correctly is to understand the rules for properly arranging letters in a word.

Do you have trouble spelling words? If so, you are not alone. Many people have trouble spelling. Despite these difficulties, it is important to work toward accurate spelling because it is an important part of effective expression. Complete the following activity and answer the question "What's the point of improving your spelling?"

What's the Point of Improving Your Spelling?

PHOTOGRAPHIC ORGANIZER: IMPROVING YOUR SPELLING

Test your spelling skills. Assume a friend of yours has applied for an internship as a nurse at your local hospital. He is going to send a follow-up letter to express his interest in the position. He has asked you to proofread the first few sentences of the letter he wants to send. Can you find the ten misspelled words in this draft? What impact would misspelled words in this follow-up letter have on your friend's chances of getting the internship?

> I submitted a letter of aplication and a résumé earler this month for a nurseing internship with Memrial Hospital. To date, I have not herd from your office. I would like to confirm reciept of my leter and agian state my intrest in the job.

What's the point of improving your spelling?

WRITING FROM LIFE

One Student Writer's Response

The following paragraph offers one writer's reaction to the spelling in the follow-up letter for the nursing internship.

> Too many misspellings makes the writer of the letter seem uneducated or careless. I would say his poor spelling could cost him the internship. I mean he is probably competing against people who will make a better first impression. It's a good thing he asked someone to read over his letter. I do seem to misspell a lot of words. I would love to be a better speller. I want to make a good impression on paper. I mean if it's worth my time to write, it's worth my time to do it correctly, right?

You can improve your spelling by identifying and correcting patterns of misspellings in your writing. Each writer develops his or her own system for learning and using correct spelling. For example, some writers keep a vocabulary journal of new words or difficult-to-spell words, and most writers use a spell checker as a last step before publishing a piece of writing. The steps, rules, and practice in this chapter are designed to help you develop a system to improve your spelling.

Five Steps to Improve Your Spelling

Five of the best ways to improve your spelling are to use a spell checker, dictionary, mnemonics, spelling error tracking, and the writing process.

1. Use a Spell Checker

Word processing programs such as Microsoft Word provide spell checkers to verify the spellings of words in a document. Beware, however, because spell checkers seldom catch all the errors in a text. In particular, spell checkers fail to spot words that sound alike but differ in meaning, such as *to*, *too*, and *two*. In addition, spell checkers sometimes flag proper nouns (nouns that name specific people, places, and things) as misspellings even though they may be spelled correctly. Thus, carefully consider the reason the spell checker highlights a word. Be cautious about clicking the "change" or "change all" button too quickly. With thoughtful use, however, a spell checker offers helpful assistance in catching commonly misspelled words.

2. Use a Dictionary

Look up misspelled words in a dictionary. Place a dot next to each word you look up in your dictionary to flag it as a word for further study.

Most print dictionaries have guide words at the top of each page to help you locate a word. For each entry, the spelling of the main word is given first in bold type. The word is also divided into syllables. The function or part of speech and the etymology, the history of the word, are also given. It is often helpful to understand the origin of a word since many words in the English language came from other languages. Additional spellings of the word appear at the end of the entry. This listing is especially helpful when letters are dropped or added to create a new word.

Online dictionaries locate words through a search box instead of using guide words. If you **misspell** a word during your search, online dictionaries usually offer alternate spellings to help you find the word you are looking for. As you study the example shown on the next page from the *Merriam-Webster Online Dictionary*, think about how you will use the information in a dictionary to improve your spelling.

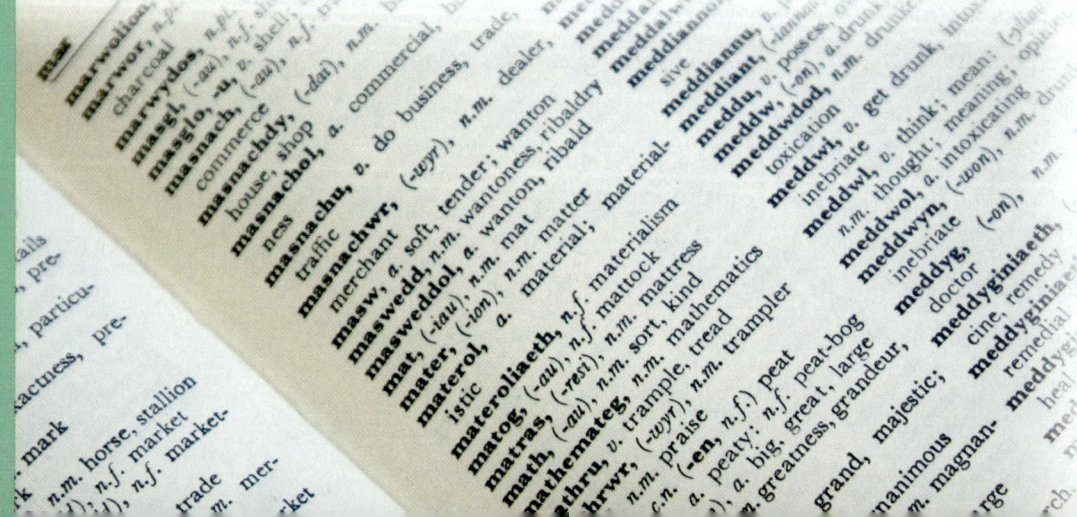

jealous

Main Entry: jeal·ous

Pronunciation: \¹je-ləs\

Function: *adjective*

Etymology: Middle English *jelous*, from Anglo-French *gelus*, from Vulgar Latin **zelosus*, from Late Latin *zelus* zeal — more at ZEAL

Date: 13th century

1 a: intolerant of rivalry or unfaithfulness **b:** disposed to suspect rivalry or unfaithfulness

2: hostile toward a rival or one believed to enjoy an advantage

3: vigilant in guarding a possession <new colonies were *jealous* of their new independence
— Scott Buchanan>

— **jeal·ous·ly** *adverb*

— **jeal·ous·ness** *noun*

Source: By permission. From *Merriam-Webster Online Dictionary* © 2015 by Merriam-Webster, Incorporated www.merriam-webster.com

3. Use Mnemonics

Mnemonics are different types of memory tricks that can help you remember the correct spelling of words. For example:

- Create a mental or visual image: Picture a person screaming "e-e-e" as he passes a cemetery.
- Chunk a word into visual parts: unforgettable = un for get table
- Color-code trouble spots in a word: rec**ei**ve (**not** recieve).
- Create a silly saying using each letter of the word: The first letters of each word in the following sentence combine to spell *geography*:
George's **E**lderly **O**ld **G**randfather **R**ode **A** **P**ig **H**ome **Y**esterday.

4. Track Spelling Errors

Identify your misspellings through teacher feedback, peer edits, or a spell checker. In a journal, create a list of words that you have misspelled. Contrast the way you misspell the word with the rule and the correct spelling. Identify information that helps you remember the correct spelling such as the word's function or etymology. Create a memory trick as needed. Choose from the headings in the following example to create your own journal system for improving your spelling.

Correct Spelling	Function	Etymology	My Misspelling	Spelling Rule	Memory Trick
argument	noun	Latin *argumentum* (from the verb *arguere*)	arguement	Drop the silent e when a vowel comes right before it.	I lost an "e" in my argument.

5. Use the Writing Process to Improve Your Spelling

As you write, use these tips to ensure accurate spelling:

☐ **Decide when during the writing process you will identify and correct misspellings.**
Some writers who compose as they type or write pause frequently to revise and edit what they just wrote. Others prefer to complete a draft and then check for misspellings during the revision and proofreading phases of the writing process.

☐ **Identify and study specialized or difficult words that are connected to your writing assignment.**
Verify the spelling and etymology (how the word originated) of these words before you begin writing. Find correctly spelled synonyms (words that have similar meanings) for these words. Use this group of correctly spelled words to brainstorm additional details for your writing.

☐ **Use one proofreading session to focus only on spelling accuracy.**
By devoting time to proofreading your spelling, you are more likely to catch errors.

☐ **During the proofreading phase, edit on a printed copy of your writing if you are using a word processor.**
It's easy to overlook text errors on a computer screen.

☐ **Decide how you will track your misspelling patterns as you write.**
Will you make a list as you go, or will you list troubling words after you have completed your final edit?

Commit to improving your spelling by creating an individual study process.

L3 Rules for Improving Your Spelling

Improving your spelling involves understanding rules about vowel and consonant patterns, as well as rules about the use of suffixes and prefixes.

Recognize Vowel and Consonant Patterns

Many spelling rules are based on the use of vowels and consonants to form words, so to improve your spelling, take note of the patterns of vowels and consonants in words. Take a moment to look at the following examples to refresh your memory about consonant (c) and vowel (v) patterns in words. Remember the vowels are *a, e, i, o, u,* and sometimes *y*. All other letters are consonants.

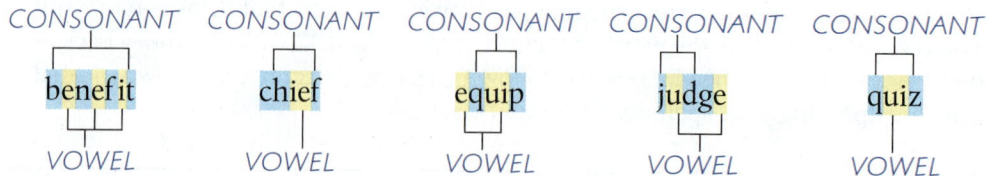

Understand How Suffixes Are Used

A **suffix** is added to the end of a **base word** (a word's original meaning) to change the use or meaning of the word. For example, the suffixes *-ing* or *-ed* can either change the tense of a verb or change the verb into a noun or an adjective. For example, *walk* is a verb, but adding *-ing* creates the present participle *walking*; adding *-ed* creates the past participle *walked*. The present and past participles can function as verbs, adjectives, or nouns depending on the context in which they are used.

Suffixes begin with either a vowel or a consonant, which affects the spelling rules for adding them to base words. You will learn about the specific ways in which vowels and consonants impact spelling throughout this chapter. The following chart lists a few common vowel and consonant suffixes, along with their meanings and examples.

Vowel Suffix	Part of Speech	Meaning	Example
-able, -ible	adj	able to	touchable, visible
-ed	verb	past tense	talked, walked
-en	verb	present or past participle	bitten, written
-en	adj	to change verbs to adjectives	fallen, frozen
-ent	adj	describes action or being	different, persistent
-er	noun	one who is or does	player, adopter
-er	adj	comparison	bigger, smaller
-es	noun	plural	dresses, boxes
-es	verb	singular present tense	washes, finishes
-ous	adj	full of	dangerous, luxurious

Consonant Suffix	Part of Speech	Meaning	Example
-ful	adj	full of	wonderful, careful
-ly or -y	adv	like	gently, weekly
-ment	noun	instance of action or process	government, statement
-ness	noun	state of being	happiness, faithfulness
-s	noun	plural	doctors, workers
-s	verb	singular present tense	runs, quits

The rules for spelling words with suffixes vary. The next several sections explain and illustrate the various spelling rules for adding suffixes.

Add -s or -es to Nouns and Verbs to Form the Plural

- Add -s to form the plural of most regular nouns, including those that end with o.

  book + s ⟶ books

  video + s ⟶ videos

- Add -es to nouns that end with a consonant immediately before a final o.

  hero + es ⟶ heroes

- Add -s to most regular verbs to form the singular present tense in the third person.

  ask + s ⟶ asks

- Add -es to form the plural of nouns and to third person present tense verbs that end in *ch, sh, s, x,* or *z*.

Nouns   **Verbs**
watch + es   watches   catch + es   catches
marsh + es   marshes   wash + es   washes
bus + es   buses   pass + es   passes
mix + es   mixes   buzz + es   buzzes

Double the Final Consonant in Words with One Syllable

Many **one-syllable** words end in a **consonant** with a **vowel** immediately **before** it. (*Hint*: Remember **CVC**.) For a word with one syllable, one consonant, and one vowel, double the final consonant when adding a vowel suffix. The final consonant is *not* doubled when adding a consonant suffix.

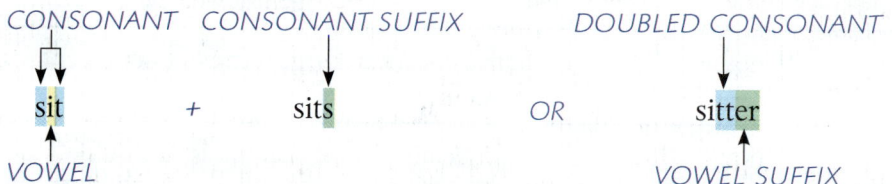

Exception: Do not double the final consonant of words that end in *w, x,* or *y* as in the following examples: snowing, boxer, obeys.

Double the Final Consonant in Words with More Than One Syllable

Words with more than one syllable often end with a vowel immediately before a **consonant**. (*Hint*: Remember **VC**.) If the final syllable is stressed or emphasized in its pronunciation, **double the final consonant**. If the final syllable is **not** stressed, do **not** double the final consonant.

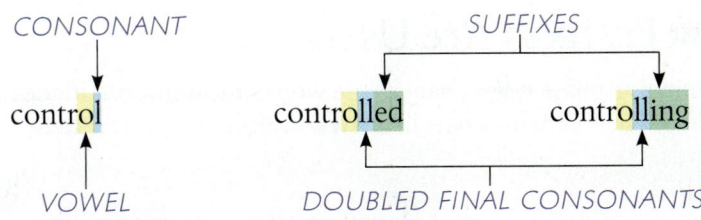

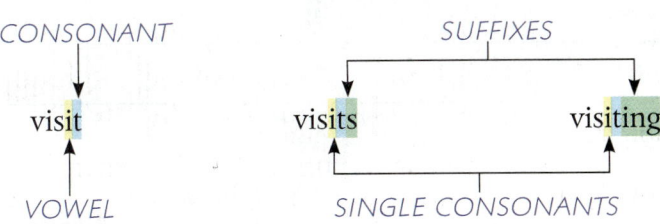

Drop or Keep the Final E

- Drop the *e* when the base *word ends* with a *silent e* and the *suffix begins* with a *vowel*.

  advance + -ing ⟶ advancing

- Drop the *e* when a *vowel comes immediately before* the silent *e*.

  true + -ly ⟶ truly

- Keep the *e* when the base *word ends* with a *silent e* and the *suffix begins* with a *consonant*.

  advance + -ment ⟶ advancement

Change or Keep the Final Y

- When a *consonant* appears before the final *y*, change the *y* to *i*.

  supply + -ies ⟶ supplies

- When a *vowel* appears before the final *y*, keep the *y*.

  obey + -ed ⟶ obeyed

- Keep the *y* when adding the suffix *-ing*.

  cry + -ing ⟶ crying

Understand How Prefixes Are Used

A prefix added to the beginning of a base word changes the word's meaning, but it does not change the word's spelling. The following chart lists a few common prefixes, their meanings, and example words.

Prefix	Meaning	Example
bi-	two	bicycle
de-	not	deregulated
dis-	not	disagree
im-	not	impossible
mis-	not	misunderstood
pre-	before	preview
re-	again	rewrite
un-	not	unknown

Adding a prefix to a word does not alter its spelling.

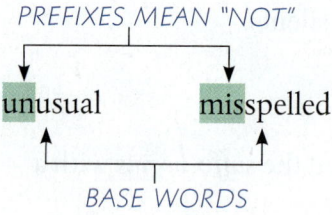

Choose *ie* or *ei*

A helpful way to remember how to use *ie* and *ei* in spelling is to think of the following rhyme:

"*i* before *e* except after *c* or when sounds like *ay* as in *neighbor* or *weigh*"

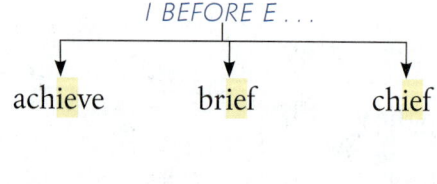

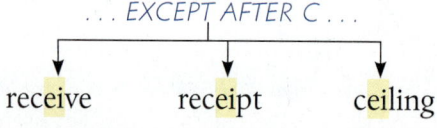

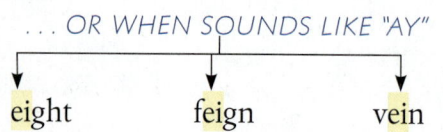

There are, however, some exceptions to the *ie, ei* rule that should be memorized:

ie: species, science, conscience

ei: height, either, neither, leisure, seize, counterfeit, foreign, forfeit, sleight, weird

Recognize and Correct Commonly Misspelled Words

To aid in your efforts to improve your vocabulary, the following chart lists 120 of the most commonly misspelled words.

120 Commonly Misspelled Words				
absence	easily	interruption	peculiar	repetition
accommodate	eight	invitation	perceive	restaurant
acquire	embarrass	irritable	permanent	ridiculous
across	environment	island	persevere	sacrifice
advertise	exaggerate	judgment	persuade	scissors
advice	excellent	knowledge	picture	secretary
apparent	except	laboratory	piece	separate
argument	exercise	length	planning	shining
becoming	experience	license	political	sincerely
beginning	experiment	loneliness	possess	soldier
believe	explanation	losing	possible	stopping
business	fascinating	mathematics	prefer	studying
calendar	finally	medicine	prejudice	succeed
ceiling	fundamental	minute	privilege	surely
cemetery	generally	miscellaneous	probably	surprise
chief	grammar	naturally	promise	temporary
coming	guarantee	necessary	proof	through
criticize	humorous	noticeable	quiet	twelfth
definite	imaginary	occasion	quit	unusual
describe	imitation	occurred	quite	using
develop	incidentally	omission	receive	village
difference	independent	optimism	recognize	weird
dilemma	intelligent	original	recommend	whether
disappoint	interesting	parallel	reference	writing

Editing Assignments

Editing for Everyday Life

Assume you recently visited an emergency clinic to get stitches, and you have contracted a Staph infection. You are writing to officially document your complaint against the clinic. Edit the misspellings in the following draft.

> On September 24 of this year, I recieve stitchs at your clinic for a deep cut on the bottom of my left foot. While I waited in the examination room for the doctor, a nurse closly examined my foot. Much later, it occured to me that she had not washed her hands. I beleive she is the source of the Staph infection that I developed within days of that visit. By writting, I am hopeing to persuade all the staff members of your clinic to wash thier hands.
>
> Sincerly, Jean Martinez

Editing for College Life

Assume you are taking a college health class. You have been assigned to write a report about the importance of hand washing. Edit the misspellings in the following draft.

> A recent survey of people in restrooms confirms that the spread of at least some infectious deseases could be curbbed if greater attention were spent on hand washing after going to the bathroom. Dirty hands can spread deseases such as colds and diarrhea and other intestinal problems. Experts say that the problem occurres across the country. Apparently, women washed up more than men; however, men used soap more often than women did.

Editing for Working Life

Assume you have been hired by a hospital to improve the quality of care. You are to present your recommendations in a PowerPoint presentation. Edit the misspellings in the following slide.

> **Monitoring Hand Hygeine**
>
> A hand hygiene audit determines health care worker (HCW) compliance with hand hygiene practice. Each department appointes a quality controller. The quality controller observes and records missed opportunites to carry out hand hygiene. Examples of hand hygiene opportunities include:
>
> - Before and after touching a pateint
> - After handleing body fluids
> - After touching objects involved in the pateint's care
> - After removeing gloves
>
> A total of 10 observations should be performed each month. Completed forms will be submitted to the Infection Control Department.

Academic Learning Log: Chapter Review

WHAT HAVE I LEARNED ABOUT IMPROVING SPELLING?

To test and track your understanding, answer the following questions.

1. Add .... to form the plural of regular nouns and regular verbs in the present tense for the singular third person.

2. Add .... to nouns that end with a consonant immediately before a final *o*.

3. Add .... to form the plural of nouns and to the third person present tense of verbs that end in *ch, sh, s, x,* or *z*.

4. When a word has one syllable, one consonant and one vowel, ... the final consonant before adding the suffix.

5. When words with more than one syllable end with a .... immediately before a consonant and the final syllable is stressed, double the final consonant.

6. Drop the *e* when the base word ends with a .... *e* and the suffix begins with a vowel.

7. Drop the *e* when a .... comes immediately before the silent *e*.

8. Keep the *e* when the word ends with a silent *e* and the suffix begins with a ....

9. When a .... appears before the final *y*, change the *y* to *i*.

10. When a .... appears before the final *y*, keep the *y*.

11. Keep the *y* when adding the suffix ....

12. Adding a .... to a word does not alter its spelling.

13. "*I* before *e* except after *c* or sounds like .... as in n*ei*ghbor or w*ei*gh."

14. **How will I use what I have learned about improving spelling?**
    In your notebook, discuss how you will apply to your own writing what you have learned about improving spelling.

15. **What do I still need to study about improving spelling?**
    In your notebook, discuss your ongoing study needs by describing how you will continue to improve your spelling.

MyWritingLab™
Complete the Post-test for Chapter 35 in MyWritingLab.

PART 8 READING SELECTIONS

- What's the Point of Reading to Write?
- Effective Strategies for Responding to Reading Selections: Annotations, Summarizing, and Reading Like a Writer
- Nineteen Reading Selections

Niagara Falls / RUPERT BROOKE 615

Maya Lin's Design Submission to the Vietnam Memorial Competition / MAYA LIN 618

Latino Heritage Month: Who We Are . . . And Why We Celebrate? / LUIS J. RODRIGUEZ 620

Confessions / AMY TAN 623

Managing Stress in College / REBECCA J. DONATELLE 625

Camping Out / ERNEST HEMINGWAY 629

Don't Call Me a Hot Tamale / JUDITH ORTIZ COFER 632

Football's Bloodiest Secret / BUZZ BISSINGER 634

The Fundamentals of Forgiveness / D. J. HENRY 636

I Am Enough / MELISSA GUITRON 640

The Talk of the Sandbox; How Johnny and Suzy's Playground Chatter Prepares Them for Life at the Office / DEBORAH TANNEN 643

The Loss of Juárez: How Has the Violence in Juárez Changed Border Culture? / SERGIO TRONCOSO 647

What is Poverty? / JO GOODWIN-PARKER 650

Cool at 13, Adrift at 23 / JAN HOFFMAN 653

Through Young Eyes / MICHAEL S. MALONE 655

Why We Crave Horror Movies / STEPHEN KING 658

The Nobel Peace Prize Lecture, 2014 / MALALA YOUSAFZAI 660

Hungry vs., Healthy: The School Lunch Controversy / BONNIE TAUB-DIX 665

Can Virtual Classrooms Beat Face-to-Face Interaction? / LIBBY PAGE 667

Reading Selections

Reading and writing are mirror reflections of the thinking process.

The connection between reading and writing is a natural one. Effective writers are often avid readers. They read and study well-written pieces by other writers as a strategy to become a better writer. To begin your thinking about the connection between reading and writing, complete the following activity.

What's the Point of Reading to Write?

By reading, writers can learn new vocabulary, see how other writers organize ideas, add information to their bank of knowledge, and find ideas to write about.

USING READING STRATEGIES TO RESPOND TO WRITING SELECTIONS

Read the following excerpt from the selection "The Fundamentals of Forgiveness" by D.J. Henry (p. 636). Answer the questions that follow.

1. Life is full of all types of hurt. A tormenting bully, an abusive or neglectful parent, an unfaithful spouse, or a careless driver ending the life of a loved one—these offenders embody just a few of the myriad types of injuries that we endure. At times, it may seem as if the hurt is insurmountable. And in its wake, we may be tempted to cling to our pain, become bitter, desire revenge, to be—in short—unforgiving.

2. However, many experts agree that an unforgiving attitude deepens the wound, as summarized in the Mayo Clinic article "Forgiveness: Letting Go of Grudges and Bitterness." Anger, bitterness, depression, anxiety, lack of purpose, spiritual conflict, and an inability to enjoy the present moment or make important connections with others often mark the lives of those who cannot or will not forgive. In fact, research indicates that we who do forgive actually lower our blood pressure, heart rate, and cholesterol levels; improve our sleep quality; and strengthen our immune system.

3. To be forgiving, we need to recognize what forgiveness is not. First, forgiveness is not a sign of weakness. Indeed, forgiveness signals strength. To forgive is to conquer anger, bitterness, and the need for revenge. As the great civil rights activist Mahatma Gandhi said in his book *All Men are Brothers: Autobiographical Reflections*, "The weak can never forgive. Forgiveness is the attribute of the strong."

1. What writing topics come to mind as you read these opening paragraphs?

2. What new words can you learn from reading this selection?

3. Based on these paragraphs, what kind of information do you need to classifiy a concept?

What's the point of reading to write?

Practice 1

PART 8 READING SELECTIONS

Effective Strategies for Responding to Reading Selections

The fundamental connection between reading and writing is thinking: thinking about the meaning of what you read and what you say, and thinking about the connection between what you read and what you write. To fully realize the connection between reading and writing, you need to be an active and focused thinker. Two active thinking-reading-writing tasks are annotating a text and writing a summary. The following discussions take you through several steps that show you how to think, read, think again, reread, and then write—as a strategy to improve your writing.

How to Annotate a Text

Use your writing skills throughout the reading process to ensure that you are an active thinker. Annotate the text, take notes, and write journal entries, summaries, and critical responses to what you read. Annotating the text before and during reading is an active thinking-reading-writing strategy. You have been taught to ask questions as a prereading thinking task. When you read, annotate your text as you find the answers to your questions.

The word *annotate* suggests that you "take notes" on the page of the text. Writing notes in the margin of the page as you read focuses your attention and improves your concentration. Annotating also will improve your understanding of the writer's purpose and point. You can note questions or answers quickly where they occur, move on in your reading, and later return to those details for clarification. In addition to writing notes, you can underline, circle, or highlight important terms, definitions, examples, or other key ideas. After reading, a review of your annotations will make responding to the material easier and more efficient. The following techniques are often used to annotate a text. Use these as guidelines to develop your own system for annotating a text.

Annotation Techniques
• Underline the main idea once.
• Underline major supporting details twice.
• Circle or highlight key words or special terms.
• Place small question marks above unknown words.
• Signal steps in a process or list by using numbers.
• Point out important concepts with symbols such as a star or a check.
• Write recall questions in the margin where the answer is found.
• Write a statement for an implied idea.
• Write a summary.

Use your annotations to guide your written response to a piece of writing. The following selection has been annotated for you as an illustration.

The Death of President Lincoln
By Walt Whitman

April 16, '65.—I find in my notes of the time, this passage on the death of Abraham Lincoln: He leaves for America's history and biography, so far, not only its most dramatic reminiscence—[memories] he leaves, in my opinion, the greatest, best, most characteristic, artistic, moral personality. Not but that he had faults, and show'd them in the Presidency; but honesty, goodness, shrewdness, conscience, and (a new virtue, unknown to other lands, and hardly yet really known here, but the foundation and tie of all, as the future will grandly develop,) UNIONISM [keeping the United States undivided!], in its truest and amplest sense, form'd the hard-pan of his character. These he seal'd with his life. The tragic splendor of his death, purging, illuminating all, throws round his form, his head, an aureole [?crown?] that will remain and will grow brighter through time, while history lives, and love of country lasts. By many has this Union been help'd; but if one name, one man, must be pick'd out, he, most of all, is the conservator [legal guardian or keeper] of it, to the future. He was assassinated—but the Union is not assassinated—ca ira! [?French expression for "it will be fine"] One falls, and another falls. The soldier drops, sinks like a wave—but the ranks of the ocean eternally press on. Death does its work, obliterates [?] literates [?] a hundred, a thousand—President, general, captain, private—but the Nation is immortal.

—Whitman, Walt. *Prose Works*. Philadelphia: David McKay, 1892; Bartleby.com, 2000. www.bartleby.com/229/. 12 August 2007.

Implied Main Idea: Lincoln preserved the UNION of the states; both he and the United States are immortal.

Source: The Death of President Lincoln By Walt Whitman. Prose Works. Philadelphia: David McKay, 1892

Practice 2

Choose a selection from the nineteen reading selections. Annotate the text. After you have annotated the text, recall and record in your notebook what you remember about the selection.

How to Write a Summary

A summary includes only the most important points of a text. A summary is a restatement of the main idea and the major supporting details. The length of the summary should reflect the length of the passage you are trying to understand. For example, a paragraph might be summarized in a sentence or two; an article might be summarized in a paragraph, and a much longer document may be summarized in several paragraphs.

Writing a summary by relying on the annotations you make during reading is an excellent way to check your understanding of what you read. Always use the writer's name and the title of the text in your summary. The following summary is based on the annotations of the Walt Whitman piece about Abraham Lincoln's death.

In his short note "The Death of President Lincoln," dated April 16, 1865, Walt Whitman honors the memory of the fallen president for his devotion to "Unionism," for being a faithful keeper of the future, and for ensuring that it will be fine and that the "Nation is immortal."

Practice 3

Write a summary based on the annotations you made for the reading selection you used in Practice 2. Use your own paper.

A Reading Strategy for a Writer

As you read the nineteen selections included in this section, use the following reading strategy to make the connection between reading and writing. Read each selection three times. Read it once just to enjoy the writing. Then, reread the piece to annotate it for understanding. Then, read a third time to study the piece more closely to prepare for a written response. The following steps are a guide to how to get the most out of your reading.

Reading Like a Writer

Before Reading Write a journal entry about the topic, title, and vocabulary. What do you already know, believe, or feel about the topic? Skim the text to identify and look up new or difficult words.

During Reading Annotate the text. Underline or highlight key terms, definitions, and main ideas. Generate questions to guide your thinking as you read; these questions will help you recall information after you read. Look for the answers to these questions and annotate the text when you come across the answers. Many college textbooks provide comprehension questions after a section of information. Feel free to use these after reading questions to focus your attention as you read.

After Reading Think, discuss, and write about what you read. Each of the nineteen reading selections has four discussion questions about the writer's main idea, relevant details, logical order, and effective expression. These directed thinking activities are called "After Reading Discussion Questions: Meaning, Structure, and Expression." Your writing will improve as you learn how other writers handle these elements.

- **Discuss it** Use your annotations to compare your views about a text with those of your classmates. Be open to ideas you had not considered. Add information to your notes. Discuss possible written responses.

- **Write about it** Respond in writing to the text. Each of the nineteen reading selections has two activities called "Thinking Prompts to Move from Reading to Writing."

Nineteen Reading Selections

Description

Niagara Falls

RUPERT BROOKE

Rupert Brooke (1887–1915) was an English poet known for his striking good looks and patriotic sonnets about war—which were inspired by his experiences in World War I—the most famous being "The Soldier." Although best known for his poetry, he was also a skilled essayist. He composed this piece of travel writing during a tour of the United States and Canada in 1913. The piece was one of a series written as letters to the *Westminster Gazette*. Two years after publishing this essay, Brooke died at the age of 27 from blood poisoning.

Before Reading Write a journal entry about a place you have visited that you think others should travel to see. Use vivid language and details to describe the striking or significant features of this place.

1 **Samuel Butler*** has a lot to answer for. But for him, a modern traveler could spend his time peacefully admiring the scenery instead of feeling himself bound to dog the simple and grotesque of the world for the sake of their too-human comments. It is his fault if a peasant's *naïveté* has come to outweigh the beauty of rivers, and the remarks of clergymen are more than mountains. It is very restful to give up all effort at observing human nature and drawing social and political deductions from trifles, and to let oneself relapse into wide-mouthed worship of the wonders of nature. And this is very easy at Niagara. Niagara means nothing. It is not leading anywhere. It does not result from anything. It throws no light on the effects of Protection, nor on the Facility for Divorce in America, nor on Corruption in Public Life, nor on Canadian character, nor even on the Navy Bill. It is merely a great deal of water falling over some cliffs. But it is very remarkably that. The human race, apt as a child to destroy what it admires, has done its best to surround the Falls with every distraction, incongruity, and vulgarity. Hotels, powerhouses, bridges, trams, picture post-cards, sham legends, stalls, booths, rifle-galleries, and side-shows frame them about. And there are Touts. Niagara is the central home and breeding-place for all the touts of earth. There are touts insinuating, and touts raucous, greasy touts, brazen touts, and upper-class, refined, gentlemanly, take-you-by-the-arm touts; touts who intimidate and touts who wheedle; professionals,

*****Samuel Butler:** A Victorian author, critic, and philosopher who examined Christian and evolutionary thought.

amateurs, and *dilettanti*, male and female; touts who would photograph you with your arm round a young lady against a faked background of the sublimest cataract, touts who would bully you into cars, char-à-bancs, elevators, or tunnels, or deceive you into a carriage and pair, touts who would sell you picture post-cards, moccasins, sham Indian beadwork, blankets, tee-pees, and crockery, and touts, finally, who have no apparent object in the world, but just purely, simply, merely, incessantly, indefatigably, and **ineffugibly*** to tout. And in the midst of all this, overwhelming it all, are the Falls. He who sees them instantly forgets humanity. They are not very high, but they are overpowering. They are divided by an island into two parts, the Canadian and the American.

Half a mile or so above the Falls, on either side, the water of the great stream begins to run more swiftly and in confusion. It descends with ever-growing speed. It begins chattering and leaping, breaking into a thousand ripples, throwing up joyful fingers of spray. Sometimes it is divided by islands and rocks, sometimes the eye can see nothing but a waste of laughing, springing, foamy waves, turning, crossing, even seeming to stand for an instant erect, but always borne impetuously forward like a crowd of triumphant feasters. Sit close down by it, and you see a fragment of the torrent against the sky, mottled, steely, and foaming, leaping onward in far-flung criss-cross strands of water. Perpetually the eye is on the point of descrying a pattern in this weaving, and perpetually it is cheated by change. In one place part of the flood plunges over a ledge a few feet high and a quarter of a mile or so long, in a uniform and stable curve. It gives an impression of almost military concerted movement, grown suddenly out of confusion. But it is swiftly lost again in the multitudinous tossing merriment. Here and there a rock close to the surface is marked by a white wave that faces backwards and seems to be rushing madly up-stream, but is really stationary in the headlong charge. But for these signs of reluctance, the waters seem to fling themselves on with some foreknowledge of their fate, in an ever wilder frenzy. But it is no **Maeterlinckian*** prescience. They prove, rather, that Greek belief that the great crashes are preceded by a louder merriment and a wilder gaiety. Leaping in the sunlight, careless, entwining, clamorously joyful, the waves riot on towards the verge.

But there they change. As they turn to the sheer descent, the white and blue and slate color, in the heart of the Canadian Falls at least, blend and deepen to a rich, wonderful, luminous green. On the edge of disaster the river seems to gather herself, to pause, top, lift a head noble in ruin, and then, with a slow grandeur, to plunge into the eternal thunder and white chaos below. Where the stream runs shallower it is a kind of violet color, but both violet and green fray and frill to white as they fall. The mass of water, striking some ever-hidden base of rock, leaps up the whole two hundred feet again in pinnacles and domes of spray. The spray falls back into the lower river once more; all but a little that fines to foam and white mist, which drifts in layers along the air, graining it, and wanders out on the wind over the trees and gardens and houses, and so vanishes.

The manager of one of the great power-stations on the banks of the river above the Falls told me that the center of the riverbed at the Canadian Falls is deep and of a saucer shape. So it may be possible to fill this up to a uniform depth, and divert a lot of water for the power-houses. And this, he said, would supply the need for more power, which will certainly soon arise, without taking away from the beauty of Niagara. This is a handsome concession of the utilitarians to ordinary sight-seers. Yet, I doubt if we shall be satisfied. The real secret of the beauty and terror of the Falls is not their height or width, but the feeling of colossal power and of unintelligible disaster caused by the plunge of that vast body of water. If that were taken away, there would be little visible change, but the heart would be gone.

The American Falls do not inspire this feeling in the same way as the Canadian. It is because they are less in volume, and because the water does not fall so much into one place. By comparison their beauty is almost delicate and fragile. They are extraordinarily level, one long curtain of lacework and woven foam. Seen from opposite, when the sun is on them, they are blindingly white, and the clouds of spray show dark against them. With both Falls the color of the water is the ever-altering wonder. Greens and blues, purples and whites, melt into one another, fade, and come again, and change with the changing sun. Sometimes they are as richly diaphanous as a precious stone, and glow from within with a deep, inexplicable light. Sometimes the white intricacies of dropping foam become opaque and creamy. And

---

***Ineffugibly** is a word made up by the author; making up words is a poetic technique often employed by writers.
****Maeterlinck,** a Belgian writer who won the Nobel Prize, was noted for his poetic use of symbolism.

always there are the rainbows. If you come suddenly upon the Falls from above, a great double rainbow, very vivid, spanning the extent of spray from top to bottom, is the first thing you see. If you wander along the cliff opposite, a bow springs into being in the American Falls, accompanies you courteously on your walk, dwindles and dies as the mist ends, and awakens again as you reach the Canadian tumult. And the bold traveler who attempts the trip under the American Falls sees, when he dare open his eyes to anything, tiny baby rainbows, some four or five yards in span, leaping from rock to rock among the foam, and gamboling beside him, barely out of hand's reach, as he goes. One I saw in that place was a complete circle, such as I have never seen before, and so near that I could put my foot on it. It is a terrifying journey, beneath and behind the Falls. The senses are battered and bewildered by the thunder of the water and the assault of wind and spray; or rather, the sound is not of falling water, but merely of falling; a noise of unspecified ruin. So, if you are close behind the endless clamor, the sight cannot recognize liquid in the masses that hurl past. You are dimly and pitifully aware that sheets of light and darkness are falling in great curves in front of you. Dull omnipresent foam washes the face. Farther away, in the roar and hissing, clouds of spray seem literally to slide down some invisible plane of air.

6 Beyond the foot of the Falls the river is like a slipping floor of marble, green with veins of dirty white, made by the scum that was foam. It slides very quietly and slowly down for a mile or two, sullenly exhausted. Then it turns to a dull sage green, and hurries more swiftly, smooth and ominous. As the walls of the ravine close in, trouble stirs, and the waters boil and eddy. These are the lower rapids, a sight more terrifying than the Falls, because less intelligible. Close in its bands of rock the river surges tumultuously forward, writhing and leaping as if inspired by a demon. It is pressed by the straits into a visibly convex form. Great planes of water slide past. Sometimes it is thrown up into a pinnacle of foam higher than a house, or leaps with incredible speed from the crest of one vast wave to another, along the shining curve between, like the spring of a wild beast. Its motion continually suggests muscular action. The power manifest in these rapids moves one with a different sense of awe and terror from that of the Falls. Here the inhuman life and strength are spontaneous, active, almost resolute; masculine vigor compared with the passive gigantic power, female, helpless and overwhelming, of the Falls. A place of fear.

7 One is drawn back, strangely, to a contemplation of the Falls, at every hour, and especially by night, when the cloud of spray becomes an immense visible ghost, straining and wavering high above the river, white and pathetic and translucent. The **Victorian*** lies very close below the surface in every man. There one can sit and let great cloudy thoughts of destiny and the passage of empires drift through the mind; for such dreams are at home by Niagara. I could not get out of my mind the thought of a friend, who said that the rainbows over the Falls were like the arts and beauty and goodness, with regard to the stream of life—caused by it, thrown upon its spray, but unable to stay or direct or affect it, and ceasing when it ceased. In all comparisons that rise in the heart, the river, with its multitudinous waves and its single current, likens itself to a life, whether of an individual or of a community. A man's life is of many flashing moments, and yet one stream; a nation's flows through all its citizens, and yet is more than they. In such places, one is aware, with an almost insupportable and yet comforting certitude, that both men and nations are hurried onwards to their ruin or ending as inevitably as this dark flood. Some go down to it unreluctant, and meet it, like the river, not without nobility. And as incessant, as inevitable, and as unavailing as the spray that hangs over the Falls, is the white cloud of human crying. . . . With some such thoughts does the platitudinous heart win from the confusion and thunder of a Niagara peace that the quietest plains or most stable hills can never give.

Source: Rupert Brooke, *Letters From America with a Preface by Henry James* (London: Sidgwick & Jackson, Ltd, 1931; repr. 1947).

*Victorian: An era from 1837–1901 in characterized by a belief in order, stability, and natural laws.
Source: *Originally published in the* Westminster Gazette, *"Niagara Falls" by Rupert Brooke was included in the collection* Letters from America *(1916). This version of the essay first appeared in* Modern Essays, *edited by Christopher Morley (Harcourt Brace, 1921).*

Vocabulary
Before, during, and after reading the selection, annotate the text and write in your journal. Create a list of vocabulary words, along with their definitions. Give examples of their use from the selection you just read.

After Reading Discussion Questions: Meaning, Structure, and Expression

1. **Central Idea:** Work as a group to write a summary that answers the following questions: What purpose did Rupert Brooke have for writing this essay? Who is his intended audience? What is the central point of the essay? What is the significance of the title?
2. **Relevant Details:** Why do you think Brooke began with a reference to Samuel Butler? What point is he making by referring to Butler? Is this reference relevant today? Why or why not?
3. **Logical Order:** Brooke concludes his essay by drawing back "to a contemplation of the Falls." What point does he make as he concludes his contemplation? Do you think this is an effective end to this essay? Why or why not?
4. **Effective Expression:** Based on Brooke's use of language, how would you describe the tone of this essay? Does his tone remain consistent throughout the essay? For example, does his attitude toward the "touts" differ from his attitude about the Falls? Identify three expressions that illustrate specific tones or attitudes. Use those quotations to explain how Brooke achieved his tone.

Thinking Prompts to Move from Reading to Writing

1. Assume you are taking a college course in geography. Your professor has asked you to choose a particular place and write a report that describes the features of the land that make it distinctive. You have chosen to report on Niagara Falls. Pull descriptive details from the reading passage to include in your report. Use your own words.
2. Assume you write a blog and you have several hundred followers. Write a description of a significant place, person, or object. For example, you may choose to describe a local soup kitchen, a popular park, a famous person, or your favorite place. Your description should reveal the significance of the subject matter you chose.

Maya Lin's Design Submission to the Vietnam Memorial Competition

MAYA LIN

Born in 1959 in Athens, Ohio, Maya Lin, as a senior at Yale University, submitted the winning design in a national competition for the Vietnam Veterans Memorial that now stands in Washington, D.C. Lin, a Chinese American, designs spaces that make room for individuals within the landscape.

Before Reading Write a journal entry about the Vietnam Memorial. What do you know about it? Have you seen it? What was its impact on you? If you have not seen it, do you want to? Why or why not? Why are monuments and memorials important?

1 Walking through this park-like area, the memorial appears as a rift in the earth—a long, polished black stone wall, emerging from and receding into the earth. Approaching the memorial, the ground slopes gently downward, and the low walls emerging on either side, growing out of the earth, extend and converge at a point below and ahead. Walking into the grassy site contained by the walls of the memorial we can barely make out the carved names upon the memorial's walls. These names,

seemingly infinite in number, convey the sense of overwhelming numbers, while unifying those individuals into a whole. For this memorial is meant not as a monument to the individual but rather, as a memorial to the men and women who died during this war, as a whole.

The memorial is composed not as an unchanging monument, but as a moving composition, to be understood as we move into and out of it; the passage itself is gradual, the descent to the origin slow, but it is at the origin that the meaning of the memorial is to be fully understood. At the intersection of these walls, on the right side, at the wall's top, is carved the date of the first death. It is followed by the names of those who have died in the war, in chronological order. These names continue on this wall, appearing to recede into the earth at the wall's end. The names resume on the left wall, as the wall emerges from the earth, continuing back to the origin, where the date of the last death is carved, at the bottom of this wall. Thus the war's beginning and end meet; the war is "complete," coming full circle, yet broken by the earth that bounds the angle's open side, and contained within the earth itself. As we turn to leave, we see these walls stretching into the distance, directing us to the Washington Monument, to the left, and the Lincoln Memorial, to the right, thus bringing the Vietnam Memorial into an historical context. We the living are brought to a concrete realization of these deaths.

Brought to a sharp awareness of such a loss, it is up to each individual to resolve or come to terms with this loss. For death, is in the end a personal and private matter, and the area contained with this memorial is a quiet place, meant for personal reflection and private reckoning. The black granite walls, each two hundred feet long, and ten feet below ground at their lowest point (gradually ascending toward ground level) effectively act as a sound barrier, yet are of such a height and length so as not to appear threatening or enclosing. The actual area is wide and shallow, allowing for a sense of privacy, and the sunlight from the memorial's southern exposure along with the grassy park surrounding and within its walls, contribute to the serenity of the area. Thus this memorial is for those who have died, and for us to remember them.

The memorial's origin is located approximately at the center of the site; its legs each extending two hundred feet towards the Washington Monument and the Lincoln Memorial. The walls, contained on one side by the earth, are ten feet below ground at their point of origin, gradually lessening in height, until they finally recede totally into the earth, at their ends. The walls are to be made of hard, polished black granite, with the names to be carved in simple Trajan letter. The memorial's construction involves recontouring the area within the wall's boundaries, so as to provide for an easily accessible descent, but as much of the site as possible should be left untouched. The area should remain as a park, for all to enjoy.

Source: Maya Lin/Vietnam Veterans Memorial Fund.

Vocabulary
Before, during, and after reading the selection, annotate the text and write in your journal. Create a list of vocabulary words, along with their definitions. Give examples of their use from the selection you just read.

After Reading Discussion Questions: Meaning, Structure, and Expression

1. **Main Idea:** Work as a group to write a summary that answers the following questions: What purpose did Maya Lin have for writing this essay? Who is her intended audience? What is the main idea of the essay?
2. **Relevant Details:** Lin writes, "For death, is in the end a personal and private matter, and the area contained with this memorial is a quiet place, meant for personal reflection and private reckoning." Based on the details in her description, how does the memorial represent this belief?
3. **Logical Order:** As Lin gives her physical description of the memorial, she explains the significance of each detail. Do her explanations help create a mental image of the memorial? Would it have been just as effective to give an uninterrupted physical description and then explain the purpose of each detail in a separate section? Why or why not?
4. **Effective Expression:** Of the 1,421 essays submitted in the design competition for the Vietnam Memorial, this essay won. In what ways did Lin use effective expression to communicate her vision? Identify three effective expressions in the essay. Discuss the reasons for your selections.

Thinking Prompts to Move from Reading to Writing

1. Just as the memorials erected in Washington, D.C. represent people and events of historical significance, many communities build memorials to honor local individuals, groups of people, or events. Describe such a memorial in your community. Use your description to convey the significance of the memorial.
2. Identify a person, place, or event that is worthy of a memorial. Design a memorial and write an essay that describes your design and the significance of the honor.

Narration

Latino Heritage Month: Who We Are . . . And Why We Celebrate?

LUIS J. RODRIGUEZ

Luis J. Rodriguez is the author of fourteen books in poetry, children's literature, fiction, and nonfiction, including the bestselling memoir *Always Running, La Vida Loca, Gang Days in L.A.* He's cofounder of Tia Chucha's Centro Cultural and Bookstore, founder/editor of Tia Chucha Press, and cofounder of Barking Rooster Entertainment. His latest book is the sequel to *Always Running*, entitled *It Calls You Back: An Odyssey Through Love, Addiction, Revolutions, and Healing*. The following essay was posted online in *The Huffington Post*. In his essay, Rodriguez uses his own story to commemorate Latino Heritage Month.

Before Reading Write a journal entry that responds to the question in Rodriguez's title: Who are Latinos? And why celebrate Latinos?

1 I recently visited Orlando, Florida, home to more Puerto Ricans on the mainland other than New York City. I was there to spend time with my grandson Ricardo, who earlier this year graduated from high school with honors and is now into his first year of college. Ricardo is part of the Puerto Rican side of my family, wonderful law-abiding Christians, who worked hard and provided a loving home for my grandson when the world around him seemed bleak.

2 For fifteen years, I lived in a mostly Puerto Rican community of Chicago, where Ricardo's mother grew up. Although I am Chicano, born on the Mexico-U.S. border, I've also lived among Mexican migrants, Central Americans, African Americans, Asians, Cuban Americans, and European Americans in Los Angeles, the San Francisco Bay Area, Miami, San Bernardino, and San Fernando. For years, I've spoken at and participated in ceremonies in Native American reservations (a Navajo medicine man and his wife around ten years ago adopted my present wife). My other grandchildren are half German, half Scottish-Irish, and half Hungarian.

3 My former wives and live-in girlfriends include a barrio-raised Chicana, an undocumented Mexican, a Mexican/Colombian, a poor white mother of two, and an African American. My own roots are with the indigenous Tarahumara (who call themselves Raramuri) of Chihuahua on my mother's side. My father—and you could see this on his face and in his hair—was native, Spanish, and African from the Mexican state of Guerrero.

In fact, Ricardo's girlfriend is from Guyana, whose family was originally from India.

To say the least, my extended family is complex and vibrant, made up of all skin colors, ethnicities, and languages . . . and as "American" as apple pie (or burritos, for that matter, since these were created on the U.S. side of that border).

Purportedly I'm a Latino, although I rarely call myself this. I mean the original Latinos are Italians, right? Yet Italian Americans are not considered Latinos in this country. And so-called Latinos have origins in Native America, Africa, Europe, Asia, and a vast array of mixtures thereof. We are known as the largest "minority" group in the United States, yet we do not constitute one ethnic group or culture.

Let me put it this way: Despite the umbrella of "Latino" above our heads, Puerto Ricans are not the same as Dominicans. And many Salvadorans I know don't want to be confused with being Mexican.

Still, today we officially launch Latino Heritage Month, configured to run from September 15 to October 15, largely to coincide with the Independence Days of countries like Mexico, El Salvador, and others. Unofficially, of course, people who claim roots in Latino countries celebrate every day—they're also into the Fourth of July, Christmas, Martin Luther King Jr. Day, Hanukah, and Native American Sun Dance ceremonies. Regardless of their country of origin, these people are central to the American soul and deeply intertwined with the social fabric.

Despite this Latinos seem to be a rumor in the country, a "middle people," neither black nor white, hardly in the popular culture, mostly shadows and shouts in the distance.

Maybe what we celebrate is the complexities, the richness, the expansiveness of who we are. Maybe we celebrate that Latinos have bled and sweated for this country. Hundreds from the Dominican Republic, Colombia, Mexico, Ecuador, Argentina, and other Latin American countries died during the 9/11 attacks. People with Spanish or Portuguese surnames garnered more medals of honor during World War II and had a disproportionate number of casualties during the Vietnam War. The first known U.S. death from the Iraq War was a young man originally from Guatemala.

Perhaps we celebrate that Latinos have worked in the auto plants of Detroit, steel mills of Chicago, cotton fields of Texas, textile centers of Massachusetts, and crop fields of California. That they are among the best in professional sports, and I'm not limiting this to soccer—they have been some of the world's best boxers, baseball players, football players, golfers, and tennis players.

Let's celebrate that Latinos have been in the forefront of the organized labor movement and fought alongside African Americans against slavery and for Civil Rights. That they are among the oldest residents of the continent, as indigenous peoples from places like Mexico, Central America or Peru. And they are the majority of this country's most recent arrivals. Let's recognize that U.S. Latinos can be found among scientists, professors, doctors, politicians, and judges. That renowned actors, musicians, and writers include Carlos Santana, Ricky Martin, Jennifer Lopez, George Lopez, Danny Trejo, Celia Cruz, Oscar Hijuelos, Sandra Cisneros, Junot Diaz, Salma Hayek, Antonio Banderas, Los Lobos, Cheech Marin, Shakira, Javier Bardem, Penelope Cruz, Eva Mendes, and Bruno Mars.

Our ancestors were former slaves and former slaveholders, peons and nobles, poets and conquistadors, African miners and native rebels. They include practitioners of the Flamenco and canto hondo with ties to the Roma people (so-called Gypsies) and the Arab/Muslim world, which once ruled Spain for close to 800 years. And so-called Latinos still use words, herbs, dance, and clothing from the wondrous civilizations of the Olmeca, Mexica (so-called Aztec), Maya, and Inca.

The fact is Latino heritage is U.S. heritage. You wouldn't have such "American" phenomena as cowboys, guitars, rubber balls, gold mining, horses, corn, and even Jazz, Rock-and-Roll, and Hip Hop, without the contribution of Latinos. And besides the hundreds of Spanish words that now grace the English language (lariat, rodeo, buckaroo, adios, cafeteria, hasta la vista, baby), there are also indigenous words that English can't do without . . . chocolate, ocelot, coyote, tomato, avocado, maize, and barbecue, among others.

Unfortunately, as we contemplate what Latino Heritage means, we have to be reminded that Latinos have been among the most scapegoated during the current financial crisis. States have established more laws against brown-skinned undocumented migrants while Arizona is trying to outlaw teachings on

Mexican/Ethnic history and culture. They are also among the poorest, least healthy, and most neglected Americans. Spanish-surnamed people are now the majority in the federal prison system and the largest single group in state penitentiaries of California, New Mexico, and Texas. And they are concentrated among this country's homeless and drug-addicted populations.

So while all Americans have much to celebrate in Latino heritage, like most Americans we also have a long way to go.

Whatever one thinks of Latinos, one thing is for sure: They have given much to this country, and have much more to give. I'm convinced any revolutionary changes in the economy, politics, technology, cultural life, social equity and justice must have Latinos (regardless of race, background, religion, social class, or political strain) at the heart of them. They are integral to the past, present, and future of this country.

And this is a beautiful thing, baby.

Source: Copyright © 2011 by Luis J. Rodriguez. First published in *The Huffington Post* on September 15, 2011. By permission of Susan Bergholtz Literary Services, New York, and Lamy, NM. all rights reserved.

Vocabulary
Before, during, and after reading the selection, annotate the text and write in your journal. Create a list of vocabulary words, along with their definitions. Give examples of their use from the selection you just read.

After Reading Discussion Questions: Meaning, Structure, and Expression

1. **Main Idea:** Work as a group to write a summary that answers the following questions: What purpose did Rodriguez have for writing this piece? Who is his intended audience? What is the main idea of the essay? What is the significance of the title of the piece?
2. **Relevant Details:** Reread the details in paragraphs 1 through 7. What is the significance of these details? How do these details relate to the main point Rodriguez is making? Would the essay be as effective if these details were deleted? Why or why not?
3. **Logical Order:** Rodriguez does not mention his topic "Latino Heritage Month" until paragraph 8, and then he doesn't state his central point until much later in the essay. Where in the essay does Rodriguez state his central point? Do you think the essay would be more effective if he had stated his topic and central point earlier in the essay? Why or why not?
4. **Effective Expression:** How would you describe the overall tone Rodriquez uses throughout his essay—admiring, critical, factual, proud, or some other attitude? Does his tone change at certain points? Identify and explain Rodriquez's tone. Support your explanation with examples from the essay.

Thinking Prompts to Move from Reading to Writing

1. In paragraph 12 of his essay, Rodriguez recognizes several "renowned actors, musicians, and writers" who have made significant contributions to American culture. Assume one of these people will be a special guest speaker on your campus during Latino Heritage Month (choose a Latino listed in paragraph 12, or you may choose another Latino not mentioned). You have been asked to introduce this person to the audience. Write a brief biography that narrates the major contributions the special guest speaker has made to American culture.
2. "Latino Heritage Month: Who We Are . . . And Why We Celebrate?" relays Rodriguez's story of Latino heritage. By narrating his family's origin and the contributions of Latinos to American culture, he celebrates Latino heritage. Write a narrative that celebrates or honors your own family or cultural heritage.

Confessions

AMY TAN

Born in 1952 to immigrant parents from China, Amy Tan is the award-winning author of several novels, including her widely popular and critically acclaimed novel *The Joy Luck Club*. Tragically, Tan's father and oldest brother both died of brain tumors within a year of each other, and Tan was in constant conflict with her mother. Tan's work has been translated into 35 languages, including Spanish, French, Chinese, Arabic, and Hebrew. The following selection is an excerpt from her autobiographical collection of essays *The Opposite of Fate*.

Before Reading Write a journal entry about the conflicts within a family. Have you ever had a terrible fight with a family member? How did it make you feel? Do mothers and daughters or fathers and sons experience a particular kind of conflict?

1. My mother's thoughts reach back like the winter tide, exposing the wreckage of a former shore. Often she's mired in 1967, 1968, the years my older brother and my father died.

2. 1968 was also the year she took me and my little brother—Didi—across the Atlantic to Switzerland, a place so preposterously different that she knew she had to give up grieving simply to survive. That year, she remembers, she was very, very sad. I too remember. I was sixteen then, and I recall a late-night hour when my mother and I were arguing in the chalet, that tinderbox of emotion where we lived.

3. She had pushed me into the small bedroom we shared, and as she slapped me about the head, I backed into a corner, by a window that looked out on the lake, the Alps, the beautiful outside world. My mother was furious because I had a boyfriend. She was shouting that he was a drug addict, a bad man who would use me for sex and throw me away like leftover garbage.

4. "Stop seeing him!" she ordered.

5. I shook my head. The more she beat me, the more implacable I became, and this in turn fueled her outrage.

6. "You didn't love you daddy or Peter! When they die you not even sad."

7. I kept my face to the window, unmoved. What does she know about sad?

8. She sobbed and beat her chest. "I rather kill myself before see you destroy you life!"

9. Suicide. How many times had she threatened that before?

10. "I wish you the one die! Not Peter, not Daddy."

11. She had just confirmed what I had always suspected. Now she flew at me with her fists.

12. "I rather kill you! I rather see you die!"

13. And then, perhaps horrified by what she had just said, she fled the room. Thank God that was over. I wished I had a cigarette to smoke. Suddenly she was back. She slammed the door shut, latched it, then locked it with a key. I saw the flash of a meat cleaver just before she pushed me to the wall and brought the blade's edge to within an inch of my throat. Her eyes were like a wild animal's, shiny, fixated on the kill. In an excited voice she said, "First, I kill you. Then Didi and me, our whole family destroy!" She smiled, her chest heaving. "Why you don't cry?" She pressed the blade closer and I could feel her breath gusting.

14. Was she bluffing? If she did kill me, so what? Who would care? While she rambled, a voice within me was whimpering, "This is sad, this is so sad."

15. For ten minutes, fifteen, longer, I straddled these two thoughts—that it didn't matter if I died, that it would be eternally sad if I did—until all at once I felt a snap, then a rush of hope into a vacuum, and I was crying, I was babbling my confession: "I want to live. I want to live."

> For twenty-five years I forgot that day, and when the memory of what happened surfaced unexpectedly at a writers' workshop in which we recalled our worst moments, I was shaking, wondering to myself, Did she really mean to kill me? If I had not pleaded with her, would she have pushed down on the cleaver and ended my life?
>
> I wanted to go to my mother and ask. Yet I couldn't, not until much later, when she became forgetful and I learned she had Alzheimer's disease. I knew that if I didn't ask her certain questions now, I would never know the real answers.
>
> So I asked.
>
> "Angry? Slap you?" she said, and laughed. "No, no, *no*. You always good girl, never even need to spank, not even one time."
>
> How wonderful to hear her say what was never true, yet now would be forever so.

Source: Amy Tan, "Confessions" Copyright © 1997 by Amy Tan. First appeared in *Confession*, PEN/Faulkner Foundation. Reprinted by permission of the author and the Sandra Dijkstra Literary Agency.

Vocabulary

Before, during, and after reading the selection, annotate the text and write in your journal. Create a list of vocabulary words, along with their definitions. Give examples of their use from the selection you just read.

After Reading Discussion Questions: Meaning, Structure, and Expression

1. **Main Idea:** Work as a group to write a summary that answers the following questions: What purpose did Amy Tan have for writing this essay? Who is her intended audience? What is the main idea of the essay? What is the significance of the title?
2. **Relevant Details:** Tan often implies a main idea through the use of well-chosen details that draw a vivid picture. Paragraph 13 describes a shocking scene. What point is Tan making with these details? How do these details fulfill her purpose and support her main idea? Why would Tan reveal so much personal and painful information?
3. **Logical Order:** Tan sets her narrative up as a flashback to an unpleasant memory. Later, in paragraph 16, she tells us she remembered this incident in a writing workshop 25 years after it occurred. Why do you think she waited to tell us when or how she remembered the incident? Would the essay be as effective if she had begun the narrative from the moment she recalled the incident in the workshop? Why or why not?
4. **Effective Expression:** Tan begins the essay with a simile, an indirect comparison between two things using *like* or *as*: "My mother's thoughts reach back like the winter tide, exposing the wreckage of a former shore." How are her mother's thoughts similar to the *winter tide*? To what do *wreckage* and *former shore* refer?

Thinking Prompts to Move from Reading to Writing

1. The conflict between parent and child is age-old and universal. In her essay, Tan shows us how this timeless conflict affected her relationship with her mother. Write a narrative about a conflict between a parent and child that shows the impact of the conflict.
2. "Confessions" is a painful admission of a "worst moment" in both Amy Tan's life and her mother's life. Her confession reveals personal and potentially embarrassing information. Often, we gain wisdom and understanding through conflict and suffering. However, not every writer feels comfortable making a point through a personal confession. Find a story in the news about a "worst moment" in someone's life. Write a narrative that makes a point about the incident.

Process

Managing Stress in College

REBECCA J. DONATELLE

Dr. Donatelle has served since 1990 as the Associate Professor and Coordinator of the Health Promotion and Health Behavior Programs in the Department of Health at Oregon State University. She has widely published in professional journals and is well known for her college textbooks on health. The following passage is an excerpt from her textbook *Health: The Basics*. In this passage, Dr. Donatelle describes ways to manage stress in college.

Before Reading Write a journal entry about managing stress. Do you or anyone you know experience stress because of school, work, or both? How do you react to stress? Describe some ways that you cope with stress. Why is learning how to manage stress important?

1. College students thrive under a certain amount of stress, but excessive stress can overwhelm many. Studies have indicated that first-year students report not only more problems with stress, but also more emotional reactivity in the form of anger, hostility, frustration, and a greater sense of being out of control. Sophomores and juniors reported fewer problems with these issues, and seniors reported the fewest problems. This may indicate students' progressive emotional growth through experience, maturity, increased awareness of support services, and more social connections.

2. Students generally report using health-enhancing methods to combat stress, but research has found that students sometimes resort to health-compromising activities to escape the stress and anxiety of college. Numerous researchers have found stress among college students to be correlated to unhealthy behaviors such as substance abuse, lack of physical activity, poor psychological and physical health, lack of social problem solving, and infrequent use of social support networks.

3. Being on your own in college may pose challenges, but it also lets you take control of and responsibility for your life. Although you can't eliminate all life stressors, you can train yourself to recognize the events that cause stress and to anticipate your reactions to them. Coping is the act of managing events or conditions to lessen the physical or psychological effects of excess stress. One of the most effective ways to combat stressors is to build coping strategies and skills, known collectively as *stress-management techniques,* such as those discussed in the following sections.

Practicing Mental Work to Reduce Stress

4. Stress management isn't something that just happens. It calls for getting a handle on what is going on in your life, taking a careful look at yourself, and coming up with a personal plan of action. Because your perceptions are often part of the problem, assessing your self-talk, beliefs, and actions are good first steps. Why are you so stressed? How much of it is due to perception rather than reality? What's a realistic plan of action for you? Think about your situation and map out a strategy for change. The tools in this section will help you.

5. **Assess Your Stressors and Solve Problems** Assessing what is really going on in your life is an important first step to solving problems and reducing your stress. Here's how:

- Make a list of the major things that you are worried about right now.
- Examine the causes of the problems and worries.
- Consider how big each problem is. What are the consequences of doing nothing? Of taking action?
- List your options, including ones that you may not like very much.
- Outline an action plan, and then *act.* Remember that even little things can sometimes make a big difference and that you shouldn't expect immediate results.
- After you act, evaluate. How did you do? Do you need to change your actions to achieve a better outcome next time? How?

One useful way of coping with your stressors, once you have identified them, is to consciously anticipate and prepare for specific stressors, a technique known as **stress inoculation.** For example, suppose speaking in front of a class scares you. Practice in front of friends or in front of a video camera to banish panic and prevent your freezing up on the day of the presentation.

Change the Way You Think and Talk to Yourself As noted earlier, our appraisal of a situation is what makes things stressful. Several types of negative self-talk can make things more stressful. Among the most common are *pessimism,* or focusing on the negative; *perfectionism,* or expecting superhuman standards; "*should-ing,*" or reprimanding yourself for things that you should have done; *blaming* yourself or others for circumstances and events; and *dichotomous thinking,* in which everything is either black or white (good or bad) instead of somewhere in between. To combat negative self-talk, we must first become aware of it, then stop it, and finally replace the negative thoughts with positive ones—a process called as **cognitive restructuring.** Once you realize that some of your thoughts may be negative, irrational, or overreactive, interrupt this self-talk by saying, "Stop" (under your breath or aloud), and make a conscious effort to think positively.

Developing a Support Network

As you plan a stress-management program, remember the importance of social networks and social bonds. Studies of college students have demonstrated the importance of social support in *buffering* individuals from the effects of stress. Different friends often serve different needs, so having more than one is usually beneficial.

Find Supportive People Family members and friends can be a steady base of support when the pressures of life seem overwhelming. People who are positive, help you to see the realities of your situation, and offer constructive suggestions can help you get through even the toughest times. Avoid "debby-downers" who continually drain you with their own issues or negative outlooks on life. If supportive friends or family are unavailable, most colleges and universities offer counseling services at no cost for short-term crises. Clergy, instructors, and residence hall supervisors also may be excellent resources. Most communities also offer low-cost counseling through mental health clinics.

Invest in Your Loved Ones As our lives get busy and obligations become overwhelming, we often don't make time for the very people who are most important to us: our friends, family, and other loved ones. In order to have a healthy social support network, we have to invest time and energy. Cultivate and nurture the relationships that matter: those built on trust, mutual acceptance and understanding, honesty, and genuine caring. In addition, treating others empathically provides them with a measure of emotional security and reduces *their* anxiety. If you want others to be there for you to help you cope with life's stressors, you need to be there for them.

Cultivating Your Spiritual Side

One of the most important factors in reducing stress in your life is taking the time and making the commitment to cultivate your spiritual side: finding your purpose in life and living your days more fully.

Managing Emotional Responses

Have you ever gotten all worked up about something only to find that your perceptions were totally wrong? We often get upset not by realities, but by our faulty perceptions. Stress management requires that you examine your emotional responses to interactions with others. With any emotional response to a stressor, you are responsible for the emotion and the resulting behaviors. Learning to tell the difference between normal emotions and emotions based on irrational beliefs or expressed and interpreted in an over the-top manner can help you stop the emotion or express it in a healthy and appropriate way.

Fight the Anger Urge Anger usually results when we feel we have lost control of a situation or are frustrated by a situation that we can do little about. Major sources of anger include (1) perceived threats to self or others we care about; (2) reactions to injustice, such as unfair actions, policies, or behaviors; (3) fear, which leads to negative responses; (4) faulty emotional reasoning, or misinterpretation of normal events; (5) low frustration tolerance, often fueled by stress, drugs, lack of sleep, and other factors; (6) unreasonable expectations about ourselves and others; and (7) people rating, or applying derogatory ratings to others.

Each of us has learned by this point in our lives that we have three main approaches to dealing with anger: *expressing it*, *suppressing it*, or *calming it*. You may be surprised to find out that, in the long run, expressing your anger is probably the healthiest thing to do, if you express anger in an assertive rather than an aggressive way. However, it's a natural reaction to want to respond aggressively, and that is what we must learn to keep at bay. To accomplish this, there are several strategies you can use:

- **Identify your anger style.** Do you express anger passively or actively? Do you hold anger in, or do you explode? Do you throw the phone, smash things, or scream at others?
- **Learn to recognize patterns in your anger responses and how to de-escalate them.** For 1 week, keep track of everything that angers you or keeps you stewing. What thoughts or feelings lead up to your boiling point? Keep a journal and listen to your anger. Try to change your self-talk. Explore how you can interrupt patterns of anger, such as counting to 10, getting a drink of water, or taking some deep breaths.
- **Find the right words to de-escalate conflict.** Communicate to de-escalate. When conflict arises, be respectful and state your needs or feelings rather than shooting zingers at the other person. Avoid "you always" or "you never" and instead say, "I feel ____ when you ____" or "I would really appreciate it if you could ____." Another approach would be to say, "I really need help understanding . . . or . . . figuring out a way to ____." If you find you are continually revved up for a battle, consider taking a class or workshop on assertiveness training or anger management.
- **Plan ahead.** Explore options to minimize your exposure to anger-provoking situations such as traffic jams. Give yourself an extra 15 minutes, and learn to "chill" when unexpected delays occur.
- **Vent to your friends.** Find a few close friends you can confide in. They can provide insight or another perspective. But, don't wear down your supporter with continual rants.
- **Develop realistic expectations of yourself and others.** Anger is often the result of unmet expectations, frustrations, resentments, and impatience. Are your expectations of yourself and others realistic? Try talking about your feelings with those involved at a time when you are calm.
- **Turn complaints into requests.** When frustrated or angry with someone, try reworking the problem into a request. Instead of screaming and pounding on the wall because your neighbors are blaring music at 2:00 A.M., talk with them. Try to reach an agreement that works for everyone. Again, think ahead about the words you will use.
- **Leave past anger in the past.** Learn to resolve issues and not bring them up over and over. Let it go. If you can't, seek the counsel of a professional to learn how.

Learn to Laugh, Be Joyful, and Cry Have you ever noticed that you feel better after a belly laugh or a good cry? Adages such as "laughter is the best medicine" and "smile and the world smiles with you" didn't evolve out of the blue. Humans have long recognized that smiling, laughing, singing, dancing, and other actions can elevate our moods, relieve stress, make us feel good, and help us improve our relationships. Learning to take yourself less seriously and laugh at yourself is a good starting place. Crying can have similar positive physiological effects in relieving tension. Several studies have indicated that laughter and joy may increase endorphin levels, increase oxygen levels in the blood, decrease stress levels, relieve pain, enhance productivity, and reduce risks of chronic disease; however, the evidence for *long-term* effects on immune functioning and protective effects for chronic diseases is only just starting to be understood.

Taking Physical Action

Feeling unbearably tense and ready to explode? Remember that the human stress response is intended to end in physical activity. Yet in today's world we usually aren't able to fight or flee. However, exercise can "burn off" stress hormones by directing them toward their intended metabolic function. Exercise can also help combat stress by raising levels of endorphins—mood-elevating, painkilling hormones—in the bloodstream, increasing energy, reducing hostility, and improving mental alertness. Go for a brisk walk, a quick run, or a dash up the stairs. Get up and get moving.

Get Enough Sleep Adequate amounts of sleep allow you to refresh your vital energy, cope with multiple stressors more effectively, and be productive when you need be. In fact, sleep is one of the biggest stress busters of them all.

Practice Self Nurturing Make time to relax. Find time each day for something fun—something that you enjoy and that calms you. Take a hot bath, get a massage, and allow yourself a set amount of guilt-free time texting or chatting with friends. Turn on your iPod or MP3 and listen to your favorite songs. Remember that taking time out for you should be a part of every day. Like exercise, relaxation can help you cope with stressful feelings, preserve your energy, and refocus your energies.

Eat Healthfully It is clear that eating a balanced, healthy diet will help provide the stamina you need to get through problems and will stress-proof you in ways that are not fully understood. It is also known that undereating, overeating, and eating the wrong kinds of foods can create distress in the body. In particular, avoid **sympathomirnetics**, substances in foods that produce (or mimic) stresslike responses, such as caffeine.

Managing Your Time

Ever put off writing a paper until the night before it was due? We all **procrastinate,** or voluntarily delay doing some task despite expecting to be worse off for the delay. These delays can result in academic difficulties, financial problems, relationship problems, and a multitude of stress-related ailments.

How can you avoid the procrastination bug? According to psychologist Peter Gollwitzer and colleagues, a key is setting clear "implementation intentions," a series of goals to be accomplished toward a specific end. For example, set a goal of spending at least 2 hours per day for the next week focusing on the review of literature for your next big term paper. Having a plan that includes deadlines and rewarding yourself for meeting those deadlines can motivate you to stay on task. Like most plans, it is important to be realistic in the number of goals you set. Start with a simple plan and be flexible. Another strategy is to get started early and set a personal end date that is well ahead of the class due date.

Learning to manage your time better overall is key to reducing stress. Keep a journal for 2 days to note how you spend your time. Write down your activities every day—everything from going to class to doing your laundry to texting your friends—and the amount of time you spend doing each. Are you completing the tasks you need to do on a daily basis? Are there any activities you can stop doing or that you would like to do more frequently? Use the following time-management tips in your stress-management program:

- Do one thing at a time. Don't try to watch television, wash clothes, and write your term paper all at once. Stay focused.
- Clean off your desk. Go through the things on your desk, toss unnecessary papers, and put into folders the papers for tasks that you must do. Read your mail, recycle what you don't need, and file what you will need later.
- Prioritize your tasks. Make a daily "to do" list and stick to it. Categorize the things you must do today; the things that you must do, but not immediately; and the things that it would be nice to do. Consider the nice-to-do items only if you finish the others or if they include something fun.
- Find a clean, comfortable place to work, and avoid interruptions. When you have a project that requires total concentration, schedule uninterrupted time. Don't answer the phone; close your door and post a "Do Not Disturb" sign; or go to a quiet room in the library or student union where you can hide and work.
- Reward yourself for work completed. When you finish a task, do something nice for yourself. Rest breaks give you time to recharge and refresh your energy levels.
- Work when you're at your best. If you're a morning person, study and write papers in the morning, and take breaks when you start to slow down.
- Break overwhelming tasks into small pieces, and allocate a certain amount of time to each. If you are floundering in a task, move on and come back to it when you're refreshed.
- Remember that time is precious. Avoid over commitment. Learn to say no and mean it. Be sympathetic but firm. Don't say you will think about it. And don't give in to guilt. Schedule time for yourself.

Source: Donatelle, Rebecca J., *Health: The Basics*, 11th Ed., © 2015, pp. 83–92. Reprinted and Electronically reproduced by permission of Pearson Education, Inc., New York, NY.

Vocabulary
Before, during, and after reading the selection, annotate the text and write in your journal. Create a list of vocabulary words, along with their definitions. Give examples of their use from the selection you just read.

After Reading Discussion Questions: Meaning, Structure, and Expression

1. Central Idea: Work as a group to write a summary that answers the following questions: What purpose did Donatelle have for writing this piece? Who is the

intended audience? What is the main idea of the essay? What is the significance of the title of the piece?
2. **Relevant Details:** The first coping technique offered by Donatelle for dealing with specific stressors is known as the *inoculation technique*. How do the details of the passage support this point?
3. **Logical Order:** Donatelle begins the passage by explaining how to assess stressors. Why is this an important first step? Identify the logical flow of her ideas by outlining how to assess stress and the coping techniques offered to solve problems. Do you agree with the order of her details?
4. **Effective Expression:** Donatelle uses questions to provoke readers to think about their personal stress, and she uses directives for actions to alleviate stress. For example, in paragraph 13, she asks the reader to identify his or her anger style. Identify two other times the author used questions to support her point. Why is the use of questioning so effective in this process?

Thinking Prompts to Move from Reading to Writing

1. Assume you are taking a college health course. Your professor has given you the following study question for an upcoming essay exam. Answer the question based on information from the passage. Use your own words. Study question: *How may one manage emotions to reduce stress?*
2. Assume you are a member of your college's student government, and you are preparing to address a group of high school seniors on what to expect in college. Using information from the passage, write an essay that explains the steps for managing stress in college.

Camping Out

ERNEST HEMINGWAY

Ernest Hemingway (1899–1961), born in Oak Park, Illinois, started his career as a writer in a newspaper office in Kansas City at the age of seventeen. He went on to win the Nobel Prize in Literature, in 1954 "for his mastery of the art of narrative, most recently demonstrated in *The Old Man and the Sea*, and for the influence that he has exerted on contemporary style." Hemingway, an avid sportsman, wrote mainly about men who were soldiers, bullfighters, fishermen, and hunters. He created heroes of action who faced danger and tragedy stoically, without complaint, with "grace under pressure." The following article first appeared in the newspaper *Toronto Daily Star* in 1920.

Before Reading Write a journal entry about an outdoor activity such as camping, hunting, fishing, or canoeing. If you do not like these types of activities, explain why. If you do like one or more of these outdoor activities, choose one and describe how you go about enjoying the experience. How do you prepare for the activity? What challenges do you face and how do you overcome them?

1   Thousands of people will go into the bush this summer to cut the high cost of living. A man who gets his two weeks' salary while he is on vacation should be able to put those two weeks in fishing and camping and be able to save one week's salary clear. He ought to be able to sleep comfortably every night, to eat well every day and to return to the city rested and in good condition.

2   But if he goes into the woods with a frying pan, an ignorance of black flies and mosquitoes, and a great and abiding lack of knowledge about cookery, the chances are that his return will be very different. He will come back with enough mosquito bites to make the back of his neck look like a relief map of the Caucasus.

His digestion will be wrecked after a valiant battle to assimilate half-cooked or charred grub. And he won't have had a decent night's sleep while he has been gone.

He will solemnly raise his right hand and inform you that he has joined the grand army of never-agains. The call of the wild may be all right, but it's a dog's life. He's heard the call of the tame with both ears. Waiter, bring him an order of milk toast.

In the first place he overlooked the insects. Black flies, no-see-ums, deer flies, gnats and mosquitoes were instituted by the devil to force people to live in cities where he could get at them better. If it weren't for them everybody would live in the bush and he would be out of work. It was a rather successful invention.

But there are lots of dopes that will counteract the pests. The simplest perhaps is oil of citronella. Two bits' worth of this purchased at any pharmacist's will be enough to last for two weeks in the worst fly and mosquito-ridden country.

Rub a little on the back of your neck, your forehead and your wrists before you start fishing, and the blacks and skeeters will shun you. The odor of citronella is not offensive to people. It smells like gun oil. But the bugs do hate it.

Oil of pennyroyal and eucalyptol are also much hated by mosquitoes, and with citronella they form the basis for many proprietary preparations. But it is cheaper and better to buy the straight citronella. Put a little on the mosquito netting that covers the front of your pup tent or canoe tent at night, and you won't be bothered.

To be really rested and get any benefit out of a vacation a man must get a good night's sleep every night. The first requisite for this is to have plenty of cover. It is twice as cold as you expect it will be in the bush four nights out of five, and a good plan is to take just double the bedding that you think you will need. An old quilt that you can wrap up in is as warm as two blankets.

Nearly all outdoor writers rhapsodize over the browse bed. It is all right for the man who knows how to make one and has plenty of time. But in a succession of one-night camps on a canoe trip all you need is level ground for your tent floor and you will sleep all right if you have plenty of covers under you. Take twice as much cover as you think that you will need, and then put two-thirds of it under you. You will sleep warm and get your rest.

When it is clear weather you don't need to pitch your tent if you are only stopping for the night. Drive four stakes at the head of your made-up bed and drape your mosquito bar over that, then you can sleep like a log and laugh at the mosquitoes.

Outside of insects and bum sleeping the rock that wrecks most camping trips is cooking. The average tyro's idea of cooking is to fry everything and fry it good and plenty. Now, a frying pan is a most necessary thing to any trip, but you also need the old stew kettle and the folding reflector baker.

A pan of fried trout can't be bettered and they don't cost any more than ever. But there is a good and bad way of frying them.

The beginner puts his trout and his bacon in and over a brightly burning fire; the bacon curls up and dries into a dry tasteless cinder and the trout is burned outside while it is still raw inside. He eats them and it is all right if he is only out for the day and going home to a good meal at night. But if he is going to face more trout and bacon the next morning and other equally well-cooked dishes for the remainder of two weeks he is on the pathway to nervous dyspepsia.

The proper way is to cook over coals. Have several cans of Crisco or Cotosuet or one of the vegetable shortenings along that are as good as lard and excellent for all kinds of shortening. Put the bacon in and when it is about half cooked lay the trout in the hot grease, dipping them in corn meal first. Then put the bacon on top of the trout and it will baste them as it slowly cooks.

The coffee can be boiling at the same time and in a smaller skillet pancakes being made that are satisfying the other campers while they are waiting for the trout.

With the prepared pancake flours you take a cupful of pancake flour and add a cup of water. Mix the water and flour and as soon as the lumps are out it is ready for cooking. Have the skillet hot and keep it well greased. Drop the batter in and as soon as it is done on one side loosen it in the skillet and flip it over. Apple butter, syrup or cinnamon and sugar go well with the cakes.

While the crowd have taken the edge from their appetites with flapjacks the trout have been cooked and they and the bacon are ready to serve. The trout are crisp outside and firm and pink inside and the bacon is well done—but not too done. If there is anything better than that combination the writer has yet to taste it in a lifetime devoted largely and studiously to eating.

18 The stew kettle will cook your dried apricots when they have resumed their predried plumpness after a night of soaking, it will serve to concoct a mulligan in, and it will cook macaroni. When you are not using it, it should be boiling water for the dishes.

19 In the baker, mere man comes into his own, for he can make a pie that to his bush appetite will have it all over the product that mother used to make, like a tent. Men have always believed that there was something mysterious and difficult about making a pie. Here is a great secret. There is nothing to it. We've been kidded for years. Any man of average office intelligence can make at least as good a pie as his wife.

20 All there is to a pie is a cup and a half of flour, one-half teaspoonful of salt, one-half cup of lard and cold water. That will make pie crust that will bring tears of joy into your camping partner's eyes.

21 Mix the salt with the flour, work the lard into the flour, make it up into a good workmanlike dough with cold water. Spread some flour on the back of a box or something flat, and pat the dough around a while. Then roll it out with whatever kind of round bottle you prefer. Put a little more lard on the surface of the sheet of dough and then slosh a little flour on and roll it up and then roll it out again with the bottle.

22 Cut out a piece of the rolled out dough big enough to line a pie tin. I like the kind with holes in the bottom. Then put in your dried apples that have soaked all night and been sweetened, or your apricots, or your blueberries, and then take another sheet of the dough and drape it gracefully over the top, soldering it down at the edges with your fingers. Cut a couple of slits in the top dough sheet and prick it a few times with a fork in an artistic manner.

23 Put it in the baker with a good slow fire for forty-five minutes and then take it out and if your pals are Frenchmen they will kiss you. The penalty for knowing how to cook is that the others will make you do all the cooking.

24 It is all right to talk about roughing it in the woods. But the real woodsman is the man who can be really comfortable in the bush.

Source: Ernest Hemingway, "Camping Out," *Toronto Daily Star*, 1920.

Vocabulary
Before, during, and after reading the selection, annotate the text and write in your journal. Create a list of vocabulary words, along with their definitions. Give examples of their use from the selection you just read.

After Reading Discussion Questions: Meaning, Structure, and Expression

1. **Main Idea:** Work as a group to write a summary that answers the following questions: What purpose did Hemingway have for writing this piece? Who is the intended audience? What is the main idea of the essay? What is the significance of the title of the piece?
2. **Relevant Details:** Hemingway identifies three major ways to enjoy camping. What are his three ways to ensure an enjoyable camping experience? Do you agree that these three phases are the keys to being "really comfortable in the bush"? For example, reread paragraphs 14 through 22. Which phase of camping does this section discuss? Why does Hemingway spend so much time on this part of the camping process?
3. **Logical Order:** The main organizational pattern for this essay is process—the steps to take to enjoy camping. However, paragraphs 1 and 2 contrast the unskilled and skilled camper. Why did Hemingway choose to begin his essay with this contrast? Is it effective or would the essay be more effective if it were left out? Explain your thinking.
4. **Effective Expression:** This essay is often praised for Hemingway's use of humor. Identify instances in the essay that are humorous. Explain why the examples you chose are amusing. Do you think this piece is as amusing today as it was in 1920? Why or why not?

Thinking Prompts to Move from Reading to Writing

1. Consider this sentence from paragraph 19: "Any man of average office intelligence can make at least as good a pie as his wife." What is Hemingway's assumption about the roles of men and women? Do current views of gender roles oppose or support this assumption? Explain how.
2. Using Hemingway's essay as a model of a process explanation, describe how to do a particular task or activity.

Illustration

Don't Call Me a Hot Tamale

JUDITH ORTIZ COFER

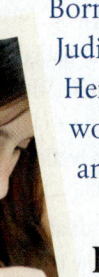

Born in 1952 in Puerto Rico and raised in Paterson, New Jersey, Judith Ortiz Cofer is an acclaimed poet, novelist, and essayist. Her writings explore the experiences of being a minority as a Hispanic woman. She is currently the Regents' and Franklin Professor of English and Creative Writing at the University of Georgia.

Before Reading Write a journal entry about your experiences with stereotypes. Have you ever been stereotyped? Describe the incident. What are some common stereotypes in our culture? How are these stereotypes harmful?

1   On a bus to London from Oxford University, where I was earning some graduate credits one summer, a young man, obviously fresh from a pub, approached my seat. With both hands over his heart, he went down on his knees in the aisle and broke into an Irish tenor's rendition of "Maria" from *West Side Story*. I was not amused. "Maria" had followed me to London, reminding me of a prime fact of my life: You can leave the island of Puerto Rico, master the English language, and travel as far as you can, but if you're a Latina, especially one who so clearly belongs to Rita Moreno's gene pool, the island travels with you.

2   Growing up in New Jersey and wanting most of all to belong, I lived in two completely different worlds. My parents designed our life as a microcosm of their *casas* on the island—we spoke in Spanish, ate Puerto Rican food bought at the *bodega*, and practiced strict Catholicism complete with Sunday mass in Spanish.

3   I was kept under tight surveillance by my parents, since my virtue and modesty were, by their cultural equation, the same as their honor. As teenagers, my friends and I were lectured constantly on how to behave as proper *señoritas*. But it was a conflicting message we received, since our Puerto Rican mothers also encouraged us to look and act like women by dressing us in clothes our Anglo schoolmates and their mothers found too "mature" and flashy. I often felt humiliated when I appeared at an American friend's birthday party wearing a dress more suitable for a semiformal. At Puerto Rican festivities, neither the music nor the colors we wore could be too loud.

4   I remember Career Day in high school, when our teachers told us to come dressed as if for a job interview. That morning, I agonized in front of my closet, trying to figure out what a "career girl" would wear, because the only model I had was Marlo Thomas on TV. To me and my Puerto Rican girlfriends, dressing up meant wearing our mother's ornate jewelry and clothing.

5   At school that day, the teachers assailed us for wearing "everything at once"—meaning too much jewelry and too many accessories. And it was painfully obvious that the other students in their tailored skirts and silk blouses thought we were hopeless and vulgar. The way they looked at us was a taste of the cultural clash that awaited us in the real world, where prospective employers and men on the street would often misinterpret our tight skirts and bright colors as a come-on.

6   It is custom, not chromosomes, that leads us to choose scarlet over pale pink. Our mothers had grown up on a tropical island where the natural environment was a riot of primary colors, where showing your skin was one way to keep cool as well as to look sexy. On the island, women felt freer to dress and move provocatively since they were protected by the traditions and laws of a Spanish/Catholic

system of morality and machismo, the main rule of which was: *You may look at my sister, but if you touch her I will kill you.* The extended family and church structure provided them with a circle of safety on the island; if a man "wronged" a girl, everyone would close in to save her family honor.

Off-island, signals often get mixed. When a Puerto Rican girl who is dressed in her idea of what is attractive meets a man from the mainstream culture who has been trained to react to certain types of clothing as a sexual signal, a clash is likely to take place. She is seen as a Hot Tamale, a sexual firebrand. I learned this lesson at my first formal dance when my date leaned over and painfully planted a sloppy, overeager kiss on my mouth. When I didn't respond with sufficient passion, he said in a resentful tone: "I thought you Latin girls were supposed to mature early." It was only the first time I would feel like a fruit or vegetable—I was supposed to *ripen,* not just grow into womanhood like other girls.

These stereotypes, though rarer, still surface in my life. I recently stayed at a classy metropolitan hotel. After having dinner with a friend, I was returning to my room when a middle-aged man in a tuxedo stepped directly into my path. With his champagne glass extended toward me, he exclaimed, "Evita!"

Blocking my way, he bellowed the song "Don't Cry for Me, Argentina." Playing to the gathering crowd, he began to sing loudly a ditty to the tune of "La Bamba"—except the lyrics were about a girl named Maria whose exploits all rhymed with her name and gonorrhea.

I knew that this same man—probably a corporate executive, even worldly by most standards—would never have regaled a white woman with a dirty song in public. But to him, I was just a character in his universe of "others," all cartoons.

Still, I am one of the lucky ones. There are thousands of Latinas without the privilege of the education that my parents gave me. For them every day is a struggle against the misconceptions perpetuated by the myth of the Latina as whore, domestic worker or criminal.

Rather than fight these pervasive stereotypes, I try to replace them with a more interesting set of realities. I travel around the U.S. reading from my books of poetry and my novel. With the stories I tell, the dreams and fears I examine in my work, I try to get my audience past the particulars of my skin color, my accent or my clothes.

I once wrote a poem in which I called Latinas "God's brown daughters." It is really a prayer, of sorts, for communication and respect. In it, Latin women pray "in Spanish to an Anglo God / with a Jewish heritage," and they are "fervently hoping / that if not omnipotent, / at least He be bilingual."

Source: Judith Ortiz Cofer, "The Myth of the Latin Woman: I Just Met a Girl Named Maria" pg 148-154 from *The Latin Deli: Telling the Lives of Barrio Women*. Copyright © 1995. Reprinted by permission of the University of Georgia Press.

Vocabulary
Before, during, and after reading the selection, annotate the text and write in your journal. Create a list of vocabulary words, along with their definitions. Give examples of their use from the selection you just read.

After Reading Discussion Questions: Meaning, Structure, and Expression

1. **Main Idea:** Work as a group to write a summary that answers the following questions: What purpose did Judith Ortiz Cofer have for writing this essay? Who is her intended audience? What is the main idea of the essay? What is the significance of the title?
2. **Relevant Details:** Cofer relies mostly on personal experience to make her point about stereotypes based on race or gender. Does she provide enough details to make her point convincingly? Would the use of facts or expert opinions strengthen her point? Why or why not?
3. **Logical Order:** Cofer opens her essay with an example from her personal life. Is this an effective opening for the essay? Why or why not? Compare the introduction of the essay to the conclusion. How does the conclusion relate to the introduction? Is this an effective conclusion? Why or why not? In what other ways could Cofer have opened or closed her essay?
4. **Effective Expression:** Based on Judith Ortiz Cofer's choice of words, how would you describe the tone of this essay? Is it angry, embarrassed, disappointed, confrontational, or candid, or does it communicate some other attitude about stereotypes? Identify three expressions that illustrate the tone of the piece. Explain the reasons for your selections.

Thinking Prompts to Move from Reading to Writing

1. Cofer makes a connection between culture and fashion. According to her description, Hispanic fashion for women is "flashy," "mature," and "sexy" with "ornate jewelry" and "tight skirts and bright colors." Write an essay in which you illustrate how fashion represents a particular culture. For example, illustrate fashion in the Hip-Hop culture.
2. Cofer's essay illustrates the stereotypes she faces as a Hispanic woman. Identify and describe a stereotype that you or someone you know has encountered. For example, what are some stereotypes that elderly people face?

Football's Bloodiest Secret

BUZZ BISSINGER

H.G. "Buzz" Bissinger is among the nation's most honored and distinguished writers. A native of New York City, Buzz is the winner of the Pulitzer Prize, the Livingston Award, the American Bar Association Silver Gavel Award, and the National Headliners Award, among others. He is the author of three highly acclaimed nonfiction books: *Friday Night Lights, A Prayer for the City,* and *Three Nights in August.* Buzz's short nonfiction pieces have appeared in a number of top U.S. magazines, including *Vanity Fair, Sports Illustrated,* and *The New York Times Magazine.* The following article was first posted in *The Daily Beast,* the online home of *Newsweek* magazine.

Before Reading Write a journal entry about sports in America. Do you think sports such as hockey, football, and basketball are too violent? Why or why not?

1. Many miles have passed in my life since I did the research for *Friday Night Lights* 21 years ago. At a certain point, an author should simply forget and move on. But the book continues to sell and the television show of the same name premiered its fourth season this week on DirecTV. The power of what I saw and what I heard still gets to me, and of all the interviews I did, the one that lingers the most took place in the living room of my rented ranch house in the dusty isolation of Odessa, Texas.

2. The man I interviewed was named Brad Allen. He was the former head of the high school booster club I was writing about, and I wanted to get some observations on why high school football had become so dominant in the culture of Odessa. I thought he would refer to the usual pop-psychology suspects—the town's hermetic location in West Texas, the lack of anything substantive to do except work and drink, the paucity of good strip clubs, the boom-and-bust cycle of the oil field economy where nothing was ever certain.

3. Today at the age of 21, one player lives with his parents, spends most of his time in a wheelchair, and struggles with short-term memory.

4. The conversation started that way. But then it veered toward the experience of his own son, Phillip. Allen was the first to admit that Phillip was not a gifted athlete, but what he lacked in skill he made up for in toughness. To prove the point, Allen told the story of when Phillip broke his arm at the beginning of a high school football game. Rather than come out, Phillip continued to play. It was only at half time, when his arm had swelled so badly that his forearm pads had to be cut off of his body, that he reluctantly went to the hospital.

5. Allen said he was not proud of the incident, but he told the story freely. What it signified was obvious: the machismo inherent to youth sports that parents crave. Football. Soccer. Baseball. Basketball. Hockey. The sport doesn't matter. The gender doesn't matter. What matters most is the vicarious thrill dad and mom get from their sons and daughters showing fearlessness and the absorption of agony in a tradition linking back to the war heroes of Sparta. No amount of studies and medical warnings are going to fully extinguish the attitude that playing hurt is all part of the price.

Yesterday, the House Judiciary Committee began hearings on the issue of brain injuries suffered in pro football. It followed a recent study commissioned by the National Football League showing that memory-related diseases have ostensibly occurred in pro players at a rate far exceeding that of the national population—19 times the normal rate for men ages 30 for 49. It was only through the superb work of *New York Times* reporter Alan Schwarz that the issue rose to the forefront at all. And almost as soon as the study was released, NFL officials tried to discredit it as inaccurate.

Mark Hyman, an expert on injuries in youth sports, feels that any awareness of the problem, regardless of the NFL's utterly self-protective stance, is a good thing. Because of the intense public pressure, there is the real possibility of changes not simply at the pro level, but all the way down the line to high school and pre-high school sports. But if past history is prologue, which it usually is (see successful conquests of Afghanistan) the changes will still be at the edges. The macho culture of sports is just too deeply embedded to be fully eradicated.

In his book *Until it Hurts,* Hyman points out that 3.5 million children under the age of 15 needed medical treatment for sport injuries each year, nearly half of which were the result of simple overuse. "Over the last 75 years, adults have staged a hostile takeover of kids' sports," he wrote. "The quest to turn children into tomorrow's superstar athletes has often led adults to push them beyond physical and emotional limits." Backs go out and young athletes continue to compete until somebody finally realizes that the ailment isn't some strain but a herniated disk and a stress fracture. High school football players have gotten concussions, been declared ready to play the following week, then suffered a far more serious second concussion.

In Odessa, a player once lost a testicle after no one bothered to thoroughly examine a groin injury he had received. It wasn't until the testicle swelled to the size of a grapefruit that he went to the emergency room. By then it was too late—the testicle had to be removed. In another instance during the Texas high school football playoffs, where all sanity goes on hiatus, an Odessa player was already suffering from a painful hip. Since he was a star going both ways, the answer was to inject him with painkillers before the game and at halftime. A hole developed, which had actually been caused by a breaking of a band of cartilage at the front of his hip joint. It had also become infected, and the player after the season had to go the hospital for six months for treatments, including scraping out the infected tissue and iodine baths.

"We go insane worrying if our kids pedal down the driveway on their bikes without a helmet," says Hyman, but then allow them to clobber each other on the field until they're seriously hurt. The NFL has actually worked to build a better protective helmet. But the pace of innovation is still too slow, according to Hyman, because looking sleek and assassin-like is more important than staving off a head injury. In hockey, former NHL great Mark Messier teamed up with a sports-equipment maker to create a helmet that cuts down on blows to the brain by 26 percent, says Hyman. The number of NHL players who are using it this season? Eight—because they don't like the shape. Were substantial changes being made at the pro level, they would probably trickle down to college, high school, and youth teams. But they're not, even though 10 to 20 percent of teen hockey players suffer a concussion each year.

Young athletes are far more vulnerable to head injuries than older ones. Just ask Cody Lehe, who in the typical tradition of football suffered a concussion in a helmet-to-helmet hit during a game. He complained of headaches the following week, but he was able return to practice on the basis of a brain scan. He suddenly collapsed the next game after a relatively mild hit to the helmet. He suffered what doctors described as a "second-impact concussion," according to a story by Dann Denny of the *Herald-Times* of Bloomington, Indiana. Lehe's second concussion took place before the symptoms of the first one had subsided, and his brain swelled rapidly. He was in a coma for three weeks. Today at the age of 21, he lives with his parents, spends most of his time in a wheelchair, and struggles with short-term memory.

Youth sports will continue to be the most vulnerable—Pop Warner football leagues, travelling soccer and basketball leagues. None of these teams routinely have a doctor or a professional trainer as part of the staff. It is a coach who will generally make the call, and don't be fooled: these coaches, woefully inexperienced, still want to win every bit as badly as their brethren in the high school, college, and pro ranks. Which means if an injury occurs, the seriousness of which cannot be immediately gauged, the coach will tell the player to shrug it off and stop being a pussy. He will undoubtedly invoke some idiotic Knute Rockne aphorism—"When the going gets tough, the tough get going!"—and parents will be right behind them, pulling their sons and daughters back into the game and implying they are weaklings if they complain. Serious injuries will continue to go undiscovered, and even when they are, too many kids will be pushed to return too soon. Some of these injuries will be excruciatingly painful down the road, some of them will be so debilitating as to ruin careers, and a few of them will even be fatal.

Because that's what too many sports are in America, whatever the age level—violent, dedicated solely to winning regardless of risk, and irresponsibly dangerous. Which is just the way we like it.

Source: Buzz Bissinger, "Football's Bloodiest Secret" from *The Daily Beast*, 10/28/2009. Copyright © 2009 The Daily Beast Company LLC. All rights reserved. Used by permission and protected under the Copyright Laws of the United States. The printing, copying, redistribution, or retransmission of this Content without express written permission is prohibited.

Vocabulary Before, during, and after reading the selection, annotate the text and write in your journal. Create a list of vocabulary words, along with their definitions. Give examples of their use from the selection you just read.

After Reading Discussion Questions: Meaning, Structure, and Expression

1. **Main Idea:** Work as a group to write a summary that answers the following questions: What purpose did Bissinger have for writing this piece? Who is the intended audience? What is the main idea of the essay? What is the significance of the title of the piece?
2. **Relevant Details:** Some of the details in this essay are very graphic, such as the illustration given in paragraph 9. Why did Bissinger include this disturbing example? Do you think the essay would be more or less effective if these details were left out? Explain your thinking.
3. **Logical Order:** Paragraphs 3 and 11 refer to the experiences of Cody Lehe. Why did Bissinger wait until paragraph 11 to tell Lehe's full story?
4. **Effective Expression:** Based on Bissinger's choice of words, would you describe the main tone of this essay as objective, sarcastic, or alarmed? Give examples with explanations to support your thoughts about the essay's tone.

Thinking Prompts to Move from Reading to Writing

1. Reread the last paragraph in the essay. Write a response to Bissinger that agrees or disagrees with his concluding view. Assume you will post your response on the *Daily Beast* comments.
2. Assume you are the parent or coach of a football player. Write an essay that takes a stand for or against the violence in the game. Suggest an action that should be taken to preserve the game as it is or to change it to make it less violent.

Classification

The Fundamentals of Forgiveness

D. J. HENRY

D. J. Henry is a veteran college English teacher with over 30 years of classroom experience. She is well known for her textbooks on reading, writing, and the reading/writing process that are used in classrooms across the country. Her philosophy and practice as a writing teacher is to engage in the same writings she assigns as a way of modeling the writing process and the ways writers think about why and how they write. To fulfill that purpose, she composed the following essay exclusively for use in this publication. In this essay, Henry contemplates the traits of forgiveness.

Before Reading Write a journal entry about your experiences with forgiveness. Do you find it easy or difficult to forgive? What are the key components of forgiveness?

Life is full of all types of hurt. A tormenting bully, an abusive or neglectful parent, an unfaithful spouse, or a careless driver ending the life of a loved one—these offenders embody just a few of the myriad types of injuries that we endure. At times, it may seem as if the hurt is insurmountable. And in its wake, we may be tempted to cling to our pain, become bitter, desire revenge, to be—in short—unforgiving.

However, many experts agree that an unforgiving attitude deepens the wound, as summarized in the Mayo Clinic article "Forgiveness: Letting Go of Grudges and Bitterness." Anger, bitterness, depression, anxiety, lack of purpose, spiritual conflict, and an inability to enjoy the present moment or make important connections with others often mark the lives of those who cannot or will not forgive. In fact, research indicates that we who do forgive actually lower our blood pressure, heart rate, and cholesterol levels; improve our sleep quality; and strengthen our immune system.

To be forgiving, we need to recognize what forgiveness is not. First, forgiveness is not a sign of weakness. Indeed, forgiveness signals strength. To forgive is to conquer anger, bitterness, and the need for revenge. As the great civil rights activist Mahatma Gandhi said in his book *All Men are Brothers: Autobiographical Reflections,* "The weak can never forgive. Forgiveness is the attribute of the strong."

Second, forgiving is not condoning. When we forgive, we do not excuse the actions of the one who harms us, nor do we deny the resulting injury or our negative feelings. In fact, only when we fully realize the extent of our injury can we then fully forgive the offender. Forgiveness does not minimize the injustice or require that we continue in a damaging situation. Sonja Lyubomirsky, Ph.D., a professor of psychology at the University of California states in her book *The How of Happiness,* "Forgiveness is not reconciliation—that is, it does not necessarily involve the reestablishment of the relationship with the transgressor."

Third, forgiving is not forgetting. The old adage "forgive and forget" is really impossible advice to follow—and for good reasons, according to Kurt Smith, Director and Lead Counselor at Guy Stuff Counseling & Coaching. In his article "4 Reasons to Forgive But Not Forget" on the Website *PsychCentral*, he explains that we remember the injustices done to us so that we can learn about ourselves, strengthen our relationships, and protect ourselves from future harm.

Most often, we think of forgiveness in view of giving forgiveness to an offender, but forgiveness also includes the offender asking for forgiveness. At times, the asking and giving of forgiveness have a reciprocal nature between the involved parties. In these instances, the wrongdoer asks for forgiveness, and the wronged gives forgiveness. Other times, forgiveness has a solitary nature. In these instances, there is no opportunity for interaction between the parties. Perhaps time, distance, or even death separates the offended from the offender. Overall, in its fundamental essence, forgiveness has three elements: recognition, reparation, and release.

Recognition of the Injury

The first and foundational aspect of forgiveness is recognition of the injustice and injury. In both giving and seeking forgiveness, the offended and the offender must admit that a wrong has indeed occurred.

As the offended, we must confront the nature of the offense and understand our own reaction to it. We need to not only clearly identify who did what to whom, but also understand the consequences of our response to the injury. For example, Janice suffered extreme child abuse at the hands of her father. At times, Janice would recount some of the more graphic details; she admits she did so mainly to excuse her own anger and justify her poor choices in given situations. Obviously, she recognized that she suffered abuse. However, she refused to carefully examine her own responses to the abuse. She spurned help from anyone, including professional counselors. She harbored bitterness and hatred. She suffered recurring anxiety attacks, high blood pressure, and insomnia. When she became a mother, she also abused her children. Janice had tried to avoid the pain by refusing to address the injury. Instead, she only deepened the wound, and she wounded innocent others as well—she, the offended, became the offender.

Ultimately, driven by the desire to escape the despair of her life, Janice made the connection between the abuse she suffered and her reactions to it. Through deliberate self-examination, she identified the various ways in which the harm done to her shaped her thinking and decisions.

As the offender seeking forgiveness, we must admit to the wrong we have committed and recognize the consequences of our wrongdoing. Janice's father, Jim, never acknowledged the harm he did to her. He consistently behaved as if he had done nothing wrong, and throughout her childhood, he painted Janice as a liar who could not be trusted. His unreasonable denial of his own wrongdoing trapped him in a life of anger and violence, deepened the wounds he inflicted on his daughter, and widened the chasm between them.

In contrast, once Janice admitted to her culpability in perpetuating the cycle of abuse, she began to heal and seek the forgiveness of those she wronged, especially her children.

Reparation for the Wronged

Reparation is a higher level of forgiveness built on recognition of the wrong. The word *reparation*, as documented by *Online Etymology Dictionary*, originates from the Latin term *reparare*, which means to make ready again, and the French term *réparation*, which means to repair. We mostly think of reparation in terms of the transgressor making amends for the transgression.

As a principle of law, reparation has existed for generations with the purpose to eliminate the consequences of the wrongdoing and re-establish the situation as if it had not occurred. In this sense, reparation is often made in the form of a monetary payment or goods. A famous example is the Civil Liberties Act of 1988. This act, signed by President Reagan, paid $20,000 to every Japanese American interned by order of President Roosevelt during World War II.

As an element in our interpersonal relationships, reparation has aspects other than monetary compensation. For one, how can the moral damage of our pain and suffering in the form of mental or emotional distress such as anxiety and fear be wiped away? How can we redress the loss of enjoyment of life?

For a good number of us, a sincere apology is the best recourse for repair. While experts vary in their language, they agree that to repair damage, a sincere apology includes certain distinct traits. A sincere apology admits the wrongdoing and its damage, expresses remorse, pledges reformed behavior, and asks for forgiveness.

When Janice wanted to repair her relationship with her teenage children, she wrote a letter to each one that exemplifies the traits of a sincere apology:

Dear Ethan,

I write this letter to apologize for all the pain I have inflicted on you and our family. I am so ashamed of every name I ever called you, every mean word I ever screamed, and every time I hit you. You are not "stupid" or "ugly" or any of the other vile things I called you. You are not a "burden," and I never meant it when I said I wished you hadn't been born. You deserve better. You deserve a mother who shows you love in her words and actions and who protects you at all costs. I have not been that kind of mother, but I want to be. My regret runs even deeper when I see how insecure, fearful, and angry you are. You have a right to be angry, but I hope you can overcome the damage I have caused. I really want to change. I have already started seeing a family counselor and hope you will join me. I hope you can find it in yourself to forgive me. I am very, very sorry!

While reparation in the form of material compensation or an apology is ideal, many offenders never offer any form of redress. When that is the case, we who are wronged are left to find a way to self-repair, to put things right in our own psyches and lives. Many of us find restoration in spiritual principles by appealing to God for recognition of and release from our injuries.

Janice never received recognition, much less an apology, or any kind of amends from her father. Instead, she sought restoration by creating a new lifestyle, unmarred by bitterness and anger, built on her new-found Christian faith, citing two scriptures as her foundation: "And we know that in all things God works for the good of those who love him, who have been called according to his purpose," Romans 8:28, NIV, and "If we confess our sins, he is faithful and just and will forgive us our sins and purify us from all unrighteousness," I John 1:9, NIV.

Release from Revenge

The need to get even is a passionate, primal drive. When we are wronged, it is our nature to experience intense feelings of vindictiveness. There is something quite satisfying about revenge—inflicting pain and making our enemy suffer just as we have suffered. According to the *Online*

Etymology Dictionary, the word *revenge* comes from two terms, the Old French *revenchier* and the Latin *vindicare*, which mean to lay claim to, to avenge, to punish, or to vindicate. We want to defend ourselves, safeguard our self-respect, and uphold social and moral order.

This need for revenge is grounded in a shared understanding of our fair and just treatment of one another. In fact, a fundamental function of a society's legal system is to establish ethical laws and objectively impose punishments for lawbreakers, thereby quenching our passionate thirst for revenge. In a sense, the punishment serves as a form of reparation by serving up a just closure. This sentiment is clearly stated in one of the most ancient legal codes to be recorded, The Code of Hammurabi, a well-preserved Babylonian law of ancient Mesopotamia, dating back to about 1754 B.C. According to the translation by L. W. King, posted online at *The Avalon Project,* The Code of Hammurabi states, "If a man put out the eye of another man, his eye shall be put out. If he break another man's bone, his bone shall be broken. . . . If a man knock out the teeth of his equal, his teeth shall be knocked out."

At times, however, legal recourse is not available, so the lust for revenge remains unsatisfied. Or the need for revenge is so urgent that we long to take matters into our own hands. This urge is particularly potent when there has been no recognition or reparation.

The highest level of forgiveness releases us from the need for revenge. The core trait of forgiveness at this level is compassion. In her book *Twelve Steps to A Compassionate Life,* Karen Armstrong shares the vision of the organization she founded called The Charter for Compassion, "The principle of compassion lies at the heart of all religious, ethical, and spiritual traditions, calling us to always treat others as we wish to be treated ourselves."

The Latin roots *com* and *patri* for the word *compassion* combine to mean, "to suffer together," as documented by the *Online Etymology Dictionary*. Compassion is the desire to alleviate the suffering of another. Compassion is grounded in our empathy—our capacity to understand what another is experiencing from his or her point of view. The hurtful behaviors of offenders are often expressions of their own past hurts and sufferings. In addition, the offenses themselves heap further damage and anguish upon the offender. Furthermore, compassion and empathy awaken us to the fact that we too cause pain and suffering. We too need forgiveness.

In her struggle to come to grips with her abuse, Janice's faith in God led her to understand the power of compassion. First, the words of Jesus on the cross about those who crucified him, "Father, forgive them for they do not know what they are doing," Luke 23:34, NIV, spoke to her on two levels—as a model of compassion for the wrongdoer and as a profound statement of forgiveness that applied to her personally. Then, as she accepted her own need for forgiveness, she abandoned all desire for revenge, guided by the prayer, "And forgive us our debts, as we also have forgiven our debtors," Mathew 6:12, NIV.

Compassion for one who has offended us releases us from the need for revenge and frees us to fully forgive. In the fundamentals of forgiveness, we find the freedom to become stronger, better people.

Vocabulary
Before, during, and after reading the selection, annotate the text and write in your journal. Create a list of vocabulary words, along with their definitions. Give examples of their use from the selection you just read.

After Reading Discussion Questions: Meaning, Structure, and Expression

1. **Central Idea:** Work as a group to write a summary that answers the following questions: What purpose did Henry have for writing this piece? Who is the intended audience? What is the central idea of the essay? What is the significance of the title of the piece?
2. **Relevant Details:** Throughout her essay, Henry shares information from various sources. Analyze her use of sources: Is each source appropriate? Explain. Is the information from a source relevant? How so? Would her essay be as effective without the use of these sources? Why or why not?

3. **Logical Order:** To make her point, Henry chose to organize her ideas using classification as her primary pattern of organization. However, she combines other patterns of organization with classification to explore the fundamentals of forgiveness. Identify and analyze her combination of patterns of organization. Which patterns does she use? Does she use transitions effectively? Is the flow of ideas smooth and logical? Explain and give examples.
4. **Effective Expression:** Henry chose to use the first person plural "we" as her primary point of view. What is the impact of this point of view on the reader? How would the impact of the essay change if she had chosen to rely on a different point of view such as the second person "you" or the third person "a person, one, he, she," and so on? Do you agree with her choice of viewpoint? Why or why not?

Thinking Prompts to Move from Reading to Writing

1. In her essay, Henry identifies and discusses the traits or elements of forgiveness, which is a moral excellence or virtue. Other virtues, or positive traits, include—but are not limited to—courage, generosity, humility, integrity, loyalty, and wisdom. Select a virtue and write an essay that identifies and explains its importance and distinguishing traits.
2. Henry asserts, "forgiveness has three elements: recognition, reparation, and release." Do you agree with this statement? Write an essay in which you agree or disagree with this statement. If you agree, include examples from what you have observed or experienced that illustrate each trait. If you disagree, identify and illustrate the traits you think best represent forgiveness.

I Am Enough

MELISSA GUITRON

Melissa Guitron is a coach at CrossFit San Mateo who is certified in Level 1 CrossFit (CF), CF Gymnastics, CF Football, and CF Kids and Mobility. She submitted the following essay to the Fashletics Website to qualify for the honor of "Fashlete of the Month." According to owner and jewelry designer Sarah Wilson, "Fashletics is a collection of handmade jewelry inspired by a passion for fitness, competition, and a strong desire to empower others who have made a commitment to a fit and healthy lifestyle. Each piece of jewelry serves a badge of honor and an expression of strength. When Guitron's essay appeared on the site, Wilson wrote "Each Fashlete of the month is presented with a custom sterling silver charm engraved with the word of her choice. In Melissa's case, this word rang loud and clear throughout her story. Not only will Melissa be receiving this custom piece, we are going to add the ENOUGH charm to the Fashletics permanent collection online later this summer. Fashletics is also donating ENOUGH charms to all of the girls who participate in Melissa's CrossFit Kids program to help her spread her important message."

Before Reading Write a journal entry about your experiences or the experiences of someone you know who struggles with self-image. Have you struggled or observed another struggle with low self-esteem or a sense of worthlessness? Do you think most people are confident in their own worth as individuals? What are some possible causes of low self-esteem?

You know what you know, and you don't know what do you don't know. Four years ago if you asked me to define beauty, I probably would have told you it involved weighing 120 pounds, wearing a size four and looking "lean and toned." Today, though I wear a size 4, I am proud to weigh a strong 150 pounds. Before Crossfit, I simply did not know. In a world that tells us who we are is not enough, not thin enough, not pretty enough, not tan enough, not strong enough, it is hard to believe that you are enough.

When did strong become the new skinny?

I discovered CrossFit three years ago through my ex-husband. When he returned from his deployment to Afghanistan, he introduced me to CrossFit and a completely new world of "you are not enough." While CrossFit motivates most people to want to be better for themselves, I embraced CrossFit to make my husband happy. For 12 months, I had spent hours on the elliptical, counting calories and skipping meals, starving myself in an attempt turn my body into what I thought was desirable. I thought exposed hip and collar bones was beauty, yet now I find myself envious of girls with muscles and strength because that is what my husband suddenly found attractive. All my hard work was now, once again, not enough. It was no longer "you are not skinny enough" but instead "you are not strong enough." I was now expected to learn to row fast, jump high, and clean massive amounts of weight all while wearing booty shorts if I wanted to be enough for him.

It is hard to openly admit that I fell in love with CrossFit for all the wrong reasons, but it's the truth. I thought that embracing CrossFit would save my marriage, that it would turn me into what my husband wanted me to be. What I didn't expect was that it would turn out to be the saving grace that gave me the strength to walk away from an abusive marriage. CrossFit for the first time taught me to embrace who I am today, not who I want to be tomorrow, as enough.

The transformation from I am too fat, to I am too skinny to, hey I am Melissa.

The transition from cardioaholic to CrossFitter was not an easy one. It's one thing to be told you don't need to do hours of cardio in order to maintain your figure. It is another to be told that you should drink whole milk instead of soy, eat bacon instead oatmeal, and yolks with your whites. I think I simply went into a state of shock and didn't wake up until I found myself stuck in the middle of a WOD with my coach screaming at me to jump up on the god damn box. Believe me, I jumped, I jumped head first into my future right in that moment. I was hooked on the personal competitive nature of every WOD, fascinated by the nutritional science behind Paleo, and mesmerized by this world of women who didn't spend all their time complaining about how unhappy they were with their bodies. I wanted to be a part of their world, and they openly let me in. Muscle quickly replaced bone protrusions, and I found myself caring less about the approval of my husband and more about how amazing I felt. For the first time, his approval of my body stopped being what I yearned for. The final straw was when we were out at dinner with friends. I had hit a good PR that day and was feeling good. His response to my success was an hour-long tirade of how CrossFit had changed me too much. I now ate too much, was bulking up too much, and stupidly cared too much about it. In that moment, I realized that maybe all along I had been too much for him, that maybe I had been enough for myself and just didn't know it.

Paying it Forward

After leaving my husband and moving home, I struggled to find a way to combine my passion for CrossFit with my desire to give others what CrossFit had given me. I started a job working with at-risk youth in a transitional group home and attempted to share my newfound sense of "enough" with the kids I worked with. While I tried my hardest to cultivate in them a sense of self-worth, I quickly realized that creating a sense of "enough" takes more than the short amount of time they spent in the transitional home. In a place where kids come and go every other week, I felt that I could make a greater impact working with my community somewhere where I could provide continuity of growth.

Enter Brendon Mahoney and CrossFit San Mateo Team Elite.

6   In the spring of 2011, I met my partner and best friend Brendon Mahoney. Not only did Brendon believe that I was enough to be a part of his team, but he believed in me so much that he gave me the freedom to make my dreams a reality. Without constraint, he handed me the power to create my own CrossFit Kids and Women Only Programs. It is through these programs I have finally been able to reach others the way I want to.

7   In the world of Pintrest boards and air brushed images, we have stopped being enough. We have been taught that you must constantly strive for more without compassion for where you are today. My goal is to change that mentality. Strong is not the new skinny in my box. You are you where are you are today, wherever that may be. Six pack abs are no more a sign of your strength than collar bones are of your beauty. My 7th grade girls don't come to my class to get in shape so that they can impress their peers; their motivational drive is to be better for themselves. We celebrate a love for ourselves, just as we are. We celebrate elbows finally touching knees on the pull up bar and graduating from dumbbells to barbells. Whether it's a teen or a retired mother, we as a CrossFit family of females are learning together that who we are is simply enough.

Source: www.fashletics.com

Source: Melissa Guitron, "I Am Enough: Fashlete of the Month." www.fashletics.com Copyright © 2012. Reprinted by permission of the author.

Vocabulary
Before, during, and after reading the selection, annotate the text and write in your journal. Create a list of vocabulary words, along with their definitions. Give examples of their use from the selection you just read.

After Reading Discussion Questions: Meaning, Structure, and Expression

1. **Main Idea:** Work as a group to write a summary that answers the following questions: What purpose did Melissa Guitron have for writing this essay? Who is her intended audience? What is the main idea of the essay? What is the significance of the title?
2. **Relevant Details:** Guitron presents two types of attitudes: "not enough" and "enough." Based on the details in the essay, what are the traits of someone who is "not enough"? What are the traits of someone who is "enough"?
3. **Logical Order:** Reread the first sentence of the essay. Why did Guitron open her essay with this statement? What was your first reaction to this statement? Do you agree with her decision to open her essay with this idea? Would Guitron's main point have been more effective if the statement were moved to the middle or end of the essay? Why or why not?
4. **Effective Expression:** Identify several words or expressions that you used as clues to identify the audience. Does the point of the essay have meaning for other audiences? What changes in words or examples would you recommend to make this essay appealing to a specific audience that is different from the one Guitron intended?

Thinking Prompts to Move from Reading to Writing

1. Throughout the essay, Guitron divides or classifies experiences and feelings into two opposite types to make her point. For example, she describes the traits of self-worth as being or feeling "enough" and "not enough." She describes two types of motivation: inner (self) motivation and outer (husband, society). She also describes two types of beauty: skinny and strong. Write a classification essay that will inspire others in which you describe the traits of self-worth, motivation, beauty, or exercise.
2. Guitron uses classification to describe her "transformation from I am too fat, to I am too skinny, to hey I am Melissa." Have you or someone you know gone through a transformation, changing from one type of person into another? For example, have you experienced or observed someone else go from being selfish to selfless, impatient to patient, immature to mature? Write an essay that will inspire others by describing a transformation you or someone you know has experienced. Be sure to describe traits and give examples.

Comparison–Contrast

The Talk of the Sandbox; How Johnny and Suzy's Playground Chatter Prepares Them for Life at the Office

DEBORAH TANNEN

Deborah Tannen is best known as the author of *You Just Don't Understand,* which was on the *New York Times* bestseller list for nearly four years, including eight months as #1, and has been translated into 30 languages. Professor Tannen serves on the linguistics department faculty at Georgetown University. She has published twenty-one books and over 100 articles, and is the recipient of five honorary doctorates. The following article first appeared in the "Outlook" section of the *Washington Post.*

Before Reading Write a journal entry about the differences between men and women. For example, do men and women differ in the ways they fight, apologize, compete, or learn? How so?

1   Bob Hoover of the Pittsburgh *Post-Gazette* was interviewing me when he remarked that after years of coaching boys' softball teams, he was now coaching girls and they were very different. I immediately whipped out my yellow pad and began interviewing him—and discovered that his observations about how girls and boys play softball parallel mine about how women and men talk at work.

2   Hoover told me that boys' teams always had one or two stars whom the other boys treated with deference. So when he started coaching a girls' team, he began by looking for the leader. He couldn't find one. "The girls who are better athletes don't lord it over the others," he said. "You get the feeling that everyone's the same." When a girl got the ball, she didn't try to throw it all the way home as a strong-armed boy would; instead, she'd throw it to another team member, so they all became better catchers and throwers. He went on, "If a girl makes an error, she's not in the doghouse for a long time, as a boy would be."

3   "But wait," I interrupted. "I've heard that when girls make a mistake at sports, they often say 'I'm sorry,' whereas boys don't."

4   That's true, he said, but then the girl forgets it—and so do her teammates. "For boys, sports is a performance art. They're concerned with how they look." When they make an error, they sulk because they've let their teammates down. Girls want to win, but if they lose, they're still all in it together—so the mistake isn't as dreadful for the individual or the team.

5   What Hoover described in these youngsters were the seeds of behavior I have observed among women and men at work.

6   The girls who are the best athletes don't "lord it over" the others—just the ethic I found among women in positions of authority. Women managers frequently told me they were good managers because they did not act in an authoritarian manner. They said they did not flaunt their power, or behave as though they were better than their subordinates. Similarly, linguist Elisabeth Kuhn found that women professors in her study informed students of course requirements as if they had magically appeared on the syllabus ("There are two papers. The first paper, ah, let's see, is due . . . . It's back here [referring to the syllabus] at the beginning"), whereas the men professors made it clear that they had set the requirements ("I have two midterms and a final").

A woman manager might say to her secretary, "Could you do me a favor and type this letter right away?" knowing that her secretary is going to type the letter. But her male boss, on hearing this, might conclude she doesn't feel she deserves the authority she has, just as a boys' coach might think the star athlete doesn't realize how good he is if he doesn't expect his teammates to treat him with deference.

I was especially delighted by Hoover's observation that, although girls are more likely to say, "I'm sorry," they are actually far less sorry when they make a mistake than boys who don't say it, but are "in the doghouse" for a long time. This dramatizes the ritual nature of many women's apologies. How often is a woman who is "always apologizing" seen as weak and lacking in confidence? In fact, for many women, saying "I'm sorry" often doesn't mean "I apologize." It means "I'm sorry that happened."

Like many of the rituals common among women, it's a way of speaking that takes into account the other person's point of view. It can even be an automatic conversational smoother. For example, you left your pad in someone's office; you knock on the door and say, "Excuse me, I left my pad on your desk," and the person whose office it is might reply, "Oh, I'm sorry. Here it is." She knows it is not her fault that you left your pad on her desk; she's just letting you know it's okay.

Finally, I was intrigued by Hoover's remark that boys regard sports as "a performance art" and worry about "how they look." There, perhaps, is the rub, the key to why so many women feel they don't get credit for what they do. From childhood, many boys learn something that is very adaptive to the workplace: Raises and promotions are based on "performance" evaluations and these depend, in large measure, on how you appear in other people's eyes. In other words, you have to worry not only about getting your job done but also about getting credit for what you do.

Getting credit often depends on the way you talk. For example, a woman told me she was given a poor evaluation because her supervisor felt she knew less than her male peers. Her boss, it turned out, reached this conclusion because the woman asked more questions: She was seeking information without regard to how her queries would make her look.

The same principle applies to apologizing. Whereas some women seem to be taking undeserved blame by saying "I'm sorry," some men seem to evade deserved blame. I observed this when a man disconnected a conference call by accidentally elbowing the speaker-phone. When his secretary re-connected the call, I expected him to say, "I'm sorry; I knocked the phone by mistake." Instead he said, "Hey, what happened?! One minute you were there, the next minute you were gone!" Annoying as this might be, there are certainly instances in which people improve their fortunes by covering up mistakes. If Hoover's observations about girls' and boys' athletic styles are fascinating, it is even more revealing to see actual transcripts of children at play and how they mirror the adult workplace. Amy Sheldon, a linguist at the University of Minnesota who studies children talking at play in a day care center, compared the conflicts of pre-school girls and boys. She found that boys who fought with one another tended to pursue their own goal. Girls tended to balance their own interests with those of the other girls through complex verbal negotiations.

Look how different the negotiations were:

Two boys fought over a toy telephone: Tony had it; Charlie wanted it. Tony was sitting on a foam chair with the base of the phone in his lap and the receiver lying beside him. Charlie picked up the receiver, and Tony protested, "No, that's my phone!" He grabbed the telephone cord and tried to pull the receiver away from Charlie, saying, "No, that—uh, it's on MY couch. It's on MY couch, Charlie. It's on MY couch. It's on MY couch." It seems he had only one point to make, so he made it repeatedly as he used physical force to get the phone back.

Charlie ignored Tony and held onto the receiver. Tony then got off the couch, set the phone base on the floor and tried to keep possession of it by overturning the chair on top of it. Charlie managed to push the chair off, get the telephone and win the fight.

This might seem like a typical kids' fight until you compare it with a fight Sheldon videotaped among girls. Here the contested objects were toy medical instruments: Elaine had them; Arlene wanted them. But she didn't just grab for them; she argued her case. Elaine, in turn, balanced her own desire to keep them with Arlene's desire to get them. Elaine lost ground gradually, by compromising.

Arlene began not by grabbing but by asking and giving a reason: "Can I have that, that thing? I'm going to take my baby's temperature." Elaine was agreeable, but cautious: "You can use it—you can use my temperature. Just make sure you can't use anything else unless you can ask." Arlene did just that; she asked for the toy syringe: "May I?" Elaine at first resisted, but gave a reason: "No, I'm gonna need to use the shot in a couple of minutes." Arlene reached for the syringe anyway, explaining in a "beseeching" tone, "But I—I need this though."

18 Elaine capitulated, but again tried to set limits: "Okay, just use it once." She even gave Arlene permission to give "just a couple of shots."

19 Arlene then pressed her advantage, and became possessive of her property: "Now don't touch the baby until I get back, because it IS MY BABY! I'll check her ears, okay?" (Even when being demanding, she asked for agreement: "okay?")

20 Elaine tried to regain some rights through compromise: "Well, let's pretend it's another day, that we have to look in her ears together." Elaine also tried another approach that would give Arlene something she wanted: "I'll have to shot her after, after, after you listen—after you look in her ears," suggested Elaine. Arlene, however, was adamant: "Now don't shot her at all!" What happened next will sound familiar to anyone who has ever been a little girl or overheard one. Elaine could no longer abide Arlene's selfish behavior and applied the ultimate sanction: "Well, then, you can't come to my birthday!" Arlene uttered the predictable retort: "I don't want to come to your birthday!"

21 The boys and girls followed different rituals for fighting. Each boy went after what he wanted; they slugged it out; one won. But the girls enacted a complex negotiation, trying to get what they wanted while taking into account what the other wanted.

22 Here is an example of how women and men at work used comparable strategies.

23 Maureen and Harold, two managers at a medium-size company, were assigned to hire a human-resources coordinator for their division. Each favored a different candidate, and both felt strongly about their preferences. They traded arguments for some time, neither convincing the other. Then Harold said that hiring the candidate Maureen wanted would make him so uncomfortable that he would have to consider resigning. Maureen respected Harold. What's more, she liked him and considered him a friend. So she said what seemed to her the only thing she could say under the circumstances: "Well, I certainly don't want you to feel uncomfortable here. You're one of the pillars of the place." Harold's choice was hired.

24 What was crucial was not Maureen's and Harold's individual styles in isolation but how they played in concert with each other's style. Harold's threat to quit ensured his triumph—when used with someone for whom it was a trump card. If he had been arguing with someone who regarded this threat as simply another move in the negotiation rather than a non-negotiable expression of deep feelings, the result might have been different. For example, had she said, "That's ridiculous; of course you're not going to quit!" or matched it ("Well, I'd be tempted to quit if we hired your guy"), the decision might well have gone the other way.

25 Like the girls at play, Maureen was balancing her perspective with those of her colleague and expected him to do the same. Harold was simply going for what he wanted and trusted Maureen to do likewise.

26 This is not to say that all women and all men, or all boys and girls, behave any one way. Many factors influence our styles, including regional and ethnic backgrounds, family experience and individual personality. But gender is a key factor, and understanding its influence can help clarify what happens when we talk.

27 Understanding the ritual nature of communication gives you the flexibility to consider different approaches if you're not happy with the reaction you're getting. Someone who tends to avoid expressing disagreement might learn to play "devil's advocate" without taking it as a personal attack. Someone who tends to avoid admitting fault might find it is effective to say "I'm sorry"—that the loss of face is outweighed by a gain in credibility.

28 There is no one way of talking that will always work best. But understanding how conversational rituals work allows individuals to have more control over their own lives.

Source: Deborah Tannen. "The Talk of the Sandbox: How Johnny and Suzy's Playground Chatter Prepares Them for Life at the Office" *The Washington Post,* December 11, 1994. Copyright Deborah Tannen. Adapted from *Talking from 9 to 5: Women and Men at Work;* HarperCollins. Reprinted with permission.

Vocabulary
Before, during, and after reading the selection, annotate the text and write in your journal. Create a list of vocabulary words, along with their definitions. Give examples of their use from the selection you just read.

After Reading Discussion Questions: Meaning, Structure, and Expression

1. Main Idea: Work as a group to write a summary that answers the following questions: What purpose did Deborah Tannen have for writing this essay? Who is the intended audience? What is the main idea of the essay?

2. **Relevant Details:** The details of this passage explain the similarities and differences in the conversation styles of four groups of people. What are those four groups? Which groups are compared to each other? Which groups are contrasted with each other? Tannen uses several comparable points such as playing sports, fighting, and apologizing. Why do you think she chose these three specific activities to make her comparisons?
3. **Logical Order:** How does Deborah Tannen organize her ideas? Does she talk about the similarities and differences between men and women point by point? Or does she organize her comparison and contrast by presenting one block of ideas (the communication styles of males) and then another (the communication styles of females)? Do you think she chose the more effective method for ordering her details? Why or why not?
4. **Effective Expression:** Deborah Tannen uses transitional words and phrases to clearly identify her specific points of comparison. For example, reread the first sentence in paragraph 6. Circle the phrase that connects the topic "girl athletes" to "women in positions of authority." Does this transitional phrase indicate a comparison or a contrast between the two groups of females? Find two additional transitional words or phrases that identify comparable points in the passage. What are the comparable points or topics? Based on the transitional words or phrases, are these topics being compared, contrasted, or both? Discuss the importance of transitional expressions in a piece of writing.

Thinking Prompts to Move from Reading to Writing

1. In this essay, Deborah Tannen reports her observation and study of human behavior. For example, reread paragraphs 13 through 28. This section objectively reports the differences between the communication styles of boys and girls—like a case study. First she narrates a fight between the boys; then she narrates a girls' fight. Simply by recording their behaviors, she illustrates their differences. Use this method of reporting to compare two topics of your choosing. For example, for a college health class report about the differences between effective and ineffective reactions to stress.
2. Deborah Tannen illustrates the differences between males and females by comparing and contrasting their communication styles as children and adults. What other differences between men and women have you observed? For example, do men and women prefer different types of movies, sports, books, cars? Do they differ in the way they act in their roles as parents, siblings, children, or friends? Write an essay using your own set of comparable points that discusses other important differences between men and women. Choose an audience and writing situation such as the following: an academic paper for a social science class or an article for the college newspaper.

The Loss of Juárez: How Has the Violence in Juárez Changed Border Culture?

SERGIO TRONCOSO

Sergio Troncoso is an award-winning American author of blogs, essays, short stories, and novels. Troncoso, the son of Mexican immigrants, was born in poverty in El Paso, Texas, and grew up in its east-side community, Ysleta. Troncoso's stories have been featured in many anthologies, newspapers, and magazines. His blog about writing, politics, and finance is at www.Chico-Lingo.com. In the following essay, posted online in *Literal, Latin American Voices,* Troncoso explores the changes in a binational, bicultural community brought about by the recent violence on the Mexican-American border.

Before Reading Write a journal entry about the relationship between the United States and Mexico. What are the conflicts about the border shared by these two countries? Do you think Mexican citizens and U.S. citizens differ in their views about border conflicts? How so?

1. Recently I returned home to El Paso, and as we drove back to Ysleta on the Border Highway a sense of sadness overtook me. My kids, Aaron and Isaac, have for two years been clamoring to go to Mexico. They have studied Spanish in New York City, where we live, and their classroom walls are covered with posters from Latin America and Spain. When we return to Ysleta to visit their abuelitos, that is the opportunity to transform the Spanish language and Mexico to more than just academic subjects, to eat an enchilada or an asadero, rather than just to lick your lips at pictures.

2. But my wife and I have said no, because of the rampant violence in Juárez. On this day we settled for stopping on the shoulder of the freeway, just after the Bridge of the Americas and on top of the Yarbrough overpass. My sons took photographs of Mexico and the infamous border fence they have studied in school. "It looks like the wall of a rusty prison," one said. My niños smiled at me, as good sons do, but theirs weren't really smiles. They were obedient, and acquiesced. Perhaps Aaron and Isaac silently questioned whether their parents were overly protective, or just old and narrow-minded.

3. I do want them to know the Juárez I knew as a child. But the current violence and the wall have separated us. It is no compensation to look at Juárez from afar, and I felt as disappointed as my children. What I know, what I want them to know, I can't show them, because I will never willingly put them in harm's way.

4. What many who have not lived on the border may not understand is how close El Paso and Juárez were, and are, even today. Close culturally. Many with families in both cities. Close in so many ways. When I was in high school in El Paso, my family always—and I mean every Sunday—had a family dinner in Juárez at one of my parents' favorite restaurants: Villa Del Mar, La Fogata, La Central, Tortas Nico, and Taqueria La Pila.

5. It was going back in time, to the city where my father and mother met and were married. But it was also to experience another set of rules and values, to a mysterious country with more bookstores than I ever saw in El Paso, to tortas and open-air mercados, to primos who would drop everything to show me their horses, and even to my first funeral—the open casket after all these years has remained vivid in my mind. A young boy, the son of a friend of my parents, had been run over by a car. Juárez for me was primal and powerful; it was my history. I thought I understood it instinctually, even spiritually, and that is just when it baffled me the most. After graduating from Harvard, I spent a year in Mexico City, a Chicano Chilango, in order to decide whether I belonged in the United States, or en el otro lado.

6. On Monday just before we left for El Paso, I was trying to explain this to friends in Boston, at a Passover Seder. How Juárez was closer to El Paso, than New York City was to New Jersey. How people went to lunch in Juárez and were able to return to the United States in a couple of hours. How we used to go to Waterfil over the Zaragoza International Bridge (on the eastern outskirts of Juárez) for Easter

picnics, clinking cases of Fantas, Sangrias and Cocas, for jarampiñados, pan dulce and pan francesito, and my personal favorite, homemade Mexican fireworks. All of what we could not find in Ysleta. Yes, it was that close, in the most trivial and profound ways.

I tried to explain to these Red Sox fans how when I went to Juárez as a child and as an adult in El Paso, it was more than just for food and tchotchkes. It was going to another possibility of being. The buildings were older than those in El Paso, and the streets more congested. The cobblestones and curbs were well-worn and shiny. The shoe shine boys snapped their red rags on shoes waiting atop hand-carved shoe-shine kits. I marveled at the men who fixed flats in Waterfil, their hands a deep brown, working quickly to snap a tire out of its rim with a few perfectly placed strikes of a tire iron.

Returning to Juárez was returning to the elemental, to a living history, to discovering an innate intelligence and workmanship that comes to be when you have to make do. Returning to Juárez was gaining an understanding of my father and mother. Despite backbreaking hardships, no money, and eking out a living in the desert of Ysleta, on weekends they would crank up their old stereo to listen to Javier Solis and Los Panchos. On their porch in Ysleta, in front of my mother's rose bushes, the sun setting behind the Franklin Mountains to the west, they were happy and in love. But their indomitable spirit had been nurtured not in America but on the other side.

So Juárez was never a joke for me, as it was for some of my Anglo friends and not a few of my Chicano friends from El Paso. It was a portal to another world that felt at once deeply familiar and strangely fascinating.

On the other hand, El Paso was littered for miles with fast food chain stores and perfectly built highways where a human being walking seemed an oddity. In grade school, I once went to an event honoring the famous Mexican-American golfer Lee Trevino, and my parents bought me a t-shirt that declared in bright green letters, 'I'm one of Lee's fleas!' But what I most remember about that day was a burly Anglo man strolling by with his wife and sniggering, "That's one fat flea." My pride turned to shame. In El Paso as in Juárez, I also fit in and did not fit in, but too often in Texas the ambiguity of this existence was laced with hurt.

Three years ago the Juárez I knew changed. An unprecedented orgy of drug violence exploded in Juárez. The government against drug cartels. Soldiers on Avenidas 16 de Septiembre and López Mateos, with machine guns anchored atop jeeps. Dozens of murders per week. Sometimes dozens of murders in one weekend. The breakdown of society, with hundreds of thousands fleeing the violence. Three years ago, we lost Juárez, as a place to show our kids where their abuelitos came from, and in so many other ways. My parents have not returned to their hometown in three years. This past that has shaped them, even though it is less than a few kilometers away, is now a forbidden, forsaken territory. It is a deeply felt loss for many of us in El Paso.

I am tired of pointing out that the billion-dollar drug habits of the United States and the millions of dollars of American guns illegally exported to Mexico are root causes of the drug violence. How often can you point out American hypocrisy and myopia on the drug violence in Mexico before you realize that you cannot force a people to understand what they do not want to see. I am tired of witnessing a corrupt local police force in Mexico, and an ineffective national government, which has failed to provide for the basic security of its citizens. For the moment, the hypocrisy, the idiocy, and the cheapness of life are too much to bear.

Thousands of lives have been lost. Neighborhoods have been abandoned. On the American side of the border, we hear precious few enlightened words from politicians, a reach even under the best of circumstances. Instead, electioneering demagogues have jumped at the opportunity to target the powerless, the dark-skinned, the other.

I just miss Juárez. I miss it as a place to show my children how their abuelitos began in this world. I miss Juárez as a place to appreciate another way to be. When will this nightmare end?

My only hope is how Juárez has, in part, come to El Paso. In relocated people, with Green Cards, who have fled the violence. In new restaurants and other businesses in El Paso, which once thrived in Juárez. Here, on this side, they wait for the darkness to pass. But even when a peaceful Juárez returns—and I know one day it will—it will not return to what it was. In the memories of those who survive will be what was lost for a few years, and perhaps forever.

Source: Sergio Troncoso, "The Loss of Juarez: How Has the Violence in Juarez Changed Border Culture," *Literal, Latin American Voices,* Issue 23. © Sergio Troncoso. Reprinted by permission of the author. Sergio Troncoso is the author of *The Last Tortilla and Other Stories, Crossing Borders: Personal Essays,* and the novels, *The Nature of Truth,* and *From This Wicked Patch of Dust.*

Vocabulary Before, during, and after reading the selection, annotate the text and write in your journal. Create a list of vocabulary words, along with their definitions. Give examples of their use from the selection you just read.

After Reading Discussion Questions: Meaning, Structure, and Expression

1. **Main Idea:** Work as a group to write a summary that answers the following questions: What purpose did Troncoso have for writing this piece? Who is the intended audience? What is the main idea of the essay? What is the significance of the title of the piece?
2. **Relevant Details:** Since the focus of the essay is on the changes to Juárez, why does Troncoso include the details given in paragraphs 12 and 13? Do you think these details are crucial to his main point? Why or why not?
3. **Logical Order:** The overall pattern of organization is a comparison and contrast between what Juárez was then and what Juárez is now. To accomplish this comparison and contrast, Troncoso used an additional main pattern of organization. Skim the essay to mark key transition words. Which additional pattern of organization did Troncoso use throughout the essay? Why did he rely also on this particular pattern?
4. **Effective Expression:** Troncoso appeals to our senses of sight, sound, smell, and taste. Find examples of his use of sensory images of Juárez. Explain the comparisons or contrasts made with sensory images you identify.

Thinking Prompts to Move from Reading to Writing

1. In paragraphs 12 and 13, Troncoso offers details about drug abuse and the violence associated with its trade. Drug abuse changes people and communities. Assume you are involved in a community service project aimed at stopping drug abuse in your community. Write an essay to post as an entry on the community's blog. Compare and contrast the healthy person or community to the drug addict or the community riddled with drug abuse. Ask your reader to take action.
2. Many people experience complete or radical changes in their mental and physical states. A profound life event or personal decision may dramatically change a person's priorities in life. For example, countless testimonials record dramatic changes in emotions, thoughts, and behaviors. Think about a dramatic change that you or someone you know has undergone. Write a personal essay that compares and contrasts the emotions, thoughts, or behaviors evident before to the change to the emotions, thoughts, or behaviors evident after the change.

Definition

What is Poverty?

JO GOODWIN-PARKER

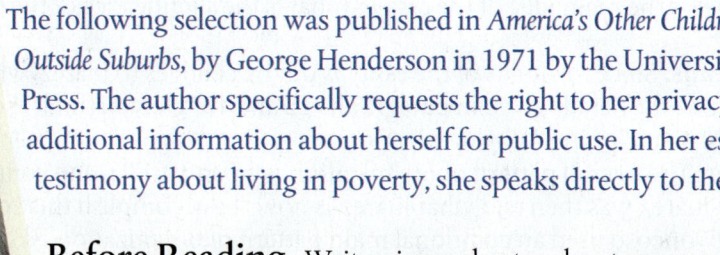

The following selection was published in *America's Other Children: Public Schools Outside Suburbs,* by George Henderson in 1971 by the University of Oklahoma Press. The author specifically requests the right to her privacy and offers no additional information about herself for public use. In her essay, a personal testimony about living in poverty, she speaks directly to the reader.

Before Reading Write a journal entry about your response to poverty. How would you define poverty? Why are people poor? How does society react to the poor? Do you think our government does enough to help poor people? What can be done to fight poverty?

1   You ask me what is poverty? Listen to me. Here I am, dirty, smelly, and with no "proper" underwear on and with the stench of my rotting teeth near you. I will tell you. Listen to me. Listen without pity. I cannot use your pity. Listen with understanding. Put yourself in my dirty, worn out, ill-fitting shoes, and hear me.

2   Poverty is getting up every morning from a dirt- and illness-stained mattress. The sheets have long since been used for diapers. Poverty is living in a smell that never leaves. This is a smell of urine, sour milk, and spoiling food sometimes joined with the strong smell of long-cooked onions. Onions are cheap. If you have smelled this smell, you did not know how it came. It is the smell of the outdoor privy. It is the smell of young children who cannot walk the long dark way in the night. It is the smell of the mattresses where years of "accidents" have happened. It is the smell of the milk which has gone sour because the refrigerator long has not worked, and it costs money to get it fixed. It is the smell of rotting garbage. I could bury it, but where is the shovel? Shovels cost money.

3   Poverty is being tired. I have always been tired. They told me at the hospital when the last baby came that I had chronic anemia caused from poor diet, a bad case of worms, and that I needed a corrective operation. I listened politely—the poor are always polite. The poor always listen. They don't say that there is no money for iron pills, or better food, or worm medicine. The idea of an operation is frightening and costs so much that, if I had dared, I would have laughed. Who takes care of my children? Recovery from an operation takes a long time. I have three children. When I left them with "Granny" the last time I had a job, I came home to find the baby covered with fly specks, and a diaper that had not been changed since I left. When the dried diaper came off, bits of my baby's flesh came with it. My other child was playing with a sharp bit of broken glass, and my oldest was playing alone at the edge of a lake. I made twenty-two dollars a week, and a good nursery school costs twenty dollars a week for three children. I quit my job.

4   Poverty is dirt. You can say in your clean clothes coming from your clean house, "Anybody can be clean." Let me explain about housekeeping with no money. For breakfast I give my children grits with no oleo or cornbread without eggs and oleo. This does not use up many dishes. What dishes there are, I wash in cold water and with no soap. Even the cheapest soap has to be saved for the baby's diapers. Look at my hands, so cracked and red. Once I saved for two months to buy a jar of Vaseline for my hands and the baby's diaper rash. When I had saved enough, I went to buy it and the price had gone up two cents. The baby and I suffered on. I have to decide every day if I can bear to put my cracked sore hands into the cold water and strong soap. But you ask, why not hot water? Fuel costs money. If you have a wood fire it costs money. If you burn electricity, it costs money. Hot water is a luxury. I do not have luxuries. I know you will be surprised when I tell you how young I am. I look so much older. My back has been

bent over the wash tubs every day for so long, I cannot remember when I ever did anything else. Every night I wash every stitch my school age child has on and just hope her clothes will be dry by morning.

Poverty is staying up all night on cold nights to watch the fire knowing one spark on the newspaper covering the walls means your sleeping child dies in flames. In summer poverty is watching gnats and flies devour your baby's tears when he cries. The screens are torn and you pay so little rent you know they will never be fixed. Poverty means insects in your food, in your nose, in your eyes, and crawling over you when you sleep. Poverty is hoping it never rains because diapers won't dry when it rains and soon you are using newspapers. Poverty is seeing your children forever with runny noses. Paper handkerchiefs cost money and all your rags you need for other things. Even more costly are antihistamines. Poverty is cooking without food and cleaning without soap.

Poverty is asking for help. Have you ever had to ask for help, knowing your children will suffer unless you get it? Think about asking for a loan from a relative, if this is the only way you can imagine asking for help. I will tell you how it feels. You find out where the office is that you are supposed to visit. You circle that block four or five times. Thinking of your children, you go in. Everyone is very busy. Finally, someone comes out and you tell her that you need help. That never is the person you need to see. You go see another person, and after spilling the whole shame of your poverty all over the desk between you, you find that this isn't the right office after all—you must repeat the whole process, and it never is any easier at the next place.

You have asked for help, and after all it has a cost. You are again told to wait. You are told why, but you don't really hear because of the red cloud of shame and the rising cloud of despair.

Poverty is remembering. It is remembering quitting school in junior high because "nice" children had been so cruel about my clothes and my smell. The attendance officer came. My mother told him I was pregnant. I wasn't, but she thought that I could get a job and help out. I had jobs off and on, but never long enough to learn anything. Mostly I remember being married. I was so young then. I am still young. For a time, we had all the things you have. There was a little house in another town, with hot water and everything. Then my husband lost his job. There was unemployment insurance for a while and what few jobs I could get. Soon, all our nice things were repossessed and we moved back here. I was pregnant then. This house didn't look so bad when we first moved in. Every week it gets worse. Nothing is ever fixed. We now had no money. There were a few odd jobs for my husband, but everything went for food then, as it does now. I don't know how we lived through three years and three babies, but we did. I'll tell you something, after the last baby I destroyed my marriage. It had been a good one, but could you keep on bringing children in this dirt? Did you ever think how much it costs for any kind of birth control? I knew my husband was leaving the day he left, but there were no goodbye between us. I hope he has been able to climb out of this mess somewhere. He never could hope with us to drag him down.

That's when I asked for help. When I got it, you know how much it was? It was, and is, seventy-eight dollars a month for the four of us; that is all I ever can get. Now you know why there is no soap, no needles and thread, no hot water, no aspirin, no worm medicine, no hand cream, no shampoo. None of these things forever and ever and ever. So that you can see clearly, I pay twenty dollars a month rent, and most of the rest goes for food. For grits and cornmeal, and rice and milk and beans. I try my best to use only the minimum electricity. If I use more, there is that much less for food.

Poverty is looking into a black future. Your children won't play with my boys. They will turn to other boys who steal to get what they want. I can already see them behind the bars of their prison instead of behind the bars of my poverty. Or they will turn to the freedom of alcohol or drugs, and find themselves enslaved. And my daughter? At best, there is for her a life like mine.

But you say to me, there are schools. Yes, there are schools. My children have no extra books, no magazines, no extra pencils, or crayons, or paper and most important of all, they do not have health. They have worms, they have infections, they have pink-eye all summer. They do not sleep well on the floor, or with me in my one bed. They do not suffer from hunger, my seventy-eight dollars keeps us alive, but they do suffer from malnutrition. Oh yes, I do remember what I was taught about health in school. It doesn't do much good.

In some places there is a surplus commodities program. Not here. The country said it cost too much. There is a school lunch program. But I have two children who will already be damaged by the time they get to school.

But, you say to me, there are health clinics. Yes, there are health clinics and they are in the towns. I live out here eight miles from town. I can walk that far (even if it is sixteen miles both ways), but can my little children? My neighbor will take me when he goes; but he expects to get paid, one way or another. I bet you know my neighbor. He is that large man who spends his time at the gas station, the barbershop, and the corner store complaining about the government spending money on the immoral mothers of illegitimate children.

Poverty is an acid that drips on pride until all pride is worn away. Poverty is a chisel that chips on honor until honor is worn away. Some of you say that you would do something in my situation, and maybe you would, for the first week or the first month, but for year after year after year?

Even the poor can dream. A dream of a time when there is money. Money for the right kinds of food, for worm medicine, for iron pills, for toothbrushes, for hand cream, for a hammer and nails and a bit of screening, for a shovel, for a bit of paint, for some sheeting, for needles and thread. Money to pay in money for a trip to town. And, oh, money for hot water and money for soap. A dream of when asking for help does not eat away the last bit of pride. When the office you visit is as nice as the offices of other governmental agencies, when there are enough workers to help you quickly, when workers do not quit in defeat and despair. When you have to tell your story to only one person, and that person can send you for other help and you don't have to prove your poverty over and over and over again.

I have come out of my despair to tell you this. Remember I did not come from another place or another time. Others like me are all around you. Look at us with an angry heart, anger that will help.

Source: America's Other Children: Public Schools Outside Suburbia by Henderson, George. Reproduced with permission of University of Oklahoma Press in the format Republish in a book via Copyright Clearance Center.

Vocabulary
Before, during, and after reading the selection, annotate the text and write in your journal. Create a list of vocabulary words, along with their definitions. Give examples of their use from the selection you just read.

After Reading Discussion Questions: Meaning, Structure, and Expression

1. **Main Idea:** Work as a group to write a summary that answers the following questions: What purpose did Jo Goodwin-Parker have for writing this essay? Who is her intended audience? What is the main idea of the essay?
2. **Relevant Details:** Parker offers her own life experiences to define poverty. Does she provide enough details to make her point convincingly? Would the use of facts or expert opinions strengthen her point? Why or why not?
3. **Logical Order:** Parker defines poverty with a series of seven statements that begin with "Poverty is." Summarize her definition of poverty using these seven statements. Do you agree with the order in which she presents these statements? Why or why not?
4. **Effective Expression:** Based on Parker's choice of words, how would you describe the tone of this essay? Is it angry, embarrassed, disappointed, reflective, sad, or optimistic, or does it communicate some other attitude about poverty? Identify three expressions that illustrate the tone of the piece. Explain the reasons for your selections.

Thinking Prompts to Move from Reading to Writing

1. Often, people do not understand what they have not experienced. Parker defines poverty for people who have never experienced it. In the last sentence in the first paragraph, she commands her readers to step into her shoes so they can learn from her experiences. Assume the view of one who understands an issue such as depression, addiction, or prejudice based on experience. Write an essay that defines the issue so that someone who has not experienced it can better understand the problem.
2. In her essay, Parker defines the problem of poverty, but she does not offer a solution, other than to say "look at us with an angry heart, anger that will help." What kind of anger will help this situation? Respond to Parker by writing an essay that defines this kind of anger. Consider using a phrase like "Anger that will help is" to reply to specific points she raises in her essay.

Cause and Effect

Cool at 13, Adrift at 23

JAN HOFFMAN

Jan Hoffman is a writer for the *New York Times*. She researches and writes about adolescent health and psychology—particularly tweens, teens, and modern family dynamics. The following article appeared in the *New York Times* blog called "Well." The article explores the surprising long-term outcomes of being a "cool kid" in school.

Before Reading Write a journal entry about your middle school experience. Describe the kind of kid you were. For example, were you outgoing and popular, or quiet and shy? Did you join any kind of team or keep to yourself? How was middle school different from elementary school and high school? Do you feel your middle school experience prepared you to navigate the social and academic world of high school?

1. At 13, they were viewed by classmates with envy, admiration and not a little awe. The girls wore makeup, had boyfriends and went to parties held by older students. The boys boasted about sneaking beers on a Saturday night and swiping condoms from the local convenience store.

2. They were cool. They were good-looking. They were so not you. Whatever happened to them?

3. "The fast-track kids didn't turn out O.K.," said Joseph P. Allen, a psychology professor at the University of Virginia. He is the lead author of a new study, published this month in the journal *Child Development*, that followed these risk-taking, socially precocious cool kids for a decade. In high school, their social status often plummeted, the study showed, and they began struggling in many ways. It was their early rush into what Dr. Allen calls pseudomature behavior that set them up for trouble. Now in their early 20s, many of them have had difficulties with intimate relationships, alcohol and marijuana, and even criminal activity. "They are doing more extreme things to try to act cool, bragging about drinking three six-packs on a Saturday night, and their peers are thinking, 'These kids are not socially competent,'" Dr. Allen said. "They're still living in their middle-school world." As fast-moving middle-schoolers, they were driven by a heightened longing to impress friends. Indeed their brazen behavior did earn them a blaze of popularity. But by high school, their peers had begun to mature, readying themselves to experiment with romance and even mild delinquency. The cool kids' popularity faded.

4. B. Bradford Brown, a professor of educational psychology at the University of Wisconsin-Madison who writes about adolescent peer relationships and was not involved in the study, said it offered a trove of data. The finding that most surprised him, he said, was that "pseudomature" behavior was an even stronger predictor of problems with alcohol and drugs than levels of drug use in early adolescence. Research on teenagers usually tracks them only through adolescence, Dr. Brown added. But this study, following a diverse group of 184 subjects in Charlottesville, Va., starting at age 13, continued into adulthood at 23.

5. Researchers took pains to document the rise and fall in social status, periodically interviewing the subjects as well as those who they felt knew them best, usually close friends. About 20 percent of the group fell into the "cool kid" category at the study's outset.

6. A constellation of three popularity-seeking behaviors characterized pseudomaturity, Dr. Allen and his colleagues found. These young teenagers sought out friends who were physically attractive; their romances were more numerous, emotionally intense and sexually exploring than those of their peers; and they dabbled in minor delinquency—skipping school, sneaking into movies, vandalism.

As they turned 23, the study found that when compared to their socially slower-moving middle-school peers, they had a 45 percent greater rate of problems resulting from alcohol and marijuana use and a 40 percent higher level of actual use of those substances. They also had a 22 percent greater rate of adult criminal behavior, from theft to assaults.

Many attributed failed adult romantic relationships to social status: they believed that their lack of cachet was the reason their partners had broken up with them. Those early attempts to act older than they were seemed to have left them socially stunted. When their peers were asked how well these young adults got along with others, the former cool kids' ratings were 24 percent lower than the average young adult.

The researchers grappled with why this cluster of behaviors set young teenagers on a downward spiral. Dr. Allen suggested that while they were chasing popularity, they were missing a critical developmental period. At the same time, other young teenagers were learning about soldering same-gender friendships while engaged in drama-free activities like watching a movie at home together on a Friday night, eating ice cream. Parents should support that behavior and not fret that their young teenagers aren't "popular," he said.

"To be truly mature as an early adolescent means you're able to be a good, loyal friend, supportive, hardworking and responsible," Dr. Allen said. "But that doesn't get a lot of airplay on Monday morning in a ninth-grade homeroom."

Dr. Brown offered another perspective about why the cool kids lost their way. The teenagers who lead the social parade in middle school—determining everyone else's choices in clothes, social media and even notebook colors—have a heavy burden for which they are not emotionally equipped. "So they gravitate towards older kids," he said. And those older teenagers, themselves possibly former cool kids, were dubious role models, he said: "In adolescence, who is open to hanging out with someone three or four years younger? The more deviant kids."

Dr. Allen offered one typical biography from the study. At 14, the boy was popular. He had numerous relationships, kissed more than six girls, flung himself into minor forms of trouble, and surrounded himself with good-looking friends.

By 22, he was a high-school dropout, had many problems associated with drinking, including work absenteeism and arrests for drunken driving. He is unemployed and still prone to minor thefts and vandalism.

But as Dr. Allen emphasized, pseudomaturity suggests a predilection; it is not a firm predictor. A teenage girl from the study initially had a similar profile, with many boyfriends at an early age, attractive friends and a fondness for shoplifting.

Yet by 23, Dr. Allen wrote in an email, "she'd earned her bachelor's degree, had not had any more trouble with criminal behavior, used alcohol only in responsible ways and was in a good job."

Dr. Mitchell J. Prinstein, a professor of psychology at the University of North Carolina at Chapel Hill who studies adolescent social development, said that while teenagers all long to be accepted by their peers studies suggest that parents can reinforce qualities that will help them withstand the pressure to be too cool, too fast.

"Adolescents also appreciate individuality and confidence," he said. "Adolescents who can stick to their own values can still be considered cool, even without doing what the others are doing."

Source: Jan Hoffman, "Cool at 13, Adrift at 23," *The New York Times,* June 23, 2014.

Vocabulary
Before, during, and after reading the selection, annotate the text and write in your journal. Create a list of vocabulary words, along with their definitions. Give examples of their use from the selection you just read.

After Reading Discussion Questions: Meaning, Structure, and Expression

1. **Central Idea:** Work as a group to write a summary that answers the following questions: What purpose did Jan Hoffman have for writing this essay? Who is her intended audience? What is the central point of the essay? What is the significance of the title?

2. **Relevant Details:** This article compares two different types of adolescent behavior and their effects on early adulthood. What are a few of the author's reasons that being cool and popular at an early age set up "fast-track kids" for early adulthood trouble? What are some healthy behaviors young teens miss out on developing while they chase popularity?
3. **Logical Order:** Hoffman concludes her essay with a quote from a professor of psychology, who states, "adolescents who can stick to their own values can still be considered cool, even without doing what the others are doing." Do you think this is an effective end to this essay? Why or why not?
4. **Effective Expression:** Why do you think Hoffman began the essay by describing what made these "cool kids" cool? What point is she making by stating, "they were so not you"? Does her tone remain consistent throughout the essay? For example, does her attitude toward the "pseudomature" kids sound positive, negative, or neutral? Identify three expressions that illustrate specific tones or attitudes and explain how Hoffman uses them.

Thinking Prompts to Move from Reading to Writing

1. Assume you are taking a college course in psychology. Your professor provided you with the following study question for an upcoming essay exam. Use information from the passage to compose your answer. Use your own words. Study question: *Explain the nature, causes, and effects of "pseudomaturity."*
2. Assume you are a parent and member of the PTA at your child's middle school. You have been asked to write a letter for the school newsletter about "fitting in." Refer to this essay and describe how the attributes of a "cool kid" can be potential signs of future trouble for the development of that child. Describe what is to be "truly mature as an early adolescent." How do those characteristics differ from those of the "cool kids"? How does developing the characteristics of "true maturity" better prepare the child for life in ways that focusing on "being cool" cannot?

Cause–Effect

Through Young Eyes

MICHAEL S. MALONE

Michael S. Malone is the author of a dozen best-selling business books including *The Virtual Corporation, Going Public, Infinite Loop* (the Apple story), and *Virtual Selling*. In addition, Malone writes *The Silicon Insider*, a popular weekly technology column for ABCNews.com. He also contributes regularly to the *Wall Street Journal, Wired,* and *Fast Company*. Currently, Malone serves as Editor-in-Chief of Edgelings.com, a news and features website founded by a team of prominent Silicon Valley media and technology executives. The following article appeared in Edgelings.com in the Consumer Electronics and Lifestyle/Culture section.

Before Reading Write a journal entry about your experiences with technology. Does technology—such as social networks, smart phones, the Web, instant messaging, online gaming—improve a person's life? In what ways? Can these forms of technology be harmful? In what ways? Does the good of technology outweigh the bad? Why or why not?

Technology in all of its forms—social networks, smart phones, the Web, instant messaging, on-line gaming—is a net loss for today's young people. At least according to one group of Silicon Valley 8th graders.

"It's bad for us, but it sure is fun," says Eric Bautista, 13, one of the students in Sister Jolene Schmitz's junior high school class at Resurrection School in Sunnyvale, California.

Admittedly, this informal survey offers, at best, only anecdotal evidence. Still, it is pretty shocking that a group of young teenagers, all of them technologically very astute, and living in the very heart of Silicon Valley, would come to such a conclusion.

These kids, born about the time the Internet became widely adopted, live within blocks of where the Intel microprocessor, the Apple computer and the Atari video game were all invented. They spend their days (and nights) surfing the web, playing on-line games and instant messaging. Most have cell phones in their backpacks. And many have at least one parent who works in the electronics industry.

Yet, when asked to weigh the benefits of having high technology in their lives versus the costs—intellectually, emotionally, socially—of that technology, the class voted 31–3 negative . . . a ratio so extreme that it argues against an aberration and towards a larger question about the overall impact of technology on the lives of our young people.

"We try to find the happy medium," says Stephanie Abreu, 13, "But we don't know where it is."

This isn't to say that the 8th graders, all of them heading off to top-tier Silicon Valley high schools, don't love their tech toys and tools. On the contrary, when asked to list all of the positives about tech, they weren't short of answers: access to information with unprecedented scope, the ability to socialize with large groups over vast distances, 24/7 multi-media communication, and perhaps best of all, whole new worlds of entertainment.

Moreover, this brave new digital world has always been part of their lives and, perhaps a bit jaded by it all, they find the idea of world without computers and cell phones surprisingly appealing: in a class vote, one-third of the students said they would prefer to have lived in the long-ago, pre-tech world of the late 1950s.

When asked what they find wrong with living in our modern Wired Web World, the students had no shortage of answers, most of which fell into a half-dozen categories. I'll let the students largely speak for themselves—voices describing the dark side of the tech revolution with a sincerity few of us adults have ever heard before:

- *Time-waster:* "Technology is the key to procrastination," says Kenny Kobetsky, 14. Eighty percent of the class said they had missed sleep due to playing on the Internet, fifty percent said they had forgotten to do homework for the same reason. "The Internet is just so tantalizing," says Nick Gregov, 14. "I actually think McDonalds is healthier than my computer," adds Blake Billiet, 13. Though the students did admit that the Web and cellphone can save time that used to be burned up driving to the store or library, few felt that these gains exceeded the many hours wasted on text or web surfing.

- *Loss of motivation:* "With all of these toys, it's hard to get out of the house," says Sybile Moser, 14. Many of the students said that while technology makes it easier to access information and learn new things, the lack of interaction with others often makes that learning biased and distorted—you only learn what you want to learn. "The students miss the give and take, the debate of learning together when they are on the Web," says Sister Jolene. Because of this, the students say, it's hard for them to keep their attention fixed on any one topic, but prefer instead to drift along in the information flow, letting it take them wherever it leads.

- *Addictive:* "The Internet is like a gateway drug," says Christine Doan, 13. Alex Nguyen, 13, compared the experience to eating ice cream—you love it even though it's bad for you. Even at their young age, many of the students already have Facebook pages and spend as much time there as watching television. Not surprisingly then, when asked if, despite all of their worries about the cost of technology in their lives, any of them would give up their laptop or their cellphone, almost no one raised a hand.

- *Second Hand Knowledge:* This answer was probably the biggest surprise. The eighth graders seemed to intuitively appreciate that the experiences and information they received from the Web and other digital sources was essentially a simulacrum of reality—a re-creation on a glowing flat screen of the three dimensional natural world . . . and that something was being lost in the translation. "We don't get as much out of things if we don't experience them ourselves," says Lauren Fahey, 13. "We seem to spend a lot of our lives as bystanders," adds Katherine Wu, 13.

- *Exposure:* The news is regularly filled with stories of Internet predators preying on naïve young people, or about the easy availability to adolescents of on-line pornography and other vices. But these eighth graders were anything but innocents about the dark side of the Web—and indeed, showed surprising maturity in their strategies for coping with threats all-but unknown to previous generations. "Look, when you're talking to a 'friend', you don't really know if it's really them—especially if they are introduced by someone else," says Peyton Yniguez, 14. "The nature of friendship changes," says Jonathon Robbins, 14. But the most astute, and disturbing, comment belonged to Jenna Kunz, 14: "You have to develop your own special conscience for the Internet."

- *Disturbed Values:* All of these forces can't help but affect a young person's sense of values. The eighth graders, in some ways sophisticated beyond their years, instinctively understand that. "We can't respect anything anymore," says Eric Bautista. Adds Jenna Kunz, "You don't care about things as much; you aren't as passionate as you should be." And yet, that said, these are still kids who are excited about graduation and the prospects of the impending four years of high school. And world-weary as they might sound, each one of the above comments provoked conversation so loud and lively that Sister Jolene spent most of the time just trying to keep the noise down to a dull roar.

In the end, if the news is surprising to us adults that teenagers believe technology is a net loss in their lives, there is consolation in knowing that these young people—themselves creations of the digital age—are not starry-eyed acolytes of the latest computer game or web site. Rather, technology is the world they casually operate within and they have a deep understanding of its rewards and its costs, what it gives and takes away. And for all of our fears for them, they themselves show an extraordinary sense of perspective.

Stephanie Abreu said it best: "Technology is like family. Sometimes it's good, sometimes bad. But you love it all the same."

Special thanks to Sr. Jolene's 8th grade class at Resurrection School, Sunnyvale, California, for its assistance in the preparation of this article.

Source: Michael S. Malone, "Through Young Eyes" Engelings.com. Reprinted by permission of the author.

Vocabulary
Before, during, and after reading the selection, annotate the text and write in your journal. Create a list of vocabulary words, along with their definitions. Give examples of their use from the selection you just read.

After Reading Discussion Questions: Meaning, Structure, and Expression

1. **Main Idea:** Work as a group to write a summary that answers the following questions: What purpose did Michael S. Malone have for writing this essay? Who is the intended audience? What is the main idea of the essay?
2. **Relevant Details:** In paragraph 9, Malone states "I'll let the students largely speak for themselves—" to signal his use of direct quotes as supporting details. Why does he use so many direct quotes? Does he use too many? Would the essay be more effective if he had paraphrased the students' ideas? Why or why not? Are these students a good source of information? Why or why not?
3. **Logical Order:** In paragraphs 10 through 15, Malone lists the things these young people think are wrong with technology—a list of six harmful effects arising from the "dark side of the tech revolution." Do you think Michael Malone presented the list in a particular order of importance? For example, is "time waster" less harmful than "disturbed values"? Are all these effects equally harmful? Assume Malone did list the effects from least to most significant. Do you agree with the given order? Would you reorder these effects based on their significance? How and why?

4. **Effective Expression:** Reread paragraph 14. In the last sentence of the paragraph, Jenna Kunz, 14, states "You have to develop your own special conscience for the Internet." Malone describes her statement as "the most astute, and disturbing." What does she imply in her use of the word "conscience" in her statement? What kind of "special conscience" is needed for the Internet? Do you agree with Malone's assessment about her comment? Why or why not?

Thinking Prompts to Move from Reading to Writing

1. "Through Young Eyes" generated numerous online comments from readers. One reader criticized the article by writing, "Interview 'normal' teens at a non-Catholic school and you will get a different answer." Do the students' views as expressed in this article represent the views of "normal" youth? Would most youth agree that technology is harmful? Work with a group of your peers and conduct your own research into this topic. Create a survey based on the information in this article. Ask students in your classes to fill out the survey. Then, write a report on your findings based on the anecdotal evidence you gather from the survey. Assume you are writing an academic paper for a sociology class.

2. Michael Malone introduces his topic in the first sentence as "technology in all of its forms." His article explores the effects of technology on a general level. Narrow this line of thought by focusing on a specific type of technology. Write an essay that explains how technology has impacted written communication for better or worse. Assume you will post your writing as a comment to Malone's article "Through Young Eyes" on Edgelings.com. Or write an academic paper for a humanities course that explains how technology in transportation has affected society for better or worse.

Why We Crave Horror Movies

STEPHEN KING

Stephen King, born in Portland, Maine, in 1947, has been writing full-time since the 1973 publication of his novel *Carrie*. He has since published over 40 books and has become one of the world's most successful writers.

Before Reading Write a journal entry about your reaction to horror movies. Do you enjoy horror movies? Why or why not? Why do you think horror movies are so popular? Do graphically violent horror movies have a harmful effect on society? Explain your reasons.

1. I think that we're all mentally ill: those of us outside the asylums only hide it a little better—and maybe not all that much better, after all. We've all known people who talk to themselves, people who sometimes squinch their faces into horrible grimaces when they believe no one is watching, people who have some hysterical fear—of snakes, the dark, the tight place, the long drop . . . and, of course, those final worms and grubs that are waiting so patiently underground.

2. When we pay our four or five bucks and seat ourselves at tenth-row center in a theater showing a horror movie, we are daring the nightmare.

3. Why? Some of the reasons are simple and obvious. To show that we can, that we are not afraid, that we can ride this roller coaster. Which is not to say that a really good horror movie may not surprise a scream out of us at some point, the way we may scream when the roller coaster twists through a complete 360 or plows through a lake at the bottom of the drop. And horror movies, like roller coasters, have always

been the special province of the young; by the time one turns 40 or 50, one's appetite for double twists or 360-degree loops may be considerably depleted.

We also go to re-establish our feelings of essential normality; the horror movie is innately conservative, even reactionary. Freda Jackson as the horrible melting woman in *Die, Monster, Die!* confirms for us that no matter how far we may be removed from the beauty of a Robert Redford or a Diana Ross, we are still light-years from true ugliness.

And we go to have fun.

Ah, but this is where the ground starts to slope away, isn't it? Because this is a very peculiar sort of fun indeed. The fun comes from seeing others menaced—sometimes killed. One critic has suggested that if pro football has become the voyeur's version of combat, then the horror film has become the modern version of the public lynching.

It is true that the mythic, "fairytale" horror film intends to take away the shades of gray.... It urges us to put away our more civilized and adult penchant for analysis and to become children again, seeing things in pure blacks and whites. It may be that horror movies provide psychic relief on this level because this invitation to lapse into simplicity, irrationality and even outright madness is extended so rarely. We are told we may allow our emotions a free rein . . . or no rein at all.

If we are all insane, then sanity becomes a matter of degree. If your insanity leads you to carve up women like Jack the Ripper or the Cleveland Torso Murderer, we clap you away in the funny farm (but neither of those two amateur-night surgeons was ever caught, heh-heh-heh); if, on the other hand your insanity leads you only to talk to yourself when you're under stress or to pick your nose on the morning bus, then you are left alone to go about your business . . . though it is doubtful that you will ever be invited to the best parties.

The potential lyncher is in almost all of us (excluding saints, past and present; but then, most saints have been crazy in their own ways), and every now and then, he has to be let loose to scream and roll around in the grass. Our emotions and our fears form their own body, and we recognize that it demands its own exercise to maintain proper muscle tone. Certain of these emotional muscles are accepted—even exalted—in civilized society; they are, of course, the emotions that tend to maintain the status quo of civilization itself. Love, friendship, loyalty, kindness—these are all the emotions that we applaud, emotions that have been immortalized in the couplets of Hallmark cards. . . .

When we exhibit these emotions, society showers us with positive reinforcement; we learn this even before we get out of diapers. When, as children, we hug our rotten little puke of a sister and give her a kiss, all the aunts and uncles smile and twit and cry, "Isn't he the sweetest little thing?" Such coveted treats as chocolate-covered graham crackers often follow. But if we deliberately slam the rotten little puke of a sister's fingers in the door, sanctions follow—angry remonstrance from parents, aunts and uncles; instead of a chocolate-covered graham cracker, a spanking.

But anticivilization emotions don't go away, and they demand periodic exercise. We have such "sick" jokes as, "What's the difference between a truckload of bowling balls and a truckload of dead babies?" (You can't unload a truckload of bowling balls with a pitchfork . . . a joke, by the way, that I heard originally from a ten-year-old.) Such a joke may surprise a laugh or a grin out of us even as we recoil, a possibility that confirms the thesis: If we share a brotherhood of man, then we also share an insanity of man. None of which is intended as a defense of either the sick joke or insanity but merely as an explanation of why the best horror films, like the best fairy tales, manage to be reactionary, anarchistic, and revolutionary all at the same time.

The mythic horror movie, like the sick joke, has a dirty job to do. It deliberately appeals to all that is worst in us. It is morbidity unchained, our most base instincts let free, our nastiest fantasies realized . . . and it all happens, fittingly enough, in the dark. For those reasons, good liberals often shy away from horror films. For myself, I like to see the most aggressive of them—*Dawn of the Dead,* for instance—as lifting a trap door in the civilized forebrain and throwing a basket of raw meat to the hungry alligators swimming around in that subterranean river beneath.

Why bother? Because it keeps them from getting out, man. It keeps them down there and me up here. It was Lennon and McCartney who said that all you need is love, and I would agree with that.

As long as you keep the gators fed.

Source: King, Stephen. "Why We Crave Horror Movies." Copyright © 1982 by Stephen King. Originally appeared in *Playboy*, 1982. Reprinted With Permissions. all rights reserved.

Vocabulary Before, during, and after reading the selection, annotate the text and write in your journal. Create a list of vocabulary words, along with their definitions. Give examples of their use from the selection you just read.

After Reading Discussion Questions: Meaning, Structure, and Expression

1. **Main Idea:** Work as a group to write a summary that answers the following questions: What purpose did Stephen King have for writing this essay? Who is his intended audience? What is the essay's main idea?
2. **Relevant Details:** In paragraphs 10 and 11, King uses children as examples to support his point. Why do you think he uses these examples? Do you think these examples are typical of most children? Do you agree that these examples effectively support his point? Why or why not?
3. **Logical Order:** King declares his thesis in paragraph 11. Locate his thesis statement. Why do you think King waited until this late in the essay to state his thesis? Reread his introduction. What is his opening point? Why do you think he opened his essay with this idea? How would the impact of the essay change if King had stated his thesis in the opening paragraph?
4. **Effective Expression:** To make his point, King appeals to our senses and prior experiences with references to roller coasters, Jack the Ripper, lynching, and alligators. Discuss how each of these images supports his point.

Thinking Prompts to Move from Reading to Writing

1. King offers reasons that explain the positive effects of horror movies. However, many disagree with this view and see the violence in horror movies as a negative factor in our society. Write an essay that explains the negative impact of horror movies.
2. King claims that we are "all mentally ill" and that horror movies appeal to the "worst in us." However, many believe that humans are basically good. The famous American essayist Emerson once encouraged us "to look into yourselves and do good because you are good." Write an essay that illustrates the goodness and positive impact of human nature. Consider, for example, the reasons and effects of Habitat for Humanity or other charities or volunteer organizations.

Persuasion

Nobel Lecture—The Nobel Peace Prize 2014

MALALA YOUSAFZAI

Malala Yousafzai, born on July 12, 1997, in Mingora, Pakistan, became an activist, speaking out for girls' education at a very young age. Named one of *Time* magazine's most influential people in 2013, she won the Nobel Peace Prize in 2014. Yousafzai is the youngest person to receive the Nobel Peace Prize. To learn more about Yousafzai, read the student narrative about her life and work on pages 87–88.

Before Reading Write a journal entry about the importance of education. Why do you think the Taliban banned education for girls? What would you do if you were told you had no right to attend school?

Bismillah hir rahman ir rahim. In the name of God, the most merciful, the most beneficent.

Your Majesties, Your royal highnesses, distinguished members of the Norwegian Nobel Committee,

Dear sisters and brothers, today is a day of great happiness for me. I am humbled that the Nobel Committee has selected me for this precious award.

Thank you to everyone for your continued support and love. Thank you for the letters and cards that I still receive from all around the world. Your kind and encouraging words strengthens and inspires me.

I would like to thank my parents for their unconditional love. Thank you to my father for not clipping my wings and for letting me fly. Thank you to my mother for inspiring me to be patient and to always speak the truth—which we strongly believe is the true message of Islam. And also thank you to all my wonderful teachers, who inspired me to believe in myself and be brave.

I am proud, well in fact, I am very proud to be the first Pashtun, the first Pakistani, and the youngest person to receive this award. Along with that, along with that, I am pretty certain that I am also the first recipient of the Nobel Peace Prize who still fights with her younger brothers. I want there to be peace everywhere, but my brothers and I are still working on that.

I am also honored to receive this award together with Kailash Satyarthi, who has been a champion for children's rights for a long time. Twice as long, in fact, than I have been alive. I am proud that we can work together, we can work together and show the world that an Indian and a Pakistani, they can work together and achieve their goals of children's rights.

Dear brothers and sisters, I was named after the inspirational Malalai of Maiwand who is the Pashtun Joan of Arc. The word Malala means "grief stricken," "sad," but in order to lend some happiness to it, my grandfather would always call me "Malala—The happiest girl in the world" and today I am very happy that we are together fighting for an important cause.

This award is not just for me. It is for those forgotten children who want education. It is for those frightened children who want peace. It is for those voiceless children who want change.

I am here to stand up for their rights, to raise their voice . . . it is not time to pity them. It is not time to pity them. It is time to take action so it becomes the last time, the last time, so it becomes the last time that we see a child deprived of education.

I have found that people describe me in many different ways.

Some people call me the girl who was shot by the Taliban.

And some, the girl who fought for her rights.

Some people, call me a "Nobel Laureate" now.

However, my brothers still call me that annoying bossy sister. As far as I know, I am just a committed and even stubborn person who wants to see every child getting quality education, who wants to see women having equal rights and who wants peace in every corner of the world.

Education is one of the blessings of life—and one of its necessities. That has been my experience during the 17 years of my life. In my paradise home, Swat, I always loved learning and discovering new things. I remember when my friends and I would decorate our hands with henna on special occasions. And instead of drawing flowers and patterns we would paint our hands with mathematical formulas and equations.

We had a thirst for education, we had a thirst for education because our future was right there in that classroom. We would sit and learn and read together. We loved to wear neat and tidy school uniforms and we would sit there with big dreams in our eyes. We wanted to make our parents proud and prove that we could also excel in our studies and achieve those goals, which some people think only boys can.

But things did not remain the same. When I was in Swat, which was a place of tourism and beauty, suddenly changed into a place of terrorism. I was just ten when more than 400 schools were destroyed. Women were flogged. People were killed. And our beautiful dreams turned into nightmares.

Education went from being a right to being a crime. Girls were stopped from going to school.

When my world suddenly changed, my priorities changed too.

I had two options. One was to remain silent and wait to be killed. And the second was to speak up and then be killed.

I chose the second one. I decided to speak up.

We could not just stand by and see those injustices of the terrorists denying our rights, ruthlessly killing people and misusing the name of Islam. We decided to raise our voice and tell them: Have you not learnt, have you not learnt that in the Holy Quran Allah says: if you kill one person it is as if you kill the whole humanity?

Do you not know that Mohammad, peace be upon him, the prophet of mercy, he says, "do not harm yourself or others."

And do you not know that the very first word of the Holy Quran is the word "Iqra," which means "read"?

The terrorists tried to stop us and attacked me and my friends who are here today, on our school bus in 2012, but neither their ideas nor their bullets could win.

We survived. And since that day, our voices have grown louder and louder. I tell my story, not because it is unique, but because it is not.

It is the story of many girls.

Today, I tell their stories too. I have brought with me some of my sisters from Pakistan, from Nigeria and from Syria, who share this story. My brave sisters Shazia and Kainat, who were also shot that day on our school bus. But they have not stopped learning. And my brave sister Kainat Soomro who went through severe abuse and extreme violence, even her brother was killed, but she did not succumb.

Also my sisters here, whom I have met during my Malala Fund campaign. My 16-year-old courageous sister, Mezon from Syria, who now lives in Jordan as refugee and goes from tent to tent encouraging girls and boys to learn. And my sister Amina, from the North of Nigeria, where Boko Haram threatens, and stops girls and even kidnaps girls, just for wanting to go to school.

Though I appear as one girl, though I appear as one girl, one person, who is 5 foot 2 inches tall, if you include my high heels. (It means I am 5 foot only) I am not a lone voice, I am not a lone voice, I am many.

I am Malala. But I am also Shazia.

I am Kainat.

I am Kainat Soomro.

I am Mezon.

I am Amina. I am those 66 million girls who are deprived of education. And today I am not raising my voice, it is the voice of those 66 million girls.

Sometimes people like to ask me why should girls go to school, why is it important for them. But I think the more important question is why shouldn't they, why shouldn't they have this right to go to school.

Dear sisters and brothers, today, in half of the world, we see rapid progress and development. However, there are many countries where millions still suffer from the very old problems of war, poverty, and injustice.

We still see conflicts in which innocent people lose their lives and children become orphans. We see many people becoming refugees in Syria, Gaza and Iraq. In Afghanistan, we see families being killed in suicide attacks and bomb blasts.

Many children in Africa do not have access to education because of poverty. And as I said, we still see, we still see girls who have no freedom to go to school in the north of Nigeria.

Many children in countries like Pakistan and India, as Kailash Satyarthi mentioned, many children, especially in India and Pakistan are deprived of their right to education because of social taboos, or they have been forced into child marriage or into child labour.

One of my very good school friends, the same age as me, who had always been a bold and confident girl, dreamed of becoming a doctor. But her dream remained a dream. At the age of 12, she was forced to get married. And then soon she had a son, she had a child when she herself was still a child—only 14. I know that she could have been a very good doctor.

But she couldn't . . . because she was a girl.

Her story is why I dedicate the Nobel Peace Prize money to the Malala Fund, to help give girls quality education, everywhere, anywhere in the world and to raise their voices. The first place this funding will go to is where my heart is, to build schools in Pakistan—especially in my home of Swat and Shangla.

In my own village, there is still no secondary school for girls. And it is my wish and my commitment, and now my challenge to build one so that my friends and my sisters can go there to school and get quality education and to get this opportunity to fulfill their dreams.

This is where I will begin, but it is not where I will stop. I will continue this fight until I see every child, every child in school.

Dear brothers and sisters, great people, who brought change, like Martin Luther King and Nelson Mandela, Mother Teresa and Aung San Suu Kyi, once stood here on this stage. I hope the steps that Kailash Satyarthi and I have taken so far and will take on this journey will also bring change—lasting change.

My great hope is that this will be the last time, this will be the last time we must fight for education. Let's solve this once and for all.

We have already taken many steps. Now it is time to take a leap.

It is not time to tell the world leaders to realize how important education is—they already know it—their own children are in good schools. Now it is time to call them to take action for the rest of the world's children.

We ask the world leaders to unite and make education their top priority.

Fifteen years ago, the world leaders decided on a set of global goals, the Millennium Development Goals. In the years that have followed, we have seen some progress. The number of children out of school has been halved, as Kailash Satyarthi said. However, the world focused only on primary education, and progress did not reach everyone.

In year 2015, representatives from all around the world will meet in the United Nations to set the next set of goals, the Sustainable Development Goals. This will set the world's ambition for the next generations.

The world can no longer accept, the world can no longer accept that basic education is enough. Why do leaders accept that for children in developing countries, only basic literacy is sufficient, when their own children do homework in Algebra, Mathematics, Science and Physics?

Leaders must seize this opportunity to guarantee a free, quality, primary and secondary education for every child.

Some will say this is impractical, or too expensive, or too hard. Or maybe even impossible. But it is time the world thinks bigger.

Dear sisters and brothers, the so-called world of adults may understand it, but we children don't. Why is it that countries which we call "strong" are so powerful in creating wars but are so weak in bringing peace?

Why is it that giving guns is so easy but giving books is so hard? Why is it, why is it that making tanks is so easy, but building schools is so hard?

We are living in the modern age and we believe that nothing is impossible. We have reached the moon 45 years ago and maybe will soon land on Mars. Then, in this 21st century, we must be able to give every child quality education.

Dear sisters and brothers, dear fellow children, we must work… not wait. Not just the politicians and the world leaders, we all need to contribute. Me. You. We. It is our duty.

Let us become the first generation to decide to be the last, let us become the first generation that decides to be the last that sees empty classrooms, lost childhoods, and wasted potentials.

Let this be the last time that a girl or a boy spends their childhood in a factory.

Let this be the last time that a girl is forced into early child marriage.

Let this be the last time that a child loses life in war.

Let this be the last time that we see a child out of school.

Let this end with us.

Let's begin this ending … together … today … right here, right now. Let's begin this ending now. Thank you so much.

Source: Nobel Lecture by Malala Yousafzai, Oslo, 10 December 2014, © The Nobel Foundation, Stockholm, 2014.

Vocabulary Before, during, and after reading the selection, annotate the text and write in your journal. Create a list of vocabulary words, along with their definitions. Give examples of their use from the selection you just read.

After Reading Discussion Questions: Meaning, Structure, and Expression

1. **Main Idea:** Work as a group to write a summary that answers the following questions: What purpose did Malala Yousafzai have for writing this piece? Who is the intended audience? What is the main idea of the speech?
2. **Relevant Details:** What detail does Yousafzai use to open her speech? How does this detail relate to her central point? Why does she use this detail as her introduction?
3. **Logical Order:** To make her argument for global support of education for women, Yousafzai organized her ideas to move from her personal story to the stories of other girls unjustly treated in her community, in her nation, and in surrounding countries. Then, she concludes with an appeal for global response and responsibility. Create an outline that shows this movement from the personal to the global. Why did she begin with her personal experience and conclude with the global appeal? Why didn't she begin by describing the scope of the problem and then end with her powerful personal experience?
4. **Effective Expression:** Throughout her speech, Yousafzai repeats certain patterns of speech. For example, in paragraph 17, she repeats the phrase "We had a thirst for education." Another example occurs in paragraph 48 with the repetition of "this will be the last time." Many other instances occur throughout her speech. Find at least three more examples of repeating patterns of speech. Describe the effect of these repetitions. Which use of repetition seems most powerful? Why?

Thinking Prompts to Move from Reading to Writing

1. Assume you are taking a college course in sociology. A key assignment is to identify a person who has made an impact on society and to analyze the significance of that impact. You have chosen to write about Malala Yousafzai. You are expected to provide a written and oral response that includes the following information: a brief biography of the person, the person's notable achievements, and the scope and significance of his or her impact on society.
2. Experts and research support Yousafzai's assertion about the importance of education. Why is formal education so important? Assume you are a volunteer peer mentor for a group of youth who are at risk of dropping out of high school. Write an essay to share with this group about the importance of education. Your purpose is to persuade group members to stay in school and excel in their studies.

Argument

Hungry vs. Healthy: The School Lunch Controversy

BONNIE TAUB-DIX

Bonnie Taub-Dix has been the Director and Owner of BTD Nutrition Consultants for more than thirty years. She is an advisor to major corporations, food companies, and fitness clubs. She has also served as a Media Spokesperson to the New York State Dietetic Association and as Spokesperson for the Academy of Nutrition and Dietetics. Taub-Dix is a prolific writer on issues related to nutrition for both popular and professional publications providing practical advice on healthy living.

Before Reading Write a journal entry about what a school lunch should offer students. How important is this issue to you? Is it more important for lunches to be nutritious or tasty? How can home life affect whether children will eat healthy options provided at school?

1. Last week, I was invited to be a guest on ABC's *20/20* to comment on a YouTube video depicting high schoolers expressing their dissatisfaction with the newest school lunch regulations. While it captured the attention of hundreds of thousands of viewers, the fact remains that although some students complain of going "hungry," boxes of food get tossed every day from school cafeterias across the country. Is it really that these kids are hungry or are they not used to foods that are healthy?

2. **The background:** The new regulations released in August, which were championed by First Lady Michelle Obama as part of her "Let's Move" campaign to fight childhood obesity, trimmed down the carbs and gave them a little color by emphasizing whole grains instead of white flour. Fruits and veggies were placed in a leading role supported by a cast of protein foods like chicken, lean meat, cheese, and so on. The calories of school lunch meals have not changed appreciably, with previous guidelines for children in grades 7 through 12 weighing in at 825 calories and the newest regs ranging from 750 to 850 calories for the same age group. What has changed significantly, however, is what's being served.

3. As hard as it might be to believe, one in three American children is overweight or obese and at risk for diabetes, meaning that so many children are overfed, yet undernourished. Previous school meal standards were developed 15 years ago and didn't meet nutritional guidelines recently established by independent health and nutrition experts. Under the watch of the Institute of Medicine and passed in December, 2010, by a bi-partisan majority in Congress, the Healthy, Hunger-Free Kids Act, was enacted to provide nutritious meals to all children across America.

4. **The Gripe:** Not everyone is happy about these healthy school-lunch makeovers, as evidenced by the YouTube video. Some hungry students and teachers are claiming that they aren't being served the calories they need—and that to compensate, they're resorting to junk food to fill up. (Ironically, that's a recipe for hunger: Unlike nutritious food, junk is only temporarily satisfying.) Adding more calories doesn't mean adding more nutritional value. For some, overeating could lead to feeling listless and weak.

5. There are, however, kids who need more food than is being served, particularly those who participate in sports and after-school programs. For these kids, schools can structure after-school snack and supper programs. Individual students and/or sports teams can also supplement with healthy snacks brought from home. Schools also have the option to give students who need additional calories seconds of

low-fat milk, fruit, and vegetables, but those are not the foods kids are requesting. Instead, they are seeking the preferred choices served in the past, which may have less to do with calories than familiarity.

The Problem: When you really weigh the difference between the calories of the old school lunch tray and the new, the bigger problem may be about giving kids the food they like, even though some of those foods, especially those that are fried and laden with unhealthy ingredients, may not like them back. Herein lies the disconnect: Our children need help in getting to a healthier place, and although science has paved the way, that doesn't mean it's easy to make sense of the science—especially when it comes to serving kids the foods they not only need, but they actually like.

And perhaps the problem goes way beyond school walls. Although the cafeteria can be a classroom through the introduction of healthier options, parents need to step up to the plate at home, too. The most important part a parent can play is that of role model. Setting up a salad bar at home and adding veggies to pizza are just some of the ways parents can bring home a healthier message.

The compromise: School lunch provides approximately one-third of the calories an average child needs for the day, but children who are active and fast-growing may require more than others. Although kids should have an adequate number of calories to support health and growth, it's important to focus on the right types of calories, not just the number of calories required. In other words, we need to look at quality and quantity. It's also unrealistic and perhaps unhealthy for kids to attempt to meet the demands of their school day, both physically and intellectually, all in one meal. Eating a balanced breakfast and including energizing snacks is key in maintaining energy levels.

Parents may need to send the right snacks with their children instead of sugary treats, which could zap their energy instead of providing it. The best snacks are composed of a combo of carbohydrate (preferably whole-grain varieties) and protein and/or fat, like cheese and whole-grain crackers, or almond butter and whole-grain bread. Even some of the energy bars on the market plus a beverage could be a great snack, but here, you have to read labels carefully to be sure that you're getting a product that's well-balanced and not full of sugar.

This is a perfect time for the government, schools, parents, and communities to join together to help healthy and tasty coexist on a child's plate. For more information on how you can help make this happen, visit www.letsmove.gov to see how family, food, and fitness come together to us raise happier and healthier children.

Source: "Hungry Vs. Healthy: The School Lunch Controversy," Bonnie Taub-Dix, *U.S. News and World Report*, October 5, 2012.

Vocabulary
Before, during, and after reading the selection, annotate the text and write in your journal. Create a list of vocabulary words, along with their definitions. Give examples of their use from the selection you just read.

After Reading Discussion Questions: Meaning, Structure, and Expression

1. **Central Idea:** Work as a group to write a summary that answers the following questions: What purpose did Bonnie Taub-Dix have for writing this essay? Who is her intended audience? What is the central point of the essay? What is the significance of the title?
2. **Relevant Details:** A strong argument refutes opposing points. Identify and explain one or more opposing points that the author refutes to persuade her audience to agree with her point. Are there other opposing points she should have addressed? If so, what are those points?
3. **Logical Order:** The author organizes her essay into four groups of information. Do you think this is an effective way to deliver this information? Why or why not?
4. **Effective Expression:** The author uses headings such as "the gripe," "the problem," and "the compromise" to describe the information she is delivering. Do these headings alter how the reader may feel about the information? Why or why not? Is this an effective way to argue a point? Why or why not?

Thinking Prompts to Move from Reading to Writing

1. Assume you read the article by Bonnie Taub-Dix in a college course in health. You are required to take a stand on one side of the issue she presents. Write an essay in which you agree or disagree with the author's point. Do you think offering a healthy lunch means children will eat healthier, or will the healthier options get thrown in the trash?
2. Assume you are the parent of children in the public school system. You are concerned about the healthfulness of the food offered to students in the cafeteria and in vending machines. Write a letter to members of your state government asking for legislation that requires healthy food to be served on campuses across the state. Explain what types of food you think should be available and why.

Argument

Can Virtual Classrooms Beat Face-to-Face Interaction?

LIBBY PAGE

Libby Page works as a content co-ordinator at Guardian Students, where she writes, commissions, and sub-edits content aimed at students. Previously, Page served as Campaigns and Policy Co-Ordinator at Intern Aware, an organization dedicated to the cause of fair internships. In this position, she campaigned for fairer, paid internships. She remains a trustee of the organization. Page has a degree in fashion journalism and previous experience at *Vogue, Cosmo*, the *Independent, Woman and Home*, and the *Evening Standard*.

Before Reading Would you prefer to take a course online or to attend a face-to-face class on campus? Explain your reasons.

1. For most students, university is a time for making friends, discovering a new city and making the most of the facilities on campus. But when you are studying online, your living room is your lecture hall and an online chat room is the equivalent of the student bar.

2. Can a computer screen make up for human interaction, and how can distance learning students avoid isolation?

3. If you are choosing to study online, chances are you have other commitments—work, children or other caring responsibilities—and you may be studying for purely academic reasons. The benefits of flexible study can outweigh the downside of not meeting people in real life.

4. But being part of an online community when studying at a distance is important, says Richard Reece, associate vice-president for teaching, learning and students at the University of Manchester.

5. He says: "Academically, support from other learners is as important on campus as it is off campus. We encourage students who are on campus to form peer-assisted study schemes. We do the same for distance learning students as well."

6. Online forums, Facebook groups and email lists with the contact details for other students can help online learners connect with their peers and ask questions about their studies.

7. Reece says: "It really benefits the learners if they have a sense of community rather than feeling like an isolated person tapping away at a computer."

Instead of tutorials or lectures, support from lecturers comes through online forums, email exchanges, phone conversations and Skype.

Tony Priest is course director for the foundation degree in drug and alcohol counseling at the University of Leicester and says his course uses "e-tutors" to support students.

He says: "Each e-tutor has a certain number of students who they follow through their comments on the discussion boards and answer their questions. They'll also contact them if they don't appear for a while and ask if they have problems and how they can help."

It might seem a little impersonal not meeting your tutor in real life, but distance learning students can sometimes have even more support than campus students, says Reece.

He says: "I would say that there are some things that you do need face-to-face interaction for, but our distance learning students do have significant access to teaching staff. In a number of cases they get even greater amounts of contact than students who are on campus and come in for a few scheduled lectures but not much more."

Amy Woodgate, project coordinator of distance education initiative and Moocs at the University of Edinburgh, agrees.

She says: "People tend to think that online learning is very detached and less of a community. It has a remote aspect so people think it is remote. But actually with online earning, students have something in common so build up good relationships."

Distance learning students can use online forums as a chance to meet their peers socially, but it can be difficult to replicate real life interactions.

"One of the biggest challenges for distance learning students is engagement with other peers," says Steve Mills, student president for education welfare at Robert Gordon University, Aberdeen.

He says: "A big part of the student experience is meeting new people, making friends, joining societies and having social events, but distance learning students don't get to experience that, so it is very academic for them."

Some distance learning courses do include an element of time on campus, and making the most of these moments to meet other students is important.

Forums and social networks are there to help connect students with their peers, but it is important to know that as a distance learning student you still have access to university support too.

"The principal that we try to work on is that the support should be the same for distance learning students as it is for campus students," says Reece. "Most of our students are studying abroad though, so obviously they can't just walk into our office and ask for help. But our services are available online and on the phone too."

Students' unions work on behalf of distance learning students too, and getting involved with your union could really help improve your life as an online student.

Mills says: "Our student helpline is there for online students, and we also deal with problems from distance learning students via Facebook and Twitter. And importantly, distance learning students have access to student counselors via Skype."

You might not be able to walk into a counselor's office as an online student, but the support is still there, and making the most of it can make all the difference to your experience of online learning.

Top tips for distance learning students:
- Make the most of online forums and social networks to meet other students and ask for help.
- Set yourself deadlines to help keep yourself motivated.
- Become a student rep. Student reps work on behalf of their peers and most universities have distance learning representatives. Being a rep is a great way to engage with your peers and see changes made to any issues you may have with your course.
- Even if you are short on time and not necessarily looking to make lots of new friends, making connections on your course can be a good networking opportunity, particularly if you are studying a business course.

Source: Page, Libby. "Can Virtual Classrooms Beat Face-to-Face Interaction?" *The Guardian.* Wednesday 13 November 2013. Copyright Guardian New & Media Ltd 2015.

Vocabulary Before, during, and after reading the selection, annotate the text and write in your journal. Create a list of vocabulary words, along with their definitions. Give examples of their use from the selection you just read.

After Reading Discussion Questions: Meaning, Structure, and Expression

1. **Central Idea:** Work as a group to write a summary that answers the following questions: What purpose did Libby Page have for writing this essay? Who is her intended audience? What is the central point of the essay? What is the significance of the title?
2. **Relevant Details:** Do you agree with the assertion by Steve Mills in paragraph 16? Identify a detail that supports his assertion. Identify a detail that counters his assertion.
3. **Logical Order:** In which paragraph does the author assert her main claim in a thesis statement? How does the concluding paragraph tie into the introduction and thesis statement?
4. **Effective Expression:** Throughout most of the essay, Page consistently uses a specific viewpoint based on her choice of pronouns. In one part of the essay, she makes an abrupt shift in viewpoint. Analyze the effectiveness of her use of viewpoint by answering the following questions: What is the viewpoint she establishes early in the essay? Where does she shift from this viewpoint into a different one? What viewpoint does she shift to? Why do you think she made this shift? Was this shift in viewpoint effective? Why or why not?

Thinking Prompt to Move from Reading to Writing

1. Assume you are taking a college course in education. Your professor requires that you write an essay taking a stand on a debatable issue. You have chosen to take a stand about distance learning versus face-to-face learning. Which of the two learning environments do you think is most effective? Be sure to address key opposing views to your stand.
2. Assume your college employs E-tutors and student representatives in the Distance Learning Program. Currently there are openings for both positions. Write a letter of application to the dean or chairperson of the program for one of these positions. In your letter, give compelling reasons to support your assertion that you are sound candidate for the position.

Text Credits

524: Winston Churchill, Speech to the House of Commons, June 4, 1940.

525: Julius Caesar, Letter to the Roman Senate, 49 BCE.

525: Franklin D. Roosevelt, Inaugural Address, March 4, 1933.

525: Dorothy Parker, from Myers, James E. "A Treasury of Victorious Women's Humor." Lincoln-Herndon Press Dec., 1999, page 184.

534, Abraham Lincoln: Attributed to ABRAHAM LINCOLN—Alexander K. McClure, "Abe" Lincoln's Yarns and Stories, p. 184 (1904).

535: Based On: Luke 6:31, *The Holy Bible*, Translated for the Latin, The New Testament first published by the English College at Rheims, A.D. 1582 (New York: P.J. Kennedy and Sons, 1914).

535: Arabic proverb: Based On: Speech is silver, silence is golden, Thomas Carlyle, *Fraser's Magazine*, June 1834, listed in George Latimer Apperson, and Martin H. Manser, Dictionary of Proverbs, (London: Wadsworth Editions Limited, 1993 and 2006).

549: "I am the good shepherd" Based On: John 10:14-15, *The Holy Bible*, Translated for the Latin, The New Testament first published by the English College at Rheims, A.D. 1582 (New York: P.J. Kennedy and Sons, 1914).

549: "Curley was flopping…" John Steinbeck, *Of Mice and Men*, Covici Friede, 1937.

549: "Dying is a wild night…" Johnson, Ward. *The Letters of Emily Dickinson*. Harvard University Press, 1986. p. 436.

549: "A good conscience…" Benjamin Franklin, *Poor Richard's Almanack*, 1733.

549: "Conscience is…" Letter to His Brother Theo, July 1880, as quoted in *Dear Theo: the Autobiography of Vincent Van Gogh* (1995) edited by Irving Stone and Jean Stone, New American Library, 1995, p. 181.

549: "Oh my love…" *The Life and Works of Robert Burns*, As Originally Edited by James Currie, M.D. to which is prefixed, A *Review of the Life of Burns, and of Various Criticisms on His Cahracter and Writings*, By Alexander Peterkin, Vol. IV (New York: S. King, 1824), p. 224.

549: "Advertising is…" Fuller, Linda K. George Orwell Quote. *Dictionary of Quotations in Communications*. Greenwood. First Edition edition (November 20, 1997).

Photo Credits

vi, 2: Image Source Plus/Alamy; 3 top: Thomas M Perkins/Shutterstock; 3 top middle: Entrieri/Shutterstock; 3 middle bottom: Naphat Rojanarangsiman/Shutterstock; 3 bottom: Andresr/Shutterstock; 18: Eugenio Marongiu/Shutterstock; 19 top left: Wavebreakmedia/Shutterstock; 19 top right: Darryl Brooks/Shutterstock; 19 bottom left: Manuel Balce Ceneta//AP Images; 19 bottom right: Zoltan Zempleni/Shutterstock; 22 top left: Aber CPC/Alamy; 22 top right: Stockbyte/Getty Images; 22 bottom left: Betsie Van der Meer/Getty Images; 20 bottom right: John Lund/Marc Romanelli/Alamy; 24 top left: Bikeriderlondon/Shutterstock; 24 top right: Moodboard/Corbis; 24 bottom left: Cardinal/Corbis; 24 bottom right: Leighton Mark/Corbis; 26 top: Bikeriderlondon/Shutterstock; 26 middle: Moodboard/Corbis; 26 bottom left: Cardinal/Corbis; 26 bottom right: Leighton Mark/Corbis; 30 Beau Lark/Fancy/Corbis; 32: DJ Henry; 34: MaszaS/Shutterstock; 35: Whitebox Media/Alamy; 50–51: KPG Payless2/Shutterstock; 52 top: David Sacks/Getty Images; 52 top middle: Bob Krist/Corbis; 52 bottom middle: Blake Little/Getty Images; 52 bottom: Image Source/Corbis; 54: NASA; 57 left: CandyBox Images/Shutterstock; 57 middle: Stephen Coburn/Shutterstock; 57 right: Tsyhun/Shutterstock; vii, 68: Mikecphoto/Shutterstock; 69, 70, 71, 73: SeaWorld/Davis; 80: Joseph Sohm/Visions of America/Corbis; 86: Douglas Kirkland/Corbis; 87 top: AP Photo/B.K. Bangash; 87 middle: AP Photo/Sherin Zada; 87 bottom: AP Photo/Heiko Junge; 100: Rebecca Emery/Corbis; 101, 103 top, top middle, bottom middle, bottom: Russell Sadur/Dorling Kindersley, Ltd.; 105: Bonnie Watton/Shutterstock; 107 left: Ghislain/Marie David de Lossy/Getty Images; 107 middle left: Cardinal/Corbis; 107 middle: Greg Daniels/Shutterstock; 107 middle: PathDoc/Shutterstock; 107 middle right: Anna Lurye/Shutterstock; 107 right: Wavebreakmedia/Shutterstock; 108 top: Tatiana Popova/Shutterstock; 108 bottom: StevenRussellSmithPhotos/Shutterstock; 116: Severija/Shutterstock; 117 top and bottom: Pearson Education; 119 top and bottom: Pearson Education; 122: InspireStock Images Photograph/Corbis; 123 left: Picturenet/Alamy; 123 middle: George Shelley/Corbis; 123 bottom: Purestock/AGE Fotostock; 126: Radius Images/Alamy; 127: ElenaGaak/Shutterstock; 132: Maksim Shmeljov/Shutterstock; 133 left: John Atashian/Corbis; 133 middle: Jessica Rinaldi/Corbis; 133 right: Chad Batka/Corbis; 135 top: John Atashian/Corbis; 135 middle: Jessica Rinaldi/Corbis; 135 bottom: Chad Batka/Corbis; 139: Dave Starbuck/Geisler-Fotopress/picture-alliance/dpa/AP Images; 141: ChooseMyPlate.gov; 148 left: Lucy Claxton/Dorling Kindersley, Ltd.; 148 right: Klaus Hackenberg/Corbis; 149 top left: Imaginechina via AP Images; 149 top right: Imaginechina via AP Images; 149 middle left: Transtock/Corbis; 149 middle right: Alison Hancock/Shutterstock; 149 bottom left: Robert Llewellyn/Corbis; 149 bottom right: Ashley Cooper/Corbis; 151 top: Imaginechina via AP Images; 151 upper middle: Imaginechina via AP Images; 151 middle: Transtock/Corbis; 151 lower middle: Alison Hancock/Shutterstock; 151 bottom: Ashley Cooper/Corbis; 156 top: Andresr/Shutterstock; 156 bottom: KieferPix/Shutterstock; 162: Graffiti with a girl walking past; 163 top: Wong Sze Yuen/Shutterstock; 163 middle left: Monkey Business Images/Shutterstock; 163 right: Tom Wang/Shutterstock; 163 bottom: Ru Bai Le/Shutterstock; 169 left: Joe Fox Dublin/Alamy; 169 middle: David Acosta Allely/Shutterstock; 169 right: Kim Karpeles/Alamy; xvi, 170: Koichi Mitsui/AFLO/Nippon News/Corbis; 176: Brian A Jackson/Shutterstock; 177 top left: Blend Images/Shutterstock; 177 top right: Andresr/Shutterstock; 177 middle: Anetlanda/Shutterstock; 177 bottom left: Syda Productions/Shutterstock; 177 bottom right: Fer Gregory/Shutterstock; 179 top: Anetlanda/Shutterstock; 179 middle top: Blend Images/Shutterstock; 179 middle bottom: Andresr/Shutterstock; 179 bottom: Fer Gregory/Shutterstock; 182: Tim Shaffer/Corbis; 183 top: Shalunts/Shutterstock; 183 bottom: Auremar/Shutterstock; 190: Hill Street Studios/Blend/Corbis; 191 top: Alan Schein Photography/Encyclopedia/Corbis; 191 middle left: Benelux/Flirt/Corbis; 191 middle right: James Leynse/Documentary Value/Corbis; 191 lower left: Lisa B./Flirt/Corbis; 191 lower right: Fancy/Corbis; 191 bottom: Ariel Skelley/Corbis; 193 top: Alan Schein Photography/Encyclopedia/Corbis; 193 upper middle: Benelux/Flirt/Corbis; 193 middle: Lisa B./Flirt/Corbis; 193 lower middle: James Leynse/Documentary Value/Corbis; 193 bottom: Fancy/Corbis; 197: Tim Barber/Chattanooga Times Free Press/AP Image; 204: Phil Klein/Corbis; 205 top left: Jonathan Ross/Dreamstime LLC; 205 top right: Zurijeta Shutterstock; 205 bottom left: Jamie Kingham/cultura/Corbis; 205 bottom right: Peter jordan/Alamy; 208: Julie Eggers/Latitude/Corbis; 210: David Crockett/Shutterstock; 211 top: Stock Connection Distribution/Alamy; 211 bottom left: Tetra/Corbis; 211 bottom middle: David Leeson/Dallas Morning News/Sygma/Corbis; 211 bottom right: 2/James Woodson/Ocean/Corbis; 214: Jennie Yundt/Crossfitfire.com; 215 top: Lisa F. Young/Shutterstock; 215 middle top: Lisa F. Young/Shutterstock; 215 middle: Christopher Mampe/Shutterstock; 215 middle: Wavebreakmedia/Shutterstock; 215 lower middle: Mediscan/Encyclopedia/Corbis; 215 bottom: Radius/Corbis; 228: Jefferson Siegel/Pool/Corbis; 229 left: Robert Paul Van Beets/Shutterstock; 229 middle: Eric J Tilford/AP Images; 229 right: Steve Heap/Shutterstock; 238: Design Pics/Corbis; 239 left: WIN-Images/CanopyCorbis; 239 middle: Ocean/Corbis; 239 right: Jorg Hackemann/Shutterstock; 242: Nicholas de Haan/Shutterstock; 246: Markus Friedrich/imageBROKER/Alamy; 249: OLJ Studio/Shutterstock; 255: Xavier ROSSI/Gamma-Rapho via Getty Images; 258 top: CBS Photo Archive/Getty Images; 258 middle: Rune Hellestad/Entertainment/Corbis; 258 bottom: Goss Images/Alamy; 264: DJ Henry; ix, 265: DJ Henry; 269 top: Library of Congress; 269 bottom: Library of Congress (Photoduplication); 270: Carl Van Vechten/Library of Congress (Photoduplication); 270 bottom: Flip Schulke/Historical Premium/Corbis; 274: Alamy; 275: Morrison/Shutterstock; 280: Corbis Images; 286: Joshua Lott/Getty Images; x, 290: Wavebreakmedia/Shutterstock; 291 top: IVY PHOTOS/Shutterstock; 291 upper middle: Leah-Anne Thompson/Shutterstock; 291 lower middle: Monkey Business Images/Shutterstock; 291 bottom: JeffreyIsaacGreenberg/Alamy; xii, 322–323: David Kadlubowski/Corbis; 325: Medioimages/Photodisc/Getty Images; 337: Bettmann/Corbis; 346: Brian Babineau/NBAE/Getty Images; 349: Comstock Images/Getty Images; xi, 364: Age fotostock/SuperStock; 383: George Marks/Getty Images, Inc.; 388: Jordan Siemens/Aurora Photos (RM)/Corbis; 389: Chris Trotman/Corbis Images; 402: RAY STUBBLEBINE/Reuters/Corbis; 403: Photo smile/Shutterstock; 407: David Frazier/Spirit/Corbis; 415: Yellow Dog Productions/Getty Images; 420–421: Doug Armand/Getty Images; 423:145/B2M Productions/Corbis; 427: Gerhardt Sisters/Historical/Corbis; 433: Fulcanelli/Shutterstock; 438: Juice Images/Corbis; 439: Africa Studio/Shutterstock; 445: Sedlacek/Shutterstock; 448: Beau Lark/Corbis; 452: Mrivserg/Shutterstock; 454: Creativa Images/Shutterstock; 455: Africa Studio/Shutterstock; 458: JordiDelgado/Shutterstock; 459: Warren Goldswain/Shutterstock; 468: Monkey Business Images/Shutterstock; 469: Alexander Raths/Shutterstock; 476: Koichi Mitsui/AFLO/Nippon News/Corbis; 482: Sripfoto/Shutterstock; 487: Tim Boyle/Getty Images; 490: Bill Varie/Cardinal/Corbis; xv, 491: Monkey Business Images/Shutterstock; 494: Eric Audras/PhotoAlto/Corbis; 505: Timothy Hiatt/FilmMagic/Getty Images; 510: Dudarev Mikhail/Shutterstock; 511: Myrleen Pearson/PhotoEdit, Inc.; 514: Lon C. Diehl/PhotoEdit, Inc.; 516: 2/Image Source/Ocean/Corbis; 522: Matthew Ward/Dorling Kindersley, Ltd.; 524: Bettmann/Corbis; 525 top left: C. Julius Caesar, full-length statue, standing, facing left/Library of Congress Prints and Photographs Division [LC-USZ62-91768]; 525 top right: Franklin D. Roosevelt/Miscellaneous Items in High Demand/Library of Congress Prints and Photographs Division [LC-USZ62-90270]; 525 bottom: Dorothy Parker/Miscellaneous Items in High Demand/Library of Congress Prints and Photographs Division [LC-USZ62-11593]; 527: Museo Nacional de Antropologia/Bridgeman Art Library; xiii, 538: LDprod/Shutterstock; 547: Spirit of america/Alamy; 554: I love photo/Shutterstock; 555: Kongsky/Shutterstock; 564: Terry Eggers/Encyclopedia/Corbis; 565: Richard Cummins/Corbis; 572: WENN Ltd/Alamy; xiv, 582: Racheal Grazias/Shutterstock; 583: Kellie L. Folkerts/Shutterstock; 590: Arena Creative/Shutterstock; 598: Kristy-Anne Glubish/Design Pics/Corbis; 600: Paul Whitfield/Dorling Kindersley Limited; 610: 68/Ocean/Corbis; 611: Mast3r/Shutterstock; 615: Mikecphoto/Shutterstock; 615, 618: Rick Mackler/Globe Photos/ZUMA/Alamy; 615: Frank Capri/Hulton Archive/Getty Images; 615: GaudiLab/Shutterstock; 615, 629: Marka/Alamy; 615, 632: Kamira/Shutterstock; 615, 634: Kathy Hutchins/Newscom; 615, 636: D. J. Henry; 615, 643: Petr Malyshev/Shutterstock; 615, 647: Chip Somodevilla/Getty Images; 615, 647: Chip Somodevilla/Getty Images; 615, 650: DJTaylor/Shutterstock; 615, 653: Creatista/Shutterstock; 615, 655: Kim Kulish/Corbis; 615, 658: Slaven Vlasic/Getty Images; 615, 660: AP Images/Heiko Junge, NTB Scanpix; 615, 665: Tammy Ljungblad/Kansas City Star/MCT/Getty Images; 615, 667: STILLFX/Shutterstock.

Index

A

-*able* endings, 352
Absolute adjectives/adverbs, 356–359
Academic course
    cause and effect use in, 185
    classification use in, 142
    comparison and contrast use in, 157
    definition use in, 171
    description use in, 80
    illustration (example) use in, 127
    narration use in, 95
    persuasion use in, 199
    prewriting for, 36
    process use in, 109
Academic learning log
    adjectives and adverbs, 363
    apostrophes, 571
    capitalization, 597
    commas, 563
    effective expression, 553
    end punctuation, 589
    essay titles, introductions, and conclusions, 237
    essays, 226–227
    fragments, 457
    modifiers, misplaced and dangling, 467
    nouns and pronouns, 345
    paragraphs, 70
    parallelism, 537
    patterns of organization, 289
    quotation marks, 581
    research writing process, 321
    sentences
        clarity, 523
        compound and complex, 419
        run-on, 437
        variety, 509
    spelling, 609
    subjects
        and verb agreement, 489
        verbs and simple sentences, 401
    verbs, 386–387
    writing, preparing to learn about, 17
    writing process, 48–49
Action verbs, 393–394
Action/being subject, 391
Active learners, 5
Active voice, 380, 543–545
Addresses, commas in, 560
Adequate details, 62–63
Adjectives, 346–363
    absolute form, 356–359
    abstract, 546
    comparative form, 356–359
    concrete, 546
    coordinate and cumulative, commas with, 560–561
    cumulative, commas with, 561
    functions and purposes, 348–349
    nouns formed as, 351–352
    order, 353–354
    participles as, 350–351
    placement, 352–353
    proper, capitalization and, 595
    spelling guidelines, 359–360
    superlative form, 356–359
    verbs formed as, 351–352
Adverbs, 346–363
    absolute form, 356–359
    abstract, 546
    common forms, 355
    comparative form, 356–359
    concrete, 546
    conjunctive, independent clauses and, 406
    functions and purposes, 348–349
    sentence openings and, 504, 505
    spelling guidelines, 359–360
    superlative form, 356–359
    use and function, 355–356
affect/effect, difference between, 184
and, 405–406, 493, 557
Annotating text, in reading/writing strategy, 12, 13, 612–613
Antecedents, 329
    pronoun agreement and, 332–335
    pronoun reference and, 329–332
    subject-verb agreement with, 485
Anthology selection, MLA citation/documentation format for, 312
Anxiety, self-evaluation by writer, 30
Apostrophes, 564–571
    for contractions, 568
    correct vs. incorrect use, 566
    misuse of, recognizing, 568–569
    for ownership, 566–567
Appositive phrase
    combining sentences with, 500–502
    fragments, 444–445
Appositives, commas and, 559–560
Articles (*a, an, the*), and nouns, 328–329
Articles (published), MLA citation/documentation format for, 312–313, 315
as, 338–339, 426
Attitude of learning, 5
    self-evaluation, 7
Audience, 20, 24–27
    questioning and, 32
Audio recordings, MLA citation/documentation format for, 313
Authors, single and multiple, MLA citation/documentation format for, 310–312

B

Base words
    prefixes for, 606
    suffixes for, 602–603
be
    passive voice, 380–381
    past tense, 370–371
    present tense, subject-verb agreement and, 475–476
Behaviors of learning, 6
Bissinger, Buzz, "Football's Bloodiest Secret," 634–636
Body
    essay, 206, 209
    paragraph, 56
Bookmark, Internet, 297
Books, MLA citation/documentation format for, 310–312
Boolean operators, 296
Brainstorming, in reading/writing strategy, 12
Broad pronoun reference, 331
Brooke, Rupert, "Niagara Falls," 615–617
Bullets, 532
Business writing, 37
but, 405–406, 426, 493, 557

C

"Camping Out" (Hemingway), 629–631
can, 382–383
"Can Virtual Classrooms Beat Face-to-Face Interaction?" (Page), 667–668
Capital letter/Capitalization, 590–597
    correcting run-on sentences with, 424–425
Case
    comparisons, 338–339
    compound constructions, 339–342
    faulty use of, 337
        correcting, 338–342
    objective, 336–337
    possessive, 336–337
    pronouns, 336–342
    subjective, 336–337
Cause
    and effect, words signaling, 61, 178, 181, 273
    identifying, 180
Cause-effect essays
    pattern of organization in, 273–277
    reading selections, 655–660
Cause-effect paragraph, 176–189
Chronological order
    narrative paragraph, 88
    process paragraph, 102, 105
Citation of sources, MLA style, 307–316
Clarity, sentence, 510–523
Classification
    defined, 136
    words signaling, 61, 137, 258
Classification essays
    pattern of organization in, 258–262
    reading selections, 636–642
Classification paragraph, 132–147
Clauses
    fragments, 450–453
    nonparallel, 529–531
    parallel, 529–531
    relative. *See* Relative clauses
    series of, commas and, 556–557
    types of, 404–405. *See also* Dependent clauses; Independent clauses
Clichés, 549–551
Climactic order, 61
    essay development and, 214, 215
Closing quotation mark, 574
Clustering. *See* Concept map/mapping
Cofer, Judith Ortiz, "Don't Call Me a Hot Tamale," 632–633
Coherence techniques, 213–215
Collective nouns, 479–480

Colon, position with quotation marks, 574
Combined pattern of organization, 283–288
Comma splices, 421
   corrective actions for, 424–433
   identifying, 422–423
   proofreading for, and eliminating, 145–146
Commas, 554–563
   appositive phrase with, 500
   appositives, 559–560
   coordinate and cumulative adjectives, 560–561
   correcting run-on sentences with, 426–427
   in dates and addresses, 560
   independent clauses, 405–406, 557–558
   introductory elements and, 557
      proofreading for, 160–161
   nonessential clauses, 413, 558–559
   with nonessential information, proofreading for, 174–175
   for parallelism, 532
   parenthetical ideas, 558
   position with quotation marks, 574
   quotations, 561
   serial, 556
   in a series, 556–557
      proofreading for, 130–131
Common nouns, 324–326
   capitalization, 594
Comparative adjectives/adverbs, 356–359
   spelling guidelines, 359–360
Comparison
   defined, 152
   pronoun case and, 338–339
   words signaling, 61, 153, 263
Comparison-contrast essays
   pattern of development in, 263–267
   reading selections, 643–649
Comparison-contrast paragraph, 148–161
Complete thoughts, independent clause and, 450
   subjects and verbs identifying, 397–399
Complex sentences, 64, 140–141, 402, 403
   combining ideas with, 503
   composing, 409–414
   compound-complex, 64, 140–141, 403, 414–416
   subordination and, 156
Compound constructions, pronoun case and, 337
   correcting faulty use, 339–342
Compound sentences, 64, 140–141, 402, 403
   combining ideas with, 503
   composing, 405–409
   compound-complex, 64, 140–141, 403, 414–416
   coordination and, 156
Compound subjects, 391
   combining simple sentences with, 494–495

Compound verbs, combining sentences with, 495–496
Compound-complex sentences, 64, 140–141, 403
   composing, 414–416
Concept charts
   comparison/contrast, 159
   definition, 168, 171, 173
   description, 77, 82
Concept map/mapping
   cause and effect, 182
   classification paragraph, 138
   as prewriting technique, 38–39
Conciseness, 540–542
Conclusions
   essay, 206, 208, 209, 229, 230, 235–237
   paragraph, 56
Concrete language, 545–548
"Confessions" (Tan), 623–624
Conjunctions
   coordinating, 405–406
   subordinating, 409–411, 412, 414
Conjunctive adverbs
   correcting run-on sentences with, 430–431
   independent clauses and, 406
Connecting paragraphs, 216–217
Consonants
   final, 604
   patterns, 602
Contractions, 568
Contrast
   in comparison-contrast essays. See Comparison-contrast essays
   in comparison-contrast paragraph, 148–161
   defined, 152
   words signaling, 61, 153, 263
"Cool at 13, Adrift at 23" (Hoffman), 653–654
Coordinate adjectives, commas with, 560–561
Coordinating conjunctions, 405–406
   correcting run-on sentences with, 426–427
   for parallelism, 532
Coordination, of ideas, 156, 493, 503
could, 382–383
Count noun, 327–328
Creative expression, 548–549
Critical thinking, 14
   questions, 14, 16
Cumulative adjectives, commas with, 560–561

D

Dangling modifiers
   correcting, 462–465
   proofreading for, 83–84
Database, electronic, 294–295
Dates, commas in, 560
Declarative sentence/statement, 492
   period and, 584
Definite article, 328
Definition, 166
   words signaling, 167, 268

Definition essays
   pattern of organization in, 268–272
   reading selections, 650–652
Definition paragraph, 162–175
Dependent clauses, 404–405, 409–411, 432, 450–451
   essential, 412, 413
   fragments, 450–451
   introductory, commas and, 557
   nonessential, 412, 413
   placement and punctuation, 412–414
Description
   creating vivid images, 69
   words signaling, 61, 76, 240
Descriptive essays
   pattern of organization in, 240–244
   reading selections, 615–620
Descriptive paragraph, 68–85
"Design Submission to the Vietnam Memorial Competition" (Lin), 618–619
Details
   in essays, 206, 208
   evaluating, 219, 223
   major and minor
      in essays, 206, 208, 209
      in paragraphs, 51
   in paragraphs
      adequate, 62–63
      relevant, 62–63
   writing plan generating, 218, 222
Dialogue, formatting and punctuating, 576–577
Dictionaries, 600–601
Direct quotes, 578
   punctuating, 575–576
   quotation marks for, 574
Distant pronoun reference, 331
do
   past tense, 370–371
   present tense, subject-verb agreement and, 473–475
Documentation of sources, MLA style, 307–316
Donatelle, Rebecca J., "Managing Stress in College," 625–628
"Don't Call Me a Hot Tamale" (Cofer), 632–633
Drafting, 28, 42–43
   essays, 224
   main idea statements, 42, 43
   paragraphs
      cause-effect paragraph, 187
      classification paragraph, 144
      comparison-contrast paragraph, 159
      definition paragraph, 173
      descriptive paragraph, 82
      illustration (example) paragraph, 129
      narrative paragraph, 97
      persuasive paragraph, 201
      process paragraph, 112
   in reading/writing strategy, 13

E

-e endings, 605
-ed endings, 350
Editing, by peers. See Peer editing

Effect, identifying, 180
effect/affect, difference between, 184
Effective expression
    elements, 63–64
    essay development and, 220
    in paragraph
        cause-effect paragraph, 178, 184
        classification paragraph, 134, 140–141
        compare-contrast paragraph, 150, 156
        definition paragraph, 164
        descriptive paragraph, 72, 78–79
        illustration (example) paragraph, 118, 126–127
        narrative paragraph, 88, 94
        persuasive paragraph, 192, 198
        process paragraph, 102, 108
    revising for, 538–555
    vs. ineffective expression, 63
ei vs. *ie* spelling, 606–607
either-or/neither-nor, 480–481
Electronic database, library, 294–295
End punctuation, 582–589
English as a second language (ESL)
    apostrophes, 567
    articles and nouns, 328
    capitalization, 592
    commas with dates, 560
    dependent clauses, 432
    fragment vs. sentence, 441
    parallel expressions, 526
    prepositions, 398
    pronoun agreement, 330, 334
    pronoun reference, 330
    subject-verb agreement in questions, 485
    verb tenses, 378
    word order, 397
-es endings, plural nouns, 603
Essays, 204–227
    cause and effect, 273–277
    classification, 258–262
    with combined patterns of organization, 283–288
    comparison and contrast, 263–267
    definition, 268–272
    descriptive, 240–244
    developmental steps, 221–227
    illustration (example), 253–257
    information levels in, 208–210
    narrative, 244–248
    parts of, 206–207
    persuasive, 278–282
    process, 248–252
    purpose for writing, 22
    research, sample in MLA style, 317–319
Essential appositive, commas and, 559
Essential clauses, commas and, 559
Example
    defined, 120
    words signaling and listing, 61, 122, 253
Example (illustration) essays
    pattern of organization in, 253–257
    reading selections, 632–636
Example paragraph, 116–131

Exchange of information, in reading-writing cycle, 8
Exclamation points, 586
Exclamatory sentence/statement, 492
    exclamation point and, 586
Exemplification, defined, 120. *See also* Example *entries*
Expression
    creative, 548–549
    effective. *See* Effective expression
    fractional, 482, 483
    grammar and, 64
    sentence structure and, 64
    word choice and, 63
Expressive writing, 22

F

Fact, identifying, 293
FANBOYS (acronym), 405–406, 426, 493, 557
Feedback
    accepting, 5
    labeling work submitted for, 15
FIL process, 398–399
First person
    pronoun agreement and, 332, 341–342
    proofreading and, 202
    singular and plural forms, 512, 515
    traits, 512
First words, capitalizing first letter of
    greetings and salutations, 592
    sentence, 592
Focused freewriting, 34, 35
"Football's Bloodiest Secret" (Bissinger), 634–636
for, 405–406, 426, 493, 557
Fractional expression, subject-verb agreement with, 482, 483
Fragments, 438–457
    clause, 450–453
    phrase, 442–449
    recognizing, 440–441
    simple sentences vs., distinguishing between, 395
    types of, 442–453
Freewriting, 34–35
    in reading/writing strategy, 12, 13
Fresh language, 549–551
-ful endings, 352
"The Fundamentals of Forgiveness" (Henry), 637–639
Fused sentence, 421
    correcting, 113
    corrective actions for, 424–433
    identifying, 422–423
    proofreading for, 112–114
Future tense
    consistent use, 517
    simple, 366–367

G

Gender, pronoun agreement and, 332, 334–335
Gerund, 447
Gerund phrase fragments, 447–448
Gerund subject, 390

Glossary, text messaging, 591
Goals, for learning to write
    portfolio and, 14
    purpose and, 20
    self-evaluation, 7
    setting, 6
good, 360, 361
Goodwin-Parker, Jo, "What is Poverty?," 650–652
Grammar, effective expression and, 64
Greetings, capitalizing first letter of first word in, 592
Groups, words and transitions signaling, 137
Guitron, Melissa, "I Am Enough," 641–642

H

had, part perfect tense, 378
has, present perfect tense, 376
have
    past tense, 370–371
    present perfect tense, 376
    present tense, subject-verb agreement and, 472–473
Helping verbs, 394–395
    commonly confused forms, 382–383
Hemingway, Ernest, "Camping Out," 629–631
Henry, D. J., "The Fundamentals of Forgiveness," 637–639
here, subject-verb agreement with, 483
Hoffman, Jan, "Cool at 13, Adrift at 23," 653–654
"Hungry vs. Healthy: The School Lunch Controversy" (Taub-Dix), 665–666

I

I, capitalizing, 592
"I Am Enough" (Guitron), 641–642
-ible endings, 352
-ic endings, 352
Ideas
    coordination, 156, 493, 503
    main. *See* Main idea
    signal words qualifying, 195
    subordination, 156, 493, 503. *See also* Dependent clauses
    supporting. *See* Supporting ideas, organizing
ie vs. *ei* spelling, 606–607
Illustration, words signaling, 61, 122, 253
Illustration (example) essays
    pattern of organization in, 253–257
    reading selections, 632–636
Illustration (example) paragraph, 116–131
Images, vivid. *See* Vivid images
Imperative sentences, 492
Imperative statement
    exclamation point and, 586
    period and, 584
Indefinite article, 328
Indefinite pronouns, subject-verb agreement with, 477–479

Independent clauses, 404, 450
    commas and, 405–406, 557–558
    coordinating conjunctions and, 405–406
    dependent clause placement and, 412–414
    semicolon and, 406
Indirect question, period and, 585
Indirect quotes, 578
Ineffective expression, 63
Infinitive, 446
    phrase fragments, 446
Information
    evaluating sources, 298–299
    exchange in reading-writing cycle, 8
    facts vs. opinion, 293
    locating, 293–295
    nonessential. *See* Nonessential clauses
    tracking sources, 297
Information levels
    essay, 208–210
    identifying, 53–55
    paragraph, 51–55
Informative writing, 22
-*ing*
    endings, 350
    phrase/fragments, 447–449
Intensive pronouns, 341–342
Interjections, exclamation point and, 586
Internet
    bookmark, 297
    information resources and sources, 296–297
Interrogative sentence/statement, 492
    question mark and, 585
Interviews, MLA citation/documentation format for, 313
In-text citations, MLA style, 308
    in sample essay, 317–318
    Web sources, 308
Introductions
    essay, 206, 208, 209, 229, 230, 233–235, 237
    paragraph, 56
Introductory elements, commas and, 557
    proofreading for, 160–161
Irregular verbs
    past participles, 373–375
    past tense, 368–370
-*ish* endings, 352
its/it's, 188
-*ive* endings, 352

J

Journals. *See* Writer's journal

K

Key verbs
    past tense, 370–371
    present tense, subject-verb agreement and, 472–476
Key words
    definition essay, 268
    definition paragraph, 167

Keywords, in Internet search, 296
King, Stephen, "Why We Crave Horror Movies," 658–659

L

Labeling, of work, 15
Language
    active, 543–545
    concise, 540–542
    concrete, 545–548
    fresh, 549–551
    positive, 543
"Latino Heritage Month: Who We Are . . . And Why We Celebrate?" (Rodriguez), 620–622
Learning
    about writing, preparation for, 3–4, 17
    attitude, 5, 7
    behaviors of, 6
-*less* endings, 352
Letters, for parallelism, 532
Library electronic database, 294–295
Library online catalogue, 293–294
Library research, information resources and sources, 293–295
Life skill, writing as, 2, 20
Lin, Maya, "Design Submission to the Vietnam Memorial Competition," 618–619
Linking verbs, 392–393
    adjective placement and, 352
List of items, commas and, 556–557
Listing
    examples, transition words for, 122
    as prewriting technique, 36–37
Listing order
    classification paragraph, 134, 137
    definition paragraph, 164, 167
    illustration (example) paragraph, 118, 122–123
Logical order, 61. *See also* Pattern of organization; *specific forms of order*
    essay development and, 213–215
    paragraphs
        cause-effect paragraph, 181
        classification paragraph, 137
        compare-contrast paragraph, 150, 153
        definition paragraph, 164, 167
        descriptive paragraph, 76
        illustration (example) paragraph, 122–123
        narrative paragraph, 91
        persuasive paragraph, 195
        process paragraph, 105
    signal words and. *See* Signal words
    supporting details, 213–215
    transition words and. *See* Transition words
"The Loss of Juárez: How Has the Violence in Juárez Changed Border Culture?" (Troncoso), 647–648
-*ly* endings, 352, 355

M

Magazine article, MLA citation/documentation format for, 312, 315

Main clauses. *See* Independent clauses
Main idea, 51, 58–60
    cause-effect paragraph, 178, 180
    classification paragraph, 134, 136
    compare-contrast paragraph, 150, 152
    definition paragraph, 164, 166
    descriptive paragraph, 72, 74–75
    illustration (example) paragraph, 118, 120
    narrative paragraph, 88, 90
    persuasive paragraph, 192, 194
    process paragraph, 102, 104
    statements, 42, 43
Major details
    essay, 206, 208, 209
    paragraph, 51
Malone, Michael S., "Through Young Eyes," 656–657
"Managing Stress in College" (Donatelle), 625–628
Metaphor, 548–549
Minor details
    essay, 206, 208, 209
    paragraph, 51
Misplaced modifiers
    correcting, 460–461, 464–465
    proofreading for, 83–84
MLA citation/documentation style. *See* Modern Language Association (MLA) citation/documentation style
Mnemonics, 601
Modern Language Association (MLA) citation/documentation style, 307–316
    sample essay, 317–319
Modifiers
    defined, 459
    misplaced and dangling, 458–467
        proofreading for, 83–84

N

Narration/Narrative
    defined, 90
    words signaling, 61, 91, 245
Narrative essays
    pattern of organization in, 244–248
    reading selections, 620–624
Narrative paragraph, 86–99
Narrowed subject, 51, 58–59
    classification and, 142
    for essay, 211, 221
Negative expression, 544
neither-nor, 480–481
Newspaper article, MLA citation/documentation format for, 313, 315
"Niagara Falls" (Brooke), 615–617
"Nobel Lecture – The Nobel Peace Prize 2014" (Yousafzai), 661–663
Noncount noun, 327–328
Nonessential appositives, commas and, 560
Nonessential clauses, commas and, 558–559
    proofreading for, 174–175
Non-Web sources
    MLA in-text citation style for, 308
    Works cited page, MLA style, 310–313

nor, 405–406, 426, 493, 557
not, and *do* contraction, 474–475
Nouns, 322–345
    abstract, 546
    as adjectives, 351–352
    articles and, 328–329
    cause/effect signaled by, 181
    collective, 479–480
    common, 324–326, 594
    concrete, 546
    count, 327–328
    noncount, 327–328
    plural, 328
    predicate, 336
    proper, 324–326, 594
    singular, 328
    types, 324–327
    uses, 326–327
Number (person)
    consistent use of, 515–516
    illogical shift in, 515
    pronoun agreement and, 332, 334
Numbers, for parallelism, 532

O

Objective case, 336–337
Objects
    compound, of preposition, 337
    compound, of verbs, 337
    of verb, 336
Online catalogue, library, 293–294
Online dictionaries, 600–601
Opening quotation mark, 574
Opinion, 58, 60
    identifying, 293
or, 405–406, 426, 493, 557
Order
    climactic, 61, 214
    logical, 61. *See also* Logical order
    topic sentence, 61
Organizational pattern. *See* Pattern of organization
Organizer. *See* Photographic organizer
-ous endings, 352
Outlining, 40–41

P

PAART guide, 298–299
PAC tips, on quoting, 304
Page, Libby, "Can Virtual Classrooms Beat Face-to-Face Interaction?", 667–668
Paragraphs, 50–67
    cause-effect, 176–189
    classification, 132–147
    compare-contrast, 148–161
    concluding, 206
    connecting, 216–217
    definition, 162–175
    descriptive, 68–85
    drafting, 43
    effective, 58
    effectiveness of, analyzing, 65–66
    essay body, 206
    illustration (example), 116–131
    information levels in, 51–55
    introductory, 206
    narrative, 86–99
    parts of, 56–58
    pattern of organization in, 58
    persuasive, 190–203
    process, 100–115
    scoring guide for, 65
Parallel language
    classification paragraph, 134
    illustration (example) paragraph, 126–127
Parallelism, 524–537
Paraphrasing, 300, 305
    direct to indirect quotation, 578
    steps for, 300–301
Parenthetical ideas, 558
Participle adjectives, 350–351
Participle phrase
    combining simple sentences with, 496–499
    fragments, 448–449
Participles, 448
Passive voice, 543–545
    verb tense and, 380–381
Past participle phrase, combining simple sentences with, 498–499
Past participles, 371–381
    irregular verbs, 373–375
    purpose of, 371
    regular verbs, 372
Past perfect tense, 378–379
Past tense, 366
    consistent use, 517
    irregular verbs in, 368–370
    key verbs in, 370–371
    regular verbs in, 367–368
    simple, 366–367
Pattern of organization
    in essay development, 214, 238–289
        cause-effect essay, 273–277
        classification essay, 258–262
        combining patterns, 283–288
        comparison-contrast essay, 263–267
        definition essay, 268–272
        descriptive essay, 240–244
        illustration (example) essay, 253–257
        narrative essay, 244–248
        persuasive essay, 278–282
        process essay, 248–252
    in paragraph, 58
    signal words and, 58, 61
    in topic sentence, 60
Peer editing
    cause-effect paragraph, 179
    classification paragraph, 135
    compare-contrast paragraph, 151
    definition paragraph, 165
    descriptive paragraph, 73
    illustration (example) paragraph, 119
    narrative paragraph, 89
    persuasive paragraph, 193
    process paragraph, 103
Period, 584–585
    correcting run-on sentences with, 424–425
    position with quotation marks, 574
Person, 512–514
    illogical shift in, 513
    pronoun agreement and, 332–333, 341–342
Personal pronouns, proofreading and, 202–203
Persuade/Persuasion
    words signaling, 61, 195, 278
    writing to, 22
Persuasive essays
    pattern of organization in, 278–282
    reading selections, 660–664
Persuasive paragraph, 190–203
Persuasive thinking map, 196, 201
Photographic organizer
    adjectives and adverbs, 347
    apostrophes, 565
    capitalization, 591
    cause-effect paragraph, 177
    classification paragraph, 133
    comma splices and fused sentences, 421
    commas, 555
    compare-contrast paragraph, 149
    compound and complex sentences, 403
    definition paragraph, 163
    descriptive paragraph, 69–71
    end punctuation, 583
    essay, 205
    fragments, 439
    illustration (example) paragraph, 117
    improving your spelling, 599
    levels of information in paragraph, 52
    modifiers, misplaced and dangling, 459
    narrative paragraph, 87
    nouns and pronouns, 323
    parallelism, 525
    patterns of organization in essays, 239
    persuasive paragraph, 191
    preparing to learn about writing, 3
    process paragraph, 101
    quotation marks, 573
    reasons to write, 19
    research, 291
    revising for effective expression, 539
    sentence clarity, 511
    sentence variety, 491
    subjects, verbs, and simple sentences, 389
    subject-verb agreement, 469
    titles, introductions, and conclusions, 229
    verb tense, 366
    verbs, 365, 389
Phrases
    fragments, 442–449
    introductory, commas and, 557
    nonparallel, 528–529
    parallel, 528–529
    series of, commas and, 556–557
Plagiarism, avoiding, 300–307
Plan. *See* Study plan; Writing plan; Writing process
Plural nouns, 47, 328
    spelling and, 603
Plural pronouns, 332
Point of view, 512, 513–514, 516
    proofreading for, 202–203
Portfolios, 14–16
Positive expression, 544

Positive self-talk, 5
Possessive case, 336–337
Possessive form, apostrophe and, 566–567
Predicate noun, 336–337
Prefixes, 606
Prepositional phrases, 397–398, 476–477
    fragments, 442–443
    sentence openings and, 504–505
Prepositions, 397, 476–477
Prereading, in reading/writing strategy, 12
Present participle phrase, combining simple sentences with, 497–498
Present perfect tense, 376–377
Present tense
    consistent use, 517
    key verbs, subject-verb agreement and, 472–476
    simple, 366–367
    subject-verb agreement in, 470–476
Prewriting, 28, 30–41
    activities, 30
    concept mapping, 38–39
    essays, 221–223
    freewriting, 34–35
    listing, 36–37
    outlining, 40–41
    paragraphs
        cause-effect paragraph, 186–187
        classification paragraph, 143–144
        comparison-contrast paragraph, 158–159
        definition paragraph, 172–173
        descriptive paragraph, 81–82
        illustration (example) paragraph, 128–129
        narrative paragraph, 96–97
        persuasive paragraph, 200–201
        process paragraph, 110–111
    questioning, 31–33
    in reading/writing strategy, 12
Primary details. *See* Major details
Print dictionaries, 600
Print sources, MLA citation/documentation format for, 310–313
Process
    defined, 104
    words signaling, 105, 249
Process essays
    pattern of organization in, 248–252
    reading selections, 625–631
Process paragraph, 100–115
Pronouns, 322–345
    agreement, 47, 332–335
    case, 336–342
    indefinite, 477–479
    intensive, 341–342
    personal
        points of view, 512, 513–514
        proofreading and, 202–203
    reference, 329–332
    reflexive, 341–342
    relative. *See* Relative pronouns
Proofreading, 29, 46–47
    essays, 226
    paragraphs
        cause-effect paragraph, 188–189

        classification paragraph, 145–146
        compare-contrast paragraph, 160–161
        definition paragraph, 174–175
        descriptive paragraph, 83–84
        illustration (example) paragraph, 130–131
        narrative paragraph, 98
        persuasive paragraph, 202–203
        process paragraph, 112–113
    in reading/writing strategy, 13
Proper nouns, 324–326
    capitalizing, 594
Punctuation
    dependent clauses, 412–414
    end, 582–589
    for parallelism, 532–533
    quotation marks with, 574–575
Purpose, 20, 22–23
Purpose (goal), 20, 22–23

Q

Question mark, 585
    position with quotation marks, 575
Questions/Questioning
    critical thinking, 14
    indirect, period and, 585
    for prewriting, 31–33
    in reading/writing strategy, 12
    reflective, 32, 33
    reporters', 31, 33
    subject-verb agreement in, 484
Quotation marks, 572–581
    general guidelines, 574–575
    in keyword searches, 296
Quotes/Quotations, 304–305
    commas and, 561
    direct. *See* Direct quotes
    indirect, 578
    PAC tips on, 304

R

Radio program, MLA in-text citation style for, 313
Reading process
    defined, 8
    SQ3R, 10–11
    thinking process and, 9
    writer's strategy for, 612, 614
    and writing, connection between, 8–9
Reading-writing cycle, 8
Reading/writing strategy, 12–13
Recite, in reading/writing strategy, 12
Reference, pronoun, 329–332
Reference librarians, 293
Reflective questions, 32, 33
Reflective writing, 14–16, 22
Reflexive pronouns, 341–342
Regular verbs
    past participles of, 372
    past tense, 367–368
Relative clauses, 412, 452–453
    fragments, 452–453
Relative pronouns, 410–411, 412, 413, 452–453
    subject-verb agreement with, 485–486

Relevant details
    essay development and, 218–219
    paragraphs, 62–63
        cause-effect paragraph, 178, 182–183
        classification paragraph, 134, 138–139
        compare-contrast paragraph, 150, 154–155
        definition paragraph, 164, 168–169
        descriptive paragraph, 72, 77–78
        illustration (example) paragraph, 118, 124–125
        narrative paragraph, 88, 92–93
        persuasive paragraph, 192, 196–197
        process paragraph, 102, 106–107
Reliability, of information source, 298–299
Reporters' questions, 31, 33
    developing relevant details with
        in essay development, 222
        in illustration (example) paragraph, 92
        in narrative paragraph, 92
        in persuasive paragraph, 196
Research writing process, 290–320
    elements, 306–307
    MLA basics for, 307–316
    plagiarism, avoiding, 300–307
    resources/sources, finding and evaluating, 292–299
    sample essay, MLA style, 317–319
Resources, finding and evaluating, 292–299
Reviewing, in reading/writing strategy, 12, 13
Revising, 29, 44–45
    for effective expression, 538–555
    essays, 224–225
    paragraphs
        cause-effect paragraph, 187–188
        classification paragraph, 145
        comparison-contrast paragraph, 160
        definition paragraph, 174
        descriptive paragraph, 82–83
        illustration (example) paragraph, 129–130
        narrative paragraph, 97–98
        persuasive paragraph, 201–202
        process paragraph, 112
    in reading/writing strategy, 13
Rodriguez, Luis J., "Latino Heritage Month: Who We Are . . . And Why We Celebrate?," 620–622
Run-on sentences, 420–437

S

-*s* endings
    plural nouns, 603
    subject-verb agreement with, 482–483
"Said" clause, 561
Salutations, capitalizing first letter of first word in, 592
Scoring guide, paragraph, 65
Search engine, 296

Second person
    pronoun agreement and, 332, 341–342
    proofreading and, 202
    singular and plural forms, 512, 515
    traits, 512
Secondary details. *See* Minor details
Self-evaluation
    attitude and behaviors of learning, 7
    reflective writing, 14
    writer anxiety, 30
-self/-selves, 341–342
Self-talk, positive, 5
Semicolons
    correcting run-on sentences with, 428–429
    independent clauses and, 406
    for parallelism, 532
    position with quotation marks, 574
Sensory verbs, adjective placement and, 352
Sentence structure
    controlled, in classification paragraph, 140–141
    definition paragraph, 170
    effective expression and, 64
Sentences
    capitalizing first letter of first word, 592
    clarity, 510–523
    complex, 64, 140–141, 156, 402, 403, 409–414
    compound, 64, 140–141, 156, 402, 403, 405–409
    compound-complex, 64, 140–141, 403, 414–416
    declarative, 492
    end punctuation for, 584–586
    exclamatory, 492
    imperative, 492
    interrogative, 492
    length, 505–506
    openings, 504–505
    purposes, 492–493
    run-on, 420–437
    simple, 64, 140–141, 389, 395–396, 403. *See also* Independent clauses
    structure. *See* Sentence structure
    variety, 490–509
Serial commas, 557
    proofreading for, 130–131
Series, commas for items in, 556–557
    proofreading for, 130–131
Shifts in tenses. *See* Tense shifts
Signal words, 58, 61
    compare-contrast paragraph, 153
    time order. *See* Time order, signal words
    transitions combined with, 137
Simile, 548–549
Simple future tense, 366–367
Simple past tense, 366–367
Simple present tense, 366–367
Simple sentences, 64, 140–141, 389, 403. *See also* Independent clauses
    combining, 494–502
    composing, 395–396
    fragment vs., distinguishing between, 395
Simple subjects, 390–391
Single quotation marks, 575
Singular nouns, 47, 328
Singular pronouns, 332
so, 405–406, 426, 493, 557
Sound recordings, MLA citation/documentation format for, 313
Sources
    finding and evaluating, 292–299
    tracking, 297
Spatial order
    descriptive paragraph, 72, 76
    essay development and, 214
Speech tag, 561
    formatting and punctuating, 575–576
Spell checkers, 600
Spelling, improving, 598–609
    adjectives and adverbs, 359–360
    rules, 602–607
    techniques, 600–602
Spelling errors, tracking, 601
SQ3R reading process, 10–11
Statements
    main idea, 42, 43
    period and, 584
    question mark and, 585
    thesis. *See* Thesis statement
Study plan
    action steps in, 6
    creating, 6–7
Study tools, 6
Subjective case, 336–337
Subjective words, for persuasion, 198
Subjects, 389, 390–392. *See also* Topic (subject)
    after verbs, 483–484
    compound, 337, 391
    FIL process identifying, 398–399
    identifying, FIL process and, 398–399
    narrowed. *See* Narrowed subject
    plural, 477–486
    separated from verbs, 476–477
    simple, 390–391
    singular, 477–486
Subject-verb agreement, 47, 468–489
    with collective nouns, 479–480
    with *either-or/neither-nor*, 480–481
    with fractions, titles and *-s* endings, 482–483
    with indefinite pronouns, 477–479
    present tense, 470–476
    with relative pronouns, 485–486
    with subjects after verbs, 484
    subjects separated from verbs, 476–477
Subordinating conjunctions, 409–411, 412, 414
    correcting clause fragments with, 450
    correcting run-on sentences with, 432–433
Subordination, of ideas, 156, 493, 503. *See also* Dependent clauses
Subsections, essay, 283

Suffixes, 602–603
    final consonant, 604–605
    final *e*, 605
    final *y*, 605
    parallel words, 526–527
    plural nouns, 604
Summary, 305, 613–614
    steps for writing, 302–304
Superlative adjectives/adverbs, 356–359
    spelling guidelines, 359–360
Supporting details
    essay development, 222
    levels, 209–210
    types, 208
Supporting ideas, organizing
    connecting paragraphs, 216–217
    logical order, 213–215
Survey, in reading/writing strategy, 12

T
"The Talk of the Sandbox; How Johnny and Suzy's Playground Chatter Prepares Them for Life at the Office" (Tannen), 643–645
Tan, Amy, "Confessions," 623–624
Tannen, Deborah, "The Talk of the Sandbox; How Johnny and Suzy's Playground Chatter prepares Them for Life at the Office," 645–645
Taub-Dix, Bonnie, "Hungry vs. Healthy: The School Lunch Controversy," 665–666
Teacher, as writing coach, 5
Television program, MLA in-text citation style for, 313
Tense. *See also individual tenses*
    consistent use, 98–99, 516–519
    primary, consistent use, 517
Tense shifts
    illogical, 517
    proofreading for, 98–99
Text messaging, capitalization and, 591
than, 338–339
their/they're/there, 188
there, subject-verb agreement with, 483
Thesaurus, using, 220
Thesis statement, 42, 43, 206, 208, 209
    drafting and revising, 212–213, 221, 223
    narrowing topic for, 211
Thinking process, 9
    persuasive thinking map, 196, 201
Third person
    pronoun agreement and, 332, 341–342
    proofreading and, 202
    singular and plural forms, 512, 515
    traits, 512
"Through Young Eyes" (Malone), 656–657
Time order
    essay development and, 214
    signal words
        narrative paragraph, 61, 91
        process paragraph, 61, 105

679

Titles (works)
    capitalizing, 593
    essay, 206, 208, 229, 230
        effective, 231–232, 237
    paragraph, 56
    quotation marks and, 575, 579
    subject-verb agreement with, 482, 483
Titles (personal), capitalizing, 595
Tools for writing, 6
Topic (subject), 20–21, 27
    comparable, in Venn diagram, 154
    narrowing, 58–59. See also Narrowed subject
    paragraph, 51
    questioning and, 32
Topic sentence, 4, 42, 56
    composing, 58–60
    essay, 209
    order, 61
    in paragraphs
        cause-effect paragraph, 180
        classification paragraph, 136
        compare-contrast paragraph, 152
        definition paragraph, 166
        descriptive paragraph, 74–75
        illustration (example) paragraph, 120–121
        narrative paragraph, 90
        persuasive paragraph, 194
        process paragraph, 104
    writing, 60
to/two/too, 188
Tracking
    information sources, 297
    spelling errors, 601
Traits
    effective essay, 211–220
    shared, by comparable topics, 154
    words and transitions signaling, 137
Transition words
    cause and effect
        essay, 273
        paragraph, 178, 181
    classification
        essay, 258
        paragraph, 137
    comparison and contrast
        essay, 263
        paragraph, 153
    definition
        essay, 268
        paragraph, 167
    description
        essay, 240
        paragraph, 76
    illustration (example)
        essay, 253
        paragraph, 122
    indicating time order
        in narrative paragraph, 91
        in process paragraph, 105
    narration
        essay, 245
        paragraph, 91
    persuasion
        essay, 278
        paragraph, 192, 195
    process
        essay, 249
        paragraph, 105
    signaling organization pattern used, 283
Troncoso, Sergio, "The Loss of Juárez: How Has the Violence in Juárez Changed Border Culture?," 647–648
Trustworthiness, of information source, 298–299
Types, words and transitions signaling, 137

V
Venn diagram, comparable topics in, 154
Verbs, 364–387, 389, 392–395
    abstract, 546
    action, 393–394
    as adjectives, 351–352
    cause/effect signaled by, 181
    concrete, 546
    FIL process identifying, 398–399
    helping, 394–395
    identifying, FIL process and, 398–399
    linking, 392–393
    object of, 336
    subjects after, 483–484
    subjects separated from, 476–477
    tenses, 366–367. See also individual tenses
        consistent use, 516–519
        primary, 517
        shifts in. See Tense shifts
    vivid, 88, 94
Visual description. transition words signaling, 76
Visual media, MLA citation/documentation format for, 313, 314
Vivid images
    definition paragraph, 164, 170
    descriptive paragraph, 69
    process paragraph, 102, 108
Vivid verbs, 88, 94
Vowel patterns, 602

W
Web sources
    MLA in-text citation style for, 308
    Works cited page, MLA style, 314–315
Webbing. See Concept map/mapping
Websites
    MLA citation/documentation format for, 314
    searching by domain, 296
well, 360–361
"What is Poverty?" (Goodwin-Parker), 650–652
whose/who's, 188
"Why We Crave Horror Movies" (King), 658–659
Word choice, 63. See also Effective expression
    affect vs. effect, 184
    concrete vs. general/vague, 78–79
Wordiness, 540–542
Words
    commonly misspelled, 607
    concrete vs. general/vague, 78–79
    confusing, proofreading for, 188–189
    correct use, 184
    introductory, commas and, 557
    nonparallel, 526–527
    order, ESL students and, 397
    parallel, 526–527
    precise use, 220
    prefixes for, 606
    series of, commas and, 556–557
    signal. See Signal words
    subjective, for persuasion, 198
    suffixes for, 602–603
    transition. See Transition words
Works cited page, MLA style, 309–310
    non-Web sources, 310–313
    in sample essay, 319
    Web sources, 314–315
would, 382–383
Writer's journal. See also Peer editing
    cause-effect paragraph, 179
    classification paragraph, 135
    compare-contrast paragraph, 151
    definition paragraph, 165
    descriptive paragraph, 73
    illustration (example) paragraph, 119
    narrative paragraph, 89
    persuasive paragraph, 193
    process paragraph, 103
    reflective entries in, 14–15
Writer/Writing
    anxiety of, self-evaluation, 30
    as life skill, 2, 20
    purpose for, 20, 22–23
    reading strategy for, 612, 614
    tools for, 6
Writing plan, generating details with, 218
    supporting details, 222
Writing process
    annotating text, 12, 13, 612–613
    defined, 8
    drafting, 13, 28, 42–43
    in everyday life, 19–20
    improving spelling with, 602
    learning about, preparation for, 3–4, 17
    prewriting, 12, 28, 30–41
    proofreading, 13, 29, 46–47
    reading and, connection between, 8–9
    revising, 13, 29, 44–45
    steps in, 28–49
    summary, 613–614
    thinking process and, 9
Writing situation, elements of, 20–27. See also Topic (subject)

Y
-y endings, 352
    adding suffix to, 605
yet, 405–406, 426, 493, 557
your/you're, 188
Yousafzai, Malala, "Nobel Lecture —The Nobel Peace Prize 2014," 661–663

Z
Zero article, 328